THE  TIMES
ATLAS
OF THE
WORLD

REFERENCE EDITION

TIMES BOOKS

The Times Atlas of the World Reference Edition

Times Books, London
77-85 Fulham Palace Road, Hammersmith,
London W6 8JB

First Published by Times Books 1995
Revised 1996

Copyright © Times Books 1996
Maps © Bartholomew 1996

Maps and index prepared by
HarperCollins*Cartographic,*
Glasgow

Design
Ivan Dodd

*The Publishers would like to extend
their grateful thanks to the following:*

Mrs J Candy, Geographical Research   Associates,
    Maidenhead
Flag information provided and authenticated
    by the Flag Institute, Chester
Mr P.J.M. Geelan, place-name consultant
Mr H.A.G. Lewis OBE, geographical
    consultant to The Times

*British Library Cataloguing in
Publication Data*
A catalogue record for
this book is available
from the British Library.

Printed by the Edinburgh Press Ltd

ISBN 0 7230 0901 5

JH8622

CONTENTS

AFGHANISTAN

STATUS: Republic
AREA: 652,225 sq km (251,825 sq miles)
POPULATION: 18,879,000
ANNUAL NATURAL INCREASE: 2.5%
CAPITAL: Kabul
LANGUAGE: Dari, Pushtu,Uzbek, Turkmen
RELIGION: Sunni Muslim, Shi'a Muslim,
Hindu, Sikh and Jewish minorities
CURRENCY: Afghani (AFA)
ORGANIZATIONS: Col. Plan, UN

Afghanistan is a mountainous landlocked country in southwest Asia with a climate of extremes. In summer the lowland southwest reaches a temperature of over 40°C (104°F); in winter this may drop to -26°C (-15°F) in the northern mountains. The country is one of the poorest in the world with barely 10 per cent of the land suitable for agriculture. Main crops are wheat, fruit and vegetables. Sheep and goats are the main livestock. Mineral resources are rich but underdeveloped with natural gas, coal and iron ore deposits predominating. The main industrial area was centred on Kabul, but both Kabul and the rural areas have been devastated by civil war.

ÅLAND

STATUS: Finnish Province
AREA: 1,527 sq km (590 sq miles)
POPULATION: 25,008
CAPITAL: Mariehamn

ALBANIA

STATUS: Republic
AREA: 28,748 sq km (11,100 sq miles)
POPULATION: 3,414,000
CAPITAL: Tirana (Tiranë)

LANGUAGE: Albanian (Gheg, Tosk), Greek
RELIGION: Sunni Muslim, Greek Orthodox,
Roman Catholic
CURRENCY: lek (ALL)
ORGANIZATIONS: Council of Europe, OSCE, UN

Albania is situated on the eastern seaboard of the Adriatic. With the exception of a coastal strip, most of the territory is mountainous and largely unfit for cultivation. The climate is Mediterranean along the coast, but cooler inland. Average temperatures in July reach 25°C (77°F) and there is 1,400 mm (55 inches) of rainfall annually. The country possesses mineral resources, notably chrome which is a major export, and deposits of coal, oil and natural gas. After decades of self-imposed political and economic isolation Albania shook off its own peculiar variant of communism in 1990. Administrative chaos and a massive fall in production ensued resulting in acute food shortages and widespread emigration. The country is one of the poorest in Europe with a backward rural economy and nearly half the labour force unemployed.

ALGERIA

STATUS: Republic
AREA: 2,381,741 sq km (919,595 sq miles)
POPULATION: 27,325,000
CAPITAL: Algiers (Alger, El-Djezaïr)
LANGUAGE: Arabic, French, Berber
RELIGION: Sunni Muslim, Roman Catholic
CURRENCY: Algerian dinar (DZD)
ORGANIZATIONS: Arab League,
OAU, OPEC, UN

Physically the country is divided between the coastal Atlas mountain ranges of the north and the Sahara to the south. Algeria is mainly hot, with negligible rainfall, but along the Mediterranean coast temperatures are more moderate, with most rain falling during the mild winters. Arable land occupies small areas of the northern valleys and coastal strip, with wheat, barley and vines the leading crops. Sheep, goats and cattle are the most important livestock. Although oil from the southern deserts dominates the economy, it is now declining and natural gas output has increased dramatically. A virtual civil war has existed between the army and Islamic extremists which has caused the economy to deteriorate.

AMERICAN SAMOA

STATUS: Unincorporated Territory of USA
AREA: 197 sq km (76 sq miles)
POPULATION: 53,000
CAPITAL: Pago Pago

ANDORRA

STATUS: Principality
AREA: 465 sq km (180 sq miles)
POPULATION: 65,000
CAPITAL: Andorra la Vella
LANGUAGE: Catalan, Spanish, French
RELIGION: Roman Catholic
CURRENCY: French franc (FRF),
Spanish peseta (ESP)
ORGANIZATIONS: Council of Europe, OSCE, UBN

Andorra, a tiny state in the Pyrenees between France and Spain, achieved fuller independence from these countries in 1993. The climate is alpine with a long winter, which lasts for six months, a mild spring and a warm summer. Tourism is the main occupation, with Andorra becoming an important skiing centre during the winter. Tobacco and potatoes are the principal crops, sheep and cattle the main livestock. Other important sources of revenue are the sale of hydro-electricity, stamps, duty-free goods and financial services.

ANGOLA

STATUS: Republic
AREA: 1,246,700 sq km (481,354 sq miles)
POPULATION: 10,674,000
CAPITAL: Luanda
LANGUAGE: Portuguese,
Tribal dialects
RELIGION: Roman Catholic, Protestant,
Traditional beliefs
CURRENCY: kwanza (AOK)
ORGANIZATIONS: OAU, SADC, UN

Independent from the Portuguese since 1975, Angola is a large country south of the equator in southwest Africa. Much of the interior is savannah plateaux with average rainfall varying from 250 mm (10 inches) in the south to 1,270 mm (50 inches) in the north. Most of the population is engaged in agriculture producing cassava, maize and coffee. Most consumer products and textiles are imported. Angola possesses vast wealth in the form of diamonds, oil, iron ore, copper and other minerals. Apart from the production of oil, which is the biggest export, the economy has collapsed as a result of many years of civil war.

ABBREVIATIONS

The following abbreviations have been used. Codes given in brackets following the name of a currency are those issued by the International Standards Organization.

ANZUS	Australia, New Zealand, United States Security Treaty
ASEAN	Association of Southeast Asian Nations
Caricom	Caribbean Community and Common Market
CACM	Central American Common Market
CIS	Commonwealth of Independent States
Col. Plan	Colombo Plan
Comm.	Commonwealth
CSCE	Council for Security and Co-operation in Europe
ECOWAS	Economic Community of West African States
EEA	European Economic Area
EFTA	European Free Trade Association
EU	European Union
G7	Group of seven industrialized nations:– (Canada, France, Germany, Italy, Japan, UK, USA)
Mercosur	Common Market of the Southern Cone
NAFTA	North American Free Trade Agreement
NATO	North Atlantic Treaty Organization
OAS	Organization of American States
OAU	Organization of African Unity
OECD	Organization for Economic Co-operation and Development
OPEC	Organization of Petroleum Exporting Countries
UN	United Nations
WEU	Western European Union

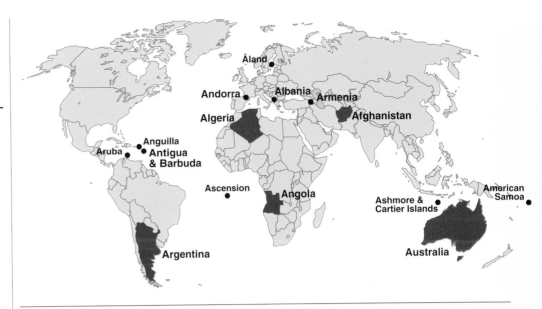

ANGUILLA

STATUS: UK Territory
AREA: 155 sq km (60 sq miles)
POPULATION: 8,000
CAPITAL: The Valley

ANTIGUA AND BARBUDA

STATUS: Monarchy
AREA: 442 sq km (171 sq miles)
POPULATION: 65,000
CAPITAL: St John's (on Antigua)
LANGUAGE: English, Creole
RELIGION: Protestant,
Roman Catholic
CURRENCY: E Caribbean dollar (XCD)
ORGANIZATIONS: Caricom, Comm., OAS, UN

The country consists of two main islands in the Leeward group in the West Indies. Tourism is the main activity. Local agriculture is being encouraged to reduce food imports and the growth of sea island cotton is making a comeback. The production of rum is the main manufacturing industry; there is also an oil refinery.

ARGENTINA

STATUS: Republic
AREA: 2,766,889 sq km
(1,068,302 sq miles)
POPULATION: 34,180,000
CAPITAL: Buenos Aires
LANGUAGE: Spanish, Italian,
Amerindian languages
RELIGION: Roman Catholic,
Protestant, Jewish
CURRENCY: peso (ARP)
ORGANIZATIONS: Aladi, Mercosur, OAS, UN

Relief is highest in the west in the Andes mountains, where altitudes exceed 6,000 m (19,500 ft). East of the Andes there are fertile plains known as the Pampas. In the northern scrub forests and grasslands of the Chaco hot tropical conditions exist. Central Argentina lies in temperate latitudes, but the southernmost regions are cold, wet and stormy. The economy of Argentina was long dominated by the produce of the rich soils of the Pampas, beef and grain. Agricultural products still account for some 40 per cent of export revenue, with grain crops predominating, despite a decline due to competition and falling world prices. Beef exports also decreased by over 50 per cent between 1970 and 1983, due to strong competition from western Europe. Industry is now the chief export earner. Industrial activity includes petrochemicals, steel, cars, and food and drink processing. There are oil and gas reserves and an abundant supply of hydroelectric power.

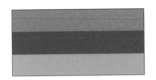

ARMENIA

STATUS: Republic
AREA: 29,800 sq km
(11,506 sq miles)
POPULATION: 3,548,000
CAPITAL: Yerevan
LANGUAGE: Armenian, Azeri, Russian
RELIGION: Armenian Orthodox,
Roman Catholic,
Shi'a Muslim
CURRENCY: dram
ORGANIZATIONS: OSCE, UN

Armenia is a country of rugged terrain, with most of the land above 1,000 m (3,300 feet). The climate, much influenced by altitude, has continental tendencies. Rainfall, although occurring throughout the year, is heaviest in summer. Agriculture is dependent upon irrigation and the main crops are vegetables, fruit and tobacco. Conflict over the disputed area of Nagornyy Karabakh, an enclave of Armenian Orthodox Christians within the territory of Azerbaijan, is casting a cloud over the immediate future of the country.

ARUBA

STATUS: Netherlands Territory
AREA: 193 sq km (75 sq miles)
POPULATION: 69,000
CAPITAL: Oranjestad
LANGUAGE: Dutch, Papiamento, English

ASCENSION

STATUS: UK Territory
AREA: 88 sq km (34 sq miles)
POPULATION: 1,192
CAPITAL: Georgetown

ASHMORE AND CARTIER ISLANDS

STATUS: Australian Territory
AREA: 5 sq km (2 sq miles)
POPULATION: no permanent population

AUSTRALIA

STATUS: Federation
AREA: 7,682,300 sq km (2,966,153 sq miles)
POPULATION: 17,843,000
CAPITAL: Canberra
LANGUAGE: English, Italian, Greek
Aboriginal languages
RELIGION: Protestant,Roman Catholic
Greek Othodox, Aboriginal beliefs
CURRENCY: Australian dollar (AUD)
ORGANIZATIONS: ANZUS, Col. Plan,
Comm., OECD, UN

The Commonwealth of Australia was founded in 1901. The British Monarch, as head of state, is represented by a governor-general. It is the sixth largest country in the world in terms of area. The western half of the country is primarily arid plateaux, ridges and vast deserts. The central-eastern area comprises lowlands of river systems draining into Lake Eyre, while to the east is the Great Dividing Range. Climate varies from cool temperate to tropical monsoon. Rainfall is high only in the northeast, where it exceeds 1,000 mm (39 inches) annually, and decreases markedly from the coast to the interior which is hot and dry. Over 50 per cent of the land area comprises desert and scrub with less than 250 mm (10 inches) of rain a year. The majority of the population live in cities concentrated along the southeast coast. Australia is rich in both agricultural and natural resources. It is the world's leading producer of wool, which together with wheat, meat, sugar and dairy products accounts for over 40 per cent of export revenue. There are vast reserves of coal, oil, natural gas, nickel, iron ore, bauxite and uranium ores. Gold, silver, lead, zinc and copper ores are also exploited. Minerals now account for over 30 per cent of Australia's export revenue. New areas of commerce have been created in eastern Asia, particularly in Japan, to counteract the sharp decline of the traditional European markets. Tourism is becoming a large revenue earner and showed a 200 per cent growth between 1983 and 1988. This has slowed recently, although the Olympics Games, due to be held in Sydney in the year 2000, are expected to attract an additional 1.5 million overseas visitors.

AUSTRALIAN CAPITAL TERRITORY
STATUS: Federal Territory
AREA: 2,400 sq km (927 sq miles)
POPULATION: 299,000
CAPITAL: Canberra

NEW SOUTH WALES
STATUS: State
AREA: 801,600 sq km (309,499 sq miles)
POPULATION: 6,009,000
CAPITAL: Sydney

NORTHERN TERRITORY
STATUS: Territory
AREA: 1,346,200 sq km (519,771 sq miles)
POPULATION: 168,000
CAPITAL: Darwin

QUEENSLAND
STATUS: State
AREA: 1,727,200 sq km (666,876 sq miles)
POPULATION: 3,113,000
CAPITAL: Brisbane

SOUTH AUSTRALIA
STATUS: State
AREA: 984,000 sq km (379,925 sq miles)
POPULATION: 1,462,000
CAPITAL: Adelaide

TASMANIA
STATUS: State
AREA: 67,800 sq km (26,178 sq miles)
POPULATION: 472,000
CAPITAL: Hobart

VICTORIA
STATUS: State
AREA: 227,600 sq km (87,877 sq miles)
POPULATION: 4,462,000
CAPITAL: Melbourne

WESTERN AUSTRALIA
STATUS: State
AREA: 2,525,500 sq km (975,101 sq miles)
POPULATION: 1,678,000
CAPITAL: Perth

AUSTRIA
STATUS: Republic
AREA: 83,855 sq km (32,377 sq miles)
POPULATION: 8,031,000
CAPITAL: Vienna (Wien)
LANGUAGE: German, Serbo-Croat,
Turkish
RELIGION: Roman Catholic, Protestant
CURRENCY: schilling (ATS)
ORGANIZATIONS: Council of Europe, EEA, EU,
OECD, OSCE, UN

Austria is an alpine, landlocked country in central Europe. The mountainous Alps which cover 75 per cent of the land consist of a series of east-west ranges enclosing lowland basins. The climate is continental with temperatures and rainfall varying with altitude. About 25 per cent of the country, in the north and northeast, is lower foreland or flat land containing most of Austria's fertile farmland. Half is arable and the remainder is mainly for root or fodder crops. Manufacturing and heavy industry, however, account for the majority of export revenues, particularly pig-iron, steel, chemicals and vehicles. Over 70 per cent of the country's power is hydro-electric. Tourism and forestry are also important to the economy.

AZERBAIJAN
STATUS: Republic
AREA: 86,600 sq km (33,436 sq miles)
POPULATION: 7,472,000
CAPITAL: Baku
LANGUAGE: Azeri, Armenian,
Russian, Lezgian
RELIGION: Shi'a Muslim,
Sunni Muslim
Russian and Armenian Orthodox
CURRENCY: manat
ORGANIZATIONS: OSCE, UN

Azerbaijan gained independence on the break-up of the USSR in 1991. It is a mountainous country that has a continental climate, greatly influenced by altitude. Arable land accounts for less than 10 per cent of the total area, with raw cotton and tobacco the leading products. Major reserves of oil and gas exist beneath and around the Caspian Sea, which are as of yet fully undeveloped. The country includes two autonomous regions: Nakhichevan, which it is cut off by a strip of intervening Armenian territory and the enclave of Nagornyy Karabakh, over which long standing tensions escalated into conflict in 1992.

AZORES
STATUS: Portuguese Territory
AREA: 2,247 sq km (868 sq miles)
POPULATION: 237,800
CAPITAL: Ponta Delgada

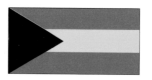

BAHAMAS
STATUS: Monarchy
AREA: 13,939 sq km (5,382 sq miles)
POPULATION: 272,000
CAPITAL: Nassau
LANGUAGE: English, Creole,
French Creole
RELIGION: Protestant,
Roman Catholic
CURRENCY: Bahamian dollar (BSD)
ORGANIZATIONS: Caricom, Comm., OAS, UN

About 700 islands and over 2,000 coral sand cays (reefs) constitute the sub-tropical Commonwealth of the Bahamas. The island group extends from the coast of Florida to Cuba and Haiti in the south. Only 29 islands are inhabited. Most of the 1,000 mm (39 inches) of rainfall falls in the summer. The tourist industry is the main source of income and, although fluctuating through recession, still employs over 70 per cent of the working population. Recent economic plans have concentrated on reducing imports by developing fishing and domestic agriculture. Other important sources of income are ship registration (the world's fourth largest open-registry fleet), income generated by offshore finance and banking, and export of rum, salt and cement.

BAHRAIN
STATUS: Monarchy
AREA: 691 sq km
(267 sq miles)
POPULATION: 549,000
CAPITAL: Manama (Al Manāmah)
LANGUAGE: Arabic, English
RELIGION: Shi'a Muslim, Sunni Muslim,
Christian
CURRENCY: Bahraini dinar (BHD)
ORGANIZATIONS: Arab League, UN

The sheikdom is a barren island in the Persian Gulf with less than 80 mm (3 inches) rainfall a year. Summer temperatures average 32°C (89°F). Bahrain was the first country in the Arabian peninsula to strike oil, in 1932. Oil still accounts for 60 per cent of revenue and gas is becoming increasingly important. Lower oil prices and decreased production is now causing the government to diversify the economy with expansion of light and heavy industry and chemical plants, and the subsequent encouragement of trade and foreign investment.

BANGLADESH
STATUS: Republic
AREA: 143,998 sq km (55,598 sq miles)
POPULATION: 117,787,000
CAPITAL: Dhaka, (Dhākā, Dacca)
LANGUAGE: Bengali, Bihari,
Hindi, English,
Local languages
RELIGION: Sunni Muslim, Hindu, Buddhist,
Christian
CURRENCY: taka (BDT)
ORGANIZATIONS: Col. Plan, Comm., UN

Bangladesh is one of the poorest and most densely populated countries of the world. Most of its territory, except for bamboo-forested hills in the southeast, comprises the vast river systems of the Ganges and Brahmaputra which drain from the Himalayan mountains into the Bay of Bengal, frequently changing course and flooding the flat delta plain. This land is, however, extremely fertile and attracts a high concentration of the population. The climate is tropical, and agriculture is dependent on monsoon rainfall. When the monsoon fails there is drought. Eighty two per cent of the population are farmers, the

main crops being rice and jute. Bangladesh is the world's leading supplier of jute, which accounts for 25 per cent of the country's exports. The main industry and number one export is clothing . Natural gas reserves, under the Bay of Bengal, are beginning to be exploited.

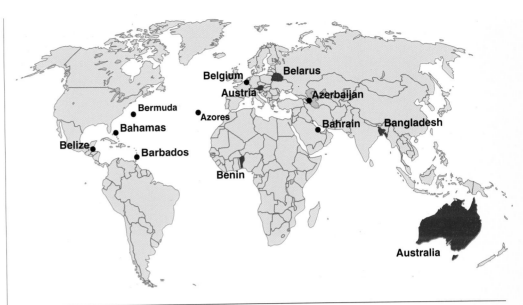

BARBADOS

STATUS: Monarchy
AREA: 430 sq km (166 sq miles)
POPULATION: 261,000
CAPITAL: Bridgetown
LANGUAGE: English,
Creole (Bajan)
RELIGION: Protestant,
Roman Catholic
CURRENCY: Barbados dollar (BBD)
ORGANIZATIONS: Caricom, Comm., OAS, UN

The former British colony of Barbados in the Caribbean is the most eastern island of the Antilles chain. The gently rolling landscape of the island is lush and fertile, the temperature ranging from 25–28°C (77–82°F) with 1270–1900 mm (50–75 inches) of rainfall per year. Sugar and its by-products, molasses and rum, are traditional cash crops. These are being overtaken in importance by tourism which provides an occupation for one-third of the population. This is a growth sector, although it has suffered recently from world recession. An oilfield supplies one-third of domestic oil requirements.

BELARUS

STATUS: Republic
AREA: 207,600 sq km (80,155 sq miles)
POPULATION: 10,355,000
CAPITAL: Minsk
LANGUAGE: Belorussian, Russian, Ukrainian
RELIGION: Belorussian Orthodox,
Roman Catholic
CURRENCY: rouble
ORGANIZATIONS: OSCE, UN

Belarus achieved independence in 1991. The country is mainly flat with forests covering more than one-third of the area. Swamps and marshlands cover large areas but, when drained, the soil is very fertile. The climate is continental with fairly cold winters (-7°C or 20°F). Grain, flax, potatoes and sugar beet are the main crops but livestock production accounts for more than half the value of agricultural output. Large areas of Belarus are thinly populated; most people live in the central area. The republic is comparatively poor in mineral resources and suffered terrible devastation during the Second World War. Postwar industrialization has been based on imported raw materials and semi-manufactured goods, concentrating on the production of trucks, tractors, agricultural machinery and other heavy engineering equipment. However, these industries are heavily reliant on imported Russian energy and output has declined since independence.

BELGIUM

STATUS: Monarchy
AREA: 30,520 sq km (11,784 sq miles)
POPULATION: 10,080,000
CAPITAL: Brussels (Bruxelles/Brussel)
LANGUAGE: Dutch (Flemish),French, German
(all official), Italian,
RELIGION: Roman Catholic ,
Protestant
CURRENCY: Belgium franc (BEF)
ORGANIZATIONS: Council of Europe, EEA,
EU, NATO, OECD, OSCE, UN, WEU

Over two-thirds of Belgium comprises the Flanders plain, a flat plateau covered by fertile wind-blown loess which extends from the North Sea coast down to the forested mountains of the Ardennes in the south. The climate is mild, maritime temperate with 720–1200 mm (28–47 inches) of rainfall a year. Over half the country is intensively farmed – cereals, root crops, vegetables and flax are the main crops and the country is nearly self-sufficient in meat and dairy products. Belgium's tradition as an industrialized nation dates back to the 19th century and Flanders has historically been famed for its textiles. The main industries now are metal-working (including motor vehicle assembly), chemicals, iron and steel, textiles, food and drink processing and diamonds. In recent years many companies have embarked on high-technology specialization including computer software, micro-electronics and telecommunications. Belgium is a trading nation, exporting more than half its national production. Most trade passes through the port of Antwerp, and an efficient communications network links it with the rest of Europe.

BELIZE

STATUS: Monarchy

AREA: 22,965 sq km (8,867 sq miles)
POPULATION: 211,000
CAPITAL: Belmopan
LANGUAGE: English, Creole,
Spanish, Mayan
RELIGION: Roman Catholic,
Protestant, Hindu
CURRENCY: Belizean dollar (BZD)
ORGANIZATIONS: CARICOM, Comm.,
OAS, UN

Bordering the Caribbean Sea, in Central America, sub-tropical Belize is dominated by its dense forest cover. Principal exports are sugar cane, citrus concentrates and bananas. Since independence from Britain in 1973 the country has developed agriculture to lessen reliance on imported food products. Other commodities produced include tropical fruits, vegetables, fish and timber.

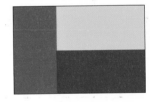

BENIN

STATUS: Republic
AREA: 112,620 sq km (43,483 sq miles)
POPULATION: 5,246,000
CAPITAL: Porto Novo
LANGUAGE: French, Fon, Yoruba, Adja,
Local languages
RELIGION: Traditional beliefs, Roman Catholic,
Sunni Muslim
CURRENCY: CFA franc (W Africa) (XOF)
ORGANIZATIONS: ECOWAS, OAU, UN

Benin, formerly Dahomey, is a small strip of country descending from the wooded savannah hills of the north to the forested and cultivated lowlands fringing the Bight of Benin. The economy is agricultural, with palm oil, cotton, cocoa, coffee, groundnuts and copra as main exports. The developing offshore oil industry has proven reserves of over 20 million barrels.

BERMUDA

STATUS: UK Territory
AREA: 54 sq km (21 sq miles)
POPULATION: 63,000
CAPITAL: Hamilton

BHUTAN

STATUS: Monarchy
AREA: 46,620 sq km (18,000 sq miles)
POPULATION: 1,614,000
CAPITAL: Thimphu
LANGUAGE: Dzongkha, Nepali,
Assamese, English
RELIGION: Buddhist, Hindu, Sunni Muslim
CURRENCY: ngultrum (BTN)
ORGANIZATIONS: Col. Plan, UN

Bhutan is a small country in the Himalayan foothills between China and India, and to the east of Nepal. Rainfall is high at over 3000 mm (118 inches) a year but temperatures vary between the extreme cold of the northern ranges to a July average of 27°C (81°F) in the southern forests. Long isolated, the economy of Bhutan is dominated by agriculture and small local industries. All manufactured goods are imported.

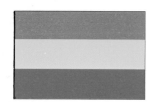

BOLIVIA

STATUS: Republic
AREA: 1,098,581 sq km (424,164 sq miles)
POPULATION: 7,237,000
CAPITAL: La Paz
LANGUAGE: Spanish, Quechua, Aymara
RELIGION: Roman Catholic,
Protestant, Baha'i
CURRENCY: Boliviano (BOB)
ORGANIZATIONS: Aladi, OAS, UN

Bolivia, where the average life expectancy is 51 years, is one of the world's poorest nations. Landlocked and isolated, the country stretches from the eastern Andes across high cool plateaux before dropping to the dense forest of the Amazon basin and the grasslands of the southeast. Bolivia was once rich, its wealth based on minerals (in recent decades tin) but in 1985 world tin prices dropped and the industry collapsed. Oil and gas and agriculture now dominate the economy. Crops include soya, cotton, coca (cocaine shrub), sugar and coffee. Mining is still important, with the emphasis on zinc.

BOSNIA-HERZEGOVINA

STATUS: Republic
AREA: 51,130 sq km (19,741 sq miles)
POPULATION: 3,527,000
CAPITAL: Sarajevo
LANGUAGE: Serbo-Croat
RELIGION: Sunni Muslim, Serbian Orthodox,
Roman Catholic, Protestant

CURRENCY: dinar
ORGANIZATIONS: OSCE, UN

Bosnia-Herzegovina achieved independence in April 1992, but international recognition did not spare the Republic from savage ethnic warfare between Muslims, Serbs and Croats. Partitioning of the country into a new federation acceptable to all warring parties appears to be a necessity for peace. Before the war Bosnia's economy was based predominantly on agriculture – sheep rearing and the cultivation of vines, olives and citrus fruits. The country is mainly mountainous with the Sava valley in the north being the only lowland of consequence. The climate is Mediterranean towards the Adriatic, but continental and cooler inland.

BOTSWANA

STATUS: Republic
AREA: 581,370 sq km (224,468 sq miles)
POPULATION: 1,443,000
CAPITAL: Gaborone
LANGUAGE: English (official), Setswana, Shona,
Local languages
RELIGION: Traditional beliefs, Protestant,
Roman Catholic
CURRENCY: pula (BWP)
ORGANIZATIONS: Comm., OAU, SADC, UN

The arid high plateau of Botswana, with its poor soils and low rainfall, supports little arable agriculture, but over 2.3 million cattle graze the dry grasslands. Diamonds are the chief export, providing 80 per cent of export earnings. Copper, nickel, potash, soda ash, salt and coal are also important. The growth of light industries around the capital has stimulated trade with neighbouring countries.

BRAZIL

STATUS: Republic
AREA: 8,511,965 sq km (3,286,488 sq miles)
POPULATION: 153,725,000
CAPITAL: Brasília
LANGUAGE: Portuguese, German, Japanese,
Italian, Amerindian languages
RELIGION: Roman Catholic, Spiritist, Protestant
CURRENCY: cruzeiro real (BRC),URV
ORGANIZATIONS: Aladi, Mercosur, OAS, UN

Brazil is the largest country in South America with the Amazon basin tropical rain forest covering roughly a third of the country. It is one of the world's leading agricultural exporters, with coffee, soya beans, sugar, bananas, cocoa, tobacco, rice and cattle major commodities. Brazil is an industrial power but with development limited to the heavily populated urban areas of the eastern coastal lowlands. Mineral resources, except for iron ore, do not play a significant role in the economy at present, but

recent economic policies have concentrated on developing the industrial base – road and rail communications, light and heavy industry and expansion of energy resources, particularly hydro-electric power harnessed from the three great river systems. Unlike other South American countries Brazil still has a serious inflation rate, introducing the 'real', on 1 July 1994 (the fifth new currency in a decade), in an attempt to slow the rate down.

BRITISH ANTARCTIC TERRITORY

STATUS: UK Territory (claim in abeyance)
AREA: 1,544,000 sq km (596,142 sq miles)
POPULATION: no permanent population

BRITISH INDIAN OCEAN TERRITORY

STATUS: UK Territory
AREA: 5,765 sq km (2,225 sq miles)
POPULATION: 2,000
LANGUAGE: English

BRUNEI

STATUS: Monarchy
AREA: 5,765 sq km
(2,226 sq miles)
POPULATION: 280,000
CAPITAL: Bandar Seri Begawan
LANGUAGE: Malay, English, Chinese
RELIGION: Sunni Muslim,
Buddhist, Christian
CURRENCY: dollar (ringgit)(BND)
ORGANIZATIONS: ASEAN, Comm, UN

The Sultanate of Brunei is situated on the northwest coast of Borneo. Its tropical climate is hot and humid with annual rainfall ranging from 2500 mm (98 inches) on the narrow coastal strip to 5000 mm (197 inches) in the mountainous interior. Oil and gas reserves, mostly offshore, are the basis of the Brunei economy. Half the oil and nearly all the natural gas (in liquefied form) are exported to Japan.

BULGARIA

STATUS: Republic
AREA: 110,994 sq km
(42,855 sq miles)
POPULATION: 8,443,000
CAPITAL: Sofia (Sofiya)
LANGUAGE: Bulgarian, Turkish, Romany,
Macedonian
RELIGION: Bulgarian Orthodox, Sunni Muslim
CURRENCY: lev (BGL)
ORGANIZATIONS: Council of Europe, EFTA,
OIEC, OSCE, UN

Bulgaria exhibits great variety in its landscape. In the north, the land from the plains of the Danube slope upwards into the Balkan mountains (Stara Planina), which run east-west through central Bulgaria. The Rhodope mountains dominate the west, with the lowlands of Thrace and the Maritsa valley in the south. Climate is continental with temperatures ranging from -5°C (23°F) in winter to 28°C (82°F) in summer. The economy is based on agricultural products, with cereals, tobacco, cotton, fruits and vines dominating. Wine is a particularly successful export. Nuclear power is the main domestic power source, however the reactors are becoming elderly and other sources of energy are being sought, in particular oil and gas in the Black Sea. The heavy industry sector, which thrived in close association with the former USSR, is declining.

BURKINA

STATUS: Republic
AREA: 274,200 sq km (105,869 sq miles)
POPULATION: 9,889,000
CAPITAL: Ouagadougou
LANGUAGE: French, Moré (Mossi), Fulani, Local languages
RELIGION: Traditional beliefs, Sunni Muslim, Roman Catholic
CURRENCY: CFA franc (W Africa) (OXF)
ORGANIZATIONS: ECOWAS, OAU, UN

Situated on the southern edge of the Sahara, Burkina, previously known as Upper Volta, is a poor, landlocked country with thin soils supporting savannah grasslands. Frequent droughts, particularly in the north, seriously affect the economy, which is mainly subsistence agriculture with livestock herding, and the export of groundnuts and cotton. There is virtually no industry. Some minerals are exported and manganese exports began in 1993.

BURMA (MYANMAR)

STATUS: Republic
AREA: 676,577 sq km (261,228 sq miles)
POPULATION: 45,555,000
CAPITAL: Rangoon (Yangon)
LANGUAGE: Burmese, Shan, Karen, Local languages
RELIGION: Buddhist, Sunni Muslim, Protestant, Roman Catholic
CURRENCY: kyat (BUK)
ORGANIZATIONS: Col. Plan, UN

Much of Burma (renamed Myanmar by its military leaders in 1989) is covered by tropical rainforest divided by the central valley of the Irrawaddy, the Sittang and the Salween rivers. The western highlands are an extension of the Himalaya mountains; hills to the east and south

are a continuation of the Yunnan plateau of China. The economy is based on the export of rice and forestry products. The irrigated central basin and the coastal region to the east of the Irrawaddy delta are the main rice-growing areas. Hardwoods, particularly teak, cover the highlands. There is potential for greater exploitation of tin, copper, gold, oil and natural gas deposits.

BURUNDI

STATUS: Republic
AREA: 27,835 sq km (10,747 sq miles)
POPULATION: 6,209,000
CAPITAL: Bujumbura
LANGUAGE: Kirundi (Hutu, Tutsi), French
RELIGION: Roman Catholic, Trad. beliefs, Protestant, Sunni Muslim
CURRENCY: Burundi franc (BIF)
ORGANIZATIONS: CEEAC, OAU, UN

This small central African republic is densely populated and one of the world's poorest nations. Although close to the equator, temperatures are modified because of altitude. Coffee is the main export, followed by tea, cotton and manufactured goods. The country has a history of ethnic fighting between the Hutu farming people, who make up 85 per cent of the population, and the Tutsi, originally pastoralists, who have dominated the army and the running of the country. Massacres of thousands of people in 1993-4 resulted from ethnic war, ignited by a Hutu election victory marking an end to 31 years of Tutsi domination.

CAMBODIA

STATUS: Monarchy
AREA: 181,000 sq km (69,884 sq miles)
POPULATION: 9,968,000

CAPITAL: Phnom Penh
LANGUAGE: Khmer, Vietnamese
RELIGION: Buddhist, Roman Catholic, Sunni Muslim
CURRENCY: riel (KHR)
ORGANIZATIONS: Col. Plan, UN

Cambodia, in southeast Asia, is mostly a lowland basin. Over 70 per cent of the country is covered by the central plain of the Mekong river. The climate is tropical, with average annual temperatures exceeding 25°C (77°F). Monsoon rainfall occurs from May to October. These provide ideal conditions for the country's rice production and fish harvesting. The economy has been damaged since the 1970s by almost constant civil war. Power shortages hamper industrial development, the roads are badly damaged and land mines buried in the countryside make farming hazardous.

CAMEROON

STATUS: Republic
AREA: 475,442 sq km(183,569 sq miles)
POPULATION: 12,871,000
CAPITAL: Yaoundé
LANGUAGE: French, English, Fang, Bamileke, many local languages
RELIGION: Trad. beliefs, Roman Catholic, Sunni Muslim, Protestant
CURRENCY: CFA franc (C Africa) (XAF)
ORGANIZATIONS: CEEAC, COMM, OAU, UN

Cameroon, in west Africa, is situated between the Gulf of Guinea in the south and the shores of Lake Chad in the north. In the south, coastal lowlands rise to densely forested plateaux, whereas further northwards savannah takes over, and aridity increases towards the Sahara. Oil products, once the main export, have declined in importance and now agricultural products account for most export revenue. Coffee, cocoa, bananas and avocados are the main cash crops. Mineral resources are underdeveloped but Cameroon is one of Africa's main producers of bauxite (aluminium ore) and aluminium is smelted at Edea.

CANADA

STATUS: Federation
AREA: 9,970,610 sq km (3,849,674 sq miles)
POPULATION: 29,248,000
CAPITAL: Ottawa
LANGUAGE: English, French, Amerindian
languages, Inuktitut (Eskimo)
RELIGION: Roman Catholic,
Protestant, Greek Orthodox, Jewish
CURRENCY: Canadian dollar (CAD)
ORGANIZATIONS: Col. Plan, Comm., G7, NAFTA,
NATO, OAS, OECD, OSCE, UN

Canada is the world's second largest country stretching from the great barren islands of the Arctic north to the vast grasslands of the central south, and from the Rocky Mountains in the west to the farmlands of the Great Lakes in the east. This huge area experiences great climatic differences but basically a continental climate prevails with extremes of heat and cold particularly in the central plains. The Arctic tundra of the far north provides summer grazing for caribou. Further south coniferous forests grow on the thin soils of the ancient shield landscape and on the extensive foothills of the Rocky Mountains. In contrast, the rich soils of the central prairies support grasslands and grain crops. The Great Lakes area provides fish, fruit, maize, root crops and dairy products; the prairies produce over 20 per cent of the worlds wheat; and the grasslands of Alberta support a thriving beef industry. Most minerals are mined and exploited in Canada with oil and natural gas, iron ore, bauxite, nickel, zinc, copper, gold and silver the major exports. Recently, diamonds have been discovered in the Northwest Territories. The country's vast rivers provide huge amounts of hydro-electric power but most industry is confined to the Great Lakes and St Lawrence margins. The principal manufactured goods for export are steel products, motor vehicles and paper for newsprint. The USA is Canada's main trading partner, taking 80 per cent of exports. Following a free trade agreement (NAFTA) in 1993 between the USA, Canada and Mexico, even closer economic ties will be made with the USA.

ALBERTA

STATUS: Province
AREA: 661,190 sq km (255,287 sq miles)
POPULATION: 2,672,000
CAPITAL: Edmonton

BRITISH COLUMBIA

STATUS: Province
AREA: 947,800 sq km (365,948 sq miles)
POPULATION: 3,570,000
CAPITAL: Victoria

MANITOBA

STATUS: Province
AREA: 649,950 sq km (250,947 sq miles)
POPULATION: 1,117,000
CAPITAL: Winnipeg

NEW BRUNSWICK

STATUS: Province
AREA: 73,440 sq km (28,355 sq miles)
POPULATION: 751,000
CAPITAL: Fredericton

NEWFOUNDLAND AND LABRADOR

STATUS: Province
AREA: 405,720 sq km (156,649 sq miles)
POPULATION: 581,000
CAPITAL: St John's

NORTHWEST TERRITORIES

STATUS: Territory
AREA: 3,426,320 sq km (1,322,910 sq miles)
POPULATION: 63,000
CAPITAL: Yellowknife

NOVA SCOTIA

STATUS: Province
AREA: 55,490 sq km (21,425 sq miles)
POPULATION: 925,000
CAPITAL: Halifax

ONTARIO

STATUS: Province
AREA: 1,068,580 sq km (412,581 sq miles)
POPULATION: 10,795,000
CAPITAL: Toronto

PRINCE EDWARD ISLAND

STATUS: Province
AREA: 5,660 sq km (2,185 sq miles)
POPULATION: 132,000
CAPITAL: Charlottetown

QUEBEC

STATUS: Province
AREA: 1,540,680 sq km (594,860 sq miles)
POPULATION: 7,226,000
CAPITAL: Quebec

SASKATCHEWAN

STATUS: Province
AREA: 652,330 sq km (251,866 sq miles)
POPULATION: 1,002,000
CAPITAL: Regina

YUKON TERRITORY

STATUS: Province
AREA: 483,450 sq km (186,661 sq miles)
POPULATION: 33,000
CAPITAL: Whitehorse

CANARY ISLANDS

STATUS: Spanish Territory
AREA: 7,273 sq km (2,808 sq miles)
POPULATION: 1,502,000
CAPITAL: Santa Cruz de Tenerife
LANGUAGE: Spanish

CAPE VERDE

STATUS: Republic
AREA: 4,033 sq km (1,557 sq miles)
POPULATION: 381,000
CAPITAL: Praia
LANGUAGE: Portuguese, Portuguese Creole
RELIGION: Roman Catholic, Protestant,
Traditional beliefs
CURRENCY: Cape Verde escudo (CVE)

ORGANIZATIONS: ECOWAS, OAU, UN

Independent since 1975, the ten inhabited volcanic islands of the republic are situated in the Atlantic 500 km (310 miles) west of Senegal. Rainfall is low but irrigation encourages growth of sugar cane, coffee, coconuts, fruit (mainly bananas) and maize. Fishing accounts for about 70 per cent of export revenue and all consumer goods are imported.

CAYMAN ISLANDS

STATUS: UK Territory
AREA: 259 sq km (100 sq miles)
POPULATION: 30,000
CAPITAL: George Town

CENTRAL AFRICAN REPUBLIC

STATUS: Republic
AREA: 622,436 sq km (240,324 sq miles)
POPULATION: 3,235,000
CAPITAL: Bangui
LANGUAGE: French, Sango, Banda,
Baya, Local languages
RELIGION: Protestant, Roman Catholic,
Traditional beliefs, Sunni Muslim
CURRENCY: CFA franc (C Africa) (XAF)
ORGANIZATIONS: CEEAC, OAU, UN

The republic is remote from both east and west Africa. It has a tropical climate with little variation in temperature. Savannah covers the rolling plateaux with rainforest in the southeast. To the north lies the Sahara Desert. Most farming is at subsistence level with a small amount of crops grown for export – cotton, coffee, groundnuts and tobacco. Hardwood forests in the southwest provide timber for export. Diamonds are the major export, accounting for over half of foreign earnings.

CHAD

STATUS: Republic
AREA: 1,284,000 sq km (495,755 sq miles)
POPULATION: 6,183,000
CAPITAL: Ndjamena
LANGUAGE: Arabic, French, local languages
RELIGION: Sunni Muslim,Traditional beliefs,
Roman Catholic
CURRENCY: CFA franc (C Africa) (XAF)
ORGANIZATIONS: CEEAC, OAU, UN

Chad is a vast state of central Africa stretching deep into the Sahara. The economy is based on agriculture but only the south, with 1,000 mm (39 in) of rainfall, can support crops for export – cotton, rice and groundnuts. Severe droughts, increasing desertification and border disputes have severely restricted development. Life expectancy at birth is still only 43 years. Salt is mined around Lake Chad where the majority of the population live.

CHANNEL ISLANDS

STATUS: UK Territory
AREA: 195 sq km (75 sq miles)
POPULATION: 147,000
CAPITAL: St Hélier (Jersey)
St Peter Port (Guernsey)

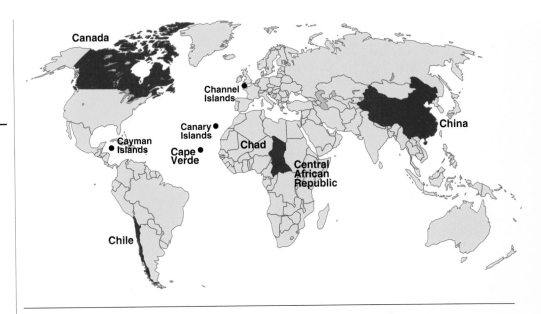

CHILE

STATUS: Republic
AREA: 756,945 sq km (292,259 sq miles)
POPULATION: 13,994,000
CAPITAL: Santiago
LANGUAGE: Spanish,
Amerindian languages
RELIGION: Roman Catholic,
Protestant
CURRENCY: Chilean peso (CLP)
ORGANIZATIONS: ALADI, OAS, UN

Chile is a long narrow country on the west coast of South America, stretching through 38° of latitude from the Atacama desert of the north to the sub-polar islands of Tierra del Fuego. Apart from a coastal strip of lowland, the country is dominated by the Andes mountains. Most energy is provided by hydro-electric power. The economy is based upon the abundance of natural resources with copper (the world's largest reserve), iron ore, nitrates, gold, timber, coal, oil and gas. Light and heavy industries are based around Concepción and Santiago. Traditional major exports are copper, fishmeal and cellulose. In the early 1990s farm production increased dramatically and food products now account for 29 per cent of export earnings.

CHINA

STATUS: Republic
AREA: 9,560,900 sq km (3,691,484 sq miles)
POPULATION: 1,208,841,000
CAPITAL: Beijing (Peking)
LANGUAGE: Chinese (Mandarin official), many
regional languages
RELIGION: Confucian, Taoist, Buddist,
Sunni Muslim, Roman Catholic
CURRENCY: yuan (CNY)
ORGANIZATIONS: UN

The land of China is one of the most diverse on Earth and has vast mineral and agricultural resources. The majority of the people live in the east where the economy is dictated by the great drainage basins of the Yellow River (Huang He) and the Yangtze (Chang Jiang). Here, intensively irrigated agriculture produces one-third of the world's rice as well as wheat, maize, sugar, cotton, soya beans and oil seeds. Pigs are reared and fish caught throughout China. The country is basically self-sufficient in foodstuffs.

Western and northern China are much less densely populated as cultivation is restricted to oases and sheltered valleys. In the southwest, the Tibetan plateau averages 4,900 m (16,000 ft) and supports scattered sheep herding. To the north are Sinkiang and the desert basins of Tarim (Tarim Pendi) and Dzungaria, and bordering Mongolia the vast dry Gobi desert. In the far north only in Manchuria does a more temperate climate allow extensive arable cultivation, of mainly wheat, barley and maize.

The natural mineral resources of China are immense, varied and under-exploited. The Yunnan plateau of the southeast is rich in tin, copper, and zinc; Manchuria possesses coal and iron ore; and oil is extracted from beneath the Yellow Sea. The main industrial centres concentrate on the production of iron, steel, cement, light engineering and textile manufacturing.

With a population of over one billion, China has made tremendous efforts since the late 1970s to erase the negative economic effects of the collectivization policy implemented from 1955, and the cultural revolution of the late 1960s. In 1978 the Chinese leader, Deng Xiaoping, launched an economic revolution (creating special economic zones and encouraging foreign investment). The country is now experiencing phenomenal economic growth, a new consumer revolution and waves of entrepreneurial activities. A growing inequality in living standards between the rural provinces and the richer urban areas has led to a surge of migrants from the countryside to the cities.

ANHUI (ANHWEI)

STATUS: Province
AREA: 139,000 sq km (53,668 sq miles)
POPULATION: 58,340,000
CAPITAL: Hefei

BEIJING (PEKING)

STATUS: Municipality
AREA: 16,800 sq km (6,487 sq miles)
POPULATION: 11,020,000

FUJIAN (FUKIEN)

STATUS: Province
AREA: 121,400 sq km (46,873 sq miles)
POPULATION: 31,160,000
CAPITAL: Fuzhou

GANSU (KANSU)

STATUS: Province
AREA: 453,700 sq km (175,175 sq miles)
POPULATION: 23,140,000
CAPITAL: Lanzhou

GUANGDONG (KWANGTUNG)

STATUS: Province
AREA: 178,000 sq km (68,726 sq miles)
POPULATION: 65,250,000
CAPITAL: Guangzhou (Canton)

GUANGXI ZHUANG (KWANGSI-CHUANG)

STATUS: Autonomous Region
AREA: 236,000 sq km (91,120 sq miles)
POPULATION: 43,800,000
CAPITAL: Nanning

GUIZHOU (KWEICHOW)

STATUS: Province
AREA: 176,000 sq km (67,954 sq miles)
POPULATION: 33,610,000
CAPITAL: Guiyang

HAINAN

STATUS: Province
AREA: 34,000 sq km (13,127 sq miles)
POPULATION: 6,860,000
CAPITAL: Haikou

HEBEI (HOPEI)

STATUS: Province
AREA: 187,700 sq km (72,471 sq miles)
POPULATION: 62,750,000
CAPITAL: Schijiazhuang

HEILONGJIANG (HEILUNGKIANG)

STATUS: Province
AREA: 454,600 sq km (175,522 sq miles)
POPULATION: 36,080,000
CAPITAL: Harbin

HENAN (HONAN)

STATUS: Province
AREA: 167,000 sq km (64,479 sq miles)
POPULATION: 88,620,000
CAPITAL: Zhengzhou

HUBEI (HUPEH)

STATUS: Province
AREA: 185,900 sq km (71,776 sq miles)
POPULATION: 55,800,000
CAPITAL: Wuhan

HUNAN
STATUS: Province
AREA: 210,000 sq km (81,081 sq miles)
POPULATION: 62,670,000
CAPITAL: Changsha

JIANGSU (KIANGSU)
STATUS: Province
AREA: 102,600 sq km (39,614 miles)
POPULATION: 69,110,000
CAPITAL: Nanjing (Nanking)

JIANGXI (KIANGSI)
STATUS: Province
AREA: 166,900 sq km (64,440 sq miles)
POPULATION: 39,130,000
CAPITAL: Nanchang

JILIN (KIRIN)
STATUS: Province
AREA: 187,000 sq km (72,201 sq miles)
POPULATION: 25,320,000
CAPITAL: Changchun

LIAONING
STATUS: Province
AREA: 147,400 sq km (56,911 sq miles)
POPULATION: 40,160,000
CAPITAL: Shenyang

NEI MONGOL (INNER MONGOLIA)
STATUS: Autonomous Region
AREA: 1,183,000 sq km (456,759 sq miles)
POPULATION: 22,070,000
CAPITAL: Hohhot

NINGXIA HUI (NINGHSIA HUI)
STATUS: Autonomous Region
AREA: 66,400 sq km (25,637 sq miles)
POPULATION: 4,870,000
CAPITAL: Yinchuan

QINGHAI (TSINGHAI)
STATUS: Province
AREA: 721,000 sq km (278,380 sq miles)
POPULATION: 4,610,000
CAPITAL: Xining

SHAANXI (SHENSI)
STATUS: Province
AREA: 205,600 sq km (79,383 sq miles)
POPULATION: 34,050,000
CAPITAL: Xian (Xi'an)

SHANDONG (SHANTUNG)
STATUS: Province
AREA: 153,300 sq km (59,189 sq miles)
POPULATION: 86,100,000
CAPITAL: Jinan

SHANGHAI
STATUS: Municipality
AREA: 6,300 sq km (2,432 sq miles)
POPULATION: 13,450,000

SHANXI (SHANSI)
STATUS: Province
AREA: 156,300 sq km (60,348 sq miles)
POPULATION: 29,790,000
CAPITAL: Taiyuan

SICHUAN (SZECHWAN)
STATUS: Province
AREA: 569,000 sq km (219,692 sq miles)
POPULATION: 109,980,000
CAPITAL: Chengdu

TIANJIN (TIENTSIN)
STATUS: Municipality
AREA: 11,300 sq km (4,363 sq miles)
POPULATION: 9,200,000

XINJIANG UYGUR (SINKIANG-UIGHUR)
STATUS: Autonomous Region
AREA: 1,600,000 sq km (617,763 sq miles)
POPULATION: 15,810,000
CAPITAL: Urumchi (Ürümqi)

XIZANG (TIBET)
STATUS: Autonomous Region
AREA: 1,228,400 sq km (474,228 sq miles)
POPULATION: 2,280,000
CAPITAL: Lhasa

YUNNAN
STATUS: Province
AREA: 394,000 sq km (152,124 sq miles)
POPULATION: 38,320,000
CAPITAL: Kunming

ZHEJIANG (CHEKIANG)
STATUS: Province
AREA: 101,800 sq km (39,305 sq miles)
POPULATION: 42,360,000
CAPITAL: Hangzhou

CHRISTMAS ISLAND
STATUS: Australian Territory
AREA: 135 sq km (52 sq miles)
POPULATION: 2,000

COCOS (KEELING) ISLANDS
STATUS: Australian Territory
AREA: 14 sq km (5 sq miles)
POPULATION: 1,000

COLOMBIA
STATUS: Republic
AREA: 1,141,748 (440,831 sq miles)
POPULATION: 34,520,000
CAPITAL: Bogotá
LANGUAGE: Spanish,
Amerindian languages
RELIGION: Roman Catholic,
Protestant
CURRENCY: Colombian peso (COP)
ORGANIZATIONS: ALADI, OAS, UN

Colombia is bounded by both the Caribbean Sea and Pacific Ocean. The northernmost peaks of the Andes chain runs from north to south through its western half and the eastern plains, beyond the Andes, contain the headwaters of the Amazon and Orinoco rivers. Almost half of Colombia is covered by the Amazon jungle. Colombia has a tropical climate and temperatures that vary with climate. The fertile river valleys in the uplands produce most of the famous Colombian coffee. Bananas, tobacco, cotton, sugar and rice are grown at lower altitudes. Coffee has always been the major export crop, but manufacturing industry and oil, coal, gold and precious stones are becoming more dominant in the economy. An oil boom is predicted following the discovery of new oil fields at Cusiana and Cupiagua. Immense illegal quantities of cocaine are exported to the US and elsewhere.

COMOROS
STATUS: Republic
AREA: 1,862 sq km (719 sq miles)
POPULATION: 630,000
CAPITAL: Moroni
LANGUAGE: Comorian,
French, Arabic
RELIGION: Sunni Muslim,
Roman Catholic
CURRENCY: Comoro franc (KMF)
ORGANIZATIONS: Arab league, AU, UN

The Comoro Islands, comprising Grand Comore, Anjouan, and Móheli, are situated between Madagascar and the east African coast. The climate is tropical and humid all year round, with a moderate average annual rainfall ranging from 1,000–1140 mm (40–45 inches). Less than half the land is cultivated and the country is dependent on imports for food supplies. The island's economy is based on the export of vanilla, copra, cloves and ylang-ylang essence (exported for the French perfume industry). Mangoes, coconuts and bananas are grown around the coastal lowlands. Timber and timber products are important to local development. There is no manufacturing of any importance.

CONGO
STATUS: Republic
AREA: 342,000 sq km (132,047 sq miles)
POPULATION: 2,516,000
CAPITAL: Brazzaville
LANGUAGE: French (official), Kongo,
Monokutuba, local languages
RELIGION: Roman Catholic, Protestant,
Traditional beliefs, Sunni Muslim
and Muslim minorities
CURRENCY: CFA franc (C Africa) (XAF)
ORGANIZATIONS: CEEAC, OAU, UN

The Congo, Africa's first communist state still has strong economic ties with the west, especially France, its former colonial ruler. Situated on the coast of west Africa, it contains over

two-thirds swamp and forest, with wooded savannah on the highlands of the Bateké plateau near the Gabon border. Its climate is hot and humid with average rainfall of 1220–1280 mm (48–50 inches). Over 60 per cent of the population is employed in subsistence farming, while sugar, coffee, palm oil and cocoa are all exported. Timber and timber products are major exports but the main source of export revenue is oil from offshore oilfields. Mineral resources are considerable, including industrial diamonds, gold, lead and zinc. Manufacturing industry is concentrated in the major towns and is primarily food processing and textiles.

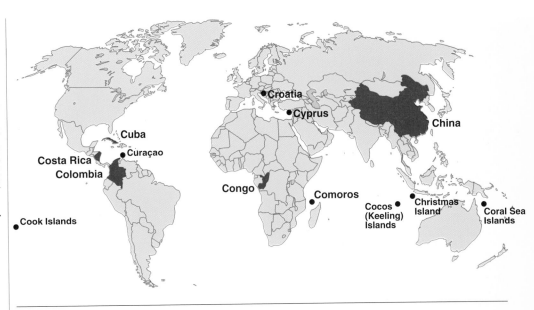

COOK ISLANDS

STATUS: New Zealand Territory
AREA: 293 sq km (113 sq miles)
POPULATION: 19,000
CAPITAL: Avarua on Rarotonga
LANGUAGE: English, Maori

CORAL SEA ISLANDS

STATUS: Australian Territory
AREA: 22 sq km (8 sq miles)
POPULATION: no permanent population

COSTA RICA

STATUS: Republic
AREA: 51,100 sq km (19,730 sq miles)
POPULATION: 3,011,000
CAPITAL: San José
LANGUAGE: Spanish
RELIGION: Roman Catholic, Protestant
CURRENCY: Costa Rican colón (CRC)
ORGANIZATIONS: CACM, OAS, UN

Costa Rica is a narrow country, situated between Nicaragua and Panama, with both a Pacific and a Caribbean coastline. Its coastal regions experience hot, humid, tropical conditions, but in upland areas its climate is more equable. The mountain chains that run the length of the country form the fertile uplands where coffee is grown and cattle are kept. Bananas, grown on the Pacific coast, and coffee are the major cash crops for export. Although gold, silver, iron ore and bauxite are mined, the principal industries are food processing and the manufacture of textiles and chemicals, fertilizers and furniture.

CROATIA

STATUS: Republic
AREA: 56,538 sq km (21,829 sq miles)
POPULATION: 4,504,000
CAPITAL: Zagreb
LANGUAGE: Serbo-Croat
RELIGION: Roman Catholic, Orthodox, Sunni Muslim
CURRENCY: kuna
ORGANIZATIONS: OSCE, UN

Croatia is an oddly shaped country which runs in a narrow strip along the Adriatic coast and extends inland in a broad curve. Its climate varies from Mediterranean along the coast to continental further inland. Once part of the Yugoslavian Federation, Croatia achieved recognition as an independent nation in 1992 following the 1991 civil war between Serb and Croat factions. The conflict left the country with a damaged economy, disruption of trade, loss of tourist revenue and a huge reconstruction bill. Traditionally the fertile plains of central and eastern Croatia have been intensively farmed, producing surplus crops, meat and dairy products. The mountainous and barren littoral has been developed for tourism. Croatia used to be the most highly developed part of Yugoslavia, concentrating on electrical engineering, metal working, machine building, chemicals and rubber. Economic recovery is dependent upon political stability and an accommodation with the Serbs over the UN-supervised areas still under ethnic Serb control.

CUBA

STATUS: Republic
AREA: 110,860 sq km (42,803 sq miles)
POPULATION: 10,960,000
CAPITAL: Havana (Habana)
LANGUAGE: Spanish
RELIGION: Roman Catholic, Protestant
CURRENCY: Cuban peso (CUP)
ORGANIZATIONS: OIEC, UN

Cuba, the largest of the Greater Antilles islands, dominates the entrance to the Gulf of Mexico. It consists of one large and over 1,500 small islands, and is a mixture of fertile plains, mountain ranges and gentle countryside. Temperatures range from 22–28°C (72–82°F) and an there is an average annual rainfall of 1,200 mm (47 inches). Sugar, tobacco and nickel are the main exports. Being a communist state, most of Cuba's trade has been with the former USSR and in the three years following the collapse of the Soviet Union the Cuban economy contracted by over 30 per cent (having lost its principal market for sugar, which it had bartered for oil, food and machinery). The economy was already suffering from US sanctions. Severe shortages of food, fuel and basic necessities were tolerated and in 1993 the government was forced to permit limited private enterprise and the use of American dollars.

CURAÇAO

STATUS: Netherlands Territory
AREA: 444 sq km (171 sq miles)
POPULATION: 143,816
CAPITAL: Willemstad

CYPRUS

STATUS: Republic
AREA: 9,251 sq km (3,572 sq miles)
POPULATION: 734,000
CAPITAL: Nicosia
LANGUAGE: Greek, Turkish, English
RELIGION: Greek (Cypriot) Orthodox , Sunni Muslim
CURRENCY: Cyprus pound (CYP),
ORGANIZATIONS: Comm., Council of Europe, OSCE, UN

Cyprus is a prosperous Mediterranean island. The summers are very hot (38°C or 100°F) and dry, and the winters warm and wet. About two-thirds of the island is under cultivation and citrus fruit, potatoes, barley, wheat and olives are produced. Sheep, goats and pigs are the principal livestock. Copper is mined but the mining industry is declining. The main exports are manufactured goods, clothing and footwear, fruit, wine and vegetables. Tourism is an important source of foreign exchange.

CZECH REPUBLIC

STATUS: Republic
AREA: 78,864 sq km
(30,450 sq miles)
POPULATION: 10,333,000
CAPITAL: Prague (Praha)
LANGUAGE: Czech, Moravian, Slovak
RELIGION: Roman Catholic,
Protestant
CURRENCY: Czech crown or koruna (CSK)
ORGANIZATIONS: Council of Europe,
OSCE, OIEC, UN

Following the break up of Czechoslovakia, the Czech Republic came into being in January 1993. It is a country that lies at the heart of central Europe and has a diversity of landscapes. In Bohemia, to the west of the country, the upper Elbe drainage basin is surrounded by mountains. Moravia, separated from Bohemia by hills and mountains, is a lowland area centred on the town of Brno. The climate is temperate but with continental characteristics. Rain falls mainly in spring and autumn. This is historically one of the most highly industrialized regions of Europe, whose heavy industry once specialized in producing arms for the Soviet Union. Now the main products include cars, aircraft, tramways and locomotive diesel engines. There are raw materials (coal, minerals and timber) and a nuclear power station is being built to replace some polluting coal-fired stations.

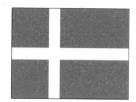

DENMARK

STATUS: Monarchy
AREA: 43,075 sq km (16,631 sq miles)
POPULATION: 5,205,000
CAPITAL: Copenhagen (København)
LANGUAGE: Danish
RELIGION: Protestant, Roman Catholic
CURRENCY: Danish krone (DKK)
ORGANIZATIONS: Council of Europe,
EEA, EU, NATO,
OECD, OSCE, UN

Denmark is the smallest of the Scandinavian countries. It consists of the Jutland Peninsula and over 400 islands of which only one quarter are inhabited. The country is low-lying with a mixture of fertile and sandy soils, generally of glacial origin. Climate is temperate, with rainfall all the year round. Denmark's economy stems traditionally from agriculture and dairy products; bacon and sugar are still particularly important. An extensive fishing industry is centred on the shallow lagoons along the western coastline. Danish North Sea oil and gas provide self-sufficiency in energy and gas exports began in 1991. Food processing, beer, pharmaceuticals and specialist biotechnological equipment contribute to the industrial sector which provides 75 per cent of Danish exports.

DJIBOUTI

STATUS: Republic
AREA: 23,200 sq km (8,958 sq miles)
POPULATION: 566,000
CAPITAL: Djibouti
LANGUAGE: Somali, French, Arabic,
Issa, Afar
RELIGION: Sunni Muslim,
Roman Catholic
CURRENCY: Djibouti franc (DJF)
ORGANIZATIONS: Arab League, OAU, UN

Situated at the mouth of the Red Sea, Djibouti consists almost entirely of low-lying desert. There are mountains in the north of which Musa Ālī Terara reaches 2,063 m (6,768 feet). Its climate is very hot all year with annual temperatures between 25–35°C (78–96°F). The annual rainfall is as low as 130 mm (5 inches). The land is barren so Djibouti's economy must rely on activities based on its deep natural port and position along a major shipping route. It therefore acts as a trade outlet for Ethiopia, as well as serving Red Sea shipping. Main exports are cattle and hides.

DOMINICA

STATUS: Republic
AREA: 750 sq km (290 sq miles)
POPULATION: 71,000
CAPITAL: Roseau
LANGUAGE: English, French creole
RELIGION: Roman Catholic, Protestant
CURRENCY: East Caribbean dollar (XCD)
ORGANIZATIONS: Caricom, Comm.,
OAS, UN

Dominica is located in the Windward Islands of the east Caribbean. It is mountainous and forested with a coastline of steep cliffs. Tropical rainforest covers nearly half of the island. The climate is tropical with average temperatures exceeding 25°C (77°F) and has abundant rainfall. Bananas are the major export, followed by citrus fruits, coconuts and timber. Coffee and cocoa production is developing. Tourism is the most rapidly expanding industry.

DOMINICAN REPUBLIC

STATUS: Republic
AREA: 48,442 sq km
(18,704 sq miles)
POPULATION: 7,769,000
CAPITAL: Santo Domingo

LANGUAGE: Spanish, French creole
RELIGION: Roman Catholic,
Protestant
CURRENCY: Dominican peso (DOP)
ORGANIZATIONS: OAS, UN

The Dominican Republic is situated on the eastern half of the Caribbean island of Hispaniola. The landscape is dominated by a series of mountain ranges, thickly covered with rainforest, reaching up to 3,000 m (9,843 feet). To the south there is a coastal plain where the capital, Santo Domingo, lies. Minerals, in particular nickel, are important but agricultural products account for 70 per cent of export earnings. The traditional dependence on sugar has diminished, with coffee, tobacco and newer products including cocoa, fruit and vegetables gaining importance.

ECUADOR

STATUS: Republic
AREA: 272,045 sq km (105,037 sq miles)
POPULATION: 11,221,000
CAPITAL: Quito
LANGUAGE: Spanish, Quechua,
Amerindian languages
RELIGION: Roman Catholic,
Protestant
CURRENCY: sucre (ECS)
ORGANIZATIONS: ALADI, OAS, UN

Ecuador falls into two distinctive geographical zones, the coastal lowlands which border the Pacific Ocean and inland, the Andean highlands. The highlands stretch about 400 km (250 miles) north-south, and here limited quantities of maize, wheat and barley are cultivated. Ecuador's main agricultural export, bananas, coffee and cocoa, are all grown on the fertile coastal lowlands. The rapidly growing fishing industry, especially shrimps, is becoming more important. Large resources of crude oil have been found in the thickly-forested lowlands on the eastern border and Ecuador has now become South America's second largest oil producer after Venezuela. Mineral reserves include silver, gold, copper and zinc.

EGYPT

STATUS: Republic
AREA: 1,000,250 sq km
(386,199 sq miles)
POPULATION: 58,326,000
CAPITAL: Cairo (El Qâhira)
LANGUAGE: Arabic,
French
RELIGION: Sunni Muslim,
Coptic Christian
CURRENCY: Egyptian pound (EGP)
ORGANIZATIONS: Arab league,
OAU, UN

The focal point of Egypt, situated on the Mediterranean coast of northeast Africa, is the fertile, irrigated Nile river valley, sandwiched between two deserts. Egypt is virtually dependent on the Nile for water as average rainfall varies between only 200 mm (8 inches) in the north and zero in the deserts. Cotton and Egyptian clover are the two most important crops, with increasing cultivation of cereals, fruits, rice, sugar cane and vegetables. Agriculture is concentrated around the Nile flood plain and delta. In spite of this, however, Egypt has to import over half the food it needs. Buffalo, cattle, sheep, goats and camels are the principal livestock. Tourism is an important source of revenue together with the tolls from the Suez Canal. Major industries include the manufacture of cement, cotton goods, iron and steel, and processed foods. The main mineral deposits are phosphates, iron ore, salt, manganese and chromium. Egypt has sufficient oil and natural gas reserves for its own needs and exports crude oil. Gas is now replacing oil in Egyptian power stations in order to release more crude oil for export.

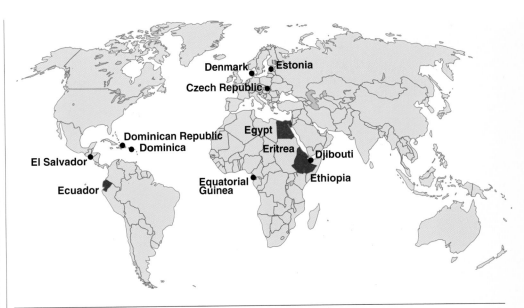

EL SALVADOR

STATUS: Republic
AREA: 21,041 sq km (8,124 sq miles)
POPULATION: 5,641,000
CAPITAL: San Salvador
LANGUAGE: Spanish
RELIGION: Roman Catholic,
Protestant
CURRENCY: El Salvador colón (SVC)
ORGANIZATIONS: CACM, OAS, UN

El Salvador is a small, densely populated country on the Pacific coast of Central America. Most of the population live around the lakes in the central plain. Temperatures range from 24–26°C (75–79°F) with an average annual rainfall of 1,780 mm (70 inches). Coffee provides about 50 per cent of export revenue. Other products include sugar, cotton, bananas and balsam. Industry has expanded considerably with the production of textiles, shoes, cosmetics, cement, processed foods, chemicals and furniture. Geothermal and hydro-electric resources are being developed and there are copper deposits as yet unexploited.

EQUATORIAL GUINEA

STATUS: Republic
AREA: 28,051 sq km (10,831 sq miles)
POPULATION: 389,000
CAPITAL: Malabo
LANGUAGE: Spanish, Fang
RELIGION: Roman Catholic,
Traditional beliefs

CURRENCY: CFA franc (C Africa) (XAF)
ORGANIZATIONS: CEEAC,
OAU, UN

Independent from Spain since 1968, Equatorial Guinea consists of two separate regions – a mainland area with a tropical, humid climate and dense rainforest but little economic development, and the volcanic island of Bioko. Agriculture is the principal source of revenue. Cocoa and coffee from the island plantations are the main exports with wood products, fish and processed foods manufactured near the coast on the mainland.

ERITREA

STATUS: Republic
AREA: 117,400 sq km (45,328 sq miles)
POPULATION: 3,437,000
CAPITAL: Asmara (Āsmera)
LANGUAGE: Tigrinya, Arabic, Tigre, English
RELIGION: Sunni Muslim, Coptic Christian
CURRENCY: Ethiopian birr
ORGANIZATIONS: OAU, UN

Eritrea gained formal recognition of its independence from Ethiopia in 1993. The landscape consists of an arid coastal plain, which borders the Red Sea, and the highlands of the central area, which rise to over 2000 m (6,562 feet). There are few natural resources, with what industry there is being concentrated around Asmara. The consequences of continuing drought and the protracted civil war will affect the population and economy for some time to come.

ESTONIA

STATUS: Republic
AREA: 45,200 sq km (17,452 sq miles)
POPULATION: 1,541,000

CAPITAL: Tallinn
LANGUAGE: Estonian, Russian
RELIGION: Protestant, Russian Orthodox
CURRENCY: kroon (EKR)
ORGANIZATIONS: Council of Europe,
OSCE, UN

With the mainland situated on the southern coast of the Gulf of Finland and encompassing a large number of islands, Estonia is the smallest and most northerly of the Baltic States. The generally flat and undulating landscape is characterised by extensive forests and many lakes. The climate is temperate. Agriculture, mainly livestock production, woodworking and textiles are also important. The economy is currently undergoing a transformation from central planning and state-ownership to a free market system based on private enterprise. Incorporated into the Soviet Union in 1940, Estonia regained its independence in 1991.

ETHIOPIA

STATUS: Republic
AREA: 1,133,880 sq km (437,794 sq miles)
POPULATION: 54,938,000
CAPITAL: Addis Ababa (Ādīs Ābeba)
LANGUAGE: Amharic (official), Oromo,
local languages
RELIGION: Ethiopian Orthodox, Sunni Muslim,
Traditional beliefs
CURRENCY: birr (ETB)
ORGANIZATIONS: OAU, UN

Ethiopia's landscape consists of heavily dissected plateaux and plains of arid desert. Rainfall in these latter areas is minimal and unreliable, and drought and starvation are ever-present problems. Farming, in the high rural areas, accounts for 90 per cent of export revenue with coffee as the principal crop and main export together with fruit and vegetables, oil-seeds, hides and skins. Gold is mined on a small scale. The most important industries are cotton textiles, cement, canned foods, construction materials and leather goods. These are concentrated around the capital. In recent years the economy has been devastated by almost constant civil war.

FAEROES

STATUS: Danish Territory
AREA: 1,399 sq km (540 sq miles)
POPULATION: 47,000
CAPITAL: Tórshavn
LANGUAGE: Danish, Faeroese

FALKLAND ISLANDS

STATUS: UK Territory
AREA: 12,170 sq km (4,699 sq miles)
POPULATION: 2,000
CAPITAL: Stanley

FIJI

STATUS: Republic
AREA: 18,330 sq km
(7,077 sq miles)
POPULATION: 771,000
CAPITAL: Suva
LANGUAGE: English, Fijian, Hindi
RELIGION: Protestant, Hindu,
Roman Catholic, Sunni Muslim
CURRENCY: Fiji dollar (FJD)
ORGANIZATIONS: Col. Plan, UN

A country of some 320 tropical islands, of which over 100 are inhabited, the Republic of Fiji is located in Melanesia, in the south-central Pacific Ocean. The islands range from tiny coral reefs and atolls to the two largest Vanua Levu and Viti Levu, which are mountainous and of volcanic origin. The climate is tropical with temperatures ranging from 16–33°C (60–90°F) and annual rainfall being 236 mm (60 inches). Fiji's economy is geared to production of sugar cane, which provides 45 per cent of export revenue. Coconuts, bananas and rice are grown and livestock raised. Main industries are sugar processing, gold-mining, copra processing and fish canning. Tourism is also an important revenue earner.

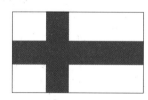

FINLAND

STATUS: Republic
AREA: 338,145 sq km
(130,559 sq miles)
POPULATION: 5,095,000
CAPITAL: Helsinki
LANGUAGE: Finnish, Swedish
RELIGION: Protestant,
Finnish (Greek) Orthodox
CURRENCY: markka (Finnmark) (FIM)
ORGANIZATIONS: Council of Europe,
EEA, EU, OECD,
OSCE, UN

Finland is a flat land of lakes and forests. Over 70 per cent of the land supports coniferous woodland with a further 10 per cent being water. The Saimaa lake area is Europe's largest inland water system. Its soils are thin and poor on ice-scarred granite plateaux. Most of Finland's population live in towns in the far south because of the harsh northern climate. In the north temperatures can range from -30°C (-22°F) in the winter to 27°C (81°F) in summer. The Baltic Sea can freeze for several miles from the coast during winter months. There is 600 mm (24 inches) of rain per annum throughout the country. Forestry products (timber, pulp and paper) once dominated the economy (80 per cent in 1980) but now account for 40 per cent of the export total and engineering, in particular shipbuilding and forest machinery, is almost equal in importance. Finland is virtually self-sufficient in basic foodstuffs. The country depends heavily on imported energy, producing only 30 per cent of its total consumption (20 per cent by its four nuclear power stations).

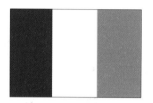

FRANCE

STATUS: Republic
AREA: 543,965 sq km (210,026 sq miles)
POPULATION: 57,747,000
CAPITAL: Paris
LANGUAGE: French, French dialects, Arabic,
German (Alsatian), Breton
RELIGION: Roman Catholic. Protestant,
Sunni Muslim
CURRENCY: French franc (FRF)
ORGANIZATIONS: Council of Europe, EEA, EU,
G7, NATO, OECD, OSCE, UN, WEU

France encompasses a great variety of landscapes, ranging from mountain ranges, high plateaux to lowland plains and river basins. The Pyrenees, in the southwest, form the border with Spain and the Jura mountains, in the west, form a border with Switzerland. The highest mountain range is the Alps, south of the Jura. The Massif Central is the highest of the plateaux, which also include the Vosges bordering the plain of Alsace, and Armorica occupying the granite moors of the Brittany peninsula. The French climate is moderated by proximity to the Atlantic, and is generally mild. The south has a Mediterranean climate with hot dry summers, the rest of the country has rain all year round (Paris has an average annual rainfall of 600 mm or 24 inches). Much of the French countryside is agricultural and it is estimated that one-third of the population derives an income from the land. France is self-sufficient in cereals, dairy products, meat, fruit and vegetables, and is a leading exporter of wheat, barley and sugar beet. Wine is also a major export. Over the past years there has been a steady drift of labour, mainly of younger people from the countryside to the industrialized areas. France is the fourth industrial power in the world after USA, Japan and Germany. It has reserves of coal, oil and natural gas, and is one of the world's leading producers of iron ore. It has large steel-making and chemical refining industries. Its vehicle, aeronautical and armaments industries are among the world's most important. Leading light industries are fashion, perfumes and luxury goods. Most of its heavy industry is concentrated in the major industrial zone of the northeast. In the past, sources of energy have been provided from its reserves of fossil fuels, however in recent years other sources have increased in importance, such as nuclear power using uranium from French mines, tidal power, and hydro-electricity. Tourism is an important source of income, that will be further encouraged by the opening of the Channel Tunnel.

FRENCH GUIANA

STATUS: French Territory
AREA: 90,000 sq km (34,749 sq miles)
POPULATION: 141,000
CAPITAL: Cayenne
LANGUAGE: French, French creole

FRENCH POLYNESIA

STATUS: French Territory
AREA: 3,265 sq km (1,261 sq miles)
POPULATION: 215,000
CAPITAL: Papeete
LANGUAGE:French, Polynesian languages

GABON

STATUS: Republic
AREA: 267,667 sq km (103,347 sq miles)
POPULATION: 1,283,000
CAPITAL: Libreville
LANGUAGE: French, Fang, Local languages
RELIGION: Roman Catholic, Protestant,
Traditional beliefs
CURRENCY: CFA franc (C Africa) (XAF)
ORGANIZATIONS: CEEAC, OAU, OPEC, UN,

Gabon, which lies on the equator, consists of the Ogooué river basin covered with tropical rain forest. It is hot and wet all year with average annual temperatures of 25°C (77°F). It is one of the most prosperous states in Africa with valuable timber (mahogany, ebony and walnut) and mineral (manganese and uranium) resources. State-run plantations growing oil palms, bananas, sugar cane and rubber are also important. Gabon's economy, however, is heavily dependent on its oil industry. It is the third largest producer in sub-Saharan Africa after Nigeria and Angola. France supplies nearly half the country's imports and French influence is evident everywhere.

GAMBIA, THE

STATUS: Republic
AREA: 11,295 sq km (4,361 sq miles)
POPULATION: 1,081,000
CAPITAL: Banjul
LANGUAGE: English (official), Malinke,
Fulani, Wolof

RELIGION: Sunni Muslim,
Protestant
CURRENCY: dalasi (GMD)
ORGANIZATIONS: Comm., ECOWAS, OAU, UN

The Gambia is the smallest country in Africa. An enclave within Senegal, it is 470 km (292 miles) long, averages 24 km (15 miles) wide and occupies land bordering the Gambia river. The climate has two distinctive seasons. November to May is dry but July to October sees monsoon rainfall of up to 1,300 mm (51 inches). The temperatures average about 23–27°C (73–81°F) throughout the year. Groundnuts and subsidiary products are the mainstay of the economy but tourism is developing rapidly. The production of cotton, livestock, fish and rice is increasing to change the present economic reliance on groundnuts.

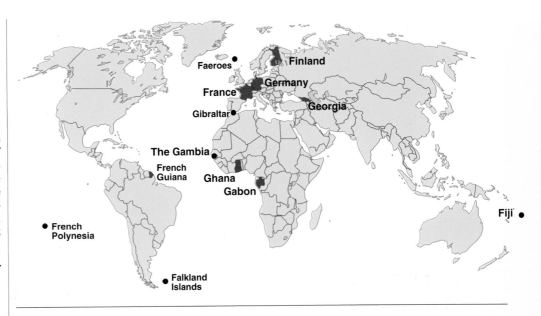

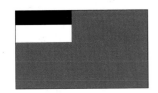

GEORGIA

STATUS: Republic
AREA: 69,700 sq km (26,911 sq miles)
POPULATION: 5,450,000
CAPITAL: Tbilisi
LANGUAGE: Georgian, Russian, Armenian,
Azeri, Ossetian, Abkhaz
RELIGION: Georgian Orthodox, Russian
Orthodox, Shi'a Muslim
CURRENCY: lari
ORGANIZATIONS: OSCE, UN

Georgia, covering part of the southern Caucasus, is a mountainous country with forests covering one-third of its area. The climate ranges from sub-tropical on the shores of the Black Sea, to perpetual ice and snow on the Caucasian crests. Rich deposits of coal are mainly unexploited. Cheap oil and gas imports, hydro-electric power and minerals, in particular rich manganese deposits, have led to industrialization successfully concentrated on metallurgy and machine-building. With the exception of the fertile plain to the east, agricultural land is in short supply and difficult to work. This is partly compensated by the cultivation of labour-intensive and profitable crops such as tea, grapes, tobacco and citrus fruit. The break-up of the Soviet Union brought independence for Georgia in 1991. The question of regional autonomy for the Abkhaz, Adzhar and South Ossetian minorities has repeatedly led to violent ethnic conflict in recent years, causing economic collapse.

GERMANY

STATUS: Republic
AREA: 357,868 sq km (138,174 sq miles)
POPULATION: 81,410,000
CAPITAL: Berlin
LANGUAGE: German, Turkish
RELIGION: Protestant, Roman Catholic
Sunni Muslim

CURRENCY: Deutsch-mark (DM)
ORGANIZATIONS: Council of Europe,
EEA, EU, G7, NATO,
OECD, OSCE, UN, WEU

Germany has three main geographical regions: the Northern plain, stretching from the rivers Oder and Neisse in the east to the Dutch border; the central uplands with elevated plateaux intersected by river valleys and relieved by isolated mountains, gradually rising to peaks of up to nearly 1500 m (5000 feet) in the Black Forest: finally the Bavarian Alps stradling the Austrian border. With exception of the Danube, all German river systems run northwards into the North or the Baltic Seas. The climate is mainly continental with temperatures ranging from -3°–1°C (27–34°F) in January to 16°–19°C (61°–66°F) in July. Only in the northwestern corner of the country does the climate become more oceanic in character. Germany on the whole has large stretches of very fertile farmland.

Politically, the division of Germany, a product of the post-1945 Cold War between the victorious Allies against Hitler, was rapidly overcome after the collapse of communism in Eastern Europe, and the unification of the two German states was effected in 1990. Economically, the legacy of 40 years of socialist rule in the East ensures that, in terms of both structure and performance, Germany will encompass two vastly different halves for a long time to come. Having lost its captive markets in what used to be the Soviet Bloc, the eastern economy then all but collapsed under the weight of superior western competition. The task of reconstruction is proving more difficult, more protracted and, most of all, more costly than expected. In the West, the Ruhr basin, historically the industrial heartland of Germany, with its emphasis on coal mining and iron and steel works, has long since been overtaken by more advanced industries elsewhere, notably in the Rhine-Main area and further south in the regions around Stuttgart and Munich. The rapidly expanding services sector apart, the German economy is now dominated by the chemical, pharmaceutical, mechanical engineering, motor and high-tech industries. To lessen the country's dependence on oil imports, an ambitious nuclear energy programme has been adopted. Although poor in minerals and other raw materials with the exception of lignite and potash, Germany has managed to become one of the world's leading manufacturers and exporters of vehicles,

machine tools, electrical and electronic products and of consumer goods of various description, in particular textiles. But the massive balance of trade surplus West Germany used to enjoy has now disappeared due to the sucking in of imports by, and the redistribution of output to, the newly acquired territories in the East.

GHANA

STATUS: Republic
AREA: 238,537 sq km (92,100 sq miles)
POPULATION: 16,944,000
CAPITAL: Accra
LANGUAGE: English (official), Hausa, Akan
Local languages
RELIGION: Protestant, Roman Catholic,
Sunni Muslim, Traditional beliefs
CURRENCY: cedi (GHC)
ORGANIZATIONS: Comm., ECOWAS, OAU, UN

Ghana, the west African state once known as the Gold Coast, gained independence from Britain in 1957. The landscape varies from tropical rainforest to dry scrubland, with the terrain becoming hillier to the north, culminating in a plateau averaging some 500 m (1,600 feet). The climate is tropical with the annual rainfall ranging from over 2,000 mm (79 inches) on the coast to less than 1,000 mm (40 inches) inland. The temperature averages 27°C (81°F) all year. Cocoa is the principal crop but although most Ghanaians farm, there is also a thriving industrial base around Tema, where local bauxite is smelted into aluminium. Tema has the largest artificial harbour in Africa. In recent years gold production has surged, Ghana having some of the world's richest gold deposits. Besides gold, Ghana's major exports are cocoa and timber. Principal imports are fuel, food and manufactured goods. Offshore oil has yet to be economically developed.

GIBRALTAR

STATUS: UK Territory
AREA: 6.5 sq km (2.51 sq miles)
POPULATION: 28,000

GREECE

STATUS: Republic
AREA: 131,957 sq km (50,949 sq miles)
POPULATION: 10,426,000
CAPITAL: Athens (Athínai)
LANGUAGE: Greek, Macedonian
RELIGION: Greek Orthodox, Sunni Muslim
CURRENCY: drachma (GRD)
ORGANIZATIONS: Council of Europe,
EEA, EU, NATO,
OECD, OSCE, UN, WEU

Greece is a mountainous country and over one-fifth of its area comprises numerous islands, 154 of which are inhabited. The climate is Mediterranean with temperatures averaging 28°C (82°F) in summer. The mountains experience some heavy snowfall during winter. Poor irrigation and drainage mean that much of the agriculture is localized. The main products of olives, fruit and vegetables, cotton, tobacco and wine are exported. The surrounding seas are important, providing two-thirds of Greece's fish requirements and supporting an active merchant fleet. Athens is the main manufacturing base and at least one quarter of the population lives there. Greece is a very popular tourist destination which helps the craft industries – tourism is a prime source of national income.

GREENLAND

STATUS: Danish Territory
AREA: 2,175,600 sq km (840,004 sq miles)
POPULATION: 58,000
CAPITAL: Nuuk (Godthåb)
LANGUAGE: Greenlandic, Danish

GRENADA

STATUS: Monarchy
AREA: 378 sq km
(146 sq miles)
POPULATION: 92,000
CAPITAL: St George's
LANGUAGE: English, Creole
RELIGION: Roman Catholic, Protestant
CURRENCY: E Caribbean dollar (XCD)
ORGANIZATIONS: Caricom, Comm., OAS, UN

The Caribbean island of Grenada, whose territory includes the southern Grenadines, is the most southern of the Windward Islands. It is mountainous and thickly forested, with a settled warm climate and an average temperature of 27°C (81°F). Rainfall varies with altitude, ranging from 760 mm (30 inches) to 3,560 mm (140 inches) on the higher ground. The island is famous for its spices and nutmeg is the main export. Cocoa and bananas are also important, together with some citrus fruits and vegetables. Tourism is important and continues to expand.

GUADELOUPE

STATUS: French Territory
AREA: 1,780 sq km (687 sq miles)
POPULATION: 421,000
CAPITAL: Basse-Terre
LANGUAGE: French, French Creole

GUAM

STATUS: US Territory
AREA: 541 sq km (209 sq miles)
POPULATION: 146,000
CAPITAL: Agaña

GUATEMALA

STATUS: Republic
AREA: 108,890 sq km
(42,043 sq miles)
POPULATION: 10,322,000
CAPITAL: Guatemala City (Guatemala)
LANGUAGE: Spanish, Mayan languages
RELIGION: Roman Catholic,
Protestant
CURRENCY: quetzal (GTQ)
ORGANIZATIONS: CACM, OAS, UN

The central American country of Guatemala has both a Pacific and a Caribbean coastline. The mountainous interior, with peaks reaching up to 4,000 m (13,120 feet), covers two-thirds of the country while to the north there is the thickly forested area known as the Petén. The northern lowland and the smaller coastal plains have a hot tropical climate, but the central highlands are more temperate. A rainy season lasts from May to October. Annual rainfall reaches up to 5,000 mm (200 inches) in some lowland areas but decreases to an average of 1,150 mm (45 inches) in the mountains. Agricultural products form the bulk of Guatemala's exports, notably coffee, sugar cane, cotton and bananas, but there is also a substantial industrial base. Manufacturing includes textiles, paper and pharmaceuticals. Mineral resources include nickel, antimony, lead, silver and in the north crude oil.

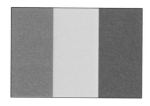

GUINEA

STATUS: Republic
AREA: 245,857 sq km
(94,926 sq miles)
POPULATION: 6,501,000
CAPITAL: Conakry
LANGUAGE: French, Fulani, Malinke,
Local languages
RELIGION: Sunni Muslim
Traditional beliefs, Roman Catholic
CURRENCY: Guinea franc (GNF)
ORGANIZATIONS: ECOWAS, OAU, UN

Guinea, a former French colony, is situated on the west African coast. Its drowned coastline, lined with mangrove swamps, contrasts strongly with its interior highlands containing the headwaters of the Gambia, Niger and Senegal rivers. Agriculture occupies 80 per cent of the workforce, the main exports being coffee, bananas, pineapple and palm products. Guinea has some of the largest resources of bauxite (aluminium ore) in the world as well as gold and diamonds. Bauxite accounts for 80 per cent of export earnings.

GUINEA-BISSAU

STATUS: Republic
AREA: 36,125 sq km
(13,948 sq miles)
POPULATION: 1,050,000
CAPITAL: Bissau
LANGUAGE: Portuguese,
Portuguese Creole, Local languages
RELIGION: Traditional beliefs, Sunni Muslim,
Roman Catholic
CURRENCY: Guinea-Bissau peso (GWP)
ORGANIZATIONS: ECOWAS, OAU, UN

Guinea-Bissau, on the west African coast, was once a centre for the Portuguese slave trade. The coast is swampy and lined with mangroves, and the interior consists of a low-lying plain densely covered with rain forest. The coast is hot and humid with annual rainfall of 2,000–3,000 mm (79–118 inches) a year, although the interior is cooler and drier. Eighty per cent of the country's exports comprise groundnut oil, palm kernels and palm oil. Fish, fish products and coconuts also make an important contribution to trade.

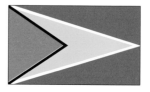

GUYANA

STATUS: Republic
AREA: 214,969 sq km
(83,000 sq miles)
POPULATION: 825,000
CAPITAL: Georgetown
LANGUAGE: English, Creole, Hindi,
Amerindian languages,
RELIGION: Protestant, Hindu, Roman Catholic,
Sunni Muslim
CURRENCY: Guyana dollar (GYD)
ORGANIZATIONS: Caricom, Comm., OAS, UN

Guyana, formerly the British colony of British Guiana, borders both Venezuela and Brazil. Its Atlantic coast, the most densely-populated area, is flat and marshy, while towards the interior the landscape gradually rises to the Guiana Highlands – a region densely covered in rainforest. The climate is tropical, with hot, wet and humid conditions, which are modified along the coast by sea breezes. Agriculture, dominated by sugar and rice, is the basis of the economy. Bauxite deposits provide a valuable export and in the mid-1990s gold production increased.

HAITI

STATUS: Republic
AREA: 27,750 sq km
(10,714 sq miles)
POPULATION: 7,041,000
CAPITAL: Port-au-Prince
LANGUAGE: French, French Creole
RELIGION: Roman Catholic,
Protestant, Voodoo
CURRENCY: gourde (HTG)
ORGANIZATIONS: OAS, UN

Haiti occupies the western part of the island of Hispaniola in the Caribbean. It is the poorest country in Central America. The country is mountainous with three main ranges, the highest reaching 2,680 m (8,793 feet). Agriculture is restricted to the plains which divide the ranges. The climate is tropical. Ninety per cent of the workforce are farmers and traditional exports have been coffee, sugar, cotton, and cocoa. In the early to mid-1990s national poverty worsened as a result of UN embargoes imposed against an illegal military regime. Thousands of Haitians fled the country. New sanctions in 1994 threatened to bring an end to all manufacturing and exporting activities.

HEARD AND McDONALD ISLANDS

STATUS: Australian Territory
AREA: 412 sq km (159 sq miles)
POPULATION: no permanent population
CAPITAL: Edmonton

HONDURAS

STATUS: Republic
AREA: 112,088 sq km
(43,277 sq miles)
POPULATION: 5,770,000
CAPITAL: Tegucigalpa
LANGUAGE: Spanish, Amerindian languages
RELIGION: Roman Catholic, Protestant
CURRENCY: lempira (HNL)
ORGANIZATIONS: CACM, OAS, UN

The central American republic of Honduras is a poor, sparsely populated country which consists substantially of rugged mountains and high plateaux with, on the Caribbean coast, an area of hot and humid plains, densely covered with tropical vegetation. These low-lying plains are subject to high annual rainfall, averaging 2,500 mm (98 inches), and it is in this region that bananas and coffee, accounting for over half the nation's exports, are grown. Other crops include sugar, rice, maize, beans and tobacco. There has been growth in new products such as shrimps, melons and tomatoes. Most industries are concerned with processing local products. Lead and zinc are exported.

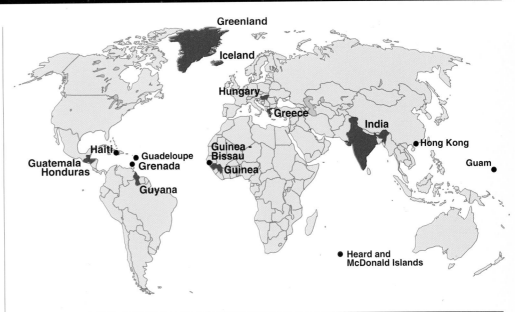

HONG KONG

STATUS: UK Territory
AREA: 1,075 sq km (415 sq miles)
POPULATION: 6,061,000

HUNGARY

STATUS: Republic
AREA: 93,030 sq km (35,919 sq miles)
POPULATION: 10,261,000
CAPITAL: Budapest
LANGUAGE: Hungarian, Romany,
German, Slovak
RELIGION: Roman Catholic,
Protestant
CURRENCY: forint (HUF)
ORGANIZATIONS: Council of Europe, OIEC,
OSCE, UN

Hungary is situated in the heartland of Europe. Its geomorphology consists mainly of undulating fertile plains with the highest terrain in the northeast of the country. The country is bisected north to south by the Danube. It has a humid continental climate, with warm summers that can become very hot on the plains, averaging 20°C (68°F), and cold winters, averaging 0°C (32°F). There is an annual rainfall of 500–750 mm (20–30 inches). Bauxite is Hungary's only substantial mineral resource, and less than 15 per cent of the gross national product is now derived from agriculture. The massive drive for industrialization has fundamentally transformed the structure of the economy since 1945. Both capital and consumer goods industries were developed, and during the 1980s engineering accounted for more than half the total industrial output. After a series of more or less unsuccessful attempts to introduce market elements into what essentially remained a centrally planned and largely state-owned economy, the communist regime finally gave up in 1989/90. However, their democratically elected successors have yet to prove that privatization and free competition will eventually bring general prosperity as well as political stability to what is now a profoundly troubled society.

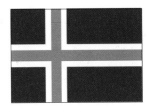

ICELAND

STATUS: Republic
AREA: 102,820 sq km (39,699 sq miles)
POPULATION: 266,000
CAPITAL: Reykjavík
LANGUAGE: Icelandic
RELIGION: Protestant, Roman Catholic
CURRENCY: Icelandic króna (ISK)
ORGANIZATIONS: Council of Europe,
EEA, EFTA, NATO,
OECD, OSCE, UN

One of the most northern islands in Europe, Iceland is 798 km (530 miles) away from Scotland, its nearest neighbour. The landscape is entirely volcanic – compacted volcanic ash has been eroded by the wind and there are substantial ice sheets and lava fields as well as many still active volcanoes, geysers and hot springs. The climate is mild for its latitude, with average summer temperatures of 9–10°C (48–50°F), and vegetation is sparse. Fishing is the traditional mainstay of the economy. An average of some 1,540,000 tonnes of fish are landed each year and 80 per cent of Iceland's exports consist of fish and fish products. Tourism is becoming an increasing source of income.

INDIA

STATUS: Republic
AREA: 3,287,263 sq km (1,269,219 sq miles)
POPULATION: 918,570,000
CAPITAL: New Delhi
LANGUAGE: Hindi, English (official),
many regional languages
RELIGION: Hindu, Sunni Muslim, Sikh,
Christian, Buddhist,
CURRENCY: Indian rupee (INR)
ORGANIZATIONS: Col. Plan, Comm., UN

Occupying most of the Indian subcontinent, India is second only to China in the size of its population. This vast country contains an extraordinary variety of landscapes, climates and resources. The Himalayas, in the north, are the world's highest mountain range with many peaks reaching over 6,000 km (19,685 feet). The Himalayan foothills, are covered with lush vegetation, water is in abundant supply (rainfall in Assam reaches 10,700 mm or 421 inches in a year) and the climate is hot, making this region a centre for tea cultivation. To the south lies the vast expanse of the Indo-Gangetic plain, 2,500 km (1,550 miles) east-west, divided by the Indus, Ganges and Brahmaputra rivers. This is one of the world's most fertile regions, although it is liable to flooding, and failure of monsoon rainfall (June to September) can result in severe drought. In the pre-monsoon season the heat becomes intense – average temperatures in New Delhi reach 38°C (110°F). Rice, wheat, cotton, jute, tobacco and sugar are the main crops. To the south lies the Deccan plateau, bordered on either side by the Eastern and Western Ghats, and in the northwest lies the barren Thar Desert. India's natural resources are immense – timber, coal, iron ore and nickel – and oil has been discovered in the Indian Ocean. There has been a rapid expansion of light industry, notably in the food processing sector, and the manufacturing of consumer goods. Nevertheless, 70 per cent of the population live by subsistence farming. Main exports by value are precious stones and jewelry, engineering goods, clothing, leather goods, chemicals and cotton. Tourism is a valuable source of revenue.

INDONESIA
STATUS: Republic
AREA: 1,919,445 sq km
(741,102 sq miles)
POPULATION: 193,017,000
CAPITAL: Jakarta
LANGUAGE: Indonesian (official),
many local languages
RELIGION: Sunni Muslim, Protestant, Roman
Catholic, Hindu, Buddhist
CURRENCY: rupiah (IDR)
ORGANIZATIONS: ASEAN, Col. Plan,
OPEC, UN

Indonesia consists of thousands of islands in equatorial southeast Asia which include Kalimantan (the central and southern parts of Borneo), Sumatera, Irian Jaya (the western part of New Guinea), Sulawesi (Celebes) and Java. The climate is tropical: hot (temperatures averaging 24°C or 75°F per year), humid and subject to monsoons. Most of its people live along the coast and river valleys of Java, leaving parts of the other islands virtually uninhabited. It is a Muslim nation and has the fourth largest population in the world. Over three-quarters of the people farm and live in small villages. Oil and gas, manufactured goods and coal are the chief exports. Indonesia is also a leading supplier of forest products, palm oil, rubber, spices, tobacco, tea, coffee and tin. With the use of modern techniques, the country has achieved self-sufficiency in rice.

IRAN
STATUS: Republic
AREA: 1,648,000 sq km (636,296 sq miles)
POPULATION: 59,778,000
CAPITAL: Tehran
LANGUAGE: Farsi (Persian), Azeri, Kurdish,
Regional languages
RELIGION: Shi'a Muslim,
Sunni Muslim, Baha'i,
Christian, Zoroastrian
CURRENCY: Iranian rial (IRR)
ORGANIZATIONS: Col. Plan, OPEC, UN

Iran is a large mountainous country north of The Gulf. The climate is one of extremes with temperatures ranging from -20–55°C (-4–131°F) and rainfall varying from 2,000 mm (79 inches) to almost zero. Iran is rich in oil and gas and the revenues have been used to improve communications and social conditions generally. The war with Iraq between 1980 and 1988 seriously restricted economic growth and particularly affected the Iranian oil industry in The Gulf. Oil is the source of 85 per cent of Iran's revenue and thus when world oil prices fall, as in the early–mid 1990s, the economy suffers. Agricultural conditions are poor, except around the Caspian Sea, and wheat is the main crop though fruit (especially dates) and nuts are grown and exported. The main livestock is sheep and goats. Iran has substantial mineral deposits relatively underdeveloped.

IRAQ
STATUS: Republic
AREA: 438,317 sq km (169,235 sq miles)
POPULATION: 19,925,000
CAPITAL: Baghdad
LANGUAGE: Arabic, Kurdish, Turkmen
RELIGION: Shi'a Muslim, Sunni Muslim,
Roman Catholic
CURRENCY: Iraqi dinar (IQD)
ORGANIZATIONS: Arab League, OPEC, UN

Iraq is mostly desert, marsh and mountain, but there are substantial areas of fertile land between the Tigris and the Euphrates. The two great rivers join and become the Shatt al-Arab which flows into The Gulf. The climate is arid with rainfall of less than 500 mm (20 inches) and summers are very hot (averaging 35°C or 95°F). Iraq has a short coastline with Basra the only port. Light industry is situated around Baghdad, and there are major petro-chemical complexes around the Basra and Kirkuk oilfields. The war with Iran (1980–8) and the Gulf conflict (1991) wrecked the economy with exports of oil and natural gas, formerly accounting for 95 per cent of export earnings, severely restricted by sanctions. Meanwhile, Arabs living in the Tigris-Euphrates marsh regions are being deprived of their livelihood as the marshes are drained in government reclamation schemes.

IRELAND, REPUBLIC OF (EIRE)
STATUS: Republic
AREA: 70,282 sq km (27,136 sq miles)
POPULATION: 3,571,000
CAPITAL: Dublin (Baile Átha Cliath)
LANGUAGE: English, Irish
RELIGION: Roman Catholic, Protestant
CURRENCY: punt or Irish pound (IEP)
ORGANIZATIONS: Council of Europe, EEA, EU,
OECD, OSCE, UN

The Republic of Ireland, forming 80 per cent of the island of Ireland, is a lowland country of wide valleys, lakes and marshes, but with some hills of significance, such as the Wicklow Mountains, south of Dublin and Macgillicuddy's Reeks, in the southwest. The Irish climate is maritime and influenced by the Gulf Stream. Temperatures average 5°C (40°F) in winter to 16°C (60°F) in summer, with annual rainfall at about 1,400 mm (55 inches) in the west and half that in the east. There is much rich pastureland and livestock farming predominates. Meat and dairy produce is processed in the small market towns where there are also breweries and mills. Large-scale manufacturing, in which food processing, electronics and textiles have shown recent growth, is centred around Dublin, the capital and main port. The Irish Republic possesses reserves of oil and natural gas, peat and deposits of lead and zinc. A large zinc mine at Galmoy is expected to come into production in 1996.

ISRAEL
STATUS: Republic
AREA: 20,770 sq km (8,019 sq miles)
POPULATION: 5,383,000
CAPITAL: Jerusalem
LANGUAGE: Hebrew, Arabic, Yiddish, English
RELIGION: Jewish, Sunni Muslim,
Christian, Druze
CURRENCY: shekel (ILS)
ORGANIZATIONS: UN

Israel, in the eastern Mediterranean littoral, contains a varied landscape – a coastal plain, interior hills, a deep valley extending from the river Jordan to the Dead Sea, and the Negev semi-desert in the south. Efficient water management is crucial as two-thirds of rainfall, which falls mostly in the mild winters, is lost by evaporation. Fuel needs to be imported (mainly oil from Egypt). Economic development in Israel is the most advanced in the Middle East. Manufacturing, particularly diamond finishing, electronics and science based products are important, although Israel also has flourishing agriculture specializing in exporting fruit, flowers and vegetables to western Europe. The only viable mineral resources are phosphates in the Negev and potash from the Dead Sea.

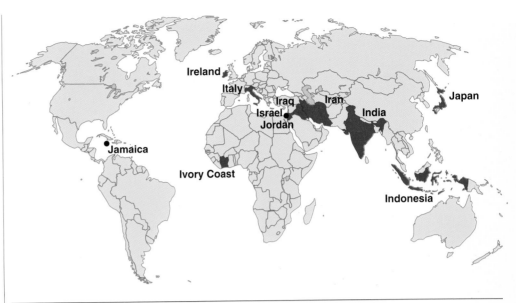

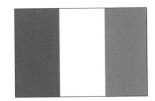

ITALY

STATUS: Republic
AREA: 301,245 sq km (116,311 sq miles)
POPULATION: 57,193,000
CAPITAL: Rome (Roma)
LANGUAGE: Italian, Italian dialects
RELIGION: Roman Catholic
CURRENCY: Italian lira (ITL)
ORGANIZATIONS: Council of Europe,
EEA, EU, G7, NATO,
OECD, OSCE, UN, WEU

Italy, separated from the rest of Europe by the great divide of the Alps, thrusts southeastwards into the Mediterranean Sea, in its famous boot-shaped peninsula. Including the large islands of Sicily and Sardinia, over 75 per cent of the land-scape is either hill or mountain. The north is dominated by the plain of the river Po rising to the high Alps. Further along the peninsula the Apennine mountains run from north to south. Climate varies with altitude, but generally there is a Mediterranean regime in the south; in the north the climate becomes more temperate. Agriculture flourishes with cereals, vegetables, olives, and cheese the principal products and Italy is the world's largest wine producer. Tourism is a major source of revenue. In spite of the lack of mineral and power resources, Italy has become a trading nation with a sound indus-trial base. Manufacturing of textiles, cars, machine tools, textile machinery and engineer-ing, mainly in the north, is expanding rapidly and accounts for nearly 50 per cent of the work force. This is increasing the imbalance between the north and south where the average income is far less per head, and where investment is lacking.

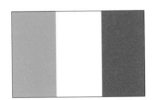

IVORY COAST (CÔTE D'IVOIRE)

STATUS: Republic
AREA: 322,463 sq km (124,504 sq miles)
POPULATION: 13,965,000
CAPITAL: Yamoussoukro
LANGUAGE: French (official), Akan,
Kru, Gur, Local languages
RELIGION: Traditional beliefs,
Sunni Muslim, Roman Catholic
CURRENCY: CFA franc (W Africa) (XOF)
ORGANIZATIONS: ECOWAS, OAU, UN,

Independent from the French since 1960, the Ivory Coast rises from low plains in the south to plateaux in the north. The climate is tropical with rainfall in two wet seasons in the south. Much of the population is engaged in subsis-tence agriculture. The two chief exports are cocoa and coffee. Other products include cot-ton, timber, fruit and tobacco. Gold mining began in 1990, diamonds are extracted and by 1995 the Ivory Coast is expected to become self-sufficient in oil and gas from the offshore fields.

JAMAICA

STATUS: Monarchy
AREA: 10,911 sq km
(4,244 sq miles)
POPULATION: 2,429,000
CAPITAL: Kingston
LANGUAGE: English, Creole
RELIGION: Protestant, Roman Catholic,
Rastafarian
CURRENCY: Jamaican dollar (JMD)
ORGANIZATIONS: Caricom, Comm., OAS, UN

Jamaica, part of the Greater Antilles chain of islands in the Caribbean, is formed from the peaks of a submerged mountain range. The cli-mate is tropical with an annual rainfall of over 5,000 mm (197 inches) on the high ground. There is a plentiful supply of tropical fruits such as melons, bananas and guavas. Principal crops include sugar cane, bananas, cocoa and coffee. Jamaica is rich in bauxite which, with the refined product alumina, is the main export. Major industries are food processing, textiles, cement and agricultural machinery. Since 1988 tourism has developed rapidly and is now the biggest single source of foreign earnings.

JAPAN

STATUS: Monarchy
AREA: 377,727 sq km
(145,841 sq miles)
POPULATION: 124,961,000
CAPITAL: Tokyo (Tōkyō)
LANGUAGE: Japanese
RELIGION: Shintoist, Buddhist,
Christian
CURRENCY: yen (JPY)
ORGANIZATIONS: Col. Plan, G7, OECD, UN

Japan consists of the main islands of Hokkaido, Honshu, Shikoku and Kyushu which stretch over 1,600 km (995 miles). The land is mountainous and heavily forested with small, fertile patches and a climate ranging from harsh to tropical. The highest mountain is Mt Fuji (Fuji-san) at 3,776 m (12,388 feet). The archipelago is also subject to monsoons, earthquakes, typhoons and tidal waves. Very little of the available land is cul-tivable. Most food has to be imported but the Japanese both catch and eat a lot of fish. The Japanese fishing fleet is the largest in the world. Japan is a leading economic power. Because of the importance of trade, industry has grown up around the major ports especially Yokohama, Osaka and Tokyo, the capital. The principal exports are motor vehicles, chemicals, iron and steel products and electronic, electric and opti-cal equipment. Japan relies heavily on imported fuel and raw materials and is developing the country's nuclear power resources to reduce this dependence. Production of coal, oil and natural gas is also being increased. In the early–mid 1990s, after four decades of phenomenal growth, industrial output declined as Japan experienced its worst recession for half a century.

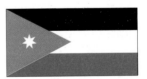

JORDAN

STATUS: Monarchy
AREA: 89,206 sq km
(34,443 sq miles)
POPULATION: 5,198,000
CAPITAL: Amman ('Ammān)
LANGUAGE: Arabic
RELIGION: Sunni Muslim, Christian,
Shi'a Muslim
CURRENCY: Jordanian dinar (JOD)
ORGANIZATIONS: Arab League, UN

Jordan, one of the few kingdoms in the Middle East, is mostly desert, but has fertile pockets. The climate is predominantly arid. Temperatures rise to 49°C (120°F) in the eastern valleys but it is cooler and wetter in the west. Fruit and veg-etables account for 20 per cent of Jordan's exports and phosphate, the most valuable min-eral, accounts for over 40 per cent of export rev-enue. Amman is the manufacturing centre, processing bromide and potash from the Dead Sea. Other important industries are food pro-cessing and textiles.

KAZAKHSTAN

STATUS: Republic
AREA: 2,717,300 sq km (1,049,155 sq miles)
POPULATION: 17,027,000
CAPITAL: Alma-Ata
LANGUAGE: Kazakh, Russian, German,
Ukrainian, Uzbek, Tatar
RELIGION: Sunni Muslim, Russian Orthodox,
Protestant
CURRENCY: tanga
ORGANIZATIONS: OSCE, UN

Stretching across central Asia, Kazakhstan is Russia's southern neighbour. Consisting of lowlands, hilly plains and plateaux, with small mountainous areas, the country has a continental climate with hot summers (30°C or 86°F in July) alternating with equally extreme winters. Exceptionally rich in raw materials, extractive industries have played a major role in the country's economy. Vast oil and gas reserves near the Caspian Sea are now being exploited. Rapid industrialization in recent years has focused on iron and steel, cement, chemicals, fertilizers and consumer goods. Although three-quarters of all agricultural land is used for pasture, the nomadic ways of the Kazakh people have all but disappeared. Economic development during the Soviet period brought a massive influx of outside labour which swamped the indigenous population. The proportion of Kazakhs employed in the industrial sector has, until recently, been small, but with the move to towns and better training, the balance is starting to be redressed. Since Kazakhstan's independence in 1991, its economic prospects appear favourable; but the Soviet legacy includes many environmental problems, such as the ruthless exploitation of the Aral Sea for irrigation.

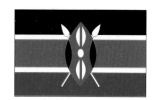

KENYA

STATUS: Republic
AREA: 582,646 sq km (224,961 sq miles)
POPULATION: 27,343,000
CAPITAL: Nairobi
LANGUAGE: Swahili (official), English,
many local languages
RELIGION: Roman Catholic, Protestant,
Traditional beliefs
CURRENCY: Kenya shilling (KES)
ORGANIZATIONS: Comm., OAU, UN

Kenya lies on the equator but as most of the country is on a high plateau the temperatures range from 10–27°C (50–81°F). Rainfall varies from 760–2,500 mm (30–98 inches) depending on altitude. Arable land is scarce but agriculture is the only source of livelihood for over three-quarters of the population. Tea, coffee, flowers and vegetables are the main products for export. Tea, however, has replaced coffee as the chief export and is second only to tourism as a source of foreign revenue. Manufacturing, centred at Nairobi and Mombasa, is dominated by food processing.

KIRGHIZIA
(KYRGYZSTAN)

STATUS: Republic
AREA: 198,500 sq km
(76,641 sq miles)
POPULATION: 4,596,000
CAPITAL: Bishkek
LANGUAGE: Kirghiz, Russian, Uzbek
RELIGION: Sunni Muslim, Russian Orthodox
CURRENCY: som
ORGANIZATIONS: OSCE, UN

Located in the heart of Asia, to the south of Kazakhstan, Kirghizia is a mountainous country. Traditionally an agrarian-based economy with stock-raising prevalent, the country underwent rapid industrialization during the Soviet period becoming a major producer of machinery and, more recently, producing consumer goods. Valuable mineral deposits include gold, silver, antimony, mercury with the gold deposits believed to be among the world's largest. The cultivation of cotton, sugar beet, tobacco and opium poppies is expanding and provides the basis for a growing processing industry. Independence came unexpectedly in 1991, although Kirghizia had long wanted to control its own affairs.

KIRIBATI

STATUS: Republic
AREA: 717 sq km (277 sq miles)
POPULATION: 77,000
CAPITAL: Bairiki
LANGUAGE: I-Kirbati (Gilbertese), English
RELIGION: Roman Catholic, Protestant,
Baha'i, Mormon
CURRENCY: Australian dollar (AUD)
ORGANIZATIONS: Comm.

Kiribati consists of 16 Gilbert Islands, eight Phoenix Islands, three Line Islands and Ocean Island. These four groups are spread over 5 million sq km (1,930,000 miles) in the central and west Pacific. The temperature is a constant 27°–32°C (80–90°F). The islanders grow coconut, breadfruit, bananas and babia (a coarse vegetable). Copra is a major export and fish, particularly tuna, accounts for one-third of total exports. Main imports are machinery and manufactured goods.

KOREA, NORTH

STATUS: Republic
AREA: 120,538 sq km (46,540 sq miles)
POPULATION: 23,483,000
CAPITAL: Pyŏngyang
LANGUAGE: Korean
RELIGION: Traditional Beliefs,
Chondoist, Buddhist,
Confucian, Taoist
CURRENCY: North Korean won (KPW)
ORGANIZATIONS: OIEC, UN

High, rugged mountains and deep valleys typify North Korea. Climate is extreme with severe winters and warm, sunny summers. Cultivation is limited to the river valley plains where rice, millet, maize and wheat are the principal crops. North Korea, rich in minerals including iron ore and copper, has developed a heavy industrial base. Industry has, however, since the early 1990s, been severely curtailed, firstly by the loss of Soviet aid following the break-up of the Soviet Union and then by losing imports through its isolationist policies and secretive nuclear industries. Its coal supplies, the main energy source for factories, are running out. Complete economic collapse is only salvaged by remittances from Koreans in Japan.

KOREA, SOUTH

STATUS: Republic
AREA: 99,274 sq km
(38,330 sq miles)
POPULATION: 44,453,000
CAPITAL: Seoul (Sŏul)
LANGUAGE: Korean
RELIGION: Buddhist, Protestant
Roman Catholic,
Confucian, Traditional beliefs
CURRENCY: won (KPW)
ORGANIZATIONS: Col. Plan, UN

The terrain of South Korea, although mountainous, is less rugged than that of North Korea. The flattest parts lie along the west coast and the extreme south of the peninsula. Its climate is continental, with an average temperature range of -5°C (23°F) in winter to 27°C (81°F) in summer. The majority of the population live in the arable river valleys and along the coastal plain. Agriculture is very primitive, with rice the principal crop. Tungsten, coal and iron ore are the main mineral deposits. Despite having to import oil and industrial materials, the country is a major industrial nation producing iron and steel, textiles, aircraft, chemicals, machinery, vehicles and, in recent years, specializing in electronics and computers. South Korea, with Japan, leads the world in ship-building.

KUWAIT

STATUS: Monarchy
AREA: 17,818 sq km (6,880 sq miles)
POPULATION: 1,620,000
CAPITAL: Kuwait City (Al Kuwayt)
LANGUAGE: Arabic
RELIGION: Sunni Muslim, Shi'a Muslim, other
Muslim, Christian, Hindu

CURRENCY: Kuwaiti dinar (KWD)
ORGANIZATIONS: Arab League, OPEC, UN

Kuwait comprises low, undulating desert, with summer temperatures as high as 52°C (126°F). Since the discovery of oil, Kuwait has been transformed into one of the world's wealthiest nations, exporting oil to Japan, France, the Netherlands and the UK since 1946. The natural gas fields have also been developed. Other industries include fishing (particularly shrimp), food processing, chemicals and building materials. In agriculture, the aim is to produce half the requirements of domestic vegetable consumption by expanding the irrigated area. The invasion and attempted annexation of Kuwait by Iraq in 1990–1 had severe effects on the country's economy, but by 1994 the oil industry was restored to its pre-Gulf war efficiency.

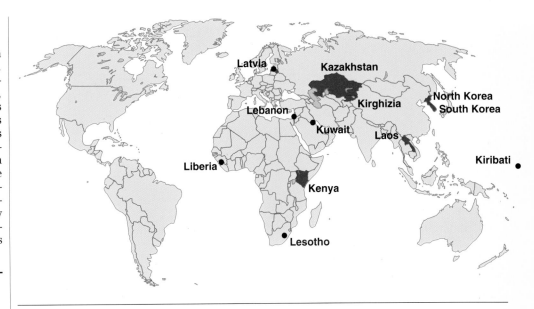

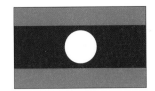

LAOS

STATUS: Republic
AREA: 236,800 sq km
(91,429 sq miles)
POPULATION: 4,742,000
CAPITAL: Vientiane (Viangchan)
LANGUAGE: Lao, local languages
RELIGION: Buddhist, Traditional beliefs,
Roman Catholic, Sunni Muslim
CURRENCY: kip (LAK)
ORGANIZATIONS: Col. Plan, UN

Laos is a landlocked, mostly mountainous and forested country in Indo-China. Temperatures range from 15°C (59°F) in winter, to 32°C (90°F) before the rains, and 26°C (79°F) during the rainy season from May to October. Most of the sparse population are subsistence farmers growing rice, maize, sweet potatoes and tobacco. Mineral resources include tin, iron ore, gold, bauxite and lignite. The major exports are coffee, tin and teak. Almost constant warfare since 1941 has hindered any possible industrial development, and Laos has become one of the world's poorest countries.

LATVIA

STATUS: Republic
AREA: 63,700 sq km (24,595 sq miles)
POPULATION: 2,548,000
CAPITAL: Riga
LANGUAGE: Latvian, Russian
RELIGION: Protestant, Roman Catholic
Russian Orthodox
CURRENCY: lat
ORGANIZATIONS: Council of Europe,
OSCE, UN

Latvia is situated on the shores of the Baltic Sea and the Gulf of Riga. Forests cover more than a third of the total territory, a second third being made up of meadows and marsh, and there are some 4,000 lakes. Farmland supports dairy and meat production and grain crops. The country

possesses no mineral resources of any value. Industrial development has been sustained by a massive influx of Russian labour since Latvia's incorporation into the Soviet Union in 1940. Under the Soviets, Latvia was assigned the production of consumer durables such as refrigerators and motorcycles as well as ships, rolling stock and power generators. Latvia regained its independence in 1991. The main industries are now radio engineering, electronics, engineering, instruments and industrial robots.

LEBANON

STATUS: Republic
AREA: 10,452 sq km
(4,036 sq miles)
POPULATION: 2,915,000
CAPITAL: Beirut (Beyrouth)
LANGUAGE: Arabic, French, Armenian
RELIGION: Shi'a, Sunni and other Muslim,
Protestant, Roman Catholic
CURRENCY: Lebanese pound (LBP)
ORGANIZATIONS: Arab League, UN

Physically, Lebanon can be divided into four main regions: a narrow coastal plain; a narrow, fertile interior plateau; the west Lebanon (Jebel Liban) and the Anti-Lebanon (Jebel esh Sharqi) mountains. It has a Mediterranean climate. Trade and tourism have been severely affected by civil war for 17 years from 1975. Agriculture accounts for nearly half of employment and cement, fertilisers, jewelry, sugar and tobacco products are all manufactured on a small scale.

LESOTHO

STATUS: Monarchy
AREA: 30,355 sq km (11,720 sq miles)

POPULATION: 1,996,000
CAPITAL: Maseru
LANGUAGE: Sesotho, English, Zulu
RELIGION: Roman Catholic, Protestant,
Traditional beliefs
CURRENCY: loti (LSL)
ORGANIZATIONS: Comm., OAU, SADC, UN

Lesotho, formerly Basutoland, is completely encircled by South Africa. This small country is rugged and mountainous, with southern Africa's highest mountain, Thabana Ntlenyana (3,482 m or 11,424 feet) to be found in the east of the Drakensberg. From these peaks the land slopes westwards in the form of dissected plateaux. The climate is generally sub-tropical although influenced by altitude; rainfall, sometimes variable, falls mainly in the summer months. Because of the terrain, agriculture is limited to the lowlands and foothills. Sorghum, wheat, barley, maize, oats and legumes are the main crops. Cattle, sheep and goats graze on the highlands.

LIBERIA

STATUS: Republic
AREA: 111,369 sq km (43,000 sq miles)
POPULATION: 2,941,000
CAPITAL: Monrovia
LANGUAGE: English,Creole,
many local languages
RELIGION: Traditional beliefs, Sunni Muslim,
Protestant, Roman Catholic
CURRENCY: Liberian dollar (LRD)
ORGANIZATIONS: ECOWAS, OAU, UN

The west African republic of Liberia is the only nation in Africa never to have been ruled by a foreign power. The hot and humid coastal plain with its savannah vegetation and mangrove swamps rises gently towards the Guinea Highlands, and the interior is densely covered by tropical rainforest. Until the civil war, which ravaged the country, broke out in 1989 the country enjoyed some prosperity from its rubber plantations, rich iron ore deposits, diamonds and gold. Liberia has the world's largest merchant fleet due to its flag of convenience register and this is the only source of revenue relatively unscathed by the war.

LIBYA

STATUS: Republic
AREA: 1,759,540 sq km (679,362 sq miles)
POPULATION: 5,225,000
CAPITAL: Tripoli (Ṭarābulus)
LANGUAGE: Arabic, Berber
RELIGION: Sunni Muslim, Roman Catholic
CURRENCY: Libyan dinar (LYD)
ORGANIZATIONS: Arab League, OAU,
OPEC, UN

Libya is situated on the lowlands of north Africa which rise southwards from the Mediterranean Sea. Ninety-five per cent of its territory is hot, dry desert or semi-desert with average rainfall of less then 130 mm (5 inches). The coastal plains, however, have a more moist Mediterranean climate with annual rainfall of around 200–610 mm (8–24 inches). In these areas, a wide range of crops are cultivated including grapes, groundnuts, oranges, wheat and barley. Only 30 years ago Libya was classed as one of the world's poorest nations but the exploitation of oil has transformed Libya's economy and now accounts for over 95 per cent of its exports.

LIECHTENSTEIN

STATUS: Monarchy
AREA: 160 sq km (62 sq miles)
POPULATION: 30,000
CAPITAL: Vaduz
LANGUAGE: German
RELIGION: Roman Catholic, Protestant
CURRENCY: franken (Swiss franc)(CHF)
ORGANIZATIONS Council of Europe,
OSCE, UN

Situated in the central Alps between Switzerland and Austria, Liechtenstein is one of the smallest states in Europe. Its territory is divided into two zones – the flood plains of the Rhine to the north and Alpine mountain ranges to the southeast, where cattle are reared. Liechtenstein's other main sources of revenue comprise light industry, chiefly the manufacture of precision instruments, and also textile production, food products, tourism, postage stamps and a fast -growing banking sector.

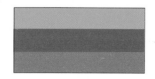

LITHUANIA

STATUS: Republic
AREA: 65,200 sq km (25,174 sq miles)
POPULATION: 3,721,000
CAPITAL: Vilnius
LANGUAGE: Lithuanian, Russian, Polish

RELIGION: Roman Catholic, Protestant,
Russian Orthodox
CURRENCY: litas
ORGANIZATIONS: Council of Europe, OSCE, UN

Lithuania is one of the three small ex-Soviet states lying on the shores of the Baltic Sea. The country consists of a low-lying plain with many lakes. Its climate is transitional, ranging between the oceanic type of western Europe and continental conditions. Temperatures range between -5– -3°C (24–28°F) in winter to 17– 18°C (62–66°F) in summer. There is on average 510 mm–610 mm (20–24 inches) of rainfall per year. Agriculture is dominated by beef and dairy produce; major crops are potatoes and flax. There is a large fishing industry. Industrial products include paper, chemicals, electronics and electrical goods. After almost 50 years' involuntary incorporation into the Soviet Union, Lithuania regained its independence in 1991. The economy is still linked to ex-Soviet countries and the change to a market economy is slow.

LUXEMBOURG

STATUS: Monarchy
AREA: 2,586 sq km (998 sq miles)
POPULATION: 401,000
CAPITAL: Luxembourg
LANGUAGE: Letzeburgish (Luxembourgian),
German, French, Portuguese
RELIGION: Roman Catholic, Protestant
CURRENCY: Luxembourg franc (LUF)
Belgian Franc (BEF)
ORGANIZATIONS: Council of Europe, EEA, EU,
NATO, OECD, OSCE, UN, WEU

The Grand Duchy of Luxembourg is situated between France, Belgium and Germany. The climate is mild and temperate with rainfall ranging from 700–1,000 mm (28–40 inches) a year. Just over half the land is arable, mainly cereals, dairy produce and potatoes. Wine is produced in the Moselle valley. Iron ore is found in the south and is the basis of the thriving steel industry. Other industries are textiles, chemicals and pharmaceutical products. Banking and financial services are growing sectors.

MACAU (MACAO)

STATUS: Portuguese Territory
AREA: 17 sq km (7 sq miles)
POPULATION: 398,000
CAPITAL: Macau
LANGUAGE: Chinese (Cantonese), Portuguese

MACEDONIA
Former Yugoslav Republic of,

STATUS: Republic
AREA: 25,713 sq km (9,928 sq miles)
POPULATION: 2,142,000

CAPITAL: Skopje
LANGUAGE: Macedonian, Albanian,
Serbo-Croat, Turkish, Romany
RELIGION: Macedonian Orthodox,
Sunni Muslim, Roman Catholic
CURRENCY: denar
ORGANIZATIONS: OSCE, UN,

The landlocked Balkan state of the Former Yugoslav Republic of Macedonia is a rugged country crossed from north to south by the Vardar valley. The climate is continental with fine hot summers but bitterly cold winters. The economy is basically agricultural. Cereals, tobacco, fruit and vegetables are grown and livestock raised. Heavy industries include chemicals and textiles, which are the county's major employers. Following a Greek economic blockade in 1994, heavy industry – which had already declined through the loss of markets in other former Yugoslav republics – suffered further collapse.

MADAGASCAR

STATUS: Republic
AREA: 587,041 sq km (226,658 sq miles)
POPULATION: 14,303,000
CAPITAL: Antananarivo
LANGUAGE: Malagasy, French,
RELIGION: Traditional beliefs, Roman Catholic,
Protestant, Sunni Muslim
CURRENCY: Malagasy franc (MGF)
ORGANIZATIONS: OAU, UN

Madagascar, the world's fourth largest island, is situated 400 km (250 miles) east of the Mozambique coast. The terrain consists largely of a high plateau with steppe and savannah vegetation and desert in the south. Much of the hot humid east coast is covered by tropical rainforest – here rainfall reaches 1,500–2,000 mm (59–79 inches) per annum. Although farming is the occupation of about 85 per cent of the population, only 3 per cent of the land is cultivated. Coffee and vanilla are the major exports, and the shellfish trade is growing rapidly. Much of Madagascar's unique plant and animal life are under increasing threat due to widespread deforestation, caused by the rapid development of forestry and soil erosion.

MADEIRA

STATUS: Portuguese Territory
AREA: 794 sq km (307 sq miles)
POPULATION: 253,000
CAPITAL: Funchal

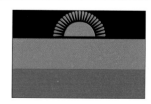

MALAWI

STATUS: Republic
AREA: 118,484 sq km (45,747 sq miles)
POPULATION: 10,843,000
CAPITAL: Lilongwe

LANGUAGE: English (official), Chichewa, Lomwe, local languages
RELIGION: Protestant, Roman Catholic, Traditional beliefs, Sunni Muslim
CURRENCY: kwacha (MWK)
ORGANIZATIONS: Comm., OAU, SADC, UN

Malawi is located at the southern end of the east African Rift Valley. The area around Lake Malawi is tropical and humid with swampy vegetation. In the highlands to the west and southeast conditions are cooler. Malawi has an intensely rural economy – 96 per cent of the population work on the land. Maize is the main subsistence crop, and tea, tobacco, sugar and groundnuts are the main exports. Malawi has deposits of both coal and bauxite, but they are under-exploited at present. Manufacturing industry concentrates on consumer goods and building and construction materials. All energy is produced by hydro-electric power.

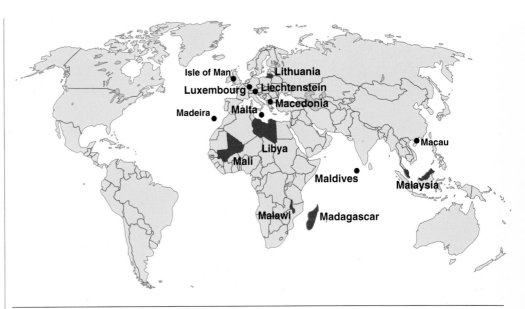

MALAYSIA

STATUS: Federation
AREA: 332,965 sq km
(128,559 sq miles)
POPULATION: 19,489,000
CAPITAL: Kuala Lumpur
LANGUAGE: Malay, English, Chinese, Tamil, local languages
RELIGION: Sunni Muslim, Buddhist, Hindu, Christian, Traditional beliefs
CURRENCY: Malaysian dollar or ringgit (MYR)
ORGANIZATIONS: ASEAN, Col. Plan, Comm., UN

The Federation of Malaysia consists of two separate parts; west Malaysia is located on the Malay Peninsula, while east Malaysia consists of Sabah and Sarawak on the island of Borneo 700 km (435 miles) across the South China Sea. Despite this distance, both areas share a similar landscape, which is mountainous and covered with lush tropical rainforest. The climate is tropical, hot and humid all the year round, with annual average rainfall of 2,500 mm (98 inches). At one time the economy was dominated by tin, rubber and timber. Now manufactured goods, in particular electronics, account for over two-thirds of the nation's exports in terms of value. Malaysia is rich in natural resources and other major exports include crude oil, timber, palm oil, pepper, rubber and tin. The fast-growing industrial sector demands increased power supplies which are being met by new power stations and hydro-electric power projects.

PENINSULAR MALAYSIA

STATUS: State
AREA: 131,585 sq km (50,790 sq miles)
POPULATION: 15,286,098
CAPITAL: Kuala Lumpur

SABAH

STATUS: State
AREA: 76,115 sq km (29,380 sq miles)
POPULATION: 1,470,902
CAPITAL: Kota Kinabalu

SARAWAK

STATUS: State
AREA: 124,965 sq km (48,235 sq miles)
POPULATION: 1,669,000
CAPITAL: Kuching

MALDIVES

STATUS: Republic
AREA: 298 sq km
(115 sq miles)
POPULATION: 246,000
CAPITAL: Male
LANGUAGE: Divehi (Maldivian)
RELIGION: Sunni Muslim
CURRENCY: rufiyaa (MVR)
ORGANIZATIONS: Col. Plan, Comm., UN

The Maldives are one of the world's poorest nations. They consist of a series of coral atolls stretching 885 km (550 miles) across the Indian Ocean. Although there are 2,000 islands, only about 215 are inhabited. The main island, Male, is only 1½ miles long. Fishing is the main activity and fish and coconut fibre are both exported. Most staple foods have to be imported but coconuts, millet, cassava, yams and fruit are grown locally. Tourism is developing and this is now the main source of revenue.

MALI

STATUS: Republic
AREA: 1,240,140 sq km (478,821 sq miles)
POPULATION: 10,462,000
CAPITAL: Bamako
LANGUAGE: French, Bambara, many local languages
RELIGION: Sunni Muslim,

Traditional beliefs, Roman Catholic
CURRENCY: CFA franc (W Africa) (XOF)
ORGANIZATIONS: ECOWAS, OAU, UN

Mali is one of the world's most underdeveloped countries. Over half the area is barren desert. South of Timbuktu (Tombouctou) the savannah-covered plains support a wide variety of wildlife. Most of the population live in the Niger valley and grow cotton, oil seeds and groundnuts. Fishing is important. Mali has few mineral resources, although a gold mine opened in 1994. Droughts have taken their toll of livestock and agriculture. Main exports are cotton, groundnuts and livestock.

MALTA

STATUS: Republic
AREA: 316 sq km (122 sq miles)
POPULATION: 364,000
CAPITAL: Valletta
LANGUAGE: Maltese, English
RELIGION: Roman Catholic
CURRENCY: Maltese lira (MTL)
ORGANIZATIONS: Comm., Council of Europe, OSCE, UN

Malta lies about 96 km (60 miles) south of Sicily, and consists of three islands; Malta, Gozo and Comino. It has a Mediterranean climate with summer temperatures averaging 25°C (77°F). About 40 per cent of the land is under cultivation with wheat, potatoes, tomatoes and vines the main crops. The large natural harbour at Valletta has made it a major transit port, and shipbuilding and repair are traditional industries. Principal exports are machinery, beverages, tobacco, flowers, wine, leather goods and potatoes. Tourism and light manufacturing are booming sectors of the economy.

MAN, ISLE OF

STATUS: UK Territory
AREA: 572 sq km (221 sq miles)
POPULATION: 73,000
CAPITAL: Douglas

MARSHALL ISLANDS

STATUS: Republic
AREA: 181 sq km
(70 sq miles)
POPULATION: 52,000
CAPITAL: Dalap-Uliga-Darrit
LANGUAGE: Marshallese, English
RELIGION: Protestant, Roman Catholic
CURRENCY: US dollar (USD)
ORGANIZATIONS: UN

The Marshall Islands, formerly UN Trust Territory under US administration, consist of over 1,000 atolls and islands which in total account for only 181 sq km (70 sq miles) but are spread over a wide area of the Pacific. The climate is hot all year round with a heavy rainfall averaging 4,050 mm (160 inches). Fishing, subsistence farming and tourism provide occupation for most. The economy is heavily dependent on grants from the USA for use of the islands as military bases.

MARTINIQUE

STATUS: French Territory
AREA: 1,079 sq km (417 sq miles)
POPULATION: 375,000
CAPITAL: Fort-de-France
LANGUAGE: French, French Creole

MAURITANIA

STATUS: Republic
AREA: 1,030,700 sq km
(397,955 sq miles)
POPULATION: 2,211,000
CAPITAL: Nouakchott
LANGUAGE: Arabic, French,
local languages
RELIGION: Sunni Muslim
CURRENCY: ouguiya (MRO)
ORGANIZATIONS: Arab League, ECOWAS,
OAU, UN

Situated on the west coast of Africa, Mauritania consists of savannah, steppes and vast areas of the Sahara desert. It has high temperatures, low rainfall and frequent droughts. There is very little arable farming except in the Senegal river valley where millet and dates are grown. Most Mauritanians raise cattle, sheep, goats or camels. The country has only one railway which is used to transport the chief export, iron ore, from the mines to the coast at Nouadhibou. Mauritania has substantial copper reserves which are mined at Akjoujt. A severe drought during the last decade decimated the livestock population and forced many nomadic tribesmen into the towns. Coastal fishing contributes nearly 50 per cent of foreign earnings. Exports are almost exclusively confined to iron ore, copper and fish products.

MAURITIUS

STATUS: Republic
AREA: 2,040 sq km
(788 sq miles)
POPULATION: 1,104,000
CAPITAL: Port Louis
LANGUAGE: English, French Creole, Hindi,
Indian languages
RELIGION: Hindu, Roman Catholic,
Sunni Muslim, Protestant
CURRENCY: Mauritian rupee (MUR)
ORGANIZATIONS: Comm., OAU, UN

Mauritius is a mountainous island in the Indian Ocean. It has a varied climate with temperatures ranging from 7–36°C (45–97°F) and annual rainfall of between 1,530–5,080 mm (60–200 inches). The economy of Mauritius once depended wholly on sugar. Although this is still important, with tea as a second crop, earnings from the manufacturing of clothing now surpass those from sugar. Tourism and financial services are also expanding.

MAYOTTE

STATUS: French Territory
AREA: 373 sq km (144 sq miles)
POPULATION: 110,000
CAPITAL: Dzaoudzi

MEXICO

STATUS: Republic
AREA: 1,972,545 sq km (761,604 sq miles)
POPULATION: 93,008,000
CAPITAL: Mexico City
LANGUAGE: Spanish,
many Amerindian languages
RELIGION: Roman Catholic, Protestant
CURRENCY: Mexican peso
ORGANISATIONS: ALADI, NAFTA, OAS, OECD, UN

Mexico consists mainly of mountain ranges and dissected plateaux. The only extensive flat lands are in the Yucatan Peninsula. Temperature and rainfall are modified by altitude – the north is arid but the south is humid and tropical. Mexico has one of the world's fastest growing populations and, with extreme poverty in many rural areas, migration to the cities continues to be prevalent. One-third of the land is used for livestock ranching and only 20 per cent farmed. Communal farms were abolished in 1991 and peasants are encouraged, with private ownership, to vary crops from the traditional corn and beans. Mexico has great mineral wealth, e.g. silver, strontium and gold, but much is still unexploited. There are considerable reserves of oil, natural gas, coal and uranium. Ten years ago petroleum products accounted for 70 per cent of exports. Now oil accounts for 30 per cent and the major exports are manufactured goods from

an industrial base of vehicle production, steel, textiles, breweries and food processing. Other exports are coffee, fruit, vegetables and shrimps. Tourism brings in important foreign revenue. Trading should be enhanced by Mexico's decision to join the USA and Canada in the North American Free Trade Association (NAFTA).

MICRONESIA
Federated States of,

STATUS: Republic
AREA: 701 sq km
(271 sq miles)
POPULATION: 121,000
CAPITAL: Palikir
LANGUAGE: English, Trukese, Pohnpeian,
local languages
RELIGION: Protestant,
Roman Catholic
CURRENCY: US dollar (USD)
ORGANIZATIONS: UN

Micronesia, a former UN Trust Territory administered by the USA, is a federation of 607 islands and atolls spread over some 3,200 km (2,000 miles) of the Pacific. Being near the equator, the climate is hot and humid all year round with a high annual rainfall of 9,300 mm (194 inches). Subsistence farming and fishing are the traditional occupations while income is derived from the export of phosphates and copper, a growing tourist industry and revenue from foreign fleets fishing within its territorial waters.

MOLDOVA

STATUS: Republic
AREA: 33,700 sq km (13,012 sq miles)
POPULATION: 4,350,000
CAPITAL: Chisinau (Kishinev)
LANGUAGE: Romanian, Russian,
Ukrainian, Gagauz
RELIGION: Moldovian Orthodox, Russian Orthodox
CURRENCY: leu
ORGANIZATIONS: Council of Europe, OSCE, UN

A country of hilly plains, Moldova enjoys a warm and dry climate with relatively mild winters. Temperatures range from 5–7°C (23–26°F) during winter , to 20–23°C (68°–72°F) for summer and rainfall averages 305–457mm (12–18 inches) per year. It has very fertile soil, so arable farming dominates agricultural output with viticulture, fruit and vegetables especially important. Sunflower seeds are the main industrial crop; wheat and maize the chief grain crops. Traditionally, food processing has been the major industry but recently light machine building and metal working industries have been expanding. Moldova, part of the Soviet Union between 1939 and 1991, has close ethnic, linguistic and historical ties with neighbouring Romania. Any moves towards re-unification have been fiercely resisted by the Russian minority in the eastern region of Trans-Dniester.

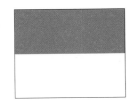

MONACO

STATUS: Monarchy
AREA: 1.95 sq km
(0.75 sq miles)
POPULATION: 31,000
CAPITAL: Monaco
LANGUAGE: French, Monegasque, Italian
RELIGION: Roman Catholic
CURRENCY: French franc (FRF)
ORGANIZATIONS: OSCE, UN

The tiny principality is the world's smallest independent state after the Vatican City. It occupies a rocky peninsula on the French Mediterranean coast near the Italian border and is backed by the Maritime Alps. The climate is Mediterranean. It comprises the towns of Monaco, la Condamine, Fontvieille and Monte Carlo. Most revenue comes from tourism, casinos, light industry and financial services. Land has been reclaimed from the sea to extend the area available for commercial development.

MONGOLIA

STATUS: Republic
AREA: 1,565,000 sq km (604,250 sq miles)
POPULATION: 2,363,000
CAPITAL: Ulan Bator (Ulaanbaatar)
LANGUAGE: Khalkha (Mongolian), Kazakh,
local languages
RELIGION: Buddhist, Sunni Muslim,
Traditional beliefs
CURRENCY: tugrik (MNT)
ORGANIZATIONS: OIEC, UN

Situated between China and the Russian Federation, Mongolia has one of the lowest population densities in the world. Much of the country consists of a high undulating plateau reaching 1,500 m (4,920 feet) covered with grassland. To the north, mountain ranges reaching 4,231 m (13,881 feet) bridge the border with the Russian Federation, and to the south is the vast Gobi desert. The climate is very extreme with January temperatures falling to -34°C (-29°F). Mongolia is predominantly a farming economy, based on rearing cattle and horses. Its natural resources include some oil, rich coal deposits, iron ore, gold , tin and copper. About half the country's exports originate from the Erdanet copper mine. The break-up of the Soviet Union in 1991 brought an end to a partnership whereby Mongolia supplied raw materials in exchange for aid. A year later communism was abandoned. The country is now forced to reform its economy, but is isolated and in need of investment.

MONTSERRAT

STATUS: UK Territory
AREA: 100 sq km (39 sq miles)
POPULATION: 11,000
CAPITAL: Plymouth

MOROCCO

STATUS: Monarchy
AREA: 446,550 sq km
(172,414 sq miles)
POPULATION: 26,590,000
CAPITAL: Rabat
LANGUAGE: Arabic, Berber,
French, Spanish,
RELIGION: Sunni Muslim,
Roman Catholic
CURRENCY: Moroccan dirham (MAD)
ORGANIZATIONS: Arab League, UN

One-third of Morocco consists of the Atlas Mountains, reaching 4,165 m (13,665 feet). Beyond the coastal plains and the mountains lies the Sahara. The north of the country has a Mediterranean climate with some winter rainfall, but elsewhere conditions are mostly desert like and arid. Agriculture has diversified in recent years and as well as tomatoes and citrus fruits exports now include a variety of fruit and vegetables. Morocco has considerable phosphate deposits, which in value account for a quarter of total exports. Manufacturing industries include textiles, leather, food processing and chemicals and a growing mechanical and electronic sector. Income from tourism and remittances from Moroccans abroad are the main sources of foreign revenue.

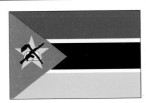

MOZAMBIQUE

STATUS: Republic
AREA: 799,380 sq km
(308,642 sq miles)
POPULATION: 15,527,000
CAPITAL: Maputo
LANGUAGE: Portuguese, Makua, Tsonga,
many local languages

RELIGION: Traditional beliefs,
Roman Catholic, Sunni Muslim
CURRENCY: metical (MZM)
ORGANIZATIONS: OAU, SADC, UN

The ex-Portuguese colony of Mozambique consists of a large coastal plain, rising towards plateaux and mountain ranges which border Malawi, Zambia and Zimbabwe. The highlands in the north reach 2,436 m (7,992 feet). The climate is tropical on the coastal plain, although high altitudes make it cooler inland. Over 90 per cent of the population are subsistence farmers cultivating coconuts, cashews, cotton, maize and rice. Cashew nuts and shrimps are the main exports. Mozambique also acts as an entrepôt, handling exports from South Africa, and landlocked Zambia and Malawi. Natural resources include large reserves of coal, also iron ore, copper, bauxite, gold and offshore gas, but most are unexploited.

NAMIBIA

STATUS: Republic
AREA: 824,292 sq km
(318,261 sq miles)
POPULATION: 1,500,000
CAPITAL: Windhoek
LANGUAGE: English, Afrikaans,
German, Ovambo, local languages
RELIGION: Protestant,
Roman Catholic
CURRENCY: Namibian dollar, SA rand
ORGANIZATIONS: Comm., OAU, SADC, UN

The southwest African country of Namibia is one of the driest in the world. The Namib desert, on the coast, has less than 50 mm (2 inches) average rainfall per year, the Kalahari, to the northeast, has 100–250 mm (4–10 inches). The vegetation is sparse. Maize and sorghum are grown in the northern highlands and sheep are reared in the south. Namibia, however, is rich in mineral resources, with large deposits of lead, tin and zinc, and the world's largest uranium mine. The rich coastal waters are the basis of a successful fishing industry.

NAURU

STATUS: Republic
AREA: 21 sq km
(8 sq miles)
POPULATION: 11,000
CAPITAL: Yaren
LANGUAGE: Nauruan, Gilbertese, English
RELIGION: Protestant, Roman Catholic
CURRENCY: Australian dollar (AUD)
ORGANIZATIONS: Comm. (special member)

Nauru, a small island only 19 km (12 miles) in circumference, is situated in the Pacific, 2,100 km (1,3000 miles) northeast of Australia. The flat coastal lowlands, encircled by coral reefs, rise gently to a central plateau. The country was once rich in phosphates which were exported to Australia and Japan. However these deposits will soon become exhausted.

NEPAL

STATUS: Monarchy
AREA: 147,181 sq km (56,827 sq miles)
POPULATION: 21,360,000
CAPITAL: Kathmandu
LANGUAGE: Nepali, Maithili, Bhojpuri, English,
many local languages
RELIGION: Hindu, Buddhist, Sunni Muslim
CURRENCY: Nepalese rupee (NPR)
ORGANIZATIONS: Col. Plan, UN

Nepal is a Himalayan kingdom sandwiched between China and India. Some of the highest mountains in the world, including Everest, are to be found along its northern borders. The climate changes sharply with altitude from the mountain peaks southwards to the Tarai plain. Central Kathmandu varies between 2–30°C (35–86°F). Most rain falls between June and October and can reach 2,500 mm (100 inches). Agriculture concentrates on rice, maize, cattle, buffaloes, sheep and goats. The small amount of industry processes local products, with carpets and clothing showing particular economic growth.

NETHERLANDS

STATUS: Monarchy
AREA: 41,526 sq km (16,033 sq miles)
POPULATION: 15,380,000
CAPITAL: Amsterdam
(seat of Government: The Hague)
LANGUAGE: Dutch, Frisian, Turkish,
Indonesian languages
RELIGION: Roman Catholic,

Protestant, Sunni Muslim
CURRENCY: guilder (NLG)
ORGANIZATIONS: Council of Europe, EEA, EU,
NATO, OECD, OSCE, UN, WEU

The Netherlands is exceptionally low-lying, with about 25 per cent of its territory being reclaimed from the sea. The wide coastal belt consists of flat marshland, mud-flats, sand-dunes and dykes. Further inland, the flat alluvial plain is drained by the Rhine, Maas and Ijssel. A complex network of dykes and canals prevents the area from flooding. To the south and east the land rises. Flat and exposed to strong winds, the Netherlands has a maritime climate with mild winters and cool summers. The Dutch are the leading world producers of dairy goods and also cultivate crops such as cereals, sugar beet and potatoes. Lacking mineral resources, much of the industry of the Netherlands is dependent on natural gas. Most manufacturing industry has developed around Rotterdam, where there are oil refineries, steel-works and chemical and food processing plants.

NETHERLANDS ANTILLES

STATUS: Netherlands Territory
AREA: 800 sq km (309 sq miles)
POPULATION: 197,000
CAPITAL: Willemstad

NEW CALEDONIA

STATUS: French Territory
AREA: 19,058 sq km (7,358 sq miles)
POPULATION: 178,000
CAPITAL: Nouméa

NEW ZEALAND

STATUS: Monarchy
AREA: 270,534 sq km
(104,454 sq miles)
POPULATION: 3,493,000
CAPITAL: Wellington
LANGUAGE: English, Maori
RELIGION: Protestant,
Roman Catholic
CURRENCY: New Zealand dollar (NZD)
ORGANIZATIONS: ANZUS, Col. Plan,
Comm., OECD, UN

New Zealand consists of two main and several smaller islands, lying in the south Pacific Ocean. South Island is mountainous, with the Southern Alps running along its length. It has many glaciers and a coast line that is indented by numerous sounds and fjords. On the more heavily populated North Island, mountain ranges, broad fertile valleys and volcanic plateaux predominate. The overall climate is temperate, with an annual average temperature of 9°C (40°F) on South Island and 15°C (59°F) on the North Island. In terms of value the chief exports are meat, dairy produce and forestry products, followed by wood, fruit and vegetables. In the mineral sector there are deposits of coal, iron ore, oil and natural gas. Hydro-electric and geothermal power are well developed. Manufacturing industries are of increasing importance and in the early 1990s tourism expanded rapidly.

NICARAGUA

STATUS: Republic
AREA: 130,000 sq km (50,193 sq miles)
POPULATION: 4,401,000
CAPITAL: Managua
LANGUAGE: Spanish,
Amerindian languages
RELIGION: Roman Catholic, Protestant
CURRENCY: córdoba (NIO)
ORGANIZATIONS: CACM, OAS, UN

Nicaragua, the largest of the Central American republics, is situated between the Caribbean and the Pacific. Active volcanic mountains run parallel with the western coast. The south is dominated by Lakes Managua and Nicaragua. Climate is tropical, with average daily temperatures in excess of 25°C (77°F) throughout the year. On the west coast wet summer months contrast with a dry period from December to April. Agriculture is the main occupation with cotton, coffee, sugar cane and fruit the main exports. Gold, silver and copper are mined.

NIGER

STATUS: Republic
AREA: 1,267,000 sq km (489,191 sq miles)
POPULATION: 8,846,000
CAPITAL: Niamey
LANGUAGE: French (official), Hausa, Fulani,
local languages
RELIGION: Sunni Muslim, Protestant, Roman
Catholic, Traditional beliefs
CURRENCY: CFA franc (W Africa) (XOF)
ORGANIZATIONS: ECOWAS, OAU, UN

Niger is a vast landlocked southern republic. Apart from savannah in the south and in the Niger valley, most of the vast country lies within the Sahara desert. Rainfall is low, and decreases from 560 mm (22 inches) in the south to near zero in the north. Temperatures are above 35°C (95°F) for much of the year. Most of the population are farmers, particularly of cattle, sheep, and goats. Recent droughts have affected both cereals and livestock. The only significant export is uranium. and phosphates, coal, and tungsten are also mined. The economy depends largely on foreign aid.

NIGERIA

STATUS: Republic
AREA: 923,768 sq km (356,669 sq miles)
POPULATION: 108,467,000
CAPITAL: Abuja
LANGUAGE: English, Creole, Hausa,

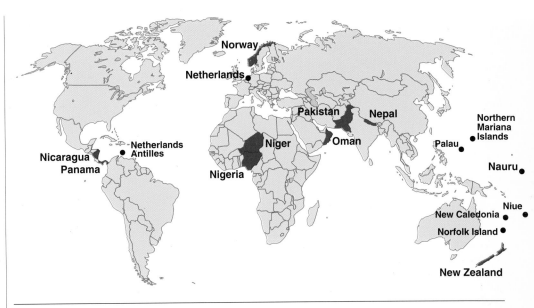

Yoruba, Ibo, Fulani
RELIGION: Sunni Muslim Protestant,
Roman Catholic, Traditional beliefs
CURRENCY: naira (NGN)
ORGANIZATIONS: Comm., ECOWAS, OAU, OPEC, UN

The most populous nation in Africa, Nigeria is bounded to the north by the Sahara and to the west, east and southeast by tropical rainforest. The southern half of the country is dominated by the Niger and its tributaries, the north by the interior plateaux. Temperatures average 32°C (90°F) with high humidity. From a basic agricultural economy, Nigeria is only slowly being transformed by the vast oil discoveries in the Niger delta and coastal regions, which account for 95 per cent of exports. Gas reserves are relatively underdeveloped.

NIUE
STATUS: New Zealand Territory
AREA: 258 sq km (100 sq miles)
POPULATION: 2,000
CAPITAL: Alofi
LANGUAGE: English, Polynesian (Niuean)

NORFOLK ISLAND
STATUS: Australian Territory
AREA: 35 sq km (14 sq miles)
POPULATION: 2,000
CAPITAL: Kingston

NORTHERN MARIANA ISLANDS
STATUS: US Territory
AREA: 477 sq km (184 sq miles)
POPULATION: 47,000
CAPITAL: Saipan

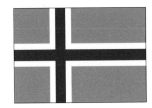

NORWAY
STATUS: Monarchy
AREA: 323,878 sq km (125,050 sq miles)
POPULATION: 4,325,000
CAPITAL: Oslo
LANGUAGE: Norwegian
RELIGION: Protestant, Roman Catholic
CURRENCY: Norwegian krone (NOK)
ORGANIZATIONS: Council of Europe,
EEA, EFTA, NATO,
OECD, OSCE, UN

Norway is a mountainous country stretching from 58° to 72°N. The climate along its indented western coast is modified by the Gulf Stream, with high rainfall and relatively mild winters. Temperatures average -3.9°C (25°F) in January and 17°C (63°F) in July. Rainfall may be as high as 1,960 mm (79 inches). Most settlements are scattered along the fjords, the coast and around Oslo in the south. Norway is rich in natural resources. Oil and natural gas predominate in exports, but are supplemented by metal products, timber, pulp and paper, fish and machinery. The advanced production of hydro-electric power has helped develop industry, particularly chemicals, metal products and paper.

OMAN
STATUS: Monarchy
AREA: 271,950 sq km (105,000 sq miles)
POPULATION: 2,077,000
CAPITAL: Muscat (Masqaṭ)
LANGUAGE: Arabic, Baluchi, Farsi, Swahili,
Indian languages
RELIGION: Ibadhi Muslim, Sunni Muslim
CURRENCY: Omani rial (OMR)
ORGANIZATIONS: Arab League, UN

The Sultanate of Oman occupies the northeast coast of the Arabian peninsula, with an enclave overlooking the Strait of Hormuz. Its desert landscape consists of a coastal plain and low hills rising to plateau in the interior, and has two fertile areas; Batinah in the north and Dhofar in the south. Copper ores are being mined and exported and oil provides over 95 per cent of export revenue. New discoveries of gas suggest that this will eventually supplant oil in importance.

PAKISTAN
STATUS: Republic
AREA: 803,940 sq km (310,403 sq miles)
POPULATION: 126,610,000
CAPITAL: Islamabad
LANGUAGE: Urdu (official), Punjabi, Sindhi,
Pushtu, English
RELIGION: Sunni Muslim, Shi'a Muslim,
Christian, Hindu
CURRENCY: Pakistan rupee (PKR)
ORGANIZATIONS Col. Plan, Comm., UN

The landscape of Pakistan is dominated by the river Indus which flows south through the country flanked by the plateau of Balochistan and the Sulaiman mountains to the west and the Thar desert to the east. The climate is arid with temperatures averaging 27°C (80°F). Rainfall can be

less than 127 mm (5 inches) in the southwest and only in the northern mountains does it reach appreciable amounts; 900 mm (36 inches). Over 50 per cent of the population are engaged in agriculture which is confined to the irrigated areas near rivers. Main crops are wheat, cotton, maize, rice and sugar cane. There are many types of low-grade mineral deposits, such as coal and copper, which are little developed. Main industries are textiles, food processing and oil refining but these only contribute about 20 per cent to the economy.

PALAU
STATUS: Republic
AREA: 497 sq km (192 sq miles)
POPULATION: 17,000
CAPITAL: Koror
LANGUAGE: Palauan, English

PANAMA
STATUS: Republic
AREA: 77,082 sq km (29,762 sq miles)
POPULATION: 2,563,000
CAPITAL: Panama City (Panamá)
LANGUAGE: Spanish, English Creole,
Amerindian languages
RELIGION: Roman Catholic, Protestant, Sunni
Muslim, Baha'i
CURRENCY: balboa (PAB), US dollar (USD)
ORGANIZATIONS: OAS, UN

Panama is situated at the narrowest part of central American isthmus. Mountain ranges, reaching heights exceeding 3,000 m (9,800 feet), run the country's length. Much of its tropical forest has now been cleared, but some remains towards the border with Colombia. Its climate is tropical with little variation throughout the year. The average temperature is around 27°C (80°F). There is a rainy season from April to December. Most of its foreign income is earned from revenues derived from the Panama Canal and from a large merchant fleet that is registered in its name. Petroleum products, bananas and shrimps are the main exports.

PAPUA NEW GUINEA

STATUS: Monarchy
AREA: 462,840 sq km (178,704 sq miles)
POPULATION: 4,205,000
CAPITAL: Port Moresby
LANGUAGE: English(official), Tok Pisin (Pidgin),
many local languages
RELIGION: Protestant, Roman Catholic,
Traditional beliefs
CURRENCY: kina (PGK)
ORGANIZATIONS: Col. Plan, Comm., UN

Papua New Guinea (the eastern half of New Guinea and neighbouring islands) is a mountainous country. It has an equatorial climate with temperatures of 21–32°C (70–90°F) and annual rainfall of over 2,000 mm (79 inches). The country is rich in minerals, in particular copper, gold and silver, but development is restricted by rainforest and lack of roads. Exports include coconuts, cocoa, coffee, rubber, tea and sugar. Logging was once dominant but exports are now being reduced in order to preserve forest resources.

PARAGUAY

STATUS: Republic
AREA: 406,752 sq km (157,048 sq miles)
POPULATION: 4,700,000
CAPITAL: Asunción
LANGUAGE: Spanish, Guaraní
RELIGION: Roman Catholic, Protestant
CURRENCY: guaraní (PYG)
ORGANIZATIONS: ALADI, MERCOSUR,
OAS, UN

Paraguay is a landlocked country in South America with hot rainy summers, when temperatures reach over 27°C (80°F), and mild winters with an average temperature of 18°C (64°F). Lush, fertile plains and heavily forested plateau east of the River Paraguay contrast with the scrubland of the Chaco to the west. Cassava, cotton, soya beans and maize are the main crops but the rearing of livestock – cattle, horses, pigs and sheep – and food processing, dominate the export trade. The largest hydro-electric power dam in the world is at Itaipú, constructed as a joint project with Brazil, and another massive hydro-electric development is being constructed at Yacyreta in conjunction with Argentina.

PERU

STATUS: Republic
AREA: 1,285,216 sq km
(496,225 sq miles)
POPULATION: 23,088,000
CAPITAL: Lima
LANGUAGE: Spanish, Quechua, Aymara
RELIGION: Roman Catholic, Protestant
CURRENCY: sol (PES)
ORGANIZATIONS: ALADI, OAS, UN

Peru exhibits three geographical regions. The Pacific coastal region is very dry but with fertile oases producing cotton, sugar, fruit and fodder crops. This is the most prosperous and heavily populated area and includes the industrial centres around Lima. In the ranges and plateaux of the Andes and in the Amazon lowlands to the northeast, the soils are thin with the inhabitants depending on cultivation and grazing. Poor communications have hindered the development of Peru and there are great differences between the rich and poor. Peru has rich mineral deposits of copper, gold, lead, zinc and silver and there are oil and gas reserves in the interior.

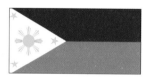

PHILIPPINES

STATUS: Republic
AREA: 300,000 sq km (115,831 sq miles)
POPULATION: 67,038,000
CAPITAL: Manila
LANGUAGE: English, Filipino (Tagalog),
Cebuano, many local languages
RELIGION: Roman Catholic, Aglipayan,
Sunni Muslim, Protestant
CURRENCY: Philippine peso (PHP)
ORGANIZATIONS: ASEAN, Col. Plan, UN

The Philippine archipelago consists of some 7,000 islands and is subject to earthquakes and typhoons. It has a monsoonal climate, with up to 6,350 mm (250 inches) of rainfall per annum in some areas. This once supported tropical rain forest but, apart from Palawan island, this has now been destroyed. Fishing is important but small farms dominate the economy, producing rice and copra for domestic consumption and other coconut and sugar products for export. Main exports are textiles, fruit and electronic products. Remittances from Filipinos working overseas are important to the economy. There is high unemployment and the extent of poverty is widespread.

PITCAIRN ISLANDS

STATUS: UK Territory
AREA: 45 sq km (17 sq miles)
POPULATION: 71
CAPITAL: Adamstown

POLAND

STATUS: Republic
AREA: 312,683 sq km
(120,728 sq miles)
POPULATION: 38,544,000
CAPITAL: Warsaw (Warszawa)
LANGUAGE: Polish, German
RELIGION: Roman Catholic, Polish Orthodox
CURRENCY: złoty (PLZ)
ORGANIZATIONS: Council of Europe,
OIEC, OSCE, UN,

Much of Poland lies in the north European plain, south of the Baltic Sea. It is a land of woods and lakes, gently rising southwards from the coast towards the Tartry mountains in the south and Sudety mountains in Silesia. The climate is continental with short, warm summers and long severe winters, when average temperatures can drop below freezing point (32°F). Rainfall occurs mainly in the summer months and averages between 520 and 730 mm (21–29 inches). Both agriculture and natural resources play an important part in the economy and Poland is nearly self-sufficient in cereals, sugar beet and potatoes. There are large reserves of coal, copper, sulphur and natural gas. Its major industries are ship-building in the north and the production of machinery, transport equipment, metals and chemicals in the major mining centres of the south. Manufacturing industries in both the private and public sectors are expanding rapidly and the government is committed to a programme of economic reforms and privatization.

PORTUGAL

STATUS: Republic
AREA: 88,940 sq km (34,340 sq miles)
POPULATION: 9,830,000
CAPITAL: Lisbon (Lisboa)
LANGUAGE: Portuguese
RELIGION: Roman Catholic, Protestant
CURRENCY: escudo (PTE)
ORGANIZATIONS: Council of Europe,
EEA, EU, NATO,
OECD, OSCE, UN, WEU

Portugal occupies the western Atlantic coast of the Iberian Peninsula. The river Tagus, on whose estuary is Lisbon, divides the country physically. In the north the land lies mainly above 4,000 m (1,220 feet) with plateaux cut by westward flowing rivers. Here, the climate is modified by westerly winds and the Gulf Stream. This is reflected in the lush mixed deciduous/coniferous forests. Land to the south is generally less than 300 m (1,000 feet) and the climate becomes progressively more arid further south, with Mediterranean scrub predominating in the far south. A quarter of the population are farmers growing vines, olives, wheat and maize. Wines, cork and fruit are important exports. In industry the chief exports are textiles, clothing, footwear and wood products. Mineral deposits include coal, copper, kaolinite and uranium. Tourism is an important source of revenue, with many visitors coming to the Algarve region in the far south of the country.

PUERTO RICO

STATUS: US Territory
AREA: 9,104 sq km (3,515 sq miles)
POPULATION: 3,646,000
CAPITAL: San Juan

QATAR
STATUS: Monarchy
AREA: 11,437 sq km (4,416 sq miles)
POPULATION: 540,000
CAPITAL: Doha (Ad Dawḥah)
LANGUAGE: Arabic, Indian languages
RELIGION: Sunni Muslim,
Christian, Hindu
CURRENCY: Qatari riyal (QAR)
ORGANIZATIONS: Arab League, OPEC, UN

The country occupies all of the Qatar peninsula in the Gulf and is a land of flat, arid desert. July temperatures average 37°C (98°F) and annual rainfall averages 62mm (2.5 inches). The main source of revenue is from the exploitation of oil and gas reserves. The North Field gas reserves are the world's largest single field and the development of these has a high priority.

RÉUNION
STATUS: French Territory
AREA: 2,551 sq km (985 sq miles)
POPULATION: 644,000
CAPITAL: St-Denis

ROMANIA
STATUS: Republic
AREA: 237,500 sq km (91,699 sq miles)
POPULATION: 22,736,000
CAPITAL: Bucharest (Bucureşti)
LANGUAGE: Romanian, Hungarian
RELIGION: Romanian Orthodox,
Roman Catholic, Protestant
CURRENCY: leu (ROL)
ORGANIZATIONS: Council of Europe,
OIEC,OSCE, UN

Romania is dominated by the great curve of the Carpathians, flanked by rich agricultural lowlands and has a continental climate. Forced industrialization has taken the economy from one based on agriculture to one dependent on heavy industry, notably chemicals, metal processing and machine-building. Since the fall of the communist dictatorship in 1989, most land has been privatized and there has been a re-emergence of Romania's traditional agriculture, with exports of cereals, fruit and wine. There are natural resources including oil, gas and minerals but industrial reform is slow and the economy is sluggish. Living standards are among the lowest in Europe.

RUSSIAN FEDERATION
STATUS: Republic
AREA: 17,075,400 sq km (6,592,849 sq miles)

POPULATION: 147,997,000
CAPITAL: Moscow (Moskva)
LANGUAGE: Russian, Tatar, Ukrainian,
many local languages
RELIGION: Russian Orthodox, Sunni Muslim,
Other Christian, Jewish
CURRENCY: rouble
ORGANIZATIONS: OSCE, UN

Covering much of east and northeast Europe and all of north Asia, the Russian Federation (Russia) displays an enormous variety of landforms and climates. The Arctic deserts of the north give way to tundra wastes and taiga which cover two-thirds of the country. In the far south, beyond the steppes, some areas assume subtropical and semi-desert landscapes. The majority of the population live west of the north-south spine of the Urals but in recent decades there has been a substantial migration eastwards to the Siberian basin in order to exploit its vast natural resources. Massive oil fields off the east coast of Sakhalin, north of Japan and also in the Russian Arctic (Timan Pechora basin) are now to be developed. Russia's extraordinary wealth of natural resources was a key factor in the country's speedy industrialization during the Soviet period. Heavy industry still plays a decisive role in the economy, while light and consumer industries have remained relatively under-developed. Agricultural land covers one-sixth of Russia's territory but there remains great potential for increase through drainage and clearance. By the mid-1980s the Soviet system was finally acknowledged to have reached an impasse, and the failure of the *perestroika* programme for reform precipitated the disintegration of the Soviet Union, which finally broke up in 1991. A transition from a state-run Communist economy to a market economy is taking place. Between 1992 and 1994 70 per cent of state-owned enterprises were privatized and farms are also starting to be re-organized.

RWANDA
STATUS: Republic
AREA: 26,338 sq km (10,169 sq miles)

POPULATION: 7,750,000
CAPITAL: Kigali
LANGUAGE: Kinyarwanda (Bantu),French
RELIGION: Roman Catholic,
Traditional beliefs,
Protestant, Sunni Muslim
CURRENCY: Rwanda franc (RWF)
ORGANIZATIONS: CEEAC,
OAU, UN

Small and isolated, Rwanda supports a high density of population on the mountains and plateaux east of the Rift Valley. It has a tropical climate with a dry season between June and August. Agriculture is basically subsistence with coffee the major export. Tin is mined and there are major natural gas reserves. Since 1990 a civil war has raged between the Tutsi and Hutu tribes, creating many thousands of casualties and well over one million refugees. The country has become reliant on foreign aid, and will require a massive international relief effort to avert disease and famine.

ST HELENA
STATUS: UK Territory
AREA: 122 sq km (47 sq miles)
POPULATION: 5,302
CAPITAL: Jamestown

ST KITTS and NEVIS
STATUS: Monarchy
AREA: 261 sq km (101 sq miles)
POPULATION: 41,000
CAPITAL: Basseterre
LANGUAGE: English, Creole
RELIGION: Protestant, Roman Catholic
CURRENCY: E Caribbean dollar (XCD)
ORGANIZATIONS: CARICOM, Comm., OAS, UN

St Kitts and Nevis, in the Leeward Islands, comprises two volcanic islands: St Kitts and Nevis. The climate is tropical with temperatures of 16–33°C (61–91°F) and an average annual rainfall of 1,400 mm (55 inches). Main exports are sugar, molasses and cotton. Tourism is an important industry.

ST LUCIA

STATUS: Monarchy
AREA: 616 sq km (238 sq miles)
POPULATION: 141,000
CAPITAL: Castries
LANGUAGE: English, French Creole
RELIGION: Roman Catholic, Protestant
CURRENCY: E. Caribbean dollar (XCD)
ORGANIZATIONS: Caricom, Comm.,
OAS, UN

Independent since 1979 this small tropical Caribbean island in the Lesser Antilles grows coconuts, cocoa and fruit. Bananas account for over 40 per cent of export earnings. Main industries are food and drink processing and all consumer goods are imported. Tourism is a major growth sector.

ST PIERRE AND MIQUELON

STATUS: French Territory
AREA: 242 sq km (93 sq miles)
POPULATION: 6,000
CAPITAL: St-Pierre

ST VINCENT AND THE GRENADINES

STATUS: Monarchy
AREA: 389 sq km (150 sq miles)
POPULATION: 111,000
CAPITAL: Kingstown
LANGUAGE: English, Creole
RELIGION: Protestant, Roman Catholic
CURRENCY: E. Caribbean dollar (XCD)
ORGANIZATIONS: Caricom, Comm., OAS, UN

St Vincent and the Grenadines in the Lesser Antilles comprises a forested main island and the northern part of the Grenadines. It has a tropical climate. Most exports are foodstuffs: arrowroot, sweet potatoes, coconut products and yams, but the principal crop is bananas. Some sugar cane is grown for the production of rum and other drinks. Tourism is well-established.

SAN MARINO

STATUS: Republic
AREA: 61 sq km (24 sq miles)
POPULATION: 25,000
CAPITAL: San Marino
LANGUAGE: Italian
RELIGION: Roman Catholic

CURRENCY: Italian lira (ITL),
San Marino coinage
ORGANIZATIONS: Council of Europe,
OSCE, UN

An independent state within Italy, San Marino straddles a limestone peak in the Apennines south of Rimini. The economy is centred around tourism and the sale of postage stamps. Most of the population are farmers growing cereals, olives and vines and tending herds of sheep and goats.

SÃO TOMÉ AND PRÍNCIPE

STATUS: Republic
AREA: 964 sq km (372 sq miles)
POPULATION: 130,000
CAPITAL: São Tomé
LANGUAGE: Portuguese, Portuguese Creole
RELIGION: Roman Catholic, Protestant
CURRENCY: dobra (STD)
ORGANIZATIONS: CEEAC, OAU, UN

This tiny state, independent from Portugal since 1975, comprises two large and several small islands near the equator, 200 km (125 miles) off west Africa. The climate is tropical with temperatures averaging 25°C (77°F) and rainfall of between 1,000–5,000 mm (40–197 inches). Cocoa (which provides 90 per cent of revenue), coconuts and palm oil are the main crops grown on the rich volcanic soil. Other foods and consumer goods are imported.

SAUDI ARABIA

STATUS: Monarchy
AREA: 2,200,000 sq km (849,425 sq miles)
POPULATION: 17,451,000
CAPITAL: Riyadh (Ar Riyāḍ)
LANGUAGE: Arabic
RELIGION: Sunni Muslim,
Shi'a Muslim
CURRENCY: Saudi riyal (SAR)
ORGANIZATIONS: Arab League,
OPEC, UN

Saudi Arabia occupies the heart of the vast arid Arabian Peninsula. The country is mostly desert and there are no rivers which flow all year round. To the west, the Hejaz and Asir mountains fringe the Red Sea but even here rainfall rarely exceeds 380 mm (15 inches). Temperatures rise beyond 44°C (111°F) in the summer. The interior plateau slopes gently eastwards down to the Gulf and supports little vegetation. The southeast of the country is well named as the 'Empty Quarter'; it is almost devoid of population. Only in the coastal strips and oases are cereals and date palms grown. Oil is the most important resource – Saudi Arabia has a quarter of the world's known oil reserves – and export commodity and economic development is dependent on its revenue.

SENEGAL

STATUS: Republic
AREA: 196,720 sq km (75,954 sq miles)
POPULATION: 8,102,000
CAPITAL: Dakar
LANGUAGE: French (official), Wolof, Fulani,
local languages
RELIGION: Sunni Muslim,
Roman Catholic, Traditional beliefs
CURRENCY: CFA franc (W Africa) (XOF)
ORGANIZATIONS: ECOWAS, OAU, UN

Senegal is a flat, dry country cut through by the Gambia, Casamance and Senegal rivers. Rainfall rarely exceeds 580 mm (23 inches) on the wetter coast. The interior savannah supports varied wildlife but little agriculture. Cultivation is mainly confined to the south where groundnuts account for nearly half of the agricultural output. Cotton and millet are also grown, but frequent droughts have reduced their value as cash crops. Phosphate mining, ship-repairing, textiles, petroleum products and food processing are the major industries. Both tourism and fishing are becoming increasingly important.

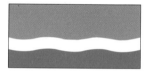

SEYCHELLES

STATUS: Republic
AREA: 455 sq km (176 sq miles)
POPULATION: 74,000
CAPITAL: Victoria
LANGUAGE: Seychellois (Seselwa, French
Creole), English
RELIGION: Roman Catholic, Protestant
CURRENCY: Seychelles rupee (SCR)
ORGANIZATIONS: Comm., OAU, UN

This archipelago in the Indian Ocean comprises over 100 granite or coral islands. Main exports are copra, coconuts and cinnamon and in recent years tea and tuna. All domestic requirements, including most foodstuffs, have to be imported. Tourism has developed rapidly in the 1990s and is now the dominant sector in the economy.

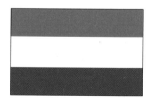

SIERRA LEONE

STATUS: Republic
AREA: 71,740 sq km
(27,699 sq miles)
POPULATION: 4,402,000
CAPITAL: Freetown
LANGUAGE: English, Creole, Mende, Temne,
local languages
RELIGION: Traditioanl beliefs, Sunni Muslim,
Protestant, Roman Catholic

CURRENCY: leone (SLL)
ORGANIZATIONS: Comm., ECOWAS, OAS, UN

Sierra Leone, a former British colony, has a coast dominated by swamps but is essentially a flat plain some 70 miles wide which extends to interior plateaux and mountains. Three-quarters of the population are employed in subsistence farming. Cash crops include cocoa and coffee but the main source of revenue is from minerals. Diamonds, gold, bauxite and iron ore are mined but the most important export is now rutile (titanium ore). Manufacturing in the form of processing local products has developed around Freetown.

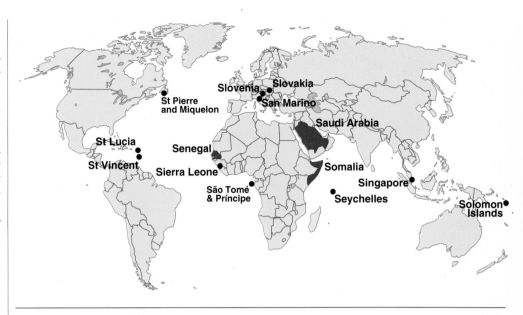

SINGAPORE
STATUS: Republic
AREA: 639 sq km
(247 sq miles)
POPULATION: 2,930,000
CAPITAL: Singapore
LANGUAGE: Chinese, English, Malay, Tamil
RELIGION: Buddhist, Taoist, Sunni Muslim, Christian, Hindu
CURRENCY: Singapore dollar (SGD)
ORGANIZATIONS: ASEAN, Col. Plan, Comm., UN

The republic of Singapore, independent from Britain since 1959, has been transformed from an island of mangrove swamps into one of the world's major entrepreneurial centres. The island, connected to Peninsular Malaysia by a man-made causeway, has a tropical, humid climate with 2,240 mm (96 inches) of rain per year. With few natural resources, Singapore depends on manufacturing precision goods, electronic products, financial services and activities associated with its port, which is one of the world's largest.

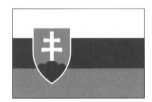

SLOVAKIA
STATUS: Republic
AREA: 49,035 sq km (18,933 sq miles)
POPULATION: 5,347,000
CAPITAL: Bratislava
LANGUAGE: Slovak, Hungarian, Czech
RELIGION: Roman Catholic, Protestant, Orthodox
CURRENCY: Slovak crown or koruna
ORGANIZATIONS: Council of Europe, OSCE, UN

On 1 January 1993 Czechoslovakia ceased to exist and Slovakia and the Czech Republic came into being. Slovakia's geomorphology is dominated by the Tatry mountains in the north. Bratislava, the capital, lies in the extreme southwest, on the north bank of the Danube. Natural resources include iron ore, copper, antimony, mercury, magnesite and oil. Under Communism large manufacturing complexes developed,

many of which specialized in arms and tanks. The end of the Cold War in 1989 brought a collapse in demand for these products. This, and a decline in trade with the Czech Republic, has forced Slovakia to restructure existing industry and look to new developments such as aluminium smelting and car assembly.

SLOVENIA
STATUS: Republic
AREA: 20,251 sq km
(7,819 sq miles)
POPULATION: 1,942,000
CAPITAL: Ljubljana
LANGUAGE: Slovene, Serbo-Croat
RELIGION: Roman Catholic, Protestant
CURRENCY: Slovenian tólar (SLT)
ORGANIZATIONS: Council of Europe, OSCE, UN

The northernmost republic of the former Yugoslav federation, Slovenia, has always been one of the key gateways from the Balkans to central and western Europe. Much of the country is mountainous, its heartland and main centre of population being the Ljubljana basin. The climate generally shows continental tendencies, with warm summers and cold winters, when snow is plentiful on the ground. The small coastal region has a Mediterranean regime. Extensive mountain pastures provide profitable dairy-farming, but the amount of cultivable land is restricted. There are large mercury mines in the northwest and, in recent decades, this area has also developed a broad range of light industries. Combined with tourism, this has given the country a well-balanced economy. After a brief military conflict Slovenia won its independence in 1991.

SOLOMON ISLANDS
STATUS: Monarchy
AREA: 28,370 sq km (10,954 sq miles)
POPULATION: 366,000
CAPITAL: Honiara
LANGUAGE: English, Soloman Islands Pidgin, many local languages
RELIGION: Protestant, Roman Catholic
CURRENCY: Solomon Islands dollar (SBD)
ORGANIZATIONS: Comm., UN

Situated in the South Pacific Ocean the Solomon Islands consist of a 1400 km (870 miles) archipelago of six main and many smaller islands. The mountainous large islands are covered by tropical rain forest reflecting the high temperatures, on average 22–34°C (72–95°F) and heavy rainfall, about 3,050 mm (120 inches). The main crops are coconuts, cocoa and rice, with copra, timber and palm oil being the main exports. Mineral deposits include reserves of bauxite, gold and phosphate, mined on the small island of Bellona south of Guadalcanal. Once a British protectorate, the Solomons became independent in 1978.

SOMALIA
STATUS: Republic
AREA: 637,657sq km
(246,201 sq miles)
POPULATION: 9,077,000
CAPITAL: Mogadishu (Muqdisho)
LANGUAGE: Somali, Arabic (official)
RELIGION: Sunni Muslim
CURRENCY: Somali shilling (SOS)
ORGANIZATIONS: Arab League, OAU, UN

Independent since 1960, Somalia is a hot and arid country in northeast Africa. The semi-desert of the northern mountains contrasts with the plains of the south where the bush country is particularly rich in wildlife. Most of the population are nomadic, following herds of camels, sheep, goats and cattle. Little land is cultivated but cotton, maize, millet and sugar cane are grown. Bananas are a major export. Iron ore, gypsum and uranium deposits are as yet unexploited. Five years of inter-clan warfare and a lack of coherent government have led to the collapse of the economy.

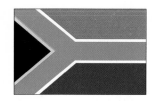

SOUTH AFRICA

STATUS: Republic
AREA: 1,219,080 sq km (470,689 sq miles)
POPULATION: 39,659,000
CAPITAL: Pretoria (administrative)
Cape Town (legislative)
LANGUAGE: Afrikaans, English,
nine local languages (all official)
RELIGION: Protestant, Roman Catholic,
Sunni Muslim, Hindu
CURRENCY: rand (ZAR)
ORGANIZATIONS: Comm., OAU,
SADC, UN

The interior of South Africa consists of a plateau of over 900 m (2,955 feet) drained by the Orange and Limpopo rivers. Surrounding the plateau is a pronounced escarpment below which the land descends by steps to the sea. Rainfall in most areas is less than 500 mm (20 inches) and the land is increasingly drier towards the west. Agriculture is limited by poor soils but sheep and cattle are extensively grazed. Main crops are maize, wheat, sugar cane, vegetables, cotton and vines. Wine is an important export commodity. South Africa abounds in minerals. Diamonds, gold, platinum, silver, uranium, copper, manganese and asbestos are mined and nearly 80 per cent of the continent's coal reserves are in South Africa. Manufacturing and engineering is concentrated in the southern Transvaal area and around the ports. In 1994 the first ever multi-racial elections were held resulting in Nelson Mandela coming to power. In a post-apartheid era, economic sanctions have been lifted, boosting exports, but the country faces adaptation, beginning with a rush of complicated land-ownership claims.

EASTERN CAPE

STATUS: Province
AREA: 169,600 sq km (65,483 sq miles)
POPULATION: 6,416,000
CAPITAL: Bisho

MPUMALANGA

STATUS: Province
AREA: 78,370 sq km (30,259 sq miles)
POPULATION: 2,953,232
CAPITAL: Nelspruit

KWAZULU-NATAL

STATUS: Province
AREA: 92,180 sq km (35,591 sq miles)
POPULATION: 8,577,779
CAPITAL: Ulundi

NORTHERN CAPE

STATUS: Province
AREA: 361,800 sq km (139,692 sq miles)
POPULATION: 739,450
CAPITAL: Kimberly

NORTHERN PROVINCE

STATUS: Province
AREA: 123,280 sq km (47,599 sq miles)
POPULATION: 5,272,583
CAPITAL: Pietersburg

NORTH WEST

STATUS: Province
AREA: 116,190 sq km (44,861 sq miles)
POPULATION: 3,315,671
CAPITAL: Mafikeng

FREE STATE

STATUS: Province
AREA: 129,480 sq km (49,993 sq miles)
POPULATION: 2,749,583
CAPITAL: Bloemfontein

GAUTENG

STATUS: Province
AREA: 18,810 sq km (7,263 sq miles)
POPULATION: 6,946,953
CAPITAL: Johannesburg

WESTERN CAPE

STATUS: Province
AREA: 123,370 sq km
(47,633 sq miles)
POPULATION: 3,676,335
CAPITAL: Cape Town

SOUTHERN AND ANTARCTIC TERRITORIES

STATUS: French Territory (claim to mainland in abeyance)
AREA: 439,580 sq km (169,680 sq miles)
POPULATION: 180

SOUTH GEORGIA AND THE SOUTH SANDWICH ISLANDS

STATUS: UK Territory
AREA: 4,091 sq km (1,580 sq miles)
POPULATION: no permanent population

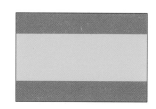

SPAIN

STATUS: Monarchy
AREA: 504,782 sq km
(194,897 sq miles)
POPULATION: 39,193,000
CAPITAL: Madrid
LANGUAGE: Spanish (Castilian), Catalan,
Galician, Basque
RELIGION: Roman Catholic
CURRENCY: Spanish peseta (ESP)
ORGANIZATIONS: Council of Europe, EEA, EU,
NATO, OECD, OSCE, UN, WEU

Spain occupies most of the Iberian Peninsula, from the Bay of Biscay and the Pyrenees mountains in the north, to the Strait of Gibraltar in the south. It includes in its territory the Balearic Islands in the Mediterranean Sea, and the Canary Islands in the Atlantic. The mainland of Spain is mostly plateaux, often forested in the north, but becoming more arid and open further south. Climate is affected regionally by latitude and proximity to the Atlantic Ocean and Mediterranean Sea. Although the climate and terrain are not always favourable, agriculture is important to the Spanish economy. Wheat and other cereals such as maize, barley and rice are cultivated while grapes, citrus fruits and olives are important cash crops. Textile manufacturing in the northeast and steel, chemicals, consumer goods and vehicle manufacturing in the towns and cities have proved a magnet for great numbers of the rural population. The main minerals found are coal, iron ore, uranium and zinc. Tourism is of vital importance to the economy.

SRI LANKA

STATUS: Republic
AREA: 65,610 sq km
(25,332 sq miles)
POPULATION: 17,865,000
CAPITAL: Colombo
LANGUAGE: Sinhalese, Tamil, English
RELIGION: Buddhist, Hindu, Sunni Muslim,
Roman Catholic
CURRENCY: Sri Lanka rupee (LKR)
ORGANIZATIONS: Col. Plan, Comm., UN

The island of Sri Lanka is situated only 19 km (12 miles) from mainland India. The climate is tropical along the coastal plain and temperate in the central highlands. Annual rainfall averages only 1,000 mm (39 inches) in the north and east while the south and west receive over 2,000 mm (79 inches). The traditional economy of Sri Lanka is based on agriculture in which rubber, coffee, coconuts and particularly tea are dominant. The nation is also self-sufficient in rice. In recent years, however, manufacturing, especially of clothing and textiles, has become the main export earner. Gemstones and tourism are also important, but the tourist industry has suffered because of the activities of Tamil separatists.

SUDAN

STATUS: Republic
AREA: 2,505,813 sq km (967,500 sq miles)
POPULATION: 27,361,000
CAPITAL: Khartoum
LANGUAGE: Arabic, Dinka, Nubian, Beja,
Nuer, local languages
RELIGION: Sunni Muslim,
Traditional beliefs, Roman Catholic, Protestant
CURRENCY: Sudanese dinar (SDD)
ORGANIZATIONS: Arab League, OAU, UN

Sudan, in the upper Nile basin, is Africa's largest country. The land is mostly flat and infertile with a hot, arid climate. The White and Blue Niles are invaluable, serving not only to irrigate cultivated land but also as a potential source of hydro-electric power. Subsistence farming accounts for 80 per cent of Sudan's total production. Major exports include cotton, groundnuts, sugar cane and sesame seed. The principal activity is nomadic herding with over 40 million cattle and sheep and 14 million goats. However, economic activity has been damaged by the effects of drought and civil war.

SURINAM

STATUS: Republic
AREA: 163,820 sq km
(63,251 sq miles)
POPULATION: 418,000
CAPITAL: Paramaribo
LANGUAGE: Dutch, Surinamese (Sranan Tongo),
English, Hindi, Javanese
RELIGION: Hindu, Roman Catholic,
Protestant, Sunni Muslim
CURRENCY: Surinam guilder (SRG)
ORGANIZATIONS: CARICOM, OAS, UN

Independent from the Dutch since 1976, Surinam is a small state lying on the northeast coast in the tropics of South America. Physically, there are three main regions: a low-lying, marshy coastal strip; undulating savannah; densely forested highlands. Rice growing takes up 75 per cent of all cultivated land; sugar and pineapples are also grown, while cattle rearing for both meat and dairy products has been introduced. Bauxite accounts for 90 per cent of Surinam's foreign earnings. Timber resources offer great potential but as yet are largely untapped.

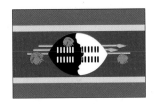

SWAZILAND

STATUS: Monarchy
AREA: 17,364 sq km (6,704 sq miles)
POPULATION: 879,000
CAPITAL: Mbabane
LANGUAGE: Swazi (Siswati), English
RELIGION: Protestant, Roman Catholic,
Traditional beliefs
CURRENCY: emalangeni (SZE),
ORGANIZATIONS: Comm., OAU,
SADC, UN

Landlocked Swaziland in southern Africa, is a sub-tropical, savannah country. It is divided into four main regions: the High, Middle and Low Velds and the Lebombo Mountains. Rainfall is abundant, promoting good pastureland for the many cattle and sheep. Major exports include sugar, meat, citrus fruits, textiles, wood products and asbestos.

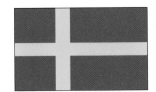

SWEDEN

STATUS: Monarchy
AREA: 449,964 sq km (173,732 sq miles)
POPULATION: 8,794,000
CAPITAL: Stockholm

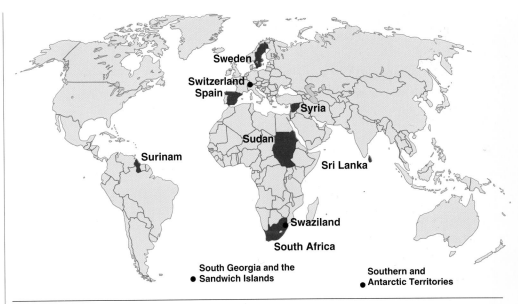

LANGUAGE: Swedish
RELIGION: Protestant, Roman Catholic
CURRENCY: Swedish krona (SED)
ORGANIZATIONS: Council of Europe,
EEA, EU, OECD,
OSCE, UN

Glacial debris, glacier-eroded valleys and thick glacial clay are all dominant features of Sweden. Physically, Sweden comprises four main regions: Norrland, the northern forested mountains; the Lake District of the centre south; the southern uplands of Jönköping; the extremely fertile Scania plain of the far south. Summers are short and hot with long, cold winters. Temperatures vary with latitude; in the south from -3–18°C (27–64°F) and in the north from -14–14°C (7–57°F). Annual rainfall varies between 2,000 mm (79 inches) in the southwest, to 500 mm (20 inches) in the east. Over half the land area is forested resulting in a thriving timber industry, but manufacturing industry, particularly cars and trucks, metal products and machine tools, is well established. Mineral resources are also rich and plentiful – iron ore production alone exceeds 17 million tons a year. There are also deposits of copper, lead and zinc.

SWITZERLAND

STATUS: Federation
AREA: 41,293 sq km
(15,943 sq miles)
POPULATION: 6,994,000
CAPITAL: Bern (Berne)
LANGUAGE: German, French, Italian, Romansch
RELIGION: Roman Catholic,
Protestant
CURRENCY: Swiss franc (CHF)
ORGANIZATIONS: Council of Europe, EFTA,
OECD, OSCE

Switzerland is a landlocked, mountainous country of great scenic beauty, situated in western Europe. The Alps traverse the southern half of the country, in which are to be found some of Europe's highest peaks. In the north the Jura mountains form a natural border with France.

Winters are cold with heavy snowfall in the highest regions. Summers are mild with an average July temperature of 18–19°C (64–66°F). Most rain falls in the summer months. Agriculture is based mainly on dairy farming. Major crops include hay, wheat, barley and potatoes. Industry plays a major role in Switzerland's economy, centred on metal engineering, watchmaking, food processing, textiles and chemicals. The high standard of living enjoyed by the Swiss owes much to the tourist industry. The financial services sector, especially banking, is also of great importance. Switzerland's history of neutrality has made it an attractive location for the headquarters of several international organizations.

SYRIA

STATUS: Republic
AREA: 185,180 sq km
(71,498 sq miles)
POPULATION: 13,844,000
CAPITAL: Damascus, (Dimashq, Esh Sham)
LANGUAGE: Arabic, Kurdish, Armenian
RELIGION: Sunni Muslim,
other Muslim, Christian
CURRENCY: Syrian pound (SYP)
ORGANIZATIONS: Arab League, UN

Syria is situated in the heart of the Middle East. Its most fertile areas lie along the coastal strip on the Mediterranean Sea which supports the bulk of its population, and in the depressions and plateaux of the northeast which are cut through by the rivers Orontes and Euphrates. In the south the Anti-Lebanon mountains (Jebel esh Sharqi) is bordered to the east by the Syrian desert. While the coast has a Mediterranean climate with dry hot summers and mild winters, the interior becomes increasingly hot and arid – average summer temperatures in the desert reach 43°C (109°F). Rainfall varies between 220–400 mm (9–16 inches). Cotton is Syria's main export crop, and wheat and barley are also grown. Cattle, sheep and goats are the main livestock. Although traditionally an agriculturally-based economy, the country is rapidly becoming industrialized as oil, natural gas, salt, gypsum and phosphate are being exploited.

TAHITI

STATUS: French Territory
AREA: 1,042 sq km (402 sq miles)
POPULATION: 213,000

TAIWAN

STATUS: Republic
AREA: 36,179 sq km
(13,969 sq miles)
POPULATION: 21,074,000
CAPITAL: Taipei (T'ai-pei)
LANGUAGE: Chinese (Mandarin (official),
Fukien, Hakka), local languages
RELIGION: Buddhist, Taoist,
Confucian, Christian
CURRENCY: New Taiwan dollar (TWD), yuan (CNY)
ORGANIZATIONS: none listed

Taiwan is separated from mainland China by the Taiwan Strait (the former Formosa Channel) in which lie the Pescadores. Two-thirds of Taiwan is mountainous, the highest point is 3,950 m (12,959 feet). The flat to rolling coastal plain in the western part of the island accommodates the bulk of the population and the national commerce, industry and agriculture. The climate is tropical marine, with persistent cloudy conditions. The monsoon rains fall in June to August, with an annual average of 2,600 mm (102 inches). Main crops are rice, tea, fruit, sugar cane and sweet potatoes. Industry has been founded on textiles but in recent years electronic products have gained in importance. The Taiwanese economy is inevitably influenced by its large neighbour and is likely to benefit from improving Chinese performance.

TAJIKISTAN

STATUS: Republic
AREA: 143,100 sq km
(55,251 sq miles)
POPULATION: 5,751,000
CAPITAL: Dushanbe
LANGUAGE: Tajik, Uzbek, Russian
RELIGION: Sunni Muslim
CURRENCY: Russian rouble
ORGANIZATIONS: OSCE, UN

Situated in the mountainous heart of Asia, more than half the territory of Tajikistan lies above 3,000 m (10,000 feet). The major settlement areas lie within the Fergana valley in the west. The climate varies from continental to subtropical according to elevation and shelter. Extensive irrigation, without which agriculture would be severely limited, has made it possible for cotton growing to develop into the leading branch of agriculture, and on that basis textiles have become the largest industry in the country. Tajikistan is rich in mineral and fuel deposits, the exploitation of which became a feature of eco-

nomic development during the Soviet era. Preceding full independence in 1991 there was an upsurge of sometimes violent Tajik nationalism as a result of which many Russians and Uzbeks have left the country.

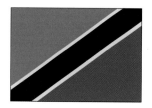

TANZANIA

STATUS: Republic
AREA: 945,087 sq km (364,900 sq miles)
POPULATION: 28,846,000
CAPITAL: Dodoma
LANGUAGE: Swahili, English, Nyamwezi,
many local languages
RELIGION: Roman Catholic, Sunni Muslim,
Traditional beliefs, Protestant
CURRENCY: Tanzanian shilling
ORGANIZATIONS: Comm., OAU, SADC, UN

Much of this east African country consists of high interior plateaux covered by scrub and grassland, bordered to the north by the volcanic Kilimanjaro region and Lake Victoria, to the west by Lake Tanganyika, by highlands to the south and by the Indian Ocean in the east. Despite its proximity to the equator, the altitude of much of Tanzania means that temperatures are reduced, and only on the narrow coastal plain is the climate truly tropical. Average temperatures vary between 19–28°C (67–82°F), and annual rainfall is around 570–1,060 mm (23–43 inches). The economy is heavily based on agriculture and subsistence farming is the main way of life for most of the population, although coffee, cotton, sisal, cashew nuts and tea are exported. Industry is limited, but gradually growing in importance, and involves textiles, food processing and tobacco. Tourism could be a future growth area.

THAILAND

STATUS: Monarchy
AREA: 513,115 sq km (198,115 sq miles)
POPULATION: 59,396,000
CAPITAL: Bangkok (Krung Thep)
LANGUAGE: Thai, Lao, Chinese, Malay,
Mon-khmer languages
RELIGION: Buddhist, Sunni Muslim
CURRENCY: baht (THB)
ORGANIZATIONS: ASEAN, Col. Plan, UN

Thailand is a land of flat undulating plains and mountains, consisting of the plains of the Chao Phraya and Mae Nam Mun river systems, fringed by mountains, a plateau in the northeast drained by the tributaries of the Mekong river, and the northern half of the Malay peninsula. From May to October, monsoon rains are heavy with an annual average rainfall of 1,500 mm (59 inches). The climate is tropical with temperatures reaching 36°C (97°F) and much of the country is forested. The central plain is well-served with irrigation canals which supply the paddy fields

for rice cultivation; Thailand is the world's leading exporter of this crop. Maize, cassava, sugar and rubber also contribute to the economy. Tin production has declined in importance in recent years and has, in part, been replaced by a small scale petro-chemical industry. Other industries of importance include textiles and clothing. Tourism, which grew at a record rate during the 1980s, has since levelled out after the military coup of 1991.

TOGO

STATUS: Republic
AREA: 56,785 sq km (21,925 sq miles)
POPULATION: 3,928,000
CAPITAL: Lomé
LANGUAGE: French, Ewe, Kabre,
many local languages
RELIGION: Traditional beliefs, Roman Catholic,
Sunni Muslim, Protestant
CURRENCY: CFA franc (West Africa) (XOF)
ORGANIZATIONS: ECOWAS, OAU, UN

Togo, formerly a German protectorate and French colony, is situated between Ghana and Benin in west Africa. A long narrow country, it has only 65 km (40 miles) of coast. The interior consists of mountains and high infertile tableland. The climate is tropical with an average temperature of 27°C (81°F). Most of Togo's farmers grow maize, cassava, yams, groundnuts and plantains, and the country is virtually self-sufficient in food stuffs. Phosphates account for half of export revenue. Cotton, cocoa and coffee are also exported.

TOKELAU ISLANDS

STATUS: New Zealand Territory
AREA: 10 sq km (4 sq miles)
POPULATION: 2,000
CAPITAL: none, each island has its own
administration centre

TONGA

STATUS: Monarchy
AREA: 748 sq km (289 sq miles)
POPULATION: 98,000
CAPITAL: Nuku'alofa
LANGUAGE: Tongan, English
RELIGION: Protestant, Roman Catholic,
Mormon
CURRENCY: pa'anga (TOP)
ORGANIZATIONS: Comm.

Tonga consists of an archipelago of 169 islands in the Pacific 180 km (112 miles) north of New Zealand. There are seven groups of islands, but the most important are Tongatapu, Ha'apai and Vava'u. All the islands are covered with dense tropical vegetation, and temperatures range from 11–29°C (52–84°F). Main exports are coconut products and bananas.

TRINIDAD & TOBAGO

STATUS: Republic
AREA: 5,130 sq km (1,981 sq miles)
POPULATION: 1,257,000
CAPITAL: Port of Spain
LANGUAGE: English, Creole, Hindi,
RELIGION: Roman Catholic, Hindu,
Protestant, Sunni Muslim
CURRENCY: Trinidad and Tobago dollar (TTD)
ORGANIZATIONS: Caricom, Comm., OAS, UN

Trinidad and Tobago, the southernmost Caribbean islands of the Lesser Antilles lie only 11 and 30 km (7 and 19 miles) respectively from the Venezuelan coast. Both islands are mountainous, the Northern Range of Trinidad reaching 940 m (3,084 feet) with its highest parts retaining tropical forest cover. The country has a humid, tropical climate with temperatures averaging 25°C (76°F) per annum. Rain falls mostly between June and December and varies between 1,300–3,000 mm (51–118 inches) annually. Sugar was once the mainstay of the economy but oil is now the leading source of revenue accounting for over 70 per cent of export revenue. There is also a petro-chemical industry based on significant gas reserves.

TRISTAN DA CUNHA

STATUS: UK Territory
AREA: 98 sq km (38 sq miles)
POPULATION: 300

TUNISIA

STATUS: Republic
AREA: 164,150 sq km
(63,379 sq miles)
POPULATION: 8,733,000
CAPITAL: Tunis
LANGUAGE: Arabic, French
RELIGION: Sunni Muslim
CURRENCY: Tunisian dinar (TND)
ORGANIZATIONS: Arab League, OAU, UN

Tunisia, on the southern shores of the Mediterranean is largely an arid, desert country of northern Africa. The eastern limits of the Atlas mountain range extend into northern parts of the country, which are separated from the Sahara desert to the south by a lowland belt of salt pans, called the Chott El Jerid. Average annual temperatures are in the range 10–27°C (50–81°F) and rainfall averages 380–500 mm (15–20 inches) in the north, but drops to virtually nothing in the south. The majority of the population live along the northeast coast. Wheat, barley, olives and citrus fruit are the main crops and oil, natural gas and sugar refining are the main industries. The tourist industry is expanding and is becoming increasingly important to the economy.

TURKEY

STATUS: Republic
AREA: 779,452 sq km
(300,948 sq miles)
POPULATION: 61,183,000
CAPITAL: Ankara
LANGUAGE: Turkish, Kurdish
RELIGION: Sunni Muslim, Shi'a Muslim
CURRENCY: Turkish lira (TRL)
ORGANIZATIONS: Council of Europe, NATO,
OECD, OSCE, UN

Turkey has always occupied a strategically important position linking Europe and Asia. It is a rugged, mountainous country particularly in the east. The central Anatolian plateau is bordered in the north by the Pontine mountains (Anadolu Dağlari) and in the south by the Taurus mountains (Toros Dağlari) which converge in the east, crowned by Mt Ararat (Büyük Ağri). Thrace, in European Turkey is flatter with rolling hills. Coastal regions exhibit Mediterranean conditions with short mild winters with some rainfall and long hot, dry summers. The interior is relatively arid with average rainfall in some places less than 250 mm (10 inches). The main crops are wheat and barley, but tobacco, olives, sugar beet, tea and fruit are also grown, and sheep, goats and cattle are raised. Turkey is becoming increasingly industrialized; textiles account for a third of exports and the car industry is developing. The nation now leads the Middle East in the production of iron, steel, chrome, coal and lignite. Tourism is a rapidly growing industry.

TURKMENISTAN

STATUS: Republic
AREA: 488,100 sq km (188,456 sq miles)
POPULATION: 4,010,000
CAPITAL: Ashkhabad

LANGUAGE: Turkmen, Russian
RELIGION: Sunni Muslim
CURRENCY: manat
ORGANIZATIONS: OSCE, UN

Situated in the far south of the former Soviet Union, Turkmenistan is a desert land except for the lowlands in the west along the Caspian shore, the mountains along its southern borders and the valley of Amudar'ya river in the north. The continental climate is responsible for great fluctuations in temperature, both during the day and throughout the year. Traditionally nomads, the Turkmen tribes under the Soviet regime, turned from pastoral farming to cotton-growing, made possible by extensive irrigation. Turk-menistan enjoys substantial natural resources, principally oil and gas but also potassium, sulphur and salt.

TURKS & CAICOS ISLANDS

STATUS: UK Territory
AREA: 430 sq km (166 sq miles)
POPULATION: 14,000
CAPITAL: Grand Turk

TUVALU

STATUS: Monarchy
AREA: 25 sq km
(10 sq miles)
POPULATION: 9,000
CAPITAL: Funafuti
LANGUAGE: Tuvaluan, English (official)
RELIGION: Protestant
CURRENCY: Australian dollar (AUD),
Tuvaluan coinage

ORGANIZATIONS: Comm., (special member)

Tuvalu consists of nine dispersed coral atolls, north of Fiji, in the Pacific Ocean. The climate is tropical; hot, with heavy annual rainfall exceeding 3,000 mm (118 inches). Fish is the staple food but coconuts and bread-fruit are cultivated. The sale of postage stamps abroad is, however, the largest source of revenue.

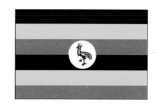

UGANDA

STATUS: Republic
AREA: 241,038 sq km (93,065 sq miles)
POPULATION: 20,621,000
CAPITAL: Kampala
LANGUAGE: English, Swahili (official), Luganda, many local languages
RELIGION: Roman Catholic, Protestant, Sunni Muslim, Traditional beliefs
CURRENCY: Uganda shilling (UGS)
ORGANIZATIONS: Comm., OAU, UN

Uganda is bordered in the west by the great Rift Valley and the Ruwenzori mountain range which reaches 5,220 m (16,765 feet). In the east it is bordered by Kenya and Lake Victoria, from which the Nile flows northwards. Most of the country is high plateau with savannah vegetation although the lands around Lake Victoria have been cleared for cultivation and have become the most populated and developed areas. The climate is warm (21–24°C or 70–75°F), and rainfall ranges from 750–1,500 mm (30–59 inches) per annum. The Ugandan economy is firmly based on agriculture with a heavy dependence on coffee, the dominant export crop, and cotton. Fishing, from the waters of Lake Victoria is also important for local consumption.

UKRAINE

STATUS: Republic
AREA: 603,700 sq km (233,090 sq miles)
POPULATION: 51,910,000
CAPITAL: Kiev (Kiyev)
LANGUAGE: Ukrainian, Russian, regional languages
RELIGION: Ukrainian Orthodox, Roman Catholic
CURRENCY: karbovanets (coupon)
ORGANIZATIONS: OSCE, UN

Ukraine consists mainly of level plains and mountainous border areas. The landscape is, however, diverse, with marshes, forests, wooded and treeless steppe. Deposits of 'black earth', among the most fertile soils, cover about 65 per cent of Ukraine. Grain, potatoes, vegetables and fruits, industrial crops (notably sugar beets and sunflower seeds) and fodder crops are grown. Food processing is important to the economy, and southern regions are renowned for wines. Ukraine is rich in mineral resources, such as iron ore, coal and lignite, and has large reserves of petroleum and gas. Extensive mining, metal production, machine-building, engineering and chemicals dominate Ukrainian industry, most of it located in the Donetsk basin and the Dnieper lowland. These two regions account for four-fifths of the urban population. Despite its natural wealth and industrial development, Ukraine has failed to respond to the economic needs of its independent status and has experienced sharp declines in agricultural and industrial output.

UNITED ARAB EMIRATES (UAE)

STATUS: Federation
AREA: 77,700 sq km (30,000 sq miles)
POPULATION: 1,861,000
CAPITAL: Abu Dhabi (Abū Ẕabī)
LANGUAGE: Arabic (official), English, Hindi, Urdu, Farsi
RELIGION: Sunni Muslim, Shi'a Muslim
CURRENCY: UAE dirham (AED)
ORGANIZATIONS: Arab League, OPEC, UN

The United Arab Emirates (UAE), comprising seven separate emirates, are stretched along the southeastern coast of the Gulf. It is a country covered mostly by flat deserts with the highest land in the Hajar mountains of the Musandam Peninsula. Summer temperatures reach 40°C (104°F); meagre rains of 130 mm (5 inches) fall mainly in the winter. Only the desert oases are fertile, producing fruit and vegetables. The economic wealth of the UAE is founded on its huge reserves of hydrocarbons, mainly within the largest Emirate, Abu Dhabi, with smaller supplies in three others – Dubai, Sharjah and Ras al Khaimah. Natural gas and oil are the major exports for which Japan and the Far East are the major markets. Revenue gained from these has allowed the economy to grow rapidly, with there being huge investment in the service industries. It has a population that is overwhelmingly made up of foreign immigrants.

ABU DHABI (ABŪ ẒABY)

STATUS: Emirate
AREA: 64,750 sq km (24,995 sq miles)
POPULATION: 670,125

AJMAN (AJMĀN)

STATUS: Emirate
AREA: 260 sq km (100 sq miles)
POPULATION: 64,318

DUBAI (DUBAYY)

STATUS: Emirate
AREA: 3,900 sq km (1,505 sq miles)
POPULATION: 419,104

FUJAIRAH (AL FUJAYRAH)

STATUS: Emirate
AREA: 1,170 sq km (452 sq miles)
POPULATION: 54,425

RAS AL KHAIMAH (RA'S AL KHAYMAH)

STATUS: Emirate
AREA: 1,690 sq km (625 sq miles)
POPULATION: 116,470

SHARJAH (ASH SHĀRIQAH)

STATUS: Emirate
AREA: 2,600 sq km (1,005 sq miles)
POPULATION: 268,722

UMM AL QAIWAIN (UMM AL QAYWAYN)

STATUS: Emirate
AREA: 780 sq km (300 sq miles)
POPULATION: 29,229

UNITED KINGDOM OF GREAT BRITAIN & NORTHERN IRELAND (UK)

STATUS: Monarchy
AREA: 244,082 sq km (94,241 sq miles)
POPULATION: 58,091,000
CAPITAL: London
LANGUAGE: English, south Indian languages, Chinese, Welsh, Gaelic
RELIGION: Protestant, Roman Catholic, Muslim, Sikh, Hindu, Jewish
CURRENCY: pound sterling (GBP)
ORGANIZATIONS: Col. Plan, Comm., Council of Europe, EEA, EU, G7, NATO, OECD, OSCE, UN, WEU

The United Kingdom, part of the British Isles, is situated off the northwest European coast, separated from France by the English Channel. It includes the countries of England and Scotland, the principality of Wales, and the region of Northern Ireland in the north of the island of Ireland.

In broad terms Britain can be divided into the upland regions of Wales, Northern England and Scotland, characterized by ancient dissected and glaciated mountain regions, and the lowland areas of southern and eastern England where low ranges of chalk, limestone and sandstone hills are interspersed with wide clay vales. The highest point in the United Kingdom is Ben Nevis in the Grampians of Scotland at 1,344 m (4,409 feet).

The climate of the British Isles is mild, wet and variable. Summer temperatures average 13–17°C (55–63°F) and winter temperatures 5–7°C (41–45°F). Annual rainfall varies between 640–5,000 mm (26–200 inches) with the highest rainfall in the Lake District and the lowest in East Anglia.

Although only a tiny percentage of the nation's workforce is employed in agriculture, farm produce is important to both home and export markets. Seventy-six per cent of the total UK land area is farmland. The main cereal crops are wheat, barley and oats. Potatoes, sugar beet and green vegetable crops are widespread.

About 20 per cent of the land is permanent pasture for raising dairy and beef stock and 28 per cent, mainly hill and mountain areas, is used for rough grazing of sheep. The best fruit-growing areas are the southeast, especially Kent, East Anglia and the central Vale of Evesham. Fishing supplies two-thirds of the nation's requirements but overfishing and encroachment into territorial waters by other countries have created problems.

The major mineral resources of the UK are coal, oil and natural gas. Over two-thirds of deep-mined coal came from the Yorkshire and East Midlands fields and substantial reserves remain. However, the coal industry, which had already been in slow decline for some 30 years, collapsed rapidly in 1993–4 when many of the remaining pits were closed. The number of employees fell from 208,000 in 1983 to 18,000 in early 1994 and by mid-1994 only 16 deep coal mines remained in operation, compared with 50 pits two years earlier.

Before the 1970s Britain relied on imports from the Middle East for its oil supplies, but in 1975 supplies of oil and gas from the vast North Sea oil fields began to provide both self-suffi-ciency and enough to export. Some of the older fields are now nearly worked out and operating costs for these are rising. The major Scott Field came on-stream in 1993 and in 1994 approval was granted for the development of the Fife and Birch oil fields and the Armada gas fields.

Wind farms as a source of energy, often the subject of controversy with environmentalists, contribute less than 1 per cent of Britain's elec-tricity.

Although the UK is an industrialized nation, the traditional mainstays of heavy industry such as coal, iron and steel and shipbuilding no longer figure prominently in the economy. Concurrent with the decline of heavy industry, there has been a substantial growth of light industries. High technology and electronic prod-ucts predominate, as well as pharmaceuticals, motor parts and food processing. Tourism is an essential part of the economy, especially in London, and in five years up to 1993 the number of visitors to the UK rose by 22 per cent. Financial services is another expanding sector, the 'City' of London having the greatest concen-tration of banks in the world.

The UK is a trading nation. The balance of trade has changed during the last 30 years because of increasingly closer economic ties with Europe and the move towards a Single European Market. Consequently, trading with Commonwealth nations, particularly Australia, has assumed lower priority. In terms of value, the most important exports from the UK are machinery, chemicals and transport equipment, followed by food, beverages and tobacco, petro-leum products, iron and steel.

The transport network in the UK is highly developed. Out of 362,357 km (225,164 miles) of public roads, 9 per cent are motorways and 13 per cent are other major roads. The railway net-work covers over 16,730 km (10,395 miles) and carries over 150 million tonnes of freight annual-ly. The opening of the Channel Tunnel in 1994 has connected the motorway and rail networks of Britain with those of northern France and southern Belgium. The inland waterway system totals only 563 navigable kilometres (350 miles) but has potential to carry more than its present 4 million tonnes of goods annually.

ENGLAND
STATUS: Constituent Country
AREA: 130,423 sq km (50,357 sq miles)
POPULATION: 48,532,700
CAPITAL: London

NORTHERN IRELAND
STATUS: Constituent Region
AREA: 14,121 sq km (5,452 sq miles)
POPULATION: 1,631,800
CAPITAL: Belfast

SCOTLAND
STATUS: Constituent Country
AREA: 78,772 sq km (30,414 sq miles)
POPULATION: 5,120,200
CAPITAL: Edinburgh

WALES
STATUS: Principality
AREA: 20,766 sq km (8,018 sq miles)
POPULATION: 2,906,500
CAPITAL: Cardiff

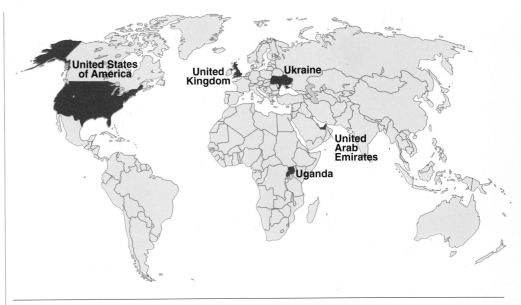

UNITED STATES OF AMERICA (USA)
STATUS: Republic
AREA: 9,809,386 sq km (3,787,425 sq miles)
POPULATION: 260,560,000
CAPITAL: Washington D.C.
LANGUAGE: English, Spanish, Amerindian laguages
RELIGION: Protestant, Roman Catholic, Sunni Muslim, Jewish, Mormon
CURRENCY: US dollar (USD)
ORGANIZATIONS: ANZUS, Col. Plan, G7, NAFTA, NATO, OAS, OECD, UN

The United States of America is the world's fourth largest country after Canada, China and Russia with the world's fourth largest population. The 19th and 20th centuries have brought 42 mil-lion immigrants to its shores, and the population of the USA now has the highest living standard of any country in the world. The large land area cov-ers a huge spectrum of different landscapes, envi-ronments and climates. The eastern coast of New England, where the European settlers first land-ed, is rocky, mountainous and richly wooded. South of New England is the Atlantic coastal plain, rising to the west towards the Appalachian mountain system. Beyond the Appalachians lie the central lowlands, a large undulating plain cut through by the Mississippi and Ohio rivers. Further west lie the Great Plains crossed by the Missouri, Red and Arkansas rivers and rising gen-tly towards the mighty Rocky Mountains, a spine of mountains running south from Alaska. Beyond these lie the Great Valley of California, the coastal ranges and the Pacific coast.

Climatic variety within the United States is enormous, ranging from the Arctic conditions of Alaska to the desert of the southwest – winter temperatures in Alaska plummet to -28°C (-19°F); in Florida they maintain a steady 19°C (66°F). The centre of the continent is dry, but both the north-west Pacific and the New England Atlantic coast are humid with heavy rainfall. Many areas of the USA fall prey to exceptional, often disastrous, weather conditions: the northeastern seaboard is susceptible to heavy blizzards, the southern low-lands are vulnerable to spring thaw flooding and the Mississippi valley is prone to tornadoes.

The natural vegetation of the USA reflects its climatic diversity. The northwest coast is rich in coniferous forest, while the Appalachian moun-tain region is well endowed with hardwoods. In the arid southwest, vegetation is limited to desert scrub whereas the Gulf and South Atlantic coast are fringed with swampy wet-lands. The central lowlands are endowed with rich black-earth soils (the agricultural heart-land), gradually supplanted, towards the Rockies, by tall-grass prairie. The northeastern states of Illinois, Iowa, Indiana and Nebraska form the 'corn belt', which produces 45 per cent of the world's corn. Further west wheat supple-ments corn as the main crop. The northeastern states are predominantly dairy country, and the south is famous for cotton and tobacco. Rice is grown in Texas, California and Louisiana, and fruit and vegetables in Florida.

The USA consumes 25 per cent of all the world's energy resources but is well endowed with energy reserves. There are substantial coal resources, particularly in the Appalachians. The great rivers have been harnessed extensively for hydro-electric power. Oil and natural gas fields are found in Texas, Alaska, Louisiana and California and new deep-sea exploratory drilling is underway in the Gulf of Mexico. Oil produc-tion, however, has declined steadily since 1983.

The industrial base is diverse, the main industries being steel, motor vehicles, aerospace, chemicals, computers, electronics, telecommu-nications and consumer goods. The service industries (encompassing tourism and finance) are by far the biggest source of employment in the United States.

ALABAMA
STATUS: State
AREA: 135,775 sq km (52,423 sq miles)
POPULATION: 4,136,000
CAPITAL: Montgomery

ALASKA
STATUS: State
AREA: 1,700,130 sq km (656,424 sq miles)
POPULATION: 587,000
CAPITAL: Juneau

ARIZONA
STATUS: State
AREA: 295,274 sq km (114,006 sq miles)
POPULATION: 3,832,000
CAPITAL: Phoenix

ARKANSAS
STATUS: State
AREA: 137,741 sq km (53,182 sq miles)
POPULATION: 2,399,000
CAPITAL: Little Rock

CALIFORNIA
STATUS: State
AREA: 423,999 sq km (163,707 sq miles)
POPULATION: 30,867,000
CAPITAL: Sacramento

COLORADO
STATUS: State
AREA: 269,618 sq km (104,100 sq miles)
POPULATION: 3,470,000
CAPITAL: Denver

CONNECTICUT
STATUS: State
AREA: 14,359 sq km (5,544 sq miles)
POPULATION: 3,281,000
CAPITAL: Hartford

DELAWARE
STATUS: State
AREA: 6,446 sq km (2,489 sq miles)
POPULATION: 689,000
CAPITAL: Dover

DISTRICT OF COLUMBIA
STATUS: Federal District
AREA: 176 sq km (68 sq miles)
POPULATION: 589,000
CAPITAL: Washington D.C.

FLORIDA
STATUS: State
AREA: 170,312 sq km (65,758 sq miles)
POPULATION: 13,488,000
CAPITAL: Tallahassee

GEORGIA
STATUS: State
AREA: 153,951 sq km (59,441 sq miles)
POPULATION: 6,751,000
CAPITAL: Atlanta

HAWAII
STATUS: State
AREA: 28,314 sq km (10,932 sq miles)
POPULATION: 1,160,000
CAPITAL: Honolulu

IDAHO
STATUS: State
AREA: 216,456 sq km (83,574 sq miles)
POPULATION: 1,067,000
CAPITAL: Boise

ILLINOIS
STATUS: State
AREA: 150,007 sq km (57,918 sq miles)
POPULATION: 11,631,000
CAPITAL: Springfield

INDIANA
STATUS: State
AREA: 94,327 sq km (36,420 sq miles)
POPULATION: 5,662,000
CAPITAL: Indianapolis

IOWA
STATUS: State
AREA: 145,754 sq km (56,276 sq miles)
POPULATION: 2,812,000
CAPITAL: Des Moines

KANSAS
STATUS: State
AREA: 213,109 sq km (82,282 sq miles)
POPULATION: 2,523,000
CAPITAL: Topeka

KENTUCKY
STATUS: State
AREA: 104,664 sq km (40,411 sq miles)
POPULATION: 3,755,000
CAPITAL: Frankfort

LOUISIANA
STATUS: State
AREA: 134,273 sq km (51,843 sq miles)
POPULATION: 4,287,000
CAPITAL: Baton Rouge

MAINE
STATUS: State
AREA: 91,652 sq km (35,387 sq miles)
POPULATION: 1,235,000
CAPITAL: Augusta

MARYLAND
STATUS: State
AREA: 32,134 sq km (12,407 sq miles)
POPULATION: 4,908,000
CAPITAL: Annapolis

MASSACHUSETTS
STATUS: State
AREA: 27,337 sq km (10,555 sq miles)
POPULATION: 5,998,000
CAPITAL: Boston

MICHIGAN
STATUS: State
AREA: 250,737 sq km (96,810 sq miles)
POPULATION: 9,437,000
CAPITAL: Lansing

MINNESOTA
STATUS: State
AREA: 225,181 sq km (86,943 sq miles)
POPULATION: 4,480,000
CAPITAL: St Paul

MISSISSIPPI
STATUS: State
AREA: 125,443 sq km (48,434 sq miles)
POPULATION: 2,614,000
CAPITAL: Jackson

MISSOURI
STATUS: State
AREA: 180,545 sq km (69,709 sq miles)
POPULATION: 5,193,000
CAPITAL: Jefferson City

MONTANA
STATUS: State
AREA: 380,847 sq km (147,046 sq miles)
POPULATION: 824,000
CAPITAL: Helena

NEBRASKA
STATUS: State
AREA: 200,356 sq km (77,358 sq miles)
POPULATION: 1,606,000
CAPITAL: Lincoln

NEVADA
STATUS: State
AREA: 286,367 sq km (110,567 sq miles)
POPULATION: 1,327,000
CAPITAL: Carson City

NEW HAMPSHIRE
STATUS: State
AREA: 24,219 sq km (9,351 sq miles)
POPULATION: 1,111,000
CAPITAL: Concord

NEW JERSEY
STATUS: State
AREA: 22,590 sq km (8,722 sq miles)
POPULATION: 7,789,000
CAPITAL: Trenton

NEW MEXICO
STATUS: State
AREA: 314,937 sq km (121,598 sq miles)
POPULATION: 1,581,000
CAPITAL: Sante Fe

NEW YORK
STATUS: State
AREA: 141,090 sq km (54,475 sq miles)
POPULATION: 18,119,000
CAPITAL: Albany

NORTH CAROLINA
STATUS: State
AREA: 139,396 sq km (53,821 sq miles)
POPULATION: 6,843,000
CAPITAL: Raleigh

NORTH DAKOTA
STATUS: State
AREA: 183,123 sq km (70,704 sq miles)
POPULATION: 638,000
CAPITAL: Bismarck

OHIO
STATUS: State
AREA: 116,104 sq km (44,828 sq miles)
POPULATION: 11,016,000
CAPITAL: Columbus

OKLAHOMA
STATUS: State
AREA: 181,048 sq km (69,903 sq miles)
POPULATION: 3,212,00
CAPITAL: Oklahoma City

OREGON
STATUS: State
AREA: 254,819 sq km (98,386 sq miles)
POPULATION: 2,977,000
CAPITAL: Salem

PENNSYLVANIA
STATUS: State
AREA: 119,290 sq km (46,058 sq miles)
POPULATION: 12,009,000
CAPITAL: Harrisburg

RHODE ISLAND
STATUS: State
AREA: 4,002 sq km (1,545 sq miles)
POPULATION: 1,005,000
CAPITAL: Providence

SOUTH CAROLINA
STATUS: State
AREA: 82,898 sq km (32,007 sq miles)
POPULATION: 3,603,000
CAPITAL: Columbia

SOUTH DAKOTA
STATUS: State
AREA: 199,742 sq km (77,121 sq miles)
POPULATION: 711,000
CAPITAL: Pierre

TENNESSEE
STATUS: State
AREA: 109,158 sq km (42,146 sq miles)
POPULATION: 5,024,000
CAPITAL: Nashville

TEXAS
STATUS: State
AREA: 695,673 sq km (268,601 sq miles)
POPULATION: 17,656,000
CAPITAL: Austin

UTAH
STATUS: State
AREA: 219,900 sq km (84,904 sq miles)
POPULATION: 1,813,000
CAPITAL: Salt Lake City

VERMONT
STATUS: State
AREA: 24,903 sq km (9,615 sq miles)
POPULATION: 570,000
CAPITAL: Montpelier

VIRGINIA
STATUS: State
AREA: 110,771 sq km (42,769 sq miles)
POPULATION: 6,377,000
CAPITAL: Richmond

WASHINGTON
STATUS: State
AREA: 184,674 sq km (71,303 sq miles)
POPULATION: 5,136,000
CAPITAL: Olympia

WEST VIRGINIA
STATUS: State
AREA: 62,758 sq km (24,231 sq miles)
POPULATION: 1,812,000
CAPITAL: Charleston

WISCONSIN
STATUS: State
AREA: 169,652 sq km (65,503 sq miles)
POPULATION: 5,007,000
CAPITAL: Madison

WYOMING
STATUS: State
AREA: 253,347 sq km (97,818 sq miles)
POPULATION: 466,000
CAPITAL: Cheyenne

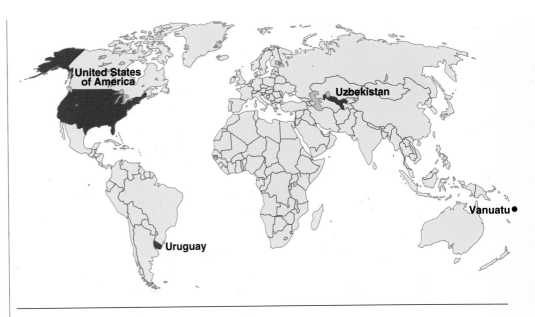

URUGUAY
STATUS: Republic
AREA: 176,215 sq km (68,037 sq miles)
POPULATION: 3,167,000
CAPITAL: Montevideo
LANGUAGE: Spanish
RELIGION: Roman Catholic, Protestant, Jewish
CURRENCY: Uruguayan peso (UYP)
ORGANIZATIONS: ALADI, Mercosur, OAS, UN

Uruguay is a small country on the southeast coast of south America. Geographically it consists firstly of a narrow plain, fringed with lagoons and dunes, skirting along the coast and the estuary of the river Plate. Further inland, rolling grassland hills are broken by minor ridges of the Brazilian highlands, which reach heights of no more than 500 m (1,600 feet). The climate is temperate and rainfall is spread evenly throughout the year at about 100 mm (4 inches) per month. Monthly temperatures average in the range of 10–22°C (50–72°F). The land has good agricultural potential, however most is given over to the grazing of sheep and cattle. The economy relies heavily on the production of meat and wool with 87 per cent of the area devoted to farming. Uruguay has no oil or gas reserves, and most of its energy requirements are obtained from hydro-electricity.

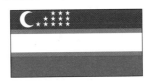

UZBEKISTAN
STATUS: Republic
AREA: 447,400 sq km (172,742 sq miles)
POPULATION: 22,349,000
CAPITAL: Tashkent
LANGUAGE: Uzbek, Russian, Tajik, Kazakh
RELIGION: Sunni Muslim, Russian Orthodox
CURRENCY: som
ORGANIZATIONS: OSCE, UN

Established in 1924 as a constituent republic of the Soviet Union, Uzbekistan became an independent state in 1991. The majority of the country consists of flat, sun-baked lowlands with mountains in the south and east. The climate is markedly continental and very dry with an abundance of sunshine and mild, short winters. The southern mountains are of great economic importance, providing ample supplies of water for hydro-electric plants and irrigation schemes. The mountain regions also contain substantial reserves of natural gas, oil, coal, iron and other metals. With its fertile soils (when irrigated) and good pastures, Uzbekistan is well situated for cattle raising and the production of cotton. It is also the largest producer of machines and heavy equipment in central Asia, and has been specializing mainly in machinery for cotton cultivation and harvesting, for irrigation projects, for road-building and textile processing. During the Soviet period the urban employment market became increasingly dominated by Russians and other outsiders. The gradual emergence of better educated and better trained Uzbeks has generated fiercely nationalist sentiments.

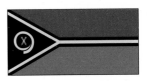

VANUATU
STATUS: Republic
AREA: 12,190 sq km (4,707 sq miles)
POPULATION: 165,000
CAPITAL: Port-Vila
LANGUAGE: English, Bislama (English Creole), French (all official)
RELIGION: Protestant, Roman Catholic, Traditional beliefs
CURRENCY: vatu (VUV)
ORGANIZATIONS: Comm., UN

Vanuatu is a chain of some 80 densely forested, mountainous, volcanic islands, situated in the Melanesian south Pacific. Its climate is tropical, with a high rainfall and a continuous threat of cyclones. Copra, cocoa and coffee are grown mainly for export, with fish, pigs and sheep as well as yams, taro, manioc and bananas important only for home consumption. Manganese is the only mineral with deposits of economic value. Tourism is becoming important, particularly with Australian and Japanese visitors.

VATICAN CITY

STATUS: Ecclesiastical State
AREA: 0.44 sq km (0.17 sq miles)
POPULATION: 1,000
LANGUAGE: Italian, Latin
RELIGION: Roman Catholic
CURRENCY: Italian lira (ITL)
ORGANIZATIONS: OSCE

The Vatican City, the headquarters of the Roman Catholic Church, is the world's smallest independent state. It is entirely surrounded by the city of Rome, occupying a hill to the west of the river Tiber. It has been the papal residence since the 5th century and a destination for pilgrims and tourists from all over the world. Most income is derived from voluntary contributions (Peter's Pence), tourism and interest on investments. The only industries are those connected with the Church.

VENEZUELA

STATUS: Republic
AREA: 912,050 sq km
(352,144 sq miles)
POPULATION: 21,177,000
CAPITAL: Caracas
LANGUAGE: Spanish,
Amerindian languages
RELIGION: Roman Catholic, Protestant
CURRENCY: bolívar (VEB)
ORGANIZATIONS: ALADI, OAS, OPEC, UN

Venezuela, one of the richest countries of Latin America, is divided into four topographical regions: the continuation of the Andes in the west; the humid lowlands around Lake Maracaibo in the north; the savannah-covered central plains (Llanos), and the extension of the Guiana Highlands covering almost half the country. The climate varies between tropical in the south to warm temperate along the northern coasts. The majority of the population live along the north coast. Venezuela's economy is built around oil production in the Maracaibo region; over three-quarters of export revenue comes from oil. Bauxite and iron ore are also important. The majority of employment is provided by industrial and manufacturing sectors of the economy.

VIETNAM

STATUS: Republic
AREA: 329,565 sq km (127,246 sq miles)

POPULATION: 72,509,000
CAPITAL: Hanoi
LANGUAGE: Vietnamese, Thai, Khmer, Chinese,
many local languages
RELIGION: Buddhist, Taoist, Roman Catholic,
Cao, Dai, Hoa Hao
CURRENCY: dong (VND)
ORGANIZATIONS: ASEAN, OIEC, UN

Situated on the eastern coast of the Indo-Chinese peninsula of southeastern Asia, Vietnam is predominantly a rugged, mountainous country. The north-south oriented mountainous spine separates two major river deltas: the Red River (Hong river) in the north and the Mekong in the south. Monsoons bring 1,500 mm (59 inches) of rain every year and temperatures average 15°C (59°F) annually. Rainforest still covers some of the central mountainous areas, but most has been cleared for agriculture and habitation. Rice is grown extensively throughout the north (Vietnam is the world's third largest exporter after the USA and Thailand) along with coffee and rubber in other parts of the country. Vietnam possesses a wide range of minerals including coal, lignite, anthracite, iron ore and tin. Industry is expanding rapidly, but decades of warfare and internal strife have impeded development. The US government has lifted its 20-year-old trade embargo, which will further help strengthen Vietnam's trade position.

VIRGIN ISLANDS (UK)

STATUS: UK Territory
AREA: 153 sq km (59 sq miles)
POPULATION: 18,000
CAPITAL: Road Town

VIRGIN ISLANDS (USA)

STATUS: US Territory
AREA: 352 sq km (136 sq miles)
POPULATION: 104,000
CAPITAL: Charlotte Amalie

WALLIS & FUTUNA ISLANDS

STATUS: French Territory
AREA: 274 sq km (106 sq miles)
POPULATION: 14,000
CAPITAL: Mata-Uta
LANGUAGE: French, Polynesian (Wallisian,
Futunian)

WESTERN SAHARA

STATUS: Territory
AREA: 266,000 sq km (102,703 sq miles)
POPULATION: 272,000
CAPITAL: Laâyoune
LANGUAGE: Arabic

WESTERN SAMOA

STATUS: Monarchy
AREA: 2,831 sq km (1,093 sq miles)
POPULATION: 164,000
CAPITAL: Apia
LANGUAGE: Samoan, English

RELIGION: Protestant, Roman Catholic,
Mormon
CURRENCY: tala (dollar) (WST)
ORGANIZATIONS: Comm., UN

Western Samoa constitutes a 160 km (100 mile) chain of nine south Pacific islands. The two largest islands, Savaii and Upolu, are mountainous and volcanic. Annual rainfall averages 2,500 mm (100 inches) per year and temperatures average 26°C (79°F) for most months. Only four of the islands are populated – Savaii, Upolu, Manono and Apolima. Main exports are copra, timber, coffee, cocoa and fruit. Western Samoa has some light industries, such as food processing, textiles and cigarette manufacture and a tourist trade is developing. Remittances from citizens abroad are, however, also very important to the economy.

YEMEN

STATUS: Republic
AREA: 527,968 sq km (203,850 sq miles)
POPULATION: 13,873,000
CAPITAL: Sana (Şan'ā')
LANGUAGE: Arabic
RELIGION: Sunni Muslim, Shi'a Muslim
CURRENCY: Yemeni dinar and rial
ORGANIZATIONS: Arab League, UN

The Yemen Arab Republic and the People's Democratic Republic of Yemen were unified in 1990 to form a single state with its capital at San'a. Situated in the southern part of the Arabian Peninsula the country comprises several contrasting physical landscapes. The north is mainly mountainous and relatively wet with rainfall reaching 890 mm (35 inches) in inland areas which helps to irrigate the cereals, cotton, fruits and vegetables grown on the windward mountain sides and along the coast. The south coast stretches for 1,100 km (685 miles) from the mouth of the Red Sea to Oman. These southern regions are generally arid except along the coastal plain where irrigation schemes support some agriculture and away from the coast in the Hadhramaut valley where sufficient rainfall occurs for cereal cultivation. To the north of the Hadhramaut lies the uninhabited Arabian Desert. The population, most of whom are subsistence farmers or nomadic herders of sheep and goats, are concentrated in western regions. Until recently the only mineral exploited commercially was salt but since the discovery of oil in 1984 and 1991, that commodity is making an important contribution to the economy. Otherwise, industrial activity is limited to small scale manufacturing.

YUGOSLAVIA

STATUS: Republic
AREA: 102,173 sq km (39,449 sq miles)
POPULATION: 10,515,000

CAPITAL: Belgrade (Beograd)
LANGUAGE: Serbo-Croat, Albanian,
Hungarian
RELIGION: Serbian Orthodox,
Montenegrin Orthodox,
Sunni Muslim
CURRENCY: Yugoslav dinar (YUD)
ORGANIZATIONS: OSCE, UN

Serbia and Montenegro are the last remaining elements of the Federal Republic of Yugoslavia. Until 1918, they were separate kingdoms. Union of the two, including Vojvodina, followed by unification with lands freed from the Turkish and Austro-Hungarian Empires, resulted in the creation of the Kingdom of Serbs, Croats and Slovenes, a name which was changed to the Kingdom of Yugoslavia in 1929. Yugoslavia became a Socialist Federal Republic in 1945. Economic difficulties from 1980 onwards, combined with regional and ethnic factors, culminated in the secession of Slovenia and Croatia in 1992. International recognition of their sovereignty did not deter Serbia, with the Serb-dominated army at its disposal, from armed incursion to secure areas inhabited by Serbians. Macedonia's claim for recognition was not so well received internationally because of Greek objection to the name Macedonia. Yet, it has ceased to be a part of Yugoslavia. No such impediment stood in the way of recognizing the independence of Bosnia-Herzegovina. Armed conflict intensified in this ethnically complex republic as rival factions fought to support their kinsfolk.

The climate is essentially continental with hot summers and cold winters. Agriculture, which is largely in private hands, features cotton and cereal cultivation on the fertile plains of Vojvodina in the north, livestock production in central Serbia and fruit and tobacco growing in Kosovo in the south. Industry, however, which had accounted for 80 per cent of economic wealth, has suffered severely from the effects of civil war and United Nations sanctions. Inflation is rife and only the black market flourishes.

MONTENEGRO
STATUS: Constituent Republic
AREA: 13,810 sq km (5,330 sq miles)
POPULATION: 616,327
CAPITAL: Podgorica

SERBIA
STATUS: Constituent Republic
AREA: 88,360 sq km (34,105 sq miles)
POPULATION: 9,815,000
CAPITAL: Belgrade (Beograd)

ZAIRE
STATUS: Republic
AREA: 2,345,410 sq km (905,568 sq miles)
POPULATION: 42,552,000
CAPITAL: Kinshasa
LANGUAGE: French, Lingala, Swahili, Kongo,
many local languages
RELIGION: Roman Catholic,

Protestant, Sunni Muslim
Traditional beliefs
CURRENCY: zaïre (ZRZ)
ORGANIZATIONS: CEEAC, OAU, UN

Zaire, formerly the Belgian Congo, lies astride the Equator and is Africa's third largest country after Sudan and Algeria. It is dominated by the drainage basin of the Zaire, Kasai, and Oubangui rivers, which join to flow into the Atlantic. The land gradually rises from these basins to the south and east, culminating in the Chaine des Mitumba or Mitumbar mountains. On its eastern border the great Rift Valley forms a natural boundary with Uganda and Tanzania. Tropical rainforest covers most of the basin. Zaire's climate is equatorial with both high temperatures, averaging 27°C (80°F) throughout the year, and high rainfall of about 1,500–2,000 (59–79 inches). The majority of the population is engaged in shifting agriculture. Cassava, cocoa, coffee, cotton, millet, rubber and sugar cane are grown. Although the nation possesses mineral wealth, particularly copper which alone has provided 40 per cent of foreign earnings, political turmoil has reduced the country to bankruptcy. The copper mines are closed and diamonds are the only source of income. Zaire faces expulsion from the IMF because of debt arrears.

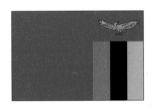

ZAMBIA
STATUS: Republic
AREA: 752,614 sq km (290,586 sq miles)
POPULATION: 9,196,000
CAPITAL: Lusaka
LANGUAGE: English, Bemba, Nyanja, Tonga,
many local languages
RELIGION: Protestant, Roman Catholic,
Traditional beliefs, Sunni Muslim
CURRENCY: kwacha (ZMK)
ORGANIZATIONS: Comm., OAU, SADC, UN

Mineral-rich Zambia, is situated in the interior of southern central Africa. Its geography consists mainly of high rolling plateaux, with mountains to the north and northeast. In the south is the Zambezi river basin and the man-made reservoir of Lake Kariba, which forms Zambia's border with

Zimbabwe. Altitude moderates the potentially tropical climate so that the summer temperature averages only 13–27°C (55–81°F). The north receives over 1,250 mm (49 inches) of rain per annum, the south less. Most of the country is grassland with some forest in the north. Farming is now mainly at subsistence level, as droughts have had an adverse effect on many crops, but some cattle rearing still takes on importance in the east. Copper remains the mainstay of the country's economy although reserves are fast running out. Lead, zinc, cobalt, cotton, groundnuts and tobacco are also exported. Wildlife is diverse and abundant and contributes to expanding tourism.

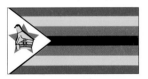

ZIMBABWE
STATUS: Republic
AREA: 390,759 sq km (150,873 sq miles)
POPULATION: 11,150,000
CAPITAL: Harare
LANGUAGE: English (official), Shona, Ndebele
RELIGION: Protestant, Roman Catholic,
Traditional beliefs
CURRENCY: Zimbabwe dollar (ZWD)
ORGANIZATIONS: Comm., OAU, SADC, UN

Landlocked Zimbabwe (formerly southern Rhodesia) in south central Africa consists predominantly of rolling plateaux and valleys. A broad ridge of upland plateaux (the high veld) crosses east-west over the greater part of the country reaching heights of 1,200–1,500 m (3,940–4,920 feet). There are lowland areas (the low veld) formed by the valleys of the Zambezi and Limpopo rivers, in the north and south respectively. The climate varies with altitude and distance from the ocean. Rainfall across the country averages between 600-1,000 mm (24-39 inches). The exploitation of mineral deposits have traditionally supported the economy although recent years have seen a shift in the decline of chrome and coal and a rise in the importance of platinum, nickel and asbestos. Maize is the most important crop as it is the staple food of a large proportion of the population. Tobacco, tea, sugar cane and fruit are also grown. Manufacturing industry is slowly developing and now provides a wide range of consumer products.

North and Central America
25 349 000
9 785 000

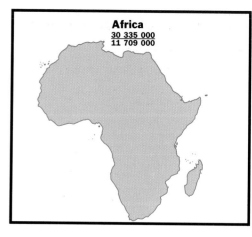

CONTINENTS

land area ⬜ = **1 000 000** sq kms / **386 000** sq miles

Europe
10 498 000
4 052 000

Asia
43 608 000
16 833 000

Europe

Asia

Africa
30 335 000
11 709 000

South America
17 611 000
6 798 000

Antarctica
13 340 000
5 149 240

Australasia
8 923 000
3 444 278

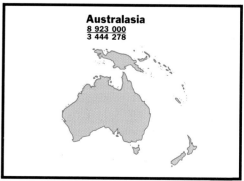

Population	City	Country
2,500,000	**Adibjan**	*Ivory Coast*
1,891,000	**Addis Ababa**	*Ethiopia*
3,297,655	**Ahmadabad**	*India*
3,380,000	**Alexandria**	*Egypt*
3,033,000	**Algiers**	*Algeria*
1,151,300	**Alma-Ata**	*Kazakhstan*
1,091,338	**Amsterdam**	*Netherlands*
3,022,236	**Ankara**	*Turkey*
1,390,000	**Anshan**	*China*
3,096,775	**Athens**	*Greece*
3,051,000	**Atlanta**	*USA*
896,700	**Auckland**	*New Zealand*
4,044,000	**Baghdad**	*Iraq*
1,779,500	**Baku**	*Azerbaijan*
2,414,000	**Baltimore**	*USA*
4,086,548	**Bangalore**	*India*
5,876,000	**Bangkok**	*Thailand*
1,625,542	**Barcelona**	*Spain*
10,900,000	**Beijing (Peking)**	*China*
1,500,000	**Beirut**	*Lebanon*
1,168,454	**Belgrade**	*Yugoslavia*
3,461,905	**Belo Horizonte**	*Brazil*
3,446,000	**Berlin**	*Germany*
2,310,900	**Birmingham**	*UK*
5,025,989	**Bogotá**	*Colombia*
12,571,720	**Bombay**	*India*
4,497,000	**Boston**	*USA*
1,803,478	**Brasília**	*Brazil*
950,339	**Brussels**	*Belgium*
2,350,984	**Bucharest**	*Romania*
2,992,000	**Budapest**	*Hungary*
12,200,000	**Buenos Aires**	*Argentina*
13,300,000	**Cairo**	*Egypt*
10,916,000	**Calcutta**	*India*
320,000	**Canberra**	*Australia*
2,350,157	**Cape Town**	*South Africa*
4,092,000	**Caracas**	*Venezuela*
3,210,000	**Casablanca**	*Morocco*
2,214,000	**Changchun**	*China*
1,362,000	**Changsha**	*China*
1,148,000	**Chelyabinsk**	*Russian Federation*
3,004,000	**Chengdu**	*China*
7,498,000	**Chicago**	*USA*
3,010,000	**Chongqing**	*China*
1,342,679	**Copenhagen**	*Denmark*
2,543,000	**Dalian**	*China*
4,135,000	**Dallas – Fort Worth**	*USA*
2,913,000	**Damascus**	*Syria*
1,657,000	**Dar-es-Salaam**	*Tanzania*
8,375,000	**Delhi**	*India*
4,285,000	**Detroit**	*USA*
6,105,160	**Dhaka**	*Bangladesh*
915,516	**Dublin**	*Republic of Ireland*
2,720,400	**Essen – Dortmund**	*Germany*
1,420,000	**Fushun**	*China*
383,900	**Geneva**	*Switzerland*
2,846,720	**Guadalajara**	*Mexico*
3,620,000	**Guangzhou (Canton)**	*China*
1,669,000	**Hamburg**	*Germany*

METROPOLITAN AREAS

Population	City	Country
1,412,000	**Hangzhou**	*China*
3,056,146	**Hanoi**	*Vietnam*
2,840,000	**Harbin**	*China*
2,099,000	**Havana**	*Cuba*
3,924,435	**Ho Chi Minh (Saigon)**	*Vietnam*
5,812,000	**Hong Kong**	*UK colony*
3,437,000	**Houston**	*USA*
4,280,000	**Hyderabad**	*India*
6,407,215	**Istanbul**	*Turkey*
9,000,000	**Jakarta**	*Indonesia*
608,000	**Jerusalem**	*Israel*
1,327,000	**Jilin**	*China*
2,415,000	**Jinan**	*China*
1,916,063	**Johannesburg**	*South Africa*
1,300,000	**Kābul**	*Afghanistan*
7,702,000	**Karachi**	*Pakistan*
1,947,000	**Khartoum**	*Sudan*
2,616,000	**Kiev**	*Ukraine*
3,505,000	**Kinshasa**	*Zaire*
1,711,000	**Kuala Lumpur**	*Malaysia*
5,689,000	**Lagos**	*Nigeria*
4,092,000	**Lahore**	*Pakistan*
1,566,000	**Lanzhou**	*China*
6,483,901	**Lima**	*Peru*
1,742,000	**Lisbon**	*Portugal*
9,277,687	**London**	*UK*
11,420,000	**Los Angeles**	*USA*
5,361,468	**Madras**	*India*
2,909,792	**Madrid**	*Spain*
2,578,900	**Manchester**	*UK*
8,475,000	**Manila – Quezon City**	*Philippines*
1,594,967	**Medellín**	*Colombia*
3,178,000	**Melbourne**	*Australia*
20,200,000	**Mexico City**	*Mexico*
1,814,000	**Miami**	*USA*
2,583,000	**Minneapolis – St Paul**	*USA*
1,633,000	**Minsk**	*Belarus*
2,521,697	**Monterrey**	*Mexico*
1,383,660	**Montevideo**	*Uruguay*
3,127,100	**Montréal**	*Canada*
8,957,000	**Moscow**	*Russian Federation*
1,236,000	**Munich**	*Germany*
2,095,000	**Nagoya**	*Japan*
1,503,000	**Nairobi**	*Kenya*
1,415,000	**Nanchang**	*China*
2,265,000	**Nanjing**	*China*
16,972,000	**New York**	*USA*
1,442,000	**Novosibirsk**	*Russian Federation*
1,106,000	**Odessa**	*Ukraine*
8,520,000	**Osaka-Kobe**	*Japan*
473,344	**Oslo**	*Norway*
921,000	**Ottawa**	*Canada*

Population	City	Country
9,318,000	**Paris**	*France*
4,941,000	**Philadelphia**	*USA*
2,287,000	**Phoenix**	*USA*
2,404,000	**Pittsburgh**	*USA*
3,015,960	**Pôrto Alegre**	*Brazil*
1,214,174	**Prague**	*Czech Republic*
3,797,566	**Pusan**	*South Korea*
2,230,000	**Pyôngyang**	*North Korea*
645,000	**Quebec**	*Canada*
2,060,000	**Qingdao**	*China*
1,281,849	**Quito**	*Ecuador*
3,295,000	**Rangoon**	*Burma*
2,859,469	**Recife**	*Brazil*
910,200	**Riga**	*Latvia*
9,871,165	**Rio de Janeiro**	*Brazil*
1,500,000	**Riyadh**	*Saudi Arabia*
2,723,327	**Rome**	*Italy*
1,388,000	**Sacramento**	*USA*
2,472,131	**Salvador**	*Brazil*
2,549,000	**San Deigo**	*USA*
5,240,000	**San Francisco**	*USA*
1,390,000	**San Juan**	*Puerto Rico*
4,628,000	**Santiago**	*Chile*
2,055,000	**Santo Domingo**	*Dominican Republic*
15,199,423	**São Paulo**	*Brazil*
10,627,000	**Seoul**	*South Korea*
13,341,896	**Shanghai**	*China*
4,763,000	**Shenyang**	*China*
2,874,000	**Singapore**	*Singapore*
1,221,000	**Sofia**	*Bulgaria*
2,507,000	**St Louis**	*USA*
5,004,000	**St Petersburg**	*Russian Federation*
1,669,840	**Stockholm**	*Sweden*
2,473,272	**Surabaya**	*Indonesia*
3,700,000	**Sydney**	*Australia*
2,228,000	**Taegu**	*South Korea*
2,720,000	**Taipei**	*Taiwan*
2,199,000	**Taiyuan**	*China*
452,000	**Tallinn**	*Estonia*
2,094,000	**Tashkent**	*Uzbekistan*
1,400,000	**Tbilisi**	*Georgia*
6,773,000	**Tehran**	*Iran*
1,135,800	**Tel Aviv**	*Israel*
9,100,000	**Tianjin**	*China*
11,609,735	**Tokyo**	*Japan*
3,893,400	**Toronto**	*Canada*
2,062,000	**Tripoli**	*Libya*
1,603,600	**Vancouver**	*Canada*
1,565,000	**Vienna**	*Austria*
593,000	**Vilnius**	*Lithuania*
1,655,700	**Warsaw**	*Poland*
4,293,000	**Washington DC**	*USA*
325,700	**Wellington**	*New Zealand*
652,000	**Winnipeg**	*Canada*
3,921,000	**Wuhan**	*China*
2,859,000	**Xian**	*China*
1,202,000	**Yerevan**	*Armenia*
726,770	**Zagreb**	*Croatia*
2,460,000	**Zibo**	*China*

MOUNTAIN HEIGHTS

metres	feet		
8,848	29,028	**Everest (Qomolangma Feng)**	
		China–Nepal	
8,611	28,250	**K2 (Qogir Feng) (Godwin Austen)**	
		India – China	
8,598	28,170	**Kangchenjunga** *India–Nepal*	
8,481	27,824	**Makalu** *China–Nepal*	
8,217	26,958	**Cho Oyu** *China–Nepal*	
8,167	26,795	**Dhaulagiri** *Nepal*	
8,156	26,758	**Manaslu** *Nepal*	
8,126	26,660	**Nanga Parbat** *India*	
8,078	26,502	**Annapurna** *Nepal*	
8,088	26,470	**Gasherbrum** *India–China*	
8,027	26,335	**Xixabangma Feng (Gosainthan)**	
		China	
7,885	25,869	**Distaghil Sar** *Kashmir, India*	
7,820	25,656	**Masherbrum** *India*	
7,817	25,646	**Nanda Devi** *India*	
7,788	25,550	**Rakaposhi** *India*	
7,756	25,446	**Kamet** *China–India*	
7,756	25,447	**Namjagbarwa Feng** *China*	
7,728	25,355	**Gurla Mandhata** *China*	
7,723	25,338	**Muztag** *China*	
7,719	25,325	**Kongur Shan (Kungur)** *China*	
7,690	25,230	**Tirich Mir** *Pakistan*	
7,556	24,790	**Gongga Shan** *China*	
7,546	24,757	**Muztagata** *China*	
7,495	24,590	**Pik Kommunizma** *Tajikistan*	
7,439	24,406	**Pik Pobedy (Tomur Feng)**	
		Kirghizia–China	
7,313	23,993	**Chomo Lhari** *Bhutan–Tibet*	
7,134	23,406	**Pik Lenina** *Kirghizia*	
6,960	22,834	**Aconcagua** *Argentina*	
6,908	22,664	**Ojos del Salado** *Argentina–Chile*	
6,872	22,546	**Bonete** *Argentina*	
6,800	22,310	**Tupungato** *Argentina–Chile*	
6,770	22,221	**Mercedario** *Argentina*	
6,768	22,205	**Huascarán** *Peru*	
6,723	22,057	**Llullaillaco** *Argentina–Chile*	
6,714	22,027	**Kangrinboqê Feng (Kailas)**	
		Tibet, China	
6,634	21,765	**Yerupaja** *Peru*	
6,542	21,463	**Sajama** *Bolivia*	
6,485	21,276	**Illampu** *Bolivia*	
6,425	21,079	**Coropuna** *Peru*	
6,402	21,004	**Illimani** *Bolivia*	
6,310	20,702	**Chimborazo** *Ecuador*	
6,194	20,320	**McKinley** *USA*	
5,959	19,551	**Logan** *Canada*	
5,896	19,344	**Cotopaxi** *Ecuador*	
5,895	19,340	**Kilimanjaro** *Tanzania*	
5,800	19,023	**Sa. Nevada de Sta. Marta**	
		(Cristobal Colon) *Columbia*	
5,775	18,947	**Bolivar** *Venezuela*	
5,699	18,697	**Citlaltépetl (Orizaba)** *Mexico*	
5,642	18,510	**El'brus** *Russian Federation*	
5,601	18,376	**Damávand** *Iran*	
5,489	18,008	**Mt St. Elias** *Canada*	
5,227	17,149	**Mt Lucania** *Canada*	
5,199	17,057	**Kenya (Kirinyaga)** *Kenya*	
5,165	16,945	**Ararat (Büyük Ağri Daği)** *Turkey*	
5,140	16,860	**Vinson Massif** *Antarctica*	
5,110	16,763	**Stanley (Margherita)** *Uganda–Zaire*	
5,029	16,499	**Jaya (Carstensz)** *Indonesia*	
5,005	16,421	**Mt Bona** *USA*	
4,949	16,237	**Sandford** *USA*	
4,936	16,194	**Mt Blackburn** *Canada*	
4,808	15,774	**Mont Blanc** *France–Italy*	
4,750	15,584	**Klyuchevskaya Sopka**	
		Russian Federation	
4,634	15,203	**Monte Rosa (Dufour)**	
		Italy–Switzerland	
4,565	14,979	**Meru** *Tanzania*	
4,545	14,910	**Dom (Mischabel group)** *Switzerland*	
4,533	14,872	**Ras Dashen** *Ethiopia*	
4,528	14,855	**Kirkpatrick** *Antarctica*	
4,508	14,790	**Wilhelm** *Papua, New Guinea*	
4,507	14,786	**Karisimbi** *Rwanda–Zaire*	
4,477	14,688	**Matterhorn** *Italy–Switzerland*	
4,418	14,495	**Whitney** *USA*	
4,398	14,431	**Elbert** *USA*	
4,392	14,410	**Rainier** *USA*	
4,351	14,275	**Markham** *Antarctica*	
4,321	14,178	**Elgon** *Kenya–Uganda*	
4,307	14,131	**Batu** *Ethiopia*	
4,169	13,677	**Mauna Loa** *USA, Hawaii*	
4,165	13,661	**Toubkal** *Morocco*	
4,095	13,435	**Cameroon (Caméroun)** *Cameroon*	
4,094	13,431	**Kinabalu** *Malaysia*	
3,794	12,447	**Erebus** *Antarctica*	
3,776	12,388	**Fuji** *Japan*	
3,754	12,316	**Cook** *New Zealand*	
3,718	12,198	**Teide** *Canary Is*	
3,482	11,424	**Thabana Ntlenyana** *Lesotho*	
3,482	11,424	**Mulhacén** *Spain*	
3,415	11,204	**Emi Koussi** *Chad*	
3,323	10,902	**Etna** *Italy, Sicily*	
2,743	9,000	**Mt Balbi**	
		Bougainville, Papua New Guinea	
2,655	8,708	**Gerlachovsky stit (Tatra)**	
		Czech Republic	
2,230	7,316	**Kosciusko** *Australia*	

ISLANDS

land area ☐ = $\dfrac{10\ 000\ \text{sq kms}}{3\ 860\ \text{sq miles}}$

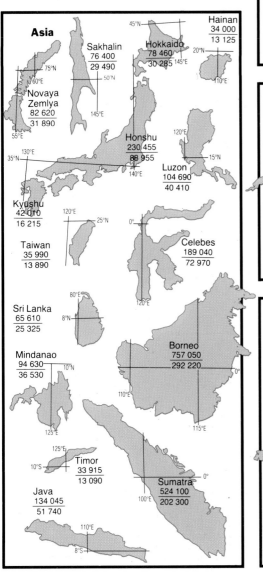

Asia

Sakhalin 76 400 / 29 490

Novaya Zemlya 82 620 / 31 890

Hokkaido 78 460 / 30 285

Hainan 34 000 / 13 125

Honshu 230 455 / 88 955

Luzon 104 690 / 40 410

Kyushu 42 010 / 16 215

Taiwan 35 990 / 13 890

Sri Lanka 65 610 / 25 325

Celebes 189 040 / 72 970

Mindanao 94 630 / 36 530

Borneo 757 050 / 292 220

Timor 33 915 / 13 090

Java 134 045 / 51 740

Sumatra 524 100 / 202 300

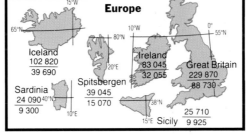

Europe

Iceland 102 820 / 39 690

Sardinia 24 090 / 9 300

Ireland 83 045 / 32 055

Spitsbergen 39 045 / 15 070

Great Britain 229 870 / 88 730

Sicily 25 710 / 9 925

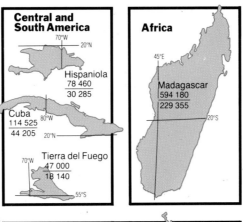

Central and South America

Hispaniola 78 460 / 30 285

Cuba 114 525 / 44 205

Tierra del Fuego 47 000 / 18 140

Africa

Madagascar 594 180 / 229 355

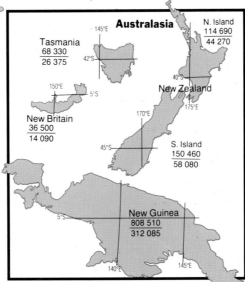

Australasia

Tasmania 68 330 / 26 375

New Britain 36 500 / 14 090

New Zealand

N. Island 114 690 / 44 270

S. Island 150 460 / 58 080

New Guinea 808 510 / 312 085

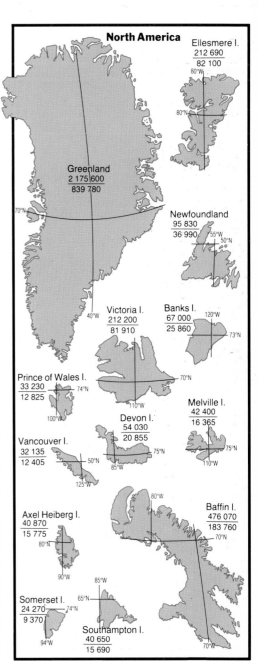

North America

Ellesmere I. 212 690 / 82 100

Greenland 2 175 600 / 839 780

Newfoundland 95 830 / 36 990

Victoria I. 212 200 / 81 910

Banks I. 67 000 / 25 860

Prince of Wales I. 33 230 / 12 825

Melville I. 42 400 / 16 365

Devon I. 54 030 / 20 855

Vancouver I. 32 135 / 12 405

Axel Heiberg I. 40 870 / 15 775

Baffin I. 476 070 / 183 760

Somerset I. 24 270 / 9 370

Southampton I. 40 650 / 15 690

OCEANS AND SEAS

water area ▮ = $\frac{1\,000\,000}{386\,000}$ sq km / sq miles

OCEAN FACTS AND FIGURES

The area of the Earth covered by sea is estimated to be 361,740,000 sq km (139,670,000 sq miles), or 70.92% of the total surface. The mean depth is estimated to be 3554 m (11,660 ft), and the volume of the oceans to be 1,285,600,000 cu. km (308,400,000 cu. miles).

INDIAN OCEAN

Mainly confined to the southern hemisphere, and at its greatest breadth (Tasmania to Cape Agulhas) 9600 km. Average depth is 4000 m; greatest depth is the Amirante Trench (9000 m).

ATLANTIC OCEAN

Commonly divided into North Atlantic (36,000,000 sq km) and South Atlantic (26,000,000 sq km). The greatest breadth in the North is 7200 km (Morocco to Florida) and in the South 9600 km (Guinea to Brazil). Average depth is 3600 m; the greatest depths are the Puerto Rico Trench 9220 m, S. Sandwich Trench 8264 m, and Romansh Trench 7728 m.

PACIFIC OCEAN

Covers nearly 40% of the world's total sea area, and is the largest of the oceans. The greatest breadth (E/W) is 16,000 km and the greatest length (N/S) 11,000 km. Average depth is 4200 m; also the deepest ocean. Generally the west is deeper than the east and the north deeper than the south. Greatest depths occur near island groups and include Mindanao Trench 11,524 m, Mariana Trench 11,022 m, Tonga Trench 10,882 m, Kuril-Kamchatka Trench 10,542 m, Philippine Trench 10,497 m, and Kermadec Trench 10,047 m.

Comparisons (where applicable)	greatest distance N/S (km)	greatest distance E/W (km)	maximum depth (m)
Indian Ocean	—	9600	9000
Atlantic Ocean	—	9600	9220
Pacific Ocean	11,000	16,000	11,524
Arctic Ocean	—	—	5450
Mediterranean Sea	960	3700	4846
S. China Sea	2100	1750	5514
Bering Sea	1800	2100	5121
Caribbean Sea	1600	2000	7100
Gulf of Mexico	1200	1700	4377
Sea of Okhotsk	2200	1400	3475
E. China Sea	1100	750	2999
Yellow Sea	800	1000	91
Hudson Bay	1250	1050	259
Sea of Japan	1500	1100	3743
North Sea	1200	550	661
Red Sea	1932	360	2246
Black Sea	600	1100	2245
Baltic Sea	1500	650	460

EARTH'S SURFACE WATERS

Total volume	c.1400 million cu. km
Oceans and seas	1370 million cu. km
Ice	24 million cu. km
Interstitial water (in rocks and sediments)	4 million cu. km
Lakes and rivers	230 thousand cu. km
Atmosphere (vapour)	c.140 thousand cu. km

to convert metric to imperial measurements:
1 m = 3.281 feet
1 km = 0.621 miles
1 sq km = 0.386 sq miles

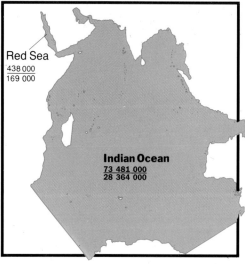

Red Sea
438 000
169 000

Indian Ocean
73 481 000
28 364 000

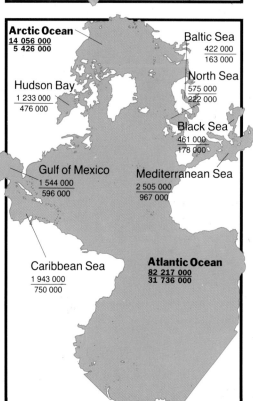

Arctic Ocean
14 056 000
5 426 000

Baltic Sea
422 000
163 000

Hudson Bay
1 233 000
476 000

North Sea
575 000
222 000

Black Sea
461 000
178 000

Gulf of Mexico
1 544 000
596 000

Mediterranean Sea
2 505 000
967 000

Caribbean Sea
1 943 000
750 000

Atlantic Ocean
82 217 000
31 736 000

FEATURES OF THE OCEAN BASIN

The majority of land drainage occurs in the Atlantic, yet this is the most saline ocean due to interchange of waters with its marginal seas. The continental margins (21% of ocean floors) are the most important economic areas.

	PACIFIC	ATLANTIC	INDIAN	WORLD
AVERAGE OCEAN DEPTH (metres)				
3000				
3500				
4000				
OCEAN AREA (million sq km)	180	107	74	361
LAND AREA DRAINED (million sq km)	19	69	13	101
AREA AS PERCENTAGE OF TOTAL				
Continental margin	15.8	27.9	14.8	20.6
Ridges, rises and fracture zones	38.4	33.3	35.6	35.8
Deep ocean floor	42.9	38.1	49.3	41.9
Island arcs and trenches	2.9	0.7	0.3	1.7

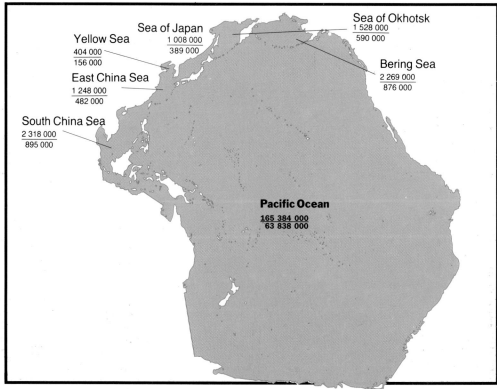

Sea of Japan
1 008 000
389 000

Sea of Okhotsk
1 528 000
590 000

Yellow Sea
404 000
156 000

Bering Sea
2 269 000
876 000

East China Sea
1 248 000
482 000

South China Sea
2 318 000
895 000

Pacific Ocean
165 384 000
63 838 000

RIVER LENGTHS

km	miles	
6,695	4,160	**Nile** *Africa*
6,515	4,050	**Amazon** *South America*
6,380	3,965	**Yangtze (Chang Jiang)** *Asia*
6,019	3,740	**Mississippi-Missouri** *North America*
5,570	3,460	**Ob'-Irtysh** *Asia*
5,550	3,450	**Yenisei-Angara** *Asia*
5,464	3,395	**Yellow River (Huang He)** *Asia*
4,667	2,900	**Congo (Zaire)** *Africa*
4,500	2,800	**Paraná** *South America*
4,440	2,775	**Irtysh** *Asia*
4,425	2,750	**Mekong** *Asia*
4,416	2,744	**Amur** *Asia*
4,400	2,730	**Lena** *Asia*
4,250	2,640	**Mackenzie** *North America*
4,090	2,556	**Yenisei** *Asia*
4,030	2,505	**Niger** *Africa*
3,969	2,466	**Missouri** *North America*
3,779	2,348	**Mississippi** *North America*
3,750	2,330	**Murray-Darling** *Australasia*
3,688	2,290	**Volga** *Europe*
3,218	2,011	**Purus** *South America*
3,200	1,990	**Madeira** *South America*
3,185	1,980	**Yukon** *North America*
3,180	1,975	**Indus** *Asia*
3,078	1,913	**Syrdar'ya** *Asia*
3,060	1,901	**Salween** *Asia*
3,058	1,900	**St Lawrence** *North America*
2,900	1,800	**São Francisco** *South America*
2,870	1,785	**Rio Grande** *North America*
2,850	1,770	**Danube** *Europe*
2,840	1,765	**Brahmaputra** *Asia*
2,815	1,750	**Euphrates** *Asia*
2,750	1,710	**Pará-Tocantins** *South America*
2,750	1,718	**Tarim** *Asia*
2,650	1,650	**Zambezi** *Africa*
2,620	1,630	**Amudar'ya** *Asia*
2,620	1,630	**Araguaia** *South America*
2,600	1,615	**Paraguay** *South America*
2,570	1,600	**Nelson-Saskatchewan** *North America*

RIVER LENGTHS & DRAINAGE BASINS

km	miles	
2,534	1,575	**Ural** *Asia*
2,513	1,562	**Kolyma** *Asia*
2,510	1,560	**Ganges (Ganga)** *Asia*
2,500	1,555	**Orinoco** *South America*
2,490	1,550	**Shabeelle** *Africa*
2,490	1,550	**Pilcomayo** *South America*
2,348	1,459	**Arkansas** *North America*
2,333	1,450	**Colorado** *North America*
2,285	1,420	**Dneper** *Europe*
2,250	1,400	**Columbia** *North America*
2,150	1,335	**Irrawaddy** *Asia*
2,129	1,323	**Pearl River (Xi Jiang)** *Asia*
2,032	1,270	**Kama** *Europe*
2,000	1,240	**Negro** *South America*
1,923	1,195	**Peace** *North America*
1,899	1,186	**Tigris** *Asia*
1,870	1,162	**Don** *Europe*
1,860	1,155	**Orange** *Africa*
1,809	1,124	**Pechora** *Europe*
1,800	1,125	**Okavango** *Africa*
1,609	1,000	**Marañón** *South America*
1,609	1,095	**Uruguay** *South America*
1,600	1,000	**Volta** *Africa*
1,600	1,000	**Limpopo** *Africa*
1,550	963	**Magdalena** *South America*
1,515	946	**Kura** *Asia*
1,480	925	**Oka** *Europe*
1,480	925	**Belaya** *Europe*
1,445	903	**Godavari** *Asia*
1,430	893	**Senegal** *Africa*
1,410	876	**Dnester** *Europe*
1,400	875	**Chari** *Africa*
1,368	850	**Fraser** *North America*
1,320	820	**Rhine** *Europe*
1,314	821	**Vyatka** *Europe*
1,183	735	**Donets** *Europe*
1,159	720	**Elbe** *Europe*
1,151	719	**Kizilirmak** *Asia*
1,130	706	**Desna** *Europe*
1,094	680	**Gambia** *Africa*
1,080	675	**Yellowstone** *North America*
1,049	652	**Tennessee** *North America*
1,024	640	**Zelenga** *Asia*
1,020	637	**Duena** *Europe*
1,014	630	**Vistula (Wisła)** *Europe*
1,012	629	**Loire** *Europe*
1,006	625	**Tagus (Tejo)** *Europe*
977	607	**Tisza** *Europe*
925	575	**Meuse (Maas)** *Europe*
909	565	**Oder** *Europe*
761	473	**Seine** *Europe*
354	220	**Severn** *Europe*
346	215	**Thames** *Europe*
300	186	**Trent** *Europe*

DRAINAGE BASINS

sq km	sq miles	
7,050,000	2,721,000	**Amazon** *South America*
3,700,000	1,428,000	**Congo** *Africa*
3,250,000	1,255,000	**Mississippi-Missouri** *North America*
3,100,000	1,197,000	**Paraná** *South America*
2,700,000	1,042,000	**Yenisei** *Asia*
2,430,000	938,000	**Ob'** *Asia*
2,420,000	934,000	**Lena** *Asia*
1,900,000	733,400	**Nile** *Africa*
1,840,000	710,000	**Amur** *Asia*
1,765,000	681,000	**Mackenzie** *North America*
1,730,000	668,000	**Ganges-Brahmaputra** *Asia*
1,380,000	533,000	**Volga** *Europe*
1,330,000	513,000	**Zambezi** *Africa*
1,200,000	463,000	**Niger** *Africa*
1,175,000	454,000	**Yangtze** *Asia*
1,020,000	394,000	**Orange** *Africa*
980,000	378,000	**Yellow River** *Asia*
960,000	371,000	**Indus** *Asia*
945,000	365,000	**Orinoco** *South America*
910,000	351,000	**Murray-Darling** *Australasia*
855,000	330,000	**Yukon** *North America*
815,000	315,000	**Danube** *Europe*
810,000	313,000	**Mekong** *Asia*
225,000	86,900	**Rhine** *Europe*

INLAND WATERS

water surface area ■ = 1 000 sq km / 386 sq miles

deepest point 229 metres / 751 feet

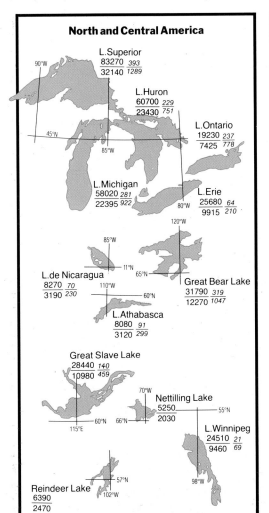

North and Central America

L.Superior 83270 *393* / 32140 *1289*

L.Huron 60700 *229* / 23430 *751*

L.Ontario 19230 *237* / 7425 *778*

L.Michigan 58020 *281* / 22395 *922*

L.Erie 25680 *64* / 9915 *210*

L.de Nicaragua 8270 *70* / 3190 *230*

Great Bear Lake 31790 *319* / 12270 *1047*

L.Athabasca 8080 *91* / 3120 *299*

Great Slave Lake 28440 *140* / 10980 *459*

Nettilling Lake 5250 / 2030

L.Winnipeg 24510 *21* / 9460 *69*

Reindeer Lake 6390 / 2470

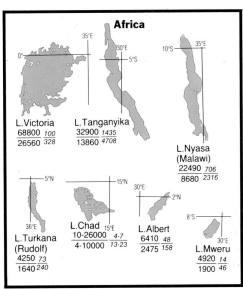

Africa

L.Victoria 68800 *100* / 26560 *328*

L.Tanganyika 32900 *1435* / 13860 *4708*

L.Nyasa (Malawi) 22490 *706* / 8680 *2316*

L.Turkana (Rudolf) 4250 *73* / 1640 *240*

L.Chad 10–26000 *4-7* / 4–10000 *13-23*

L.Albert 6410 *48* / 2475 *158*

L.Mweru 4920 *14* / 1900 *46*

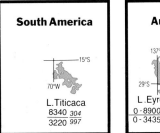

South America

L.Titicaca 8340 *304* / 3220 *997*

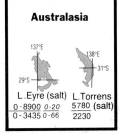

Australasia

L.Eyre (salt) 0 – 8900 *0-20* / 0 – 3435 *0-66*

L.Torrens 5780 (salt) / 2230

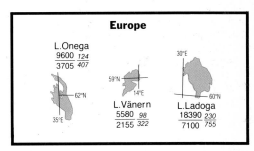

Europe

L.Onega 9600 *124* / 3705 *407*

L.Vänern 5580 *98* / 2155 *322*

L.Ladoga 18390 *230* / 7100 *755*

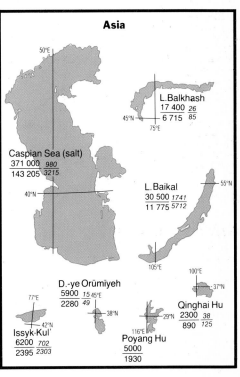

Asia

L.Balkhash 17 400 *26* / 6 715 *85*

Caspian Sea (salt) 371 000 *980* / 143 205 *3215*

L.Baikal 30 500 *1741* / 11 775 *5712*

D.-ye Orūmīyeh 5900 *15* / 2280 *49*

Issyk-Kul' 6200 *702* / 2395 *2303*

Qinghai Hu 2300 *38* / 890 *125*

Poyang Hu 5000 / 1930

ABBREVIATIONS	FULL FORM	ENGLISH FORM
A		
a.d.	an der	on the
Akr.	Ákra, Akrotírion	cape
Appno	Appennino	mountain range
Arch.	Archipelago	
	Archipiélago	archipelago
B		
B.	1. Bahía, Baía, Baie, Bay, Bucht, Bukhta, Bugt	bay
	2. Ban	village
	3. Barrage,	dam
	4. Bir, Bîr, Bi'r	well
Bol.	Bol'sh, -oy	big
Br.	1. Branch	branch
	2. Bridge, Brücke	bridge
	3. Burun	cape
Brj	Baraj, -i	dam
C		
C.	Cabo, Cap, Cape	cape
Can.	Canal	canal
Cd	Ciudad	town
Chan.	Channel	channel
Ck	Creek	creek
Co., Cord.	Cordillera	mountain chain
D		
D.	1. Dağ, Dagh, Daği, Dağları	mountain, range
	2. Daryācheh	lake
Dj.	Djebel	mountain
Dr.	doctor	doctor
E		
E.	East	east
Emb.	Embalse	reservoir
Escarp.	Escarpment	escarpment
Estr.	Estrecho	strait
F		
F.	Firth	estuary
Fj.	Fjord, Fjörður	fjord
Ft	Fort	fort
G		
G.	1. Gebel	mountain
	2. Göl, Gölü	lake
	3. Golfe, Golfo, Gulf	Gulf
	4. Gora, -gory	mountain, range
	5. Gunung	mountain
Gd, Gde	Grand, Grande	grand
Geb.	Gebirge	mountain range
Gl.	Glacier	glacier
Grl	General	general
Gt, Gtr	Great, Groot, -e, Greater	greater
H		
Har.	Harbour, Harbor	harbour
Hd	Head	head
I		
I.	Ile, Ilha, Insel, Isla, Island, Isle Isola,	island
	Isole	islands
In.	1. Inner	inner
	2. Inlet	inlet
Is	Iles, Ilhas, Islands, Isles, Islas	islands
Isth.	Isthmus	isthmus
J		
J.	Jabal, Jebel,	mountain
K		
K.	1. Kaap, Kap, Kapp	cape
	2. Kūh(hā)	mountain(s)
	3. Kólpos	gulf
Kep.	Kepulauan	islands
Khr.	Khrebet	mountain range
Kör.	Körfez, -i	gulf, bay
L		
L.	Lac, Lago, Lagoa, Lake, Liman, Limni, Loch, Lough	lake
Lag.	Lagoon, Laguna, Lagune, Lagoa	lagoon
Ld.	Land	land
Lit.	Little	little
M		
M.	1. Muang	town
	2. Mys	cape
m	metre, -s	metre(s)
Mal.	Malyy	small
Mf	Massif	mountain group
Mgne	Montagne(s)	mountain(s)
Mt	Mont, Mount	mountain
Mte	Monte	mountain
Mti	Monti	mountains, range
Mtn	Mountain	mountain
Mts	Monts, Mountains, Montañas, Montes	mountains
N		
N.	1. Neu-, Ny-	new
	2. Noord, Nord, Norte, North, Norra, Nørre	north
	3. Nos	cape
Nat.	National	national
Nat. Pk	National Park	national park
Ndr	Nieder	lower
N.E.	North East	north east
N.M.	National Monument	national monument
N.P.	National Park	national park
N.W.	North West	north west
O		
O.	1. Oost, Ost	east
	2. Ostrov	island
Ø	-øy	island
Oz.	Ózero, Ozera	lake(s)
P		
P.	1. Pass, Passo	pass
	2. Pic, Pico, Pizzo	peak
	3. Pulau	island
Pass.	Passage	passage
Peg.	Pegunungan	mountains
Pen.	Peninsula, Penisola	peninsula
Pk	1. Park	park
	2. Peak, Pik	peak
Plat.	Plateau, Planalto	plateau
Pov	Poluostrov	peninsula
Pr.	Prince	prince
P.P.	Pulau-pulau	islands
Pres.	Presidente	president
Promy	Promontory	promontory
Pt	Point	point
Pta	1. Ponta, Punta	point
	2. Puerta	pass
Pte	Pointe	point
Pto	Porto, Puerto	port
R		
R.	Rio, Río, River, Rivière	river
Ra.	Range	range
Rap.	Rapids	rapids
Res.	Reserve, Reservation	reserve, reservation
Resp.	Respublika	Republic
Resr	Reservoir	reservoir
S		
S.	1. Salar, Salina	salt marsh
	2. San, São	saint
	3. See	sea, lake
	4. South, Sud	south
s.	sur	on
Sa	Serra, Sierra	mountain range
Sd	Sound, Sund	sound
S.E.	South East	south east
Sev.	Severo-, Severnaya, -nyy	north peak
Sp.	Spitze	saint
St	Saint	saint
Sta	Santa	saint
Ste	Sainte	saint
Sto	Santo	strait
Str.	Strait	south west
S.W.	South West	
T		
T.	Tall, Tell	hill, mountain
Tg	Tanjung	cape
Tk	Teluk	bay
Tr.	Trench, Trough	trench, trough
U		
U.	Uad	wadi
Ug	Ujung	cape
Upr	Upper	upper
V		
V.	1. Val, Valle	valley
	2. Ville	town
Va	Villa	town
Vdkhr.	Vodokhranilishche	reservoir
Vol.	Volcán, Volcano, Vulkan	volcano
Vozv.	Vozvyshennost'	upland
W		
W.	1. Wadi	wadi
	2. Water	water
	3. Well	well
	4. West	west
Y		
Yuzh.	Yuzhno-, Yuzhnyy	south
Z		
Z	1. Zaliv	gulf, bay
	2. Zatoka	
Zap.	Zapad-naya, Zapadno-, Zapadnyy	western
Zem.	Zemlya	country, land

This page explains the main symbols, lettering style and height/depth colours used on the reference maps on pages 2 to 76. The scale of each map is indicated at the foot of each page. Abbreviations used on the maps appear at the beginning of the index.

BOUNDARIES

————————	International
— — — — —	International under Dispute
· · · · · · · ·	Cease Fire Line
————————	Autonomous or State
————————	Administrative
— — — —	Maritime (National)
– – – – –	International Date Line

COMMUNICATIONS

————————	Motorway/Express Highway
==========	Under Construction
————————	Major Highway
————————	Other Roads
– – – – –	Under Construction
- - - - - -	Track
⇒═══⇒═══	Road Tunnel
– – – – –	Car Ferry
———•————	Main Railway
————————	Other Railway
– – – – –	Under Construction
→—–—–—←	Rail Tunnel
– – – – – –	Rail Ferry
—+—+—+—	Canal
⊕	International Airport
✦	Other Airport

LAKE FEATURES

	Freshwater
	Saltwater
	Seasonal
	Salt Pan

LANDSCAPE FEATURES

	Glacier, Ice Cap
	Marsh, Swamp
	Sand Desert, Dunes

OTHER FEATURES

～～～	River
– · – ·→	Seasonal River
⋈	Pass, Gorge
	Dam, Barrage
～～	Waterfall, Rapid
—→—	Aqueduct
～～～～～	Reef
▲ 4231	Summit, Peak
· 217	Spot Height, Depth
◡	Well
△	Oil Field
▲	Gas Field
—Gas/Oil—	Oil/Natural Gas Pipeline
Gemsbok Nat. Pk	National Park
∴UR	Historic Site

LETTERING STYLES

CANADA	Independent Nation
FLORIDA	State, Province or Autonomous Region
Gibraltar (U.K.)	Sovereignty of Dependent Territory
Lothian	Administrative Area
LANGUEDOC	Historic Region
Loire *Vosges*	Physical Feature or Physical Region

TOWNS AND CITIES

Square symbols denote capital cities. Each settlement is given a symbol according to its relative importance, with type size to match.

▣	◉	**New York**	Major City
■	●	**Montréal**	City
◻	○	Ottawa	Small City
■	●	Québec	Large Town
◻	○	St John's	Town
◻	○	Yorkton	Small Town
◻	○	Jasper	Village
			Built-up-area

Height

	6000m
	5000m
	4000m
	3000m
	2000m
	1000m
	500m
	200m
0	0 Sea Level
	200m
	2000m
	4000m
	6000m
	8000m

Depth

Map labels (major): ARCTIC OCEAN, RUSSIAN FEDERATION, KAZAKHSTAN, MONGOLIA, CHINA, ASIA, JAPAN, INDIA, AFRICA, AUSTRALIA, AUSTRALASIA, INDIAN OCEAN, PACIFIC OCEAN, NEW ZEALAND

1:70 000 000 (45° N & S)

ARCTIC

A B 40 C 2 30 D E 20 70 D 10 E 0 F 10 G

Greenland (Dan.)
Cape Farewell

Jan Mayen (Nor.)

ICELAND
Reykjavík

Arctic Circle

NORWEGIAN

SEA

Vesterålen
Lofoten
Narvik

③

N O R W A Y

Sundsvall

Faeroes

Trondheim

Rockall

Bergen

Shetland

Stavanger

Oslo

Uppsala
Västerås

S W E D E N
Örebro
Borås
Linköping

Stockholm

Norrköping

Göteborg
Jönköping

Gotland

ATLANTIC

50

Orkney

UNITED KINGDOM
OF GREAT BRITAIN AND
NORTHERN IRELAND
Dundee
Glasgow
Aberdeen
Edinburgh

NORTH

Ålborg
Helsingborg
Århus

DENMARK
Copenhagen
(København)
Odense
Malmö

Öland

OCEAN

Belfast

IRELAND
Dublin
Cork

Blackpool
Liverpool

SEA

Bornholm

Baltic

Kiel
Lübeck
Schwerin
Rostock
Hamburg

Gdańsk

Newcastle
Middlesborough

Bremerhaven
Wilhelmshaven

Szczecin

Leeds
Hull
Manchester
Sheffield
Derby
Wolverhampton
Birmingham
Northampton Leicester Norwich
Swansea Cardiff Oxford Luton Ipswich
Bristol Reading

Gronigen
Amsterdam
The Hague
's-Gravenhage NETHERLANDS
Rotterdam
Antwerp
Brussels
Bruxelles BELGIUM
Düsseldorf
Cologne
(Köln)

Bremen
Hannover Wolfsburg
Enschede Hildesheim
Paderborn
Essen Dortmund Kassel
Göttingen

Berlin

Gorzów Wlkp.
Poznań

P O L

Cottbus
Zielona Góra
Leipzig Dresden Wrocław

④

Isles of Scilly
Plymouth
Southampton
Brighton

English Channel

London

Boulogne
Valenciennes
Channel Islands
Le Havre
Amiens
Brest
Caen
Rouen
Rennes
Seine
Paris
Lorient
Le Mans
St. Nazaire
Angers
Orléans
Nantes
Loire
Tours

Namur
Koblenz
Luxembourg
LUXEMBOURG
Metz
Reims
Troyes
Nancy

Bonn
Frankfurt
Mainz
Darmstadt Offenbach
Heidelberg
Karlsruhe
Strasbourg
Stuttgart
Heilbronn

Jena
Zwickau
Chemnitz

Erlangen
Nürnberg

Regensburg

Prague
(Praha)
Plzeň

CZECH REP.
Brno

SLO

Bay of
Biscay

F R A N C E

Dijon
Besançon Berne
Montbéliard (Bern)
Freiburg
Mulhouse
Basle
Zurich

Ulm
Augsburg
Munich
(München)

Salzburg

Vienna
(Wien)

Bratislava

Győr

40

Limoges
Clermont-
Ferrand

Lyon
St-Étienne
Villeurbanne
Valence

Geneva
(Genève)
Lausanne
SWITZERLAND
LIECHTENSTEIN
Bolzano

Innsbruck

A U S T R I A

Graz

HUNG

La Coruña
Vigo
Oporto
(Porto)

Gijón
Oviedo Santander
León Baracaldo
Bilbao
Burgos Vitoria
San Sebastián
Bayonne
Pau
Toulouse

Bordeaux

Rhône
Nîmes
Montpellier

Novara
Bergamo Brescia
Milan Verona
(Milano)
Turin Piacenza
(Torino) Parma Reggio
Alessandria
Genoa
(Genova)
Nice

Udine
SLOVENIA
Venice
(Venezia)
Padova
Bologna
Florence
(Firenze)

Trieste
Ljubljana

CROATIA

Zagreb

BOSNIA-
HERZEGOVINA

La
Spezia
Pisa
Livorno

Rimini
Ancona

SAN
MARINO

Adriatic sea

Split
Sarajevo

Valladolid

Salamanca

Logroño
Zaragoza
ANDORRA
Sabadell
Tarrasa

Marseilles
(Marseille)
Perpignan
Toulon

MONACO

PORTUGAL
Lisbon
(Lisboa)

Madrid
SPAIN
Badajoz

Alcalá de H.
Toledo

Badalona
Barcelona
Tarragona

Corsica
(Corse)
Ajaccio
Bastia

Perugia
Terni

Pescara

⑤

Faro
Huelva
Sevilla
Jerez de la F.
Cádiz

Córdoba

Albacete

Castellon
de la P.

Valencia

Balearic
Islands
Minorca
(Menorca)
Majorca
(Mallorca)
Ibiza

Sassari

Sardinia
(Sardegna)

Olbia

Rome
(Roma)

I T A L Y

Naples
(Napoli)
Salerno

Foggia
Bari

Taranto

Granada
Málaga
Murcia
Elche
Cartagena

Alicante

Almería

TYRRHENIAN
SEA

Cagliari

Cosenza

Tangiers
(Tanger)
Tetouan
Gibraltar (U.K.)
Ceuta (Sp.)
Melilla
(Sp.)
Oran

M E D I T E R R A N E A N

Algiers
(Alger)

Palermo
Messina
Sicily
(Sicilia)
Reggio di Calabria
Syracuse

Casablanca
Rabat

MALTA

SEA

M O R O C C O
Marrakech

A L G E R I A

Tunis

TUNISIA

Canary Is.

D 10 E 0 F 10 G

1:15M 200 400 600 km
        100 200 300 mls

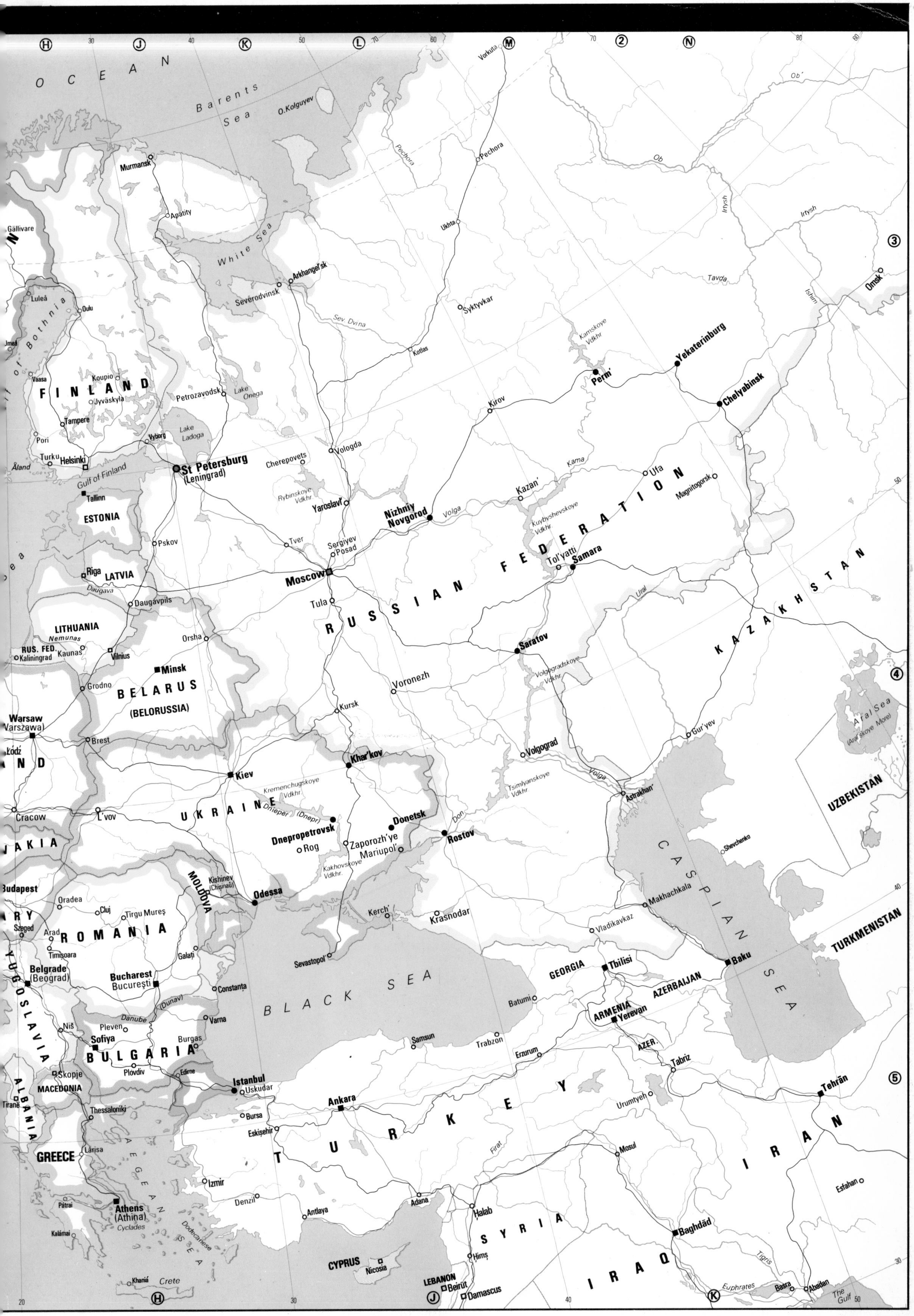

OCEAN

Barents Sea

O.Kolguyev

Pechora

Pechora

Vorkuta

Ob'

Irtysh

Irtysh

Ob'

N

White Sea

Sev Dvina

Syktyvkar

Ukhta

Tavda

Omsk

Ishim

Murmansk

Apatity

Arkhangel'sk

Severodvinsk

Kotlas

Kamskoye Vdkhr.

Yekaterinburg

Perm'

Chelyabinsk

Luleå

Oulu

Jmeå

Gällivare

Vaasa

Kuopio

Jyväskylä

Tampere

Petrozavodsk

Lake Onega

Kirov

Kazan'

Ufa

Magnitogorsk

Pori

Vyborg

Lake Ladoga

Cherepovets

Vologda

FINLAND

Åland

Turku

Helsinki

Gulf of Finland

St Petersburg (Leningrad)

Tallinn

Rybinskoye Vdkhr.

Yaroslavl'

Nizhniy Novgorod

Volga

Kuybyshevskoye Vdkhr.

Tol'yatti

Samara

RUSSIAN FEDERATION

Kama

Ural

50

ESTONIA

Pskov

Tver

Sergiyev Posad

KAZAKHSTAN

Sea

Riga

LATVIA

Daugava

Daugávpils

Moscow

Tula

Orsha

LITHUANIA

Nemunas

Kaunas

RUS. FED.

Kaliningrad

Vilnius

Grodno

Minsk

BELARUS

(BELORUSSIA)

Voronezh

Saratov

Volgogradskoye Vdkhr.

Aral Sea (Aral'skoye More)

Warsaw

Varszawa

Łódź

Brest

Kursk

UZBEKISTAN

AND

Cracow

L'vov

UKRAINE

Kiev

Kremenchugskoye Vdkhr.

Dnieper (Dnepr)

Khar'kov

Volgograd

Volga

Gur'yev

AKIA

Dnepropetrovsk

Rog

Donetsk

Zaporozh'ye

Mariupol'

Rostov

Don

Tsimlyanskoye Vdkhr.

Astrakhan'

CASPIAN

SEA

Shevchenko

Budapest

Oradea

Cluj

Tirgu Mureş

MOLDOVA

Kishinev (Chişinău)

Kakhovskoye Vdkhr.

Odessa

ARY

Szeged

Arad

ROMANIA

Galaţi

Kerch'

Krasnodar

Makhachkala

40

Timişoara

YUGOSLAVIA

Belgrade (Beograd)

Bucharest

Bucureşti

(Dunav)

Sevastopol'

Vladikavkaz

TURKMENISTAN

Niš

Pleven

Danube

Constanţa

BLACK SEA

GEORGIA

Tbilisi

AZERBAIJAN

Baku

Sofiya

Varna

Batumi

ARMENIA

Yerevan

AZER.

Skopje

Plovdiv

Burgas

Samsun

Trabzon

ALBANIA

MACEDONIA

Edirne

Istanbul

Üsküdar

Erzurum

Tabriz

Tirane

Thessaloniki

Ankara

TURKEY

IRAN

GREECE

Lárisa

Bursa

Eskişehir

Firat

Mosul

Tehrān

Izmir

Denzil

Adana

Esfahan

Pátrai

Athens (Athína)

Antalya

Halab

SYRIA

Baghdād

Tigris

Kalámai

Cyclades

Khaniá

Crete

SEA

Denzil

CYPRUS

Nicosia

Hims

LEBANON

Beirūt

Damascus

IRAQ

Euphrates

Basra

Abadan

The Gulf

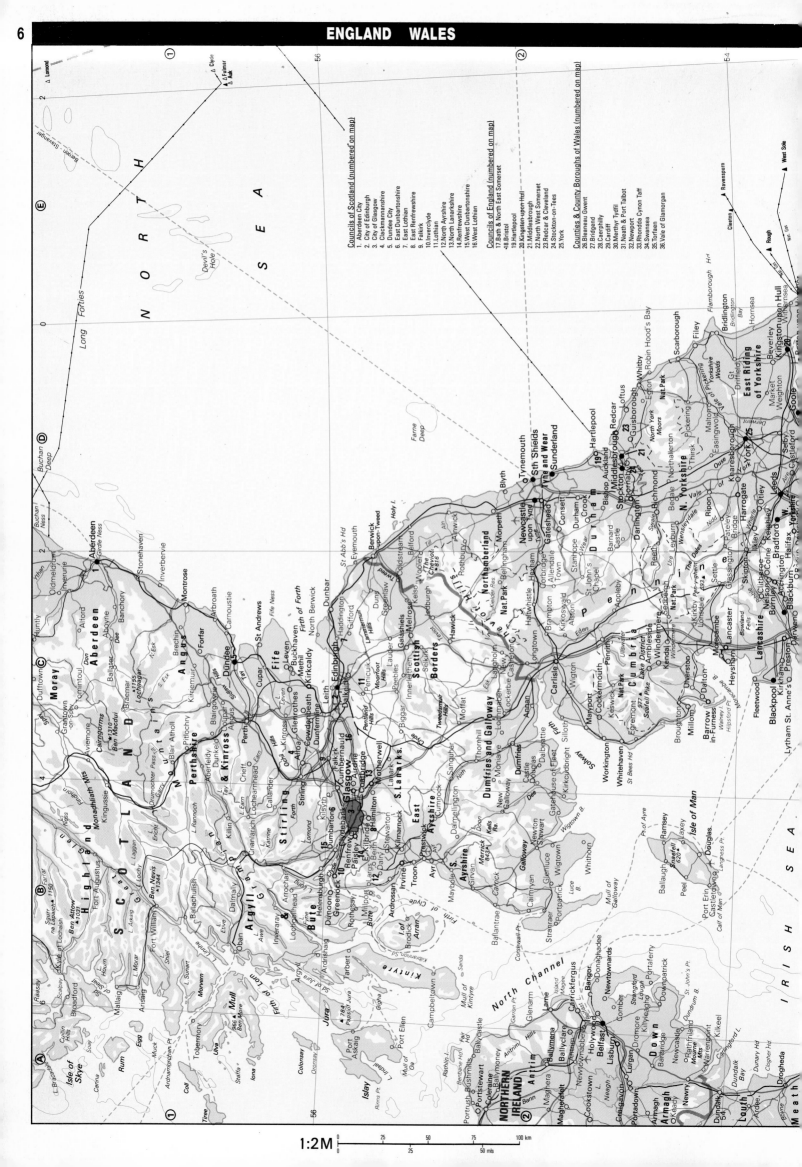

Councils of Scotland (numbered on map)
1. Aberdeen City
2. City of Edinburgh
3. City of Glasgow
4. Clackmannanshire
5. Dundee City
6. East Dunbartonshire
7. East Lothian
8. East Renfrewshire
9. Falkirk
10. Inverclyde
11. Lothian
12. North Ayrshire
13. North Lanarkshire
14. Renfrewshire
15. West Dunbartonshire
16. West Lothian

Councils of England (numbered on map)
17. Bath & North East Somerset
18. Bristol
19. Hartlepool
20. Kingston upon Hull
21. Middlesbrough
22. North West Somerset
23. Redcar & Cleveland
24. Stockton-on-Tees
25. York

Counties & County Boroughs of Wales (numbered on map)
26. Bleaneau Gwent
27. Bridgend
28. Caerphilly
29. Cardiff
30. Merthyr Tydfil
31. Neath & Port Talbot
32. Newport
33. Rhondda Cynon Taff
34. Swansea
35. Torfaen
36. Vale of Glamorgan

1:2M

0   25   50   75   100 km
0   25   50 mls

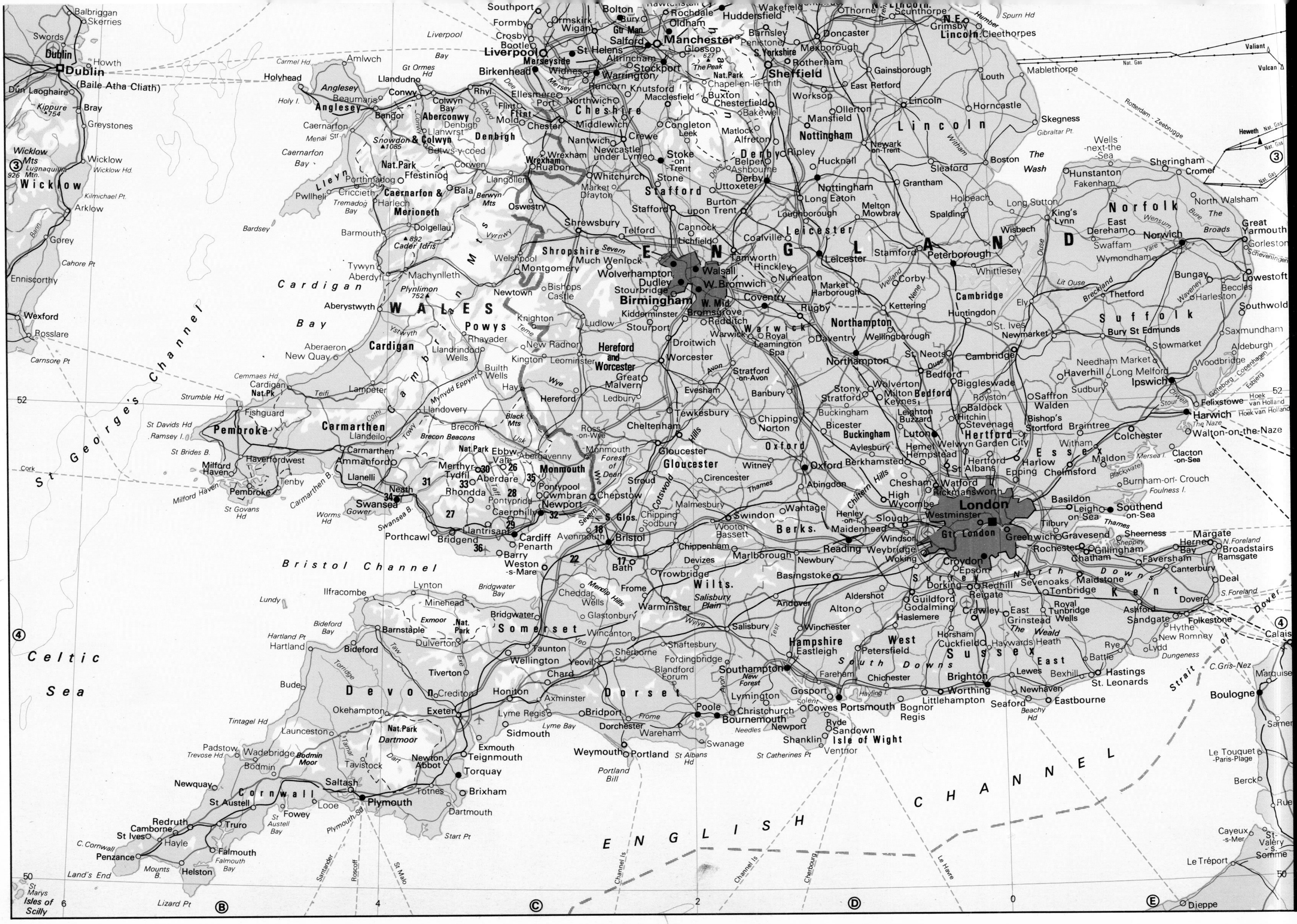
ENGLAND
WALES
ENGLISH CHANNEL
Bristol Channel
Cardigan Bay
St George's Channel
Celtic Sea
The Wash
Strait of Dover
London
Gt London
Birmingham
Manchester
Liverpool
Sheffield
Leeds
Bristol
Cardiff
Swansea
Newport
Plymouth
Southampton
Portsmouth
Brighton
Norwich
Ipswich
Cambridge
Oxford
Reading
Northampton
Leicester
Nottingham
Derby
Coventry
Peterborough
Lincoln
Dover
Canterbury
Exeter
Bournemouth
Gloucester
Worcester
Hereford
Shrewsbury
Stoke-on-Trent
Wolverhampton
Dublin
Dublin (Baile Atha Cliath)
Wicklow
Wexford
Rosslare
Boulogne
Calais
Dieppe
Le Touquet-Paris-Plage
Norfolk
Suffolk
Essex
Kent
Sussex
Surrey
Hampshire
Dorset
Devon
Cornwall
Somerset
Wilts.
Berks.
Oxford
Buckingham
Hertford
Bedford
Northampton
Warwick
Gloucester
Hereford and Worcester
Shropshire
Stafford
Cheshire
Derby
Nottingham
Leicester
Lincoln
Cambridge
Powys
Cardigan
Carmarthen
Pembroke
Merioneth
Caernarfon & Colwyn
Denbigh
Anglesey
Isle of Wight
Isles of Scilly
Cambrian Mts
Brecon Beacons
Cotswold Hills
Chiltern Hills
North Downs
South Downs
Salisbury Plain
Exmoor Nat. Park
Dartmoor Nat. Park
Bodmin Moor
The Peak Nat. Park
Snowdon ▲1085
Cader Idris ▲892
Plynlimon 752▲
Land's End
Lizard Pt
Start Pt
Portland Bill
St Catherines Pt
Beachy Hd
S. Foreland
N. Foreland
Spurn Hd
Gibraltar Pt
Nat. Gas
Rotterdam - Zeebrugge
Hoek van Holland
Esbjerg
Göteborg Copenhagen
Le Havre
Cherbourg
Channel Is
St Malo
Roscoff
Santander
Cork
B
C
D
E
3
4
52
50
6
4
2
0

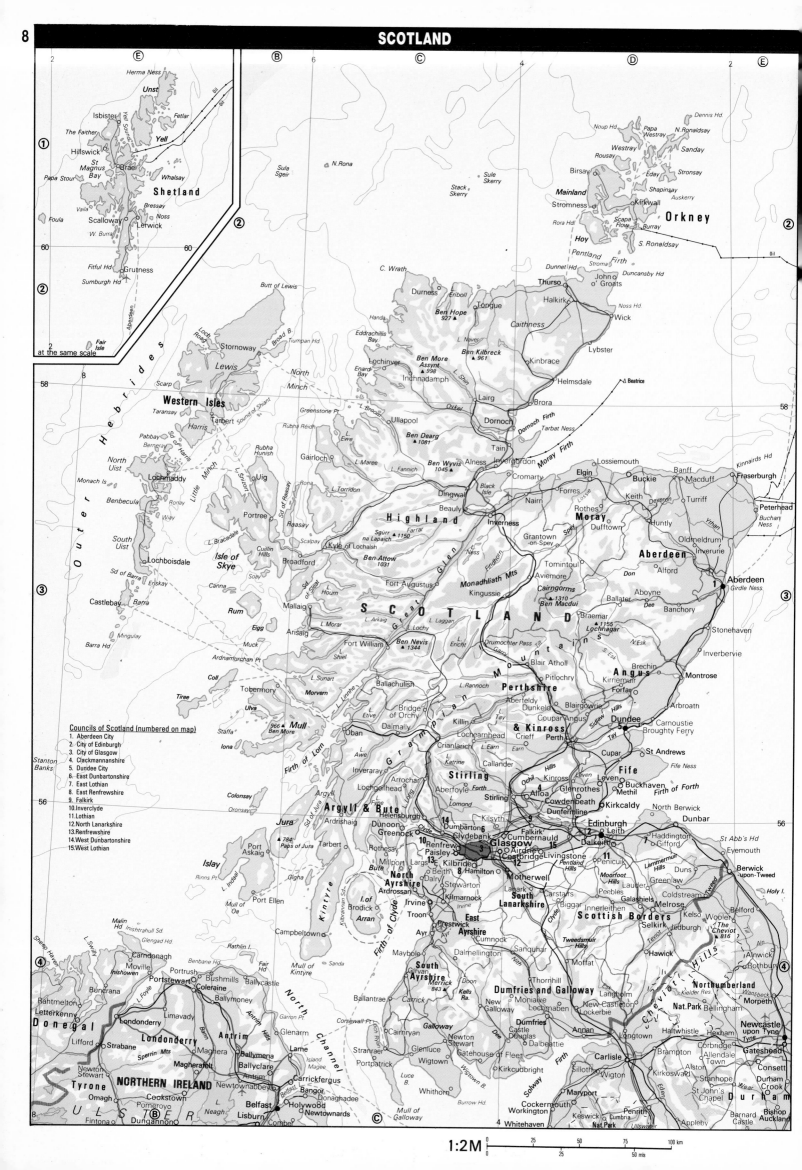

Shetland

Unst
Herma Ness
Isbister
The Faither
Fetlar
Yell Sound
Yell
Hillswick
St Magnus Bay
Brae
Whalsay
Papa Stour
Bressay
Noss
Foula
Vaila
W. Burra
Scalloway
Lerwick

60

Fitful Hd
Fair Isle
Grutness
Sumburgh Hd

at the same scale

Orkney

Noup Hd
Papa Westray
N. Ronaldsay
Westray
Sanday
Rousay
Stronsay
Birsay
Eday
Shapinsay
Auskerry
Mainland
Kirkwall
Stromness
Scapa Flow
Burray
Hoy
S. Ronaldsay
Pentland Firth
Rora Hd
Dennis Hd

Oil

Western Isles

Butt of Lewis
Stornoway
Broad B.
Tiumpan Hd
Lewis
North Minch
Loch Roag
Scarp
Tarbert
Sound of Shiant
Harris
Greenstone Pt
Taransay
Rubha Reidh
Pabbay
Berneray
Sd of Harris
North Uist
Monach Is
Lochmaddy
Benbecula
Wiay
Ronay
L. Snizort
Rona
Sd of Raasay
Uig
South Uist
Lochboisdale
Eriskay
Barra
Castlebay
Mingulay
Barra Hd

Outer Hebrides
Little Minch

Isle of Skye
Portree
Raasay
Cuillin Hills
Broadford
Scalpay
Kyle of Lochalsh
Sd of Sleat
L. Bracadale
Soay
Canna
Rum
Eigg
Muck
Coll
Tiree
Staffa
Iona
Ulva
Mull
Ben More 966
Tobermory
Morvern

C. Wrath
Durness
Eriboll
Tongue
Ben Hope 927
Handa
Eddrachillis Bay
Lochinver
Ben More Assynt 998
Inchnadamph
Enard Bay
L. Shin
Ben Kilbreck 961
Kinbrace
Caithness
Thurso
Halkirk
John o' Groats
Duncansby Hd
Dunnet Hd
Wick
Lybster
Helmsdale
L. Naver
Oykel
Lairg
Brora
Beatrice
Dornoch
Dornoch Firth
Tarbat Ness
Tain
Moray Firth
Ullapool
L. Broom
Ben Dearg 1081
L. Ewe
Gairloch
L. Maree
L. Fannich
Ben Wyvis 1045
Alness
Invergordon
Cromarty
Black Isle
Dingwall
Beauly
Nairn
Lossiemouth
Elgin
Buckie
Banff
Macduff
Fraserburgh
Forres
Rothes
Keith
Deveron
Turriff
Peterhead
Buchan Ness
Kinnairds Hd
L. Torridon
Rubha Hunish

Moray
Inverness
L. Ness
Grantown-on-Spey
Spey
Dufftown
Huntly
Oldmeldrum
Inverurie

Highland
Sgurr na Lapaich 1150
Farrar
Ben Attow 1031
Great Glen
Fort Augustus
Monadhliath Mts
Aviemore
Kingussie
Cairngorms
Ben Macdui 1310
Tomintoul
Findhorn
Don
Alford

Aberdeen
Aberdeen 1
Girdle Ness
Aboyne
Ballater
Dee
Banchory
Braemar
Lochnagar 1155
Stonehaven
Inverbervie

L. Arkaig
Mallaig
L. Morar
Arisaig
L. Lochy
L. Laggan
Fort William
Ben Nevis 1344
L. Shiel
Ardnamurchan Pt
L. Sunart
L. Linnhe
Ballachulish
Bridge of Orchy
L. Etive
Dalmally
Oban
L. Awe
L. Rannoch
L. Ericht
Drumochter Pass
Garry
Blair Atholl
Pitlochry
Aberfeldy
Dunkeld
Blairgowrie
N. Esk
S. Esk
Brechin
Angus
Kirriemuir
Forfar
Montrose
Arbroath
Carnoustie
Broughty Ferry

Perthshire & Kinross
Killin
Lochearnhead
Crieff
L. Tay
Coupar Angus
Sidlaw Hills
Dundee 5
Perth
Cupar
St Andrews
Fife Ness
L. Katrine
L. Earn
Callander
Crianlarich
Stirling
Aberfoyle
L. Lomond
L. Voil
Forth
Stirling
Ochil Hills
Kinross
Leven
Glenrothes
Leven
Buckhaven
Methil
Fife
Firth of Forth
Alloa
Cowdenbeath
Dunfermline
Kirkcaldy
North Berwick
Dunbar

Grampian Mountains

SCOTLAND

Inveraray
Arrochar
Lochgoilhead
L. Fyne
L. Long
Helensburgh
Dunoon
Greenock
Argyll & Bute
Ardrishaig
Rothesay
Bute
Millport
Largs
Gigha
Jura
Paps of Jura 784
Sd of Jura
Tarbert
Kintyre
Islay
Port Askaig
Rinns Pt
Port Ellen
Mull of Oa
Colonsay
Oronsay
Campbeltown
Mull of Kintyre
Sanda
Gigha

Dumbarton 14
Clydebank
Renfrew 10
Paisley
Glasgow 3
Airdrie
Coatbridge 12
E. Kilbride 13
Beith
Hamilton 8
Motherwell
Kilsyth
Cumbernauld
Falkirk 9
Grangemouth 15
Edinburgh 2
Leith
Dalkeith
Livingstone
Penicuik 11
Haddington 7
Gifford
Eyemouth
St Abb's Hd
Pentland Hills
Moorfoot Hills
Lammermuir Hills
Duns
Greenlaw
Lauder
Galashiels
Melrose
Kelso
Scottish Borders
Peebles
Biggar
Innerleithen
Selkirk
Jedburgh
Coldstream
Tweed
Berwick-upon-Tweed
Holy I.

North Ayrshire
Ardrossan
Irvine
Troon
Prestwick
East Ayrshire
Kilmarnock
Stewarton
Dalry
Lanark
Carstairs
South Lanarkshire
Clyde
Cumnock
Ayr
Maybole
Dalmellington
South Ayrshire
Girvan
Ballantrae
Merrick 843
Kells Ra.
Carrick
Doon
Thornhill
Sanquhar
Moffat
Tweedsmuir Hills
Langholm
Hawick
The Cheviot 816
Cheviot Hills
Rothbury
Alnwick
Northumberland
Nat. Park
Bellingham
Kielder Res.
Wansbeck
Morpeth

Dumfries and Galloway
New Galloway
Monaiaive
Lochmaben
Lockerbie
New Castleton
Dumfries
Castle Douglas
Dalbeattie
Annan
Longtown
Carlisle
Brampton
Corbridge
Allendale Town
Hexham
Haltwhistle
Alston
Consett
Newcastle upon Tyne
Gateshead
Durham
Stanhope
Wear
Crook
Bishop Auckland
Barnard Castle
Appleby
Penrith
Keswick
Cumbria
Ullswater
Nat. Park

Galloway
Newton Stewart
Gatehouse of Fleet
Kirkcudbright
Wigtown
Whithorn
Burrow Hd
Cairnryan
Stranraer
Portpatrick
Luce B.
Wigtown B.
Solway Firth
Workington
Maryport
Cockermouth
Siloth
Wigton
St John's Chapel

NORTHERN IRELAND
Donegal
Rahtmelton
Letterkenny
Lifford
Strabane
Newton Stewart
Tyrone
Omagh
Dungannon
Cookstown
Fintona
Londonderry
Londonderry
Limavady
Coleraine
Portstewart
Portrush
Bushmills
Ballycastle
Ballymoney
Maghera
Magherafelt
Antrim
Antrim Hills
Ballymena
Ballyclare
Ballycare
Larne
Island Magee
Carrickfergus
Newtownabbey
Belfast
Lisburn
Holywood
Bangor
Donaghadee
Newtownards
Comber
L. Neagh
Moville
Inishowen
Buncrana
Carndonagh
Malin Hd
Inishtrahull Sd.
Benbane Hd
Fair Hd
Glengad Hd
Rathlin I.
Garron Pt.
Glenarm
Newton Stewart
Barn
Sperrin Mts
ULSTER

Sheep Haven
L. Swilly
L. Foyle
North Channel
Mull of Galloway
Corsewall Pt
Loch Ryan

Stanton Banks

1:2M

0   25   50   75   100 km
0   25   50 mls

1:2M

1:5M

| 0 | 50 | 100 | 150 | 200 km |
| 0 | | 50 | | 100 mls |

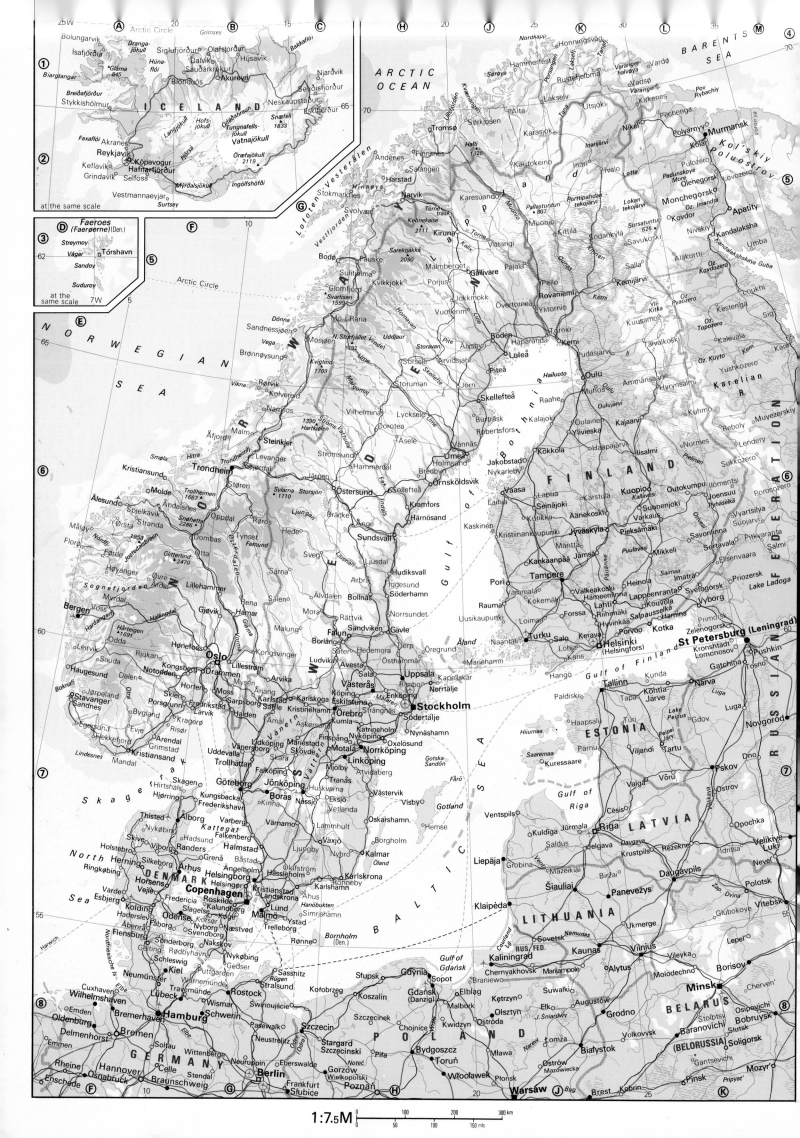

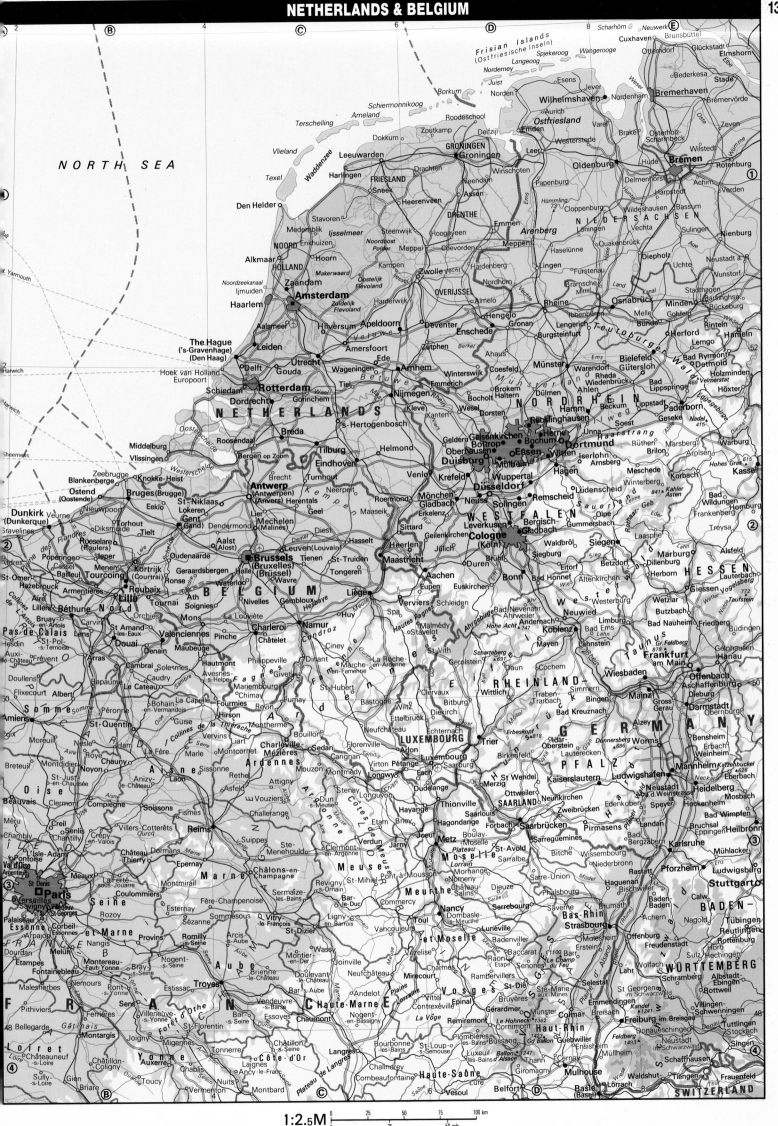

NORTH SEA

Frisian Islands
(Ostfriesische Inseln)

NETHERLANDS

NOORD HOLLAND

FRIESLAND

DRENTHE

OVERIJSSEL

NIEDERSACHSEN

NORDRHEIN

WESTFALEN

HESSEN

RHEINLAND-

GERMANY

PFALZ

BELGIUM

LUXEMBOURG

SAARLAND

FRANCE

Ardennes

Pas-de-Calais

WÜRTTEMBERG

BADEN-

SWITZERLAND

1:2.5M

1:5M

0   50   100   150   200 km

0   50   100 mls

1:5M

| 0 | 50 | 100 | 150 | 200 km |

| 0 | 50 | 100 mls |

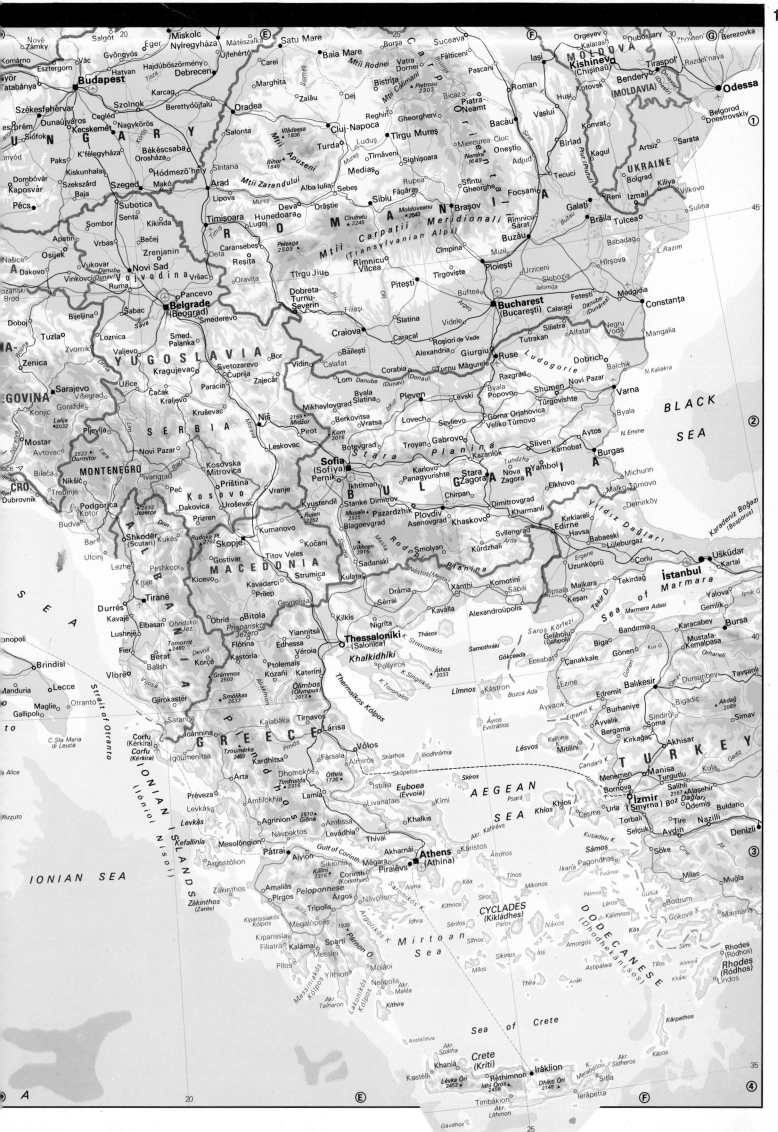

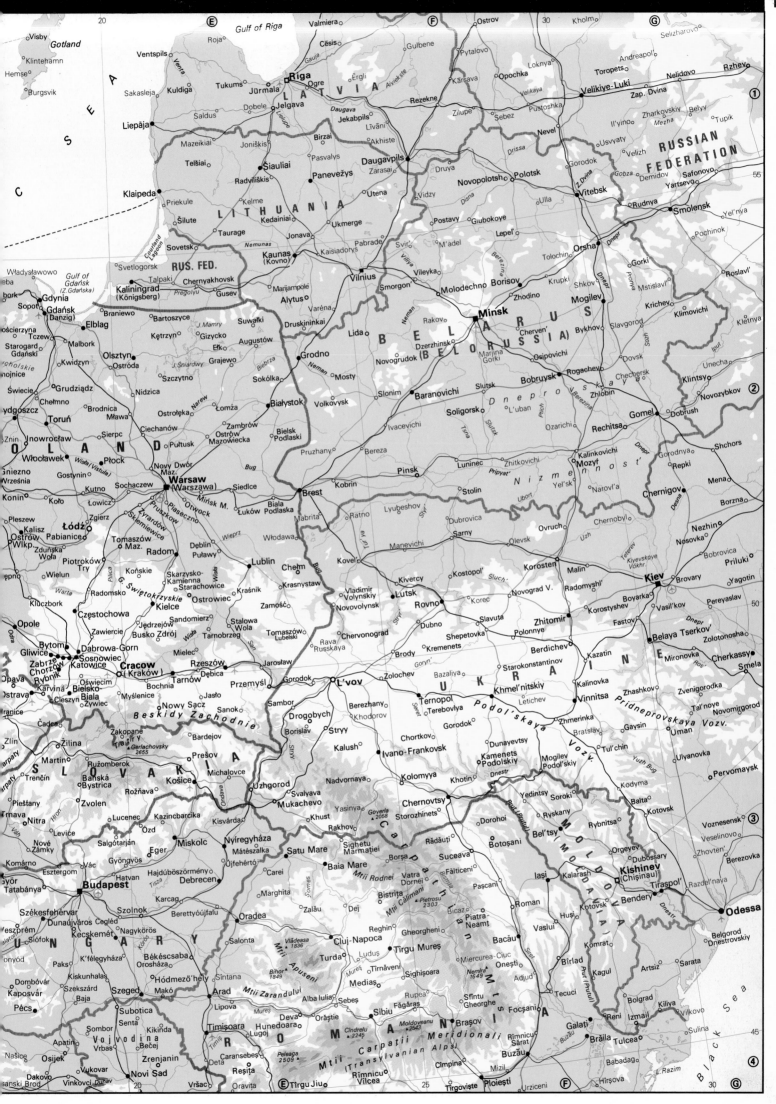

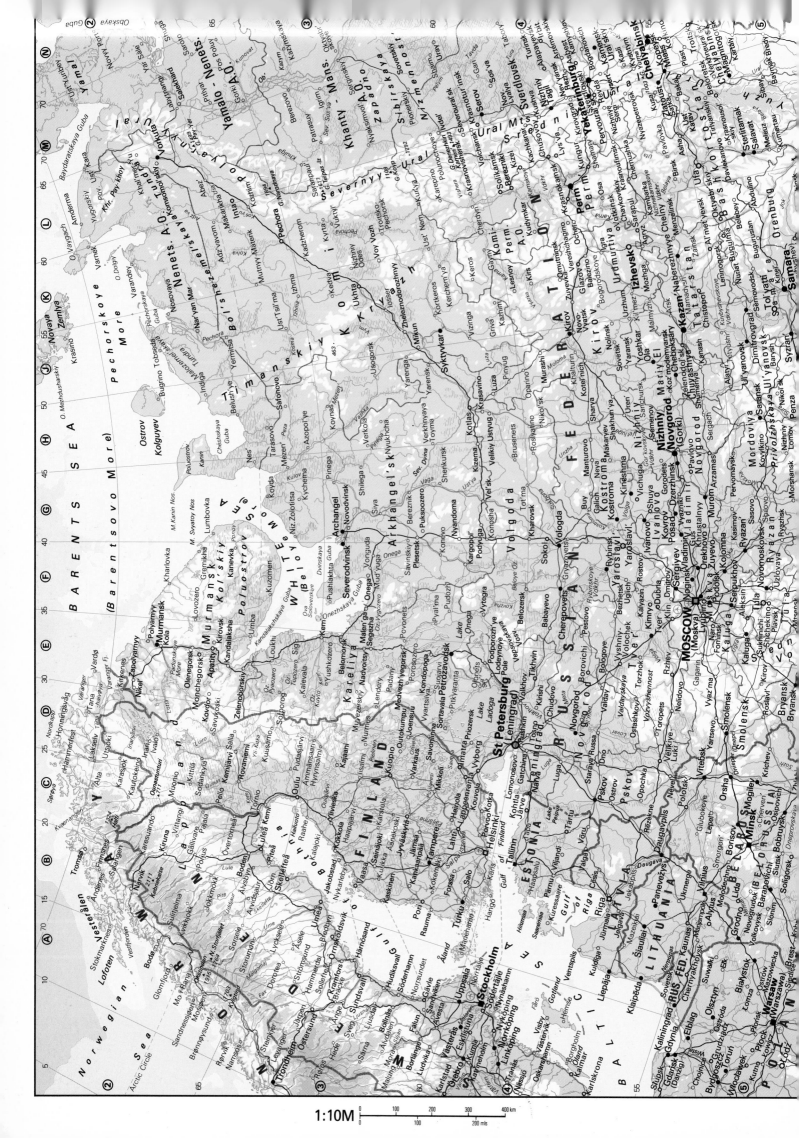

1:10M

Map labels

Countries / major regions: KAZAKHSTAN, UZBEKISTAN, TURKMENISTAN, RUSSIA, UKRAINE, MOLDOVA, ROMANIA, BULGARIA, YUGOS., GREECE, TURKEY, SYRIA, IRAQ, IRAN, GEORGIA, ARMENIA, AZERBAIJAN, SLOVAKIA, HUNGARY, CRIMEA, Dagestan, Kalmykiya-Khal'mg Tangch, Chechnya

Seas / water: CASPIAN SEA, BLACK SEA, Sea of Azov, Mediterranean Sea, Aegean Sea, Sea of Marmara, Sea of Crete

Cities (selection): Orenburg, Aktyubinsk, Saratov, Engels, Volgograd (Stalingrad), Astrakhan, Baku, Sumgait, Makhachkala, Groznyy, Vladikavkaz, Tbilisi, Yerevan, Rostov, Stavropol', Krasnodar, Sochi, Novorossiysk, Simferopol', Sevastopol', Yalta, Odessa, Kiev (Kiyev), Khar'kov, Donetsk, Dnepropetrovsk, Zaporozh'ye, Mariupol', Kishinev (Chişinău), Bucharest (Bucureşti), Constanţa, Varna, Burgas, Sofia (Sofiya), Plovdiv, Thessaloniki, Athens (Athinai), Istanbul (Üsküdar), Ankara, Izmir, Bursa, Konya, Adana, Kayseri, Sivas, Erzurum, Trabzon, Samsun, Malatya, Gaziantep, Halab (Aleppo), Hamah, Hims, Latakia, Nicosia, CYPRUS, Limassol, Mosul, Arbil, Kirkūk, Tehrān, Qom, Qazvīn, Rasht, Tabrīz, Urumīyeh, Ardabīl

Physical features: Caucasus, Lesser Caucasus, Elbrus, Mt. Ararat, Reshteh ye Alborz (Elburz Mts), Anadolu Dağları, Kuzey Anadolu Dağları, Toros Dağları (Taurus Mts), Rodopi Planina, Ustyurt Plateau, Mugodzhary

Legend
1 Severnaya Osetiya
2 Alaria
3 Chechnya
4 Kabardino-Balkariya
5 Nakhichevan (to Azerbaijan)
6 Karachayevo-Cherkesiya
7 Adygeya
8 Ingushetiya

ICELAND

ARCTIC OCEAN

Greenland (Den.)

Svalbard (Nor.)

Zemlya Frantsa Iosifa

Severnaya Zemlya

Novosibirskiye Ostrova

Barents Sea

Novaya Zemlya

Arctic Circle

IRELAND
UNITED KINGDOM
London
Dublin
Edinburgh
DENMARK
NORWAY
SWEDEN
FINLAND
Faeroes (Den.)
Oslo
Stockholm
Helsinki
Copenhagen
Baltic Sea
Riga
Tallinn
EST.
LAT.
LITH.
Vilnius

PORT.
SPAIN
FRANCE
Paris
Marseilles
Corsica
Sardinia
ITALY
Rome
Sicily
Tunis
ALB.
GREECE
Athens
Crete
MAC.
YUG.
BULGARIA
BOS. HERZ.
CROATIA
SLOVENIA
AUSTRIA
HUNGARY
SWITZ.
GERMANY
NETH.
BEL.
LUX.
CZECH REP.
SLOVAKIA
POLAND
Warsaw
ROMANIA
Bucuresti
MOLD.
UKRAINE
Kiev
Dnepropetrovsk
Khar'kov
BELARUS (BELORUSSIA)
Minsk
Moscow
St Petersburg (Leningrad)
Yaroslavl'
Nizhniy Novgorod
Voronezh
Rostov
Volgograd
Astrakhan
Saratov
Samara
Kazan'
Perm'
Ufa
Yekaterinburg
Chelyabinsk
Murmansk
Arkhangel'sk
White Sea
L. Ladoga
L. Onega
Vorkuta
Noril'sk
Lena
Yakutsk
Volga
Ural'sk

RUSSIAN FEDERATION

Krasnoyarsk
Bratsk
Novosibirsk
Barnaul
Omsk
Karaganda
Semipalatinsk
Irkutsk
Ulan Ude
L. Baikal
Yenisey
Ob'

KAZAKHSTAN
Aral Sea
L. Balkhash
Aral'sk

Black Sea
TURKEY
Istanbul
Ankara
Adana
Izmir
CYPRUS
GEO.
Tbilisi
Yerevan
ARM.
AZER.
Baku
Caspian Sea
Tabriz
Mosul
Basra
Abadan
IRAQ
Baghdad
Kerman
Esfahan
Tehran
Mashhad
IRAN
Herat
Kabul
AFGHANISTAN
Islamabad
Kashmir

UZBEKISTAN
TURKMENISTAN
Ashkhabad
TAJIKISTAN
Dushanbe
Tashkent
KYRGYZSTAN
Bishkek
Oz. Issyk Kul'
Almaty
Ürümqi
SINKIANG

LIBYA
Alexandria
Cairo
EGYPT
Aswan
Nile
SUDAN
Khartoum
RED SEA
Asmara
ERITREA
DJIBOUTI
Adis Abeba
ETHIOPIA
SOMALIA
KENYA
Mogadishu (Muqdisho)
Mombasa
Dar es Salaam
TANZANIA
SEYCHELLES
COMOROS
MOZAMBIQUE
MADAGASCAR
Antananarivo

SAUDI ARABIA
Makkah
Riyadh
KUWAIT
BAHRAIN
QATAR
U.A.E.
Abu Dhabi
Muscat
OMAN
YEMEN
San'a'
Aden
G. of Aden
Socotra (Yemen)
ARABIAN SEA

Beirut
LEB.
ISRAEL
Jerusalem
JOR.
Amman
SYRIA
Damascus
Halab

PAKISTAN
Karachi
Hyderabad
Lahore
Delhi
Agra
Jaipur
Ahmadabad
Bombay
INDIA
Nagpur
Hyderabad
Jabalpur
Allahabad
Kanpur
Lucknow
Patna
Ganga
Godavari
Krishna
Bangalore
Madras
Madurai
Jaffna
SRI LANKA
Colombo
Kandy
Laccadive Is. (Ind.)
MALDIVES
Indus

NEPAL
Kathmandu
BHUTAN
Thimphu
BANGLA-DESH
Dhaka
Calcutta
Chittagong
Brahmaputra
Imphal

TIBET
Lhasa
Qinghai Hu
CHINA
Chengdu
Chongqing
Kunming
Guiyang
Changsha
Wuhan
Zhengzhou
Xi'an
Lanzhou
Taiyuan
Tianjin
Beijing
Qiqi
INNER MONGOLIA
MONGOLIA
Ulaanbaatar (Ulan Bator)
Chang Jiang
Huang

MYANMAR (BURMA)
Mandalay
Rangoon (Yangon)
Moulmein
Irrawaddy
Chiang Mai
THAILAND
Bangkok
Surat Thani
Vientiane
LAOS
VIETNAM
Hanoi
Haiphong
Da Nang
Hainan
CAMBODIA
Phnom Penh
Ho Chi Minh City (Saigon)
Mekong
Guangzhou
Macao
Bay of Bengal
Andaman Is. (Ind.)
Nicobar Is. (Ind.)

Equator
INDIAN OCEAN
Chagos Arch. (U.K.)
Aldabra Is (Sey.)

George Town
Kota Bharu
Kuala Lumpur
SINGAPORE
MALAYSIA
Medan
SUMATERA
Padang
Palembang
Jakarta
JAVA
Christmas I. (Aust.)
Cocos Is (Aust.)

1:40M
400   800   1200   1600 km
400   800 mls

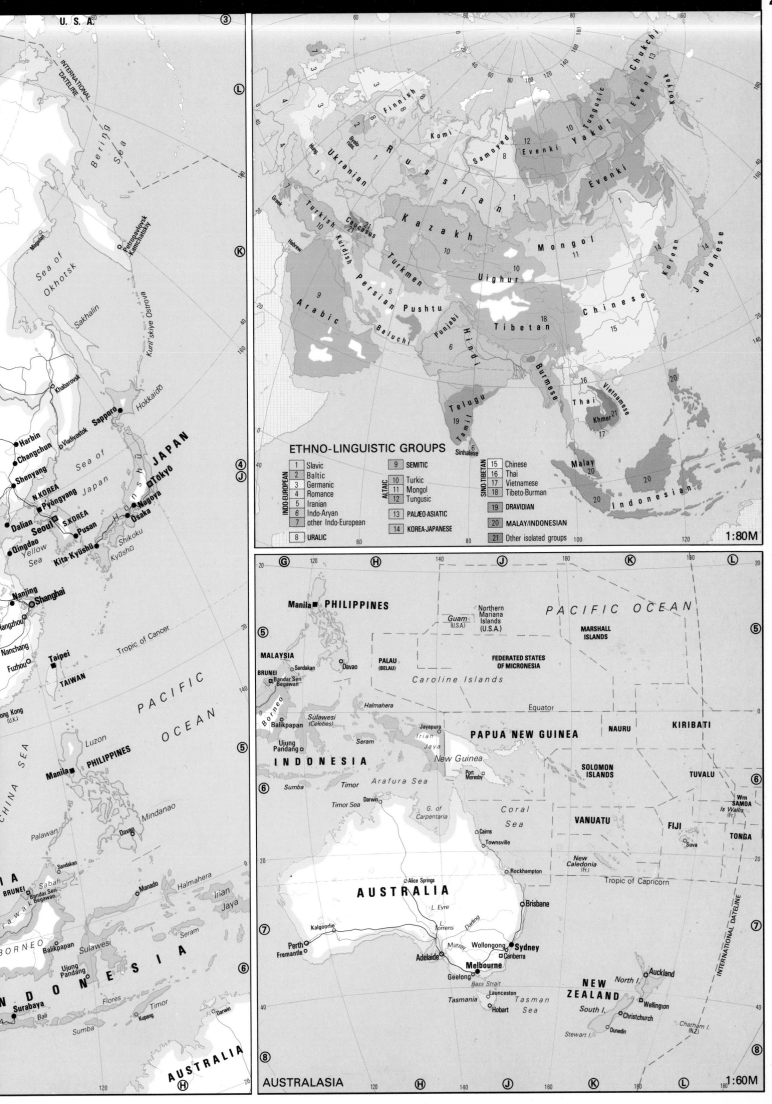

U.S.A. ③

INTERNATIONAL DATELINE

Bering Sea

Sea of Okhotsk

Sakhalin

Kuril'skiye Ostrova

Petropavlovsk-Kamchatskiy

Magadan

Ⓛ

Ⓚ

Khabarovsk

Vladivostok

Sapporo

Hokkaidō

JAPAN

Harbin
Changchun
Shenyang
N.KOREA
Pyŏngyang
Dalian
Seoul
S.KOREA
Pusan
Qingdao
Yellow Sea
Kita-Kyūshū
Kyūshū
Tōkyō
Nagoya
Osaka
Shikoku

Sea of Japan

Ⓙ ④

Nanjing
Shanghai
Hangzhou
Nanchang
Fuzhou
Taipei
TAIWAN

Tropic of Cancer

PACIFIC OCEAN

Hong Kong (U.K.)

CHINA SEA

Luzon

Manila ■ **PHILIPPINES**

Mindanao

Palawan

Davao

Sandakan

Sabah

BRUNEI
Bandar Seri Begawan

BORNEO

Balikpapan

Ujung Pandang

Sulawesi

Surabaya
Bali
Flores
Timor
Sumba
Kupang
Darwin

INDONESIA

Irian Jaya

Halmahera

Manado

Seram

AUSTRALIA

⑤

⑥

ETHNO-LINGUISTIC GROUPS

Finnish
Komi
Samoyed
Evenki
Yakut
Tungusic
Chukchi
Koryak
Evenki
Evenki
Russian
Ukranian
Byelorussian
Greek
Turkish
Caucasus
Hebrew
Kurdish
Persian
Arabic
Kazakh
Turkmen
Pushtu
Baluchi
Punjabi
Hindi
Telugu
Tamil
Sinhalese
Uighur
Mongol
Tibetan
Burmese
Chinese
Korean
Japanese
Thai
Vietnamese
Khmer
Malay
Indonesian

INDO-EUROPEAN						
1	Slavic	9	SEMITIC	15	Chinese	
2	Baltic			16	Thai	
3	Germanic	10	Turkic	17	Vietnamese	
4	Romance	11	Mongol	18	Tibeto-Burman	
5	Iranian	12	Tungusic			
6	Indo-Aryan			19	DRAVIDIAN	
7	other Indo-European	13	PALÆO-ASIATIC	20	MALAY/INDONESIAN	
8	URALIC	14	KOREA-JAPANESE	21	Other isolated groups	

ALTAIC — 10, 11, 12
SINO-TIBETAN — 15, 16, 17, 18

1:80M

Ⓖ Ⓗ Ⓙ Ⓚ Ⓛ

Manila ■ **PHILIPPINES**

Guam (U.S.A.)

Northern Mariana Islands (U.S.A.)

PACIFIC OCEAN

MARSHALL ISLANDS

⑤

MALAYSIA

Sandakan
Davao

BRUNEI
Bandar Seri Begawan

Borneo

Balikpapan

Ujung Pandang

PALAU (BELAU)

Sulawesi (Celebes)

Seram

Halmahera

Caroline Islands

FEDERATED STATES OF MICRONESIA

Equator

INDONESIA

Jayapura

Irian Jaya

New Guinea

PAPUA NEW GUINEA

Port Moresby

NAURU

KIRIBATI

SOLOMON ISLANDS

TUVALU

⑥

Sumba
Timor
Timor Sea
Darwin

Arafura Sea

G. of Carpentaria

Coral Sea

Cairns
Townsville

VANUATU

New Caledonia (Fr.)

Wm SAMOA
Is Wallis (Fr.)

FIJI
Suva

TONGA

Rockhampton

Tropic of Capricorn

⑦

Alice Springs

AUSTRALIA

Kalgoorlie

L. Eyre
L. Torrens

Murray
Darling

Brisbane

Perth
Fremantle

Adelaide

Geelong

Wollongong
Sydney
Canberra

MELBOURNE

Bass Strait

Launceston

Tasmania

Hobart

Tasman Sea

NEW ZEALAND

North I.

Auckland

Wellington

South I.

Christchurch

Dunedin

Stewart I.

Chatham I. (N.Z.)

INTERNATIONAL DATELINE

⑧

AUSTRALASIA

1:60M

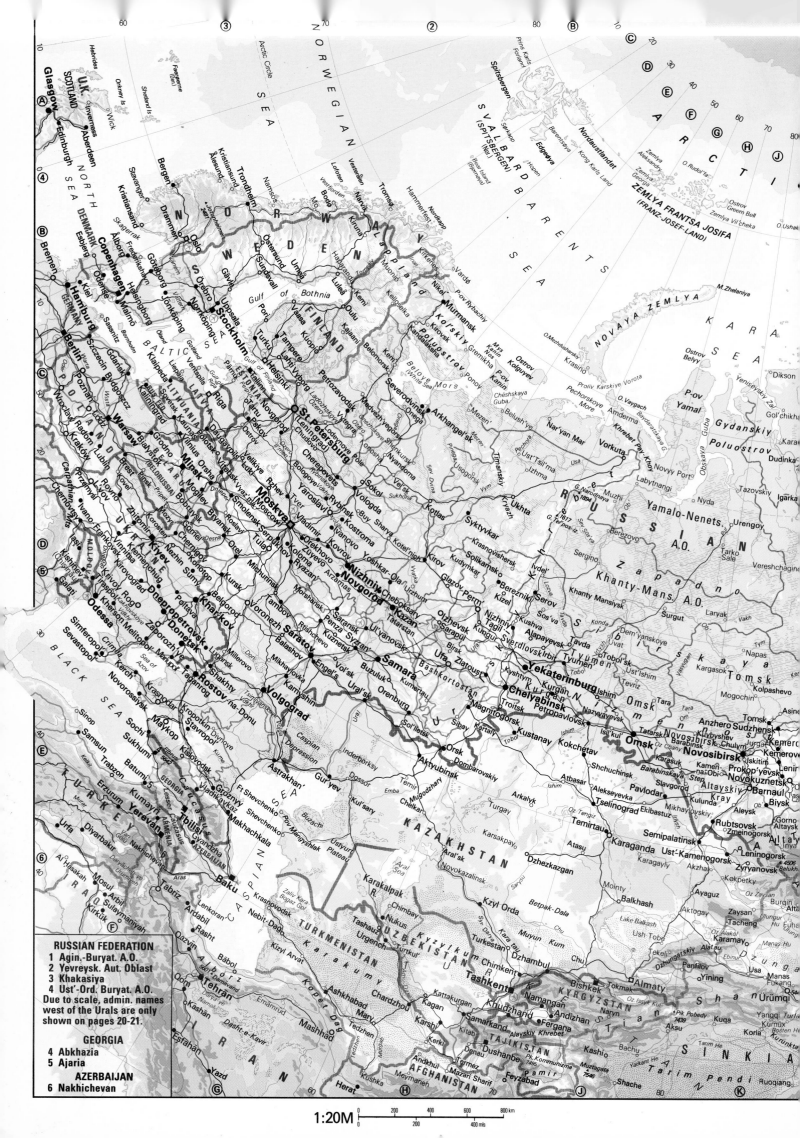

O C E A N
SEVERNAYA ZEMLYA
(NORTH LAND)
NOVOSIBIRSKYE OSTROVA
(NEW SIBERIAN ISLANDS)
LAPTEV SEA
EAST SIBERIAN SEA
CHUKCHI SEA
BERING SEA
Bering Str.
Wrangel I.
Chukot. A.O.
Koryak A.O.
KAMCHATKA
Petropavlovsk-Kamchatskiy
SEA OF OKHOTSK
Magadan
Sakha
(Yakutiya)
Yakutsk
Verkhoyanskiy Khrebet
Khrebet Cherskogo
Taymyr A.O.
Poluostrov Taymyr
Gory Byrranga
Noril'sk
Evenk. A.O.
Sredne Sibirskoye Ploskogor'ye
F E D E R A T I O N
S I B E R I A
Krasnoyarsk
Irkutsk
Ulan Ude
Chita
Buryatiya
Tyva
Khabarovsk
Komsomol'sk-na-Amure
SAKHALIN
Kuril Islands
(Kuril'skiye Ostrova)
HOKKAIDO
Sapporo
SEA OF JAPAN
J A P A N
Tokyo
Yokohama
Nagoya
Osaka
Kobe
Kyoto
Hiroshima
Fukuoka
Kita-Kyushu
Kyushu
Shikoku
NORTH KOREA
SOUTH KOREA
P'yongyang
Seoul
(Soul)
Pusan
Taegu
Vladivostok
MANCHURIA
Harbin
Changchun
Shenyang
Dalian
Beijing
(Peking)
Tianjin
(Tientsin)
YELLOW SEA
Korea Bay
Bo Hai
INNER MONGOLIA
M O N G O L I A
Ulaanbaatar
G O B I
Hohhot
Baotou
Datong
Jinan
Qingdao
Yinchuan
Taiyuan
Hami
Turpan
Altun Shan
Qilian Shan
GREAT WALL

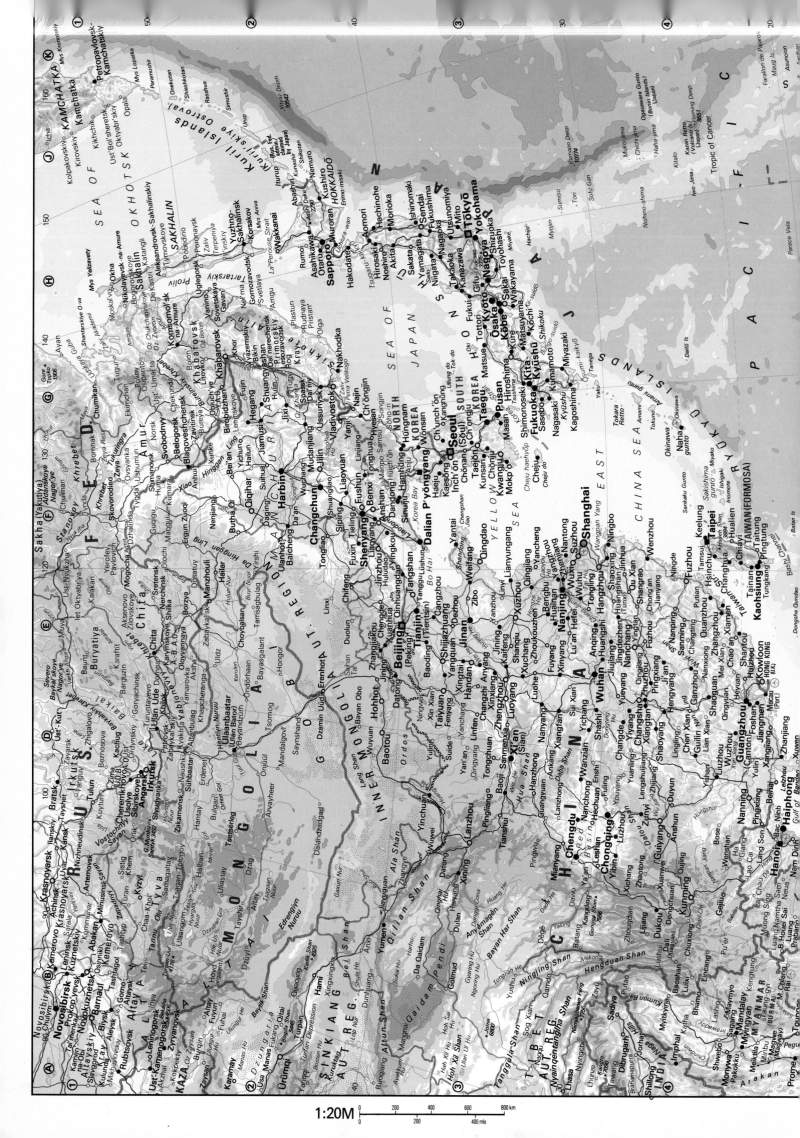

1:20M

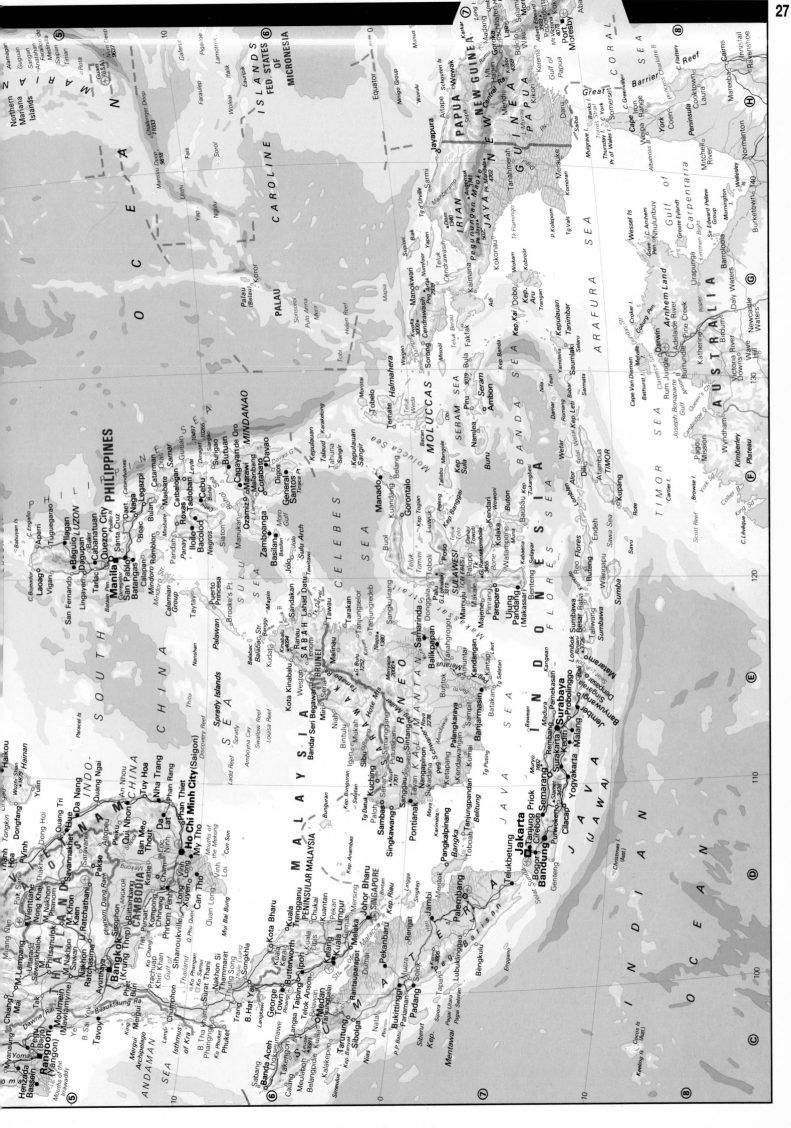

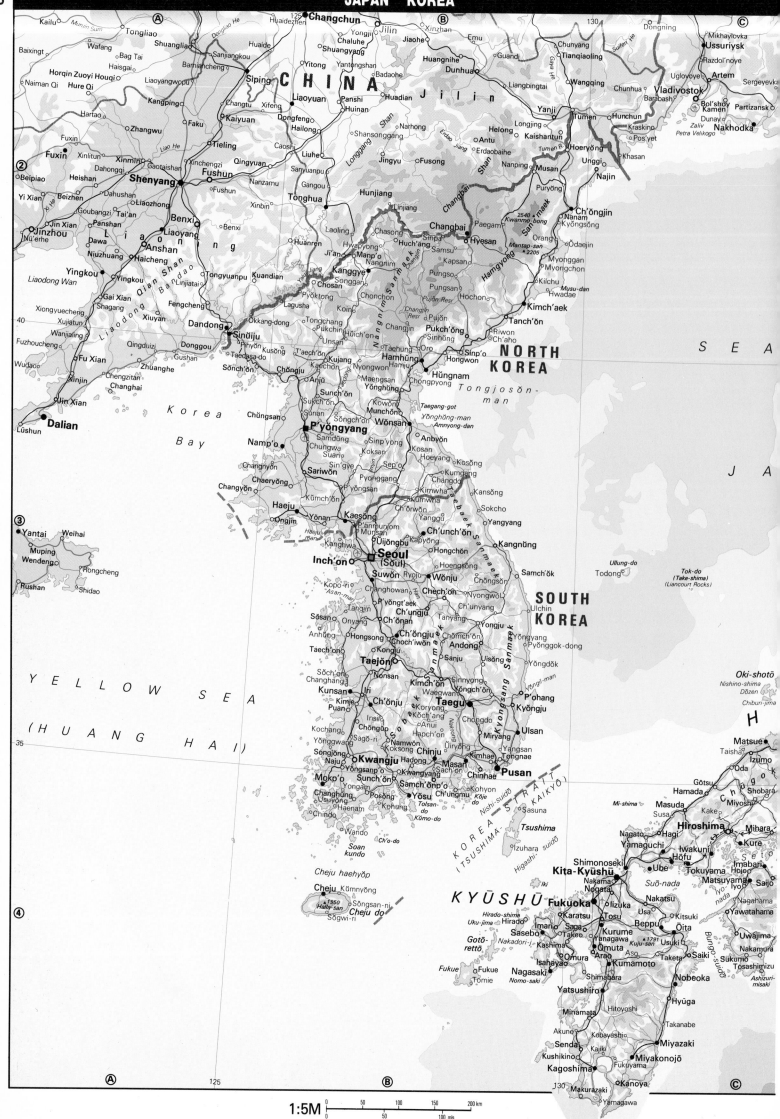

1:5M

| 0 | 50 | 100 | 150 | 200 km |

50   100 mils

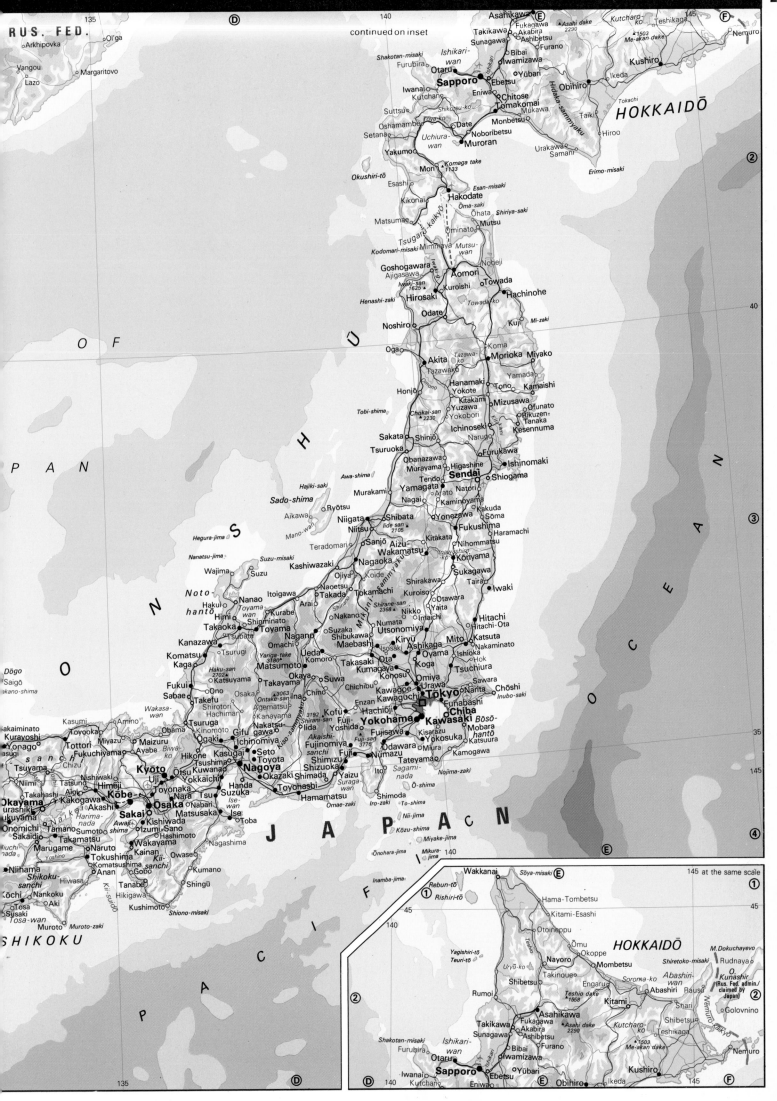

RUS. FED.

HOKKAIDŌ

JAPAN

PACIFIC OCEAN

SHIKOKU

145 at the same scale

HOKKAIDŌ

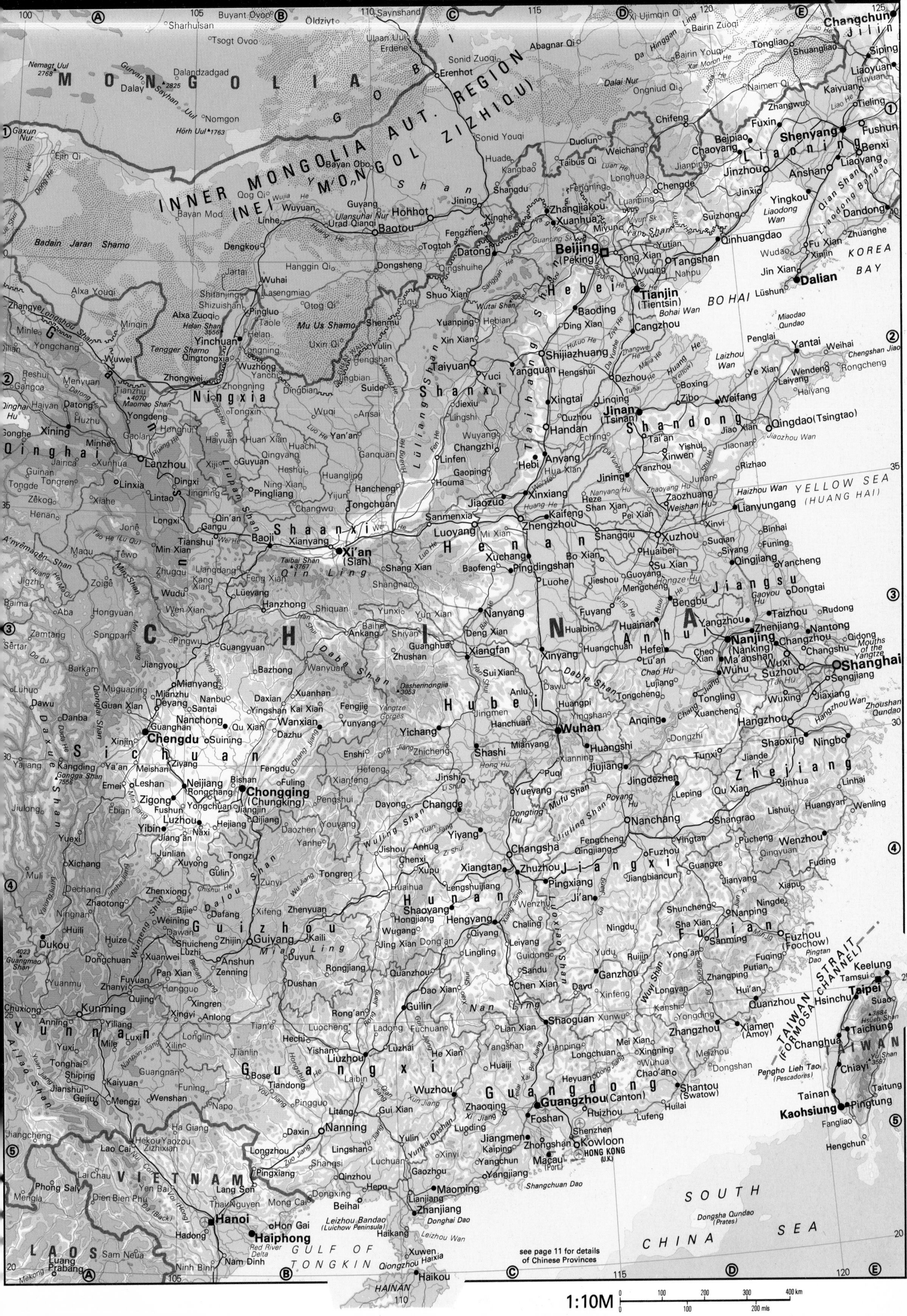

MONGOLIA

GOBI

INNER MONGOLIA AUT. REGION (NEI MONGOL ZIZHIQU)

Jilin

Changchun

Siping
Liaoyuan

Shenyang
Fushun
Benxi
Liaoning
Anshan
Liaoyang

Jinzhou
Yingkou
Dalian
Lüshun

KOREA BAY

BO HAI

Beijing (Peking)

Tianjin (Tientsin)
Tangshan
Qinhuangdao

Hebei

Baoding
Cangzhou

Shijiazhuang
Hengshui

Taiyuan

Shanxi

Handan

Jinan (Tsinan)

Shandong

Qingdao (Tsingtao)
Yantai
Weihai
Weifang
Zibo

YELLOW SEA (HUANG HAI)

Lianyungang

Qinghai

Lanzhou
Xining

Ningxia

Yinchuan

Yan'an

Shaanxi

Xi'an (Sian)

Baoji
Xianyang

Luoyang
Zhengzhou
Kaifeng

Henan

Nanyang

Xuzhou

Jiangsu

Bengbu
Huainan
Hefei

Anhui

Nanjing (Nanking)

Changzhou
Wuxi
Suzhou
Shanghai

Hangzhou

CHINA

Chengdu

Sichuan

Chongqing (Chungking)

Hubei

Wuhan

Yichang
Shashi
Huangshi

Nanchang

Jiangxi

Zhejiang

Ningbo
Wenzhou

Changsha

Hunan

Hengyang
Zhuzhou
Xiangtan

Guizhou

Guiyang

Yunnan

Kunming

Guangxi

Nanning
Liuzhou
Guilin

Guangdong

Guangzhou (Canton)

Shenzhen
Kowloon
HONG KONG (U.K.)
Macau (Port.)

Shantou (Swatow)

Fujian

Fuzhou (Foochow)
Xiamen (Amoy)

TAIWAN (FORMOSA)

Taipei
Taichung
Chiayi
Tainan
Kaohsiung
Pingtung

TAIWAN STRAIT (FORMOSA CHANNEL)

VIETNAM

Hanoi
Haiphong

LAOS

GULF OF TONGKIN

HAINAN

Haikou

SOUTH CHINA SEA

see page 11 for details of Chinese Provinces

1:10M

0   100   200   300   400 km
0   100   200 mls

Map of Australia and surrounding regions

Scale
1:20M

0 200 400 600 800 km
0 200 400 mils

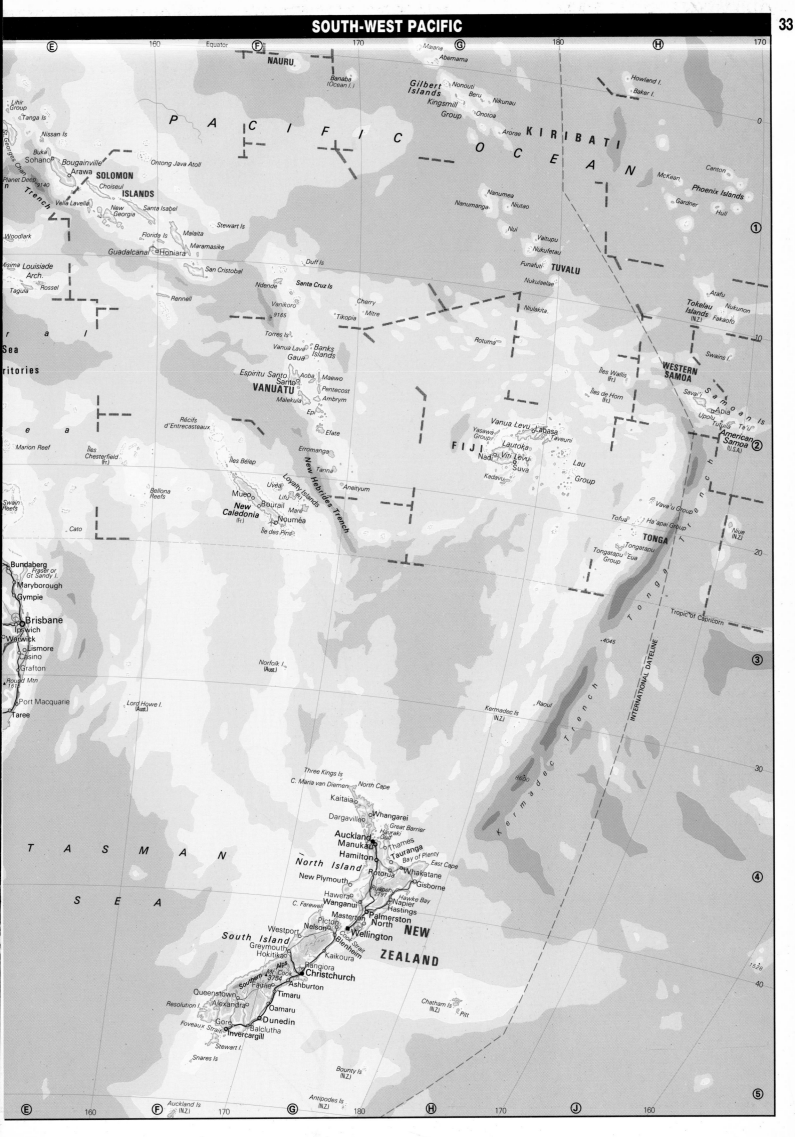

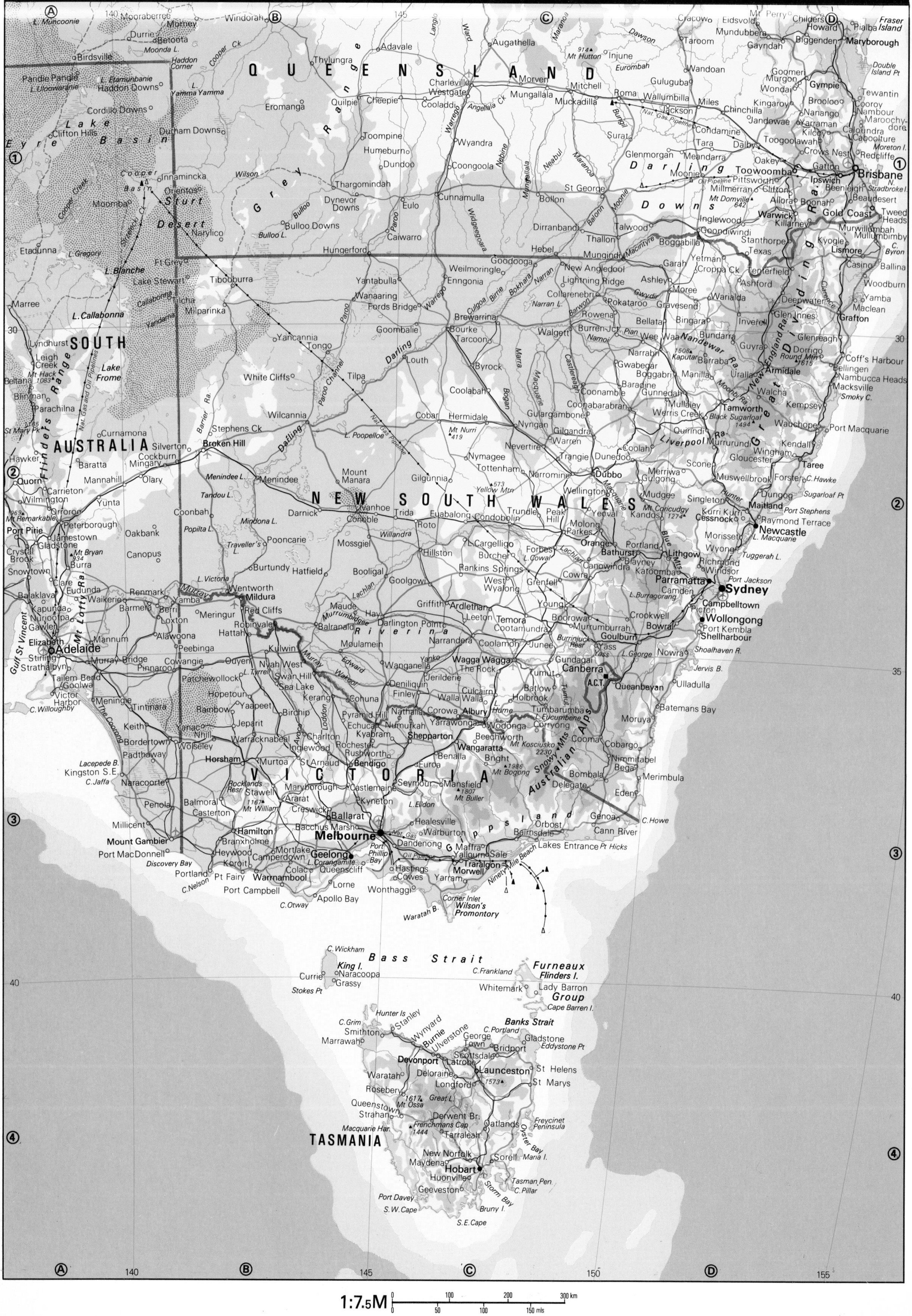

QUEENSLAND

SOUTH AUSTRALIA

NEW SOUTH WALES

VICTORIA

TASMANIA

Lake Eyre Basin

Sturt Desert

Grey Range

Darling Downs

Flinders Range

Mt Lofty Ra.

Riverina

Snowy Mts

Australian Alps

Gippsland

Great Dividing Range

New England Range

Liverpool Ra.

Brisbane
Gold Coast
Toowoomba
Maryborough
Gympie

Sydney
Parramatta
Wollongong
Newcastle
Canberra
A.C.T.

Adelaide
Port Pirie
Broken Hill
Dubbo
Tamworth
Armidale
Coff's Harbour
Grafton

Melbourne
Geelong
Ballarat
Bendigo
Mildura
Wagga Wagga
Albury
Shepparton
Wangaratta
Traralgon
Morwell
Sale

Mount Gambier
Horsham
Hamilton
Warrnambool

Mt Kosciusko 2230

Bass Strait
King I.
Furneaux Flinders I.
Group
Banks Strait

Burnie
Devonport
Launceston
Hobart

Mt Ossa 1617

Wilson's Promontory

Gulf St Vincent

1:7.5M   0 50 100 200 300 km
         0 50 100 150 mls

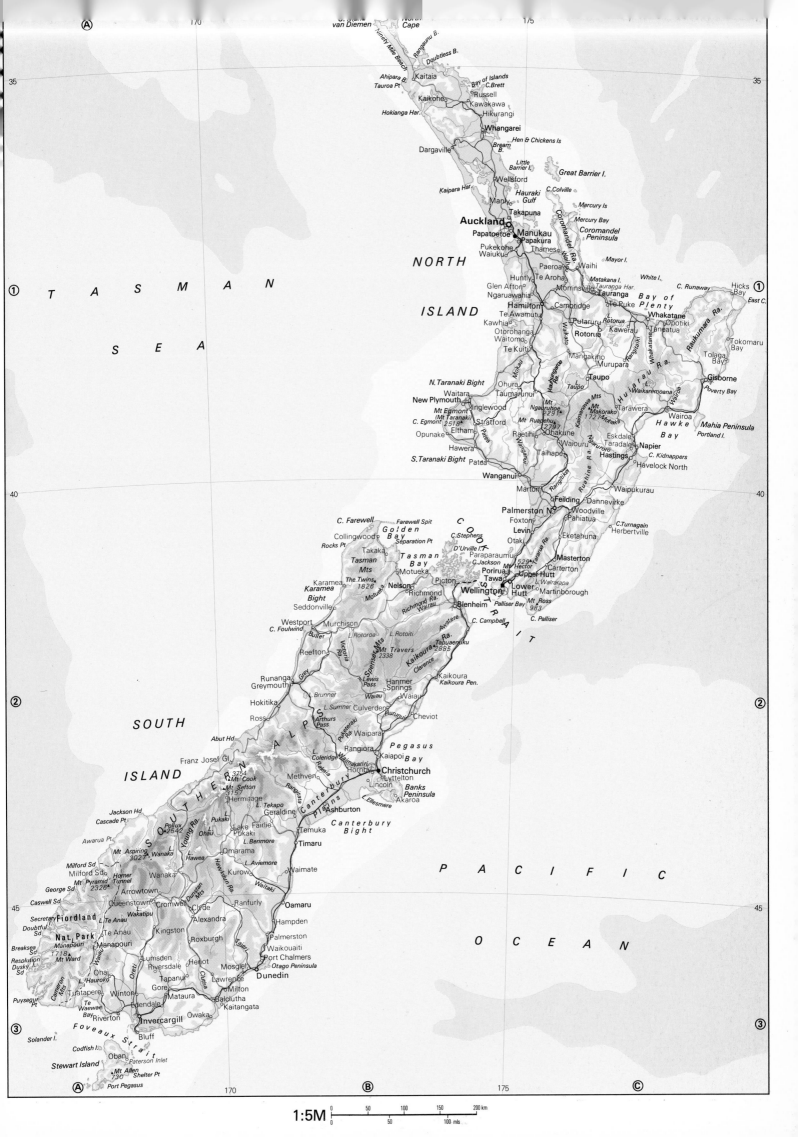

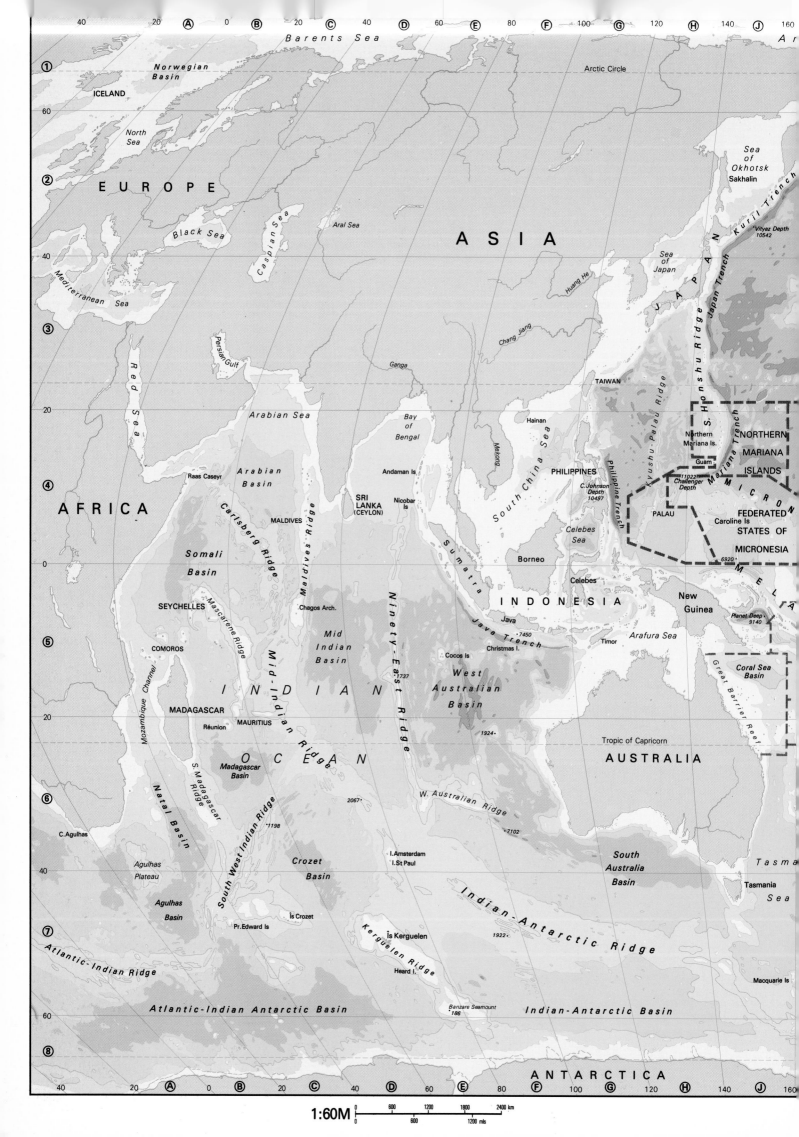

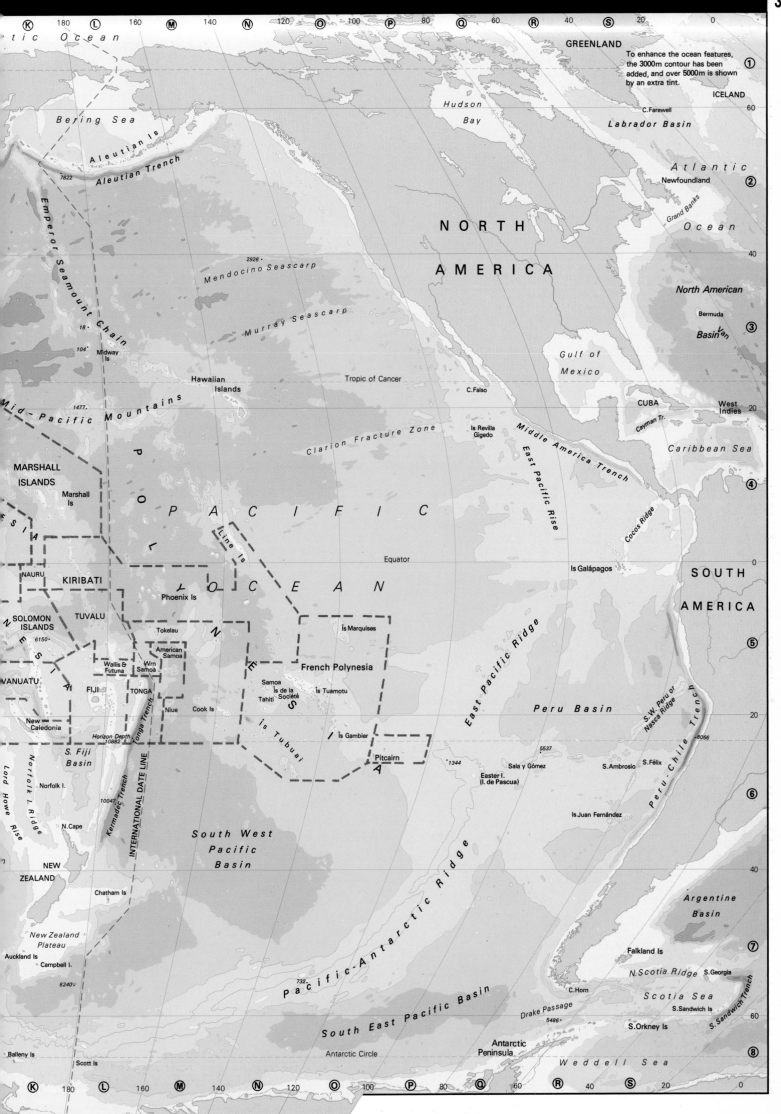

K 180 L 160 M 140 N 120 O 100 P 80 Q 60 R 40 S 20 0

...tic *Ocean*

GREENLAND

To enhance the ocean features, the 3000m contour has been added, and over 5000m is shown by an extra tint.

ICELAND

①

Bering Sea

Hudson Bay

C.Farewell

60

Labrador Basin

Atlantic

Newfoundland

②

Aleutian Is

7822 •

Aleutian Trench

Grand Banks

Ocean

N O R T H

A M E R I C A

40

2926 •

Mendocino Seascarp

North American

Emperor Seamount Chain

Bermuda

Van

③

Basin

18 •

Murray Seascarp

Gulf of Mexico

104 • Midway Is

Mid - Pacific Mountains

Hawaiian Islands

Tropic of Cancer

C.Falso

CUBA

West Indies

20

1477 •

Cayman Tr.

Caribbean Sea

Clarion Fracture Zone

Is Revilla Gigedo

Middle America Trench

④

MARSHALL ISLANDS

P

East Pacific Rise

Cocos Ridge

Marshall Is

O

P A C I F I C

L

S I A

Y

NAURU

N

Line Is

Equator

Is Galápagos

S O U T H

0

KIRIBATI

E

O C E A N

A M E R I C A

Phoenix Is

S

⑤

6150 •

SOLOMON ISLANDS

TUVALU

Tokelau

N

Îs Marquises

E

East Pacific Ridge

NESIA

American Samoa

French Polynesia

Wallis & Futuna

Wrn Samoa

S

Samoa

Îs de la Société

Îs Tuamotu

VANUATU

FIJI

TONGA

Tahiti

Peru Basin

S.W. Peru or Nasca Ridge

20

New Caledonia

Niue

Cook Is

I

Îs Gambier

8066 •

Horizon Depth 10882

Îs Tubuai

A

Pitcairn

Peru - Chile Trench

Norfolk I. Ridge

S. Fiji Basin

Norfolk I.

Tonga Trench

1344 •

5537 •

Sala y Gómez

S.Ambrosio

S.Félix

Lord Howe Rise

10047 •

Easter I. (I. de Pascua)

⑥

N.Cape

INTERNATIONAL DATE LINE

Kermadec Trench

Is Juan Fernández

South West Pacific Basin

NEW ZEALAND

Chatham Is

Argentine Basin

⑦

Pacific-Antarctic Ridge

Falkland Is

New Zealand Plateau

Auckland Is

N.Scotia Ridge

S.Georgia

Campbell I.

C.Horn

Scotia Sea

732 •

6240 •

S.Sandwich Is

60

South East Pacific Basin

Drake Passage

5486 •

S.Orkney Is

S. Sandwich Trench

Balleny Is

Antarctic Circle

Antarctic Peninsula

Weddell Sea

⑧

Scott Is

K 180 L 160 M 140 N 120 O 100 P 80 Q 60 R 40 S 20 0

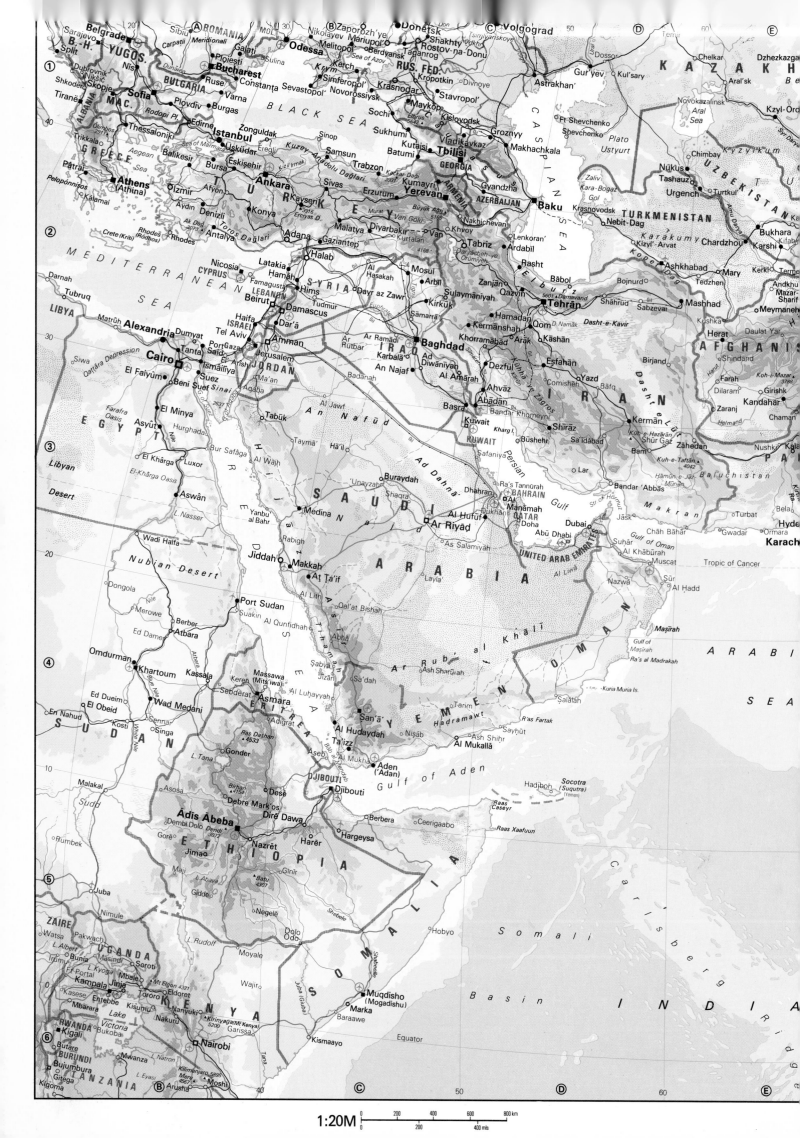

1:20M
0 200 400 600 800 km
0   200   400 mls

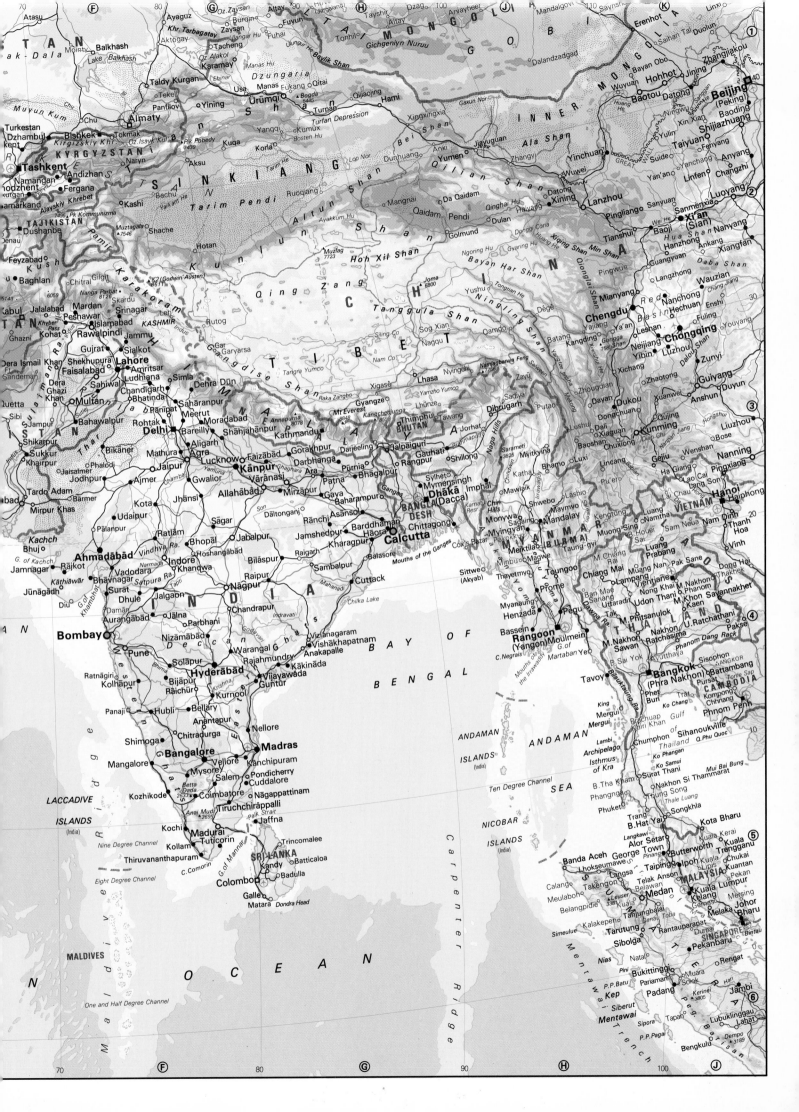

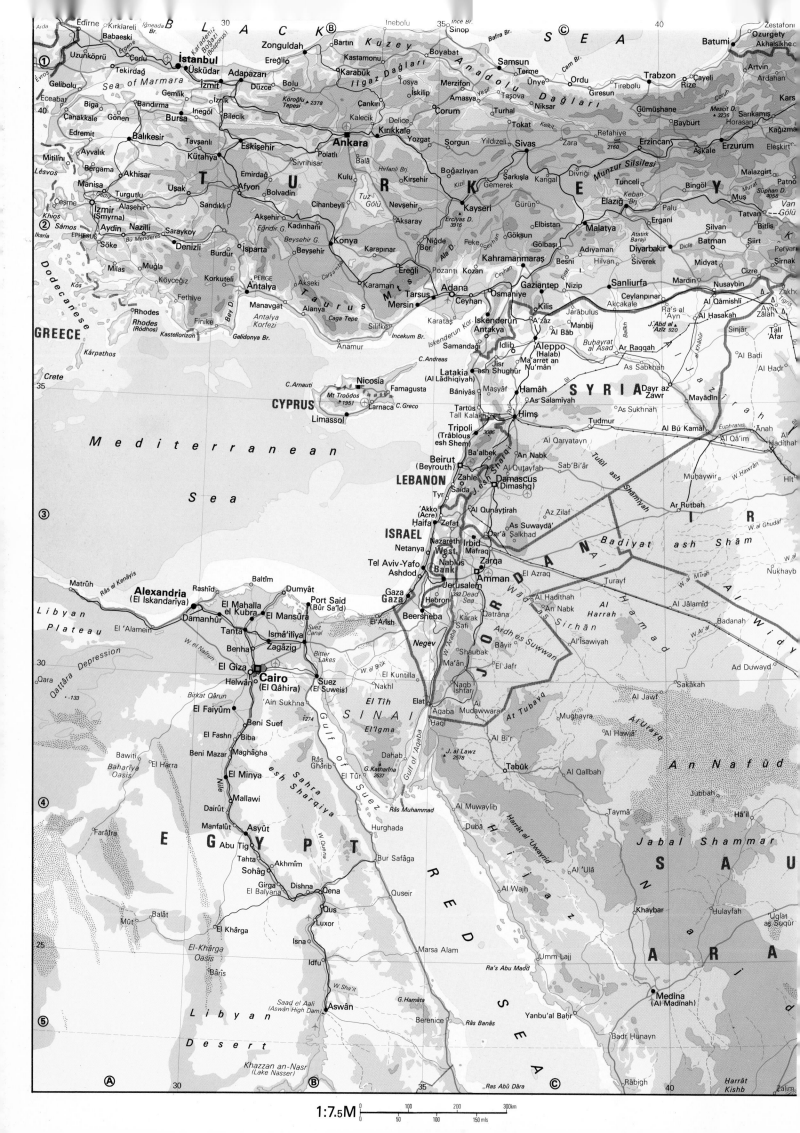

1:7.5M

100   200   300km

50   100   150mls

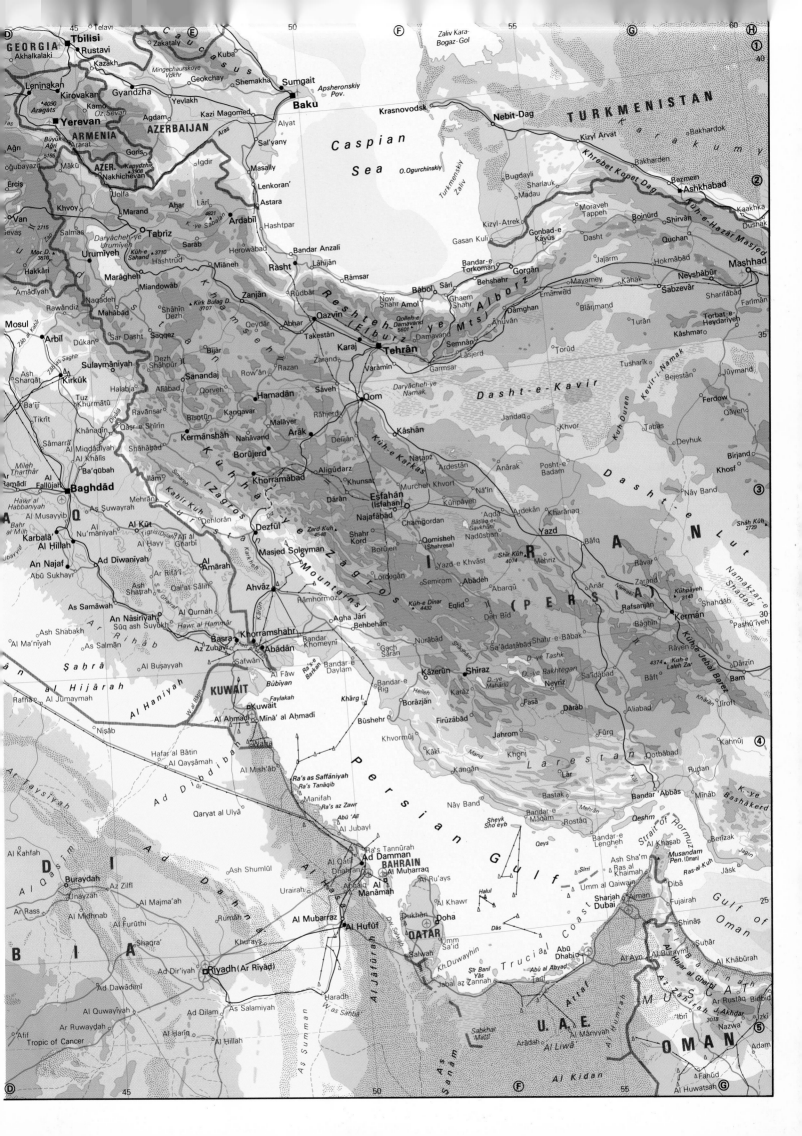

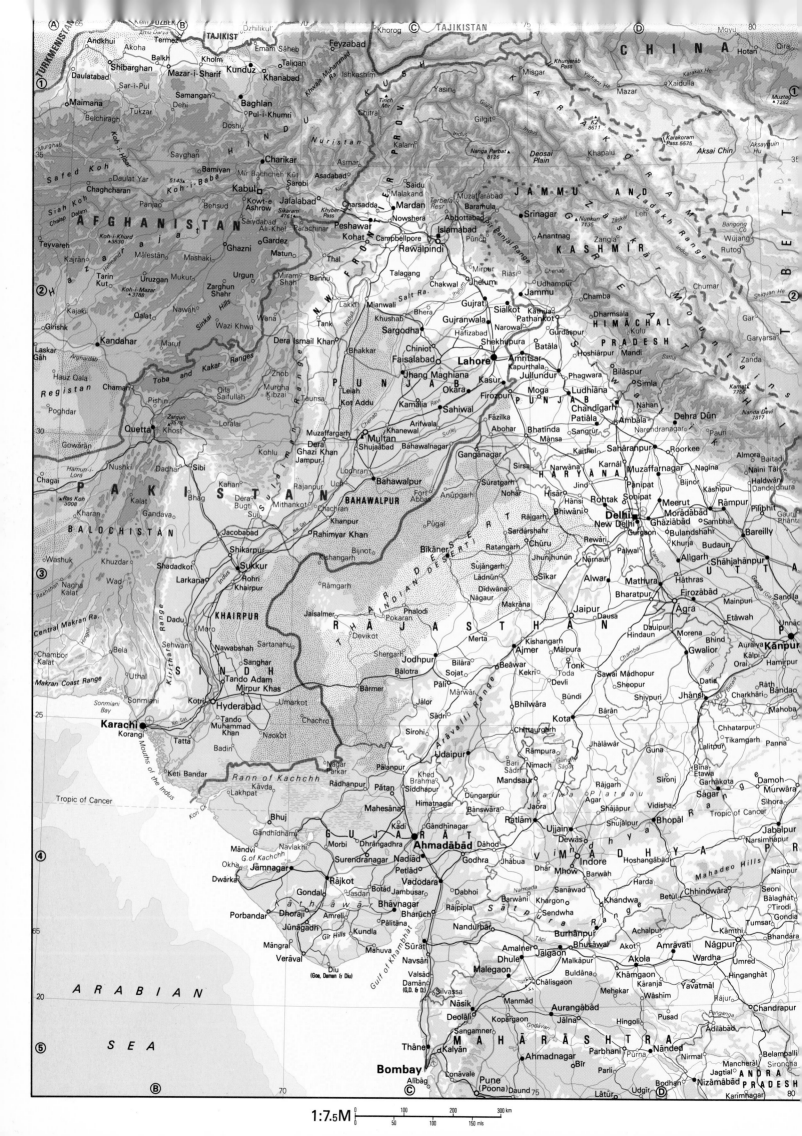

1:7.5M

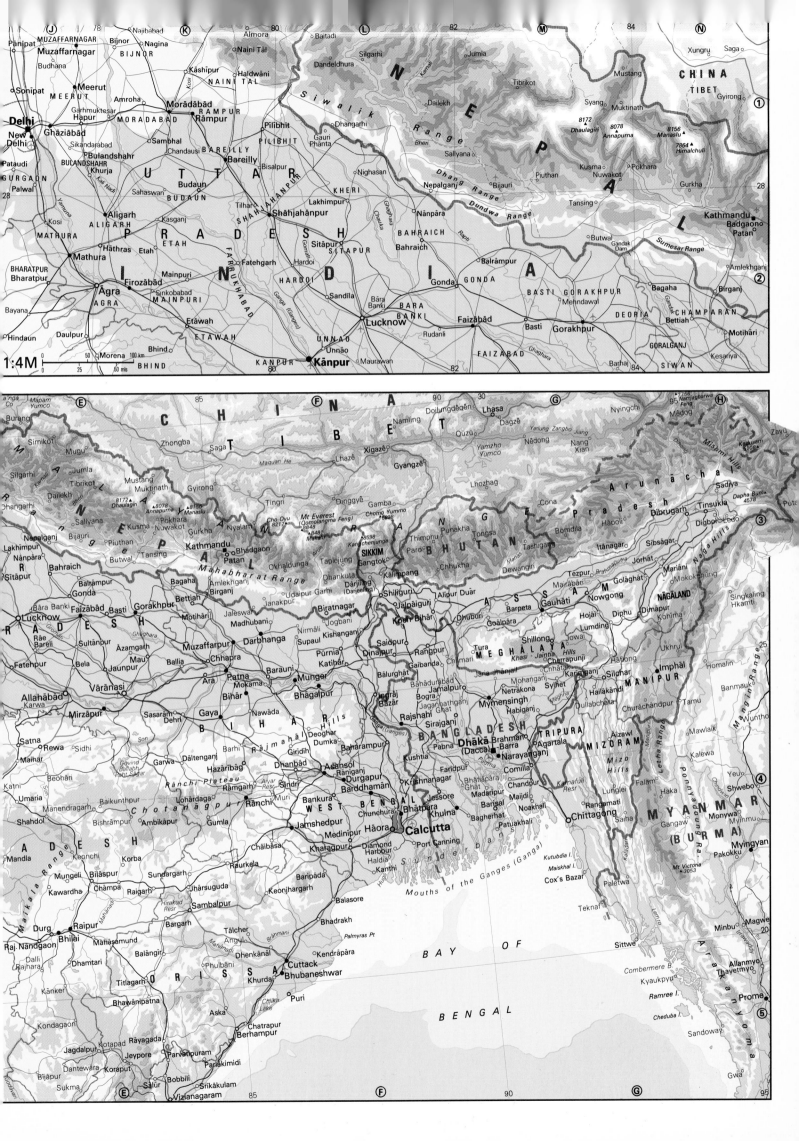

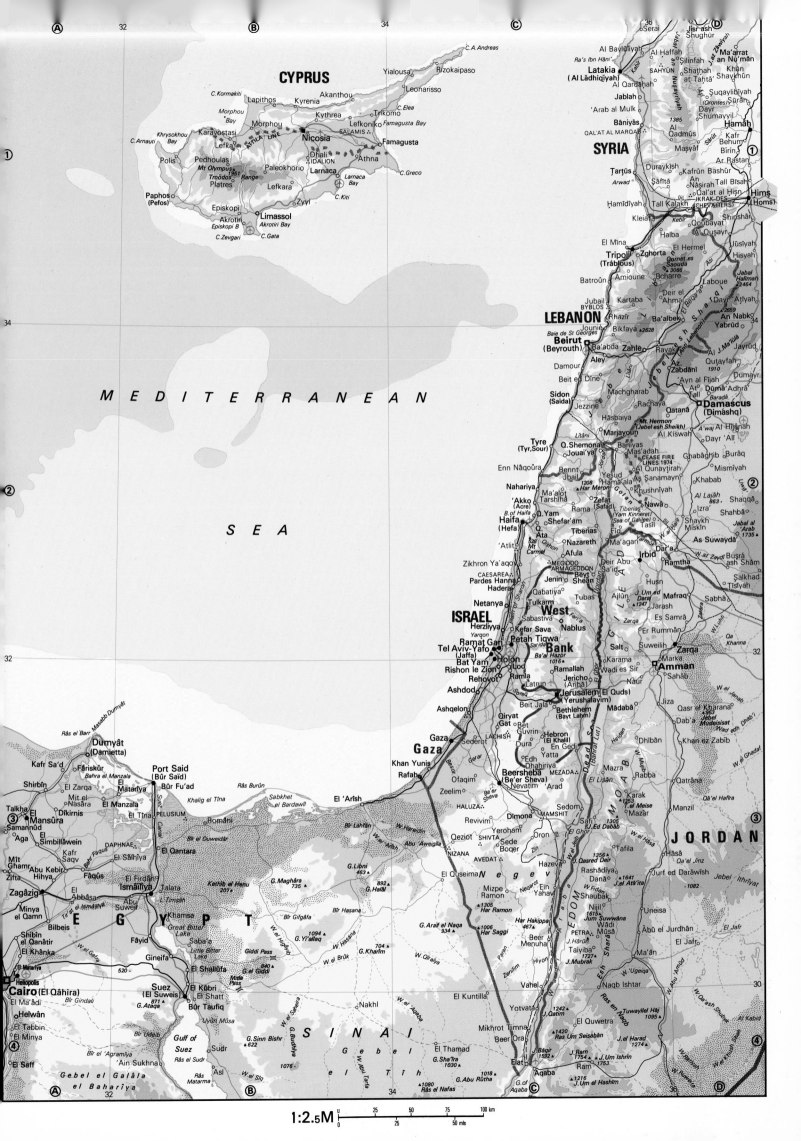

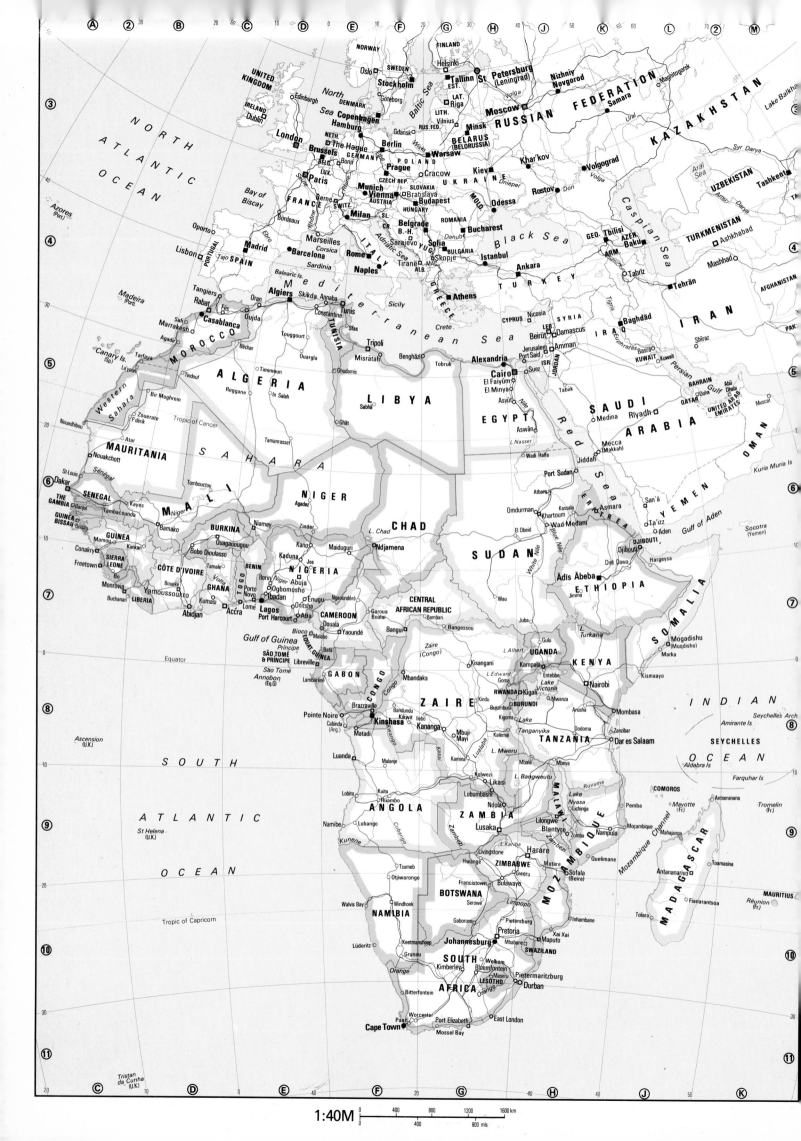

1:7.5M

| 0 | 100 | 200 | 300 km |
| 50 | 100 | 150 mls | |

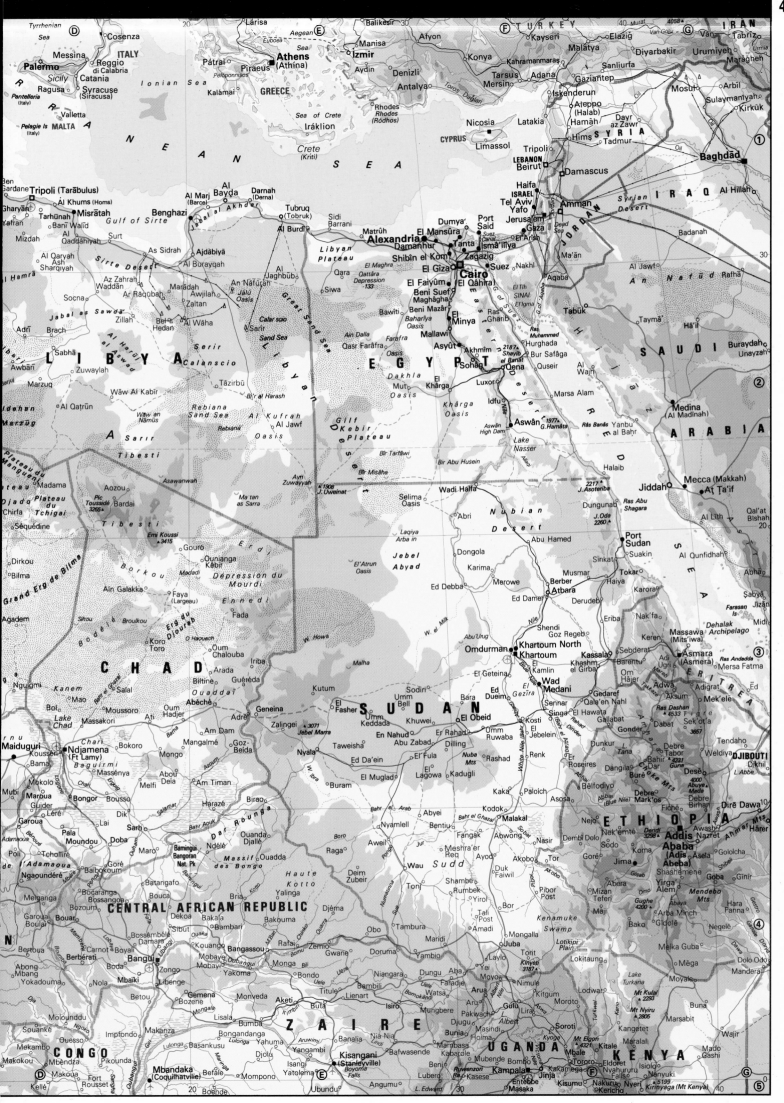

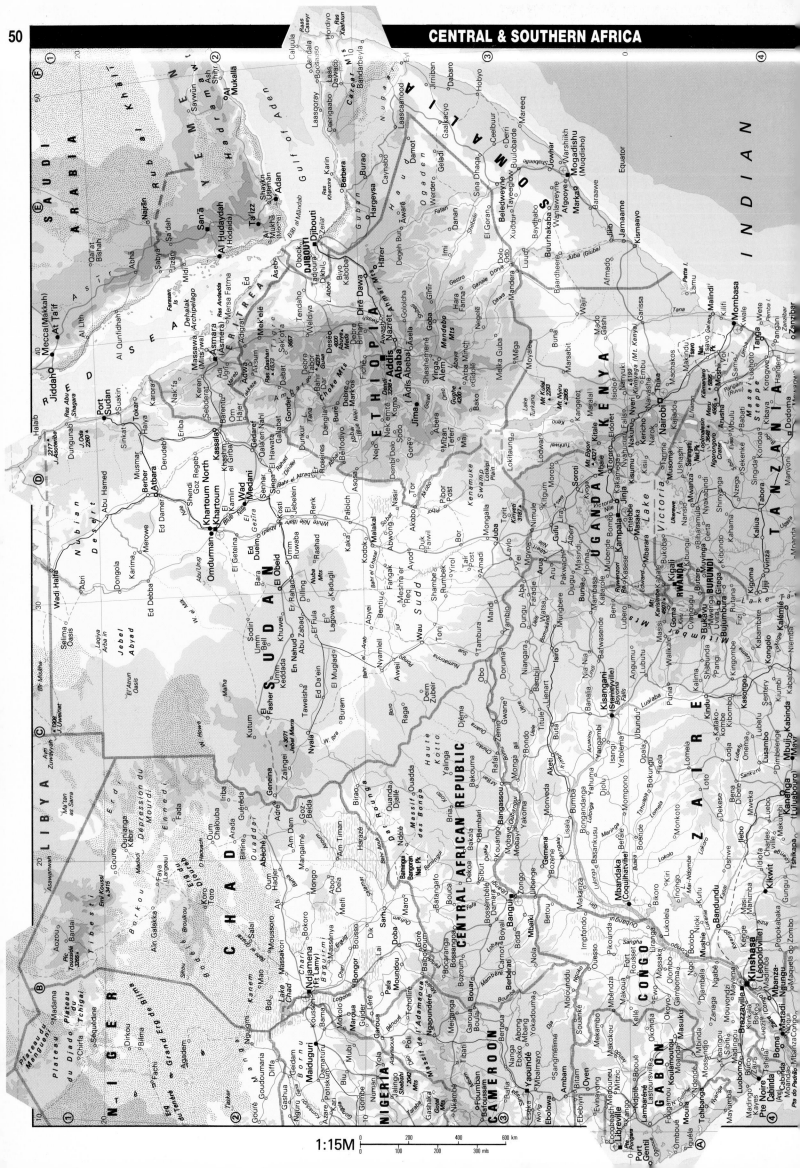

1:15M

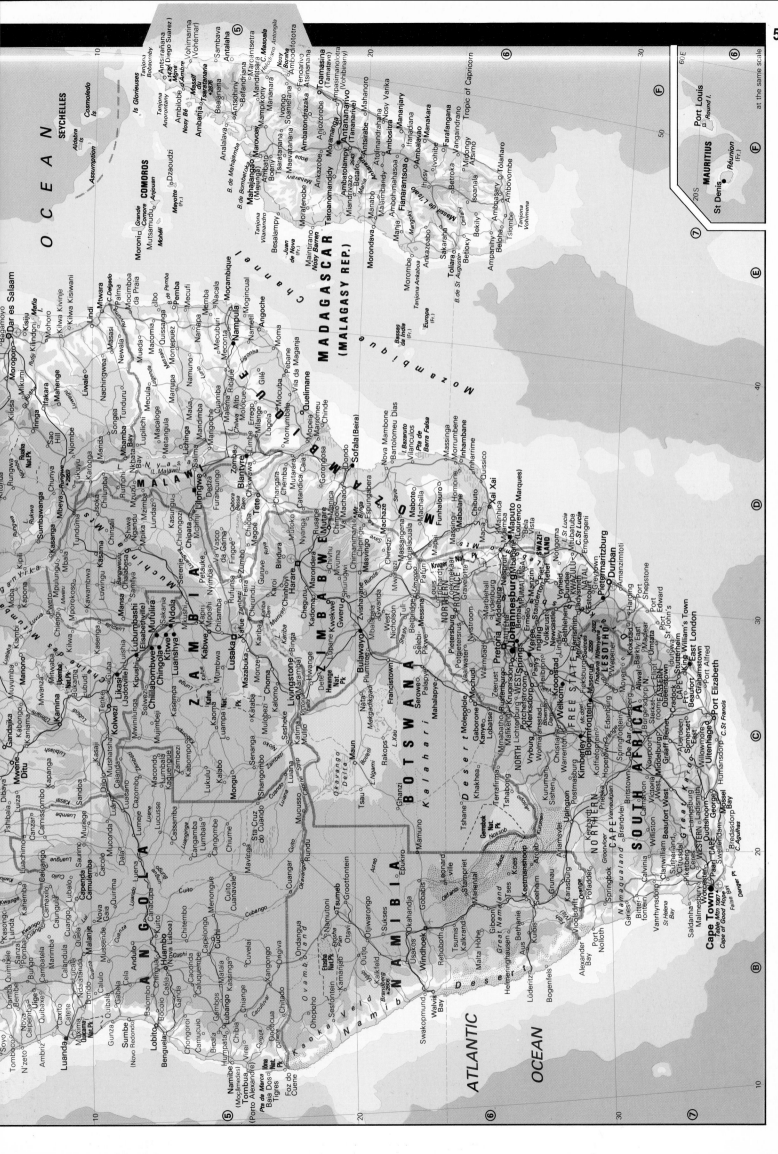

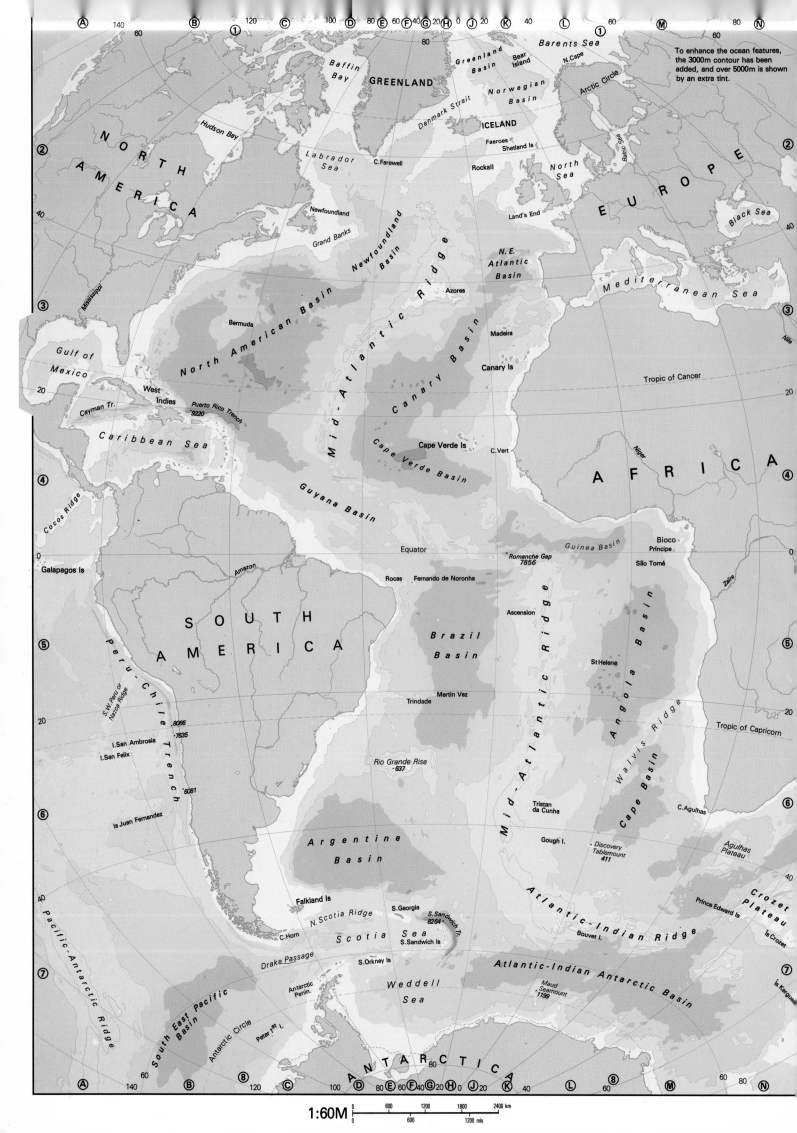

To enhance the ocean features, the 3000m contour has been added, and over 5000m is shown by an extra tint.

A 140 60 B 120 C 100 D 80 E 60 F 40 G 20 H J 20 K 40 L 60 M 80 N

Baffin Bay

GREENLAND

Greenland Basin

Bear Island

Barents Sea

N. Cape

Arctic Circle

Baltic Sea

Hudson Bay

Denmark Strait

Norwegian Basin

ICELAND

Faeroes

Shetland Is

Labrador Sea

C. Farewell

Rockall

North Sea

NORTH AMERICA

Newfoundland

Land's End

EUROPE

Grand Banks

Newfoundland Basin

N.E. Atlantic Basin

Mediterranean Sea

Black Sea

Mid-Atlantic Ridge

Azores

Bermuda

North American Basin

Madeira

Canary Basin

Nile

Gulf of Mexico

Canary Is

Tropic of Cancer

West Indies

Puerto Rico Trench •9220

Cayman Tr.

Cape Verde Is

C. Vert

AFRICA

Caribbean Sea

Cape Verde Basin

Guyana Basin

Cocos Ridge

Guinea Basin

Bioco

Príncipe

Galapagos Is

Amazon

Equator

Romanche Gap 7856

São Tomé

Zaïre

Rocas

Fernando de Noronha

Niger

SOUTH AMERICA

Brazil Basin

Ascension

Mid-Atlantic Ridge

St Helena

Angola Basin

Peru-Chile Trench

S.W. Peru or Nazca Ridge

•8066

•7635

I.San Ambrosia

I.San Felix

•6081

Martin Vaz

Trindade

Walvis Ridge

Tropic of Capricorn

Rio Grande Rise •637

Cape Basin

Is Juan Fernandez

Tristan da Cunha

C. Agulhas

Agulhas Plateau

Argentine Basin

Gough I.

Discovery Tablemount 411

Crozet Plateau

Falkland Is

N. Scotia Ridge

S. Georgia

S.Sandwich Tr. 8264

Bouvet I.

Prince Edward Is

Is Crozet

Atlantic-Indian Ridge

C. Horn

Scotia Sea

S.Sandwich Is

Drake Passage

S. Orkney Is

Weddell Sea

Atlantic-Indian Antarctic Basin

Pacific-Antarctic Ridge

Antarctic Penin.

Maud Seamount 1199

Is Kerguelen

South East Pacific Basin

Antarctic Circle

Peter 1st I.

ANTARCTICA

A 140 60 B 120 C 100 D 80 E 60 F 40 G 20 H J 20 K 40 L 60 M 80 N

1:60M

0 600 1200 1800 2400 km

0 600 1200 mls

Arctic Ocean

Chukchi Sea

Bering Strait

Bering Sea

Beaufort Sea

Aleutian Islands

Yukon

A l a s k a

Anchorage

Fairbanks

Whitehorse

Dawson

Inuvik

Prudhoe Bay

Banks I.

Victoria I.

Great Bear L.

Mackenzie

Queen Elizabeth Islands

Ellesmere I.

Thule

Resolute

Devon I.

Baffin Bay

G R E E N L A N D (KALAALLIT NUNAAT) (Denmark)

Denmark Strait

ICELAND

Reykjavik

Gothåb (Nuuk)

Davis Strait

Baffin I.

Labrador Sea

Hudson Strait

Southampton I.

Arctic Circle

Hudson Bay

James Bay

Churchill

Inukjuak

Schefferville

Churchill Falls

Goose Bay

Newfoundland

Anticosti I.

St John's

Sept-Iles

Chibougamau

Moosonee

Chicoutimi

Charlottetown

Alexander Arch.

Juneau

Prince Rupert

Q. Charlotte Is

Prince George

Vancouver I.

Fraser

C A N A D A

Peace

Dawson Creek

Athabasca

Uranium City

Athabasca

L. Athabasca

Yellowknife

Hay River

Great Slave L.

Edmonton

Calgary

Saskatchewan

Saskatoon

Regina

Medicine Hat

L. Winnipeg

Winnipeg

Kenora

Thunder Bay

Victoria

Vancouver

Seattle

Columbia

Portland

Spokane

Great Falls

Butte

Snake

Fargo

Duluth

L. Superior

Sault Ste Marie

Sudbury

Québec

Moncton

Fredericton

St. John

Halifax

Minneapolis

St Paul

Milwaukee

L. Michigan

Chicago

Detroit

L. Huron

Ottawa

Toronto

L. Ontario

Montréal

St Lawrence

Boston

San Francisco

Sacramento

Reno

Salt Lake City

Omaha

Denver

Colorado

U N I T E D   S T A T E S

Kansas City

St Louis

Indianapolis

Cincinatti

Cleveland

Buffalo

L. Erie

New York

Philadelphia

Baltimore

Washington

Newport News

Norfolk

ATLANTIC OCEAN

Los Angeles

San Diego

Tijuana

San Bernadino

Phoenix

Tucson

Albuquerque

Amarillo

Pueblo

Arkansas

Wichita

Oklahoma City

O F   A M E R I C A

Nashville

Memphis

Red

Ohio

Mississippi

Birmingham

Atlanta

Charleston

Savannah

Bermuda (U.K)

Ciudad Juárez

El Paso

Hermosillo

Chihuahua

M E X I C O

Fort Worth

Dallas

Austin

San Antonio

Jackson

Baton Rouge

Mobile

Tallahassee

Jacksonville

Houston

New Orleans

Tropic of Cancer

Guadalupe (Mex.)

G. de California

Monterrey

Torreón

Durango

Rio Grande

Corpus Christi

Tampa

Miami

Nassau

THE BAHAMAS

Sargasso Sea

Mazatlán

Revilla Gigedo Is. (Mex.)

Tampico

Gulf of Mexico

Habana

CUBA

Guantánamo

DOMINICAN REP.

Pto Rico (U.S.A.)

San Juan

ANTIGUA & BARBUDA

PACIFIC

Guadalajara

Mexico

Veracruz

Mérida

HAITI

Port-au-Prince

Santo Domingo

DOMINICA

Acapulco

JAMAICA

Kingston

ST KITTS-NEVIS

ST LUCIA

BAR-BADOS

Clipperton (Fr.)

BELIZE

Belmopan

CARIBBEAN SEA

ST VINCENT & THE GRENADINES

GRENADA

TRINIDAD & TOBAGO

O C E A N

GUATEMALA

Guatemala

S.Salvador

EL SALVADOR

HONDURAS

Tegucigalpa

NICARAGUA

Managua

Netherlands Antilles

Sta Marta

Barranquilla

Maracaibo

Caracas

Cd Guayana

COSTA RICA

S.José

P A N A M A

Panamá

VENEZUELA

I.del Coco (C.R)

Malpelo (Col.)

Bueraventura

Medellín

Bogotá

COLOMBIA

Cali

Orinoco

B R A Z I L

Equator

Galapagos Is. (Ecu.)

Quito

ECUADOR

PERU

Negro

1:35M

0   250   500   750   1000   1250 km

0   250   500   750 mls

ARCTIC OCEAN

BEAUFORT SEA

BERING SEA

Bering Str.

PACIFIC OCEAN

Gulf of Alaska

ALASKA (U.S.A.)

Brooks Range

Alaska Range

Aleutian Ra.

Kodiak Island

YUKON TERRITORY

BRITISH COLUMBIA

Queen Charlotte Islands

Vancouver Island

NORTHWEST TERRITORIES

Banks Island

Victoria Island

Prince of Wales Island

Parry Island

Melville Island

CANADA

ALBERTA

SASKATCHEWAN

MANITOBA

Great Bear Lake

Great Slave Lake

Lake Athabasca

Wood Buffalo Nat Pk

Whitehorse

Dawson

Inuvik

Tuktoyaktuk

Yellowknife

Fort Simpson

Fort Nelson

Fort St John

Prince George

Prince Rupert

Kitimat

Vancouver

Victoria

New Westminster

Nanaimo

Port Alberni

Powell River

Campbell River

Kamloops

Kelowna

Penticton

Vernon

Edmonton

Calgary

Red Deer

Lethbridge

Medicine Hat

Saskatoon

Regina

Prince Albert

Moose Jaw

Swift Current

Yorkton

Winnipeg

Brandon

Portage la Prairie

Jasper

Banff

WASHINGTON

OREGON

IDAHO

MONTANA

WYOMING

NORTH DAKOTA

SOUTH DAKOTA

U. S.

Seattle

Tacoma

Olympia

Portland

Spokane

Salem

Eugene

Helena

Butte

Billings

Great Falls

Bismarck

Fargo

Grand Forks

Rapid City

Pierre

1:15M

0   200   400   600 km
0   100   200   300 mls

Names underlined indicate Province/State capitals

Map — Canada, Greenland, Northeastern United States

GREENLAND (KALAALLIT NUNAAT) (Denmark)

ICELAND · Reykjavík

BAFFIN BAY · **DAVIS STRAIT** · **DENMARK STRAIT**

Baffin Island · Foxe Basin · Foxe Peninsula · Cumberland Peninsula · Cumberland Sound

Devon Island · Lancaster Sound · Ellesmere Island · Arctic Bay · Pond Inlet · Clyde · Pangnirtung

HUDSON STRAIT · Cape Dorset · Frobisher Bay · Resolution I. · Salluit · Kangiqsujuaq

HUDSON BAY · Churchill · York Factory · Belcher Is. · King George Is. · Inukjuak · Kuujjuarapik

Labrador Sea · **NEWFOUNDLAND** · Labrador · Nain · Hopedale · Makkovik · Rigolet · Goose Bay · Cartwright · St Anthony · Labrador City · Wabush · Churchill Falls · Corner Brook · Gander · St John's · Avalon Pen.

UNGAVA BAY · Kangiqsualujjuaq · Kuujjuaq · Schefferville

QUEBEC · Rés. Caniapiscau · Rés. Manicouagan · Sept-Îles · Baie-Comeau · Gaspé · Gulf of Saint Lawrence · Chicoutimi · Québec · Trois Rivières · Montréal

PRINCE EDWARD I. · Charlottetown · **NEW BRUNSWICK** · Fredericton · Saint John · Moncton · **NOVA SCOTIA** · Truro · Halifax · Dartmouth · Sydney · Cape Breton I. · Sable I.

ONTARIO · Thunder Bay · Sudbury · Sault Ste Marie · Timmins · Kapuskasing · Ottawa · Toronto · Hamilton · London · Windsor · Kenora · Dryden

MAINE · **NEW HAMPSHIRE** · **VERMONT** · **MASS.** · **CONN.** · Boston · Providence · Hartford · New Haven · Portland · Augusta · Concord · Montpelier · Albany · Syracuse · Rochester · Buffalo · **NEW YORK**

LAKE SUPERIOR · **LAKE MICHIGAN** · **LAKE HURON** · **L. Erie** · **L. Ontario**

Duluth · Superior · St Paul · Minneapolis · Milwaukee · Madison · Detroit · **MINNESOTA** · **WISCONSIN** · **MICHIGAN**

ATLANTIC OCEAN

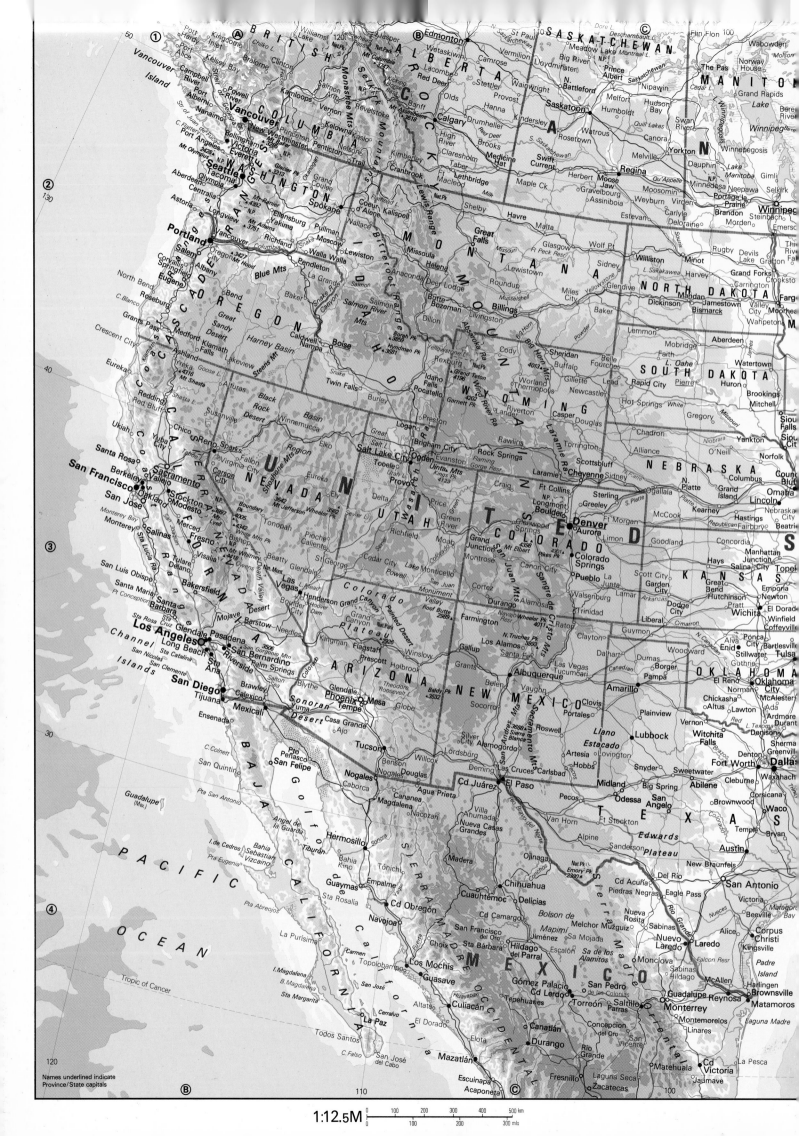

1:12.5M

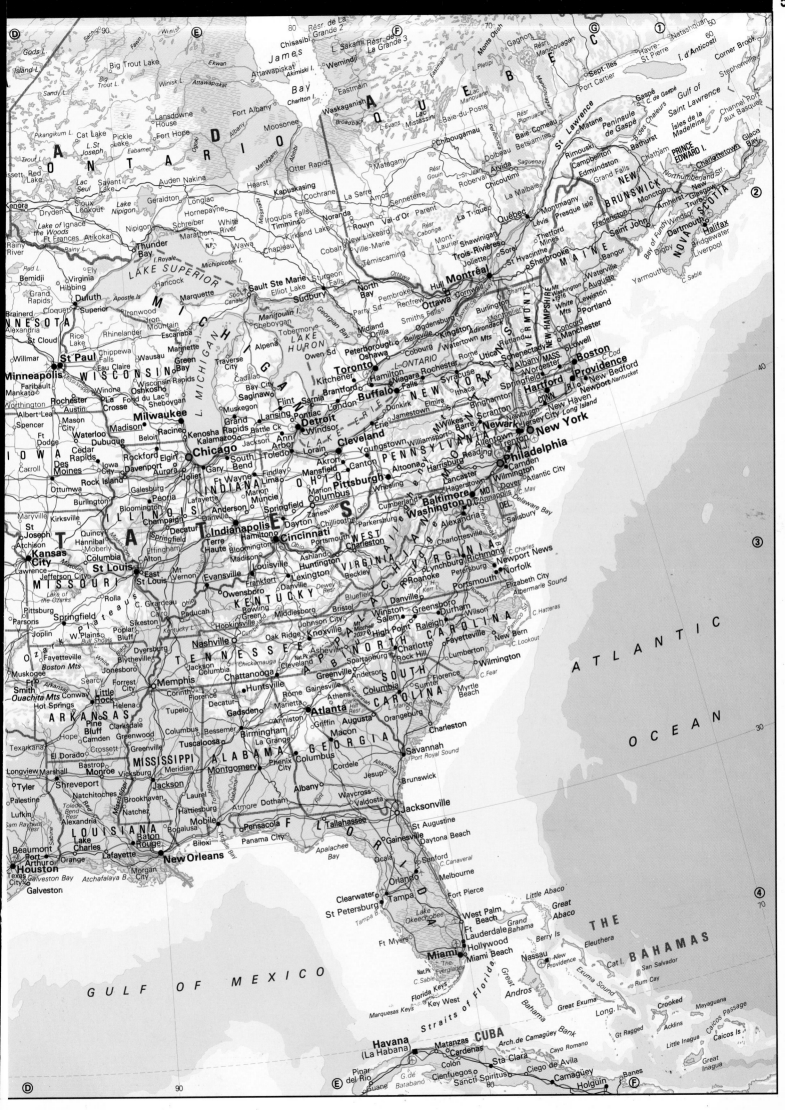

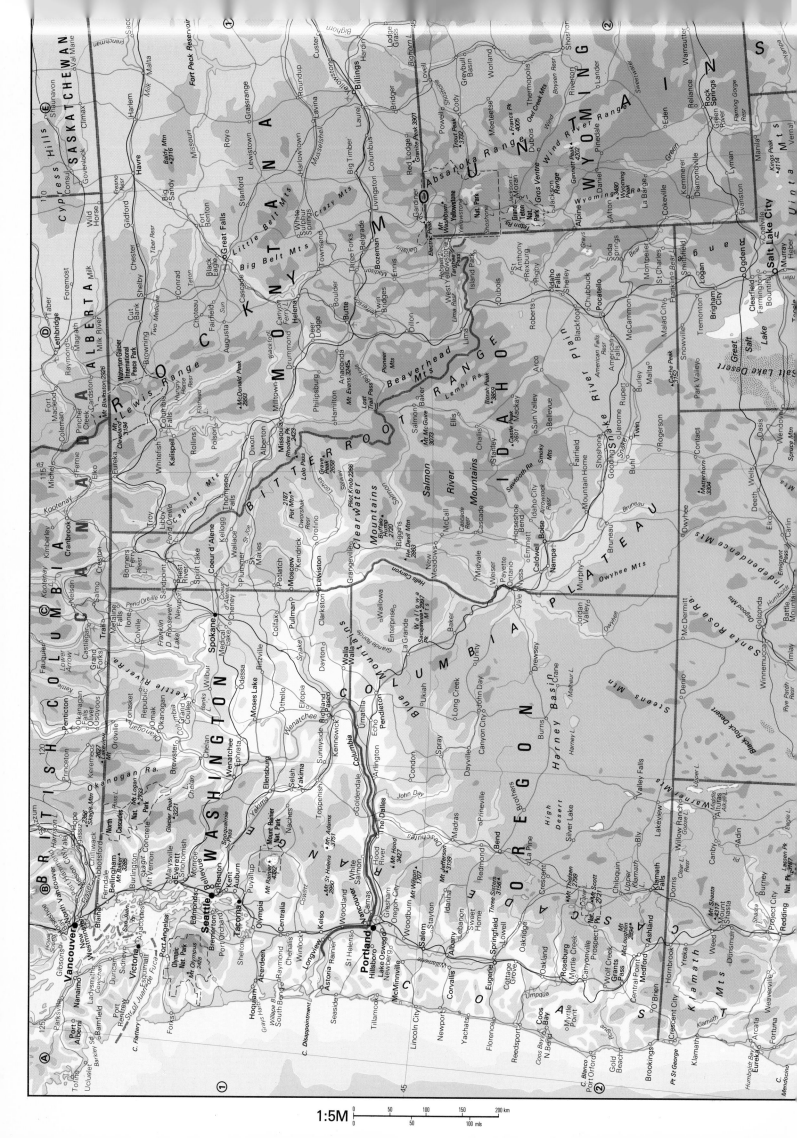

1:5M

0 50 100 150 200 km
0 50 100 mils

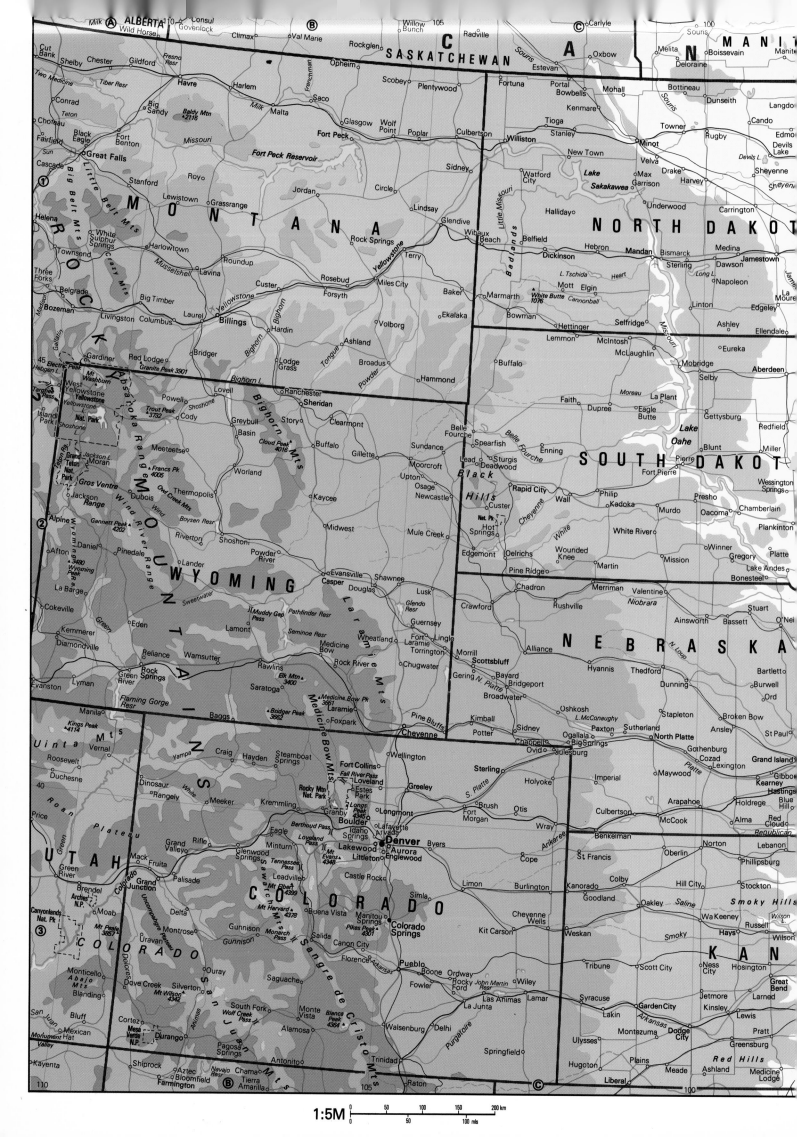

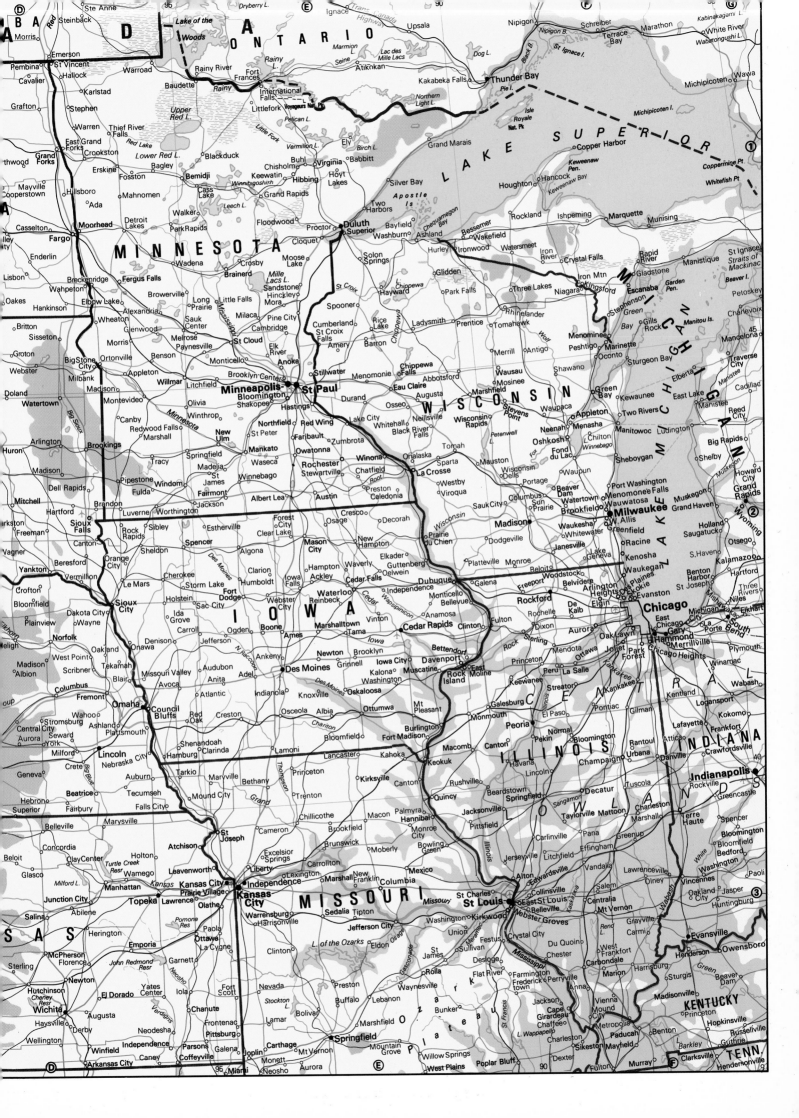

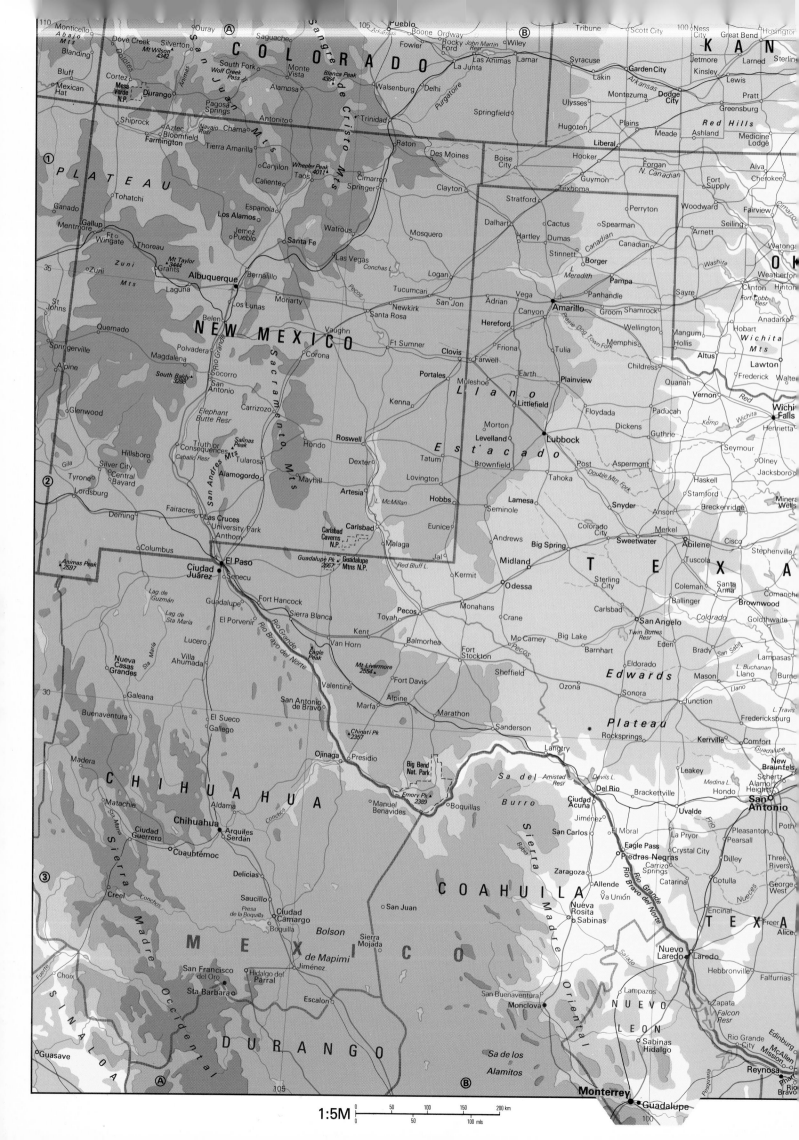

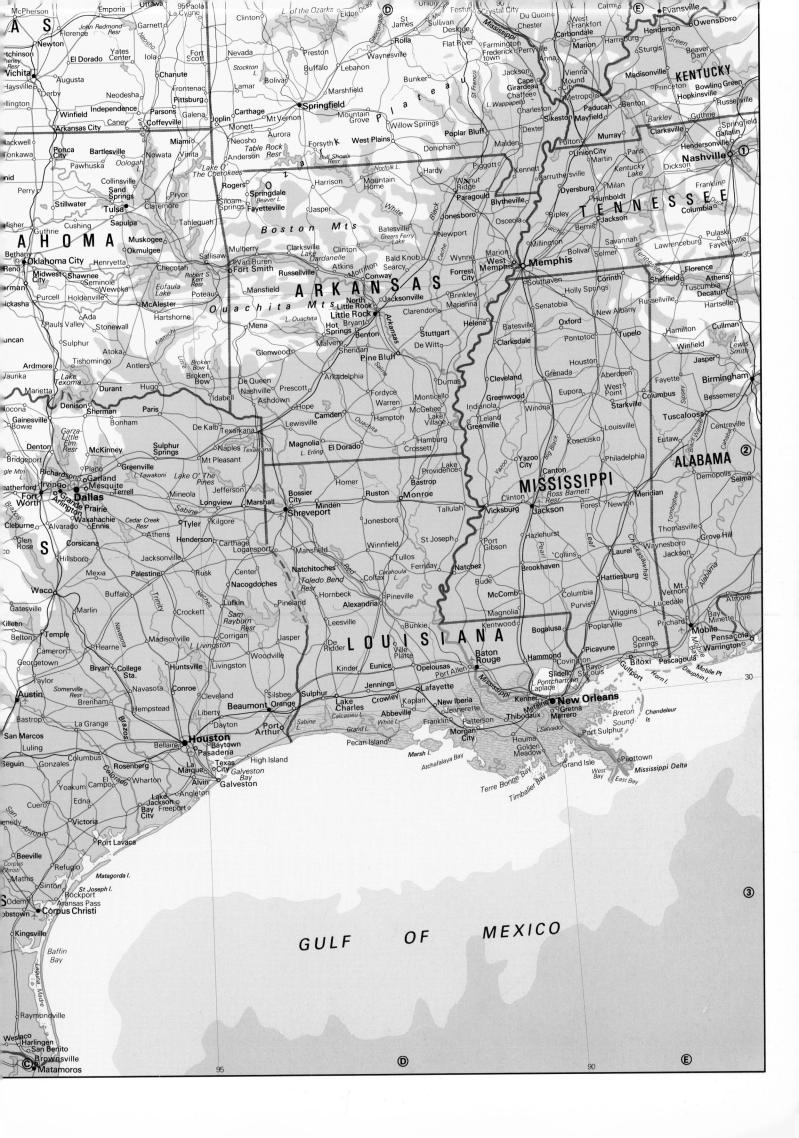

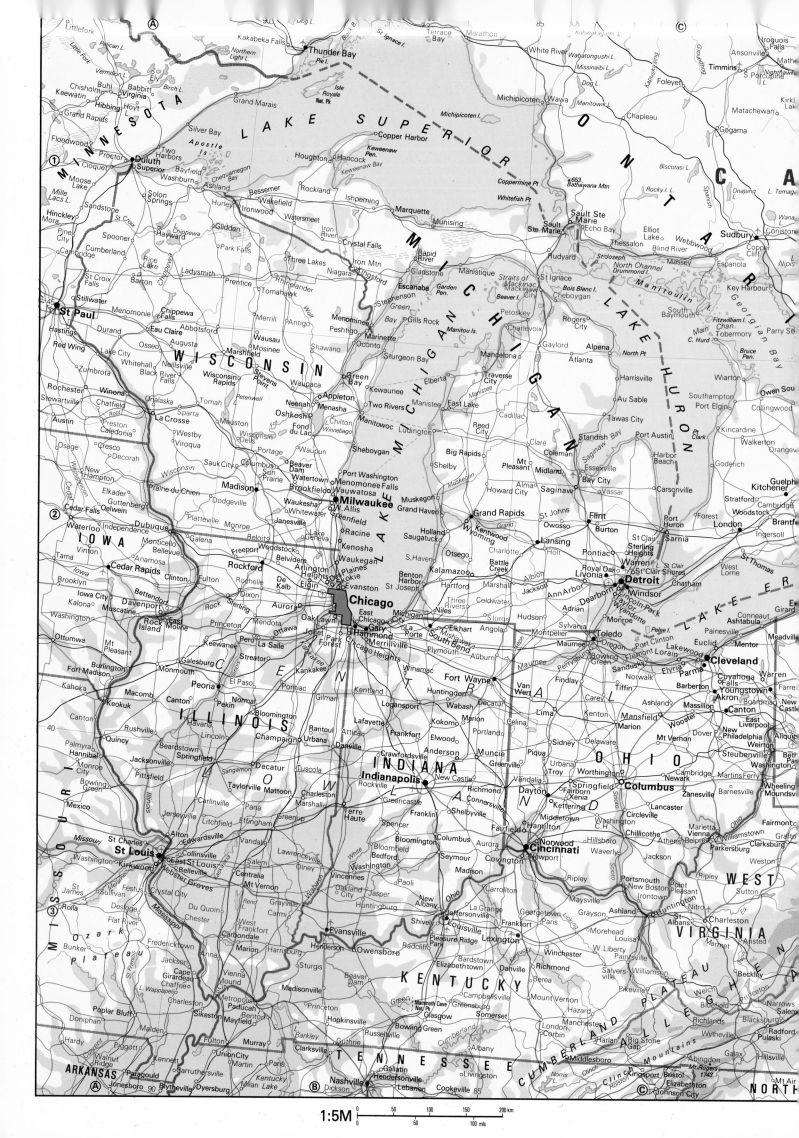

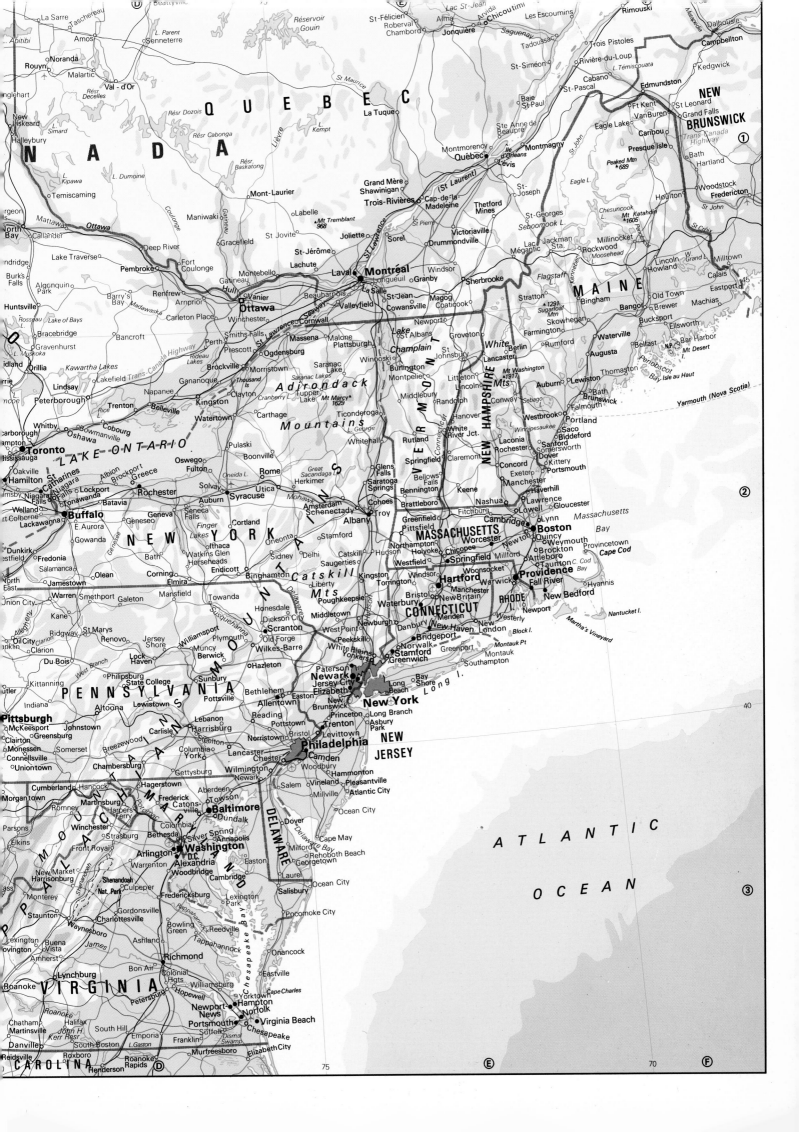

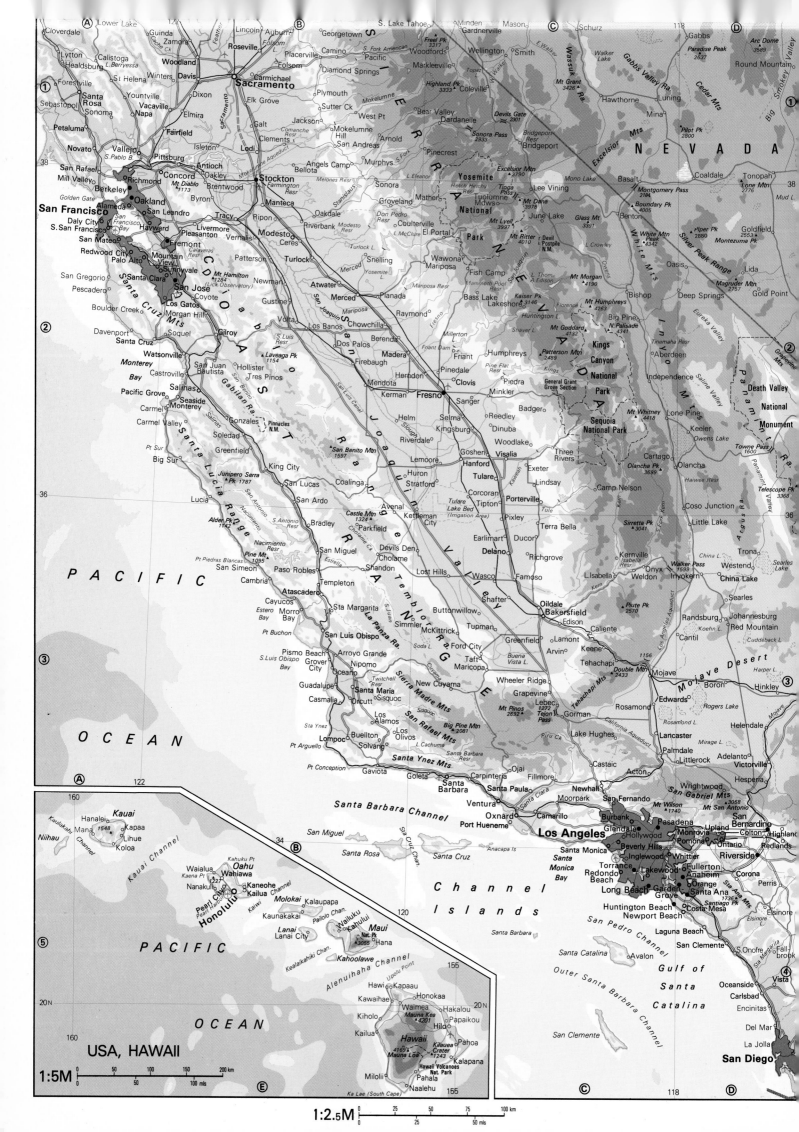

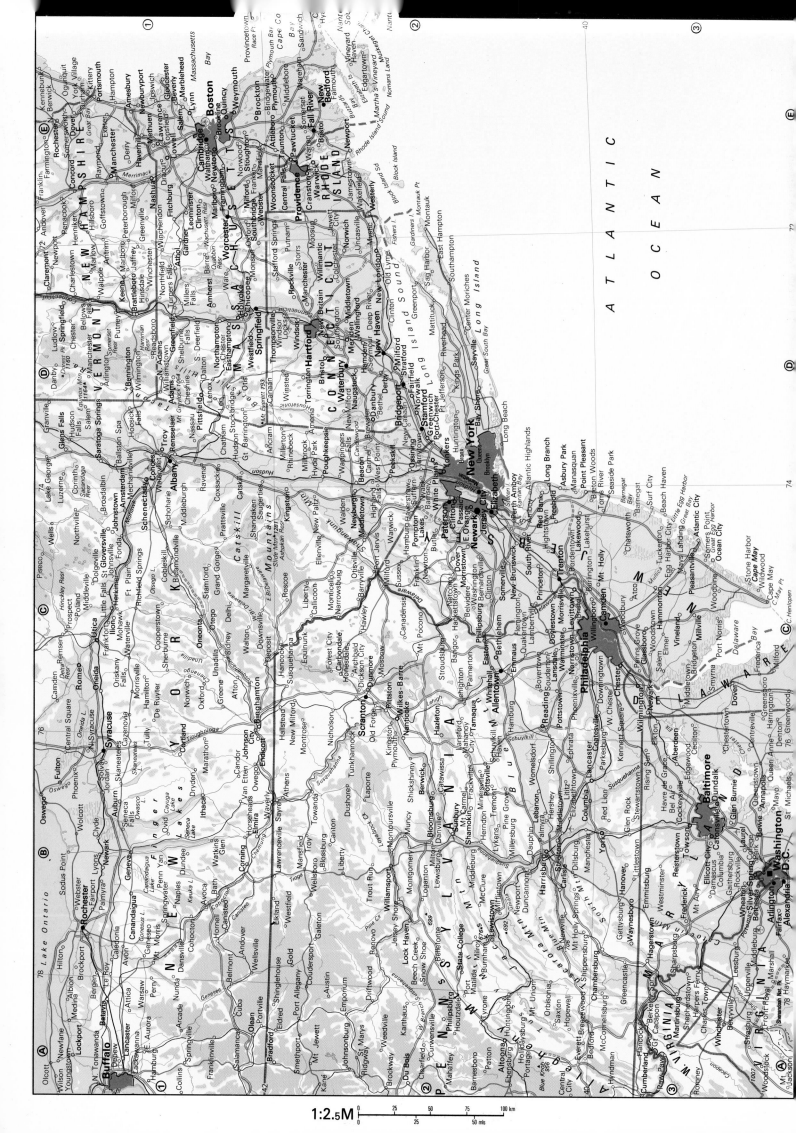

1:2.5M

25   50   75   100 km

25   50 mls

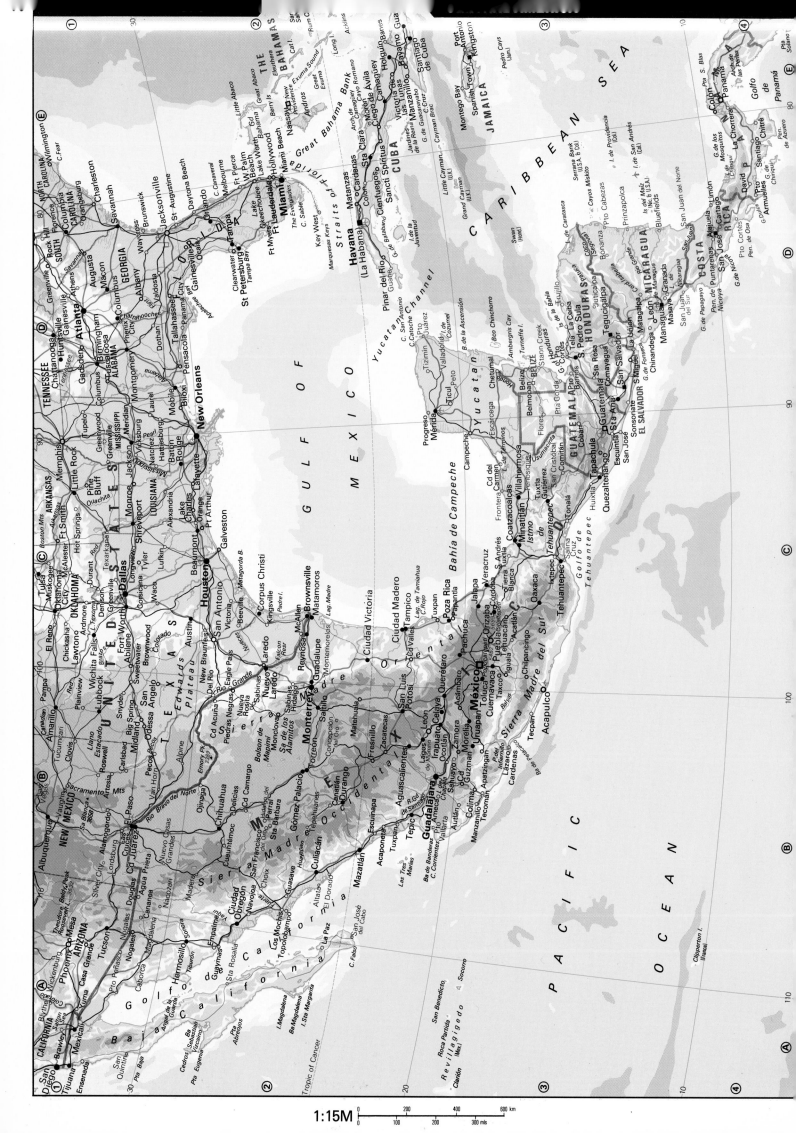

1:15M

Map of South America and Central America

Top border coordinates (left to right): Ⓐ 90 Ⓑ U.S.A. 80 Ⓒ 70 Ⓓ 60 Ⓔ 50 Ⓕ 40 Ⓖ 30

Gulf of Mexico

Miami

THE BAHAMAS

Tropic of Cancer

Ⓐ①

Mérida

Habana

CUBA

MEXICO

BELIZE
Belmopan

GUATEMALA
Guatemala
HONDURAS
Tegucigalpa
S.Salvador
EL SALVADOR
NICARAGUA
Managua
COSTA RICA
S.José
Colón
Panamá
PANAMA

Santiago de Cuba
Guantanamo
HAITI
JAMAICA
Kingston
Port-au-Prince
DOMINICAN REP.
Santiago
Santo Domingo
Pto Rico (U.S.A.)
San Juan
ST KITTS-NEVIS
ANTIGUA & BARBUDA
Guadeloupe (Fr.)
DOMINICA
Martinique (Fr.)
ST LUCIA
ST VINCENT & THE GRENADINES
GRENADA
BARBADOS
Port of Spain
TRINIDAD & TOBAGO

CARIBBEAN SEA

I. del Coco (C.R.)

Malpelo (Col.)

Barranquilla
Sta Marta
Cartagena
Maracaibo
Neth. Antilles
Curaçao
Caracas
Barcelona
Barquisimeto
Cd. Bolívar
Cd. Guayana
Georgetown
Paramaribo
Cayenne

S.Cristóbal
Medellín
Manizales
Bogotá
VENEZUELA
GUYANA
SURINAM
FR. GUIANA

Buenaventura
Cali
COLOMBIA
Popayán
S.Lorenzo
Pasto
Boa Vista

Orinoco
Branco
Macapá
I. de Marajó
Equator
S.Pedro e S.Paulo (Braz.)

Galapagos Is (Ecu.)

Quito
ECUADOR
Guayaquil
Iquitos
Negro
Manaus
Santarém
Belém
São Luís
Codó
Sobral
Fortaleza
Rocas
I. Fernando de Noronha (Braz.)

Piura
PERU
Marañón
Ucayali
Juruá
Purús
Amazon
Madeira
Tapajós
Xingú
Tocantins
Araguaia
Teresina
Natal

Chiclayo
Trujillo
Chimbote
Pto Velho
Rio Branco
João Pessoa
Juazeiro
Recife
Maceió

Callao
Lima
Huancayo
Pto Maldonado
BRAZIL
Alagoinhas
Aracajú

Cuzco
Arequipa
La Paz
Oruro
Cochabamba
BOLIVIA
Sucre
Sta Cruz
Arica
Iquique
Cáceres
Cuiabá
Goiânia
Brasília
São Francisco
Montes Claros
Ilhéus
Salvador

Corumbá
Corinto
Belo Horizonte
Vitória

SOUTH PACIFIC OCEAN

Tropic of Capricorn

S.Félix (Chile)

Antofagasta
Campo Grande
Dourados
Paraná
Ribeirão Prêto
Juiz de Fora
Campos
Campinas
Santos
Rio de Janeiro
São Paulo
Trindade (Braz.)

Salta
Concepción
PARAGUAY
Asunción
Foz do Iguaçu
Ponta Grossa
Curitiba
Florianópolis

S.Miguel de Tucumán
Salado
Resistencia
Posadas
Uruguay

Córdoba
CHILE
ARGENTINA
Santa Fe
Paraná
Rivera
Paysandu
Pto Alegre
Pelotas
Rio Grande

Juan Fernández Is. (Chile)

Viña del Mar
Valparaíso
Santiago
Mendoza
Rosario
URUGUAY
Montevideo

Talca
Concepción
Colorado
Negro
Bahía Blanca
Mar del Plata
R.de la Plata

SOUTH ATLANTIC OCEAN

Temuco
Valdivia
Pto Montt

Chico

Cmd. Rivadavia
G.San Jorge
Deseado

Falkland Is (U.K.)
Stanley

Pto Natales
Rio Gallegos

Punta Arenas
Tierra del Fuego
Cape Horn

S.Georgia (U.K.)

S.Shetland Is (U.K.)
S.Orkney Is (U.K.)
S.Sandwich Is (U.K.)

ANTARCTICA

1:35M

0 250 500 750 1000 1250 km

0 250 500 750mls

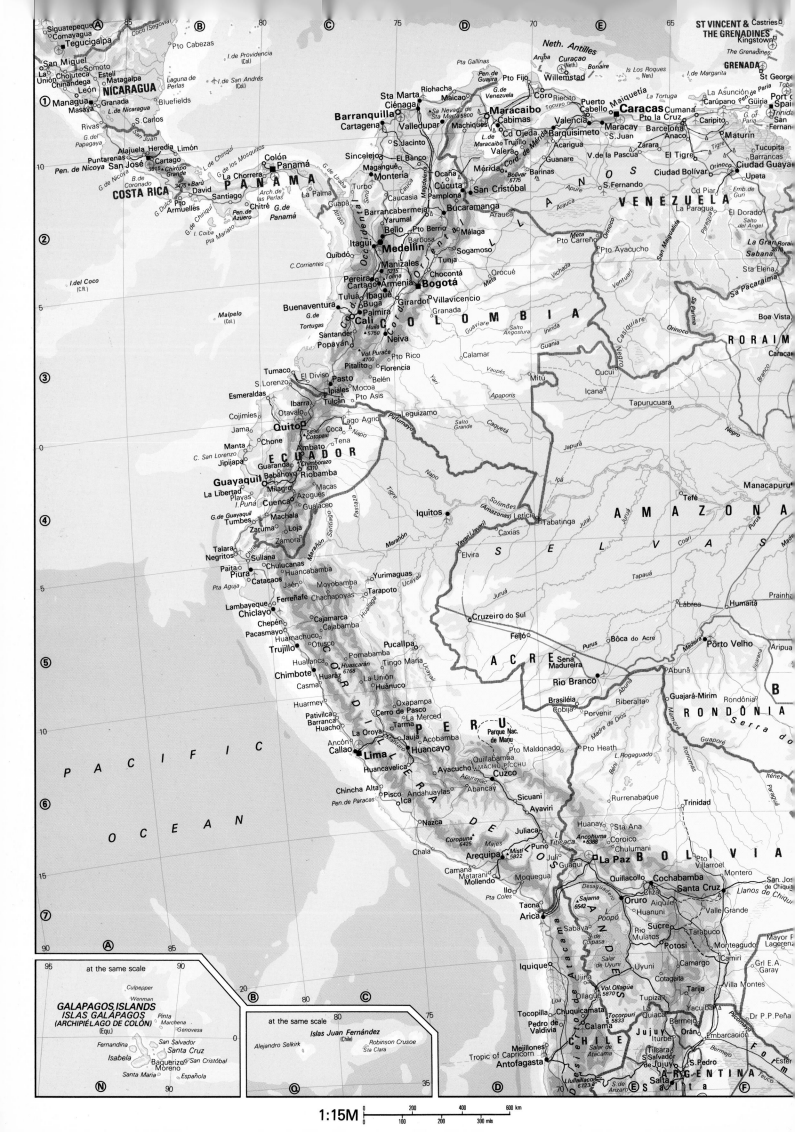

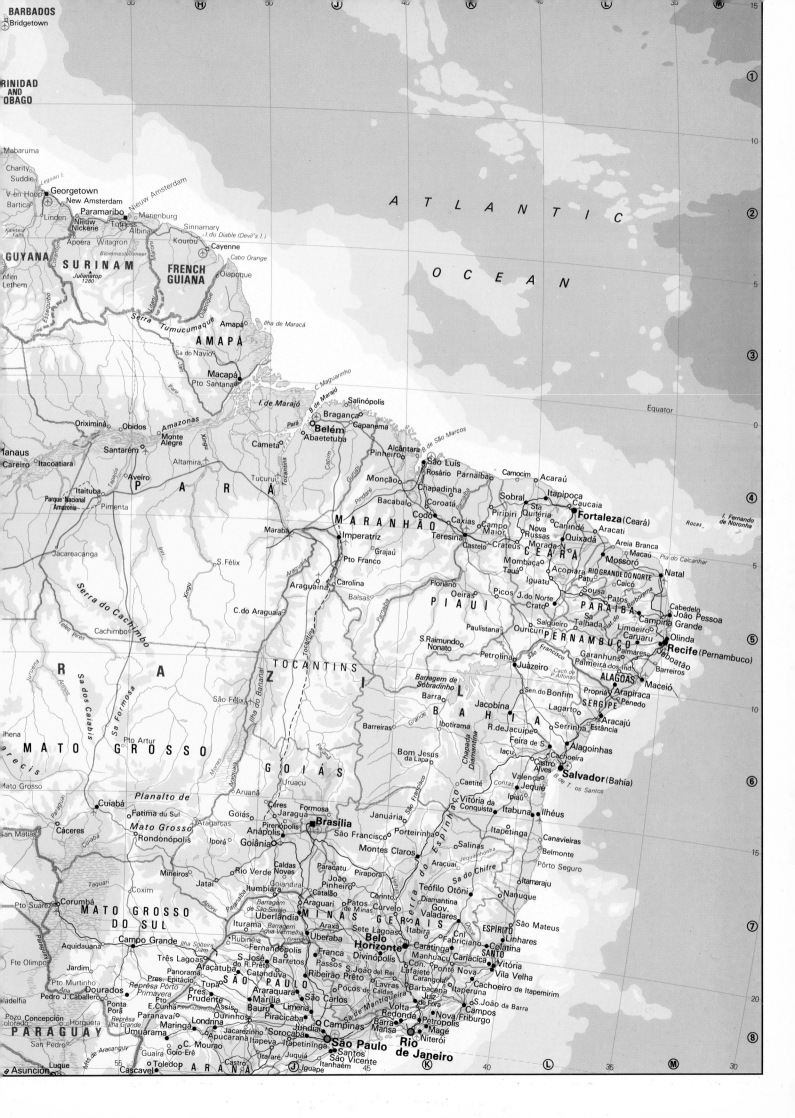

1:7.5M

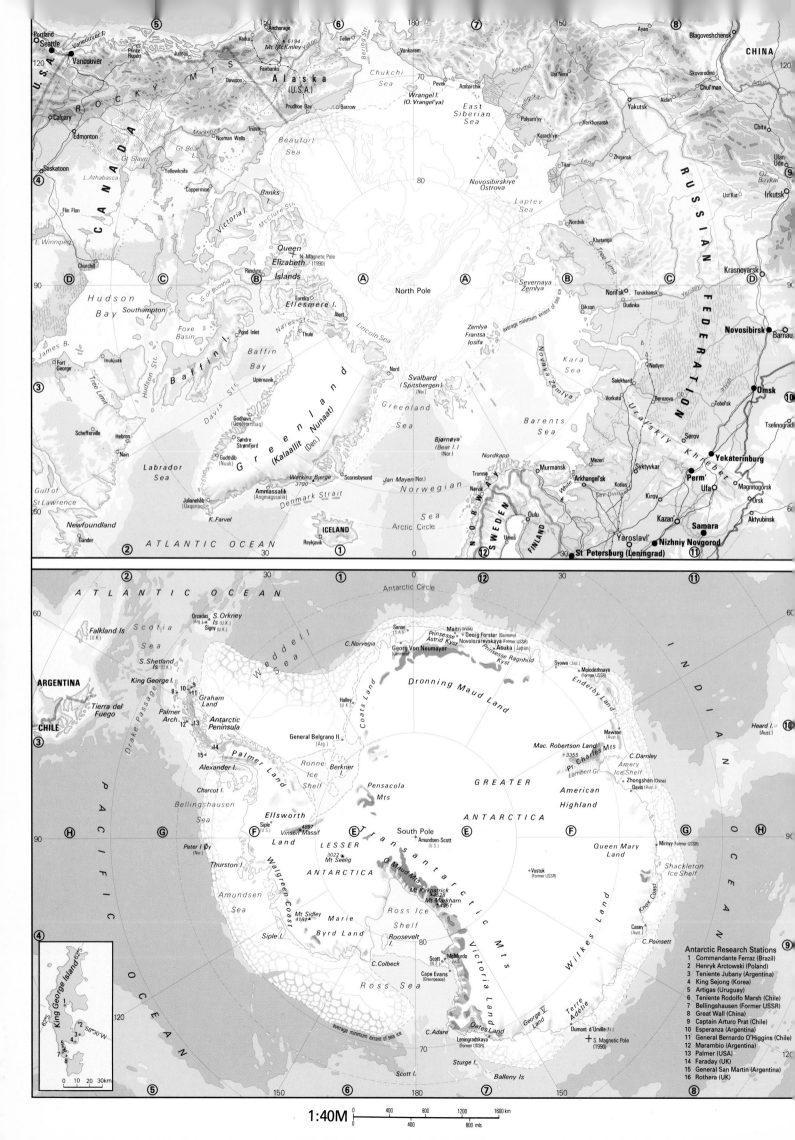

1:40M

Introduction to the index

In the index, the first number refers to the page, and the following letter and number to the section of the map in which the index entry can be found.
For example, 14C2 **Paris** means that Paris can be found on page 14 where column C and row 2 meet.

Abbreviations used in the index

Arch	Archipelago
B	Bay
C	Cape
Chan	Channel
Gl	Glacier
I(s)	Island(s)
Lg	Lagoon
L	Lake
Mt(s)	Mountain(s)
P	Pass
Pass	Passage
Pen	Peninsula
Plat	Plateau
Pt	Point
Res	Reservoir
R	River
S	Sea
Sd	Sound
Str	Strait
UAE	United Arab Emirates
UK	United Kingdom
USA	United States of America
V	Valley

A

18B2 **Aachen** Germany
13C1 **Aalsmeer** Netherlands
13C2 **Aalst** Belgium
12K6 **Äänekoski** Finland
31A3 **Aba** China
48C4 **Aba** Nigeria
50D3 **Aba** Zaïre
41E3 **Abādān** Iran
41F3 **Abādeh** Iran
48B1 **Abadla** Algeria
75C2 **Abaeté** Brazil
75C2 **Abaeté** *R* Brazil
73J4 **Abaetetuba** Brazil
31D1 **Abagnar Qi** China
59E3 **Abajo Mts** USA
48C4 **Abakaliki** Nigeria
25L4 **Abakan** Russian Federation
48C3 **Abala** Niger
48C2 **Abalessa** Algeria
72D6 **Abancay** Peru
41F3 **Abarqū** Iran
29E2 **Abashiri** Japan
29E2 **Abashiri-wan** *B* Japan
27H7 **Abau** Papua New Guinea
50D3 **Abaya, L** Ethiopia
50D2 **Abbai** *R* Ethiopia/Sudan
50E2 **Abbe, L** Djibouti/Ethiopia
14C1 **Abbeville** France
63D3 **Abbeville** Louisiana, USA
67B2 **Abbeville** S Carolina, USA
58B1 **Abbotsford** Canada
64A2 **Abbotsford** USA
42C2 **Abbottabad** Pakistan
40D2 **'Abd al 'Azīz, Jebel** *Mt* Syria
20J5 **Abdulino** Russian Federation
50C2 **Abéché** Chad
48B4 **Abengourou** Ivory Coast
18B1 **Åbenrå** Denmark
48C4 **Abeokuta** Nigeria
50D3 **Abera** Ethiopia
7B3 **Aberaeron** Wales
6C3 **Aberconwy and Colwyn** *County* Wales
7C4 **Aberdare** Wales
66C2 **Aberdeen** California, USA
65D3 **Aberdeen** Maryland, USA
63E2 **Aberdeen** Mississippi, USA
47C3 **Aberdeen** South Africa
8D3 **Aberdeen** Scotland
8D3 **Aberdeen** *Division* Scotland
56D2 **Aberdeen** S Dakota, USA
56A2 **Aberdeen** Washington, USA
54J3 **Aberdeen L** Canada
7B3 **Aberdyfi** Wales
8D3 **Aberfeldy** Scotland
8C3 **Aberfoyle** Scotland
7C4 **Abergavenny** Wales
7B3 **Aberystwyth** Wales
20L2 **Abez'** Russian Federation
50E2 **Abhā** Saudi Arabia
41E2 **Abhar** Iran
48B4 **Abidjan** Ivory Coast
61D3 **Abilene** Kansas, USA
62C2 **Abilene** Texas, USA
7D4 **Abingdon** England
64C3 **Abingdon** USA
55K4 **Abitibi** *R* Canada
55L5 **Abitibi,L** Canada
21G7 **Abkhazia** *Division* Georgia
42C2 **Abohar** India
48C4 **Abomey** Benin
50B3 **Abong Mbang** Cameroon
50B2 **Abou Deïa** Chad
8D3 **Aboyne** Scotland
41E4 **Abqaiq** Saudi Arabia
15A2 **Abrantes** Portugal
70A2 **Abreojos, Punta** *Pt* Mexico
50D1 **'Abri** Sudan
32A3 **Abrolhos** *I* Australia
75E2 **Abrolhos, Arquipélago dos** *Is* Brazil
56B2 **Absaroka Range** *Mts* USA
41F5 **Abū al Abyaḑ** *I* UAE
41E4 **Abū 'Alī** *I* Saudi Arabia
45D3 **Abu 'Amūd, Wadi** Jordan
45C3 **Abu 'Aweigīla** *Well* Egypt
41F5 **Abū Dhabi** UAE
45C3 **Abū el Jurdhān** Jordan
50D2 **Abu Hamed** Sudan
48C4 **Abuja** Nigeria
45A3 **Abu Kebir Hihya** Egypt
72E5 **Abunã** Brazil
72E6 **Abunã** *R* Bolivia/Brazil
45C4 **Abu Rûtha, Gebel** *Mt* Egypt
41D3 **Abú Sukhayr** Iraq
45B3 **Abu Suweir** Egypt
45B4 **Abu Tarfa, Wadi** Egypt
35B2 **Abut Head** *C* New Zealand
40B4 **Abu Tig** Egypt
50D2 **Abu'Urug** *Well* Sudan
50D2 **Abuye Meda** *Mt* Ethiopia
50C2 **Abu Zabad** Sudan
50D3 **Abwong** Sudan
18B1 **Åby** Denmark
50C3 **Abyei** Sudan
65F2 **Acadia Nat Pk** USA
70B2 **Acámbaro** Mexico
69B5 **Acandí** Colombia
70B2 **Acaponeta** Mexico
70B3 **Acapulco** Mexico
73L4 **Acaraú** Brazil
72E2 **Acarigua** Venezuela
70C3 **Acatlán** Mexico
48B4 **Accra** Ghana
6C3 **Accrington** England
42D4 **Achalpur** India
74B6 **Achao** Chile
13E3 **Achern** Germany
9A3 **Achill Hd** *Pt* Irish Republic
10A3 **Achill I** Irish Republic
13E1 **Achim** Germany
25L4 **Achinsk** Russian Federation
16D3 **Acireale** Sicily, Italy
61E2 **Ackley** USA
69C2 **Acklins** *I* The Bahamas
72D6 **Acobamba** Peru
74B4 **Aconcagua** *Mt* Chile
73L5 **Acopiara** Brazil
Açores *Is* **= Azores**
A Coruña = La Coruña
Acre = 'Akko
72D5 **Acre** *State* Brazil
66C3 **Acton** USA
63C2 **Ada** USA
15B1 **Adaja** *R* Spain
41G5 **Adam** Oman
50D3 **Adama** Ethiopia
75B3 **Adamantina** Brazil
50B3 **Adamaoua** *Region* Cameroon/Nigeria
50B3 **Adamaoua, Massif de l'** *Mts* Cameroon
68D1 **Adams** USA
44B4 **Adam's Bridge** India/Sri Lanka
56A2 **Adams,Mt** USA
44C4 **Adam's Peak** *Mt* Sri Lanka
'Adan = Aden
21F8 **Adana** Turkey
21E7 **Adapazarı** Turkey
76F7 **Adare,C** Antarctica
34B1 **Adavale** Australia
41E4 **Ad Dahnā'** *Region* Saudi Arabia
41F4 **Ad Damman** Saudi Arabia
41D5 **Ad Dawādimī** Saudi Arabia
41E4 **Ad Dibdibah** *Region* Saudi Arabia
41E5 **Ad Dilam** Saudi Arabia
41E5 **Ad Dir'iyah** Saudi Arabia
50D3 **Addis Ababa** Ethiopia
41D3 **Ad Dīwanīyah** Iraq
40D3 **Ad Duwayd** Saudi Arabia
61E2 **Adel** USA
32C4 **Adelaide** Australia
67C4 **Adelaide** Bahamas
76G3 **Adelaide** *Base* Antarctica
54J3 **Adelaide Pen** Canada
27G8 **Adelaide River** Australia
66D3 **Adelanto** USA
38C4 **Aden** Yemen
38C4 **Aden,G of** Somalia/Yemen
48C3 **Aderbissinat** Niger
45D2 **Adhrā'** Syria
27G7 **Adi** *I* Indonesia
16C1 **Adige** *R* Italy
50D2 **Adigrat** Ethiopia
42D5 **Adilābād** India
58B2 **Adin** USA
65E2 **Adirondack Mts** USA
50D2 **Adi Ugrī** Eritrea
40C2 **Adıyaman** Turkey
17F1 **Adjud** Romania
54E4 **Admiralty I** USA
55K2 **Admiralty Inlet** *B* Canada
32D1 **Admiralty Is** Papua New Guinea
44B2 **Ādoni** India
14B3 **Adour** *R* France
48B2 **Adrar** Algeria
48C2 **Adrar** *Mts* Algeria
48A2 **Adrar** *Region* Mauritius
48A2 **Adrar Soutouf** *Region* Morocco
50C2 **Adré** Chad
49D2 **Adri** Libya
64C2 **Adrian** Michigan, USA
62B1 **Adrian** Texas, USA
16C2 **Adriatic S** Italy/Yugoslavia
50D2 **Adwa** Ethiopia
25P3 **Adycha** *R* Russian Federation
21G7 **Adygeya** *Division* Russian Federation
48B4 **Adzopé** Ivory Coast
20K2 **Adz'va** *R* Russian Federation
20K2 **Adz'vavom** Russian Federation
17E3 **Aegean Sea** Greece
38E2 **Afghanistan** *Republic* Asia
50E3 **Afgooye** Somalia
41D5 **'Afif** Saudi Arabia
48C4 **Afikpo** Nigeria
12G6 **Åfjord** Norway
48C1 **Aflou** Algeria
50E3 **Afmado** Somalia
48A3 **Afollé** *Region* Mauritius
68C1 **Afton** New York, USA
58D2 **Afton** Wyoming, USA
45C2 **Afula** Israel
21E8 **Afyon** Turkey
45A3 **Aga** Egypt
50B2 **Agadem** Niger
48C3 **Agadez** Niger
48B1 **Agadir** Morocco
42D4 **Agar** India
43G4 **Agartala** India
58B1 **Agassiz** Canada
48B4 **Agboville** Ivory Coast
40E1 **Agdam** Azerbaijan
29C3 **Agematsu** Japan
14C3 **Agen** France
41E3 **Agha Jārī** Iran
25N4 **Aginskiy-Buryatskiy Avt. Okrug** *Division* Russian Federation
48B4 **Agnibilékrou** Ivory Coast
14C3 **Agout** *R* France
42D3 **Āgra** India
41D2 **Ağrı** Turkey
16D2 **Agri** *R* Italy
16C3 **Agrigento** Sicily, Italy
26H5 **Agrihan** *I* Marianas
17E3 **Agrínion** Greece
16C2 **Agropoli** Italy
20J4 **Agryz** Russian Federation
55N3 **Agto** Greenland
75B3 **Agua Clara** Brazil
69D3 **Aguadilla** Puerto Rico
70B1 **Agua Prieta** Mexico
75A3 **Aguaray Guazú** Paraguay
70B2 **Aguascalientes** Mexico
75D2 **Aguas Formosas** Brazil
75C2 **Agua Vermelha, Barragem** Brazil
15A1 **Agueda** Portugal
48C3 **Aguelhok** Mali
48A2 **Agüenit** *Well* Morocco
15B2 **Águilas** Spain
72B5 **Aguja, Puerta** Peru
36C7 **Agulhas Basin** Indian Ocean
51C7 **Agulhas,C** South Africa
36C6 **Agulhas Plat** Indian Ocean
Ahaggar = Hoggar
21H8 **Ahar** Iran
13D1 **Ahaus** Germany
35B1 **Ahipara B** New Zealand
13D2 **Ahlen** Germany
42C4 **Ahmadābād** India
44A2 **Ahmadnagar** India
50E3 **Ahmar Mts** Ethiopia
67C1 **Ahoskie** USA
13D2 **Ahr** *R* Germany
13D2 **Ahrgebirge** *Mts* Germany
12G7 **Åhus** Sweden
41F2 **Āhuvān** Iran
41E3 **Ahvāz** Iran
69A4 **Aiajuela** Costa Rica
14C3 **Aigoual, Mount** France
29C3 **Aikawa** Japan
67B2 **Aiken** USA
31A5 **Ailao Shan** *Upland* China
75D2 **Aimorés** Brazil
16B3 **Aïn Beïda** Algeria
48B1 **Aïn Beni Mathar** Morocco
49E2 **Aïn Dalla** *Well* Egypt
15C2 **Aïn el Hadjel** Algeria
50B2 **Aïn Galakka** Chad
15C2 **Aïn Oussera** Algeria
48B1 **Aïn Sefra** Algeria
40B4 **'Ain Sukhna** Egypt
60D2 **Ainsworth** USA
15B2 **Aïn Témouchent** Algeria
29B4 **Aioi** Japan
48B2 **Aïoun Abd el Malek** *Well* Mauritius
48B3 **Aïoun El Atrouss** Mauritius
72E7 **Aiquile** Bolivia
48C3 **Aïr** *Desert Region* Niger
8D4 **Airdrie** Scotland
13B2 **Aire** France
6D3 **Aire** *R* England
13C3 **Aire** *R* France
55L3 **Airforce I** Canada
54E3 **Aishihik** Canada
13B3 **Aisne** *Department* France
14C2 **Aisne** *R* France
27H7 **Aitape** Papua New Guinea
19F1 **Aiviekste** *R* Latvia
14D3 **Aix-en-Provence** France
14D2 **Aix-les-Bains** France
43F4 **Aiyar Res** India
17E3 **Aíyion** Greece
17E3 **Aíyna** *I* Greece
43G4 **Āīzawl** India
51B6 **Aizeb** *R* Namibia
29D3 **Aizu-Wakamatsu** Japan
16B2 **Ajaccio** Corsica, Italy
16B2 **Ajaccio, G d'** Corsica, Italy
21G7 **Ajaria** *Division* Georgia
49E1 **Ajdābiyā** Libya
29E2 **Ajigasawa** Japan
45C2 **Ajlūn** Jordan
41G4 **Ajman** UAE
42C3 **Ajmer** India
59D4 **Ajo** USA
15B1 **Ajo, Cabo de** *C* Spain
17F3 **Ak** *R* Turkey
29D2 **Akabira** Japan
29C3 **Akaishi-sanchi** *Mts* Japan
44B2 **Akalkot** India
45B1 **Akanthou** Cyprus
35B2 **Akaroa** New Zealand
29B4 **Akashi** Japan
21K5 **Akbulak** Russian Federation
40C2 **Akçakale** Turkey
48A2 **Akchar** *Watercourse* Mauritius
50C3 **Aketi** Zaïre
41D1 **Akhalkalaki** Georgia
40D1 **Akhalsikhe** Georgia
17E3 **Akharnaí** Greece
49E1 **Akhdar, Jabal al** *Mts* Libya
41G5 **Akhdar, Jebel** *Mt* Oman
40A2 **Akhisar** Turkey
19F1 **Akhiste** Latvia
49F2 **Akhmîm** Egypt
21H6 **Akhtubinsk** Russian Federation
21E5 **Akhtyrka** Ukraine
29B4 **Aki** Japan
55K4 **Akimiski I** Canada
29E3 **Akita** Japan
48A3 **Akjoujt** Mauritius
45C2 **'Akko** Israel
54E3 **Aklavik** Canada
48B3 **Aklé Aouana** *Desert Region* Mauritius
50D3 **Akobo** Ethiopia
50D3 **Akobo** *R* Ethiopia/Sudan
42B1 **Akoha** Afghanistan
42D4 **Akola** India
42D4 **Akot** India
55M3 **Akpatok I** Canada
17E3 **Ákra Kafirévs** *C* Greece
17E4 **Ákra Líthinon** *C* Greece
17E3 **Ákra Maléa** *C* Greece
12A2 **Akranes** Iceland
17F3 **Ákra Sídheros** *C* Greece
17E3 **Ákra Spátha** *C* Greece
17E3 **Ákra Taínaron** *C* Greece
57E2 **Akron** USA
45B1 **Akrotiri** Cyprus
45B1 **Akrotiri B** Cyprus
42D1 **Aksai Chin** *Mts* China
21E8 **Aksaray** Turkey
21J5 **Aksay** Kazakhstan
42D1 **Aksayquin Hu** *L* China
40B2 **Akşehir** Turkey
40B2 **Akseki** Turkey
25N4 **Aksenovo Zilovskoye** Russian Federation
26E1 **Aksha** Russian Federation
39G1 **Aksu** China
50D2 **Aksum** Ethiopia
24J5 **Aktogay** Kazakhstan
21K6 **Aktumsyk** Kazakhstan
21K5 **Aktyubinsk** Kazakhstan
12B1 **Akureyri** Iceland
Akyab = Sittwe
24K5 **Akzhal** Kazakhstan
63E2 **Alabama** *R* USA
57E3 **Alabama** *State* USA
67A2 **Alabaster** USA
40C2 **Ala Dağları** *Mts* Turkey
21G7 **Alagir** Russian Federation
73L5 **Alagoas** *State* Brazil
73L6 **Alagoinhas** Brazil
15B1 **Alagón** Spain
41E4 **Al Ahmadi** Kuwait
70D3 **Alajuela** Costa Rica
54B3 **Alakanuk** USA
24K5 **Alakol, Ozero** *L* Kazakhstan/Russian Federation
12L5 **Alakurtti** Russian Federation
27H5 **Alamagan** *I* Pacific Ocean
41E3 **Al Amārah** Iraq
59B3 **Alameda** USA
59C3 **Alamo** USA
62A2 **Alamogordo** USA
62C3 **Alamo Heights** USA
62A1 **Alamosa** USA
12H6 **Åland** *I* Finland
21E8 **Alanya** Turkey
67B2 **Alapaha** *R* USA
42L4 **Alapayevsk** Russian Federation
15B2 **Alarcón, Embalse de** *Res* Spain
40A2 **Alaşehir** Turkey
26D3 **Ala Shan** *Mts* China
54C3 **Alaska** *State* USA
54D4 **Alaska,G of** USA
54C3 **Alaska Range** *Mts* USA
16B2 **Alassio** Italy
20H5 **Alatyr'** Russian Federation
34B2 **Alawoona** Australia
41G5 **Al'Ayn** UAE
39F2 **Alayskiy Khrebet** *Mts* Tajikistan
25R3 **Alazeya** *R* Russian Federation
14D3 **Alba** Italy
15B2 **Albacete** Spain
15A1 **Alba de Tormes** Spain
40D2 **Al Badi** Iraq
17E1 **Alba Iulia** Romania
17D2 **Albania** *Republic* Europe
32A4 **Albany** Australia
67B2 **Albany** Georgia, USA
64B3 **Albany** Kentucky, USA
65E2 **Albany** New York, USA
56A2 **Albany** Oregon, USA
55K4 **Albany** *R* Canada
15B1 **Albarracin, Sierra de** *Mts* Spain
41G5 **Al Bātinah** *Region* Oman
27H8 **Albatross B** Australia
49E1 **Al Bayḑa** Libya
45C1 **Al Baylūlīyah** Syria
67B1 **Albemarle** USA
67C1 **Albemarle Sd** USA
15B1 **Alberche** *R* Spain
13B2 **Albert** France
54G4 **Alberta** *Province* Canada
27H7 **Albert Edward** *Mt* Papua New Guinea
47C3 **Albertinia** South Africa
50D3 **Albert,L** Uganda/Zaïre
57D2 **Albert Lea** USA
50D3 **Albert Nile** *R* Uganda
58D1 **Alberton** USA
14D2 **Albertville** France
14C3 **Albi** France
61E2 **Albia** USA
73H2 **Albina** Surinam
64C2 **Albion** Michigan, USA
61D2 **Albion** Nebraska, USA
65D2 **Albion** New York, USA
40C4 **Al Bi'r** Saudi Arabia
15B2 **Alborán** *I* Spain
12G7 **Ålborg** Denmark
13E3 **Albstadt-Ebingen** Germany
40D3 **Al Bū Kamāl** Syria
56C3 **Albuquerque** USA
41G5 **Al Buraymī** Oman
49D1 **Al Burayqah** Libya
49E1 **Al Burdī** Libya

Albury Angul

32D4 **Albury** Australia
41E3 **Al Buşayyah** Iraq
15B1 **Alcalá de Henares** Spain
16C3 **Alcamo** Sicily, Italy
15B1 **Alcañiz** Spain
73K4 **Alcântara** Brazil
15A2 **Alcántara, Embalse de** *Res* Spain
15B2 **Alcaraz** Spain
15B2 **Alcaraz, Sierra de** *Mts* Spain
15B2 **Alcázar de San Juan** Spain
15B2 **Alcira** Spain
75E2 **Alcobaça** Brazil
15B1 **Alcolea de Pinar** Spain
15B2 **Alcoy** Spain
15C2 **Alcudia** Spain
46J8 **Aldabra Is** Indian Ocean
62A3 **Aldama** Mexico
25O4 **Aldan** Russian Federation
25P4 **Aldan** *R* Russian Federation
25O4 **Aldanskoye Nagor'ye** *Upland* Russian Federation
7E3 **Aldeburgh** England
14B2 **Alderney** *I* Channel Islands
7D4 **Aldershot** England
48A3 **Aleg** Mauritius
75A2 **Alegre** *R* Brazil
74E3 **Alegrete** Brazil
25Q4 **Aleksandrovsk Sakhalinskiy** Russian Federation
24J4 **Alekseyevka** Kazakhstan
20F5 **Aleksin** Russian Federation
18D1 **Ålem** Sweden
75D3 **Além Paraíba** Brazil
14C2 **Alençon** France
66E5 **Alenuihaha Chan** Hawaiian Islands
21F8 **Aleppo** Syria
55M1 **Alert** Canada
14C3 **Alès** France
16B2 **Alessandria** Italy
24B3 **Ålesund** Norway
54C4 **Aleutian Ra** *Mts* USA
37L2 **Aleutian Trench** Pacific Ocean
54E4 **Alexander Arch** USA
47B2 **Alexander Bay** South Africa
67A2 **Alexander City** USA
76G3 **Alexander I** Antarctica
35A3 **Alexandra** New Zealand
74J8 **Alexandra,C** South Georgia
55L2 **Alexandra Fjord** Canada
49E1 **Alexandria** Egypt
57D3 **Alexandria** Louisiana, USA
57D2 **Alexandria** Minnesota, USA
57F3 **Alexandria** Virginia, USA
17F2 **Alexandroúpolis** Greece
45C2 **Aley** Lebanon
24K4 **Aleysk** Russian Federation
41D3 **Al Fallūjah** Iraq
15B1 **Alfaro** Spain
17F2 **Alfatar** Bulgaria
41E4 **Al Fāw** Iraq
75C3 **Alfensas** Brazil
17E3 **Alfiós** *R* Greece
75D3 **Alfonso Cláudio** Brazil
8D3 **Alford** Scotland
75D3 **Alfredo Chaves** Brazil
7D3 **Alfreton** England
41E4 **Al Furūthī** Saudi Arabia
21K6 **Alga** Kazakhstan
15A2 **Algeciras** Spain
Alger = Algiers
48B2 **Algeria** *Republic* Africa
16B2 **Alghero** Sardinia, Italy
15C2 **Algiers** Algeria
61E2 **Algona** USA
65D1 **Algonquin Park** Canada
38D3 **Al Ḩadd** Oman
40D3 **Al Ḩadīthah** Iraq
40C3 **Al Ḩadīthah** Saudi Arabia
40D2 **Al Ḩaḑr** Iraq
45D1 **Al Haffah** Syria
41G5 **Al Ḩajar al Gharbī** *Mts* Oman
40C3 **Al Hamad** *Desert Region* Jordan/Saudi Arabia
41E4 **Al Haniyah** *Desert Region* Iraq
41E5 **Al Ḩariq** Saudi Arabia
40C3 **Al Harrah** *Desert Region* Saudi Arabia
49D2 **Al Harūj al Aswad** *Upland* Libya
41E4 **Al Hasa** *Region* Saudi Arabia
40D2 **Al Ḩasakah** Syria
40C4 **Al Hawjā'** Saudi Arabia
41E3 **Al Hayy** Iraq
45D2 **Al Hījānah** Syria
41D3 **Al Ḩillah** Iraq
41E5 **Al Ḩillah** Saudi Arabia
15B2 **Al Hoceima** Morocco
50E2 **Al Ḩudaydah** Yemen
41E4 **Al Hufūf** Saudi Arabia
41F5 **Al Humrah** *Region* UAE
41G5 **Al Huwatsah** Oman
41E2 **Alīābad** Iran
41G4 **Aliabad** Iran
17E2 **Aliákmon** *R* Greece
41E3 **Alī al Gharbī** Iraq
44A2 **Alībāg** India
15B2 **Alicante** Spain
56D4 **Alice** USA
16D3 **Alice, Punta** *Pt* Italy
32C3 **Alice Springs** Australia
16C3 **Alicudi** *I* Italy
42D3 **Aligarh** India
41E3 **Aligūdarz** Iran
42B2 **Ali-Khel** Afghanistan
17F3 **Alimniá** *I* Greece
43F3 **Alīpur Duār** India
64C2 **Aliquippa** USA
40C3 **Al' Isawiyah** Saudi Arabia
47D3 **Aliwal North** South Africa
49E2 **Al Jaghbūb** Libya
40D3 **Al Jālamīd** Saudi Arabia
49E2 **Al Jawf** Libya
40C4 **Al Jawf** Saudi Arabia
40D2 **Al Jazīrah** *Desert Region* Iraq/Syria
15A2 **Aljezur** Portugal
41E4 **Al Jubayl** Saudi Arabia
41D4 **Al Jumaymah** Saudi Arabia
45D4 **Al Kabid** *Desert* Jordan
41D4 **Al Kahfah** Saudi Arabia
41E4 **Al Kāmil** Oman
40D2 **Al Khābūr** *R* Syria
41G5 **Al Khābūrah** Oman
41D3 **Al Khālis** Iraq
41G4 **Al Khaşab** Oman
41F4 **Al Khawr** Qatar
49D1 **Al Khums** Libya
41F5 **Al Kidan** *Region* Saudi Arabia
45D2 **Al Kiswah** Syria
18A2 **Alkmaar** Netherlands
49E2 **Al Kufrah Oasis** Libya
41E3 **Al Kūt** Iraq
Al Lādhiqīyah = Latakia
43E3 **Allahābād** India
45D2 **Al Lajāh** *Mt* Syria
54C3 **Allakaket** USA
30B2 **Allanmyo** Burma
67B2 **Allatoona L** USA
47D1 **Alldays** South Africa
65D2 **Allegheny** *R* USA
57F3 **Allegheny Mts** USA
67B2 **Allendale** USA
6C2 **Allendale Town** England
9B2 **Allen, Lough** *L* Irish Republic
35A3 **Allen,Mt** New Zealand
65D2 **Allentown** USA
44B4 **Alleppey** India
14C2 **Aller** *R* France
60C2 **Alliance** USA
50E1 **Al Līth** Saudi Arabia
41F5 **Al Liwā'** *Region* UAE
8D3 **Alloa** Scotland
34D1 **Allora** Australia
65E1 **Alma** Canada
64C2 **Alma** Michigan, USA
60D2 **Alma** Nebraska, USA
39F1 **Alma Ata** Kazakhstan
15A2 **Almada** Portugal
41E4 **Al Majma'ah** Saudi Arabia
41F4 **Al Manāmah** Bahrain
41D3 **Al Ma'nīyah** Iraq
59B2 **Almanor,L** USA
15B2 **Almansa** Spain
41F5 **Al Māriyyah** UAE
49E1 **Al Marj** Libya
75C2 **Almas** *R* Brazil
15B1 **Almazán** Spain
13E2 **Alme** *R* Germany
13D1 **Almelo** Netherlands
75D2 **Almenara** Brazil
15A1 **Almendra, Embalse de** *Res* Spain
15B2 **Almería** Spain
15B2 **Almería, Golfo de** Spain
20J5 **Al'met'yevsk** Russian Federation
18C1 **Älmhult** Sweden
41D4 **Al Midhnab** Saudi Arabia
41E3 **Al Miqdādīyah** Iraq
17E3 **Almirós** Greece
41E4 **Al Mish'āb** Saudi Arabia
15A2 **Almodôvar** Portugal
42D3 **Almora** India
41E4 **Al Mubarraz** Saudi Arabia
40C4 **Al Mudawwara** Jordan
41F4 **Al Muḩarraq** Bahrain
38C4 **Al Mukallā** Yemen
50E2 **Al Mukhā** Yemen
41D3 **Al Musayyib** Iraq
40C4 **Al Muwayliḩ** Saudi Arabia
8C3 **Alness** Scotland
6D2 **Aln, R** England
41E3 **Al Nu'mānīyah** Iraq
6D2 **Alnwick** England
27F7 **Alor** *I* Indonesia
30C4 **Alor Setar** Malaysia
Alost = Aalst
32E2 **Alotau** Papua New Guinea
32B3 **Aloysius,Mt** Australia
64C1 **Alpena** USA
16C1 **Alpi Dolomitiche** *Mts* Italy
59E4 **Alpine** Arizona, USA
62B2 **Alpine** Texas, USA
58D2 **Alpine** Wyoming, USA
16B1 **Alps** *Mts* Europe
49D1 **Al Qaddāhiyah** Libya
45D1 **Al Qadmūs** Syria
40D3 **Al Qā'im** Iraq
40C4 **Al Qalībah** Saudi Arabia
40D2 **Al Qāmishlī** Syria
45D1 **Al Qardāḩah** Syria
49D1 **Al Qaryah Ash Sharqiyah** Libya
40C3 **Al Qaryatayn** Syria
41D4 **Al Qasīm** *Region* Saudi Arabia
41E4 **Al Qatīf** Saudi Arabia
49D2 **Al Qatrūn** Libya
41E4 **Al Qayşāmah** Saudi Arabia
15A2 **Alquera** *Res* Portugal/Spain
40C3 **Al Qunayţirah** Syria
50E2 **Al Qunfidhah** Saudi Arabia
41E3 **Al Qurnah** Iraq
45D1 **Al Quşayr** Syria
45D2 **Al Quţayfah** Syria
41E5 **Al Quwayīyah** Saudi Arabia
18B1 **Als** *I* Denmark
14D2 **Alsace** *Region* France
13D3 **Alsace, Plaine d'** France
18B2 **Alsfeld** Germany
6C2 **Alston** England
12J5 **Alta** Norway
74D4 **Alta Gracia** Argentina
69D5 **Altagracia de Orituco** Venezuela
26B2 **Altai** *Mts* Mongolia
67B2 **Altamaha** *R* USA
73H4 **Altamira** Brazil
16D2 **Altamura** Italy
26D1 **Altanbulag** Mongolia
70B2 **Altata** Mexico
24K5 **Altay** China
25L5 **Altay** Mongolia
24K4 **Altay** *Division* Russian Federation
24K4 **Altay** *Mts* Russian Federation
24K4 **Altayskiy Kray** *Division* Russian Federation
13D2 **Altenkirchen** Germany
75B2 **Alto Araguaia** Brazil
51D5 **Alto Molócue** Mozambique
7D4 **Alton** England
64A3 **Alton** USA
65D2 **Altoona** USA
75B2 **Alto Sucuriú** Brazil
7C3 **Altrincham** England
39G2 **Altun Shan** *Mts* China
58B2 **Alturas** USA
62C2 **Altus** USA
40C4 **Al'Ulā** Saudi Arabia
40C4 **Al Urayq** *Desert Region* Saudi Arabia
62C1 **Alva** USA
63C2 **Alvarado** USA
12G6 **Älvdalen** Sweden
63C3 **Alvin** USA
12J5 **Älvsbyn** Sweden
49D2 **Al Wāha** Libya
40C4 **Al Wajh** Saudi Arabia
42D3 **Alwar** India
40D3 **Al Widyān** *Desert Region* Iraq/Saudi Arabia
31A2 **Alxa Youqi** China
31B2 **Alxa Zuoqi** China
41E2 **Alyat** Azerbaijan
12J8 **Alytus** Lithuania
13E3 **Alzey** Germany
50D3 **Amadi** Sudan
41D2 **Amādīyah** Iraq
55L3 **Amadjuak L** Canada
12G7 **Åmål** Sweden
25N4 **Amalat** *R* Russian Federation
17E3 **Amaliás** Greece
42C4 **Amalner** India
75A3 **Amambaí** Brazil
75B3 **Amambaí** *R* Brazil
75A3 **Amamba, Serra** *Mts* Brazil/Paraguay
26F4 **Amami** *I* Japan
26F4 **Amami gunto** *Arch* Japan
73H3 **Amapá** Brazil
73H3 **Amapá** *State* Brazil
62B1 **Amarillo** USA
21F7 **Amasya** Turkey
73H4 **Amazonas** *R* Brazil
72E4 **Amazonas** *State* Brazil
42D2 **Ambāla** India
44C4 **Ambalangoda** Sri Lanka
51E6 **Ambalavao** Madagascar
50B3 **Ambam** Cameroon
51E5 **Ambanja** Madagascar
25S3 **Ambarchik** Russian Federation
72C4 **Ambato** Ecuador
51E5 **Ambato-Boeny** Madagascar
51E5 **Ambatolampy** Madagascar
51E5 **Ambatondrazaka** Madagascar
18C3 **Amberg** Germany
70D3 **Ambergris Cay** *I* Belize
43E4 **Ambikāpur** India
51E5 **Ambilobe** Madagascar
6C2 **Ambleside** England
51E6 **Amboasary** Madagascar
51E5 **Ambodifototra** Madagascar
51E6 **Ambohimahasoa** Madagascar
Amboina = Ambon
27F7 **Ambon** Indonesia
51E6 **Ambositra** Madagascar
51E6 **Ambovombe** Madagascar
27E6 **Amboyna Cay** *I* S China Sea
51E5 **Ambre, Montagne d'** *Mt* Madagascar
51B4 **Ambriz** Angola
33F2 **Ambrym** *I* Vanuatu
50C2 **Am Dam** Chad
20L2 **Amderma** Russian Federation
70B2 **Ameca** Mexico
18B2 **Ameland** *I* Netherlands
68D2 **Amenia** USA
58D2 **American Falls** USA
58D2 **American Falls Res** USA
59D2 **American Fork** USA
76F10 **American Highland** *Upland* Antarctica
37L5 **American Samoa** *Is* Pacific Ocean
67B2 **Americus** USA
18B2 **Amersfoort** Netherlands
47D2 **Amersfoort** South Africa
61E1 **Amery** USA
76G10 **Amery Ice Shelf** Antarctica
61E2 **Ames** USA
68E1 **Amesbury** USA
17E3 **Amfilokhía** Greece
17E3 **Amfissa** Greece
25P3 **Amga** Russian Federation
25P3 **Amgal** *R* Russian Federation
26G2 **Amgu** Russian Federation
26G1 **Amgun'** *R* Russian Federation
50D2 **Amhara** *Region* Ethiopia
55M5 **Amherst** Canada
68D1 **Amherst** Massachusetts, USA
65D3 **Amherst** Virginia, USA
44B3 **Amhūr** India
16C2 **Amiata, Monte** *Mt* Italy
14C2 **Amiens** France
29C3 **Amino** Japan
45C1 **Amioune** Lebanon
46K8 **Amirante Is** Indian Ocean
62B3 **Amistad Res** Mexico
43F3 **Amlekhganj** Nepal
7B3 **Amlwch** Wales
40C3 **Amman** Jordan
7C4 **Ammanford** Wales
12K6 **Ämmänsaari** Finland
55P3 **Ammassalik** Greenland
28A3 **Amnyong-dan** *C* N Korea
41F2 **Amol** Iran
17F3 **Amorgós** *I* Greece
55L5 **Amos** Canada
Amoy = Xiamen
51E6 **Ampanihy** Madagascar
75C3 **Amparo** Brazil
51E5 **Ampasimanolotra** Madagascar
15C1 **Amposta** Spain
42D4 **Amrāvati** India
42C4 **Amreli** India
42C2 **Amritsar** India
43K1 **Amroha** India
36E6 **Amsterdam** *I* Indian Ocean
18A2 **Amsterdam** Netherlands
47E2 **Amsterdam** South Africa
65E2 **Amsterdam** USA
50C2 **Am Timan** Chad
24H5 **Amu Darya** *R* Uzbekistan
55J2 **Amund Ringnes I** Canada
54F2 **Amundsen G** Canada
76E **Amundsen-Scott** *Base* Antarctica
76F4 **Amundsen Sea** Antarctica
27E7 **Amuntai** Indonesia
25O4 **Amur** *Division* Russian Federation
26F1 **Amur** *R* Russian Federation
25N2 **Anabar** *R* Russian Federation
66C4 **Anacapa Is** USA
72F2 **Anaco** Venezuela
56B2 **Anaconda** USA
58B1 **Anacortes** USA
62C1 **Anadarko** USA
25T3 **Anadyr'** Russian Federation
25T3 **Anadyr'** *R* Russian Federation
25U3 **Anadyrskiy Zaliv** *S* Russian Federation
25T3 **Anadyrskoye Ploskogor'ye** *Plat* Russian Federation
17F3 **Anáfi** *I* Greece
75D1 **Anagé** Brazil
40D3 **'Ānah** Iraq
59C4 **Anaheim** USA
44B3 **Anaimalai Hills** India
44C2 **Anakāpalle** India
51E5 **Analalava** Madagascar
27D6 **Anambas, Kepulauan** *Is* Indonesia
64A2 **Anamosa** USA
21E8 **Anamur** Turkey
29B4 **Anan** Japan
44B3 **Anantapur** India
42D2 **Anantnag** India
73J7 **Anápolis** Brazil
41G3 **Anār** Iran
41F3 **Anārak** Iran
27H5 **Anatahan** *I* Pacific Ocean
74D3 **Añatuya** Argentina
28B3 **Anbyŏn** N Korea
54D3 **Anchorage** USA
72E7 **Ancohuma** *Mt* Bolivia
72C6 **Ancón** Peru
16C2 **Ancona** Italy
68D1 **Ancram** USA
74B6 **Ancud** Chile
74B6 **Ancud, Golfo de** *G* Chile
13C4 **Ancy-le-Franc** France
72D6 **Andahuaylas** Peru
12F6 **Åndalsnes** Norway
15A2 **Andalucia** *Region* Spain
67A2 **Andalusia** USA
39H4 **Andaman Is** India
75D1 **Andaraí** Brazil
13C3 **Andelot** France
12H5 **Andenes** Norway
18B2 **Andernach** Germany
64B2 **Anderson** Indiana, USA
63D1 **Anderson** Missouri, USA
67B2 **Anderson** S Carolina, USA
54F3 **Anderson** *R* Canada
72C5 **Andes, Cordillera de los** *Mts* Peru
44B2 **Andhra Pradesh** *State* India
17E3 **Andikíthira** *I* Greece
24J5 **Andizhan** Uzbekistan
24H6 **Andkhui** Afghanistan
28B3 **Andong** S Korea
15C1 **Andorra** *Principality* SW Europe
15C1 **Andorra-La-Vella** Andorra
7D4 **Andover** England
68E1 **Andover** New Hampshire, USA
68B1 **Andover** New York, USA
75B3 **Andradina** Brazil
19G1 **Andreapol'** Russian Federation
40B2 **Andreas,C** Cyprus
62B2 **Andrews** USA
16D2 **Andria** Italy
17E3 **Ándros** *I* Greece
57F4 **Andros** *I* The Bahamas
67C4 **Andros Town** Bahamas
44A3 **Androth** *I* India
15B2 **Andújar** Spain
51B5 **Andulo** Angola
48C3 **Anéfis** Mali
48C4 **Aného** Togo
33F3 **Aneityum** *I* Vanuatu
25M4 **Angarsk** Russian Federation
20A3 **Ånge** Sweden
70A2 **Angel de la Guarda** *I* Mexico
12G7 **Ängelholm** Sweden
34C1 **Angellala Creek** *R* Australia
66B1 **Angels Camp** USA
27G7 **Angemuk** *Mt* Indonesia
14B2 **Angers** France
13B3 **Angerville** France
30C3 **Angkor** *Hist Site* Cambodia
10C3 **Anglesey** *County* Wales
10C3 **Anglesey** *I* Wales
63C3 **Angleton** USA
Angmagssalik = Ammassalik
51E5 **Angoche** Mozambique
74B5 **Angol** Chile
64C2 **Angola** Indiana, USA
51B5 **Angola** *Republic* Africa
52J5 **Angola Basin** Atlantic Ocean
14C2 **Angoulême** France
48A1 **Angra do Heroismo** Azores
75D3 **Angra dos Reis** Brazil
69E3 **Anguilla** *I* Caribbean Sea
69B2 **Anguilla Cays** *Is* Caribbean Sea
43F4 **Angul** India

Astorga
Ban Aranyaprathet

15A1 **Astorga** Spain
56A2 **Astoria** USA
21H6 **Astrakhan'** Russian Federation
21H6 **Astrakhan'** *Division* Russian Federation
15A1 **Asturias** *Region* Spain
76F12 **Asuka** *Base* Antarctica
74E3 **Asunción** Paraguay
26H5 **Asuncion** *I* Marianas
50D3 **Aswa** *R* Uganda
40B5 **Aswân** Egypt
49F2 **Aswân High Dam** Egypt
49F2 **Asyût** Egypt
74C2 **Atacama, Desierto de** *Desert* Chile
33H1 **Atafu** *I* Tokelau Islands
45C3 **Atā'ita, Jebel el** *Mt* Jordan
48C4 **Atakpamé** Togo
27F7 **Atambua** Indonesia
55N3 **Atangmik** Greenland
45B4 **Ataqa, Gebel** *Mt* Egypt
48A2 **Atar** Mauritius
40C2 **Atatirk Baraji** *Res* Turkey
66B3 **Atascadero** USA
24J5 **Atasu** Kazakhstan
50D2 **Atbara** Sudan
24H4 **Atbasar** Kazakhstan
57D4 **Atchafalaya B** USA
57D3 **Atchison** USA
68C3 **Atco** USA
16C2 **Atessa** Italy
13B2 **Ath** Belgium
54G4 **Athabasca** Canada
54G4 **Athabasca** *R* Canada
54H4 **Athabasca,L** Canada
67A2 **Athens** Alabama, USA
57E3 **Athens** Georgia, USA
17E3 **Athens** Greece
64C3 **Athens** Ohio, USA
68B2 **Athens** Pennsylvania, USA
67B1 **Athens** Tennessee, USA
63C2 **Athens** Texas, USA
Athína = Athens
10B3 **Athlone** Irish Republic
45B1 **Athna** Cyprus
68D1 **Athol** USA
17E2 **Áthos** *Mt* Greece
9C3 **Athy** Irish Republic
50B2 **Ati** Chad
55J5 **Atikoken** Canada
25R3 **Atka** Russian Federation
21G5 **Atkarsk** Russian Federation
63D1 **Atkins** USA
57E3 **Atlanta** Georgia, USA
64C2 **Atlanta** Michigan, USA
61D2 **Atlantic** USA
57F3 **Atlantic City** USA
68C2 **Atlantic Highlands** USA
52H8 **Atlantic-Indian Antarctic Basin** Atlantic Ocean
52H7 **Atlantic Indian Ridge** Atlantic Ocean
Atlas Mts = Haut Atlas, Moyen Atlas
48C1 **Atlas Saharien** *Mts* Algeria
54E4 **Atlin** Canada
54E4 **Atlin L** Canada
45C2 **'Atlit** Israel
57E3 **Atmore** USA
51E6 **Atofinandrahana** Madagascar
63C2 **Atoka** USA
72C2 **Atrato** *R* Colombia
41F5 **Attaf** *Region* UAE
50E1 **Aṭ Ṭā'if** Saudi Arabia
45D2 **At Tall** Syria
67A2 **Attalla** USA
55K4 **Attawapiskat** Canada
55K4 **Attawapiskat** *R* Canada
41D3 **At Taysīyah** *Desert Region* Saudi Arabia
64B2 **Attica** Indiana, USA
68A1 **Attica** New York, USA
13C3 **Attigny** France
45B1 **Attila Line** Cyprus
65E2 **Attleboro** Massachusetts, USA
30D3 **Attopeu** Laos
40C4 **At Tubayq** *Upland* Saudi Arabia
12H7 **Atvidaberg** Sweden
66B2 **Atwater** USA
14D3 **Aubagne** France
13C3 **Aube** *Department* France
13C3 **Aube** *R* France
14C3 **Aubenas** France
67A2 **Auburn** Alabama, USA
59B3 **Auburn** California, USA
64B2 **Auburn** Indiana, USA
65E2 **Auburn** Maine, USA
61D2 **Auburn** Nebraska, USA
65D2 **Auburn** New York, USA
58B1 **Auburn** Washington, USA
14C3 **Auch** France
33G4 **Auckland** New Zealand
37K7 **Auckland Is** New Zealand
14C3 **Aude** *R* France
55K4 **Auden** Canada
61E2 **Audubon** USA
34C1 **Augathella** Australia
9C2 **Aughnacloy** Northern Ireland
47B2 **Aughrabies Falls** South Africa
18C3 **Augsburg** Germany
32A4 **Augusta** Australia
57E3 **Augusta** Georgia, USA
63C1 **Augusta** Kansas, USA
57G2 **Augusta** Maine, USA
58D1 **Augusta** Montana, USA
64A2 **Augusta** Wisconsin, USA
19E2 **Augustów** Poland
32A3 **Augustus,Mt** Australia
47B1 **Auob** *R* Namibia
42D3 **Auraiya** India
42D5 **Aurangābād** India
48C1 **Aurès** *Mts* Algeria
16B3 **Aurès, Mt de l'** Algeria
13D1 **Aurich** Germany
14C3 **Aurillac** France
56C3 **Aurora** Colorado, USA
64B2 **Aurora** Illinois, USA
64C3 **Aurora** Indiana, USA
63D1 **Aurora** Mississippi, USA
61D2 **Aurora** Nebraska, USA
47B2 **Aus** Namibia
64C2 **Au Sable** USA
48A2 **Ausert** *Well* Morocco
8D2 **Auskerry, I** Scotland
57D2 **Austin** Minnesota, USA
59C3 **Austin** Nevada, USA
68A2 **Austin** Pennsylvania, USA
56D3 **Austin** Texas, USA
32D4 **Australian Alps** *Mts* Australia
18C3 **Austria** *Federal Republic* Europe
70B3 **Autlán** Mexico
14C2 **Autun** France
14C2 **Auvergne** *Region* France
14C2 **Auxerre** France
13A2 **Auxi-le-Château** France
14C2 **Avallon** France
66C4 **Avalon** USA
55N5 **Avalon Pen** Canada
75C3 **Avaré** Brazil
13E1 **Ave** *R* Germany
45C3 **Avedat** *Hist Site* Israel
73G4 **Aveíro** Brazil
15A1 **Aveiro** Portugal
74E4 **Avellaneda** Argentina
16C2 **Avellino** Italy
66B3 **Avenal** USA
13B2 **Avesnes-sur-Helpe** France
12H6 **Avesta** Sweden
16C2 **Avezzano** Italy
8D3 **Aviemore** Scotland
35B2 **Aviemore,L** New Zealand
14C3 **Avignon** France
15B1 **Avila** Spain
15A1 **Avilés** Spain
61D2 **Avoca** Iowa, USA
68B1 **Avoca** New York, USA
34B3 **Avoca** *R* Australia
68B1 **Avon** USA
7D4 **Avon** *R* Dorset, England
7D3 **Avon** *R* Warwick, England
59D4 **Avondale** USA
7C4 **Avonmouth** Wales
67B3 **Avon Park** USA
13B3 **Avre** *R* France
17D2 **Avtovac** Bosnia-Herzegovina
45D2 **A'waj** *R* Syria
29D4 **Awaji-shima** *I* Japan
50E3 **Awarē** Ethiopia
35A2 **Awarua Pt** New Zealand
50E3 **Awash** Ethiopia
50E3 **Awash** *R* Ethiopia
29C3 **Awa-shima** *I* Japan
35B2 **Awatere** *R* New Zealand
49D2 **Awbārī** Libya
50C3 **Aweil** Sudan
8C3 **Awe, Loch** *L* Scotland
49E2 **Awjilah** Libya
55J1 **Axel Heiberg I** Canada
7C4 **Axminster** England
29C3 **Ayabe** Japan
74E5 **Ayacucho** Argentina
69C5 **Ayacucho** Colombia
72D6 **Ayacucho** Peru
24K5 **Ayaguz** Kazakhstan
39G2 **Ayakkum Hu** *L* China
15A2 **Ayamonte** Spain
25P4 **Ayan** Russian Federation
72D6 **Ayaviri** Peru
21D8 **Aydın** Turkey
17F3 **Áyios Evstrátios** *I* Greece
25N3 **Aykhal** Russian Federation
7D4 **Aylesbury** England
45D2 **'Ayn al Fījah** Syria
40D2 **Ayn Zālah** Iraq
49E2 **Ayn Zuwayyah** *Well* Libya
50D3 **Ayod** Sudan
32D2 **Ayr** Australia
8C4 **Ayr** Scotland
8C4 **Ayr** *R* Scotland
6B2 **Ayre,Pt of** Isle of Man, British Islands
17F2 **Aytos** Bulgaria
30C3 **Ayutthaya** Thailand
17F3 **Ayvacık** Turkey
17F3 **Ayvalık** Turkey
43E3 **Āzamgarh** India
48B3 **Azaouad** *Desert Region* Mali
48C3 **Azaouak, Vallée de l'** Niger
48D3 **Azare** Nigeria
40C2 **A'zāz** Syria
Azbine = Aïr
48A2 **Azeffal** *Watercourse* Mauritius
21H7 **Azerbaijan** *Republic* Europe
72C4 **Azogues** Ecuador
20H2 **Azopol'ye** Russian Federation
46B4 **Azores** *Is* Atlantic Ocean
50C2 **Azoum** *R* Chad
21F6 **Azov, S of** Russian Federation/Ukraine
48B1 **Azrou** Morocco
62A1 **Aztec** USA
72B2 **Azuero,Pen de** Panama
74E5 **Azul** Argentina
75B1 **Azul, Serra** *Mts* Brazil
16B3 **Azzaba** Algeria
45D2 **Az-Zabdānī** Syria
41G5 **Aẓ Ẓāhirah** *Mts* Oman
49D2 **Az Zahrah** Libya
40C3 **Az Zilaf** Syria
41D4 **Az Zilfī** Saudi Arabia
41E3 **Az Zubayr** Iraq

B

45C2 **Ba'abda** Lebanon
40C3 **Ba'albek** Lebanon
45C3 **Ba'al Hazor** *Mt* Israel
50E3 **Baardheere** Somalia
17F2 **Babadag** Romania
40A1 **Babaeski** Turkey
72C4 **Babahoyo** Ecuador
50E2 **Bāb al Mandab** *Str* Djibouti/Yemen
32B1 **Babar, Kepulauan** *I* Indonesia
50D4 **Babati** Tanzania
20F4 **Babayevo** Russian Federation
61E1 **Babbitt** USA
64C2 **Baberton** USA
54F4 **Babine L** Canada
32C1 **Babo** Indonesia
41F2 **Bābol** Iran
27F5 **Babuyan Is** Philippines
73J4 **Bacabal** Brazil
27F7 **Bacan** *I* Indonesia
21D6 **Bacău** Romania
30D1 **Bac Can** Vietnam
13D3 **Baccarat** France
34B3 **Bacchus Marsh** Australia
39F2 **Bachu** China
54J3 **Back** *R* Canada
30D1 **Bac Ninh** Vietnam
27F5 **Bacolod** Philippines
6C3 **Bacup** England
44B3 **Badagara** India
31A1 **Badain Jaran Shamo** *Desert* China
15A2 **Badajoz** Spain
15C1 **Badalona** Spain
40D3 **Badanah** Saudi Arabia
28B2 **Badaohe** China
13E3 **Bad Bergzabern** Germany
13D2 **Bad Ems** Germany
18B3 **Baden-Baden** Germany
13D3 **Badenviller** France
18B3 **Baden-Württemberg** *State* Germany
18C3 **Badgastein** Austria
66C2 **Badger** USA
18B2 **Bad-Godesberg** Germany
18B2 **Bad Hersfeld** Germany
13D2 **Bad Honnef** Germany
42B4 **Badin** Pakistan
16C1 **Bad Ischl** Austria
40C3 **Badiyat ash Sham** *Desert Region* Iraq/Jordan
18B3 **Bad-Kreuznach** Germany
60C1 **Badlands** *Region* USA
13E2 **Bad Lippspringe** Germany
13E2 **Bad Nauheim** Germany
13D2 **Bad Nevenahr-Ahrweiler** Germany
40C5 **Badr Ḩunayn** Saudi Arabia
13E2 **Bad Ryrmont** Germany
18C3 **Bad Tolz** Germany
44C4 **Badulla** Sri Lanka
13E2 **Bad Wildungen** Germany
13E3 **Bad Wimpfen** Germany
15B2 **Baena** Spain
48A3 **Bafatá** Guinea-Bissau
55L2 **Baffin B** Canada/Greenland
63C3 **Baffin B** USA
55L2 **Baffin I** Canada
50B3 **Bafia** Cameroon
48A3 **Bafing** *R* Mali
48A3 **Bafoulabé** Mali
50B3 **Bafoussam** Cameroon
41G3 **Bāfq** Iran
21F7 **Bafra Burun** *Pt* Turkey
41G4 **Bāft** Iran
50C3 **Bafwasende** Zaïre
43E3 **Bagaha** India
44B2 **Bāgalkot** India
51D4 **Bagamoyo** Tanzania
59D4 **Bagdad** USA
74F4 **Bagé** Brazil
60B2 **Baggs** USA
41D3 **Baghdād** Iraq
43F4 **Bagherhat** Bangladesh
41G3 **Bāghīn** Iran
42B1 **Baghlan** Afghanistan
61D1 **Bagley** USA
48B4 **Bagnoa** Ivory Coast
14C3 **Bagnols-sur-Cèze** France
Bago = Pegu
48B3 **Bagoé** *R* Mali
28A2 **Bag Tai** China
27F5 **Baguio** Philippines
43F3 **Bāhādurābād** Bangladesh
57F4 **Bahamas,The** *Is* Caribbean Sea
43F4 **Baharampur** India
40A4 **Baharîya Oasis** Egypt
42C3 **Bahawalnagar** Pakistan
42C3 **Bahawalpur** Pakistan
42C3 **Bahawalpur** *Division* Pakistan
Bahia = Salvador
73K6 **Bahia** *State* Brazil
74D5 **Bahía Blanca** Argentina
70D3 **Bahía, Islas de la** Honduras
56B4 **Bahia Kino** Mexico
74C6 **Bahias, Cabo dos** Argentina
50D2 **Bahir Dar** Ethiopia
45A3 **Bahra el Manzala** *L* Egypt
43E3 **Bahraich** India
38D3 **Bahrain** *Sheikhdom* Arabian Pen
41D3 **Bahr al Milh** *L* Iraq
50C3 **Bahr Aouk** *R* Chad/Central African Republic
Bahrat Lut = Dead Sea
Bahr el Abiad = White Nile
50C3 **Bahr el Arab** *Watercourse* Sudan
Bahr el Azraq = Blue Nile
50D3 **Bahr el Ghazal** *R* Sudan
50B2 **Bahr el Ghazal** *Watercourse* Chad
45A3 **Bahr Fâqûs** *R* Egypt
15A2 **Baia de Setúbal** *B* Portugal
51B5 **Baia dos Tigres** Angola
21C6 **Baia Mare** Romania
50B3 **Baïbokoum** Chad
26F2 **Baicheng** China
55M5 **Baie-Comeau** Canada
45C2 **Baie de St Georges** *B* Lebanon
55L4 **Baie-du-Poste** Canada
65E1 **Baie St Paul** Canada
55N5 **Baie-Verte** Canada
31B3 **Baihe** China
31C3 **Bai He** *R* China
41D3 **Ba'ījī** Iraq
25M4 **Baikal, L** Russian Federation
43E4 **Baikunthpur** India
Baile Atha Cliath = Dublin
17E2 **Băileşti** Romania
13B2 **Bailleul** France
31A3 **Baima** China
67B2 **Bainbridge** USA
54B3 **Baird Mts** USA
31D1 **Bairin Youqi** China
31D1 **Bairin Zuoqi** China
32D4 **Bairnsdale** Australia
43E3 **Baitadi** Nepal
28A2 **Baixingt** China
17D1 **Baja** Hungary
70A1 **Baja California** *Pen* Mexico
59C4 **Baja California** *State* Mexico
70A2 **Baja, Punta** *Pt* Mexico
20K5 **Bakal** Russian Federation
50C3 **Bakala** Central African Republic
48A3 **Bakel** Senegal
59C3 **Baker** California, USA
56C2 **Baker** Montana, USA
56B2 **Baker** Oregon, USA
55J3 **Baker Foreland** *Pt* Canada
54J3 **Baker L** Canada
54J3 **Baker Lake** Canada
56A2 **Baker,Mt** USA
56B3 **Bakersfield** USA
7D3 **Bakewell** England
41G2 **Bakharden** Turkmenistan
41G2 **Bakhardok** Turkmenistan
21E5 **Bakhmach** Ukraine
12C1 **Bakkaflói** *B* Iceland
50D3 **Bako** Ethiopia
50C3 **Bakouma** Central African Republic
21H7 **Baku** Azerbaijan
40B2 **Balâ** Turkey
7C3 **Bala** Wales
27E6 **Balabac** *I* Philippines
27E6 **Balabac Str** Malaysia/Philippines
43E4 **Bālāghāt** India
34A2 **Balaklava** Australia
21H5 **Balakovo** Russian Federation
43E4 **Balāngīr** India
21G5 **Balashov** Russian Federation
43F4 **Balasore** India
17D1 **Balaton** *L* Hungary
9C3 **Balbriggan** Irish Republic
74E5 **Balcarce** Argentina
17F2 **Balchik** Bulgaria
33F5 **Balclutha** New Zealand
63D1 **Bald Knob** USA
7D4 **Baldock** England
67B2 **Baldwin** USA
58E1 **Baldy Mt** USA
56C3 **Baldy Peak** *Mt* USA
15C2 **Balearic Is** Spain
75E2 **Baleia, Ponta da** *Pt* Brazil
55M4 **Baleine, Rivière de la** *R* Canada
27F5 **Baler** Philippines
20J4 **Balezino** Russian Federation
32A1 **Bali** *I* Indonesia
40A2 **Balıkesir** Turkey
40C2 **Balīkh** *R* Syria/Turkey
27E7 **Balikpapan** Indonesia
75B2 **Baliza** Brazil
42B1 **Balkh** Afghanistan
24J5 **Balkhash** Kazakhstan
24J5 **Balkhash, L** Kazakhstan
8C3 **Ballachulish** Scotland
8C4 **Ballantrae** Scotland
54G2 **Ballantyne Str** Canada
44B3 **Ballāpur** India
32D4 **Ballarat** Australia
8D3 **Ballater** Scotland
6B2 **Ballaugh** England
76G7 **Balleny Is** Antarctica
43E3 **Ballia** India
34D1 **Ballina** Australia
10B3 **Ballina** Irish Republic
62C2 **Ballinger** USA
9A4 **Ballinskelligis B** Irish Republic
13D4 **Ballon d'Alsace** *Mt* France
17D2 **Ballsh** Albania
68D1 **Ballston Spa** USA
9C2 **Ballycastle** Northern Ireland
9D2 **Ballyclare** Northern Ireland
9C4 **Ballycotton B** Irish Republic
9B3 **Ballyhaunis** Northern Ireland
9C2 **Ballymena** Northern Ireland
9C2 **Ballymoney** Northern Ireland
9C2 **Ballynahinch** Northern Ireland
9B2 **Ballyshannon** Irish Republic
9C3 **Ballyteige B** Irish Republic
34B3 **Balmoral** Australia
62B2 **Balmorhea** USA
42B3 **Balochistān** *Region* Pakistan
51B5 **Balombo** Angola
34C1 **Balonn** *R* Australia
42C3 **Bālotra** India
43E3 **Balrāmpur** India
32D4 **Balranald** Australia
73J5 **Balsas** Brazil
70B3 **Balsas** *R* Mexico
21D6 **Balta** Ukraine
12H7 **Baltic S** N Europe
40B3 **Baltîm** Egypt
57F3 **Baltimore** USA
43F3 **Bālurghāt** India
21J6 **Balykshi** Kazakhstan
41G4 **Bam** Iran
50B2 **Bama** Nigeria
48B3 **Bamako** Mali
50C3 **Bambari** Central African Republic
67B2 **Bamberg** USA
18C3 **Bamberg** Germany
50C3 **Bambili** Zaïre
75C3 **Bambuí** Brazil
50B3 **Bamenda** Cameroon
28A2 **Bamiancheng** China
50B3 **Bamingui** *R* Central African Republic
50B3 **Bamingui Bangoran National Park** Central African Republic
42B2 **Bamiyan** Afghanistan
33F1 **Banaba** *I* Kiribati
50C3 **Banalia** Zaïre
48B3 **Banamba** Mali
44E4 **Bananga** Nicobar Is, Indian Ocean
30C3 **Ban Aranyaprathet** Thailand

Ban Ban Belchiragh

30C2 **Ban Ban** Laos
30C4 **Ban Betong** Thailand
9C2 **Banbridge** Northern Ireland
7D3 **Banbury** England
8D3 **Banchory** Scotland
70D3 **Banco Chinchorro** *Is* Mexico
65D1 **Bancroft** Canada
43E3 **Bānda** India
27C6 **Banda Aceh** Indonesia
27G7 **Banda, Kepulauan** *Arch* Indonesia
48B4 **Bandama** *R* Ivory Coast
41G4 **Bandar 'Abbās** Iran
21H8 **Bandar Anzalī** Iran
41F4 **Bandar-e Daylam** Iran
41F4 **Bandar-e Lengheh** Iran
41F4 **Bandar-e Māqām** Iran
41F4 **Bandar-e Rig** Iran
21J8 **Bandar-e Torkoman** Iran
41E3 **Bandar Khomeynī** Iran
27E6 **Bandar Seri Begawan** Brunei
27F7 **Banda S** Indonesia
75D3 **Bandeira** *Mt* Brazil
75B1 **Bandeirantes** Brazil
70B2 **Banderas, B de** Mexico
48B3 **Bandiagara** Mali
21D7 **Bandırma** Turkey
47D1 **Bandolier Kop** South Africa
50B4 **Bandundu** Zaïre
27D7 **Bandung** Indonesia
21H8 **Baneh** Iran
70E2 **Banes** Cuba
8D3 **Banff** Scotland
54G4 **Banff** *R* Canada
44B3 **Bangalore** India
50C3 **Bangassou** Central African Republic
32B1 **Banggai, Kepulauan** *I* Indonesia
27E6 **Banggi** *I* Malaysia
30D2 **Bang Hieng** *R* Laos
27D7 **Bangka** *I* Indonesia
30C3 **Bangkok** Thailand
30C3 **Bangkok, Bight of** *B* Thailand
39G3 **Bangladesh** *Republic* Asia
42D2 **Bangong Co** *L* China
57G2 **Bangor** Maine, USA
9D2 **Bangor** Northern Ireland
68C2 **Bangor** Pennsylvania, USA
7B3 **Bangor** Wales
30B3 **Bang Saphan Yai** Thailand
50B3 **Bangui** Central African Republic
51D5 **Bangweulu, L** Zambia
30C4 **Ban Hat Yai** Thailand
30C2 **Ban Hin Heup** Laos
30C1 **Ban Houei Sai** Laos
30B3 **Ban Hua Hin** Thailand
48B3 **Bani** *R* Mali
48C3 **Bani Bangou** Niger
49D1 **Banī Walīd** Libya
40C2 **Bāniyās** Syria
16D2 **Banja Luka** Bosnia-Herzegovina
27E7 **Banjarmasin** Indonesia
48A3 **Banjul** The Gambia
30B4 **Ban Kantang** Thailand
30D2 **Ban Khemmarat** Laos
30B4 **Ban Khok Kloi** Thailand
27H8 **Banks I** Australia
54E4 **Banks I** British Columbia, Canada
54F2 **Banks I** Northwest Territories, Canada
33F2 **Banks Is** Vanuatu
58C1 **Banks L** USA
35B2 **Banks Pen** New Zealand
34C4 **Banks Str** Australia
43F4 **Bankura** India
30B2 **Ban Mae Sariang** Thailand
30B2 **Ban Mae Sot** Thailand
43H4 **Banmauk** Burma
30D3 **Ban Me Thuot** Vietnam
9C3 **Bann** *R* Irish Republic
9C2 **Bann** *R* Northern Ireland
30B4 **Ban Na San** Thailand
42C2 **Bannu** Pakistan
30C2 **Ban Pak Neun** Laos
30C4 **Ban Pak Phanang** Thailand
30D3 **Ban Pu Kroy** Cambodia
30B3 **Ban Sai Yok** Thailand
30C3 **Ban Sattahip** Thailand
19D3 **Banská Bystrica** Slovakia
42C4 **Bānswāra** India
30B4 **Ban Tha Kham** Thailand
30D2 **Ban Thateng** Laos
30C2 **Ban Tha Tum** Thailand
10B3 **Bantry** Irish Republic
10A3 **Bantry** *B* Irish Republic
27C6 **Banyak, Kepulauan** *Is* Indonesia
30D3 **Ban Ya Soup** Vietnam
27E7 **Banyuwangi** Indonesia
36E7 **Banzare Seamount** Indian Ocean
31D2 **Baoding** China
31C3 **Baofeng** China
30C1 **Bao Ha** Vietnam
31B3 **Baoji** China
30D3 **Bao Loc** Vietnam
26C4 **Baoshan** China
31C1 **Baotou** China
44C2 **Bāpatla** India
13B2 **Bapaume** France
45C4 **Bāqir, Jebel** *Mt* Jordan
41D3 **Ba'qūbah** Iraq
17D2 **Bar** Montenegro, Yugoslavia
50D2 **Bara** Sudan
50E3 **Baraawe** Somalia
43E3 **Bāra Banki** India
28C2 **Barabash** Russian Federation
24J4 **Barabinsk** Kazakhstan/Russian Federation
24J4 **Barabinskaya Step** *Steppe* Kazakhstan/Russian Federation
15B1 **Baracaldo** Spain
69C2 **Baracoa** Cuba
45D2 **Baradá** *R* Syria
34C2 **Baradine** Australia
44A2 **Bārāmati** India
42C2 **Baramula** Pakistan
42D3 **Bārān** India
54E4 **Baranof I** USA
20D5 **Baranovichi** Belarus
34A2 **Baratta** Australia
43F3 **Barauni** India
73K8 **Barbacena** Brazil
69F4 **Barbados** *I* Caribbean Sea
15C1 **Barbastro** Spain
47E2 **Barberton** South Africa
14B2 **Barbezieux** France
72D2 **Barbosa** Colombia
69E3 **Barbuda** *I* Caribbean Sea
32D3 **Barcaldine** Australia
Barce = Al Marj
16D3 **Barcellona** Sicily, Italy
15C1 **Barcelona** Spain
72F1 **Barcelona** Venezuela
32D3 **Barcoo** *R* Australia
50B1 **Bardai** Chad
74C5 **Bardas Blancas** Argentina
43F4 **Barddhamān** India
19E3 **Bardejov** Slovakia
7B3 **Bardsey** *I* Wales
64B3 **Bardstown** USA
42D3 **Bareilly** India
Barentsovo More *S* = **Barents Sea**
24D2 **Barentsøya** *I* Svalbard
20F1 **Barents S** Russian Federation
50D2 **Barentu** Eritrea
14B2 **Barfleur, Pointe de** France
43E4 **Bargarh** India
25M4 **Barguzin** Russian Federation
25N4 **Barguzin** *R* Russian Federation
65F2 **Bar Harbor** USA
43F4 **Barhi** India
16D2 **Bari** Italy
15D2 **Barika** Algeria
72D2 **Barinas** Venezuela
43F4 **Baripāda** India
40B5 **Bârîs** Egypt
42C4 **Bari Sādri** India
43G4 **Barisal** Bangladesh
27D7 **Barisan, Pegunungan** *Mts* Indonesia
27E7 **Barito** *R* Indonesia
49D2 **Barjuj** *Watercourse* Libya
31A3 **Barkam** China
64B3 **Barkley,L** USA
47D3 **Barkly East** South Africa
32C2 **Barkly Tableland** *Mts* Australia
13C3 **Bar-le-Duc** France
32A3 **Barlee,L** Australia
32A3 **Barlee Range** *Mts* Australia
16D2 **Barletta** Italy
42C3 **Bārmer** India
34B2 **Barmera** Australia
7B3 **Barmouth** Wales
6D2 **Barnard Castle** England
24K4 **Barnaul** Russian Federation
68C3 **Barnegat** USA
68C3 **Barnegat B** USA
68A2 **Barnesboro** USA
55L2 **Barnes Icecap** Canada
67B2 **Barnesville** Georgia, USA
64C3 **Barnesville** Ohio, USA
62B2 **Barnhart** USA
7D3 **Barnsley** England
7B4 **Barnstaple** England
48C4 **Baro** Nigeria
43G3 **Barpeta** India
72E1 **Barquisimeto** Venezuela
13D3 **Barr** France
73K6 **Barra** Brazil
8B3 **Barra** *I* Scotland
34D2 **Barraba** Australia
75D1 **Barra da Estiva** Brazil
75A2 **Barra do Bugres** Brazil
75B2 **Barra do Garças** Brazil
75D3 **Barra do Piraí** Brazil
51D6 **Barra Falsa, Punta de** *Pt* Mozambique
73K6 **Barragem de Sobradinho** *Res* Brazil
15A2 **Barragem do Castelo do Bode** *Res* Portugal
15A2 **Barragem do Maranhão** *Res* Portugal
8B3 **Barra Head** *Pt* Scotland
73K8 **Barra Mansa** Brazil
72C6 **Barranca** Peru
72D2 **Barrancabermeja** Colombia
72F2 **Barrancas** Venezuela
74E3 **Barranqueras** Argentina
72D1 **Barranquilla** Colombia
8B3 **Barra,Sound of** *Chan* Scotland
68D1 **Barre** USA
73J6 **Barreiras** Brazil
15A2 **Barreiro** Portugal
73L5 **Barreiros** Brazil
32D5 **Barren,C** Australia
73J8 **Barretos** Brazil
65D2 **Barrie** Canada
34B2 **Barrier Range** *Mts* Australia
32E4 **Barrington,Mt** Australia
75C2 **Barro Alto** Brazil
27G8 **Barroloola** Australia
64A1 **Barron** USA
69N2 **Barrouallie** St Vincent
54C2 **Barrow** USA
9C3 **Barrow** *R* Irish Republic
32C3 **Barrow Creek** Australia
32A3 **Barrow I** Australia
6C2 **Barrow-in-Furness** England
54C2 **Barrow,Pt** USA
55J2 **Barrow Str** Canada
7C4 **Barry** Wales
65D1 **Barry's Bay** Canada
68C2 **Barryville** USA
44B2 **Barsi** India
13E1 **Barsinghausen** Germany
56B3 **Barstow** USA
14C2 **Bar-sur-Aube** France
13C3 **Bar-sur-Seine** France
73G2 **Bartica** Guyana
40B1 **Bartın** Turkey
32D2 **Bartle Frere,Mt** Australia
56D3 **Bartlesville** USA
60D2 **Bartlett** USA
51D6 **Bartolomeu Dias** Mozambique
6D3 **Barton-upon-Humber** England
19E2 **Bartoszyce** Poland
72B2 **Barú** *Mt* Panama
42D4 **Barwāh** India
42C4 **Barwāni** India
34C1 **Barwon** *R* Australia
20H5 **Barysh** Russian Federation
66C1 **Basalt** USA
50B3 **Basankusu** Zaïre
Basel = Basle
16D2 **Basento** *R* Italy
26F4 **Bashi Chan** Philippines/Taiwan
20J5 **Bashkortostan** *Division* Russian Federation
27F6 **Basilan** Philippines
27F6 **Basilan** *I* Philippines
7E4 **Basildon** England
58E2 **Basin** USA
7D4 **Basingstoke** England
56B2 **Basin Region** USA
65D1 **Baskatong, Réservoir** Canada
16B1 **Basle** Switzerland
41E3 **Basra** Iraq
13D3 **Bas-Rhin** *Department* France
30D3 **Bassac** *R* Cambodia
16C1 **Bassano** Italy
48C4 **Bassar** Togo
51D6 **Bassas da India** *I* Mozambique Channel
30A2 **Bassein** Burma
69E3 **Basse Terre** Guadeloupe
60D2 **Bassett** USA
48C4 **Bassila** Benin
66C2 **Bass Lake** USA
32D5 **Bass Str** Australia
13E1 **Bassum** Germany
12G7 **Båstad** Sweden
41F4 **Bastak** Iran
43E3 **Basti** India
16B2 **Bastia** Corsica, Italy
18B3 **Bastogne** Belgium
63D2 **Bastrop** Louisiana, USA
63C2 **Bastrop** Texas, USA
48C4 **Bata** Equatorial Guinea
27F5 **Bataan Pen** Philippines
69A2 **Batabanó, G de** Cuba
27E7 **Batakan** Indonesia
42D2 **Batāla** India
26C3 **Batang** China
50B3 **Batangafo** Central African Republic
27F5 **Batangas** Philippines
26F4 **Batan Is** Philippines
75C3 **Batatais** Brazil
65D2 **Batavia** USA
34D3 **Batemans Bay** Australia
67B2 **Batesburg** USA
63D1 **Batesville** Arkansas, USA
63E2 **Batesville** Mississippi, USA
65F1 **Bath** Canada
7C4 **Bath** England
65F2 **Bath** Maine, USA
65D2 **Bath** New York, USA
50B2 **Batha** *R* Chad
7C4 **Bath and North East Somerset** *County* England
64C1 **Bathawana Mt** Canada
32D4 **Bathurst** Australia
55M5 **Bathurst** Canada
54F2 **Bathurst,C** Canada
32C2 **Bathurst I** Australia
54H2 **Bathurst I** Canada
54H3 **Bathurst Inlet** *B* Canada
48B4 **Batié** Burkina
41E4 **Bāṭin, Wadi al** *Watercourse* Iraq
41F3 **Bāṭlāq-e-Gavkhūnī** *Salt Flat* Iran
34C3 **Batlow** Australia
40D2 **Batman** Turkey
16B3 **Batna** Algeria
57D3 **Baton Rouge** USA
45C1 **Batroûn** Lebanon
30C3 **Battambang** Cambodia
44C4 **Batticaloa** Sri Lanka
44E4 **Batti Malv** *I* Nicobar Is, Indian Ocean
7E4 **Battle** England
57E2 **Battle Creek** USA
55N4 **Battle Harbour** Canada
58C2 **Battle Mountain** USA
21G7 **Batumi** Georgia
30C5 **Batu Pahat** Malaysia
45C2 **Bat Yam** Israel
32B1 **Baubau** Indonesia
48C3 **Bauchi** Nigeria
61E1 **Baudette** USA
55N4 **Bauld,C** Canada
25N4 **Baunt** Russian Federation
73J8 **Bauru** Brazil
75B2 **Baús** Brazil
18C2 **Bautzen** Germany
27E7 **Bawean** *I* Indonesia
49E2 **Bawîti** Egypt
48B3 **Bawku** Ghana
30B2 **Bawlake** Burma
34A2 **Bawlen** Australia
67B2 **Baxley** USA
70E2 **Bayamo** Cuba
43J2 **Bayana** India
26D2 **Bayandzürh** Mongolia
26C3 **Bayan Har Shan** *Mts* China
31A1 **Bayan Mod** China
31B1 **Bayan Obo** China
60C2 **Bayard** Nebraska, USA
62A2 **Bayard** New Mexico, USA
25N2 **Bayasgalant** Mongolia
40D1 **Bayburt** Turkey
57E2 **Bay City** Michigan, USA
63C3 **Bay City** Texas, USA
20M2 **Baydaratskaya Guba** *B* Russian Federation
50E3 **Baydhabo** Somalia
18C3 **Bayern** *State* Germany
14B2 **Bayeux** France
64A1 **Bayfield** USA
40C3 **Bāyir** Jordan
Baykal, Ozero *L* = **Baikal, L**
26D1 **Baykalskiy Khrebet** *Mts* Russian Federation
25L3 **Baykit** Russian Federation
25L5 **Baylik Shan** *Mts* China/Mongolia
20K5 **Baymak** Russian Federation
63E2 **Bay Minette** USA
14B3 **Bayonne** France
18C3 **Bayreuth** Germany
63E2 **Bay St Louis** USA
65E2 **Bay Shore** USA
65D1 **Bays,L of** Canada
26B2 **Baytik Shan** *Mts* China
Bayt Lahm = Bethlehem
63D3 **Baytown** USA
15B2 **Baza** Spain
19F3 **Bazaliya** Ukraine
21H7 **Bazar-Dyuzi** *Mt* Azerbaijan
51D6 **Bazaruto, Ilha** Mozambique
14B3 **Bazas** France
31B3 **Bazhong** China
45D1 **Bcharre** Lebanon
60C1 **Beach** USA
68C3 **Beach Haven** USA
7E4 **Beachy Head** England
68D2 **Beacon** USA
51E5 **Bealanana** Madagascar
58D2 **Bear** *R* USA
64A2 **Beardstown** USA
24C2 **Bear I** Barents Sea
58D2 **Bear L** USA
66B1 **Bear Valley** USA
69C3 **Beata, Cabo** *C* Dominican Republic
69C3 **Beata, Isla** Dominican Republic
56D2 **Beatrice** USA
8D2 **Beatrice** *Oilfield* N Sea
54F4 **Beatton River** Canada
56B3 **Beatty** USA
65D1 **Beattyville** Canada
74E8 **Beauchene Is** Falkland Islands
34D1 **Beaudesert** Australia
67B2 **Beaufort** USA
54D2 **Beaufort S** Canada/USA
47C3 **Beaufort West** South Africa
65E1 **Beauharnois** Canada
8C3 **Beauly** Scotland
7B3 **Beaumaris** Wales
59C4 **Beaumont** California, USA
57D3 **Beaumont** Texas, USA
14C2 **Beaune** France
14C2 **Beauvais** France
54D3 **Beaver** USA
59D3 **Beaver** Utah, USA
54G4 **Beaver** *R* Canada
54D3 **Beaver Creek** Canada
64B3 **Beaver Dam** Kentucky, USA
64B2 **Beaver Dam** Wisconsin, USA
58D1 **Beaverhead Mts** USA
64B1 **Beaver I** USA
63D1 **Beaver L** USA
42C3 **Beāwar** India
75C3 **Bebedouro** Brazil
7E3 **Beccles** England
17E1 **Bečej** Serbia, Yugoslavia
48B1 **Béchar** Algeria
57E3 **Beckley** USA
13E2 **Beckum** Germany
6D2 **Bedale** England
13E1 **Bederkesa** Germany
7D3 **Bedford** England
64B3 **Bedford** Indiana, USA
68A3 **Bedford** Pennsylvania, USA
7D3 **Bedford** *County* England
69M2 **Bedford Pt** Grenada
68B2 **Beech Creek** USA
54D2 **Beechey Pt** USA
34C3 **Beechworth** Australia
34D1 **Beenleigh** Australia
45C3 **Beer Menuha** Israel
45C4 **Beer Ora** Israel
40B3 **Beersheba** Israel
Be'er Sheva = Beersheba
45C3 **Be'er Sheva** *R* Israel
56D4 **Beeville** USA
50C3 **Befale** Zaïre
51E5 **Befandriana** Madagascar
34C3 **Bega** Australia
Begicheva, Ostrov *I* = **Bol'shoy Begichev, Ostrov**
15C1 **Begur, C de** Spain
41F3 **Behbehān** Iran
41F2 **Behshahr** Iran
42B2 **Behsud** Afghanistan
26F2 **Bei'an** China
31B5 **Beihai** China
31D2 **Beijing** China
30E1 **Beiliu** China
31B4 **Beipan Jiang** *R* China
31E1 **Beipiao** China
Beira = Sofala
40C3 **Beirut** Lebanon
26C2 **Bei Shan** *Mts* China
47E1 **Beitbridge** Zimbabwe
45C2 **Beit ed Dīne** Lebanon
8C4 **Beith** Scotland
45C3 **Beit Jala** West Bank
28A2 **Beizhen** China
15A2 **Beja** Portugal
16B3 **Béja** Tunisia
15C2 **Bejaïa** Algeria
15A1 **Béjar** Spain
41G3 **Bejestān** Iran
19E3 **Békéscsaba** Hungary
51E6 **Bekily** Madagascar
43E3 **Bela** India
42B3 **Bela** Pakistan
68B3 **Bel Air** USA
44B2 **Belampalli** India
27F6 **Belang** Indonesia
27C6 **Belangpidie** Indonesia
20D5 **Belarus** *Republic* Europe
Belau = Palau
75A3 **Bela Vista** Brazil/Paraguay
47E2 **Bela Vista** Mozambique
27C6 **Belawan** Indonesia
20K4 **Belaya** *R* Russian Federation
19G3 **Belaya Tserkov'** Ukraine
55J2 **Belcher Chan** Canada
55L4 **Belcher Is** Canada
42B1 **Belchiragh** Afghanistan

Belebey Biwa-ko

20J5 **Belebey** Russian Federation
50E3 **Beledweyne** Somalia
73J4 **Belém** Brazil
72C3 **Belén** Colombia
75A3 **Belén** Paraguay
56C3 **Belen** USA
33F2 **Bélep, Îles** Nouvelle Calédonie
16B3 **Belezma, Mts de** Algeria
9C2 **Belfast** Northern Ireland
47E2 **Belfast** South Africa
9C2 **Belfast Lough** *Estuary* Northern Ireland
60C1 **Belfield** USA
50D2 **Bēlfodiyo** Ethiopia
6D2 **Belford** England
14D2 **Belfort** France
44A2 **Belgaum** India
18A2 **Belgium** *Kingdom* NW Europe
21F5 **Belgorod** Russian Federation
21F5 **Belgorod** *Division* Russian Federation
21E6 **Belgorod Dnestrovskiy** Ukraine
58D1 **Belgrade** USA
17E2 **Belgrade** Serbia, Yugoslavia
49D2 **Bel Hedan** Libya
27D7 **Belitung** *I* Indonesia
70D3 **Belize** Belize
70D3 **Belize** *Republic* Central America
25P2 **Bel'kovskiy, Ostrov** *I* Russian Federation
14C2 **Bellac** France
54F4 **Bella Coola** Canada
63C3 **Bellaire** USA
44B2 **Bellary** India
34C1 **Bellata** Australia
68B2 **Bellefonte** USA
56C2 **Belle Fourche** USA
60C2 **Belle Fourche** *R* USA
14D2 **Bellegarde** France
13B4 **Bellegarde** France
67B3 **Belle Glade** USA
55N4 **Belle I** Canada
14B2 **Belle-Ile** *I* France
55N4 **Belle Isle,Str of** Canada
55L5 **Belleville** Canada
64B3 **Belleville** Illinois, USA
61D3 **Belleville** Kansas, USA
58D2 **Bellevue** Idaho, USA
64A2 **Bellevue** Iowa, USA
58B1 **Bellevue** Washington, USA
34D2 **Bellingen** Australia
6C2 **Bellingham** England
56A2 **Bellingham** USA
76G2 **Bellingshausen** *Base* Antarctica
76G3 **Bellingshausen S** Antarctica
16B1 **Bellinzona** Switzerland
72C2 **Bello** Colombia
33E3 **Bellona Reefs** Nouvelle Calédonie
66B1 **Bellota** USA
65E2 **Bellows Falls** USA
55K3 **Bell Pen** Canada
16C1 **Belluno** Italy
74D4 **Bell Ville** Argentina
68B1 **Belmont** USA
73L7 **Belmonte** Brazil
70D3 **Belmopan** Belize
26F1 **Belogorsk** Russian Federation
51E6 **Beloha** Madagascar
73K7 **Belo Horizonte** Brazil
61D3 **Beloit** Kansas, USA
57E2 **Beloit** Wisconsin, USA
20E3 **Belomorsk** Russian Federation
20K5 **Beloretsk** Russian Federation
Belorussia = Belarus
51E5 **Belo-Tsiribihina** Madagascar
Beloye More *S* **= White Sea**
20F3 **Beloye Ozero** *L* Russian Federation
20F3 **Belozersk** Russian Federation
7D3 **Belper** England
64C3 **Belpre** USA
34A2 **Beltana** Australia
63C2 **Belton** USA
19F3 **Bel'tsy** Moldavia
24K5 **Belukha** *Mt* Russian Federation
20H2 **Belush'ye** Russian Federation
64B2 **Belvidere** Illinois, USA
68C2 **Belvidere** New Jersey, USA
24J2 **Belyy, Ostrov** *I* Russian Federation
51B4 **Bembe** Angola
48C3 **Bembéréké** Benin
57D2 **Bemidji** USA
63E1 **Bemis** USA
50C4 **Bena Dibele** Zaïre
34C3 **Benalla** Australia
8C3 **Ben Attow** *Mt* Scotland
15A1 **Benavente** Spain
8B3 **Benbecula** *I* Scotland
32A4 **Bencubbin** Australia
56A2 **Bend** USA
8C3 **Ben Dearg** *Mt* Scotland
50E3 **Bendarbeyla** Somalia
19F3 **Bendery** Moldavia
32D4 **Bendigo** Australia
18C3 **Benešov** Czech Republic
16C2 **Benevento** Italy
39G4 **Bengal,B of** Asia
49D1 **Ben Gardane** Tunisia
31D3 **Bengbu** China
49E1 **Benghazi** Libya
27D7 **Bengkulu** Indonesia
51B5 **Benguela** Angola
40B3 **Benha** Egypt
8C2 **Ben Hope** *Mt* Scotland
50C3 **Beni** Zaïre
72E6 **Béni** *R* Bolivia
48B1 **Beni Abbès** Algeria
15C1 **Benicarló** Spain
15B2 **Benidorm** Spain
15C2 **Beni Manṣour** Algeria
49F2 **Beni Mazâr** Egypt
48B1 **Beni Mellal** Morocco
48C4 **Benin** *Republic* Africa
48C4 **Benin City** Nigeria
15B2 **Beni-Saf** Algeria
49F2 **Beni Suef** Egypt
60C3 **Benkelman** USA
8C2 **Ben Kilbreck** *Mt* Scotland
10C2 **Ben Lawers** *Mt* Scotland
8D3 **Ben Macdui** *Mt* Scotland
8B3 **Ben More** Scotland
8C2 **Ben More Assynt** *Mt* Scotland
35B2 **Benmore,L** New Zealand
25R2 **Bennetta, Ostrov** *I* Russian Federation
8C3 **Ben Nevis** *Mt* Scotland
65E2 **Bennington** USA
45C2 **Bennt Jbail** Lebanon
50B3 **Bénoué** *R* Cameroon
13E3 **Bensheim** Germany
56B3 **Benson** Arizona, USA
61D1 **Benson** Minnesota, USA
27F7 **Benteng** Indonesia
50C3 **Bentiu** Sudan
75A2 **Bento Gomes** *R* Brazil
63D2 **Benton** Arkansas, USA
66C2 **Benton** California, USA
64B3 **Benton** Kentucky, USA
64B2 **Benton Harbor** USA
48C4 **Benue** *R* Nigeria
8C3 **Ben Wyvis** *Mt* Scotland
31E1 **Benxi** China
Beograd = Belgrade
43E4 **Beohāri** India
28C4 **Beppu** Japan
17D2 **Berat** Albania
27G7 **Berau, Teluk** *B* Indonesia
50D2 **Berber** Sudan
50E2 **Berbera** Somalia
50B3 **Berbérati** Central African Republic
19F3 **Berdichev** Ukraine
21F6 **Berdyansk** Ukraine
64C3 **Berea** USA
48B4 **Berekum** Ghana
66B2 **Berenda** USA
40C5 **Berenice** Egypt
54J4 **Berens** *R* Canada
54J4 **Berens River** Canada
61D2 **Beresford** USA
19E3 **Berettyóújfalu** Hungary
19E2 **Bereza** Belarus
19E3 **Berezhany** Ukraine
19F2 **Berezina** *R* Belarus
20G3 **Bereznik** Russian Federation
20K4 **Berezniki** Russian Federation
21E6 **Berezovka** Ukraine
20L3 **Berezovo** Russian Federation
40A2 **Bergama** Turkey
16B1 **Bergamo** Italy
12F6 **Bergen** Norway
68B1 **Bergen** USA
13C2 **Bergen op Zoom** Netherlands
14C3 **Bergerac** France
13D2 **Bergisch-Gladbach** Germany
44C2 **Berhampur** India
25S4 **Beringa, Ostrov** *I* Russian Federation
25T3 **Beringovskiy** Russian Federation
37K2 **Bering S** Russian Federation/USA
76C6 **Bering Str** Russian Federation/USA
41G4 **Berīzak** Iran
15B2 **Berja** Spain
13D1 **Berkel** *R* Germany/ Netherlands
56A3 **Berkeley** USA
68A3 **Berkeley Spring** USA
7D4 **Berkhamsted** England
76F2 **Berkner I** Antarctica
17E2 **Berkovitsa** Bulgaria
7D4 **Berkshire** *County* England
68D1 **Berkshire Hills** USA
18C2 **Berlin** Germany
18C2 **Berlin** *State* Germany
65E2 **Berlin** New Hampshire, USA
72F8 **Bermejo** Bolivia
74E3 **Bermejo** *R* Argentina
53M5 **Bermuda** *I* Atlantic Ocean
Bern = Berne
62A1 **Bernalillo** USA
75B4 **Bernardo de Irigoyen** Argentina
68C2 **Bernardsville** USA
18C2 **Bernburg** Germany
16B1 **Berne** Switzerland
8B3 **Berneray, I** Scotland
55K2 **Bernier B** Canada
18C3 **Berounka** *R* Czech Republic
34B2 **Berri** Australia
48C1 **Berriane** Algeria
14C2 **Berry** *Region* France
66A1 **Berryessa,L** USA
57F4 **Berry Is** The Bahamas
68B3 **Berryville** USA
47B2 **Berseba** Namibia
60B3 **Berthoud P** USA
50B3 **Bertoua** Cameroon
33G1 **Beru** *I* Kiribati
65D2 **Berwick** USA
6C2 **Berwick-upon-Tweed** England
7C3 **Berwyn Mts** Wales
51E5 **Besalampy** Madagascar
14D2 **Besançon** France
19E3 **Beskidy Zachodnie** *Mts* Poland
40C2 **Besni** Turkey
45C3 **Besor** *R* Israel
67A2 **Bessemer** Alabama, USA
64B1 **Bessemer** Michigan, USA
51E5 **Betafo** Madagascar
15A1 **Betanzos** Spain
45C3 **Bet Guvrin** Israel
47D2 **Bethal** South Africa
47B2 **Bethanie** Namibia
61E2 **Bethany** Missouri, USA
63C1 **Bethany** Oklahoma, USA
54B3 **Bethel** Alaska, USA
68D2 **Bethel** Connecticut, USA
64C2 **Bethel Park** USA
65D3 **Bethesda** USA
45C3 **Bethlehem** West Bank
47D2 **Bethlehem** South Africa
65D2 **Bethlehem** USA
47D3 **Bethulie** South Africa
14C1 **Béthune** France
51E6 **Betioky** Madagascar
34B1 **Betoota** Australia
50B3 **Betou** Congo
39E1 **Betpak Dala** *Steppe* Kazakhstan
51E6 **Betroka** Madagascar
55M5 **Betsiamites** Canada
64A2 **Bettendorf** USA
43E3 **Bettiah** India
42D4 **Betūl** India
13C2 **Betuwe** *Region* Netherlands
42D3 **Betwa** *R* India
7C3 **Betws-y-coed** Wales
13D2 **Betzdorf** Germany
7D3 **Beverley** England
68E1 **Beverly** USA
66C3 **Beverly Hills** USA
7E4 **Bexhill** England
40B2 **Bey Dağları** Turkey
48B4 **Beyla** Guinea
44B3 **Beypore** India
Beyrouth = Beirut
40B2 **Beyşehir** Turkey
21E8 **Beyşehir Gölü** *L* Turkey
45C2 **Beyt Shean** Israel
20F4 **Bezhetsk** Russian Federation
14C3 **Béziers** France
41G2 **Bezmein** Turkmenistan
26D1 **Beznosova** Russian Federation
43F3 **Bhadgaon** Nepal
44C2 **Bhadrāchalam** India
43F4 **Bhadrakh** India
44B3 **Bhadra Res** India
44B3 **Bhadrāvati** India
42B3 **Bhag** Pakistan
43F3 **Bhāgalpur** India
42C2 **Bhakkar** Pakistan
42D4 **Bhandāra** India
42D3 **Bharatpur** India
42C4 **Bharūch** India
43F4 **Bhātiāpāra Ghat** Bangladesh
42C2 **Bhatinda** India
44A3 **Bhatkal** India
43F4 **Bhātpāra** India
42C4 **Bhāvnagar** India
43E5 **Bhawānipatna** India
42C2 **Bhera** Pakistan
43E3 **Bheri** *R* Nepal
43E4 **Bhilai** India
42C3 **Bhīlwāra** India
44C2 **Bhīmavaram** India
42D3 **Bhind** India
42D3 **Bhiwāni** India
44B2 **Bhongir** India
42D4 **Bhopāl** India
43F4 **Bhubaneshwar** India
42B4 **Bhuj** India
42D4 **Bhusāwal** India
39H3 **Bhutan** *Kingdom* Asia
27G7 **Biak** *I* Indonesia
19E2 **Biala Podlaska** Poland
18D2 **Białogard** Poland
19E2 **Bialystok** Poland
12A1 **Biargtangar** *C* Iceland
41G2 **Biārjmand** Iran
14B3 **Biarritz** France
40B4 **Biba** Egypt
29E2 **Bibai** Japan
51B5 **Bibala** Angola
18B3 **Biberach** Germany
48B4 **Bibiani** Ghana
17F1 **Bicaz** Romania
7D4 **Bicester** England
59D3 **Bicknell** USA
48C4 **Bida** Nigeria
44B2 **Bīdar** India
41G5 **Bidbid** Oman
65E2 **Biddeford** USA
7C6 **Bideford** England
7B4 **Bideford B** England
48C2 **Bidon 5** Algeria
19E2 **Biebrza** *R* Poland
16B1 **Biel** Switzerland
18D2 **Bielawa** Poland
18B2 **Bielefeld** Germany
16B1 **Biella** Italy
19E2 **Bielsk Podlaski** Poland
30D3 **Bien Hoa** Vietnam
55L4 **Bienville, Lac** Canada
16C2 **Biferno** *R* Italy
40A1 **Biga** Turkey
17F3 **Bigadiç** Turkey
58D1 **Big Belt Mts** USA
62B3 **Big Bend Nat Pk** USA
63E2 **Big Black** *R* USA
61D2 **Big Blue** *R* USA
67B3 **Big Cypress Swamp** USA
54D3 **Big Delta** USA
8D4 **Biggar** Scotland
54H4 **Biggar Kindersley** Canada
34D1 **Biggenden** Australia
7D3 **Biggleswade** England
58D1 **Big Hole** *R* USA
60B1 **Bighorn** *R* USA
60B1 **Bighorn L** USA
60B2 **Bighorn Mts** USA
48C4 **Bight of Benin** *B* W Africa
48C4 **Bight of Biafra** *B* Cameroon
55L3 **Big I** Canada
62B2 **Big Lake** USA
48A3 **Bignona** Senegal
59C3 **Big Pine** USA
67B4 **Big Pine Key** USA
66C3 **Big Pine Mt** USA
64B2 **Big Rapids** USA
54H4 **Big River** Canada
58D1 **Big Sandy** USA
61D2 **Big Sioux** *R* USA
66D1 **Big Smokey V** USA
56C3 **Big Spring** USA
60C2 **Big Springs** USA
61D1 **Big Stone City** USA
64C3 **Big Stone Gap** USA
66B2 **Big Sur** USA
58E1 **Big Timber** USA
55J4 **Big Trout L** Canada
55K4 **Big Trout Lake** Canada
16D2 **Bihać** Bosnia-Herzegovina
43F3 **Bihār** India
43F4 **Bihār** *State* India
50D4 **Biharamulo** Tanzania
21C6 **Bihor** *Mt* Romania
48A3 **Bijagós, Arquipélago dos** *Is* Guinea-Bissau
44B2 **Bijāpur** India
44C2 **Bījāpur** India
41E2 **Bījār** Iran
43E3 **Bijauri** Nepal
17D2 **Bijeljina** Bosnia-Herzegovina
31B4 **Bijie** China
42D3 **Bijnor** India
42C3 **Bijnot** Pakistan
42C3 **Bīkāner** India
45C2 **Bikfaya** Lebanon
26G2 **Bikin** Russian Federation
50B4 **Bikoro** Zaïre
Bilbo = Bilbao
42C3 **Bilāra** India
42D2 **Bilāspur** India
43E4 **Bilāspur** India
30B3 **Bilauktaung Range** *Mts* Burma/Thailand
15B1 **Bilbao** Spain
45A3 **Bilbeis** Egypt
18D3 **Bílé** *R* Czech Republic/ Slovakia
17D2 **Bileća** Bosnia-Herzegovina
40B1 **Bilecik** Turkey
50C3 **Bili** *R* Zaïre
25S3 **Bilibino** Russian Federation
56C2 **Billings** USA
50B2 **Bilma** Niger
57E3 **Biloxi** USA
50C2 **Biltine** Chad
67C3 **Bimini Is** Bahamas
42D4 **Bīna-Etawa** India
51D5 **Bindura** Zimbabwe
51C5 **Binga** Zimbabwe
51D5 **Binga, Mt** Mozambique/ Zimbabwe
34D1 **Bingara** Australia
18B3 **Bingen** Germany
65F1 **Bingham** USA
57F2 **Binghamton** USA
40D2 **Bingöl** Turkey
31D3 **Binhai** China
15C2 **Binibeca, Cabo** *C* Spain
27D6 **Bintan** *I* Indonesia
27E6 **Bintulu** Malaysia
74B5 **Bió Bió** *R* Chile
48C4 **Bioco** *I* Equatorial Guinea
44B2 **Bīr** India
49E2 **Bîr Abu Husein** *Well* Egypt
49E2 **Bi'r al Harash** *Well* Libya
50C2 **Birao** Central African Republic
43F3 **Biratnagar** Nepal
34B3 **Birchip** Australia
61E1 **Birch L** USA
54G4 **Birch Mts** Canada
55J4 **Bird** Canada
32C3 **Birdsville** Australia
32C2 **Birdum** Australia
45A4 **Bîr el 'Agramîya** *Well* Egypt
45B3 **Bîr el Duweidâr** *Well* Egypt
43E3 **Birganj** Nepal
45B3 **Bîr Gifgâfa** *Well* Egypt
45A4 **Bîr Gindali** *Well* Egypt
45B3 **Bîr Hasana** *Well* Egypt
75B3 **Birigui** Brazil
45D1 **Bīrīn** Syria
41G3 **Bīrjand** Iran
40B4 **Birkat Qârun** *L* Egypt
13D3 **Birkenfeld** Germany
7C3 **Birkenhead** England
21D6 **Bîrlad** Romania
45B3 **Bîr Lahfân** *Well* Egypt
7C3 **Birmingham** England
57E3 **Birmingham** USA
49E2 **Bîr Misâha** *Well* Egypt
48A2 **Bir Moghrein** Mauritius
48C3 **Birnin-Kebbi** Nigeria
26G2 **Birobidzhan** Russian Federation
9C3 **Birr** Irish Republic
15C2 **Bir Rabalou** Algeria
34C1 **Birrie** *R* Australia
8D2 **Birsay** Scotland
20K4 **Birsk** Russian Federation
49E2 **Bîr Tarfâwi** *Well* Egypt
45B4 **Bîr Udelb** *Well* Egypt
25L4 **Biryusa** *R* Russian Federation
12J7 **Biržai** Lithuania
48B2 **Bir Zreigat** *Well* Mauritius
43K1 **Bisalpur** India
59E4 **Bisbee** USA
14A2 **Biscay,B of** France/Spain
67B3 **Biscayne B** USA
13D3 **Bischwiller** France
64C1 **Biscotasi L** Canada
31B4 **Bishan** China
39F1 **Bishkek** Kirgizia
56B3 **Bishop** USA
6D2 **Bishop Auckland** England
7C3 **Bishops Castle** England
7E4 **Bishop's Stortford** England
43E4 **Bishrāmpur** India
48C1 **Biskra** Algeria
56C2 **Bismarck** USA
32D1 **Bismarck Arch** Papua New Guinea
32D1 **Bismarck Range** *Mts* Papua New Guinea
32D1 **Bismarck S** Papua New Guinea
41E3 **Bīsotūn** Iran
48A3 **Bissau** Guinea-Bissau
57D1 **Bissett** Canada
54G4 **Bistcho L** Canada
17F1 **Bistrita** *R* Romania
50B3 **Bitam** Gabon
18B3 **Bitburg** Germany
13D3 **Bitche** France
40D2 **Bitlis** Turkey
17E2 **Bitola** Macedonia, Yugoslavia
18C2 **Bitterfeld** Germany
47B3 **Bitterfontein** South Africa
40B3 **Bitter Lakes** Egypt
56B2 **Bitteroot Range** *Mts* USA
48D3 **Biu** Nigeria
29D3 **Biwa-ko** *L* Japan

Biyo Kaboba Brecon

50E2 **Biyo Kaboba** Ethiopia
24K4 **Biysk** Russian Federation
16B3 **Bizerte** Tunisia
16D1 **Bjelovar** Croatia
48B2 **Bj Flye Ste Marie** Algeria
Bjørnøya *I* = **Bear I**
63D1 **Black** *R* USA
32D3 **Blackall** Australia
64B1 **Black B** Canada
6C3 **Blackburn** England
54D3 **Blackburn, Mt** USA
59D4 **Black Canyon City** USA
61E1 **Blackduck** USA
58D1 **Black Eagle** USA
58D2 **Blackfoot** USA
58D1 **Blackfoot** *R* USA
9B3 **Black Hd** *Pt* Irish Republic
54H5 **Black Hills** USA
8C3 **Black Isle** *Pen* Scotland
69Q2 **Blackman's** Barbados
59D3 **Black Mts** USA
7C4 **Black Mts** Wales
47B1 **Black Nosob** *R* Namibia
6C3 **Blackpool** England
69H1 **Black River** Jamaica
64A2 **Black River Falls** USA
56B2 **Black Rock Desert** USA
21D7 **Black S** Asia/Europe
64C3 **Blacksburg** USA
34D2 **Black Sugarloaf** *Mt* Australia
48B4 **Black Volta** *R* W Africa
63E2 **Black Warrior** *R* USA
7E4 **Blackwater** *R* England
10B3 **Blackwater** *R* Irish Republic
63C1 **Blackwell** USA
17E2 **Blagoevgrad** Bulgaria
25O4 **Blagoveshchensk** Russian Federation
58D1 **Blaikiston,Mt** Canada
58B1 **Blaine** USA
61D2 **Blair** USA
8D3 **Blair Atholl** Scotland
8D3 **Blairgowrie** Scotland
67C2 **Blakely** USA
74D5 **Blanca, Bahía** *B* Argentina
62A1 **Blanca Peak** *Mt* USA
16B3 **Blanc, C** Tunisia
34A1 **Blanche** *L* Australia
16B1 **Blanc, Mont** *Mt* France/Italy
56A2 **Blanco,C** USA
55N4 **Blanc Sablon** Canada
7C4 **Blandford Forum** England
59E3 **Blanding** USA
13B2 **Blankenberge** Belgium
69E4 **Blanquilla, Isla** Venezuela
51D5 **Blantyre** Malawi
9A3 **Blasket Sd** Irish Republic
14B2 **Blaye** France
34C2 **Blayney** Australia
7C4 **Bleaneau Gwent** *County* Wales
33G5 **Blenheim** New Zealand
15C2 **Blida** Algeria
64C1 **Blind River** Canada
34A2 **Blinman** Australia
65E2 **Block I** USA
68E2 **Block Island Sd** USA
47D2 **Bloemfontein** South Africa
47D2 **Bloemhof** South Africa
47D2 **Bloemhof Dam** *Res* South Africa
73G3 **Blommesteinmeer** *L* Surinam
12A1 **Blönduós** Iceland
64B3 **Bloomfield** Indiana, USA
61E2 **Bloomfield** Iowa, USA
61D2 **Bloomfield** Nebraska,USA
62A1 **Bloomfield** New Mexico, USA
64B2 **Bloomington** Illinois, USA
64B3 **Bloomington** Indiana, USA
61E2 **Bloomington** Minnesota, USA
68B2 **Bloomsburg** USA
68B2 **Blossburg** USA
55Q3 **Blosseville Kyst** *Mts* Greenland
47D1 **Blouberg** *Mt* South Africa
18B3 **Bludenz** Austria
57E3 **Bluefield** USA
72B1 **Bluefields** Nicaragua
60D2 **Blue Hill** USA
68A2 **Blue Knob** *Mt* USA
69J1 **Blue Mountain Peak** *Mt* Jamaica
68B2 **Blue Mt** USA
34D2 **Blue Mts** Australia
56A2 **Blue Mts** USA
69J1 **Blue Mts, The** Jamaica
50D2 **Blue Nile** *R* Sudan
54G3 **Bluenose L** Canada
67C2 **Blue Ridge** USA
57E3 **Blue Ridge Mts** USA
9C2 **Blue Stack** *Mt* Irish Republic
35A3 **Bluff** New Zealand
59E3 **Bluff** USA
32A4 **Bluff Knoll** *Mt* Australia
74G3 **Blumenau** Brazil
60D2 **Blunt** USA
58B2 **Bly** USA
6D2 **Blyth** England
56B3 **Blythe** USA
57E3 **Blytheville** USA
48A4 **Bo** Sierra Leone
27F5 **Boac** Philippines
75D1 **Boa Nova** Brazil
64C2 **Boardman** USA
72F3 **Boa Vista** Brazil
48A4 **Boa Vista** *I* Cape Verde
30E1 **Bobai** China
44C2 **Bobbili** India
48B3 **Bobo Dioulasso** Burkina
19G2 **Bobrovica** Ukraine
20D5 **Bobruysk** Belarus
67B4 **Boca Chica Key** *I* USA
72E5 **Bôca do Acre** Brazil
75D2 **Bocaiúva** Brazil
50B3 **Bocaranga** Central African Republic
67B3 **Boca Raton** USA
19E3 **Bochnia** Poland
18B2 **Bocholt** Germany
13D2 **Bochum** Germany
51B5 **Bocoio** Angola
50B3 **Boda** Central African Republic
25N4 **Bodaybo** Russian Federation
59B3 **Bodega Head** *Pt* USA
50B2 **Bodélé** *Desert Region* Chad
12J5 **Boden** Sweden
9C3 **Boderg, L** Irish Republic
44B2 **Bodhan** India
44B3 **Bodināyakkanūr** India
7B4 **Bodmin** England
7B4 **Bodmin Moor** *Upland* England
12G5 **Bodø** Norway
17F3 **Bodrum** Turkey
50C4 **Boende** Zaïre
48A3 **Boffa** Guinea
30B2 **Bogale** Burma
63E2 **Bogalusa** USA
34C2 **Bogan** *R* Australia
48B3 **Bogande** Burkina
40C2 **Boğazlıyan** Turkey
20L4 **Bogdanovich** Russian Federation
26B2 **Bogda Shan** *Mt* China
47B2 **Bogenfels** Namibia
34D1 **Boggabilla** Australia
34C2 **Boggabri** Australia
7D4 **Bognor Regis** England
34C3 **Bogong** *Mt* Australia
27D7 **Bogor** Indonesia
25Q4 **Bogorodskoye** Russian Federation
20J4 **Bogorodskoye** Russian Federation
72D3 **Bogotá** Colombia
25K4 **Bogotol** Russian Federation
43F4 **Bogra** Bangladesh
31D2 **Bo Hai** *B* China
13B3 **Bohain-en-Vermandois** France
31D2 **Bohai Wan** *B* China
18C3 **Bohmer-wald** *Upland* Germany
27F6 **Bohol** *I* Philippines
27F6 **Bohol S** Philippines
75E1 **Boipeba, Ilha de** Brazil
75B2 **Bois** *R* Brazil
64C1 **Bois Blanc I** USA
56B2 **Boise** USA
62B1 **Boise City** USA
54F3 **Bois, Lac des** Canada
60C1 **Boissevain** Canada
48A2 **Bojador,C** Morocco
27F5 **Bojeador, C** Philippines
41G2 **Bojnūrd** Iran
48A3 **Boké** Guinea
34C1 **Bokhara** *R* Australia
12F7 **Boknafjord** *Inlet* Norway
50B4 **Boko** Congo
30C3 **Bokor** Cambodia
50B2 **Bokoro** Chad
50C4 **Bokungu** Zaïre
50B2 **Bol** Chad
48A3 **Bolama** Guinea-Bissau
14C2 **Bolbec** France
48B4 **Bole** Ghana
18D2 **Bolesławiec** Poland
48B3 **Bolgatanga** Ghana
21D6 **Bolgrad** Ukraine
63D1 **Bolivar** Missouri, USA
63E1 **Bolivar** Tennessee, USA
72D2 **Bolívar** *Mt* Venezuela
72E7 **Bolivia** *Republic* S America
12H6 **Bollnäs** Sweden
34C1 **Bollon** Australia
50B4 **Bolobo** Zaïre
16C2 **Bologna** Italy
20E4 **Bologoye** Russian Federation
26G1 **Bolon'** Russian Federation
26G2 **Bolon', Oz** *L* Russian Federation
16C2 **Bolsena, L di** Italy
25M2 **Bol'shevik, Ostrov** *I* Russian Federation
20J2 **Bol'shezemel'skaya Tundra** *Plain* Russian Federation
25S3 **Bol'shoy Anyuy** *R* Russian Federation
25N2 **Bol'shoy Begichev, Ostrov** *I* Russian Federation
21H5 **Bol'shoy Irgiz** *R* Russian Federation
28C2 **Bol'shoy Kamen** Russian Federation
25Q2 **Bol'shoy Lyakhovskiy, Ostrov** *I* Russian Federation
21H6 **Bol'shoy Uzen** *R* Kazakhstan
56C4 **Bolson de Mapimí** *Desert* Mexico
7C3 **Bolton** England
40B1 **Bolu** Turkey
12A1 **Bolungarvik** Iceland
9A4 **Bolus Hd** *Pt* Irish Republic
40B2 **Bolvadin** Turkey
16C1 **Bolzano** Italy
50B4 **Boma** Zaïre
32D4 **Bombala** Australia
44A2 **Bombay** India
51E5 **Bombetoka, Baie de** *B* Madagascar
50D3 **Bombo** Uganda
75C2 **Bom Despacho** Brazil
43G3 **Bomdila** India
48A4 **Bomi Hills** Liberia
73K6 **Bom Jesus da Lapa** Brazil
25O4 **Bomnak** Russian Federation
50C3 **Bomokāndi** *R* Zaïre
50C3 **Bomu** *R* Central African Republic/Zaïre
65D3 **Bon Air** USA
69D4 **Bonaire** *I* Caribbean Sea
70D3 **Bonanza** Nicaragua
55N5 **Bonavista** Canada
16C3 **Bon, C** Tunisia
50C3 **Bondo** Zaïre
48B4 **Bondoukou** Ivory Coast
Bône = **'Annaba**
60D2 **Bonesteel** USA
73G3 **Bonfim** Guyana
50C3 **Bongandanga** Zaïre
50C3 **Bongo, Massif des** *Upland* Central African Republic
50B2 **Bongor** Chad
63C2 **Bonham** USA
16B2 **Bonifacio** Corsica, France
16B2 **Bonifacio,Str of** *Chan* Corsica, France/Sardinia, Italy
Bonin Is = **Ogasawara Gunto**
67B3 **Bonita Springs** USA
75A3 **Bonito** Brazil
18B2 **Bonn** Germany
58C1 **Bonners Ferry** USA
48C4 **Bonny** Nigeria
32A1 **Bonthain** Indonesia
48A4 **Bonthe** Sierra Leone
50E2 **Booaaso** Somalia
34B2 **Booligal** Australia
34D1 **Boonah** Australia
62B1 **Boone** Colorado, USA
61E2 **Boone** Iowa, USA
67B1 **Boone** North Carolina, USA
65D2 **Boonville** USA
34C2 **Boorowa** Australia
55J2 **Boothia,G of** Canada
55J2 **Boothia Pen** Canada
7C3 **Bootle** England
50B4 **Booué** Gabon
62B3 **Boquillas** Mexico
50D3 **Bor** Sudan
40B2 **Bor** Turkey
17E2 **Bor** Serbia, Yugoslavia
56B2 **Borah Peak** *Mt* USA
12G7 **Borås** Sweden
41F4 **Borāzjān** Iran
14B3 **Bordeaux** France
54G2 **Borden I** Canada
55K2 **Borden Pen** Canada
68C2 **Bordentown** USA
34B3 **Bordertown** Australia
15C2 **Bordj bou Arréidj** Algeria
48C2 **Bordj Omar Driss** Algeria
Borgå = **Porvoo**
55Q3 **Borgarnes** Iceland
56C3 **Borger** USA
12H7 **Borgholm** Sweden
19E3 **Borislav** Ukraine
21G5 **Borisoglebsk** Russian Federation
20D5 **Borisov** Belarus
21F5 **Borisovka** Russian Federation
75A4 **Borja** Paraguay
50B2 **Borkou** *Desert Region* Chad
13D1 **Borkum** *I* Germany
12H6 **Borlänge** Sweden
27E6 **Borneo** *I* Indonesia/Malaysia
12H7 **Bornholm** *I* Denmark
17F3 **Bornova** Turkey
48D3 **Bornu** *Region* Nigeria
50C3 **Boro** *R* Sudan
25P3 **Borogontsy** Russian Federation
48B3 **Boromo** Burkina
66D3 **Boron** USA
20E4 **Borovichi** Russian Federation
32C2 **Borroloola** Australia
17E1 **Borsa** Romania
41F3 **Borūjen** Iran
41E3 **Borūjerd** Iran
18D2 **Bory Tucholskie** *Region* Poland
19G2 **Borzna** Ukraine
25N4 **Borzya** Russian Federation
31B5 **Bose** China
47D2 **Boshof** South Africa
17D2 **Bosna** *R* Bosnia-Herzegovina
17D2 **Bosnia-Herzegovina** *Republic* Europe
29D3 **Bōsō-hantō** *B* Japan
Bosporus = **Karadeniz Boğazi**
15C2 **Bosquet** Algeria
50B3 **Bossangoa** Central African Republic
50B3 **Bossèmbélé** Central African Republic
63D2 **Bossier City** USA
24K5 **Bosten Hu** *L* China
7D3 **Boston** England
57F2 **Boston** USA
57D3 **Boston Mts** USA
42C4 **Botād** India
17E2 **Botevgrad** Bulgaria
47D2 **Bothaville** South Africa
20B3 **Bothnia,G of** Finland/Sweden
51C6 **Botletli** *R* Botswana
21D6 **Botoşani** Romania
51C6 **Botswana** *Republic* Africa
16D3 **Botte Donato** *Mt* Italy
60C1 **Bottineau** USA
13D2 **Bottrop** Germany
75C3 **Botucatu** Brazil
75D1 **Botuporã** Brazil
55N5 **Botwood** Canada
48B4 **Bouaké** Ivory Coast
50B3 **Bouar** Central African Republic
48B1 **Bouârfa** Morocco
50B3 **Bouca** Central African Republic
15C2 **Boufarik** Algeria
33E1 **Bougainville** *I* Papua New Guinea
16B3 **Bougaroun, C** Algeria
Bougie = **Bejaïa**
48B3 **Bougouni** Mali
15A2 **Bouhalla, Djebel** *Mt* Morocco
13C3 **Bouillon** France
15C2 **Bouïra** Algeria
48B2 **Bou Izakarn** Morocco
13D3 **Boulay-Moselle** France
56C2 **Boulder** Colorado, USA
58D1 **Boulder** Montana, USA
56B3 **Boulder City** USA
66A2 **Boulder Creek** USA
14C1 **Boulogne** France
50B3 **Boumba** *R* Cameroon/Central African Republic
48B4 **Bouna** Ivory Coast
56B3 **Boundary Peak** *Mt* USA
48B4 **Boundiali** Ivory Coast
58D2 **Bountiful** USA
33G5 **Bounty Is** New Zealand
33F3 **Bourail** New Caledonia
13C4 **Bourbonne-les-Bains** France
48B3 **Bourem** Mali
14D2 **Bourg** France
14D2 **Bourg de Péage** France
14C2 **Bourges** France
14C3 **Bourg-Madame** France
14C2 **Bourgogne** *Region* France
34C2 **Bourke** Australia
7D4 **Bournemouth** England
15C2 **Bou Saâda** Algeria
50B2 **Bousso** Chad
48A3 **Boutilimit** Mauritius
52J7 **Bouvet I** Atlantic Ocean
60C1 **Bowbells** USA
32D2 **Bowen** Australia
59E4 **Bowie** Arizona, USA
63C2 **Bowie** Texas, USA
6C3 **Bowland Fells** England
57E3 **Bowling Green** Kentucky, USA
63D1 **Bowling Green** Missouri, USA
64C2 **Bowling Green** Ohio, USA
65D3 **Bowling Green** Virginia, USA
60C1 **Bowman** USA
65D2 **Bowmanville** Canada
9C3 **Bowna, L** Irish Republic
34D2 **Bowral** Australia
31D3 **Bo Xian** China
31D2 **Boxing** China
40B1 **Boyabat** Turkey
50B3 **Boyali** Central African Republic
19G2 **Boyarka** Ukraine
54J4 **Boyd** Canada
68C2 **Boyertown** USA
10B3 **Boyle** Irish Republic
9C3 **Boyne** *R* Irish Republic
67B3 **Boynton Beach** USA
50C3 **Boyoma Falls** Zaïre
58E2 **Boysen Res** USA
17D1 **Bozanski Brod** Bosnia-Herzegovina/Croatia
17F3 **Bozca Ada** *I* Turkey
17F3 **Boz Dağları** *Mts* Turkey
56B2 **Bozeman** USA
Bozen = **Bolzano**
50B3 **Bozene** Zaïre
50B3 **Bozoum** Central African Republic
16D2 **Brač** *I* Croatia
8B3 **Bracadale, Loch** *Inlet* Scotland
16C2 **Bracciano, L di** Italy
65D1 **Bracebridge** Canada
49D2 **Brach** Libya
12H6 **Bräcke** Sweden
62B3 **Brackettville** USA
67B3 **Bradenton** USA
6D3 **Bradford** England
68A2 **Bradford** USA
66B3 **Bradley** USA
62C2 **Brady** USA
8E1 **Brae** Scotland
8D3 **Braemar** Scotland
15A1 **Braga** Portugal
73J4 **Bragança** Brazil
15A1 **Bragança** Portugal
75C3 **Bragança Paulista** Brazil
43G4 **Brahman-Baria** Bangladesh
43F4 **Brāhmani** *R* India
43G3 **Brahmaputra** *R* Bangladesh/India
21D6 **Brăila** Romania
57D2 **Brainerd** USA
7E4 **Braintree** England
47C3 **Brak** *R* South Africa
47D1 **Brak** *R* South Africa
13E1 **Brake** Germany
48A3 **Brakna** *Region* Mauritius
54F4 **Bralorne** Canada
65D2 **Brampton** Canada
6C2 **Brampton** England
13D1 **Bramsche** Germany
72F3 **Branco** *R* Brazil
51B6 **Brandberg** *Mt* Namibia
18C2 **Brandenburg** Germany
18C2 **Brandenburg** *State* Germany
47D2 **Brandfort** South Africa
56D2 **Brandon** Canada
61D2 **Brandon** USA
47C3 **Brandvlei** South Africa
18C2 **Brandýs-nad-Laben** Czech Republic
19D2 **Braniewo** Poland
57F2 **Brantford** Canada
34B3 **Branxholme** Australia
55M5 **Bras d'Or Lakes** Canada
72E6 **Brasiléia** Brazil
73J7 **Brasília** Brazil
75D2 **Brasília de Minas** Brazil
17F1 **Braşov** Romania
18D3 **Bratislava** Slovakia
25M4 **Bratsk** Russian Federation
19F3 **Bratslav** Ukraine
65E2 **Brattleboro** USA
18C2 **Braunschweig** Germany
48A4 **Brava** *I* Cape Verde
56B3 **Brawley** USA
9C3 **Bray** Irish Republic
55L3 **Bray I** Canada
13B3 **Bray-sur-Seine** France
71E5 **Brazil** *Republic* S America
52G5 **Brazil Basin** Atlantic Ocean
56D3 **Brazos** *R* USA
50B4 **Brazzaville** Congo
18C3 **Brdy** *Upland* Czech Republic
35A3 **Breaksea Sd** New Zealand
35B1 **Bream B** New Zealand
8D3 **Brechin** Scotland
13C2 **Brecht** Belgium
61D1 **Breckenridge** Minnesota, USA
62C2 **Breckenridge** Texas, USA
7E3 **Breckland** England
18D3 **Břeclav** Czech Republic
7C4 **Brecon** Wales

Brecon Beacons Cairngorms

7C4 **Brecon Beacons** *Mts* Wales
7B3 **Brecon Beacons Nat Pk** Wales
18A2 **Breda** Netherlands
47C3 **Bredasdorp** South Africa
12H6 **Bredbyn** Sweden
20K5 **Bredy** Russian Federation
47B3 **Breede** *R* South Africa
65D2 **Breezewood** USA
12A1 **Breiethafjörethur** *B* Iceland
13D3 **Breisach** Germany
67A2 **Bremen** USA
18B2 **Bremen** Germany
18B2 **Bremerhaven** Germany
58B1 **Bremerton** USA
13E1 **Bremervörde** Germany
59E3 **Brendel** USA
63C2 **Brenham** USA
18C3 **Brenner** *P* Austria/Italy
66B2 **Brentwood** USA
16C1 **Brescia** Italy
Breslau = Wrocław
8E1 **Bressay** *I* Scotland
14B2 **Bressuire** France
14B2 **Brest** France
19E2 **Brest** Belarus
14B2 **Bretagne** *Region* France
13B3 **Breteuil** France
63E3 **Breton Sd** USA
68C2 **Breton Woods** USA
35B1 **Brett,C** New Zealand
67B1 **Brevard** USA
34C1 **Brewarrina** Australia
65F2 **Brewer** USA
68D2 **Brewster** New York, USA
58C1 **Brewster** Washington, USA
67A2 **Brewton** USA
47D2 **Breyten** South Africa
16D1 **Brežice** Slovenia
50C3 **Bria** Central African Republic
14D3 **Briançon** France
14C2 **Briare** France
7C4 **Bridgend** Wales
7C4 **Bridgend** *County* Wales
8C3 **Bridge of Orchy** Scotland
67A2 **Bridgeport** Alabama, USA
59C3 **Bridgeport** California, USA
65E2 **Bridgeport** Connecticut, USA
60C2 **Bridgeport** Nebraska, USA
63C2 **Bridgeport** Texas, USA
66C1 **Bridgeport Res** USA
58E1 **Bridger** USA
60B2 **Bridger Peak** USA
68C3 **Bridgeton** USA
69R3 **Bridgetown** Barbados
55M5 **Bridgewater** Canada
68E2 **Bridgewater** USA
7C4 **Bridgwater** England
7C4 **Bridgwater B** England
6D2 **Bridlington** England
6E3 **Bridlington Bay** England
34C4 **Bridport** Australia
7C4 **Bridport** England
13C3 **Brienne-le-Château** France
13C3 **Briey** France
16B1 **Brig** Switzerland
56B2 **Brigham City** USA
34C3 **Bright** Australia
7D4 **Brighton** England
75A3 **Brilhante** *R* Brazil
13E2 **Brilon** Germany
17D2 **Brindisi** Italy
63D2 **Brinkley** USA
33E3 **Brisbane** Australia
65E2 **Bristol** Connecticut, USA
7C4 **Bristol** *County* England
7C4 **Bristol** England
65E2 **Bristol** Pennsylvania, USA
68E2 **Bristol** Rhode Island, USA
57E3 **Bristol** Tennessee, USA
64C3 **Bristol** USA
7B4 **Bristol Chan** England/Wales
54F4 **British Columbia** *Province* Canada
55K1 **British Empire Range** *Mts* Canada
54E3 **British Mts** Canada
47D2 **Brits** South Africa
47C3 **Britstown** South Africa
61D1 **Britton** USA
14C2 **Brive** France
7C4 **Brixham** England
18D3 **Brno** Czech Republic
67B2 **Broad** *R* USA
68C1 **Broadalbin** USA
55L4 **Broadback** *R* Canada
8B2 **Broad Bay** *Inlet* Scotland
8C3 **Broadford** Scotland
9B2 **Broad Haven, B** Irish Republic
7E4 **Broadstairs** England
60B1 **Broadus** USA
60C2 **Broadwater** USA
54H4 **Brochet** Canada
54G2 **Brock I** Canada
65D2 **Brockport** USA
68E1 **Brockton** USA
65D2 **Brockville** Canada
68A2 **Brockway** USA
55K2 **Brodeur Pen** Canada
8C4 **Brodick** Scotland
19D2 **Brodnica** Poland
21D5 **Brody** Ukraine
13D2 **Brokem Haltern** Germany
60D2 **Broken Bow** Nebraska, USA
63D2 **Broken Bow** Oklahoma, USA
63D2 **Broken Bow L** USA
32D4 **Broken Hill** Australia
7C3 **Bromsgrove** England
12G5 **Brønnøysund** Norway
68D2 **Bronx** *Borough* New York, USA
27E6 **Brooke's Pt** Philippines
61E3 **Brookfield** Missouri, USA
64B2 **Brookfield** Wisconsin, USA
57D3 **Brookhaven** USA
58B2 **Brookings** Oregon, USA
56D2 **Brookings** South Dakota, USA
68E1 **Brookline** USA
61E2 **Brooklyn** USA
68D2 **Brooklyn** *Borough* New York, USA
61E1 **Brooklyn Center** USA
54G4 **Brooks** Canada
54C3 **Brooks Range** *Mts* USA
67B3 **Brooksville** USA
34D1 **Brooloo** Australia
32B2 **Broome** Australia
8C3 **Broom, Loch** *Estuary* Scotland
8D2 **Brora** Scotland
58B2 **Brothers** USA
6C2 **Broughton** England
8D3 **Broughty Ferry** Scotland
50B2 **Broulkou** *Well* Chad
19G2 **Brovary** Ukraine
61E1 **Browerville** USA
62B2 **Brownfield** USA
56D4 **Brownsville** USA
56D3 **Brownwood** USA
27F8 **Browse I** Australia
13B2 **Bruay-en-Artois** France
32A3 **Bruce,Mt** Australia
64C1 **Bruce Pen** Canada
13E3 **Bruchsal** Germany
18D3 **Bruck an der Mur** Austria
Bruges = Brugge
13B2 **Brugge** Belgium
13D2 **Brühl** Germany
45B3 **Brûk, Wadi el** Egypt
75D1 **Brumado** Brazil
13D3 **Brumath** France
58C2 **Bruneau** USA
58C2 **Bruneau** *R* USA
27E6 **Brunei** *State* Borneo
16C1 **Brunico** Italy
35B2 **Brunner,L** New Zealand
13E1 **Brunsbüttel** Germany
57E3 **Brunswick** Georgia, USA
65F2 **Brunswick** Maine, USA
61E3 **Brunswick** Mississippi, USA
74B8 **Brunswick,Pen de** Chile
34C4 **Bruny I** Australia
20G3 **Brusenets** Russian Federation
60C2 **Brush** USA
69A3 **Brus Laguna** Honduras
Brüssel = Brussels
18A2 **Brussels** Belgium
Bruxelles = Brussels
13D3 **Bruyères** France
56D3 **Bryan** USA
34A2 **Bryan,Mt** Australia
20E5 **Bryansk** Russian Federation
20E5 **Bryansk** *Division* Russian Federation
63D2 **Bryant** USA
59D3 **Bryce Canyon Nat Pk** USA
18D2 **Brzeg** Poland
41E4 **Būbīyan** *I* Kuwait
50D4 **Bubu** *R* Tanzania
47E1 **Bubye** *R* Zimbabwe
72D2 **Bucaramanga** Colombia
8E3 **Buchan** *Oilfield* N Sea
48A4 **Buchanan** Liberia
62C2 **Buchanan,L** USA
8E3 **Buchan Deep** N Sea
55L2 **Buchan G** Canada
10C2 **Buchan Ness** *Pen* Scotland
55N5 **Buchans** Canada
17F2 **Bucharest** Romania
66B3 **Buchon,Pt** USA
13E1 **Bückeburg** Germany
59D4 **Buckeye** USA
8D3 **Buckhaven** Scotland
8D3 **Buckie** Scotland
7D3 **Buckingham** England
65F2 **Bucksport** USA
50B4 **Buco Zau** Congo
Bucureşti = Bucharest
19D3 **Budapest** Hungary
42D3 **Budaun** India
7B4 **Bude** England
63D2 **Bude** USA
21G7 **Budennovsk** Russian Federation
43J1 **Budhana** India
45B4 **Budhīya, Gebel** Egypt
13E2 **Büdingen** Germany
17D2 **Budva** Montenegro, Yugoslavia
48C4 **Buéa** Cameroon
66B3 **Buellton** USA
72C3 **Buenaventura** Colombia
62A3 **Buenaventura** Mexico
60B3 **Buena Vista** Colorado, USA
65D3 **Buena Vista** Virginia, USA
66C3 **Buena Vista L** USA
74E4 **Buenos Aires** Argentina
74E5 **Buenos Aires** *State* Argentina
74B7 **Buenos Aires, Lago** Argentina
63D1 **Buffalo** Mississipi, USA
57F2 **Buffalo** New York, USA
60C1 **Buffalo** S Dakota, USA
63C2 **Buffalo** Texas, USA
56C2 **Buffalo** Wyoming, USA
47E2 **Buffalo** *R* South Africa
58C1 **Buffalo Hump** *Mt* USA
54G3 **Buffalo L** Canada
54H4 **Buffalo Narrows** Canada
67B2 **Buford** USA
17F2 **Buftea** Romania
19E2 **Bug** *R* Poland/Ukraine
72C3 **Buga** Colombia
41F2 **Bugdayli** Turkmenistan
20H2 **Bugrino** Russian Federation
20J5 **Bugulma** Russian Federation
20J5 **Buguruslan** Russian Federation
40C2 **Buḩayrat al Asad** *Res* Syria
58D2 **Buhl** Idaho, USA
61E1 **Buhl** Minnesota, USA
7C3 **Builth Wells** Wales
50C4 **Bujumbura** Burundi
33E1 **Buka** *I* Papua New Guinea
51C4 **Bukama** Zaïre
50C4 **Bukavu** Zaïre
38E2 **Bukhara** Uzbekistan
27D7 **Bukittinggi** Indonesia
50D4 **Bukoba** Tanzania
27G7 **Bula** Indonesia
27F5 **Bulan** Philippines
42D3 **Bulandshahr** India
51C6 **Bulawayo** Zimbabwe
17F3 **Buldan** Turkey
42D4 **Buldāna** India
26D2 **Bulgan** Mongolia
17E2 **Bulgaria** *Republic* Europe
35B2 **Buller** *R* New Zealand
34C3 **Buller,Mt** Australia
32A4 **Bullfinch** Australia
34B1 **Bulloo** *R* Australia
34B1 **Bulloo Downs** Australia
34B1 **Bulloo L** Australia
63D1 **Bull Shoals Res** USA
32D1 **Bulolo** Papua New Guinea
47D2 **Bultfontein** South Africa
27E6 **Bulu, Gunung** *Mt* Indonesia
50C3 **Bumba** Zaïre
21D8 **Bu Menderes** *R* Turkey
30B2 **Bumphal Dam** Thailand
50D3 **Buna** Kenya
32A4 **Bunbury** Australia
9C2 **Buncrana** Irish Republic
33E3 **Bundaberg** Australia
34D2 **Bundarra** Australia
13E1 **Bünde** Germany
42D3 **Būndi** India
7E3 **Bungay** England
34C1 **Bungil** *R* Australia
51B4 **Bungo** Angola
28B4 **Bungo-suidō** *Str* Japan
27D6 **Bunguran** *I* Indonesia
27D6 **Bunguran, Kepulauan** *I* Indonesia
50D3 **Bunia** Zaïre
63D1 **Bunker** USA
63D2 **Bunkie** USA
67B3 **Bunnell** USA
27E7 **Buntok** Indonesia
27F6 **Buol** Indonesia
50C2 **Buram** Sudan
43E2 **Burang** China
50E3 **Burao** Somalia
45D2 **Burāq** Syria
41D4 **Buraydah** Saudi Arabia
59C4 **Burbank** USA
34C2 **Burcher** Australia
21E8 **Burdur** Turkey
50D2 **Burē** Ethiopia
7E3 **Bure** *R* England
26G1 **Bureinskiy Khrebet** *Mts* Russian Federation
26F2 **Bureya** *R* Russian Federation
45B3 **Bûr Fu'ad** Egypt
18C2 **Burg** Germany
17F2 **Burgas** Bulgaria
67C2 **Burgaw** USA
47D3 **Burgersdorp** South Africa
15B1 **Burgos** Spain
13D1 **Burgsteinfurt** Germany
19D1 **Burgsvik** Sweden
17F3 **Burhaniye** Turkey
42D4 **Burhānpur** India
30C2 **Buriram** Thailand
75C2 **Buritis** Brazil
32C2 **Burketown** Australia
48B3 **Burkina** *Republic* W Africa
65D1 **Burk's Falls** Canada
56B2 **Burley** USA
60C3 **Burlington** Colorado, USA
57D2 **Burlington** Iowa, USA
68C2 **Burlington** New Jersey, USA
67C1 **Burlington** North Carolina, USA
57F2 **Burlington** Vermont, USA
58B1 **Burlington** Washington, USA
Burma = Myanmar
62C2 **Burnet** USA
58B2 **Burney** USA
68B2 **Burnham** USA
7E4 **Burnham-on-Crouch** England
32D5 **Burnie** Australia
6C3 **Burnley** England
58C2 **Burns** USA
54F4 **Burns Lake** Canada
24K5 **Burqin** China
34A2 **Burra** Australia
34D2 **Burragorang,L** Australia
8D2 **Burray** *I* Scotland
34C2 **Burren Junction** Australia
34C2 **Burrinjuck Res** Australia
62B3 **Burro, Serranías del** *Mts* Mexico
8C4 **Burrow Head** *Pt* Scotland
27G8 **Burrundie** Australia
21D7 **Bursa** Turkey
40B4 **Bur Safâga** Egypt
Bûr Saîd = Port Said
45B4 **Bûr Taufiq** Egypt
64C2 **Burton** USA
7D3 **Burton upon Trent** England
12J6 **Burtrask** Sweden
34B2 **Burtundy** Australia
27F7 **Buru** *I* Indonesia
50C4 **Burundi** *Republic* Africa
60D2 **Burwell** USA
7C3 **Bury** England
25N4 **Buryatiya** *Division* Russian Federation
21J6 **Burynshik** Kazakhstan
7E3 **Bury St Edmunds** England
28A3 **Bushan** China
41F4 **Būshehr** Iran
9C2 **Bushmills** Northern Ireland
50B4 **Busira** *R* Zaïre
19E2 **Busko Zdrój** Poland
45D2 **Buşrá ash Shām** Syria
13D4 **Bussang** France
32A4 **Busselton** Australia
16B1 **Busto Arsizio** Italy
50C3 **Buta** Zaïre
50C4 **Butare** Rwanda
8C4 **Bute** *I* Scotland
27B2 **Butha Qi** China
65D2 **Butler** USA
32B1 **Buton** *I* Indonesia
48C4 **Butta** Togo
56B2 **Butte** USA
30C4 **Butterworth** Malaysia
47D3 **Butterworth** South Africa
10B2 **Butt of Lewis** *C* Scotland
55M3 **Button Is** Canada
66C3 **Buttonwillow** USA
27F6 **Butuan** Philippines
21G5 **Buturlinovka** Russian Federation
43E3 **Butwal** Nepal
13E2 **Butzbach** Germany
50E3 **Buulobarde** Somalia
50E3 **Buurhakaba** Somalia
7D3 **Buxton** England
20G4 **Buy** Russian Federation
31B1 **Buyant Ovoo** Mongolia
21H7 **Buynaksk** Russian Federation
25N5 **Buyr Nuur** *L* Mongolia
21G8 **Büyük Ağrı Dağı** *Mt* Turkey
40A2 **Büyük Menderes** *R* Turkey
17F1 **Buzău** Romania
17F1 **Buzău** *R* Romania
75D3 **Búzios, Ponta dos** *Pt* Brazil
20J5 **Buzuluk** Russian Federation
68E2 **Buzzards B** USA
17F2 **Byala** Bulgaria
17E2 **Byala Slatina** Bulgaria
54H2 **Byam Martin Channel** Canada
54H2 **Byam Martin I** Canada
45C1 **Byblos** *Hist site* Lebanon
19D2 **Bydgoszcz** Poland
60C3 **Byers** USA
12F7 **Bygland** Norway
19G2 **Bykhov** Belarus
55L2 **Bylot I** Canada
34C2 **Byrock** Australia
66B2 **Byron** USA
34D1 **Byron** *C* Australia
25P3 **Bytantay** *R* Russian Federation
19D2 **Bytom** Poland

C

74E3 **Caacupú** Paraguay
75A4 **Caaguazú** Paraguay
51B5 **Caála** Angola
75A4 **Caapucú** Paraguay
75B3 **Caarapó** Brazil
74E3 **Caazapá** Paraguay
15C1 **Caballería, Cabo de** *C* Spain
62A2 **Caballo Res** USA
27F5 **Cabanatuan** Philippines
65F1 **Cabano** Canada
73M5 **Cabedelo** Brazil
15A2 **Cabeza del Buey** Spain
72D1 **Cabimas** Venezuela
50B4 **Cabinda** Angola
50B4 **Cabinda** *Province* Angola
58C1 **Cabinet Mts** USA
75D3 **Cabo Frio** Brazil
55L5 **Cabonga,Réservoire** Canada
34D1 **Caboolture** Australia
51D5 **Cabora Bassa Dam** Mozambique
70A1 **Caborca** Mexico
55M5 **Cabot Str** Canada
15B2 **Cabra** Spain
75D2 **Cabral, Serra do** *Mts* Brazil
15A1 **Cabreira** *Mt* Portugal
15C2 **Cabrera** *I* Spain
15B2 **Cabriel** *R* Spain
17E2 **Čačak** Serbia, Yugoslavia
68A3 **Cacapon** *R* USA
73G7 **Cáceres** Brazil
15A2 **Cáceres** Spain
63D1 **Cache** *R* USA
66A1 **Cache Creek** *R* USA
58D2 **Cache Peak** *Mt* USA
74C3 **Cachi** Argentina
73G5 **Cachimbo** Brazil
73G5 **Cachimbo, Serra do** *Mts* Brazil
73L6 **Cachoeira** Brazil
75B2 **Cachoeira Alta** Brazil
73L5 **Cachoeira de Paulo Afonso** *Waterfall* Brazil
74F4 **Cachoeira do Sul** Brazil
73K8 **Cachoeiro de Itapemirim** Brazil
66C3 **Cachuma,L** USA
51B5 **Cacolo** Angola
51B5 **Caconda** Angola
62B1 **Cactus** USA
75B2 **Caçu** Brazil
75D1 **Caculé** Brazil
51B5 **Caculuvar** *R* Angola
19D3 **Čadca** Slovakia
7C3 **Cader Idris** *Mt* Wales
57E2 **Cadillac** USA
15A2 **Cádiz** Spain
15A2 **Cádiz, Golfo de** *G* Spain
14B2 **Caen** France
7B3 **Caernarfon** Wales
7B3 **Caernarfon and Merioneth** *County* Wales
7B3 **Caernarfon B** Wales
7C4 **Caerphilly** Wales
7C4 **Caerphilly** *County* Wales
45C2 **Caesarea** *Hist Site* Israel
75D1 **Caetité** Brazil
74C3 **Cafayate** Argentina
40B2 **Caga Tepe** *Mt* Turkey
27F6 **Cagayan de Oro** Philippines
16B3 **Cagliari** Sardinia, Italy
16B3 **Cagliari, G di** Sardinia, Italy
69D3 **Caguas** Puerto Rico
67A2 **Cahaba** *R* USA
9C3 **Cahir** Irish Republic
9C3 **Cahore Pt** Irish Republic
14C3 **Cahors** France
51D5 **Caia** Mozambique
73G6 **Caiabis, Serra dos** *Mts* Brazil
51C5 **Caianda** Angola
75B2 **Caiapó** *R* Brazil
75B2 **Caiapônia** Brazil
75B2 **Caiapó, Serra do** *Mts* Brazil
73L5 **Caicó** Brazil
69C2 **Caicos Is** Caribbean Sea
57F4 **Caicos Pass** The Bahamas
8D3 **Cairngorms** *Mts* Scotland

Cairnryan Caungula

8C4 **Cairnryan** Scotland
32D2 **Cairns** Australia
40B3 **Cairo** Egypt
57E3 **Cairo** USA
8D2 **Caithness** Scotland
34B1 **Caiwarro** Australia
72C5 **Cajabamba** Peru
72C5 **Cajamarca** Peru
48C4 **Calabar** Nigeria
69D5 **Calabozo** Venezuela
17E2 **Calafat** Romania
74B8 **Calafate** Argentina
15B1 **Calahorra** Spain
14C1 **Calais** France
65F1 **Calais** USA
74C2 **Calama** Chile
72D3 **Calamar** Colombia
27E5 **Calamian Group** *Is* Philippines
51B4 **Calandula** Angola
27C6 **Calang** Indonesia
49E2 **Calanscio Sand Sea** Libya
27F5 **Calapan** Philippines
17F2 **Calarasi** Romania
15B1 **Calatayud** Spain
66B2 **Calaveras Res** USA
63D3 **Calcasieu L** USA
43F4 **Calcutta** India
15A2 **Caldas da Rainha** Portugal
73J7 **Caldas Novas** Brazil
74B3 **Caldera** Chile
56B2 **Caldwell** USA
47B3 **Caledon** South Africa
47D3 **Caledon** *R* South Africa
64A2 **Caledonia** Minnesota, USA
68B1 **Caledonia** New York, USA
74C7 **Caleta Olivia** Argentina
56B3 **Calexico** USA
54G4 **Calgary** Canada
67B2 **Calhoun** USA
67B2 **Calhoun Falls** USA
72C3 **Cali** Colombia
66C3 **Caliente** California, USA
56B3 **Caliente** Nevada, USA
62A1 **Caliente** New Mexico, USA
56A3 **California** *State* USA
66C3 **California Aqueduct** USA
70A1 **California, G de** Mexico
44B3 **Calimera,Pt** India
59C4 **Calipatria** USA
47C3 **Calitzdorp** South Africa
34B1 **Callabonna** *R* Australia
34A1 **Callabonna,L** Australia
65D1 **Callander** Canada
8C3 **Callander** Scotland
72C6 **Callao** Peru
68C2 **Callicoon** USA
67B3 **Caloosahatchee** *R* USA
34D1 **Caloundra** Australia
16C3 **Caltanissetta** Sicily, Italy
51B4 **Caluango** Angola
51B5 **Calulo** Angola
51B5 **Caluquembe** Angola
50F2 **Caluula** Somalia
16B2 **Calvi** Corsica, France
47B3 **Calvinia** South Africa
13E3 **Calw** Germany
75E1 **Camacari** Brazil
70E2 **Camagüey** Cuba
70E2 **Camagüey,Arch de** *Is* Cuba
75E1 **Camamu** Brazil
72D7 **Camaná** Peru
75B2 **Camapuã** Brazil
72E8 **Camargo** Bolivia
66C3 **Camarillo** USA
74C6 **Camarones** Argentina
58B1 **Camas** USA
51B4 **Camaxilo** Angola
51B4 **Cambatela** Angola
30C3 **Cambodia** *Republic* SE Asia
7B4 **Camborne** England
14C1 **Cambrai** France
66B3 **Cambria** USA
7C3 **Cambrian Mts** Wales
64C2 **Cambridge** Canada
7E3 **Cambridge** England
69H1 **Cambridge** Jamaica
65D3 **Cambridge** Maryland, USA
65E2 **Cambridge** Massachussets, USA
61E1 **Cambridge** Minnesota, USA
35C1 **Cambridge** New Zealand
64C2 **Cambridge** Ohio, USA
7D3 **Cambridge** *County* England
54H3 **Cambridge Bay** Canada
27F8 **Cambridge G** Australia
21F7 **Cam Burun** *Pt* Turkey
57D3 **Camden** Arkansas, USA
34D2 **Camden** Australia
65E3 **Camden** New Jersey, USA
68C1 **Camden** New York, USA
67B2 **Camden** South Carolina, USA
61E3 **Cameron** Missouri, USA
63C2 **Cameron** Texas, USA
54H2 **Cameron I** Canada
35A3 **Cameron Mts** New Zealand
50B3 **Cameroon** *Federal Republic* Africa
48C4 **Cameroun, Mt** Cameroon
73J4 **Cametá** Brazil
67B2 **Camilla** USA
66B1 **Camino** USA
72F8 **Camiri** Bolivia
51C4 **Camissombo** Angola
73K4 **Camocim** Brazil
32C2 **Camooweal** Australia
44E4 **Camorta** *I* Nicobar Is, Indian Ocean
74A7 **Campana** *I* Chile
47C2 **Campbell** South Africa
35B2 **Campbell,C** New Zealand
37K7 **Campbell I** New Zealand
54E3 **Campbell,Mt** Canada
42C2 **Campbellpore** Pakistan
54F5 **Campbell River** Canada
64B3 **Campbellsville** USA
55M5 **Campbellton** Canada
34D2 **Campbelltown** Australia
8C4 **Campbeltown** Scotland
70C3 **Campeche** Mexico
70C2 **Campeche, B de** Mexico
34B3 **Camperdown** Australia
73L5 **Campina Grande** Brazil
73J8 **Campinas** Brazil
75C2 **Campina Verde** Brazil
66C2 **Camp Nelson** USA
48C4 **Campo** Cameroon
16C2 **Campobasso** Italy
75C3 **Campo Belo** Brazil
75C2 **Campo Florido** Brazil
74D3 **Campo Gallo** Argentina
74F2 **Campo Grande** Brazil
73K4 **Campo Maior** Brazil
74F2 **Campo Mourão** Brazil
75D3 **Campos** Brazil
75C2 **Campos Altos** Brazil
59D4 **Camp Verde** USA
30D3 **Cam Ranh** Vietnam
54G4 **Camrose** Canada
51B5 **Camucuio** Angola
69K1 **Canaan** Tobago
68D1 **Canaan** USA
51B5 **Canacupa** Angola
53F3 **Canada** *Dominion* N America
74D4 **Cañada de Gómez** Argentina
68C2 **Canadensis** USA
62B1 **Canadian** USA
56C3 **Canadian** *R* USA
21D7 **Çanakkale** Turkey
68B1 **Canandaigua** USA
68B1 **Canandaigua L** USA
70A1 **Cananea** Mexico
75C4 **Cananeia** Brazil
Canarias, Islas = Canary Islands
52G3 **Canary Basin** Atlantic Ocean
48A2 **Canary Is** *Atlantic Ocean*
75C3 **Canastra, Serra da** *Mts* Brazil
70B2 **Canatlán** Mexico
57E4 **Canaveral,C** USA
73L7 **Canavieiras** Brazil
32D4 **Canberra** Australia
58B2 **Canby** California, USA
61D2 **Canby** Minnesota, USA
17F3 **Çandarlı Körfezi** *B* Turkey
68D2 **Candlewood,L** USA
60D1 **Cando** USA
68B1 **Candor** USA
74E4 **Canelones** Uruguay
63C1 **Caney** USA
51C5 **Cangamba** Angola
51C5 **Cangombe** Angola
31D2 **Cangzhou** China
55M4 **Caniapiscau** *R* Canada
55M4 **Caniapiscau, Réservoir** *Res* Canada
16C3 **Canicatti** Sicily, Italy
73L4 **Canindé** Brazil
68B1 **Canisteo** USA
68B1 **Canisteo** *R* USA
62A1 **Canjilon** USA
40B1 **Çankırı** Turkey
8B3 **Canna** *I* Scotland
44B3 **Cannanore** India
14D3 **Cannes** France
7C3 **Cannock** England
60C1 **Cannonball** *R* USA
34C3 **Cann River** Australia
74F3 **Canõas** Brazil
75B4 **Canoinhas** Brazil
60B3 **Canon City** USA
34B2 **Canopus** Australia
54H4 **Canora** Canada
34C2 **Canowindra** Australia
15B1 **Cantabria** *Region* Spain
14A3 **Cantabrica, Cord** *Mts* Spain
7E4 **Canterbury** England
35B2 **Canterbury Bight** *B* New Zealand
35B2 **Canterbury Plains** New Zealand
30D4 **Can Tho** Vietnam
66D3 **Cantil** USA
Canton = Guangzhou
63E2 **Canton** Mississippi, USA
64A2 **Canton** Missouri, USA
57E2 **Canton** Ohio, USA
68B2 **Canton** Pensylvania, USA
61D2 **Canton** S Dakota, USA
33H1 **Canton** *I* Phoenix Islands
75B3 **Cantu, Serra do** *Mts* Brazil
62B2 **Canyon** USA
58C2 **Canyon City** USA
58D1 **Canyon Ferry L** USA
59E3 **Canyonlands Nat Pk** USA
58B2 **Canyonville** USA
51C4 **Canzar** Angola
30D1 **Cao Bang** Vietnam
28B2 **Caoshi** China
73J4 **Capanema** Brazil
75C3 **Capão Bonito** Brazil
75D3 **Caparaó, Serra do** *Mts* Brazil
14B3 **Capbreton** France
16B2 **Cap Corse** *C* Corsica, France
14B2 **Cap de la Hague** *C* France
65E1 **Cap-de-la-Madeleine** Canada
15C2 **Capdepera** Spain
34C4 **Cape Barren I** Australia
52J6 **Cape Basin** Atlantic Ocean
55N5 **Cape Breton I** Canada
Cape, Cabo etc: see also individual cape names
48B4 **Cape Coast** Ghana
65E2 **Cape Cod B** USA
55M3 **Cape Dyer** Canada
76F7 **Cape Evans** *Base* Antarctica
67C2 **Cape Fear** *R* USA
63E1 **Cape Girardeau** USA
74C8 **Cape Horn** Chile
36H4 **Cape Johnson Depth** Pacific Ocean
75D2 **Capelinha** Brazil
54B3 **Cape Lisburne** USA
51B5 **Capelongo** Angola
65E3 **Cape May** USA
54F5 **Cape Mendocino** USA
51B4 **Capenda Camulemba** Angola
54F2 **Cape Parry** Canada
47B3 **Cape Town** South Africa
52G4 **Cape Verde** *Is* Atlantic Ocean
52G4 **Cape Verde Basin** Atlantic Ocean
32D2 **Cape York Pen** Australia
69C3 **Cap-Haïtien** Haiti
73J4 **Capim** *R* Brazil
75A3 **Capitán Bado** Paraguay
59E3 **Capitol Reef Nat Pk** USA
75A2 **Capivari** *R* Brazil
9C3 **Cappoquin** Irish Republic
69P2 **Cap Pt** St Lucia
16C2 **Capri** *I* Italy
51C5 **Caprivi Strip** *Region* Namibia
72D4 **Caquetá** *R* Colombia
17E2 **Caracal** Romania
72F3 **Caracaraí** Brazil
72E1 **Caracas** Venezuela
75A3 **Caracol** Brazil
75C3 **Caraguatatuba** Brazil
74B5 **Carahue** Chile
75D2 **Caraí** Brazil
75D3 **Carandaí** Brazil
75A2 **Carandazal** Brazil
73K8 **Carangola** Brazil
17E1 **Caransebeş** Romania
69A3 **Caratasca** Honduras
70D3 **Caratasca, L de** *Lg* Honduras
75D2 **Caratinga** Brazil
15B2 **Caravaca de la Cruz** Spain
75E2 **Caravelas** Brazil
16B3 **Carbonara, C** Sardinia, Italy
64B3 **Carbondale** Illinois, USA
68C2 **Carbondale** Pennsylvania, USA
55N5 **Carbonear** Canada
16B3 **Carbonia** Sardinia, Italy
54G4 **Carcajou** Canada
50E2 **Carcar Mts** Somalia
14C3 **Carcassonne** France
54E3 **Carcross** Canada
30C3 **Cardamomes, Chaîne des** *Mts* Cambodia
70D2 **Cardenas** Cuba
7C4 **Cardiff** Wales
7C4 **Cardiff** *County* Wales
7B3 **Cardigan** Wales
7B3 **Cardigan** *County* Wales
7B3 **Cardigan B** Wales
75C4 **Cardoso, Ilha do** Brazil
17E1 **Carei** Romania
73G4 **Careiro** Brazil
64C2 **Carey** USA
14B2 **Carhaix-Plouguer** France
74D5 **Carhué** Argentina
73K8 **Cariacíca** Brazil
71C2 **Caribbean S** Central America
54J4 **Caribou** Canada
65F1 **Caribou** USA
54G4 **Caribou Mts** Alberta, Canada
54F4 **Caribou Mts** British Columbia, Canada
13C3 **Carignan** France
75D1 **Carinhanha** Brazil
75D1 **Carinhanha** *R* Brazil
72F1 **Caripito** Venezuela
65D1 **Carleton Place** Canada
47D2 **Carletonville** South Africa
58C2 **Carlin** USA
9C2 **Carlingford, L** Northern Ireland
64B3 **Carlinville** USA
6C2 **Carlisle** England
65D2 **Carlisle** USA
75D2 **Carlos Chagas** Brazil
9C3 **Carlow** Irish Republic
9C3 **Carlow** *County* Irish Republic
59C4 **Carlsbad** California, USA
56C3 **Carlsbad** New Mexico, USA
62B2 **Carlsbad Caverns Nat Pk** USA
36E4 **Carlsberg Ridge** Indian Ocean
54H5 **Carlyle** Canada
54E3 **Carmacks** Canada
7B4 **Carmarthen** Wales
7B4 **Carmarthen** *County* Wales
7B4 **Carmarthen B** Wales
66B2 **Carmel** California, USA
68D2 **Carmel** New York, USA
7B3 **Carmel Hd** *Pt* Wales
45C2 **Carmel,Mt** Israel
66B2 **Carmel Valley** USA
56B4 **Carmen** *I* Mexico
74D6 **Carmen de Patagones** Argentina
64B3 **Carmi** USA
59B3 **Carmichael** USA
75C2 **Carmo do Paranaiba** Brazil
15A2 **Carmona** Spain
75E2 **Carnacá** Brazil
32A3 **Carnarvon** Australia
47C3 **Carnarvon** South Africa
9C2 **Carndonagh** Irish Republic
32B3 **Carnegie,L** Australia
44E4 **Car Nicobar** *I* Nicobar Is, Indian Ocean
50B3 **Carnot** Central African Republic
8D3 **Carnoustie** Scotland
9C3 **Carnsore Pt** Irish Republic
67B3 **Carol City** USA
73J5 **Carolina** Brazil
47E2 **Carolina** South Africa
67C2 **Carolina Beach** USA
27H6 **Caroline Is** Pacific Ocean
19F3 **Carpathian Mts** Romania
21C6 **Carpathians** *Mts* E Europe
32C2 **Carpentaria,G of** Australia
39H5 **Carpenter Ridge** Indian Ocean
14D3 **Carpentras** France
16C2 **Carpi** Italy
66C3 **Carpinteria** USA
67B3 **Carrabelle** USA
16C2 **Carrara** Italy
10B3 **Carrauntoohill** *Mt* Irish Republic
8C4 **Carrick** Scotland
9D2 **Carrickfergus** Northern Ireland
9C3 **Carrickmacross** Irish Republic
9C3 **Carrick-on-Suir** Irish Republic
34A2 **Carrieton** Australia
54J5 **Carrington** USA
15B1 **Carrión** *R* Spain
62C3 **Carrizo Springs** USA
62A2 **Carrizozo** USA
57D2 **Carroll** USA
67A2 **Carrollton** Georgia, USA
64B3 **Carrollton** Kentucky, USA
61E3 **Carrollton** Missouri, USA
9B2 **Carrowmore,L** *Irish Republic*
63E1 **Carruthersville** USA
21F7 **Carşamba** Turkey
21E8 **Carşamba** *R* Turkey
56B3 **Carson City** USA
64C2 **Carsonville** USA
8D4 **Carstairs** Scotland
69B4 **Cartagena** Colombia
15B2 **Cartagena** Spain
72C3 **Cartago** Colombia
70D4 **Cartago** Costa Rica
66C2 **Cartago** USA
35C2 **Carterton** New Zealand
63D1 **Carthage** Missouri, USA
65D2 **Carthage** New York, USA
63D2 **Carthage** Texas, USA
32B2 **Cartier I** Timor Sea
55N4 **Cartwright** Canada
73L5 **Caruaru** Brazil
72F1 **Carúpano** Venezuela
13B2 **Carvin** France
15A2 **Carvoeiro, Cabo** *C* Portugal
67C1 **Cary** USA
48B1 **Casablanca** Morocco
75C3 **Casa Branca** Brazil
56B3 **Casa Grande** USA
16B1 **Casale Monferrato** Italy
58D1 **Cascade** USA
35A2 **Cascade Pt** New Zealand
56A2 **Cascade Range** *Mts* USA
58C2 **Cascade Res** USA
74F2 **Cascavel** Brazil
16C2 **Caserta** Italy
76G9 **Casey** *Base* Antarctica
9C3 **Cashel** Irish Republic
33E3 **Casino** Australia
72C5 **Casma** Peru
66B3 **Casmalia** USA
15C1 **Caspe** Spain
56C2 **Casper** USA
21H6 **Caspian Depression** *Region* Kazakhstan
21H7 **Caspian S** Asia/Europe
65D3 **Cass** USA
51C5 **Cassamba** Angola
13B2 **Cassel** France
61D1 **Casselton** USA
54E3 **Cassiar Mts** Canada
75B2 **Cassilândia** Brazil
16C2 **Cassino** Italy
61E1 **Cass Lake** USA
66C3 **Castaic** USA
14D3 **Castellane** France
16C2 **Castello, Città di** Italy
15C1 **Castellón de la Plana** Spain
73K5 **Castelo** Brazil
15A2 **Castelo Branco** Portugal
14C3 **Castelsarrasin** France
16C3 **Castelvetrano** Sicily, Italy
34B3 **Casterton** Australia
15B2 **Castilla la Mancha** *Region* Spain
15B1 **Castilla y León** *Region* Spain
10B3 **Castlebar** Irish Republic
8B3 **Castlebay** Scotland
9C2 **Castleblayney** Irish Republic
59D3 **Castle Dale** USA
8D4 **Castle Douglas** Scotland
6D3 **Castleford** England
58C1 **Castlegar** Canada
34B3 **Castlemaine** Australia
66B3 **Castle Mt** USA
58D2 **Castle Peak** *Mt* USA
34C2 **Castlereagh** *R* Australia
60C3 **Castle Rock** USA
6B2 **Castletown** England
9B4 **Castletown Bere** Irish Republic
14C3 **Castres-sur-l'Agout** France
69P2 **Castries** St Lucia
74B6 **Castro** Argentina
74F2 **Castro** Brazil
73L6 **Castro Alves** Brazil
16D3 **Castrovillari** Italy
66B2 **Castroville** USA
35A2 **Caswell Sd** New Zealand
70E2 **Cat** *I* The Bahamas
72B5 **Catacaos** Peru
75D3 **Cataguases** Brazil
63D2 **Catahoula L** USA
75C2 **Catalão** Brazil
15C1 **Cataluña** *Region* Spain
74C3 **Catamarca** Argentina
74C3 **Catamarca** *State* Argentina
51D5 **Catandica** Mozambique
27F5 **Catanduanes** *I* Philippines
74G2 **Catanduva** Brazil
75B4 **Catanduvas** Brazil
16D3 **Catania** Sicily, Italy
16D3 **Catanzaro** Italy
62C3 **Catarina** USA
27F5 **Catarman** Philippines
69C5 **Catatumbo** *R* Venezuela
68B2 **Catawissa** USA
27F5 **Catbalogan** Philippines
16B2 **Cateraggio** Corsica, France
51B4 **Catete** Angola
47D3 **Cathcart** South Africa
48A3 **Catio** Guinea-Bissau
55J4 **Cat Lake** Canada
33E3 **Cato** *I* Australia
70D2 **Catoche,C** Mexico
68B3 **Catoctin Mt** USA
65D3 **Catonsville** USA
65E2 **Catskill** USA
65E2 **Catskill Mts** USA
72D2 **Cauca** *R* Colombia
73L4 **Caucaia** Brazil
72C2 **Caucasia** Colombia
21G7 **Caucasus** *Mts* Georgia
13B2 **Caudry** France
51B4 **Caungula** Angola

Cauquenes Chirfa

74B5 **Cauquenes** Chile
65F1 **Causapscal** Canada
44B3 **Cauvery** *R* India
14D3 **Cavaillon** France
75C1 **Cavalcante** Brazil
61D1 **Cavalier** USA
48B4 **Cavally** *R* Liberia
9C3 **Cavan** Irish Republic
9C3 **Cavan** *County* Irish Republic
72D4 **Caxias** Brazil
73K4 **Caxias** Brazil
74F3 **Caxias do Sul** Brazil
51B4 **Caxito** Angola
67B2 **Cayce** USA
40D1 **Çayeli** Turkey
73H3 **Cayenne** French Guiana
70E3 **Cayman Brac** *I* Cayman Is, Caribbean Sea
69A3 **Cayman Is** Caribbean Sea
69A3 **Cayman Trench** Caribbean Sea
50E3 **Caynabo** Somalia
70E2 **Cayo Romano** *I* Cuba
70D3 **Cayos Miskito** *Is* Nicaragua
69A2 **Cay Sal** *I* Caribbean Sea
66B3 **Cayucos** USA
68B1 **Cayuga L** USA
68C1 **Cazenovia** USA
51C5 **Cazombo** Angola
Ceará = Fortaleza
73K5 **Ceará** *State* Brazil
27F5 **Cebu** Philippines
27F5 **Cebu** *I* Philippines
68C3 **Cecilton** USA
16C2 **Cecina** Italy
61E2 **Cedar** *R* USA
56B3 **Cedar City** USA
63C2 **Cedar Creek Res** USA
61E2 **Cedar Falls** USA
54H4 **Cedar L** Canada
66D1 **Cedar Mts** USA
57D2 **Cedar Rapids** USA
67A2 **Cedartown** USA
70A2 **Cedros** *I* Mexico
56B4 **Cedros, Isla de** Mexico
32C4 **Ceduna** Australia
50E3 **Ceelbuur** Somalia
50E2 **Ceerigaabo** Somalia
16C3 **Cefalù** Sicily, Italy
19D3 **Cegléd** Hungary
51B5 **Cela** Angola
70B2 **Celaya** Mexico
Celebes = Sulawesi
27F6 **Celebes S** SE Asia
64C2 **Celina** USA
16D1 **Celje** Slovenia
18C2 **Celle** Germany
7A4 **Celtic S** British Islands
7B3 **Cemmaes Hd** *Pt* Wales
27G7 **Cendrawasih** *Pen* Indonesia
63D2 **Center** USA
67A1 **Center Hill L** USA
68D2 **Center Moriches** USA
67A2 **Center Point** USA
62A2 **Central** USA
50B3 **Central African Republic** Africa
61D2 **Central City** Nebraska, USA
68A2 **Central City** Pennsylvania, USA
68E2 **Central Falls** USA
64B3 **Centralia** Illinois, USA
56A2 **Centralia** Washington, USA
47C1 **Central Kalahari Game Res** Botswana
42A3 **Central Makran Ra** *Mts* Pakistan
58B2 **Central Point** USA
27H7 **Central Range** *Mts* Papua New Guinea
68B1 **Central Square** USA
67A2 **Centreville** Alabama, USA
68B3 **Centreville** Maryland, USA
Ceram = Seram
Ceram Sea = Seram Sea
73J7 **Ceres** Brazil
47B3 **Ceres** South Africa
66B2 **Ceres** USA
14C2 **Cergy-Pontoise** France
16D2 **Cerignola** Italy
21D7 **Cernavodă** Romania
13D4 **Cernay** France
56C4 **Cerralvo** *I* Mexico
72C6 **Cerro de Pasco** Peru
69D3 **Cerro de Punta** *Mt* Puerto Rico
69C4 **Cerron** *Mt* Venezuela
74C5 **Cerros Colorados, Embalse** *Res* Argentina
16C2 **Cesena** Italy
20D4 **Cēsis** Latvia
18C3 **České Budějovice** Czech Republic
18D3 **Českomoravská Vyosina** *Region* Czech Republic
17F3 **Çeşme** Turkey
32E4 **Cessnock** Australia
16D2 **Cetina** *R* Croatia
15A2 **Ceuta** NW Africa
40C2 **Ceyhan** Turkey
40C2 **Ceyhan** *R* Turkey
40C2 **Ceylanpınar** Turkey
44C4 **Ceylon** *I* Indian Oc
Ceylon *Republic* **= Sri Lanka**
25L4 **Chaa-Khol** Russian Federation
14C2 **Chaâteaudun** France
13B4 **Chablis** France
72C5 **Chachapoyas** Peru
42C3 **Chachran** Pakistan
42C3 **Chachro** Pakistan
74D3 **Chaco** *State* Argentina
50B2 **Chad** *Republic* Africa
50B2 **Chad, L** C Africa
56C2 **Chadron** USA
28B3 **Chaeryŏng** N Korea
63E1 **Chaffee** USA
42A3 **Chagai** Pakistan
25P4 **Chagda** Russian Federation
42B2 **Chaghcharan** Afghanistan
36E5 **Chagos Arch** Indian Ocean
69L1 **Chaguanas** Trinidad
38E3 **Chāh Bahār** Iran
28A2 **Ch'aho** N Korea
30C2 **Chai Badan** Thailand
43F4 **Chāībāsa** India
30C2 **Chaiyaphum** Thailand
42C2 **Chakwal** Pakistan
72D7 **Chala** Peru
51D5 **Chalabesa** Zambia
42A2 **Chalap Dalam** *Mts* Afghanistan
57G2 **Chaleurs, B des** Canada
13C4 **Chalindrey** France
31C4 **Chaling** China
42D4 **Chālisgaon** India
27H5 **Challenger Deep** Pacific Ocean
13C3 **Challerange** France
58D2 **Challis** USA
13C3 **Châlons-en-Champagne** France
14C2 **Chalon sur Saône** France
28B2 **Chaluhe** China
18C3 **Cham** Germany
62A1 **Chama** USA
42B2 **Chaman** Pakistan
42D2 **Chamba** India
42D3 **Chambal** *R* India
60D2 **Chamberlain** USA
65D3 **Chambersburg** USA
14D2 **Chambéry** France
13B3 **Chambly** France
65E1 **Chambord** Canada
42A3 **Chambor Kalat** Pakistan
41F3 **Chamgordan** Iran
43E4 **Chāmpa** India
14C2 **Champagne** *Region* France
47D2 **Champagne Castle** *Mt* Lesotho
57E2 **Champaign** USA
43N2 **Champaran** *District* India
30D3 **Champassak** Laos
57F2 **Champlain,L** USA
44B3 **Chāmrājnagar** India
74B3 **Chañaral** Chile
54D3 **Chandalar** USA
54D3 **Chandalar** *R* USA
63E3 **Chandeleur Is** USA
42D2 **Chandīgarh** India
59D4 **Chandler** USA
43G4 **Chandpur** Bangladesh
42D5 **Chandrapur** India
47E1 **Changane** *R* Mozambique
51D5 **Changara** Mozambique
28B2 **Changbai** China
28B2 **Changbai Shan** *Mts* China
28B2 **Changchun** China
31C4 **Changde** China
28A3 **Changdo** N Korea
28A3 **Changhai** China
28A3 **Changhang** S Korea
28A3 **Changhowan** S Korea
26E4 **Changhua** Taiwan
28A4 **Changhŭng** S Korea
30D2 **Changjiang** China
31D3 **Chang Jiang** *R* China
28B2 **Changjin** N Korea
28A2 **Changjin** *R* N Korea
28A2 **Changjin Res** N Korea
28B3 **Changnyŏn** N Korea
31C4 **Changsha** China
31E3 **Changshu** China
31B2 **Changwu** China
28A3 **Changyŏn** N Korea
31C2 **Changzhi** China
31E3 **Changzhou** China
14B2 **Channel Is** British Isles
56B3 **Channel Is** USA
55N5 **Channel Port-aux-Basques** Canada
30C3 **Chanthaburi** Thailand
13B3 **Chantilly** France
55J3 **Chantrey Inlet** *B* Canada
63C1 **Chanute** USA
24J4 **Chany, Ozero** *L* Russian Federation
31D5 **Chao'an** China
31D3 **Chao Hu** *L* China
30C3 **Chao Phraya** *R* Thailand
15A2 **Chaouen** Morocco
31E1 **Chaoyang** China
73K6 **Chapada Diamantina** *Mts* Brazil
73K4 **Chapadinha** Brazil
70B2 **Chapala, L de** Mexico
21J5 **Chapayevo** Kazakhstan
74F3 **Chapecó** Brazil
7D3 **Chapel-en-le-Frith** England
67C1 **Chapel Hill** USA
69H1 **Chapeltown** Jamaica
55K5 **Chapleau** Canada
25U3 **Chaplino, Mys** *C* Russian Federation
20G5 **Chaplygin** Russian Federation
60C2 **Chappell** USA
76G3 **Charcot I** Antarctica
7C4 **Chard** England
38E2 **Chardzhou** Turkmenistan
14C2 **Charente** *R* France
50B2 **Chari** *R* Chad
50B2 **Chari Baguirmi** *Region* Chad
42B1 **Charikar** Afghanistan
61E2 **Chariton** *R* USA
73G2 **Charity** Guyana
42D3 **Charkhāri** India
13C2 **Charleroi** Belgium
57F3 **Charles,C** USA
64B3 **Charleston** Illinois, USA
63E1 **Charleston** Missouri, USA
57F3 **Charleston** S Carolina, USA
57E3 **Charleston** W Virginia, USA
59C3 **Charleston Peak** *Mt* USA
68B3 **Charles Town** USA
68D1 **Charlestown** USA
50C4 **Charlesville** Zaïre
32D3 **Charleville** Australia
14C2 **Charleville-Mézières** France
64B1 **Charlevoix** USA
64C2 **Charlotte** Michigan, USA
57E3 **Charlotte** N Carolina, USA
67B3 **Charlotte Harbor** *B* USA
57F3 **Charlottesville** USA
55M5 **Charlottetown** Canada
69K1 **Charlotteville** Tobago
34B3 **Charlton** Australia
57F1 **Charlton I** Canada
13D3 **Charmes** France
42C2 **Charsadda** Pakistan
32D3 **Charters Towers** Australia
14C2 **Chartres** France
74E5 **Chascomús** Argentina
28B2 **Chasong** N Korea
14B2 **Châteaubriant** France
14B2 **Châteaulin** France
13B4 **Châteauneuf-sur-Loire** France
14C2 **Châteauroux** France
13D3 **Château-Salins** France
14C2 **Château-Thierry** France
13C2 **Châtelet** Belgium
14C2 **Châtellerault** France
61E2 **Chatfield** USA
7F6 **Chatham** England
68E2 **Chatham** Massachusetts, USA
55M5 **Chatham** New Brunswick, Canada
68D1 **Chatham** New York, USA
64C2 **Chatham** Ontario, Canada
65D3 **Chatham** Virginia, USA
33H5 **Chatham Is** New Zealand
54E4 **Chatham Str** USA
14C2 **Châtillon** France
13B4 **Châtillon-Coligny** France
13C4 **Châtillon-sur-Seine** France
43E5 **Chatrapur** India
68C3 **Chatsworth** USA
67B2 **Chattahoochee** USA
67A2 **Chattahoochee** *R* USA
57E3 **Chattanooga** USA
30A1 **Chauk** Burma
43L2 **Chauka** *R* India
14D2 **Chaumont** France
13B3 **Chauny** France
30D3 **Chau Phu** Vietnam
44E4 **Chaura** *I* Nicobar Is, Indian Ocean
15A1 **Chaves** Portugal
20J4 **Chaykovskiy** Russian Federation
18C2 **Cheb** Czech Republic
20H4 **Cheboksary** Russian Federation
57E2 **Cheboygan** USA
21H7 **Chechnya** *Division* Russian Federation
19G2 **Chechersk** Belarus
28B3 **Chech'on** S Korea
63C1 **Checotah** USA
7C4 **Cheddar** England
30A2 **Cheduba I** Burma
34B1 **Cheepie** Australia
48B2 **Chegga** Mauritius
51D5 **Chegutu** Zimbabwe
58B1 **Chehalis** USA
28B4 **Cheju** S Korea
28B4 **Cheju Do** *I* S Korea
28B4 **Cheju Haehyŏp** *Str* S Korea
25P4 **Chekunda** Russian Federation
58B1 **Chelan,L** USA
21J8 **Cheleken** Turkmenistan
16B3 **Chélia, Dj** *Mt* Algeria
15C2 **Cheliff** *R* Algeria
38D1 **Chelkar** Kazakhstan
19E2 **Chełm** Poland
19D2 **Chełmno** Poland
7E4 **Chelmsford** England
7C4 **Cheltenham** England
20L4 **Chelyabinsk** Russian Federation
20L5 **Chelyabinsk** *Division* Russian Federation
25M2 **Chelyuskin, Mys** *C* Russian Federation
51D5 **Chemba** Mozambique
18C2 **Chemnitz** Germ
68B1 **Chemung** *R* USA
42D2 **Chenab** *R* India/Pakistan
48B2 **Chenachen** Algeria
68C1 **Chenango** *R* USA
58C1 **Cheney** USA
63C1 **Cheney Res** USA
31D1 **Chengde** China
31A3 **Chengdu** China
31E2 **Chengshan Jiao** *Pt* China
28A3 **Chengzitan** China
31C4 **Chenxi** China
31C4 **Chen Xian** China
31D3 **Cheo Xian** China
72C5 **Chepén** Peru
7C4 **Chepstow** Wales
64A1 **Chequamegon B** USA
14C2 **Cher** *R* France
67C2 **Cheraw** USA
14B2 **Cherbourg** France
15C2 **Cherchell** Algeria
20K3 **Cherdyn** Russian Federation
25M4 **Cheremkhovo** Russian Federation
20F4 **Cherepovets** Russian Federation
21E6 **Cherkassy** Ukraine
21G7 **Cherkessk** Russian Federation
21E5 **Chernigov** Ukraine
19G2 **Chernobyl** Ukraine
21D6 **Chernovtsy** Ukraine
20K4 **Chernushka** Russian Federation
20C5 **Chernyakhovsk** Russian Federation
21H6 **Chernyye Zemli** *Region* Russian Federation
61D2 **Cherokee** Iowa, USA
62C1 **Cherokee** Oklahoma, USA
63D1 **Cherokees,L o'the** USA
43G3 **Cherrapunji** India
33F2 **Cherry** *I* Solomon Islands
25S3 **Cherskiy** Russian Federation
25Q3 **Cherskogo, Khrebet** *Mts* Russian Federation
20D5 **Cherven'** Belarus
19E2 **Chervonograd** Ukraine
65D3 **Chesapeake** USA
65D3 **Chesapeake B** USA
7D4 **Chesham** England
68D1 **Cheshire** USA
7C3 **Cheshire** *County* England
20H2 **Chëshskaya Guba** *B* Russian Federation
59B2 **Chester** California, USA
7C3 **Chester** England
64B3 **Chester** Illinois, USA
68D1 **Chester** Massachusetts, USA
58D1 **Chester** Montana, USA
65D3 **Chester** Pennsylvania, USA
67B2 **Chester** S Carolina, USA
68D1 **Chester** Vermont, USA
68B3 **Chester** *R* USA
7D3 **Chesterfield** England
33E2 **Chesterfield, Îles** Nouvelle Calédonie
55J3 **Chesterfield Inlet** Canada
68B3 **Chestertown** USA
65F1 **Chesuncook L** USA
70D3 **Chetumal** Mexico
35B2 **Cheviot** New Zealand
10C2 **Cheviots** *Hills* England/ Scotland
60C2 **Cheyenne** USA
60C2 **Cheyenne** *R* USA
60C3 **Cheyenne Wells** USA
43E3 **Chhapra** India
43G3 **Chhātak** Bangladesh
42D4 **Chhatarpur** India
42D4 **Chhindwāra** India
43F3 **Chhukha** Bhutan
51B5 **Chiange** Angola
30C2 **Chiang Kham** Thailand
30B2 **Chiang Mai** Thailand
31E5 **Chiayi** Taiwan
29E3 **Chiba** Japan
51B5 **Chibia** Angola
55L4 **Chibougamau** Canada
28B3 **Chiburi-jima** *I* Japan
47E1 **Chibuto** Mozambique
57E2 **Chicago** USA
64B2 **Chicago Heights** USA
54E4 **Chichagof I** USA
7D4 **Chichester** England
29C3 **Chichibu** Japan
26H4 **Chichi-jima** *I* Japan
57E3 **Chickamauga L** USA
63E2 **Chickasawhay** *R* USA
56D3 **Chickasha** USA
54D3 **Chicken** USA
72B5 **Chiclayo** Peru
56A3 **Chico** USA
74C6 **Chico** *R* Argentina
51D5 **Chicoa** Mozambique
65E2 **Chicopee** USA
55L5 **Chicoutimi** Canada
51D6 **Chicualacuala** Mozambique
44B3 **Chidambaram** India
55M3 **Chidley,C** Canada
67B3 **Chiefland** USA
48B4 **Chiehn** Liberia
51C4 **Chiengi** Zambia
13C3 **Chiers** *R* France
16C2 **Chieti** Italy
31D1 **Chifeng** China
73K7 **Chifre, Serra do** *Mts* Brazil
54C3 **Chigmit Mts** USA
47E1 **Chigubo** Mozambique
70B2 **Chihuahua** Mexico
62A3 **Chihuahua** *State* Mexico
44B3 **Chik Ballāpur** India
44B3 **Chikmagalūr** India
51D5 **Chikwawa** Malawi
30A1 **Chi-kyaw** Burma
44C2 **Chilakalūrupet** India
44B4 **Chilaw** Sri Lanka
34D1 **Childers** Australia
62B2 **Childress** USA
71C6 **Chile** *Republic* S America
51C5 **Chililabombwe** Zambia
43F5 **Chilka L** India
54F4 **Chilko L** Canada
74B5 **Chillán** Chile
61E3 **Chillicothe** Missouri, USA
64C3 **Chillicothe** Ohio, USA
43G3 **Chilmari** India
74B6 **Chiloé, Isla de** Chile
51D5 **Chilongozi** Zambia
58B2 **Chiloquin** USA
70C3 **Chilpancingo** Mexico
7D4 **Chiltern Hills** *Upland* England
64B2 **Chilton** USA
51D5 **Chilumba** Malawi
Chi-lung = Keelung
51D5 **Chilwa, L** Malawi
51D5 **Chimanimani** Zimbabwe
13C2 **Chimay** Belgium
24G5 **Chimbay** Uzbekistan
72C4 **Chimborazo** *Mt* Ecuador
72C5 **Chimbote** Peru
24H5 **Chimkent** Kazakhstan
51D5 **Chimoio** Mozambique
22F4 **China** *Republic* Asia
66D3 **China L** USA
66D3 **China Lake** USA
China, National Republic of = Taiwan
70D3 **Chinandega** Nicaragua
62B3 **Chinati Peak** *Mt* USA
72C6 **Chincha Alta** Peru
34D1 **Chinchilla** Australia
51D5 **Chinde** Mozambique
28A4 **Chindo** S Korea
43G4 **Chindwin** *R* Burma
51C5 **Chingola** Zambia
51B5 **Chinguar** Angola
48A2 **Chinguetti** Mauritius
28B3 **Chinhae** S Korea
51D5 **Chinhoyi** Zimbabwe
42C2 **Chiniot** Pakistan
28B3 **Chinju** S Korea
50C3 **Chinko** *R* Central African Republic
29C3 **Chino** Japan
51D5 **Chinsali** Zambia
16C1 **Chioggia** Italy
51D5 **Chipata** Zambia
51D6 **Chipinge** Zimbabwe
44A2 **Chiplūn** India
7C4 **Chippenham** England
64A1 **Chippewa** *R* USA
57D2 **Chippewa Falls** USA
64A1 **Chippewa,L** USA
7D4 **Chipping Norton** England
7C4 **Chipping Sodbury** England
72B4 **Chira** *R* Peru
44C2 **Chīrāla** India
51D6 **Chiredzi** Zimbabwe
50B1 **Chirfa** Niger

Chiricahua Peak Concepción

59E4 **Chiricahua Peak** *Mt* USA
70D4 **Chiriquí, G de** Panama
72B2 **Chiriquí, Lago de** Panama
17F2 **Chirpan** Bulgaria
72B2 **Chirripó Grande** *Mt* Costa Rica
51C5 **Chirundu** Zimbabwe
51C5 **Chisamba** Zambia
55L4 **Chisasibi** Canada
61E1 **Chisholm** USA
31B4 **Chishui He** *R* China
Chisimaio = Kismaayo
Chişinău = Kishinev
20H4 **Chistopol** Russian Federation
26E1 **Chita** Russian Federation
25N4 **Chita** *Division* Russian Federation
51B5 **Chitado** Angola
51B5 **Chitembo** Angola
29D2 **Chitose** Japan
44B3 **Chitradurga** India
42C1 **Chitral** Pakistan
72B2 **Chitré** Panama
43G4 **Chittagong** Bangladesh
42C4 **Chittaurgarh** India
44B3 **Chittoor** India
51C5 **Chiume** Angola
74D4 **Chivilcoy** Argentina
51D5 **Chivu** Zimbabwe
29B3 **Chizu** Japan
28A3 **Choch'iwŏn** S Korea
72D2 **Chocontá** Colombia
28A4 **Ch'o-do** *I* S Korea
74C5 **Choele Choel** Argentina
33E1 **Choiseul** *I* Solomon Islands
70B2 **Choix** Mexico
19D2 **Chojnice** Poland
29D3 **Chokai-san** *Mt* Japan
50D2 **Choke Mts** Ethiopia
25Q2 **Chokurdakh** Russian Federation
66B3 **Cholame** USA
66B3 **Cholame Creek** *R* USA
14B2 **Cholet** France
72A1 **Choluteca** Honduras
51C5 **Choma** Zambia
28A3 **Chŏmch'ŏn** S Korea
43F3 **Chomo Yummo** *Mt* China/India
18C2 **Chomutov** Czech Republic
25M3 **Chona** *R* Russian Federation
28B3 **Ch'ŏnan** S Korea
30C3 **Chon Buri** Thailand
28A2 **Chonchon** N Korea
72C4 **Chone** Ecuador
74B6 **Chones, Archipiélago de las** Chile
28A3 **Chongdo** S Korea
28B2 **Ch'ŏngjin** N Korea
28B3 **Chŏngju** N Korea
28B3 **Ch'ŏngju** S Korea
51B5 **Chongoroi** Angola
28A3 **Chongpyong** N Korea
31B4 **Chongqing** China
28A3 **Chŏngsŏn** S Korea
28B3 **Chŏngŭp** S Korea
28B3 **Ch'ŏnju** S Korea
43F3 **Cho Oyu** *Mt* China/Nepal
75B4 **Chopim** *R* Brazil
6C3 **Chorley** England
19F3 **Chortkov** Ukraine
28B3 **Ch'ŏrwŏn** S Korea
19D2 **Chorzów** Poland
28A2 **Chosan** N Korea
29E3 **Chōshi** Japan
18D2 **Choszczno** Poland
43E4 **Chotanāgpur** *Region* India
58D1 **Choteau** USA
48C1 **Chott ech Chergui** *L* Algeria
15C2 **Chott El Hodna** *L* Algeria
48C1 **Chott Melrhir** *L* Algeria
66B2 **Chowchilla** USA
25N5 **Choybalsan** Mongolia
7D4 **Christchurch** England
35B2 **Christchurch** New Zealand
47D2 **Christiana** South Africa
55M2 **Christian,C** Canada
55N3 **Christianshåb** Greenland
27D8 **Christmas I** Indian Ocean
24J5 **Chu** Kazakhstan
24J5 **Chu** *R* Kazakhstan
58D2 **Chubbuck** USA
74C6 **Chubut** *R* Argentina
74C6 **Chubut** *State* Argentina
20E4 **Chudovo** Russian Federation
54D3 **Chugach Mts** USA
28B3 **Chūgoku-sanchi** *Mts* Japan
60C2 **Chugwater** USA
74F4 **Chui** Uruguay
30C5 **Chukai** Malaysia
26G1 **Chukchagirskoye, Ozero** *L* Russian Federation
25S3 **Chukotskiy Avt. Okrug** *Division* Russian Federation
25T3 **Chukotskiy Khrebet** *Mts* Russian Federation
25U3 **Chukotskiy Poluostrov** *Pen* Russian Federation
30D2 **Chu Lai** Vietnam
59C4 **Chula Vista** USA
26F1 **Chulman** Russian Federation
72B5 **Chulucanas** Peru
72E7 **Chulumani** Bolivia
24K4 **Chulym** Russian Federation
25K4 **Chulym** *R* Russian Federation
25L4 **Chuma** *R* Russian Federation
42D2 **Chumar** India
25P4 **Chumikan** Russian Federation
30B3 **Chumphon** Thailand
28B3 **Ch'unch'ŏn** S Korea
43F4 **Chunchura** India
28B3 **Ch'ungju** S Korea
Chungking = Chongqing
28A4 **Ch'ungmu** S Korea
28B3 **Chŭngsan** N Korea
28A3 **Chungwa** N Korea
28C2 **Chunhua** China
51D4 **Chunya** Tanzania
25M3 **Chunya** *R* Russian Federation
28B2 **Chunyang** China
28A3 **Ch'unyang** S Korea
69L1 **Chupara Pt** Trinidad
74C2 **Chuquicamata** Chile
16B1 **Chur** Switzerland
43G4 **Churāchāndpur** India
25P3 **Churapcha** Russian Federation
55J4 **Churchill** Canada
55M4 **Churchill** *R* Labrador, Canada
55J4 **Churchill** *R* Manitoba, Canada
55J4 **Churchill,C** Canada
55M4 **Churchill Falls** Canada
54H4 **Churchill L** Canada
42C3 **Chūru** India
20K4 **Chusovoy** Russian Federation
20H4 **Chuvashiya** *Division* Russian Federation
26D4 **Chuxiong** China
30D3 **Chu Yang Sin** *Mt* Vietnam
75B3 **Cianorte** Brazil
19E2 **Ciechanów** Poland
70E2 **Ciego de Ávila** Cuba
72D1 **Ciénaga** Colombia
70D2 **Cienfuegos** Cuba
19D3 **Cieszyn** Poland
15B2 **Cieza** Spain
40B2 **Cihanbeyli** Turkey
15B2 **Cijara, Embalse de** *Res* Spain
27D7 **Cilacap** Indonesia
62B1 **Cimarron** USA
62C1 **Cimarron** *R* USA
16C2 **Cimone, Monte** *Mt* Italy
17F1 **Cimpina** Romania
15C1 **Cinca** *R* Spain
16D2 **Cincer** *Mt* Bosnia-Herzegovina
57E3 **Cincinnati** USA
17E1 **Cindrelu** *Mt* Romania
17F3 **Cine** *R* Turkey
13C2 **Ciney** Belgium
16B2 **Cinto, Monte** *Mt* Corsica, France
54D3 **Circle** Alaska, USA
60B1 **Circle** Montana, USA
64C3 **Circleville** USA
27D7 **Cirebon** Indonesia
7D4 **Cirencester** England
62C2 **Cisco** USA
70C3 **Citlaltepetl** *Vol* Mexico
47B3 **Citrusdal** South Africa
8D4 **City of Edinburgh** *Division* Scotland
8C4 **City of Glasgow** *Division* Scotland
70B2 **Ciudad Acuña** Mexico
72F2 **Ciudad Bolívar** Venezuela
70B2 **Ciudad Camargo** Mexico
70C3 **Ciudad del Carmen** Mexico
15C2 **Ciudadela** Spain
72F2 **Ciudad Guayana** Venezuela
70B3 **Ciudad Guzman** Mexico
70B1 **Ciudad Juárez** Mexico
56C4 **Ciudad Lerdo** Mexico
70C2 **Ciudad Madero** Mexico
70B2 **Ciudad Obregon** Mexico
69C4 **Ciudad Ojeda** Venezuela
72F2 **Ciudad Piar** Venezuela
15B2 **Ciudad Real** Spain
15A1 **Ciudad Rodrigo** Spain
70C2 **Ciudad Valles** Mexico
70C2 **Ciudad Victoria** Mexico
16C2 **Civitavecchia** Italy
40D2 **Cizre** Turkey
8D3 **Clackmannanshire** *Division* Scotland
7E4 **Clacton-on-Sea** England
54G4 **Claire,L** Canada
65D2 **Clairton** USA
67A2 **Clanton** USA
47B3 **Clanwilliam** South Africa
9C3 **Clara** Irish Republic
64C2 **Clare** USA
65E2 **Claremont** USA
63C1 **Claremore** USA
34D1 **Clarence** *R* Australia
35B2 **Clarence** *R* New Zealand
32C2 **Clarence Str** Australia
63D2 **Clarendon** USA
55N5 **Clarenville** Canada
54G4 **Claresholm** Canada
61D2 **Clarinda** USA
61E2 **Clarion** Iowa, USA
65D2 **Clarion** Pennsylvania, USA
70A3 **Clarión** *I* Mexico
65D2 **Clarion** *R* USA
37M4 **Clarion Fracture Zone** Pacific Ocean
57E3 **Clark Hill Res** USA
59C3 **Clark Mt** USA
64C2 **Clark,Pt** Canada
64C3 **Clarksburg** USA
57D3 **Clarksdale** USA
58C1 **Clarkston** USA
63D1 **Clarksville** Arkansas, USA
67A1 **Clarksville** Tennessee, USA
75B2 **Claro** *R* Brazil
74E5 **Claromecó** Argentina
61D3 **Clay Center** USA
8E2 **Claymore** *Oilfield* N Sea
56C3 **Clayton** New Mexico, USA
65D2 **Clayton** New York, USA
10B3 **Clear, C** Irish Republic
68A2 **Clearfield** Pennsylvania, USA
58D2 **Clearfield** Utah, USA
59B3 **Clear L** USA
61E2 **Clear Lake** USA
58B2 **Clear Lake Res** USA
60B2 **Clearmont** USA
57E4 **Clearwater** USA
58C1 **Clearwater Mts** USA
56D3 **Cleburne** USA
7D3 **Cleethorpes** England
6E2 **Cleeton** *Oilfield* N Sea
66B1 **Clements** USA
32D3 **Clermont** Australia
13B3 **Clermont** France
13C3 **Clermont-en-Argonne** France
14C2 **Clermont-Ferrand** France
13D2 **Clervaux** Luxembourg
63D2 **Cleveland** Mississippi, USA
57E2 **Cleveland** Ohio, USA
67B1 **Cleveland** Tennessee, USA
63C2 **Cleveland** Texas, USA
75B4 **Clevelândia** Brazil
58D1 **Cleveland,Mt** USA
10B3 **Clew B** Irish Republic
59E4 **Clifton** Arizona, USA
34D1 **Clifton** Australia
68C2 **Clifton** New Jersey, USA
34A1 **Clifton Hills** Australia
67B1 **Clinch** *R* USA
67B1 **Clinch Mts** USA
63D1 **Clinton** Arkansas, USA
54F4 **Clinton** Canada
68D2 **Clinton** Connecticut, USA
64A2 **Clinton** Iowa, USA
68E1 **Clinton** Massachusetts, USA
63D2 **Clinton** Mississippi, USA
63D1 **Clinton** Missouri, USA
67C2 **Clinton** N Carolina, USA
68C2 **Clinton** New Jersey, USA
62C1 **Clinton** Oklahoma, USA
54H3 **Clinton-Colden L** Canada
70B3 **Clipperton I** Pacific Ocean
6C3 **Clitheroe** England
72E7 **Cliza** Bolivia
9C3 **Clogher Hd** *Pt* Irish Republic
9B4 **Clonakilty B** Irish Republic
32D3 **Cloncurry** Australia
9C3 **Clones** Irish Republic
9C3 **Clonmel** Irish Republic
13E1 **Cloppenburg** Germany
57D2 **Cloquet** USA
75A4 **Clorinda** Argentina
60B2 **Cloud Peak** *Mt* USA
66A1 **Cloverdale** USA
66C2 **Clovis** California, USA
56C3 **Clovis** New Mexico, USA
21C6 **Cluj** Romania
17E1 **Cluj-Napoca** Romania
35A3 **Clutha** *R* New Zealand
7C3 **Clwyd** *R* Wales
55M2 **Clyde** Canada
35A3 **Clyde** New Zealand
6F1 **Clyde** *Oilfield* N Sea
68B1 **Clyde** USA
8C4 **Clyde** *R* Scotland
8C4 **Clydebank** Scotland
59C4 **Coachella** USA
62B3 **Coahuila** *State* Mexico
59C3 **Coaldale** USA
59B3 **Coalinga** USA
7D3 **Coalville** England
58D2 **Coalville** USA
75E1 **Coaraci** Brazil
72F5 **Coari** *R* Brazil
67A2 **Coastal Plain** USA
54E4 **Coast Mts** Canada
56A2 **Coast Ranges** *Mts* USA
8C4 **Coatbridge** Scotland
68C3 **Coatesville** USA
65E1 **Coaticook** Canada
55K3 **Coats I** Canada
76F1 **Coats Land** *Region* Antarctica
70C3 **Coatzacoalcas** Mexico
55L5 **Cobalt** Canada
70C3 **Cobán** Guatemala
32D4 **Cobar** Australia
34C3 **Cobargo** Australia
72E6 **Cobija** Bolivia
68C1 **Cobleskill** USA
55L5 **Cobourg** Canada
32C2 **Cobourg Pen** Australia
18C2 **Coburg** Germany
72C4 **Coca** Ecuador
75B1 **Cocalinho** Brazil
72E7 **Cochabamba** Bolivia
13D2 **Cochem** Germany
55K5 **Cochrane** Ontario, Canada
74B7 **Cochrane, Lago** Argentina/Chile
34B2 **Cockburn** Australia
6C2 **Cockermouth** England
68B3 **Cockeysville** USA
69H1 **Cockpit Country,The** Jamaica
47C3 **Cockscomb** *Mt* South Africa
70D3 **Coco** *R* Honduras/Nicaragua
67B3 **Cocoa** USA
48C4 **Cocobeach** Equatorial Guinea
44E3 **Coco Channel** Andaman Is/Burma
53K8 **Coco, Isla del** Costa Rica
75D1 **Côcos** Brazil
69L1 **Cocos B** Trinidad
27C8 **Cocos Is** Indian Ocean
37P4 **Cocos Ridge** Pacific Ocean
57F2 **Cod,C** USA
35A3 **Codfish I** New Zealand
55M4 **Cod I** Canada
15C1 **Codi, Sierra del** *Mts* Spain
73K4 **Codó** Brazil
56C2 **Cody** USA
27H8 **Coen** Australia
18B2 **Coesfeld** Germany
56B2 **Coeur d'Alene** USA
58C1 **Coeur d'Alene L** USA
13D1 **Coevorden** Netherlands
56D3 **Coffeyville** USA
34D2 **Coff's Harbour** Australia
47D3 **Cofimvaba** South Africa
16B2 **Coghinas, Lago del** Sardinia, Italy
14B2 **Cognac** France
68B1 **Cohocton** USA
68B1 **Cohocton** *R* USA
65E2 **Cohoes** USA
34B3 **Cohuna** Australia
72B2 **Coiba, Isla** Panama
74B7 **Coihaique** Chile
44B3 **Coimbatore** India
15A1 **Coimbra** Portugal
72B3 **Cojimies** Ecuador
58D2 **Cokeville** USA
32D4 **Colac** Australia
73K7 **Colatina** Brazil
76F6 **Colbeck,C** Antarctica
14B2 **Colby** USA
7E4 **Colchester** England
68D2 **Colchester** USA
8D4 **Coldstream** Scotland
64C2 **Coldwater** USA
58D1 **Coleman** Canada
64C2 **Coleman** Michigan, USA
62C2 **Coleman** Texas, USA
47D2 **Colenso** South Africa
9C2 **Coleraine** Northern Ireland
35B2 **Coleridge,L** New Zealand
47D3 **Colesberg** South Africa
72D7 **Coles, Puerta** Peru
66C1 **Coleville** USA
59B3 **Colfax** California, USA
63D2 **Colfax** Louisiana, USA
58C1 **Colfax** Washington, USA
74C7 **Colhué Huapí, Lago** Argentina
70B3 **Colima** Mexico
8B3 **Coll** *I* Scotland
34C1 **Collarenebri** Australia
67B2 **College Park** Georgia, USA
68B3 **College Park** Washington DC, USA
63C2 **College Station** USA
32A4 **Collie** Australia
32B2 **Collier B** Australia
13A2 **Collines de l'Artois** *Hills* France
13B3 **Collines de la Thiérache** *Hills* France
64C2 **Collingwood** Canada
35B2 **Collingwood** New Zealand
63E2 **Collins** Mississippi, USA
68A1 **Collins** New York, USA
54H2 **Collinson Pen** Canada
32D3 **Collinsville** Australia
64B3 **Collinsville** Illinois, USA
63C1 **Collinsville** Oklahoma, USA
14D2 **Colmar** France
6C3 **Colne** England
56B3 **Colnett, Cabo** *C* Mexico
18B2 **Cologne** Germany
75C3 **Colômbia** Brazil
65D3 **Colombia** USA
72D3 **Colombia** *Republic* S America
44B4 **Colombo** Sri Lanka
74E4 **Colón** Argentina
70D2 **Colon** Cuba
72C2 **Colón** Panama
Colón, Arch. de = Galapagos Islands
74E4 **Colonia** Uruguay
74C7 **Colonia Las Heras** Argentina
65D3 **Colonial Heights** USA
8B3 **Colonsay** *I* Scotland
69E5 **Coloradito** Venezuela
74D5 **Colorado** *R* Buenos Aires, Argentina
56D3 **Colorado** *R* Texas, USA
56B3 **Colorado** *R* Mexico/USA
56C3 **Colorado** *State* USA
62B2 **Colorado City** USA
56B3 **Colorado Plat** USA
56C3 **Colorado Springs** USA
68B3 **Columbia** Maryland, USA
63E2 **Columbia** Mississippi, USA
57D3 **Columbia** Missouri, USA
65D2 **Columbia** Pennsylvania, USA
57E3 **Columbia** S Carolina, USA
57E3 **Columbia** Tennessee, USA
56A2 **Columbia** *R* USA
58D1 **Columbia Falls** USA
54G4 **Columbia,Mt** Canada
58C1 **Columbia Plat** USA
47B3 **Columbine,C** South Africa
15C2 **Columbretes, Islas** Spain
57E3 **Columbus** Georgia, USA
64B3 **Columbus** Indiana, USA
57E3 **Columbus** Mississippi, USA
58E1 **Columbus** Montana, USA
56D2 **Columbus** Nebraska, USA
62A2 **Columbus** New Mexico, USA
57E2 **Columbus** Ohio, USA
63C3 **Columbus** Texas, USA
64B2 **Columbus** Wisconsin, USA
58C1 **Colville** USA
54C3 **Colville** *R* USA
35C1 **Colville,C** New Zealand
54F3 **Colville L** Canada
7C3 **Colwyn Bay** Wales
62C2 **Comanche** USA
66B1 **Comanche Res** USA
76G2 **Comandante Ferraz** *Base* Antarctica
70D3 **Comayagua** Honduras
13C4 **Combeaufontaine** France
9D2 **Comber** Northern Ireland
43G5 **Combermere B** Burma
9C3 **Comeragh Mts** Irish Republic
62C2 **Comfort** USA
43G4 **Comilla** Bangladesh
70C3 **Comitán** Mexico
13C3 **Commercy** France
55K3 **Committee B** Canada
16B1 **Como** Italy
74C7 **Comodoro Rivadavia** Argentina
16B1 **Como, L di** Italy
44B4 **Comorin,C** India
51E5 **Comoros** *Is, Republic* Indian Ocean
14C2 **Compiègne** France
75C3 **Comprida, Ilha** Brazil
15B2 **Comunidad Valenciana** *Region* Spain
43G3 **Cona** China
48A4 **Conakry** Guinea
14B2 **Concarneau** France
75E2 **Conceiçao da Barra** Brazil
73J5 **Conceição do Araguaia** Brazil
75D2 **Conceiçao do Mato Dentro** Brazil
74E4 **Concepción** Argentina
75A3 **Concepción** Brazil/Paraguay
74B5 **Concepción** Chile

Divnoye **East Riding of Yorkshire**

21G6 **Divnoye** Russian Federation
40C2 **Divriği** Turkey
66B1 **Dixon** California, USA
64B2 **Dixon** Illinois, USA
58D1 **Dixon** Montana, USA
54E4 **Dixon Entrance** *Sd* Canada/USA
41E3 **Diyālā** *R* Iraq
21G8 **Diyarbakır** Turkey
41E3 **Diz** *R* Iran
50B3 **Dja** *R* Cameroon
50B1 **Djado,Plat du** Niger
50B4 **Djambala** Congo
48C2 **Djanet** Algeria
48C1 **Djedi** *Watercourse* Algeria
48C1 **Djelfa** Algeria
50C3 **Djéma** Central African Republic
48B3 **Djenné** Mali
48B3 **Djibo** Burkina
50E2 **Djibouti** Djibouti
50E2 **Djibouti** *Republic* E Africa
50C3 **Djolu** Zaïre
48C4 **Djougou** Benin
50B2 **Djourab, Erg du** *Desert Region* Chad
50D3 **Djugu** Zaïre
12C2 **Djúpivogur** Iceland
15C2 **Djurdjura** *Mts* Algeria
25P2 **Dmitriya Lapteva, Proliv** *Str* Russian Federation
20F4 **Dmitrov** Russian Federation
Dnepr *R* Ukraine = **Dnieper**
21E6 **Dneprodzerzhinsk** Ukraine
21F6 **Dnepropetrovsk** Ukraine
20D5 **Dneprovskaya Nizmennost'** *Region* Belarus
21C6 **Dnestr** *R* Ukraine = **Dniester**
21E6 **Dnieper** *R* Ukraine
21C6 **Dniester** *R* Ukraine
20E4 **Dno** Russian Federation
50B3 **Doba** Chad
19E1 **Dobele** Latvia
32C1 **Dobo** Indonesia
17D2 **Doboj** Bosnia-Herzegovina
17F2 **Dobrich** Bulgaria
21E5 **Dobrush** Belarus
73K7 **Doce** *R* Brazil
74D2 **Doctor P P Peña** Paraguay
44B3 **Dod** India
44B3 **Doda Betta** *Mt* India
17F3 **Dodecanese** *Is* Greece
56C3 **Dodge City** USA
64A2 **Dodgeville** USA
50D4 **Dodoma** Tanzania
64B1 **Dog L** Canada
64C1 **Dog L** Canada
29B3 **Dōgo** *I* Japan
48C3 **Dogondoutchi** Niger
41D2 **Doğubayazit** Turkey
41F4 **Doha** Qatar
43G3 **Doilungdêqên** China
13D1 **Dokkum** Netherlands
29F2 **Dokuchayevo, Mys** *C* Russian Federation
32C1 **Dolak** *I* Indonesia
61D2 **Doland** USA
55L5 **Dolbeau** Canada
14D2 **Dole** France
Dolgano-Nenetskiy Avt. Okrug = Taymytskiy Avt. Okrug
7C3 **Dolgellau** Wales
68C1 **Dolgeville** USA
20K2 **Dolgiy, Ostrov** *I* Russian Federation
50E3 **Dolo Odo** Ethiopia
74E5 **Dolores** Argentina
60B3 **Dolores** *R* USA
54G3 **Dolphin and Union Str** Canada
74E8 **Dolphin,C** Falkland Islands
27G7 **Dom** *Mt* Indonesia
21K5 **Dombarovskiy** Russian Federation
12F6 **Dombås** Norway
13D3 **Dombasle-sur-Meurthe** France
17D1 **Dombóvár** Hungary
14B2 **Domfront** France
69E3 **Dominica** *I* Caribbean Sea
69C3 **Dominican Republic** Caribbean Sea
55L3 **Dominion,C** Canada
55N4 **Domino** Canada
26E1 **Domna** Russian Federation
16B1 **Domodossola** Italy
74B5 **Domuyo, Vol** Argentina
34D1 **Domville,Mt** Australia
8D3 **Don** *R* Scotland
21G6 **Don** *R* Russian Federation
9C2 **Donaghadee** Northern Ireland
Donau *R* Bulgaria = **Danube**
Donau *R* Austria/Germany = **Danube**
13E4 **Donaueschingen** Germany
18C3 **Donauwörth** Germany
15A2 **Don Benito** Spain
7D3 **Doncaster** England
51B4 **Dondo** Angola
51D5 **Dondo** Mozambique
44C4 **Dondra Head** *C* Sri Lanka
10B3 **Donegal** Irish Republic
9C2 **Donegal** *County* Irish Republic
10B3 **Donegal B** Irish Republic
9C2 **Donegal Mts** Irish Republic
9B3 **Donegal Pt** Irish Republic
21F6 **Donetsk** Ukraine
31C4 **Dong'an** China
32A3 **Dongara** Australia
31A4 **Dongchuan** China
30D2 **Dongfang** China
28B2 **Dongfeng** China
32A1 **Donggala** Indonesia
26C3 **Donggi Cona** *L* China
28A3 **Donggou** China
31C5 **Donghai Dao** *I* China
31A1 **Dong He** *R* China
30D2 **Dong Hoi** Vietnam
31C5 **Dong Jiang** *R* China
28A2 **Dongliao He** *R* China
28C2 **Dongning** China
50D2 **Dongola** Sudan
31D5 **Dongshan** China
26E4 **Dongsha Qundao** *I* China
31C2 **Dongsheng** China
31E3 **Dongtai** China
31C4 **Dongting Hu** *L* China
31B5 **Dongxing** China
31D3 **Dongzhi** China
63D1 **Doniphan** USA
16D2 **Donji Vakuf** Bosnia-Herzegovina
12G5 **Dönna** *I* Norway
59B3 **Donner P** USA
13D3 **Donnersberg** *Mt* Germany
47D2 **Donnybrook** South Africa
Donostia = San Sebatián
66B2 **Don Pedro Res** USA
8C4 **Doon, Loch** *L* Scotland
31A3 **Do Qu** *R* China
14D2 **Dorbirn** Austria
7C4 **Dorchester** England
55L3 **Dorchester,C** Canada
14C2 **Dordogne** *R* France
18A2 **Dordrecht** Netherlands
47D3 **Dordrecht** South Africa
68D1 **Dorest Peak** *Mt* USA
48B3 **Dori** Burkina
47B3 **Doring** *R* South Africa
7D4 **Dorking** England
13B3 **Dormans** France
18B3 **Dornbirn** Austria
8C3 **Dornoch** Scotland
8D3 **Dornoch Firth** *Estuary* Scotland
12H6 **Dorotea** Sweden
34D2 **Dorrigo** Australia
58B2 **Dorris** USA
7C4 **Dorset** *County* England
55L3 **Dorset, Cape** Canada
13D2 **Dorsten** Germany
18B2 **Dortmund** Germany
50C3 **Doruma** Zaïre
25N4 **Dosatuy** Russian Federation
42B1 **Doshi** Afghanistan
66B2 **Dos Palos** USA
48C3 **Dosso** Niger
24G5 **Dossor** Kazakhstan
57E3 **Dothan** USA
14C1 **Douai** France
50A3 **Douala** Cameroon
34D1 **Double Island Pt** Australia
62B2 **Double Mountain Fork** *R* USA
66C3 **Double Mt** USA
14D2 **Doubs** *R* France
35A3 **Doubtful Sd** New Zealand
48B3 **Douentza** Mali
56C3 **Douglas** Arizona, USA
67B2 **Douglas** Georgia, USA
6B2 **Douglas** Isle of Man, British Islands
47C2 **Douglas** South Africa
56C2 **Douglas** Wyoming, USA
67B1 **Douglas L** USA
13C2 **Doulevant-le-Château** France
13B2 **Doullens** France
75B2 **Dourada, Serra** *Mts* Brazil
75C1 **Dourada, Serra** *Mts* Brazil
73H8 **Dourados** Brazil
75B3 **Dourados** *R* Brazil
75B3 **Dourados, Serra dos** *Mts* Brazil
13B3 **Dourdan** France
15A1 **Douro** *R* Portugal
7D3 **Dove** *R* England
62A1 **Dove Creek** USA
65D3 **Dover** Delaware, USA
7E4 **Dover** England
65E2 **Dover** New Hampshire, USA
68C2 **Dover** New Jersey, USA
64C2 **Dover** Ohio, USA
7E4 **Dover,Str of** England/France
19G2 **Dovsk** Belarus
9C2 **Down** *County* Northern Ireland
68C3 **Downingtown** USA
9D2 **Downpatrick** Northern Ireland
68C1 **Downsville** USA
68C2 **Doylestown** USA
28B3 **Dözen** *I* Japan
65D1 **Dozois, Réservoir** Canada
48A2 **Dr'aa** *Watercourse* Morocco
75B3 **Dracena** Brazil
13D1 **Drachten** Netherlands
68E1 **Dracut** USA
14D3 **Draguignan** France
60C1 **Drake** USA
51D6 **Drakensberg** *Mts* South Africa
47D2 **Drakensberg** *Mt* South Africa
52E7 **Drake Passage** Atlantic O/Pacific Ocean
17E2 **Dráma** Greece
12G7 **Drammen** Norway
12A1 **Drangajökull** *Ice cap* Iceland
16D1 **Drava** *R* Slovenia
13D1 **Drenthe** *Province* Netherlands
18C2 **Dresden** Germany
14C2 **Dreux** France
58C2 **Drewsey** USA
68A2 **Driftwood** USA
17E2 **Drin** *R* Albania
17D2 **Drina** *R* Bosnia-Herzegovina/Serbia, Yugoslavia
19F1 **Drissa** *R* Belarus
9C3 **Drogheda** Irish Republic
19E3 **Drogobych** Ukraine
9C3 **Droihead Nua** Irish Republic
7C3 **Droitwich** England
9C2 **Dromore** Northern Ireland
76F12 **Dronning Maud Land** *Region* Antarctica
54G4 **Drumheller** Canada
58D1 **Drummond** USA
64C1 **Drummond I** USA
65E1 **Drummondville** Canada
8C3 **Drumochter Pass** Scotland
19E2 **Druskininkai** Lithuania
25Q3 **Druzhina** Russian Federation
61E1 **Dryberry L** Canada
55J5 **Dryden** Canada
68B1 **Dryden** USA
69H1 **Dry Harbour Mts** Jamaica
30B3 **Duang** *I* Burma
40C4 **Dubā** Saudi Arabia
41G4 **Dubai** UAE
54H3 **Dubawnt** *R* Canada
54H3 **Dubawnt L** Canada
32D4 **Dubbo** Australia
9C3 **Dublin** Irish Republic
67B2 **Dublin** USA
9C3 **Dublin** *County* Irish Republic
20F4 **Dubna** Russian Federation
21D5 **Dubno** Ukraine
58D2 **Dubois** Idaho, USA
65D2 **Du Bois** USA
58E2 **Dubois** Wyoming, USA
19F3 **Dubossary** Moldavia
19F2 **Dubrovica** Ukraine
17D2 **Dubrovnik** Croatia
57D2 **Dubuque** USA
59D2 **Duchesne** USA
67A1 **Duck** *R* USA
66C3 **Ducor** USA
13D3 **Dudelange** Luxembourg
24K3 **Dudinka** Russian Federation
7C3 **Dudley** England
25L2 **Dudypta** *R* Russian Federation
48B4 **Duekoué** Ivory Coast
15B1 **Duero** *R* Spain
33F1 **Duff Is** Solomon Islands
8D3 **Dufftown** Scotland
16C2 **Dugi Otok** *I* Croatia
18B2 **Duisburg** Germany
47E1 **Duiwelskloof** South Africa
41E3 **Dūkan** Iraq
50D3 **Duk Faiwil** Sudan
41F4 **Dukhān** Qatar
31A4 **Dukou** China
26C3 **Dulan** China
70D4 **Dulce, Golfo** Costa Rica
43G4 **Dullabchara** India
13D2 **Dülmen** Germany
57D2 **Duluth** USA
7C4 **Dulverton** England
45D2 **Dūmā** Syria
27D6 **Dumai** Indonesia
56C3 **Dumas** USA
45D2 **Ḑumayr** Syria
8C4 **Dumbarton** Scotland
48B1 **Dumer Rbia** Morocco
8D4 **Dumfries** Scotland
8C4 **Dumfries and Galloway** *Division* Scotland
43F4 **Dumka** India
65D1 **Dumoine,L** Canada
76G8 **Dumont d'Urville** *Base* Antarctica
49F1 **Dumyat** Egypt
Dunărea *R* Romania = **Danube**
9C3 **Dunary Head** *Pt* Irish Republic
Dunav *R* Bulgaria = **Danube**
Dunav *R* Croatia/Serbia = **Danube**
28C2 **Dunay** Russian Federation
19F3 **Dunayevtsy** Ukraine
8D4 **Dunbar** Scotland
63C2 **Duncan** USA
68B2 **Duncannon** USA
44E3 **Duncan Pass** *Chan* Andaman Islands
8D2 **Duncansby Head** *Pt* Scotland
9C2 **Dundalk** Irish Republic
68B3 **Dundalk** USA
9C3 **Dundalk B** Irish Republic
55M2 **Dundas** Greenland
54G2 **Dundas Pen** Canada
27G8 **Dundas Str** Australia
47E2 **Dundee** South Africa
8D3 **Dundee** Scotland
8D3 **Dundee City** *Division* Scotland
68B1 **Dundee** USA
34B1 **Dundoo** Australia
9D2 **Dundrum B** Northern Ireland
43M2 **Dundwa Range** *Mts* Nepal
33G5 **Dunedin** New Zealand
67B3 **Dunedin** USA
34C2 **Dunedoo** Australia
8D3 **Dunfermline** Scotland
9C2 **Dungannon** Northern Ireland
42C4 **Dūngarpur** India
9C3 **Dungarvan** Irish Republic
7E4 **Dungeness** *Pen* England
34D2 **Dungog** Australia
50C3 **Dungu** Zaïre
50D1 **Dungunab** Sudan
28B2 **Dunhua** China
26C2 **Dunhuang** China
8D3 **Dunkeld** Scotland
Dunkerque = Dunkirk
13B2 **Dunkirk** France
57F2 **Dunkirk** USA
50D2 **Dunkur** Ethiopia
48B4 **Dunkwa** Ghana
10B3 **Dun Laoghaire** Irish Republic
9B4 **Dunmanus** Irish Republic
68C2 **Dunmore** USA
69B1 **Dunmore Town** The Bahamas
67C1 **Dunn** USA
8D2 **Dunnet Head** *Pt* Scotland
60C2 **Dunning** USA
8C4 **Dunoon** Scotland
8D4 **Duns** Scotland
60C1 **Dunseith** USA
58B2 **Dunsmuir** USA
35A2 **Dunstan Mts** New Zealand
13C3 **Dun-sur-Meuse** France
31D1 **Duolun** China
60C1 **Dupree** USA
64B3 **Du Quoin** USA
45C3 **Dura** West Bank
14D3 **Durance** *R* France
64A2 **Durand** USA
70B2 **Durango** Mexico
15B1 **Durango** Spain
56C3 **Durango** USA
56D3 **Durant** USA
45D1 **Duraykish** Syria
74E4 **Durazno** Uruguay
47E2 **Durban** South Africa
13D2 **Duren** Germany
43E4 **Durg** India
43F4 **Durgapur** India
6D2 **Durham** England
57F3 **Durham** N Carolina, USA
68E1 **Durham** New Hampshire, USA
6D2 **Durham** *County* England
34B1 **Durham Downs** Australia
17D2 **Durmitor** *Mt* Montenegro, Yugoslavia
8C2 **Durness** Scotland
17D2 **Durrës** Albania
34B1 **Durrie** Australia
17F3 **Dursunbey** Turkey
35B2 **D'Urville I** New Zealand
41H2 **Dushak** Turkmenistan
31B4 **Dushan** China
39E2 **Dushanbe** Tajikistan
68B2 **Dushore** USA
35A3 **Dusky Sd** New Zealand
18B2 **Düsseldorf** Germany
59D3 **Dutton,Mt** USA
31B4 **Duyun** China
40B1 **Düzce** Turkey
20F2 **Dvinskaya Guba** *B* Russian Federation
42B4 **Dwārka** India
58C1 **Dworshak Res** USA
57E3 **Dyersburg** USA
21G7 **Dykh Tau** *Mt* Russian Federation
34B1 **Dynevor Downs** Australia
26C2 **Dzag** Mongolia
26E2 **Dzamïn Üüd** Mongolia
51E5 **Dzaoudzi** Mayotte, Indian Ocean
26C2 **Dzavhan Gol** *R* Mongolia
20G4 **Dzerzhinsk** Russian Federation
25O4 **Dzhalinda** Russian Federation
24J5 **Dzhambul** Kazakhstan
21E6 **Dzhankoy** Ukraine
24H5 **Dzhezkazgan** Kazakhstan
42B1 **Dzhilikul'** Tajikistan
25P4 **Dzhugdzhur, Khrebet** *Mts* Russian Federation
24J5 **Dzhungarskiy Alatau** *Mts* Kazakhstan
18D2 **Dzierzoniów** Poland
39G1 **Dzungaria Basin** China
25L5 **Dzüyl** Mongolia

E

55K4 **Eabamet L** Canada
60B3 **Eagle** Colorado, USA
60C1 **Eagle Butte** USA
58B2 **Eagle L** California, USA
65F1 **Eagle L** Maine, USA
65F1 **Eagle Lake** USA
63C2 **Eagle Mountain L** USA
56C4 **Eagle Pass** USA
62A2 **Eagle Peak** *Mt* USA
54E3 **Eagle Plain** Canada
59C3 **Earlimart** USA
8D3 **Earn** *R* Scotland
8C3 **Earn, Loch** *L* Scotland
59D4 **Earp** USA
62B2 **Earth** USA
6D2 **Easingwold** England
67B2 **Easley** USA
65D2 **East Aurora** USA
8C4 **East Ayrshire** *Division* Scotland
63E2 **East B** USA
7E4 **Eastbourne** England
68C1 **East Branch Delaware** *R* USA
33G4 **East C** New Zealand
64B2 **East Chicago** USA
26F3 **East China Sea** China/Japan
7E3 **East Dereham** England
8C4 **East Dunbartonshire** *Division* Scotland
37O6 **Easter I** Pacific Ocean
51C7 **Eastern Cape** *Province* South Africa
43E5 **Eastern Ghats** *Mts* India
Eastern Transvaal = Mpumalanga
74E8 **East Falkland** *Is* Falkland Islands
59C3 **Eastgate** USA
61D1 **East Grand Forks** USA
7D4 **East Grinstead** England
68D1 **Easthampton** USA
68D2 **East Hampton** USA
8C4 **East Kilbride** Scotland
64B2 **East Lake** USA
7D4 **Eastleigh** England
64C2 **East Liverpool** USA
8C4 **East Lanarkshire** *Division* Scotland
47D3 **East London** South Africa
8D4 **East Lothian** *Division* Scotland
55L4 **Eastmain** Canada
55L4 **Eastmain** *R* Canada
67B2 **Eastman** USA
64A2 **East Moline** USA
65D3 **Easton** Maryland, USA
65D2 **Easton** Pennsylvania, USA
68C2 **East Orange** USA
37O5 **East Pacific Ridge** Pacific Ocean
37O4 **East Pacific Rise** Pacific Ocean
67B2 **East Point** USA
65F2 **Eastport** USA
8C4 **East Renfrewshire** *Division* Scotland
7D3 **East Retford** England
67A1 **East Ridge** USA
6D3 **East Riding of Yorkshire** *County* England

Espinhaço, Serra do
Fortaleza

75D2 **Espinhaço, Serra do** *Mts* Brazil
75D2 **Espírito Santo** *State* Brazil
33F2 **Espiritu Santo** *I* Vanuatu
51D6 **Espungabera** Mozambique
74B6 **Esquel** Argentina
58B1 **Esquimalt** Canada
45D2 **Es Samrā** Jordan
48B1 **Essaouira** Morocco
18B2 **Essen** Germany
73G3 **Essequibo** *R* Guyana
7E4 **Essex** *County* England
64C2 **Essexville** USA
18B3 **Esslingen** Germany
13B3 **Essonne** *Department* France
13C3 **Essoyes** France
74D8 **Estados, Isla de los** Argentina
73L6 **Estância** Brazil
47D2 **Estcourt** South Africa
72A1 **Esteí** Nicaragua
13B3 **Esternay** France
66B3 **Estero B** USA
74D2 **Esteros** Paraguay
60B2 **Estes Park** USA
54H5 **Estevan** Canada
61E2 **Estherville** USA
67B2 **Estill** USA
13B3 **Estissac** France
20C4 **Estonia** *Republic* Europe
66B3 **Estrella** *R* USA
15A2 **Estremoz** Portugal
19D3 **Esztergom** Hungary
34A1 **Etadunna** Australia
55L2 **Etah** Canada
43K2 **Etah** India
13C3 **Etam** France
14C2 **Étampes** France
34A1 **Etamunbanie,L** Australia
42D3 **Etāwah** India
50D3 **Ethiopia** *Republic* Africa
8C3 **Etive, Loch** *Inlet* Scotland
16C3 **Etna** *Vol* Sicily, Italy
51B5 **Etosha Nat Pk** Namibia
51B5 **Etosha Pan** *Salt L* Namibia
67B2 **Etowah** *R* USA
13C3 **Ettelbruck** Luxembourg
33H3 **Eua** *I* Tonga
34C2 **Euabalong** Australia
17E3 **Euboea** *I* Greece
64C2 **Euclid** USA
34C3 **Eucumbene,L** Australia
34A2 **Eudunda** Australia
63C1 **Eufala L** USA
67A2 **Eufaula** USA
56A2 **Eugene** USA
70A2 **Eugenia, Punta** *Pt* Mexico
34C1 **Eulo** Australia
63D2 **Eunice** Louisiana, USA
62B2 **Eunice** New Mexico, USA
13D2 **Eupen** Germany
40D3 **Euphrates** *R* Iraq/Syria
63E2 **Eupora** USA
14C2 **Eure** *R* France
58B2 **Eureka** California, USA
55K1 **Eureka** Canada
58C1 **Eureka** Montana, USA
56B3 **Eureka** Nevada, USA
60D1 **Eureka** S Dakota, USA
59D3 **Eureka** Utah, USA
55K2 **Eureka Sd** Canada
66D2 **Eureka V** USA
34C3 **Euroa** Australia
34C1 **Eurombah** *R* Australia
51E6 **Europa** *I* Mozambique Channel
13C2 **Europoort** Netherlands
18B2 **Euskirchen** Germany
63E2 **Eutaw** USA
55K1 **Evans,C** Canada
55L4 **Evans,L** Canada
60B3 **Evans,Mt** Colorado, USA
58D1 **Evans,Mt** Montana, USA
55K3 **Evans Str** Canada
64B2 **Evanston** Illinois, USA
56B2 **Evanston** Wyoming, USA
57E3 **Evansville** Indiana, USA
60B2 **Evansville** Wyoming, USA
47D2 **Evaton** South Africa
25L3 **Evenkiyskiy Avt. Okrug** *Division* Russian Federation
32C4 **Everard,L** Australia
39G3 **Everest,Mt** China/Nepal
68A2 **Everett** Pennsylvania, USA
56A2 **Everett** Washington, USA
68D1 **Everett,Mt** USA
57E4 **Everglades,The** *Swamp* USA
67A2 **Evergreen** USA
7D3 **Evesham** England
50B3 **Evinayong** Equatorial Guinea
12F7 **Evje** Norway
15A2 **Évora** Portugal
14C2 **Evreux** France
Évvoia = Euboea
8C3 **Ewe, Loch** *Inlet* Scotland
50B4 **Ewo** Congo
66C1 **Excelsior Mt** USA
66C1 **Excelsior Mts** USA
61E3 **Excelsior Springs** USA
7C4 **Exe** *R* England
59C3 **Exeter** California, USA
7C4 **Exeter** England
65E2 **Exeter** New Hampshire, USA
7C4 **Exmoor** England
7C4 **Exmouth** England
15A2 **Extremadura** *Region* Spain
70E2 **Exuma Sd** The Bahamas
50D4 **Eyasi, L** Tanzania
8D4 **Eyemouth** Scotland
50E3 **Eyl** Somalia
32B4 **Eyre** Australia
32C3 **Eyre Creek** *R* Australia
32C3 **Eyre,L** Australia
32C4 **Eyre Pen** Australia
17F3 **Ezine** Turkey

F

54G3 **Faber L** Canada
12F7 **Fåborg** Denmark
16C2 **Fabriano** Italy
50B2 **Fachi** Niger
50C2 **Fada** Chad
48C3 **Fada N'Gourma** Burkina
25Q2 **Faddeyevskiy, Ostrov** *I* Russian Federation
16C2 **Faenza** Italy
55N3 **Færingehavn** Greenland
12D3 **Faeroes** *Is* N Atlantic Oc
50B3 **Fafa** *R* Central African Republic
50E3 **Fafan** *R* Ethiopia
17E1 **Făgăraş** Romania
13C2 **Fagnes** *Region* Belgium
48B3 **Faguibine,L** Mali
41G5 **Fahūd** Oman
48A1 **Faiol** *I* Azores
62A2 **Fairacres** USA
54D3 **Fairbanks** USA
64C3 **Fairborn** USA
56D2 **Fairbury** USA
68B3 **Fairfax** USA
59B3 **Fairfield** California, USA
68D2 **Fairfield** Connecticut, USA
58D2 **Fairfield** Idaho, USA
58D1 **Fairfield** Montana, USA
64C3 **Fairfield** Ohio, USA
9C2 **Fair Head** *Pt* Northern Ireland
10C2 **Fair Isle** *I* Scotland
35B2 **Fairlie** New Zealand
61E2 **Fairmont** Minnesota, USA
64C3 **Fairmont** W Virginia, USA
68B1 **Fairport** USA
62C1 **Fairview** USA
54E4 **Fairweather,Mt** USA
27H6 **Fais** *I* Pacific Ocean
42C2 **Faisalabad** Pakistan
60C1 **Faith** USA
8E1 **Faither,The** *Pen* Scotland
33H1 **Fakaofo** *I* Tokelau Islands
7E3 **Fakenham** England
32C1 **Fakfak** Indonesia
28A2 **Faku** China
43G4 **Falam** Burma
70C2 **Falcon Res** Mexico/USA
48A3 **Falémé** *R* Mali/Senegal/Guinea
62C3 **Falfurrias** USA
12G7 **Falkenberg** Sweden
8D4 **Falkirk** Scotland
8D4 **Falkirk** *Division* Scotland
74D8 **Falkland Is** *Dependency* S Atlantic
74E8 **Falkland Sd** Falkland Islands
12G7 **Falköping** Sweden
66D4 **Fallbrook** USA
56B3 **Fallon** USA
65E2 **Fall River** USA
60B2 **Fall River P** USA
61D2 **Falls City** USA
7B4 **Falmouth** England
69H1 **Falmouth** Jamaica
65E2 **Falmouth** Maine, USA
68E2 **Falmouth** Massachusetts, USA
7B4 **Falmouth Bay** England
47B3 **False B** South Africa
70A2 **Falso,C** Mexico
18C2 **Falster** *I* Denmark
17F1 **Fălticeni** Romania
12H6 **Falun** Sweden
40B2 **Famagusta** Cyprus
45B1 **Famagusta B** Cyprus
13C2 **Famenne** *Region* Belgium
66C3 **Famoso** USA
30B2 **Fang** Thailand
50D3 **Fangak** Sudan
31E5 **Fangliao** Taiwan
8C3 **Fannich, L** Scotland
16C2 **Fano** Italy
45A3 **Fâqûs** Egypt
76G3 **Faraday** *Base* Antarctica
50C3 **Faradje** Zaïre
51E6 **Farafangana** Madagascar
49E2 **Farafra Oasis** Egypt
38E2 **Farah** Afghanistan
27H5 **Farallon de Medinilla** *I* Pacific Ocean
26H4 **Farallon de Pajaros** *I* Marianas
48A3 **Faranah** Guinea
50E2 **Farasan Is** Saudi Arabia
27H6 **Faraulep** *I* Pacific Ocean
55J5 **Farbault** USA
7D4 **Fareham** England
55O4 **Farewell,C** Greenland
33G5 **Farewell,C** New Zealand
35B2 **Farewell Spit** *Pt* New Zealand
56D2 **Fargo** USA
45C2 **Fari'a** *R* Israel
57D2 **Faribault** USA
43F4 **Faridpur** Bangladesh
41G2 **Farīmān** Iran
45A3 **Fâriskûr** Egypt
65E2 **Farmington** Maine, USA
63D1 **Farmington** Missouri, USA
68E1 **Farmington** New Hampshire, USA
56C3 **Farmington** New Mexico, USA
58D2 **Farmington** Utah, USA
66B2 **Farmington Res** USA
6D2 **Farne Deep** N Sea
15A2 **Faro** Portugal
12H7 **Fårö** *I* Sweden
46K9 **Farquhar Is** Indian Ocean
8C3 **Farrar** *R* Scotland
64C2 **Farrell** USA
43K2 **Farrukhabad** *District* India
17E3 **Fársala** Greece
75B4 **Fartura, Serra de** *Mts* Brazil
62B2 **Farwell** USA
41F4 **Fasā** Iran
21D5 **Fastov** Ukraine
43K2 **Fatehgarh** India
43E3 **Fatehpur** India
73H7 **Fatima du Sul** Brazil
58C1 **Fauquier** Canada
47D2 **Fauresmith** South Africa
12H5 **Fauske** Norway
7E4 **Faversham** England
55K4 **Fawn** *R* Canada
12H6 **Fax** *R* Sweden
12A2 **Faxaflói** *B* Iceland
50B2 **Faya** Chad
63E2 **Fayette** USA
57D3 **Fayetteville** Arkansas, USA
57F3 **Fayetteville** N Carolina, USA
67A1 **Fayetteville** Tennessee, USA
45B3 **Fâyid** Egypt
41E4 **Faylakah** *I* Kuwait
42C2 **Fāzilka** India
48A2 **Fdérik** Mauritius
57F3 **Fear,C** USA
66B1 **Feather** *R* USA
59B3 **Feather Middle Fork** *R* USA
14C2 **Fécamp** France
18C2 **Fehmarn** *I* Germany
75D3 **Feia, Lagoa** Brazil
72D5 **Feijó** Brazil
31C5 **Feilai Xai Bei Jiang** *R* China
35C2 **Feilding** New Zealand
51D5 **Feira** Zambia
73L6 **Feira de Santan** Brazil
40C2 **Feke** Turkey
13D4 **Feldberg** *Mt* Germany
18B3 **Feldkirch** Austria
10D3 **Felixstowe** England
12G6 **Femund** *L* Norway
28A2 **Fengcheng** China
31B4 **Fengdu** China
31B3 **Fengjie** China
31D1 **Fengning** China
31B3 **Feng Xian** China
31C1 **Fengzhen** China
31C2 **Fen He** *R* China
51E5 **Fenoarivo Atsinanana** Madagascar
21F7 **Feodosiya** Ukraine
41G3 **Ferdow** Iran
13B3 **Fère-Champenoise** France
39F1 **Fergana** Uzbekistan
61D1 **Fergus Falls** USA
48B4 **Ferkessedougou** Ivory Coast
9C2 **Fermanagh** *County* Northern Ireland
67B2 **Fernandina Beach** USA
73M4 **Fernando de Noronha, Isla** Brazil
75B3 **Fernandópolis** Brazil
Fernando Poo *I* **=Bioko**
58B1 **Ferndale** USA
58C1 **Fernie** Canada
59C3 **Fernley** USA
16C2 **Ferrara** Italy
15B2 **Ferrat, Cap** *C* Algeria
72C5 **Ferreñafe** Peru
63D2 **Ferriday** USA
13B3 **Ferrières** France
48B1 **Fès** Morocco
63D1 **Festus** USA
17F2 **Feteşti** Romania
9C3 **Fethard** Irish Republic
40A2 **Fethiye** Turkey
21J7 **Fetisovo** Kazakhstan
8E1 **Fetlar** *I* Scotland
55L4 **Feuilles, Rivière aux** *R* Canada
24J6 **Feyzabad** Afghanistan
7C3 **Ffestiniog** Wales
51E6 **Fianarantsoa** Madagascar
50D3 **Fichē** Ethiopia
47D2 **Ficksburg** South Africa
45C3 **Fidan, Wadi** Jordan
17D2 **Fier** Albania
8D3 **Fife** *Division* Scotland
8D3 **Fife Ness** *Pen* Scotland
14C3 **Figeac** France
15A1 **Figueira da Foz** Portugal
Figueres = Figueras
15C1 **Figueras** Spain
48B1 **Figuig** Morocco
33G2 **Fiji** *Is* Pacific Ocean
15B2 **Filabres, Sierra de los** *Mts* Spain
73G8 **Filadelfia** Paraguay
6D2 **Filey** England
17E2 **Filiaşi** Romania
17E3 **Filiatrá** Greece
16C3 **Filicudi** *I* Italy
59C4 **Fillmore** California, USA
59D3 **Fillmore** Utah, USA
8C3 **Findhorn** *R* Scotland
57E2 **Findlay** USA
65D2 **Finger Lakes** USA
51D5 **Fingoè** Mozambique
21E8 **Finike** Turkey
15A1 **Finisterre, Cabo** *C* Spain
32C3 **Finke** *R* Australia
20C3 **Finland** *Republic* N Europe
12J7 **Finland,G of** N Europe
54F4 **Finlay** *R* Canada
54F4 **Finlay Forks** Canada
34C3 **Finley** Australia
9C2 **Finn** *R* Irish Republic
12H5 **Finnsnes** Norway
27H7 **Finschhafen** Papua New Guinea
12H7 **Finspång** Sweden
18C2 **Finsterwalde** Germany
9C2 **Fintona** Northern Ireland
35A3 **Fiordland Nat Pk** New Zealand
45C2 **Fiq** Syria
21F8 **Firat** *R* Turkey
66B2 **Firebaugh** USA
Firenze = Florence
42D3 **Firozābād** India
42C2 **Firozpur** India
8C4 **Firth of Clyde** *Estuary* Scotland
8D3 **Firth of Forth** *Estuary* Scotland
8B3 **Firth of Lorn** *Estuary* Scotland
10C2 **Firth of Tay** *Estuary* Scotland
41F4 **Firūzābād** Iran
47B2 **Fish** *R* Namibia
47C3 **Fish** *R* South Africa
66C2 **Fish Camp** USA
68D2 **Fishers I** USA
55K3 **Fisher Str** Canada
7B4 **Fishguard** Wales
55N3 **Fiskenæsset** Greenland
13B3 **Fismes** France
65E2 **Fitchburg** USA
8E2 **Fitful Head** *Pt* Scotland
67B2 **Fitzgerald** USA
32B2 **Fitzroy** *R* Australia
32B2 **Fitzroy Crossing** Australia
64C1 **Fitzwilliam I** Canada
Fiume = Rijeka
50C4 **Fizi** Zaïre
47D3 **Flagstaff** South Africa
56B3 **Flagstaff** USA
65E1 **Flagstaff L** USA
6D2 **Flamborough Head** *C* England
56C2 **Flaming Gorge Res** USA
27G7 **Flamingo, Teluk** *B* Indonesia
13B2 **Flandres, Plaine des** Belgium/France
8B2 **Flannan Isles** Scotland
56B2 **Flathead L** USA
63D1 **Flat River** USA
27H8 **Flattery,C** Australia
56A2 **Flattery,C** USA
6C3 **Fleetwood** England
12F7 **Flekkefjord** Norway
26H4 **Fleming Deep** Pacific Ocean
68C2 **Flemington** USA
18B2 **Flensburg** Germany
32C4 **Flinders** *I* Australia
32D5 **Flinders** *I* Australia
32D2 **Flinders** *R* Australia
32C4 **Flinders Range** *Mts* Australia
54H4 **Flin Flon** Canada
57E2 **Flint** USA
7C3 **Flint** Wales
7C3 **Flint** *County* Wales
57E3 **Flint** *R* USA
13B2 **Flixecourt** France
64A1 **Floodwood** USA
67A2 **Florala** USA
57E3 **Florence** Alabama, USA
59D4 **Florence** Arizona, USA
60B3 **Florence** Colorado, USA
16C2 **Florence** Italy
63C1 **Florence** Kansas, USA
58B2 **Florence** Oregon, USA
57F3 **Florence** S Carolina, USA
66C2 **Florence L** USA
72C3 **Florencia** Colombia
74C6 **Florentine Ameghino, Embalse** *Res* Argentina
13C3 **Florenville** Belgium
70D3 **Flores** Guatemala
48A1 **Flores** *I* Azores
32B1 **Flores** *I* Indonesia
27E7 **Flores S** Indonesia
73K5 **Floriano** Brazil
74G3 **Florianópolis** Brazil
74E4 **Florida** Uruguay
70D2 **Florida** *State* USA
67B3 **Florida B** USA
67B3 **Florida City** USA
33E1 **Florida Is** Solomon Islands
57E4 **Florida Keys** *Is* USA
57E4 **Florida,Strs of** USA
17E2 **Flórina** Greece
12F6 **Florø** Norway
62B2 **Floydada** USA
32D1 **Fly** *R* Papua New Guinea
17F1 **Focşani** Romania
16D2 **Foggia** Italy
48A4 **Fogo** *I* Cape Verde
14C3 **Foix** France
64C1 **Foleyet** Canada
55L3 **Foley I** Canada
16C2 **Foligno** Italy
7E4 **Folkestone** England
67B2 **Folkston** USA
16C2 **Follonica** Italy
66B1 **Folsom** USA
68C1 **Fonda** USA
54H4 **Fond-du-Lac** Canada
57E2 **Fond du Lac** USA
70D3 **Fonseca, G de** Honduras
14C2 **Fontainbleau** France
14B2 **Fontenay-le-Comte** France
17D1 **Fonyód** Hungary
Foochow = Fuzhou
54C3 **Foraker, Mt** USA
13D3 **Forbach** France
34C2 **Forbes** Australia
48C4 **Forcados** Nigeria
66C3 **Ford City** USA
12F6 **Førde** Norway
7D4 **Fordingbridge** England
34C1 **Fords Bridge** Australia
63D2 **Fordyce** USA
48A4 **Forécariah** Guinea
55P3 **Forel,Mt** Greenland
58D1 **Foremost** Canada
64C2 **Forest** Canada
63E2 **Forest** USA
61E2 **Forest City** Iowa, USA
68C2 **Forest City** Pennsylvania, USA
7C4 **Forest of Dean** England
67B2 **Forest Park** USA
66A1 **Forestville** USA
13B3 **Forêt d'Othe** France
8D3 **Forfar** Scotland
62B1 **Forgan** USA
58B1 **Forks** USA
16C2 **Forlì** Italy
7C3 **Formby** England
15C2 **Formentera** *I* Spain
15C1 **Formentor, Cabo** *C* Spain
16C2 **Formia** Italy
48A1 **Formigas** *I* Azores
Formosa = Taiwan
74E3 **Formosa** Argentina
73J7 **Formosa** Brazil
74D2 **Formosa** *State* Argentina
Formosa Channel = Taiwan Str
73G6 **Formosa, Serra** *Mts* Brazil
75C1 **Formoso** Brazil
75C1 **Formoso** *R* Brazil
8D3 **Forres** Scotland
32B4 **Forrest** Australia
57D3 **Forrest City** USA
32D2 **Forsayth** Australia
12J6 **Forssa** Finland
34D2 **Forster** Australia
63D1 **Forsyth** Missouri, USA
60B1 **Forsyth** Montana, USA
42C3 **Fort Abbas** Pakistan
55K4 **Fort Albany** Canada
73L4 **Fortaleza** Brazil

Fort Augustus **General Pico**

8C3 **Fort Augustus** Scotland
47D3 **Fort Beaufort** South Africa
58D1 **Fort Benton** USA
59B3 **Fort Bragg** USA
62C1 **Fort Cobb Res** USA
56C2 **Fort Collins** USA
65D1 **Fort Coulonge** Canada
62B2 **Fort Davis** USA
69E4 **Fort-de-France** Martinique
67A2 **Fort Deposit** USA
57D2 **Fort Dodge** USA
32A3 **Fortescue** *R* Australia
57D2 **Fort Frances** Canada
54F3 **Fort Franklin** Canada
54F3 **Fort Good Hope** Canada
34B1 **Fort Grey** Australia
8C3 **Forth** *R* Scotland
62A2 **Fort Hancock** USA
55K4 **Fort Hope** Canada
8F3 **Forties** *Oilfield* N Sea
65F1 **Fort Kent** USA
48C1 **Fort Lallemand** Algeria
Fort Lamy = Ndjamena
60C2 **Fort Laramie** USA
57E4 **Fort Lauderdale** USA
54F3 **Fort Liard** Canada
54G4 **Fort Mackay** Canada
54G5 **Fort Macleod** Canada
54G4 **Fort McMurray** Canada
54E3 **Fort McPherson** Canada
64A2 **Fort Madison** USA
56C2 **Fort Morgan** USA
57E4 **Fort Myers** USA
54F4 **Fort Nelson** Canada
54F3 **Fort Norman** Canada
67A2 **Fort Payne** USA
60B1 **Fort Peck** USA
56C2 **Fort Peck Res** USA
57E4 **Fort Pierce** USA
60C2 **Fort Pierre** USA
68C1 **Fort Plain** USA
54G3 **Fort Providence** Canada
54G3 **Fort Resolution** Canada
50B4 **Fort Rousset** Congo
54F4 **Fort St James** Canada
54F4 **Fort St John** Canada
63D1 **Fort Scott** USA
54E3 **Fort Selkirk** Canada
55K4 **Fort Severn** Canada
21J7 **Fort Shevchenko** Kazakhstan
54F3 **Fort Simpson** Canada
54G3 **Fort Smith** Canada
57D3 **Fort Smith** USA
54F3 **Fort Smith** *Region* Canada
56C3 **Fort Stockton** USA
62B2 **Fort Sumner** USA
62C1 **Fort Supply** USA
58B2 **Fortuna** California, USA
60C1 **Fortuna** N Dakota, USA
54G4 **Fort Vermilion** Canada
67A2 **Fort Walton Beach** USA
57E2 **Fort Wayne** USA
8C3 **Fort William** Scotland
62A1 **Fort Wingate** USA
56D3 **Fort Worth** USA
54D3 **Fort Yukon** USA
31C5 **Foshan** China
55K2 **Fosheim Pen** Canada
61D1 **Fosston** USA
50B4 **Fougamou** Gabon
14B2 **Fougères** France
8D1 **Foula** *I* Scotland
7E4 **Foulness I** England
35B2 **Foulwind,C** New Zealand
50B3 **Foumban** Cameroon
48B2 **Foum el Alba** *Region* Mali
14C1 **Fourmies** France
17F3 **Foúrnoi** *I* Greece
48A3 **Fouta Djallon** *Mts* Guinea
33F5 **Foveaux Str** New Zealand
7B4 **Fowey** England
62B1 **Fowler** USA
64B2 **Fox** *R* USA
55K3 **Foxe Basin** *G* Canada
55K3 **Foxe Chan** Canada
55L3 **Foxe Pen** Canada
60B2 **Foxpark** USA
35C2 **Foxton** New Zealand
10B2 **Foyle, Lough** *Estuary* Irish Republic/Northern Ireland
51B5 **Foz do Cuene** Angola
74F3 **Foz do Iguaçu** Brazil
68B2 **Frackville** USA
15C1 **Fraga** Spain
68E1 **Framingham** USA
73J8 **Franca** Brazil
14C2 **France** *Republic* Europe
14D2 **Franche Comté** *Region* France
47D1 **Francistown** Botswana
58E2 **Francs Peak** *Mt* USA
13E2 **Frankenberg** Germany
64B2 **Frankfort** Indiana, USA
57E3 **Frankfort** Kentucky, USA
68C1 **Frankfort** New York, USA
47D2 **Frankfort** South Africa
18B2 **Frankfurt am Main** Germany
18C2 **Frankfurt an-der-Oder** Germany
18C3 **Fränkischer Alb** *Upland* Germany
58D2 **Franklin** Idaho, USA
64B3 **Franklin** Indiana, USA
63D3 **Franklin** Louisiana, USA
68E1 **Franklin** Massachusetts, USA
67B1 **Franklin** N Carolina, USA
68E1 **Franklin** New Hampshire, USA
68C2 **Franklin** New Jersey, USA
65D2 **Franklin** Pennsylvania, USA
67A1 **Franklin** Tennessee, USA
65D3 **Franklin** Virginia, USA
54F2 **Franklin B** Canada
58C1 **Franklin D Roosevelt** *L* USA
54F3 **Franklin Mts** Canada
54J2 **Franklin Str** Canada
68A1 **Franklinville** USA
35B2 **Franz Josef Glacier** New Zealand
Franz-Josef-Land = Zemlya Frantsa Josifa
54F5 **Fraser** *R* Canada
47C3 **Fraserburg** South Africa
8D3 **Fraserburgh** Scotland
34D1 **Fraser I** Australia
68C3 **Frederica** USA
18B1 **Fredericia** Denmark
65D3 **Frederick** Maryland, USA
62C2 **Frederick** Oklahoma, USA
62C2 **Fredericksburg** Texas, USA
65D3 **Fredericksburg** Virginia, USA
64A3 **Fredericktown** USA
55M5 **Fredericton** Canada
55N3 **Frederikshåp** Greenland
12G7 **Frederikshavn** Denmark
65D2 **Fredonia** USA
12G7 **Fredrikstad** Norway
68C2 **Freehold** USA
66C1 **Freel Peak** *Mt* USA
61D2 **Freeman** USA
64B2 **Freeport** Illinois, USA
63C3 **Freeport** Texas, USA
69B1 **Freeport** The Bahamas
62C3 **Freer** USA
47D2 **Free State** *Province* South Africa
48A4 **Freetown** Sierra Leone
18B3 **Freiburg** Germany
13D3 **Freiburg im Breisgau** Germany
18C3 **Freistadt** Austria
32A4 **Fremantle** Australia
66B2 **Fremont** California, USA
61D2 **Fremont** Nebraska, USA
64C2 **Fremont** Ohio, USA
73H3 **French Guiana** *Dependency* S America
60B1 **Frenchman** *R* USA
34C4 **Frenchmans Cap** *Mt* Australia
37M5 **French Polynesia** *Is* Pacific Ocean
15C2 **Frenda** Algeria
70B2 **Fresnillo** Mexico
56B3 **Fresno** USA
66C2 **Fresno** *R* USA
58D1 **Fresno Res** USA
13E3 **Freudenstadt** Germany
13B2 **Frévent** France
34C4 **Freycinet Pen** Australia
48A3 **Fria** Guinea
66C2 **Friant** USA
66C2 **Friant Dam** USA
16B1 **Fribourg** Switzerland
13E2 **Friedberg** Germany
18B3 **Friedrichshafen** Germany
13C1 **Friesland** *Province* Netherlands
62C3 **Frio** *R* USA
75D3 **Frio, Cabo** *C* Brazil
62B2 **Friona** USA
55M3 **Frobisher B** Canada
55M3 **Frobisher Bay** Canada
54H4 **Frobisher L** Canada
21G6 **Frolovo** Russian Federation
7C4 **Frome** England
7C4 **Frome** *R* England
32C4 **Frome,L** Australia
63D1 **Frontenac** USA
70C3 **Frontera** Mexico
65D3 **Front Royal** USA
16C2 **Frosinone** Italy
60B3 **Fruita** USA
31C5 **Fuchuan** China
31E4 **Fuding** China
70B2 **Fuerte** *R* Mexico
75A3 **Fuerte Olimpo** Brazil
74E2 **Fuerte Olimpo** Paraguay
48A2 **Fuerteventura** *I* Canary Islands
31C2 **Fugu** China
26B2 **Fuhai** China
41G4 **Fujairah** UAE
29C3 **Fuji** Japan
31D4 **Fujian** *Province* China
26G2 **Fujin** China
29C3 **Fujinomiya** Japan
29D3 **Fuji-san** *Mt* Japan
29C3 **Fujisawa** Japan
29C3 **Fuji-Yoshida** Japan
29D2 **Fukagawa** Japan
24K5 **Fukang** China
29D3 **Fukuchiyama** Japan
28A4 **Fukue** Japan
28A4 **Fukue** *I* Japan
29D3 **Fukui** Japan
28C4 **Fukuoka** Japan
29E3 **Fukushima** Japan
29C4 **Fukuyama** Japan
61D2 **Fulda** USA
18B2 **Fulda** Germany
18B2 **Fulda** *R* Germany
31B4 **Fuling** China
69L1 **Fullarton** Trinidad
66D4 **Fullerton** USA
6F1 **Fulmar** *Oilfield* N Sea
64A2 **Fulton** Illinois, USA
64B3 **Fulton** Kentucky, USA
65D2 **Fulton** New York, USA
13C2 **Fumay** France
29D3 **Funabashi** Japan
33G1 **Funafuti** *I* Tuvalu
48A1 **Funchal** Madeira
75D2 **Fundão** Brazil
55M5 **Fundy,B of** Canada
51D6 **Funhalouro** Mozambique
31B5 **Funing** China
31D3 **Funing** China
48C3 **Funtua** Nigeria
31D4 **Fuqing** China
51D5 **Furancungo** Mozambique
29D2 **Furano** Japan
41G4 **Fūrg** Iran
75B2 **Furnas, Serra das** *Mts* Brazil
32D5 **Furneaux Group** *Is* Australia
13D1 **Furstenau** Germany
18C2 **Fürstenwalde** Germany
18C3 **Fürth** Germany
29D2 **Furubira** Japan
29E3 **Furukawa** Japan
55K3 **Fury and Hecla Str** Canada
28A2 **Fushun** China
31A4 **Fushun** Sichuan, China
28B2 **Fusong** China
18C3 **Füssen** Germany
31E2 **Fu Xian** China
31E1 **Fuxin** China
31D3 **Fuyang** China
31E1 **Fuyuan** Liaoning, China
31A4 **Fuyuan** Yunnan, China
26B2 **Fuyun** China
31D4 **Fuzhou** China
28A3 **Fuzhoucheng** China
18C1 **Fyn** *I* Denmark
8C3 **Fyne, Loch** *Inlet* Scotland

G

50E3 **Gaalkacyo** Somalia
59C3 **Gabbs** USA
66C1 **Gabbs Valley Range** *Mts* USA
51B5 **Gabela** Angola
48D1 **Gabès, G de** Tunisia
66B2 **Gabilan Range** *Mts* USA
50B4 **Gabon** *Republic* Africa
47D1 **Gaborone** Botswana
15A1 **Gabriel y Galán, Embalse** *Res* Spain
17F2 **Gabrovo** Bulgaria
41F3 **Gach Sārān** Iran
44B2 **Gadag** India
67A2 **Gadsden** Alabama, USA
59D4 **Gadsden** Arizona, USA
16C2 **Gaeta** Italy
27H6 **Gaferut** *I* Pacific Ocean
67B1 **Gaffney** USA
45A3 **Gafra, Wadi el** Egypt
48C1 **Gafsa** Tunisia
20E4 **Gagarin** Russian Federation
55M4 **Gagnon** Canada
21G7 **Gagra** Georgia
43F3 **Gaibanda** Bangladesh
74C6 **Gaimán** Argentina
67B3 **Gainesville** Florida, USA
67B2 **Gainesville** Georgia, USA
63C2 **Gainesville** Texas, USA
7D3 **Gainsborough** England
32C4 **Gairdner, L** Australia
8C3 **Gairloch** Scotland
68B3 **Gaithersburg** USA
28A2 **Gai Xian** China
44B2 **Gajendragarh** India
31D4 **Ga Jiang** *R* China
47C2 **Gakarosa** *Mt* South Africa
50D4 **Galana** *R* Kenya
72N **Galapagos Is** Pacific Ocean
Gálápagos, Islas = Galapagos Islands
8D4 **Galashiels** Scotland
17F1 **Galaţi** Romania
64C3 **Galax** USA
62A2 **Galeana** Mexico
54C3 **Galena** Alaska, USA
64A2 **Galena** Illinois, USA
63D1 **Galena** Kansas, USA
69L1 **Galeota Pt** Trinidad
69L1 **Galera Pt** Trinidad
64A2 **Galesburg** USA
68B2 **Galeton** USA
20G4 **Galich** Russian Federation
15A1 **Galicia** *Region* Spain
Galilee,S of = Tiberias,L
69J1 **Galina Pt** Jamaica
50D2 **Gallabat** Sudan
67A1 **Gallatin** USA
58D1 **Gallatin** *R* USA
44C4 **Galle** Sri Lanka
62A3 **Gallego** Mexico
15B1 **Gállego** *R* Spain
72D1 **Gallinas, Puerta** Colombia
Gallipolī = Gelibolu
17D2 **Gallipoli** Italy
20C2 **Gällivare** Sweden
8C4 **Galloway** *District* Scotland
8C4 **Galloway,Mull of** *C* Scotland
62A1 **Gallup** USA
66B1 **Galt** USA
9B3 **Galty Mts** Irish Republic
70C2 **Galveston** USA
57D4 **Galveston B** USA
10B3 **Galway** Irish Republic
10B3 **Galway B** Irish Republic
43F3 **Gamba** China
48B3 **Gambaga** Ghana
54A3 **Gambell** USA
48A3 **Gambia** *R* Senegal/The Gambia
48A3 **Gambia,The** *Republic* Africa
37N6 **Gambier, Îles** Pacific Ocean
50B4 **Gamboma** Congo
51B5 **Gambos** Angola
44C4 **Gampola** Sri Lanka
59E3 **Ganado** USA
50E3 **Ganale Dorya** *R* Ethiopia
65D2 **Gananoque** Canada
Gand = Gent
51B5 **Ganda** Angola
51C4 **Gandajika** Zaïre
43N2 **Gandak** *R* India/Nepal
43M2 **Gandak Dam** Nepal
42B3 **Gandava** Pakistan
55N5 **Gander** Canada
42B4 **Gāndhīdhām** India
42C4 **Gāndhīnagar** India
42D4 **Gāndhi Sāgar** *L* India
15B2 **Gandia** Spain
75E1 **Gandu** Brazil
Ganga *R* **=Ganges**
42C3 **Gangānagar** India
43G4 **Gangaw** Burma
31A2 **Gangca** China
39G2 **Gangdise Shan** *Mts* China
22F4 **Ganges** *R* India
43F4 **Ganges, Mouths of the** Bangladesh/India
28B2 **Gangou** China
43F3 **Gangtok** India
31B3 **Gangu** China
58E2 **Gannett Peak** *Mt* USA
31B2 **Ganquan** China
12K8 **Gantsevichi** Belarus
31D4 **Ganzhou** China
48C3 **Gao** Mali
31A2 **Gaolan** China
31C2 **Gaoping** China
48B3 **Gaoua** Burkina
48A3 **Gaoual** Guinea
31D3 **Gaoyou Hu** *L* China
31C5 **Gaozhou** China
14D3 **Gap** France
42D2 **Gar** China
9C3 **Gara,L** Irish Republic
34C1 **Garah** Australia
73L5 **Garanhuns** Brazil
59B2 **Garberville** USA
75C3 **Garça** Brazil
15A2 **Garcia de Sola, Embalse de** *Res* Spain
75B3 **Garcias** Brazil
16C1 **Garda, L di** Italy
62B1 **Garden City** USA
64B1 **Garden Pen** USA
42B2 **Gardez** Afghanistan
58D1 **Gardiner** USA
68D2 **Gardiners I** USA
68E1 **Gardner** USA
33H1 **Gardner** *I* Phoenix Islands
66C1 **Gardnerville** USA
16D2 **Gargano, Monte** *Mt* Italy
16D2 **Gargano, Prom. del** Italy
42D4 **Garhākota** India
43K1 **Garhmuktesar** India
20L4 **Gari** Russian Federation
47B3 **Garies** South Africa
50D4 **Garissa** Kenya
63C2 **Garland** USA
18C3 **Garmisch-Partenkirchen** Germany
41F2 **Garmsar** Iran
63C1 **Garnett** USA
56B2 **Garnett Peak** *Mt* USA
14C3 **Garonne** *R* France
49D4 **Garoua** Cameroon
49D4 **Garoua Boulai** Cameroon
60C1 **Garrison** USA
9D2 **Garron** *Pt* Northern Ireland
8C3 **Garry** *R* Scotland
54H3 **Garry L** Canada
43E4 **Garwa** India
64B2 **Gary** USA
39G2 **Garyarsa** China
63C2 **Garza-Little Elm** *Res* USA
41F2 **Gasan Kuli** Turkmenistan
14B3 **Gascogne** *Region* France
63D1 **Gasconade** *R* USA
32A3 **Gascoyne** *R* Australia
50B3 **Gashaka** Nigeria
48D3 **Gashua** Nigeria
57G2 **Gaspé** Canada
57G2 **Gaspé,C de** Canada
57G2 **Gaspé, Peninsule de** Canada
67B1 **Gastonia** USA
67C1 **Gaston,L** USA
45B1 **Gata, C** Cyprus
15B2 **Gata, Cabo de** *C* Spain
20D4 **Gatchina** Russian Federation
8C4 **Gatehouse of Fleet** Scotland
6D2 **Gateshead** England
63C2 **Gatesville** USA
13B3 **Gâtinais** *Region* France
65D1 **Gatineau** Canada
65D1 **Gatineau** *R* Canada
67B1 **Gatlinburg** USA
34D1 **Gatton** Australia
33F2 **Gaua** *I* Vanuatu
43G3 **Gauhāti** India
19E1 **Gauja** *R* Latvia
43E3 **Gauri Phanta** India
51C6 **Gauteng** *Provence* South Africa
17E4 **Gávdhos** *I* Greece
75D1 **Gavião** *R* Brazil
66B3 **Gaviota** USA
12H6 **Gävle** Sweden
32C4 **Gawler Ranges** *Mts* Australia
31A1 **Gaxun Nur** *L* China
43E4 **Gaya** India
48C3 **Gaya** Niger
48C3 **Gaya** Nigeria
28B2 **Gaya He** *R* China
64C1 **Gaylord** USA
34D1 **Gayndah** Australia
20J3 **Gayny** Russian Federation
19F3 **Gaysin** Ukraine
40B3 **Gaza** Gaza
45C3 **Gaza Autonomous Region** SW Asia
40C2 **Gaziantep** Turkey
48B4 **Gbaringa** Liberia
48D1 **Gbbès** Tunisia
19D2 **Gdańsk** Poland
19D2 **Gdańsk,G of** Poland
12K7 **Gdov** Russian Federation
19D2 **Gdynia** Poland
45A4 **Gebel el Galâla el Bahariya** *Desert* Egypt
50D2 **Gedaref** Sudan
17F3 **Gediz** *R* Turkey
18C2 **Gedser** Denmark
13C2 **Geel** Belgium
34B3 **Geelong** Australia
34C4 **Geeveston** Australia
48D3 **Geidam** Nigeria
13D2 **Geilenkirchen** Germany
50D4 **Geita** Tanzania
31A5 **Gejiu** China
16C3 **Gela** Italy
50E3 **Geladī** Ethiopia
13D2 **Geldern** Germany
17F2 **Gelibolu** Turkey
40B2 **Gelidonya Burun** Turkey
13E2 **Gelnhausen** Germany
13D2 **Gelsenkirchen** Germany
12F8 **Gelting** Germany
30C5 **Gemas** Malaysia
13C2 **Gembloux** Belgium
50B3 **Gemena** Zaïre
40C2 **Gemerek** Turkey
40A1 **Gemlik** Turkey
16C1 **Gemona** Italy
47C2 **Gemsbok Nat Pk** Botswana
50C2 **Geneina** Sudan
74C5 **General Alvear** Argentina
76F2 **General Belgrano** *Base* Antarctica
76G2 **General Bernardo O'Higgins** *Base* Antarctica
74B7 **General Carrera, Lago** Chile
74D2 **General Eugenio A Garay** Paraguay
66C2 **General Grant Grove Section** *Region* USA
74C3 **General Manuel Belgrano** *Mt* Argentina
74D5 **General Pico** Argentina

General Roca **Grapevine**

74C5 **General Roca** Argentina
27F6 **General Santos** Philippines
65D2 **Genesee** *R* USA
65D2 **Geneseo** USA
61D2 **Geneva** Nebraska, USA
68B1 **Geneva** New York, USA
16B1 **Geneva** Switzerland
Geneva,L of = Léman, L
Genève = Geneva
15B2 **Genil** *R* Spain
16B2 **Gennargentu, Monti del** *Mt* Sardinia, Italy
34C3 **Genoa** Australia
16B2 **Genoa** Italy
Genova = Genoa
16B2 **Genova, G di** Italy
13B2 **Gent** Belgium
27D7 **Genteng** Indonesia
18C2 **Genthin** Germany
21H7 **Geokchay** Azerbaijan
47C3 **George** South Africa
55M4 **George** *R* Canada
34C2 **George,L** Australia
67B3 **George,L** Florida, USA
65E2 **George,L** New York, USA
35A2 **George Sd** New Zealand
34C4 **George Town** Australia
66B1 **Georgetown** California, USA
65D3 **Georgetown** Delaware, USA
73G2 **Georgetown** Guyana
64C3 **Georgetown** Kentucky, USA
30C4 **George Town** Malaysia
69N2 **Georgetown** St Vincent
67C2 **Georgetown** S Carolina, USA
63C2 **Georgetown** Texas, USA
48A3 **Georgetown** The Gambia
76G8 **George V Land** *Region* Antarctica
62C3 **George West** USA
21G7 **Georgia** *Republic* Europe
76F12 **Georg Forster** *Base* Antarctica
67B2 **Georgia** *State* USA
64C1 **Georgian B** Canada
54F5 **Georgia, Str of** Canada
32C3 **Georgina** *R* Australia
21F5 **Georgiu-Dezh** Russian Federation
21G7 **Georgiyevsk** Russian Federation
76F1 **Georg von Neumayer** *Base* Antarctica
18C2 **Gera** Germany
13B2 **Geraardsbergen** Belgium
75C1 **Geral de Goiás, Serra** *Mts* Brazil
35B2 **Geraldine** New Zealand
75C2 **Geral do Paraná, Serra** *Mts* Brazil
32A3 **Geraldton** Australia
57E2 **Geraldton** Canada
75D2 **Geral, Serra** *Mts* Bahia, Brazil
75B4 **Geral, Serra** *Mts* Paraná, Brazil
45C3 **Gerar** *R* Israel
13D3 **Gérardmer** France
54C3 **Gerdine,Mt** USA
30C4 **Gerik** Malaysia
60C2 **Gering** USA
21C6 **Gerlachovsky** *Mt* Poland
47D2 **Germiston** South Africa
13D2 **Gerolstein** Germany
15C1 **Gerona** Spain
13E2 **Geseke** Germany
50E3 **Gestro** *R* Ethiopia
15B1 **Getafe** Spain
68B3 **Gettysburg** Pennsylvania, USA
60D1 **Gettysburg** S Dakota, USA
41D2 **Gevaş** Turkey
17E2 **Gevgeliija** Macedonia, Yugoslavia
45D2 **Ghabāghib** Syria
45D3 **Ghadaf, Wadi el** Jordan
48C1 **Ghadamis** Libya
41F2 **Ghaem Shahr** Iran
43E3 **Ghāghara** *R* India
48B4 **Ghana** *Republic* Africa
47C1 **Ghanzi** Botswana
48C1 **Ghardaïa** Algeria
49D1 **Gharyān** Libya
49D2 **Ghāt** Libya
15B2 **Ghazaouet** Algeria
42D3 **Ghāziābād** India
42B2 **Ghazni** Afghanistan
17F1 **Gheorgheni** Romania
40D3 **Ghudāf, Wadi al** *Watercourse* Iraq
16D3 **Giarre** Sicily, Italy
60D2 **Gibbon** USA
47B2 **Gibeon** Namibia
15A2 **Gibraltar** *Colony* SW Europe
7E7 **Gibraltar** *Pt* England
15A2 **Gibraltar,Str of** Africa/Spain
32B3 **Gibson Desert** Australia
58B1 **Gibsons** Canada
44B2 **Giddalūr** India
45B3 **Giddi, Gebel el** *Mt* Egypt
45B3 **Giddi Pass** Egypt
50D3 **Gīdolē** Ethiopia
13B4 **Gien** France
18B2 **Giessen** Germany
8D4 **Gifford** Scotland
67B3 **Gifford** USA
29D3 **Gifu** Japan
8C4 **Gigha** *I* Scotland
16C2 **Giglio** *I* Italy
15A1 **Gijón** Spain
59D4 **Gila** *R* USA
59D4 **Gila Bend** USA
59D4 **Gila Bend Mts** USA
32D2 **Gilbert** *R* Australia
33G1 **Gilbert Is** Pacific Ocean
58D1 **Gildford** USA
51D5 **Gilé** Mozambique
45C2 **Gilead** *Region* Jordan
49E2 **Gilf Kebir Plat** Egypt
34C2 **Gilgandra** Australia
42C1 **Gilgit** Pakistan
42C1 **Gilgit** *R* Pakistan
34C2 **Gilgunnia** Australia
55J4 **Gillam** Canada
60B2 **Gillette** USA
7E4 **Gillingham** England
64B1 **Gills Rock** USA
64B2 **Gilman** USA
66B2 **Gilroy** USA
69P2 **Gimie, Mont** St Lucia
45B3 **Gineifa** Egypt
47E2 **Gingindlovu** South Africa
50E3 **Gīnīr** Ethiopia
17E3 **Gióna** *Mt* Greece
34C3 **Gippsland** *Mts* Australia
64C2 **Girard** USA
72D3 **Girardot** Colombia
8D3 **Girdle Ness** *Pen* Scotland
40C1 **Giresun** Turkey
40B4 **Girga** Egypt
42C4 **Gīr Hills** India
50B3 **Giri** *R* Zaïre
43F4 **Girīdīh** India
42A2 **Girishk** Afghanistan
13D4 **Giromagny** France
Girona = Gerona
14B2 **Gironde** *R* France
8C4 **Girvan** Scotland
35C1 **Gisborne** New Zealand
50C4 **Gitega** Burundi
Giuba,R = Juba,R
17F2 **Giurgiu** Romania
13C2 **Givet** France
25S3 **Gizhiga** Russian Federation
19E2 **Gizycko** Poland
17E2 **Gjirokastër** Albania
54J3 **Gjoatlaven** Canada
12G6 **Gjøvik** Norway
55M5 **Glace Bay** Canada
58B1 **Glacier Peak** *Mt* USA
55K2 **Glacier Str** Canada
32E3 **Gladstone** Queensland, Australia
34A2 **Gladstone** S Aust, Australia
34C4 **Gladstone** Tasmania, Australia
64B1 **Gladstone** USA
12A1 **Gláma** *Mt* Iceland
12G6 **Glåma** *R* Norway
13D3 **Glan** *R* Germany
61D3 **Glasco** USA
64B3 **Glasgow** Kentucky, USA
60B1 **Glasgow** Montana, USA
8C4 **Glasgow** Scotland
68C3 **Glassboro** USA
66C2 **Glass Mt** USA
7C4 **Glastonbury** England
20J4 **Glazov** Russian Federation
18D3 **Gleisdorf** Austria
35C1 **Glen Afton** New Zealand
9D2 **Glenarm** Northern Ireland
68B3 **Glen Burnie** USA
47E2 **Glencoe** South Africa
59D4 **Glendale** Arizona, USA
66C3 **Glendale** California, USA
60C1 **Glendive** USA
60C2 **Glendo Res** USA
9C2 **Glengad Hd** *Pt* Irish Republic
34D1 **Glen Innes** Australia
8C4 **Glenluce** Scotland
34C1 **Glenmorgan** Australia
34D2 **Glenreagh** Australia
68B3 **Glen Rock** USA
63C2 **Glen Rose** USA
8D3 **Glenrothes** Scotland
68D1 **Glens Falls** USA
63D2 **Glenwood** Arkansas, USA
61D1 **Glenwood** Minnesota, USA
62A2 **Glenwood** New Mexico, USA
60B3 **Glenwood Springs** USA
64A1 **Glidden** USA
12F6 **Glittertind** *Mt* Norway
19D2 **Gliwice** Poland
59D4 **Globe** USA
18D2 **Głogów** Poland
12G5 **Glomfjord** Norway
51E5 **Glorieuses, Isles** Madagascar
7C3 **Glossop** England
34D2 **Gloucester** Australia
7C4 **Gloucester** England
68E1 **Gloucester** USA
7C4 **Gloucester** *County* England
68C1 **Gloversville** USA
19F1 **Glubokoye** Belarus
13E1 **Glückstadt** Germany
21E5 **Glukhov** Ukraine
18D3 **Gmünd** Austria
18C3 **Gmunden** Austria
19D2 **Gniezno** Poland
44A2 **Goa, Daman and Diu** *Union Territory* India
47B2 **Goageb** Namibia
43G3 **Goālpāra** India
50D3 **Goba** Ethiopia
47B1 **Gobabis** Namibia
31B1 **Gobi** *Desert* China/Mongolia
29C4 **Gobo** Japan
19G1 **Gobza** *R* Russian Federation
47B1 **Gochas** Namibia
7D4 **Godalming** England
44C2 **Godāvari** *R* India
66C2 **Goddard,Mt** USA
64C2 **Goderich** Canada
55N3 **Godhavn** Greenland
42C4 **Godhra** India
57D1 **Gods L** Canada
55N3 **Godthåb** Greenland
Godwin Austen *Mt* **=K2**
68E1 **Goffstown** USA
64C1 **Gogama** Canada
13E1 **Gohfeld** Germany
75C2 **Goiandira** Brazil
75C2 **Goianésia** Brazil
75C2 **Goiânia** Brazil
75B2 **Goiás** Brazil
73J6 **Goiás** *State* Brazil
75B3 **Goio-Erê** Brazil
50D3 **Gojab** *R* Ethiopia
17F2 **Gökçeada** *I* Turkey
17F3 **Gökova Körfezi** *B* Turkey
21F8 **Goksu** *R* Turkey
40C2 **Göksun** Turkey
43G3 **Golāghāt** India
9B2 **Gola, I** Irish Republic
40C2 **Gölbaşı** Turkey
24K2 **Gol'chikha** Russian Federation
58C2 **Golconda** USA
68B2 **Gold** USA
58B2 **Gold Beach** USA
34D1 **Gold Coast** Australia
35B2 **Golden B** New Zealand
58B1 **Goldendale** USA
66A2 **Golden Gate** *Chan* USA
63D3 **Golden Meadow** USA
59C3 **Goldfield** USA
66D2 **Gold Point** USA
67C1 **Goldsboro** USA
62C2 **Goldthwaite** USA
18C2 **Goleniów** Poland
66C3 **Goleta** USA
26C3 **Golmud** China
50E3 **Gololcha** Ethiopia
29F2 **Golovnino** Russian Federation
50C4 **Goma** Zaïre
43L2 **Gomati** India
48D3 **Gombe** Nigeria
19G2 **Gomel** Belarus
48A2 **Gomera** *I* Canary Islands
70B2 **Gómez Palacio** Mexico
25O4 **Gonam** *R* Russian Federation
69C3 **Gonâve, Isla de la** Cuba
41G2 **Gonbad-e Kāvūs** Iran
43E3 **Gonda** India
42C4 **Gondal** India
50D2 **Gonder** Ethiopia
43E4 **Gondia** India
40A1 **Gönen** Turkey
17F3 **Gonen** *R* Turkey
31A4 **Gongga Shan** *Mt* China
31A2 **Gonghe** China
75D1 **Gongogi** *R* Brazil
48D3 **Gongola** *R* Nigeria
66B2 **Gonzales** California, USA
63C3 **Gonzales** Texas, USA
47B3 **Good Hope,C of** South Africa
58D2 **Gooding** USA
60C3 **Goodland** USA
34C1 **Goodooga** *R* Australia
7D3 **Goole** England
34C2 **Goolgowi** Australia
34A3 **Goolwa** Australia
32A4 **Goomalling** Australia
34C2 **Goombalie** Australia
34D1 **Goomeri** Australia
34D1 **Goondiwindi** Australia
55N4 **Goose Bay** Canada
67C2 **Goose Creek** USA
58B2 **Goose L** USA
44B2 **Gooty** India
32D1 **Goraka** Papua New Guinea
43E3 **Gorakhpur** India
20K3 **Gora Koyp** *Mt* Russian Federation
25M4 **Gora Munku Sardyk** *Mt* Mongolia/Russian Federation
20K3 **Gora Narodnaya** *Mt* Russian Federation
20L2 **Gora Pay-Yer** *Mt* Russian Federation
20K3 **Gora Telpos-Iz** *Mt*
17D2 **Goražde** Bosnia-Herzegovina
54D2 **Gordon** USA
65D3 **Gordonsville** USA
50B3 **Goré** Chad
50D3 **Gorē** Ethiopia
35A3 **Gore** New Zealand
25P4 **Gore Topko** *Mt* Russian Federation
9C3 **Gorey** Irish Republic
41F2 **Gorgān** Iran
13C2 **Gorinchem** Netherlands
41E2 **Goris** Armenia
16C1 **Gorizia** Italy
19G2 **Gorki** Belarus
20M2 **Gorki** Russian Federation
Gorki = Novgorod
20G4 **Gor'kovskoye Vodokhranilishche** *Res* Russian Federation
7E3 **Gorleston** England
18C2 **Görlitz** Germany
21F6 **Gorlovka** Ukraine
66C3 **Gorman** USA
17F2 **Gorna Orjahovica** Bulgaria
26B1 **Gorno-Altaysk** Russian Federation
26H2 **Gornozavodsk** Russian Federation
20K3 **Goro Denezhkin Kamen'** *Mt* Russian Federation
20G4 **Gorodets** Russian Federation
19G2 **Gorodnya** Ukraine
19F1 **Gorodok** Belarus
19E3 **Gorodok** Ukraine
19F3 **Gorodok** Ukraine
27H7 **Goroka** Papua New Guinea
51D5 **Gorongosa** Mozambique
27F6 **Gorontalo** Indonesia
20L4 **Goro Yurma** *Mt* Russian Federation
75D2 **Gorutuba** *R* Brazil
25M4 **Goryachinsk** Russian Federation
21J7 **Gory Akkyr** *Upland* Turkmenistan
25L2 **Gory Byrranga** *Mts* Russian Federation
19F3 **Goryn'** *R* Ukraine
25L3 **Gory Putorana** *Mts* Russian Federation
19E2 **Góry Świętokrzyskie** *Upland* Poland
12H8 **Gorzów Wielkopolski** Poland
66C2 **Goshen** USA
29E2 **Goshogawara** Japan
16D2 **Gospić** Croatia
7D4 **Gosport** England
17E2 **Gostivar** Macedonia, Yugoslavia
19D2 **Gostynin** Poland
12G7 **Göteborg** Sweden
50B3 **Gotel Mts** Nigeria
60C2 **Gothenburg** USA
12H7 **Gotland** *I* Sweden
28B4 **Gotō-rettō** *Is* Japan
12H7 **Gotska Sandön** *I* Sweden
28C4 **Gōtsu** Japan
18B2 **Göttingen** Germany
28A2 **Goubangzi** China
13C2 **Gouda** Netherlands
50B2 **Goudoumaria** Niger
52H7 **Gough I** Atlantic Ocean
55L5 **Gouin, Réservoire** Canada
34C2 **Goulburn** Australia
48B3 **Goumbou** Mali
48B3 **Goundam** Mali
50B2 **Gouré** Niger
48B3 **Gourma Rharous** Mali
50B2 **Gouro** Chad
58E1 **Govenlock** Canada
27G8 **Gove Pen** Australia
21C6 **Goverla** *Mt* Ukraine
75D2 **Governador Valadares** Brazil
43E4 **Govind Ballabh Paht Sāgar** *L* India
42B3 **Gowārān** Afghanistan
7B4 **Gower** Wales
74E3 **Goya** Argentina
50C2 **Goz-Beïda** Chad
16C3 **Gozo** *I* Malta
50D2 **Goz Regeb** Sudan
47C3 **Graaff-Reinet** South Africa
65D1 **Gracefield** Canada
69A4 **Gracias à Dios, Cabo** Honduras
34D1 **Grafton** Australia
61D1 **Grafton** N Dakota, USA
64C3 **Grafton** W Virginia, USA
54E4 **Graham I** Canada
59E4 **Graham,Mt** USA
47D3 **Grahamstown** South Africa
73J5 **Grajaú** Brazil
19E2 **Grajewo** Poland
17E2 **Grámmos** *Mt* Albania/Greece
8C3 **Grampian** *Mts* Scotland
8D3 **Grampian** *Region* Scotland
72D3 **Granada** Colombia
72A1 **Granada** Nicaragua
15B2 **Granada** Spain
65E1 **Granby** Canada
60B2 **Granby** USA
48A2 **Gran Canaria** *I* Canary Islands
74D3 **Gran Chaco** *Region* Argentina
64B2 **Grand** *R* Michigan, USA
61E2 **Grand** *R* Missouri, USA
69Q2 **Grand B** Dominica
57F4 **Grand Bahama** *I* The Bahamas
13D4 **Grand Ballon** *Mt* France
55N5 **Grand Bank** Canada
52F2 **Grand Banks** Atlantic Ocean
48B4 **Grand Bassam** Ivory Coast
59D3 **Grand Canyon** USA
59D3 **Grand Canyon Nat Pk** USA
69A3 **Grand Cayman** *I* Cayman Is, Caribbean Sea
58C1 **Grand Coulee** USA
73K6 **Grande** *R* Bahia, Brazil
75C2 **Grande** *R* Minas Gerais/São Paulo, Brazil
55L4 **Grande 2, Rēservoir de la** Canada
55L4 **Grande 3, Rēservoir de la** Canada
55L4 **Grande 4, Rēservoir de la** Canada
74C8 **Grande, Bahía** *B* Argentina
51E5 **Grande Comore** *I* Comoros
75D3 **Grande, Ilha** Brazil
63C2 **Grande Prairie** USA
50B2 **Grand Erg de Bilma** *Desert Region* Niger
48C1 **Grand Erg Occidental** *Desert* Algeria
48C2 **Grand Erg Oriental** *Desert* Algeria
55L4 **Grande Rivière de la Baleine** *R* Canada
58C1 **Grande Ronde** *R* USA
59D4 **Gran Desierto** USA
55M5 **Grand Falls** New Brunswick, Canada
55N5 **Grand Falls** Newfoundland, Canada
58C1 **Grand Forks** Canada
61D1 **Grand Forks** USA
68C1 **Grand Gorge** USA
64B2 **Grand Haven** USA
60D2 **Grand Island** USA
63E2 **Grand Isle** USA
60B3 **Grand Junction** USA
63D3 **Grand L** USA
64A1 **Grand Marais** USA
65E1 **Grand Mère** Canada
15A2 **Grândola** Portugal
54G4 **Grand Prairie** Canada
54J4 **Grand Rapids** Canada
64B2 **Grand Rapids** Michigan, USA
64A1 **Grand Rapids** Minnesota, USA
16B1 **Grand St Bernard, Col du** *P* Italy/Switzerland
56B2 **Grand Teton** *Mt* USA
58D2 **Grand Teton Nat Pk** USA
60B3 **Grand Valley** USA
58C1 **Grangeville** USA
58E1 **Granite Peak** *Mt* Montana, USA
59D2 **Granite Peak** *Mt* Utah, USA
15C1 **Granollérs** Spain
16B1 **Gran Paradiso** *Mt* Italy
7D3 **Grantham** England
66C1 **Grant,Mt** USA
8D3 **Grantown-on-Spey** Scotland
62A1 **Grants** USA
58B2 **Grants Pass** USA
14B2 **Granville** France
68D1 **Granville** USA
54H4 **Granville L** Canada
75D2 **Grão Mogol** Brazil
66C3 **Grapevine** USA

Ignace James

57D2 **Ignace** Canada
40A1 **Iğneada Burun** *Pt* Turkey
48C1 **Ignil-Izane** Algeria
44E3 **Ignoitijala** Andaman Islands
17E3 **Igoumenítsa** Greece
20J4 **Igra** Russian Federation
20L3 **Igrim** Russian Federation
74F3 **Iguaçu, Quedas do** *Falls* Argentina/Brazil
70C3 **Iguala** Mexico
74G2 **Iguape** Brazil
75C3 **Iguatama** Brazil
75B3 **Iguatemi** Brazil
75A3 **Iguatemi** *R* Brazil
73L5 **Iguatu** Brazil
50A4 **Iguéla** Gabon
51E6 **Ihosy** Madagascar
29D3 **Iida** Japan
29C3 **Iide-san** *Mt* Japan
12K6 **Iisalmi** Finland
28B4 **Iisuka** Japan
48C4 **Ijebu** Nigeria
13C1 **Ijmuiden** Netherlands
13C1 **Ijssel** *R* Netherlands
18B2 **Ijsselmeer** *S* Netherlands
17F3 **Ikaría** *I* Greece
29E2 **Ikeda** Japan
50C4 **Ikela** Zaïre
17E2 **Ikhtiman** Bulgaria
28A4 **Iki** *I* Japan
51E5 **Ikopa** *R* Madagascar
27F5 **Ilagan** Philippines
41E3 **Ilām** Iran
26C1 **Ilanskiy** Russian Federation
50C4 **Ilebo** Zaïre
13B3 **Île De France** *Region* France
65E1 **Ile d'Orleans** Canada
21K5 **Ilek** *R* Russian Federation
7B4 **Ilfracombe** England
40B1 **Ilgaz Dağları** *Mts* Turkey
73H6 **Ilha do Bananal** *Region* Brazil
75D3 **Ilha Grande, B de** Brazil
73H8 **Ilha Grande, Reprêsa** Brazil/Paraguay
75B3 **Ilha Solteira Dam** Brazil
73L6 **Ilhéus** Brazil
54C4 **Iliamna L** USA
25M4 **Ilim** *R* Russian Fed
25M4 **Ilimsk** Russian Federation
25M4 **Ilin** *R* Russian Federation
26H2 **Il'inskiy** Russian Federation
17E3 **Iliodhrómia** *I* Greece
68C1 **Ilion** USA
6D3 **Ilkley** England
74B4 **Illapel** Chile
48C3 **Illéla** Niger
64A3 **Illinois** *R* USA
64B2 **Illinois** *State* USA
48C2 **Illizi** Algeria
20E4 **Il'men, Ozero** *L* Russian Federation
72D7 **Ilo** Peru
27F5 **Iloilo** Philippines
12L6 **Ilomantsi** Finland
48C4 **Ilorin** Nigeria
19G1 **Il'yino** Russian Federation
28B4 **Imabari** Japan
29C3 **Imaichi** Japan
12L5 **Imandra, Ozero** *L* Russian Federation
28A4 **Imari** Japan
20D3 **Imatra** Finland
74G3 **Imbituba** Brazil
75B4 **Imbituva** Brazil
50E3 **Imi** Ethiopia
28A3 **Imjin** *R* N Korea
58C2 **Imlay** USA
16C2 **Imola** Italy
73J5 **Imperatriz** Brazil
16B2 **Imperia** Italy
60C2 **Imperial** USA
59C4 **Imperial V** USA
50B3 **Impfondo** Congo
43G4 **Imphāl** India
29C3 **Ina** Japan
48C2 **In Afaleleh** *Well* Algeria
29C4 **Inamba-jima** *I* Japan
48C2 **In Amenas** Algeria
12K5 **Inari** Finland
12K5 **Inarijärvi** *L* Finland
29D3 **Inawashiro-ko** *L* Japan
48C2 **In Belbel** Algeria
21F7 **Ince Burun** *Pt* Turkey
40B2 **Incekum Burun** *Pt* Turkey
8C2 **Inchnadamph** Scotland
28B3 **Inch'on** S Korea
8B4 **Indaal, Loch** *Inlet* Scotland
48B2 **In Dagouber** *Well* Mali
75C2 **Indaiá** *R* Brazil
12H6 **Indals** *R* Sweden
66C2 **Independence** California, USA
61E2 **Independence** Iowa, USA
63C1 **Independence** Kansas, USA
61E3 **Independence** Missouri, USA
58C2 **Independence Mts** USA
21J6 **Inderborskiy** Kazakhstan
39F3 **India** *Federal Republic* Asia
65D2 **Indiana** USA
64B2 **Indiana** *State* USA
36F7 **Indian-Antarctic Basin** Indian Ocean
36F7 **Indian-Antarctic Ridge** Indian Ocean
64B3 **Indianapolis** USA
Indian Desert = Thar Desert
55N4 **Indian Harbour** Canada
36E5 **Indian O**
61E2 **Indianola** Iowa, USA
63D2 **Indianola** Mississippi, USA
75C2 **Indianópolis** Brazil
59C3 **Indian Springs** USA
20H2 **Indiga** Russian Federation
25Q3 **Indigirka** *R* Russian Federation
30D2 **Indo-China** *Region* SE Asia
27F7 **Indonesia** *Republic* SE Asia
42D4 **Indore** India
14C2 **Indre** *R* France
42B3 **Indus** *R* Pakistan
42B4 **Indus, Mouths of the** Pakistan
48C2 **In Ebeggi** *Well* Algeria
21E7 **Inebolu** Turkey
48C2 **In Ecker** Algeria
40A1 **Inegöl** Turkey
48D2 **In Ezzane** Algeria
47C3 **Infantta, C** South Africa
70B3 **Infiernillo, Pico del** *Mt* Mexico
48C3 **Ingal** Niger
64C2 **Ingersoll** Canada
32D2 **Ingham** Australia
55M2 **Inglefield Land** *Region* Greenland
35B1 **Inglewood** New Zealand
34D1 **Inglewood** Queensland, Australia
66C4 **Inglewood** USA
34B3 **Inglewood** Victoria, Australia
12B2 **Ingólfshöfdi** *I* Iceland
18C3 **Ingolstadt** Germany
43F4 **Ingrāj Bāzār** India
21G7 **Ingushetiya** *Division* Russian Federation
48C3 **In Guezzam** *Well* Algeria
47E2 **Inhaca** *I* Mozambique
47E2 **Inhaca Pen** Mozambique
51D6 **Inhambane** Mozambique
51D6 **Inharrime** Mozambique
75C2 **Inhumas** Brazil
72E3 **Inirida** *R* Colombia
9C2 **Inishowen** *District* Irish Republic
9C2 **Inishtrahull Sd** Irish Republic
34C1 **Injune** Australia
34B1 **Innamincka** Australia
8D4 **Innerleithen** Scotland
31B1 **Inner Mongolia Aut. Region** China
32D2 **Innisfail** Australia
18C3 **Innsbruck** Austria
50B4 **Inongo** Zaïre
19D2 **Inowrocław** Poland
48C2 **In Salah** Algeria
28A3 **Insil** S Korea
20L2 **Inta** Russian Federation
16B1 **Interlaken** Switzerland
33H3 **International Date Line**
61E1 **International Falls** USA
29D3 **Inubo-saki** *C* Japan
55L4 **Inukjuak** Canada
54E3 **Inuvik** Canada
54E3 **Inuvik** *Region* Canada
8C3 **Inveraray** Scotland
8D3 **Inverbervie** Scotland
35A3 **Invercargill** New Zealand
8C4 **Inverclyde** *Division* Scotland
34D1 **Inverell** Australia
8C3 **Invergordon** Scotland
8C3 **Inverness** Scotland
8D3 **Inverurie** Scotland
32C4 **Investigator Str** Australia
26B1 **Inya** Russian Federation
25Q3 **Inya** *R* Russian Federation
51D5 **Inyanga** Zimbabwe
66D3 **Inyokern** USA
66C2 **Inyo Mts** USA
50B4 **Inzia** *R* Zaïre
17E3 **Ioánnina** Greece
63C1 **Iola** USA
8B3 **Iona** *I* Scotland
51B5 **Iôna Nat Pk** Angola
58C1 **Ione** USA
17E3 **Ionian Is** Greece
17D3 **Ionian S** Greece/Italy
Iónioi Nísoi *Is* = **Ionian Islands**
17F3 **Íos** *I* Greece
20J3 **Iosser** Russian Federation
61E2 **Iowa** *R* USA
61E2 **Iowa** *State* USA
64A2 **Iowa City** USA
61E2 **Iowa Falls** USA
75C2 **Ipameri** Brazil
75D2 **Ipanema** Brazil
21G6 **Ipatovo** Russian Federation
72C3 **Ipiales** Colombia
75E1 **Ipiaú** Brazil
75B4 **Ipiranga** Brazil
30C5 **Ipoh** Malaysia
73H7 **Iporá** Brazil
17F2 **Ipsala** Turkey
34D1 **Ipswich** Australia
7E3 **Ipswich** England
68E1 **Ipswich** USA
19G2 **Iput** *R* Russian Federation
75C3 **Iquape** Brazil
74B2 **Iquique** Chile
72D4 **Iquitos** Peru
17F3 **Iráklion** Greece
38D2 **Iran** *Republic* SW Asia
70B2 **Irapuato** Mexico
40D3 **Iraq** *Republic* SW Asia
75B4 **Irati** Brazil
49D2 **Irāwan** *Watercourse* Libya
45C2 **Irbid** Jordan
20L4 **Irbit** Russian Federation
10B3 **Ireland, Republic of** NW Europe
73G3 **Ireng** *R* Guyana
28B3 **Iri** S Korea
27G7 **Irian Jaya** *Province* Indonesia
50C2 **Iriba** Chad
51D4 **Iringa** Tanzania
26F4 **Iriomote** *I* Ryukyu Is, Japan
69A3 **Iriona** Honduras
73H5 **Iriri** *R* Brazil
10B3 **Irish S** England/Ire
25M4 **Irkutsk** Russian Federation
25M4 **Irkutsk** *Division* Russian Federation
32C4 **Iron Knob** Australia
64B1 **Iron Mountain** USA
32D2 **Iron Range** Australia
64B1 **Iron River** USA
64C3 **Irontown** USA
64A1 **Ironwood** USA
57E2 **Iroquois Falls** Canada
29C4 **Iro-zaki** *C* Japan
30B2 **Irrawaddy** *R* Burma
30A2 **Irrawaddy,Mouths of the** Burma
24H4 **Irtysh** *R* Russian Federation
15B1 **Irún** Spain
8C4 **Irvine** Scotland
8C4 **Irvine** *R* Scotland
63C2 **Irving** USA
66C3 **Isabella Res** USA
54H2 **Isachsen** Canada
54H2 **Isachsen,C** Canada
55Q3 **Ísafjörður** Iceland
28C4 **Isahaya** Japan
50C3 **Isangi** Zaïre
8E1 **Isbister** Scotland
16C2 **Ischia** *I* Italy
29C4 **Ise** Japan
13D2 **Iserlohn** Germany
16C2 **Isernia** Italy
29C4 **Ise-wan** *B* Japan
Isfahan = Esfahan
26F4 **Ishigaki** *I* Ryukyu Is, Japan
29E2 **Ishikari** *R* Japan
29E2 **Ishikari-wan** *B* Japan
24H4 **Ishim** Russian Federation
24H4 **Ishim** *R* Kazakhstan
29E3 **Ishinomaki** Japan
29D3 **Ishioka** Japan
42C1 **Ishkashim** Afghanistan
64B1 **Ishpeming** USA
24J4 **Isil'kul'** Russian Federation
50D3 **Isiolo** Kenya
50C3 **Isiro** Zaïre
40C2 **Iskenderun** Turkey
40C2 **Iskenderun Körfezi** *B* Turkey
40B1 **İskilip** Turkey
24K4 **Iskitim** Russian Federation
17E2 **Iskur** *R* Bulgaria
42C2 **Islamabad** Pakistan
67B4 **Islamorada** USA
57D1 **Island L** Canada
9D2 **Island Magee** Northern Ireland
58D2 **Island Park** USA
35B1 **Islands,B of** New Zealand
Islas Baleares = Balearic Islands
Islas Malvinas = Falkland Islands
8B4 **Islay** *I* Scotland
14C2 **Isle** *R* France
Isle, Island, Isola etc : see also individual island names
7D4 **Isle of Wight** *County* England
64B1 **Isle Royale Nat Pk** USA
7A5 **Isles of Scilly** England
66B1 **Isleton** USA
40B3 **Ismâ'ilîya** Egypt
40B4 **Isna** Egypt
51E6 **Isoanala** Madagascar
51D5 **Isoka** Zambia
16D3 **Isola de Correnti, C** Sicily, Italy
29C3 **Isosaki** Japan
40B2 **Isparta** Turkey
45C2 **Israel** *Republic* SW Asia
15C2 **Isser** *R* Algeria
14C2 **Issoire** France
14C2 **Issoudun** France
39F1 **Issyk Kul', Ozero** *L* Kirgizia
40A1 **İstanbul** Turkey
17E3 **Istiáia** Greece
67B3 **Istokpoga,L** USA
16C1 **Istra** *Pen* Croatia
75C2 **Itaberai** Brazil
75D2 **Itabira** Brazil
75D3 **Itabirito** Brazil
75E1 **Itabuna** Brazil
75E1 **Itacaré** Brazil
73G4 **Itacoatiara** Brazil
75A3 **Itacurubí del Rosario** Paraguay
75C1 **Itaguari** *R* Brazil
72C2 **Itagui** Colombia
75B4 **Itaipu, Reprêsa** *Res* Brazil/Paraguay
73G4 **Itaituba** Brazil
74G3 **Itajaí** Brazil
75C3 **Itajuba** Brazil
16C2 **Italy** *Republic* Europe
75E2 **Itamaraju** Brazil
75D2 **Itamarandiba** Brazil
75D2 **Itambacuri** Brazil
75D2 **Itambé** Brazil
75D2 **Itambé** *Mt* Brazil
43G3 **Itānagar** India
75C3 **Itanhaém** Brazil
75D2 **Itanhém** Brazil
75D2 **Itanhém** *R* Brazil
75D2 **Itaobím** Brazil
75C1 **Itapaci** Brazil
75C3 **Itapecerica** Brazil
75D3 **Itaperuna** Brazil
73K7 **Itapetinga** Brazil
75C3 **Itapetininga** Brazil
75C3 **Itapeva** Brazil
73L4 **Itapipoca** Brazil
75C2 **Itapuranga** Brazil
74E3 **Itaqui** Brazil
75D2 **Itarantim** Brazil
75C3 **Itararé** Brazil
75C3 **Itararé** *R* Brazil
75D3 **Itaúna** Brazil
72F6 **Iténez** *R* Bolivia/Brazil
65D2 **Ithaca** USA
45D3 **Ithrīyat, Jebel** *Mt* Jordan
50C3 **Itimbiri** *R* Zaïre
75D2 **Itinga** Brazil
75A2 **Itiquira** *R* Brazil
55N3 **Itivdleq** Greenland
29C4 **Ito** Japan
29D3 **Itoigawa** Japan
72F6 **Itonomas** *R* Bolivia
75C3 **Itu** Brazil
75E1 **Ituberá** Brazil
75C2 **Ituiutaba** Brazil
75C2 **Itumbiara** Brazil
75B2 **Iturama** Brazil
74C2 **Iturbe** Argentina
26H2 **Iturup** *I* Russian Federation
18B2 **Itzehoe** Germany
25U3 **Iul'tin** Russian Federation
19F2 **Ivacevichi** Belarus
75B3 **Ivai** *R* Brazil
12K5 **Ivalo** Finland
17D2 **Ivangrad** Montenegro, Yugoslavia
34B2 **Ivanhoe** Australia
19E3 **Ivano-Frankovsk** Ukraine
20G4 **Ivanovo** Russian Federation
20G4 **Ivanova** *Division* Russian Federation
20L3 **Ivdel'** Russian Federation
50B3 **Ivindo** *R* Gabon
75B3 **Ivinhema** Brazil
75B3 **Ivinhema** *R* Brazil
51E6 **Ivohibe** Madagascar
51E5 **Ivongo Soanierana** Madagascar
Ivory Coast = Côte d'Ivoire
16B1 **Ivrea** Italy
55L3 **Ivujivik** Canada
29E3 **Iwaki** Japan
29D2 **Iwaki** *R* Japan
29D2 **Iwaki-san** *Mt* Japan
28C4 **Iwakuni** Japan
29D2 **Iwamizawa** Japan
29E2 **Iwanai** Japan
48C4 **Iwo** Nigeria
26H4 **Iwo Jima** *I* Japan
70C3 **Ixtepec** Mexico
28B4 **Iyo** Japan
28B4 **Iyo-nada** *B* Japan
24G4 **Izhevsk** Russian Federation
20J2 **Izhma** Russian Federation
20J2 **Izhma** *R* Russian Federation
41G5 **Izkī** Oman
19F3 **Izmail** Ukraine
40A2 **İzmir** Turkey
17F3 **İzmir Körfezi** *B* Turkey
40A1 **İzmit** Turkey
40A1 **İznik** Turkey
17F2 **Iznik Golü** *L* Turkey
45D2 **Izra'** Syria
28A4 **Izuhara** Japan
29C4 **Izumi-sano** Japan
28B3 **Izumo** Japan

J

41F5 **Jabal az Zannah** UAE
43E4 **Jabalpur** India
40D4 **Jabal Shammar** *Region* Saudi Arabia
45C1 **Jablah** Syria
18D2 **Jablonec nad Nisou** Czech Republic
73L5 **Jaboatão** Brazil
75C3 **Jaboticabal** Brazil
15B1 **Jaca** Spain
73G5 **Jacareacanga** Brazil
73H8 **Jacarezinho** Brazil
75C3 **Jacarie** Brazil
74C4 **Jáchal** Argentina
75B2 **Jaciara** Brazil
75D2 **Jacinto** Brazil
65E1 **Jackman Station** USA
62C2 **Jacksboro** USA
68B2 **Jacks Mt** USA
67A2 **Jackson** Alabama, USA
34C1 **Jackson** Australia
66B1 **Jackson** California, USA
64C2 **Jackson** Michigan, USA
61E2 **Jackson** Minnesota, USA
63D2 **Jackson** Mississippi, USA
64B3 **Jackson** Missouri, USA
64C3 **Jackson** Ohio, USA
63E2 **Jackson** Tennessee, USA
58D2 **Jackson** Wyoming, USA
35B2 **Jackson,C** New Zealand
35A2 **Jackson Head** *Pt* New Zealand
58D2 **Jackson L** USA
63D2 **Jacksonville** Arkansas, USA
67B2 **Jacksonville** Florida, USA
64A3 **Jacksonville** Illinois, USA
67C2 **Jacksonville** N Carolina, USA
63C2 **Jacksonville** Texas, USA
67B2 **Jacksonville Beach** USA
69C3 **Jacmel** Haiti
42B3 **Jacobabad** Pakistan
73K6 **Jacobina** Brazil
Jadotville = Likasi
72C5 **Jaén** Peru
15B2 **Jaén** Spain
Jaffa = Tel Aviv-Yafo
34A3 **Jaffa,C** Australia
44B4 **Jaffna** Sri Lanka
68D1 **Jaffrey** USA
43F4 **Jagannathganj Ghat** Bangladesh
44C2 **Jagdalpur** India
41G4 **Jagin** *R* Iran
44B2 **Jagtial** India
75E1 **Jaguaquara** Brazil
74F4 **Jaguarão** *R* Brazil/Uruguay
75C3 **Jaguariaiva** Brazil
21H8 **Jahan Dāgh** *Mt* Iran
41F4 **Jahrom** Iran
31A2 **Jainca** China
42D3 **Jaipur** India
42C3 **Jaisalmer** India
41G2 **Jajarm** Iran
16D2 **Jajce** Bosnia-Herzegovina
27D7 **Jakarta** Indonesia
55N3 **Jakobshavn** Greenland
12J6 **Jakobstad** Finland
62B2 **Jal** USA
42C2 **Jalalabad** Afghanistan
70C3 **Jalapa** Mexico
75B3 **Jales** Brazil
43F3 **Jaleswar** Nepal
42D4 **Jalgaon** India
48D4 **Jalingo** Nigeria
42D5 **Jālna** India
15B1 **Jalón** *R* Spain
49E2 **Jalo Oasis** Libya
42C3 **Jālor** India
43F3 **Jalpāiguri** India
49E2 **Jālū Oasis** Libya
72B4 **Jama** Ecuador
50E3 **Jamaame** Somalia
69B3 **Jamaica** *I* Caribbean Sea
69B3 **Jamaica Chan** Haiti/Jamaica
43F4 **Jamalpur** Bangladesh
27D7 **Jambi** Indonesia
42C4 **Jambusar** India
60D1 **James** *R* N Dakota, USA

James Kamchatka

65D3 **James** *R* Virginia, USA
55K4 **James B** Canada
34A2 **Jamestown** Australia
60D1 **Jamestown** N Dakota, USA
65D2 **Jamestown** New York, USA
68E2 **Jamestown** Rhode Island, USA
47D3 **Jamestown** South Africa
54J5 **Jamestown** USA
44B2 **Jamkhandi** India
42C2 **Jammu** India
42D2 **Jammu and Kashmīr** *State* India
42B4 **Jāmnagar** India
42C3 **Jampur** Pakistan
20C3 **Jämsä** Finland
43F4 **Jamshedpur** India
45D3 **Janab, Wadi el** Jordan
43F3 **Janakpur** Nepal
75D2 **Janaúba** Brazil
41F3 **Jandaq** Iran
34D1 **Jandowae** Australia
64B2 **Janesville** USA
76B1 **Jan Mayen** *I* Norwegian Sea
75D2 **Januária** Brazil
42D4 **Jaora** India
26G3 **Japan, S of** Japan
36J3 **Japan Trench** Pacific Ocean
72E4 **Japurá** *R* Brazil
40C2 **Jarābulus** Syria
75C2 **Jaraguá** Brazil
75B3 **Jaraguari** Brazil
15B1 **Jarama** *R* Spain
45C2 **Jarash** Jordan
75A3 **Jardim** Brazil
69B2 **Jardines de la Reina** *Is* Cuba
Jargalant = Hovd
73H3 **Jari** *R* Brazil
43G3 **Jaria Jhānjail** Bangladesh
13C3 **Jarny** France
18D2 **Jarocin** Poland
19E2 **Jarosław** Poland
12G6 **Järpen** Sweden
31B2 **Jartai** China
42C4 **Jasdan** India
48C4 **Jasikan** Ghana
41G4 **Jāsk** Iran
19E3 **Jasło** Poland
74D8 **Jason Is** Falkland Islands
63E2 **Jasper** Alabama, USA
63D1 **Jasper** Arkansas, USA
54G4 **Jasper** Canada
67B2 **Jasper** Florida, USA
64B3 **Jasper** Indiana, USA
63D2 **Jasper** Texas, USA
18D2 **Jastrowie** Poland
75B2 **Jataí** Brazil
15B2 **Játiva** Spain
75C3 **Jau** Brazil
72C6 **Jauja** Peru
43E3 **Jaunpur** India
44B3 **Javadi Hills** India
27D7 **Java,I** Indonesia
Javari *R* **= Yavari**
27D7 **Java S** Indonesia
32A2 **Java Trench** Indonesia
Jawa = Java
27G7 **Jaya, Pk** Indonesia
27H7 **Jayapura** Indonesia
45D2 **Jayrūd** Syria
63D3 **Jeanerette** USA
48C4 **Jebba** Nigeria
50C2 **Jebel Abyad** *Desert Region* Sudan
Jebel esh Sheikh = Hermon, Mt
8D4 **Jedburgh** Scotland
Jedda = Jiddah
19E2 **Jędrzejów** Poland
61E2 **Jefferson** Iowa, USA
63D2 **Jefferson** Texas, USA
58D1 **Jefferson** *R* USA
57D3 **Jefferson City** USA
56B3 **Jefferson,Mt** USA
64B3 **Jeffersonville** USA
45C3 **Jeib, Wadi el** Israel/Jordan
75A3 **Jejui-Guazú** *R* Paraguay
20D4 **Jekabpils** Latvia
18D2 **Jelena Góra** Poland
20C4 **Jelgava** Latvia
27E7 **Jember** Indonesia
62A1 **Jemez Pueblo** USA
18C2 **Jena** Germany
16B3 **Jendouba** Tunisia
45C2 **Jenin** West Bank
63D2 **Jennings** USA
55O3 **Jensen Nunatakker** *Mt* Greenland
55K3 **Jens Munk** *I* Canada
34B3 **Jeparit** Australia
73L6 **Jequié** Brazil
75D2 **Jequitai** *R* Brazil
75D2 **Jequitinhonha** Brazil
73K7 **Jequitinhonha** *R* Brazil
48D1 **Jerba, I de** Tunisia
15A2 **Jerez de la Frontera** Spain
15A2 **Jerez de los Caballeros** Spain
45C3 **Jericho** West Bank
34C3 **Jerilderie** Australia
58D2 **Jerome** USA
14B2 **Jersey** *I* Channel Islands
57F2 **Jersey City** USA
65D2 **Jersey Shore** USA
64A3 **Jerseyville** USA
40C3 **Jerusalem** Israel/West Bank
34D3 **Jervis B** Australia
16C1 **Jesenice** Slovenia
18D2 **Jeseniky** *Upland* Czech Republic
43F4 **Jessore** Bangladesh
57E3 **Jesup** USA
62C1 **Jetmore** USA
13D1 **Jever** Germany
68E2 **Jewett City** USA
44C2 **Jeypore** India
17D2 **Jezerce** *Mt* Albania
19E2 **Jezioro Mamry** *L* Poland
19E2 **Jezioro Śniardwy** *L* Poland
45C2 **Jezzine** Lebanon
42C4 **Jhābua** India
42D4 **Jhālāwār** India
42C2 **Jhang Maghiana** Pakistan
42D3 **Jhānsi** India
43E4 **Jhārsuguda** India
42C2 **Jhelum** Pakistan
42C2 **Jhelum** *R* Pakistan
42D3 **Jhunjhunūn** India
31B3 **Jialing Jiang** *R* China
26G2 **Jiamusi** China
28B2 **Ji'an** China
31C4 **Ji'an** Jiangxi, China
31D4 **Jiande** China
31B4 **Jiang'an** China
31D4 **Jiangbiancun** China
31A5 **Jiangcheng** China
31C5 **Jiangmen** China
31D3 **Jiangsu** *Province* China
31C4 **Jiangxi** *Province* China
31A3 **Jiangyou** China
31D1 **Jianping** China
31A5 **Jianshui** China
31D4 **Jian Xi** *R* China
31D4 **Jianyang** China
28B2 **Jiaohe** China
31E2 **Jiaonan** China
31E2 **Jiao Xian** China
31E2 **Jiaozhou Wan** *B* China
31C2 **Jiaozuo** China
31E3 **Jiaxiang** China
26C3 **Jiayuguan** China
75C2 **Jibão, Serra do** *Mts* Brazil
50D1 **Jiddah** Saudi Arabia
31D3 **Jieshou** China
31C2 **Jiexiu** China
31A3 **Jigzhi** China
18D3 **Jihlava** Czech Republic
16B3 **Jijel** Algeria
50E3 **Jilib** Somalia
28B2 **Jilin** China
28B2 **Jilin** *Province* China
15B1 **Jiloca** *R* Spain
50D3 **Jima** Ethiopia
62B3 **Jiménez** Coahuila, Mexico
31D2 **Jinan** China
42D3 **Jind** India
31B2 **Jingbian** China
31D4 **Jingdezhen** China
30C1 **Jinghong** China
31C3 **Jingmen** China
31B2 **Jingning** China
31B4 **Jing Xian** China
28B2 **Jingyu** China
31D4 **Jinhua** China
31C1 **Jining** Inner Mongolia, China
31D2 **Jining** Shandong, China
50D3 **Jinja** Uganda
30C1 **Jinping** China
31A4 **Jinsha Jiang** *R* China
31C4 **Jinshi** China
31E1 **Jinxi** China
28A2 **Jin Xian** China
31E1 **Jinzhou** China
72F5 **Jiparaná** *R* Brazil
72B4 **Jipijapa** Ecuador
41G4 **Jiroft** Iran
50E3 **Jirriiban** Somalia
31B4 **Jishou** China
40C2 **Jisr ash Shughūr** Syria
17E2 **Jiu** *R* Romania
31D4 **Jiujiang** China
31C4 **Jiuling Shan** *Hills* China
31A4 **Jiulong** China
31D4 **Jiulong Jiang** *R* China
26G2 **Jixi** China
45C3 **Jiza** Jordan
50E2 **Jīzān** Saudi Arabia
48A3 **Joal** Senegal
75D2 **João Monlevade** Brazil
73M5 **João Pessoa** Brazil
73J7 **João Pinheiro** Brazil
42C3 **Jodhpur** India
12K6 **Joensuu** Finland
13C3 **Joeuf** France
43F3 **Jogbani** India
44A3 **Jog Falls** India
47D2 **Johannesburg** South Africa
59C3 **Johannesburg** USA
55L2 **Johan Pen** Canada
58C2 **John Day** USA
58B1 **John Day** *R* USA
57F3 **John H Kerr L** USA
65D3 **John H. Kerr Res** USA
62B1 **John Martin Res** USA
8D2 **John o'Groats** Scotland
63C1 **John Redmond Res** USA
68A2 **Johnsonburg** USA
68C1 **Johnson City** New York, USA
67B1 **Johnson City** Tennessee, USA
67B2 **Johnston** USA
69N2 **Johnston Pt** St Vincent
68C1 **Johnstown** New York, USA
65D2 **Johnstown** Pennsylvania, USA
30C5 **Johor Bharu** Malaysia
14C2 **Joigny** France
74G3 **Joinville** Brazil
13C3 **Joinville** France
20J5 **Jok** *R* Russian Federation
12H5 **Jokkmokk** Sweden
21H8 **Jolfa** Iran
57E2 **Joliet** USA
55L5 **Joliette** Canada
27F6 **Jolo** Philippines
27F6 **Jolo** *I* Philippines
39H2 **Joma** *Mt* China
19E1 **Jonava** Lithuania
31A3 **Jonê** China
57D3 **Jonesboro** Arkansas, USA
63D2 **Jonesboro** Louisiana, USA
55K2 **Jones Sd** Canada
19E1 **Joniškis** Lithuania
12G7 **Jönköping** Sweden
65E1 **Jonquière** Canada
57D3 **Joplin** USA
60B1 **Jordan** Montana, USA
68B1 **Jordan** New York, USA
40C3 **Jordan** *Kingdom* SW Asia
45C2 **Jordan** *R* Israel
58C2 **Jordan Valley** USA
75B4 **Jordão** *R* Brazil
43G3 **Jorhāt** India
20C2 **Jörn** Sweden
12F7 **Jørpeland** Norway
48C3 **Jos** Nigeria
32B2 **Joseph Bonaparte G** Australia
59D3 **Joseph City** USA
55M4 **Joseph, Lac** Canada
24B3 **Jotunheimen** *Mt* Norway
45C2 **Jouai'ya** Lebanon
45C2 **Jounié** Lebanon
43G3 **Jowai** India
50E3 **Jowhar** Somalia
54F5 **Juan de Fuca,Str of** Canada/USA
51E5 **Juan de Nova** *I* Mozambique Channel
72Q **Juan Fernández, Islas** Pacific Ocean
73K5 **Juàzeiro** Brazil
73L5 **Juàzeiro do Norte** Brazil
50D3 **Juba** Sudan
50E3 **Juba** *R* Somalia
45C1 **Jubail** Lebanon
76G2 **Jubany** *Base* Antarctica
40D4 **Jubbah** Saudi Arabia
15B2 **Júcar** *R* Spain
18C3 **Judenburg** Austria
13D1 **Juist** *I* Germany
73K8 **Juiz de Fora** Brazil
74C2 **Jujuy** *State* Argentina
60C2 **Julesburg** USA
72E7 **Juli** Peru
72D7 **Juliaca** Peru
73G3 **Julianatop** *Mt* Surinam
55O3 **Julianehåb** Greenland
13D2 **Jülich** Germany
42D2 **Jullundur** India
43E3 **Jumla** Nepal
45C3 **Jum Suwwāna** *Mt* Jordan
42C4 **Jūnāgadh** India
31D2 **Junan** China
62C2 **Junction** Texas, USA
59D3 **Junction** Utah, USA
56D3 **Junction City** USA
74G2 **Jundiaí** Brazil
54E4 **Juneau** USA
32D4 **Junee** Australia
66C2 **June Lake** USA
16B1 **Jungfrau** *Mt* Switzerland
68B2 **Juniata** *R* USA
74D4 **Junín** Argentina
66B2 **Junipero Serra Peak** *Mt* USA
31A4 **Junlian** China
75D2 **Juparanã, Lagoa** Brazil
74G2 **Juquiá** Brazil
50C3 **Jur** *R* Sudan
8C4 **Jura** *I* Scotland
14D2 **Jura** *Mts* France
8C3 **Jura,Sound of** *Chan* Scotland
45C3 **Jurf ed Darāwīsh** Jordan
24K4 **Jurga** Russian Federation
20C4 **Jūrmala** Latvia
72E4 **Juruá** *R* Brazil
73G6 **Juruena** *R* Brazil
45D1 **Jūsīyah** Syria
72E4 **Jutaí** *R* Brazil
70D3 **Juticalpa** Honduras
Jutland *Pen* **= Jylland**
69A2 **Juventud, Isla de la** Cuba
41G3 **Jūymand** Iran
18B1 **Jylland** *Pen* Denmark
12K6 **Jyväskylä** Finland

K

39F2 **K2** *Mt* China/India
41G2 **Kaakhka** Turkmenistan
47E2 **Kaapmuiden** South Africa
27F7 **Kabaena** Indonesia
32B1 **Kabaena** *I* Indonesia
48A4 **Kabala** Sierra Leone
50D4 **Kabale** Uganda
50C4 **Kabalo** Zaïre
50C4 **Kabambare** Zaïre
21G7 **Kabardino-Balkariya** *Division* Russian Federation
50D3 **Kabarole** Uganda
64C1 **Kabinakagami L** Canada
50C4 **Kabinda** Zaïre
45C1 **Kabīr** *R* Syria
41E3 **Kabir Kuh** *Mts* Iran
51C5 **Kabompo** Zambia
51C5 **Kabompo** *R* Zambia
51C4 **Kabongo** Zaïre
42B2 **Kabul** Afghanistan
42B4 **Kachchh,G of** India
20K4 **Kachkanar** Russian Federation
25M4 **Kachug** Russian Federation
30B3 **Kadan** *I* Burma
42C4 **Kadi** India
40B2 **Kadınhanı** Turkey
44B3 **Kadiri** India
21F6 **Kadiyevka** Ukraine
60C2 **Kadoka** USA
51C5 **Kadoma** Zimbabwe
50C2 **Kadugli** Sudan
48C3 **Kaduna** Nigeria
48C3 **Kaduna** *R* Nigeria
44B3 **Kadūr** India
43H3 **Kadusam** *Mt* China
20K3 **Kadzherom** Russian Federation
28A3 **Kaechon** N Korea
48A3 **Kaédi** Mauritius
66E5 **Kaena Pt** Hawaiian Islands
28B3 **Kaesŏng** N Korea
48C4 **Kafanchan** Nigeria
48A3 **Kaffrine** Senegal
45D1 **Kafr Behum** Syria
45A3 **Kafr Sa'd** Egypt
45A3 **Kafr Saqv** Egypt
45D1 **Kafrūn Bashūr** Syria
51C5 **Kafue** Zambia
51C5 **Kafue** *R* Zambia
51C5 **Kafue Nat Pk** Zambia
29D3 **Kaga** Japan
24H6 **Kagan** Uzbekistan
21G7 **Kağızman** Turkey
19F3 **Kagul** Moldavia
41G2 **Kāhak** Iran
50D4 **Kahama** Tanzania
42B3 **Kahan** Pakistan
51B4 **Kahemba** Zaïre
13E2 **Kahler Asten** *Mt* Germany
41G4 **Kahnūj** Iran
64A2 **Kahoka** USA
66E5 **Kahoolawe** *I* Hawaiian Islands
40C2 **Kahramanmaraş** Turkey
66E5 **Kahuku Pt** Hawaiian Islands
66E5 **Kahului** Hawaiian Islands
35B2 **Kaiapoi** New Zealand
59D3 **Kaibab Plat** USA
73G2 **Kaieteur Falls** Guyana
31C3 **Kaifeng** China
27G7 **Kai, Kepulauan** *Arch* Indonesia
35B1 **Kaikohe** New Zealand
33G5 **Kaikoura** New Zealand
35B2 **Kaikoura Pen** New Zealand
35B2 **Kaikoura Range** *Mts* New Zealand
31B4 **Kaili** China
28A2 **Kailu** China
66E5 **Kailua** Hawaii
66E5 **Kailua** Oahu, Hawaiian Islands
27G7 **Kaimana** Indonesia
35C1 **Kaimenawa Mts** New Zealand
29C4 **Kainan** Japan
48C3 **Kainji Res** Nigeria
35B1 **Kaipara Harbour** *B* New Zealand
31C5 **Kaiping** China
16C3 **Kairouan** Tunisia
66C2 **Kaiser Peak** *Mt* USA
14D2 **Kaiserslautern** Germany
28B2 **Kaishantun** China
19E2 **Kaisiadorys** Lithuania
35B1 **Kaitaia** New Zealand
35A3 **Kaitangata** New Zealand
42D3 **Kaithal** India
66E5 **Kaiwi Chan** Hawaiian Islands
31B3 **Kai Xian** China
28A2 **Kaiyuan** Liaoning, China
31A5 **Kaiyuan** Yunnan, China
12K6 **Kajaani** Finland
42B2 **Kajaki** Afghanistan
50D4 **Kajiado** Kenya
42B2 **Kajrān** Afghanistan
50D2 **Kaka** Sudan
64B1 **Kakabeka Falls** Canada
50D3 **Kakamega** Kenya
28B4 **Kake** Japan
21E6 **Kakhovskoye Vodokhranilishche** *Res* Ukraine
41F4 **Kākī** Iran
44C2 **Kākināda** India
29B4 **Kakogawa** Japan
54D2 **Kaktovik** USA
29D3 **Kakuda** Japan
16B3 **Kalaat Khasba** Tunisia
17E3 **Kalabáka** Greece
51C5 **Kalabo** Zambia
21G5 **Kalach** Russian Federation
21G6 **Kalach-na-Donu** Russian Federation
43G4 **Kaladan** *R* Burma/India
66E5 **Ka Lae** *C* Hawaiian Islands
51C6 **Kalahari Desert** Botswana
47C2 **Kalahari Gemsbok Nat Pk** South Africa
20C3 **Kalajoki** Finland
25N4 **Kalakan** Russian Federation
27C6 **Kalakepen** Indonesia
42C1 **Kalam** Pakistan
17E3 **Kalámai** Greece
57E2 **Kalamazoo** USA
66E5 **Kalapana** Hawaiian Islands
19F3 **Kalarash** Moldavia
42B3 **Kalat** Pakistan
66E5 **Kalaupapa** Hawaiian Islands
40B1 **Kalecik** Turkey
50C4 **Kalémié** Zaïre
20E2 **Kalevala** Russian Federation
43G4 **Kalewa** Burma
32B4 **Kalgoorlie** Australia
43E3 **Kali** *R* India/Nepal
50C4 **Kalima** Zaïre
27E7 **Kalimantan** *Terr* Indonesia
17F3 **Kálimnos** *I* Greece
43F3 **Kālimpang** India
43K1 **Kali Nadi** *R* India
12J8 **Kaliningrad** Russian Federation
21D5 **Kalinkovichi** Belarus
19F3 **Kalinovka** Ukraine
56B2 **Kalispell** USA
19D2 **Kalisz** Poland
50D4 **Kaliua** Tanzania
12J5 **Kalix** *R* Sweden
51B6 **Kalkfeld** Namibia
47C1 **Kalkfontein** Botswana
12K6 **Kallavesi** *L* Finland
17F3 **Kallonis Kólpos** *B* Greece
12H7 **Kalmar** Sweden
21H6 **Kalmykiya-Khal'mg Tangh** *Division* Russian Federation
51C5 **Kalomo** Zambia
64A2 **Kalona** USA
44A3 **Kalpeni** *I* India
42D3 **Kālpi** India
20F5 **Kaluga** Russian Federation
20F4 **Kaluga** *Division* Russian Federation
12G7 **Kalundborg** Denmark
19E3 **Kalush** Ukraine
44A2 **Kalyān** India
44B3 **Kalyandurg** India
20F4 **Kalyazin** Russian Federation
20J3 **Kama** *R* Russian Federation
29E3 **Kamaishi** Japan
42C2 **Kamalia** Pakistan
51B5 **Kamanjab** Namibia
25O4 **Kamara** China
42D2 **Kamat** *Mt* China/India
44B4 **Kambam** India
20J4 **Kambarka** Russian Federation
48A4 **Kambia** Sierra Leone
25S4 **Kamchatka** *Pen* Russian Federation

Kólpos Toronaíos Kwanmo-bong

17E2 **Kólpos Toronaíos** *G* Greece
20F2 **Kol'skiy Poluostrov** *Pen* Russian Federation
20K2 **Kolva** *R* Russian Federation
12G6 **Kolvereid** Norway
51C5 **Kolwezi** Zaïre
25R3 **Kolyma** *R* Russian Federation
25R3 **Kolymskaya Nizmennost'** *Lowland* Russian Federation
25S3 **Kolymskoye Nagor'ye** *Mts* Russian Federation
17E2 **Kom** *Mt* Bulgaria/Serbia, Yugoslavia
50D3 **Koma** Ethiopia
29D3 **Koma** Japan
48D3 **Komadugu Gana** *R* Nigeria
29D2 **Komaga take** *Mt* Japan
25S4 **Komandorskiye Ostrova** *Is* Russian Federation
19D3 **Komárno** Slovakia
47E2 **Komati** *R* South Africa/ Swaziland
47E2 **Komati Poort** South Africa
29D3 **Komatsu** Japan
29B4 **Komatsushima** Japan
20J3 **Komi** *Division* Russian Federation
20J4 **Komi-Permyatskiy Avt. Okrug** *Division* Russian Federation
26B1 **Kommunar** Russian Federation
27E7 **Komodo** *I* Indonesia
27G7 **Komoran** *I* Indonesia
29C3 **Komoro** Japan
17F2 **Komotiní** Greece
47C3 **Kompasberg** *Mt* South Africa
30D3 **Kompong Cham** Cambodia
30C3 **Kompong Chhnang** Cambodia
30C3 **Kompong Som = Sihanoukville**
30D3 **Kompong Thom** Cambodia
30D3 **Kompong Trabek** Cambodia
19F3 **Komrat** Moldavia
47C3 **Komsberg** *Mts* South Africa
25L1 **Komsomolets, Ostrov** *I* Russian Federation
20L2 **Komsomol'skiy** Russian Federation
25P4 **Komsomol'sk na Amure** Russian Federation
24H4 **Konda** *R* Russian Federation
43E5 **Kondagaon** India
50D4 **Kondoa** Tanzania
20E3 **Kondopoga** Russian Federation
44B2 **Kondukūr** India
20F3 **Konevo** Russian Federation
55P3 **Kong Christian IX Land** *Region* Greenland
55O3 **Kong Frederik VI Kyst** *Region* Greenland
28A3 **Kongju** S Korea
24D2 **Kong Karls Land** *Is* Svalbard
50C4 **Kongolo** Zaïre
12F7 **Kongsberg** Norway
12G6 **Kongsvinger** Norway
Königsberg = Kaliningrad
19D2 **Konin** Poland
17D2 **Konjic** Bosnia-Herzegovina
20G3 **Konosha** Russian Federation
29C3 **Konosu** Japan
21E5 **Konotop** Ukraine
19E2 **Końskie** Poland
18B3 **Konstanz** Germany
48C3 **Kontagora** Nigeria
30D3 **Kontum** Vietnam
21E8 **Konya** Turkey
58C1 **Kootenay L** Canada
42C5 **Kopargaon** India
55R3 **Kópasker** Iceland
12A2 **Kópavogur** Iceland
16C1 **Koper** Slovenia
38D2 **Kopet Dag** *Mts* Iran/ Turkmenistan
20L4 **Kopeysk** Russian Federation
30C4 **Ko Phangan** *I* Thailand
30B4 **Ko Phuket** *I* Thailand
12H7 **Köping** Sweden
28A3 **Kopo-ri** S Korea
44B2 **Koppal** India
16D1 **Koprivnica** Croatia
42B4 **Korangi** Pakistan
44C2 **Koraput** India
43E4 **Korba** India
18B2 **Korbach** Germany
17E2 **Korçë** Albania
16D2 **Korčula** *I* Croatia
31E2 **Korea B** China/Korea
28B2 **Korea, North** *Republic* Asia
28B3 **Korea, South** *Republic* Asia
26F3 **Korea Strait** Japan/Korea
19F2 **Korec** Ukraine
25S3 **Korf** Russian Federation
40B1 **Körğlu Tepesi** *Mt* Turkey
48B4 **Korhogo** Ivory Coast
42B4 **Kori Creek** India
Kórinthos = Corinth
29E3 **Kōriyama** Japan
20L5 **Korkino** Russian Federation
25R3 **Korkodon** Russian Federation
25R3 **Korkodon** *R* Russian Federation
40B2 **Korkuteli** Turkey
39G1 **Korla** China
45B1 **Kormakiti, C** Cyprus
16D2 **Kornat** *I* Croatia
21E7 **Köroğlu Tepesi** *Mt* Turkey
50D4 **Korogwe** Tanzania
34B3 **Koroit** Australia
27G6 **Koror** Palau, Pacific Ocean
19E3 **Körös** *R* Hungary
21D5 **Korosten** Ukraine
19F2 **Korostyshev** Ukraine
50B2 **Koro Toro** Chad
26H2 **Korsakov** Russian Federation
12G7 **Korsør** Denmark
20J3 **Kortkeros** Russian Federation
18A2 **Kortrijk** Belgium
25S3 **Koryakskiy Avt. Okrug** *Division* Russian Federation
25S3 **Koryakskoye Nagor'ye** *Mts* Russian Federation
28A3 **Koryong** S Korea
17F3 **Kós** *I* Greece
30C4 **Ko Samui** *I* Thailand
28A3 **Kosan** N Korea
19D2 **Kościerzyna** Poland
63E2 **Kosciusko** USA
32D4 **Kosciusko** *Mt* Australia
43J2 **Kosi** India
43K1 **Kosi** *R* India
19E3 **Košice** Slovakia
20J2 **Kosma** *R* Russian Federation
28B3 **Kosŏng** N Korea
17E2 **Kosovo** *Region* Serbia, Yugoslavia
17E2 **Kosovska Mitrovica** Serbia, Yugoslavia
48B4 **Kossou** *L* Ivory Coast
47D2 **Koster** South Africa
50D2 **Kosti** Sudan
19F2 **Kostopol'** Ukraine
20G4 **Kostroma** *Division* Russian Federation
20G4 **Kostroma** *Division* Rusian Federation
18C2 **Kostrzyn** Poland
20K2 **Kos'yu** *R* Russian Federation
12H8 **Koszalin** Poland
42D3 **Kota** India
30C4 **Kota Baharu** Malaysia
42C2 **Kot Addu** Pakistan
27E6 **Kota Kinabalu** Malaysia
44C2 **Kotapad** India
20H4 **Kotel'nich** Russian Federation
21G6 **Kotel'nikovo** Russian Federation
25P2 **Kotel'nyy, Ostrov** *I* Russian Federation
12K6 **Kotka** Finland
20H3 **Kotlas** Russian Federation
54B3 **Kotlik** USA
17D2 **Kotor** Montenegro, Yugoslavia
21D6 **Kotovsk** Ukraine
42B3 **Kotri** Pakistan
44C2 **Kottagūdem** India
44B4 **Kottayam** India
50C3 **Kotto** *R* Central African Republic
44B3 **Kottūru** India
25L3 **Kotuy** *R* Russian Federation
54B3 **Kotzebue** USA
54B3 **Kotzebue Sd** USA
48C3 **Kouandé** Benin
50C3 **Kouango** Central African Republic
48B3 **Koudougou** Burkina
47C3 **Kougaberge** *Mts* South Africa
50B4 **Koulamoutou** Gabon
48B3 **Koulikoro** Mali
48B3 **Koupéla** Burkina
73H2 **Kourou** French Guiana
48B3 **Kouroussa** Guinea
50B2 **Kousséri** Cameroon
12K6 **Kouvola** Finland
12L5 **Kovdor** Russian Federation
12L5 **Kovdozero, Ozero** *L* Russian Federation
19E2 **Kovel** Ukraine
Kovno = Kaunas
20G4 **Kovrov** Russian Federation
20G5 **Kovylkino** Russian Federation
20F3 **Kovzha** *R* Russian Federation
30C4 **Ko Way** *I* Thailand
31C5 **Kowloon** Hong Kong
28A3 **Kowŏn** N Korea
42B2 **Kowt-e-Ashrow** Afghanistan
40A2 **Köycegğiz** Turkey
20G2 **Koyda** Russian Federation
44A2 **Koyna Res** India
20H3 **Koynas** Russian Federation
54C3 **Koyukuk** USA
40C2 **Kozan** Turkey
17E2 **Kozańi** Greece
44B3 **Kozhikode** India
20K2 **Kozhim** Russian Federation
20H4 **Koz'modemyansk** Russian Federation
29C4 **Kōzu-shima** *I* Japan
48C4 **Kpalimé** Togo
47D3 **Kraai** *R* South Africa
12F7 **Kragerø** Norway
17E2 **Kragujevac** Serbia, Yugoslavia
30B3 **Kra,Isthmus of** Burma/ Malaysia
45D1 **Krak des Chevaliers** *Hist Site* Syria
Kraków = Cracow Poland
17E2 **Kraljevo** Serbia, Yugoslavia
21F6 **Kramatorsk** Ukraine
12H6 **Kramfors** Sweden
16C1 **Kranj** Slovenia
20H3 **Krasavino** Russian Federation
20J1 **Krasino** Russian Federation
28C2 **Kraskino** Russian Federation
19E2 **Kraśnik** Poland
21H5 **Krasnoarmeysk** Russian Federation
21F6 **Krasnodar** Russian Federation
21F6 **Krasnodar** *Division* Russian Federation
20K4 **Krasnokamsk** Russian Federation
20L4 **Krasnotur'insk** Russian Federation
20K4 **Krasnoufimsk** Russian Federation
20K5 **Krasnousol'skiy** Russian Federation
20K3 **Krasnovishersk** Russian Federation
21J7 **Krasnovodsk** Turkmenistan
25L4 **Krasnoyarsk** Russian Federation
25L4 **Krasnoyarsk** *Division* Russian Federation
19E2 **Krasnystaw** Poland
21H5 **Krasnyy Kut** Russian Federation
21F6 **Krasnyy Luch** Ukraine
21H6 **Krasnyy Yar** Russian Federation
30D3 **Kratie** Cambodia
55N2 **Kraulshavn** Greenland
18B2 **Krefeld** Germany
21E6 **Kremenchug** Ukraine
21E6 **Kremenchugskoye Vodokhranilische** *Res* Ukraine
19F2 **Kremenets** Ukraine
60B2 **Kremming** USA
48C4 **Kribi** Cameroon
20E5 **Krichev** Belarus
44B2 **Krishna** *R* India
44B3 **Krishnagiri** India
43F4 **Krishnanagar** India
12F7 **Kristiansand** Norway
12G7 **Kristianstad** Sweden
24B3 **Kristiansund** Norway
12J6 **Kristiinankaupunki** Finland
12G7 **Kristinehamn** Sweden
Kríti = Crete
21E6 **Krivoy Rog** Ukraine
16C1 **Krk** *I* Croatia
47D1 **Krokodil** *R* South Africa
25S4 **Kronotskaya Sopka** *Mt* Russian Federation
25S4 **Kronotskiy, Mys** *C* Russian Federation
55P3 **Kronprins Frederik Bjerge** *Mts* Greenland
12K7 **Kronshtadt** Russian Federation
47D2 **Kroonstad** South Africa
21G6 **Kropotkin** Russian Federation
47E1 **Kruger Nat Pk** South Africa
47D2 **Krugersdorp** South Africa
17D2 **Kruje** Albania
Krung Thep = Bangkok
19F2 **Krupki** Belarus
17E2 **Kruševac** Serbia, Yugoslavia
12K7 **Krustpils** Latvia
Krym = Crimea
21F7 **Krymsk** Russian Federation
18D2 **Krzyz** Poland
15C2 **Ksar El Boukhari** Algeria
15A2 **Ksar-el-Kebir** Morocco
48C1 **Ksour, Mts des** Algeria
27C6 **Kuala** Indonesia
30C5 **Kuala Dungun** Malaysia
30C4 **Kuala Kerai** Malaysia
30C5 **Kuala Kubu Baharu** Malaysia
30C5 **Kuala Lipis** Malaysia
30C5 **Kuala Lumpur** Malaysia
30C4 **Kuala Trengganu** Malaysia
27F6 **Kuandang** Indonesia
28A2 **Kuandian** China
30C5 **Kuantan** Malaysia
21H7 **Kuba** Azerbaijan
27H7 **Kubor** *Mt* Papua New Guinea
27E6 **Kuching** Malaysia
27E6 **Kudat** Malaysia
20J4 **Kudymkar** Russian Federation
18C3 **Kufstein** Austria
41G3 **Kuh Duren** *Upland* Iran
41F3 **Kūh-e Dinar** *Mt* Iran
41G2 **Kūh-e-Hazār Masjed** *Mts* Iran
41G4 **Kūh-e Jebāl Barez** *Mts* Iran
41F3 **Kūh-e Karkas** *Mts* Iran
41G4 **Kūh-e Laleh Zar** *Mt* Iran
41E2 **Kūh-e Sahand** *Mt* Iran
38E3 **Kuh-e-Taftān** *Mt* Iran
21H9 **Kūhhaye Alvand** *Mts* Iran
21H8 **Kūhhaye Sabalan** *Mts* Iran
41E3 **Kūhhā-ye Zāgros** *Mts* Iran
12K6 **Kuhmo** Finland
41F3 **Kūhpāyeh** Iran
41G3 **Kūhpāyeh** *Mt* Iran
41G4 **Kūh-ye Bashākerd** *Mts* Iran
41E2 **Kūh-ye Sabalan** *Mt* Iran
47B2 **Kuibis** Namibia
47B1 **Kuiseb** *R* Namibia
51B5 **Kuito** Angola
28A3 **Kujang** N Korea
29E2 **Kuji** Japan
28B4 **Kuju-san** *Mt* Japan
17E2 **Kukës** Albania
30C5 **Kukup** Malaysia
41G4 **Kūl** *R* Iran
17F3 **Kula** Turkey
21K6 **Kulakshi** Kazakhstan
50D3 **Kulal,Mt** Kenya
17E2 **Kulata** Bulgaria
20C4 **Kuldīga** Latvia
20G2 **Kulov** *R* Russian Federation
21J6 **Kul'sary** Kazakhstan
42D2 **Kulu** India
40B2 **Kulu** Turkey
24J4 **Kulunda** Russian Federation
34B2 **Kulwin** Australia
21H7 **Kuma** *R* Russian Federation
29C3 **Kumagaya** Japan
27E7 **Kumai** Indonesia
21L5 **Kumak** Russian Federation
28C4 **Kumamoto** Japan
29C4 **Kumano** Japan
17E2 **Kumanovo** Macedonia, Yugoslavia
48B4 **Kumasi** Ghana
21G7 **Kumayri** Armenia
48C4 **Kumba** Cameroon
44B3 **Kumbakonam** India
28A3 **Kūmch'ŏn** N Korea
20K5 **Kumertau** Russian Federation
28A3 **Kumgang** N Korea
12H7 **Kumla** Sweden
28A4 **Kūmnyŏng** S Korea
28A4 **Kūmo-do** *I* S Korea
44A3 **Kumta** India
39G1 **Kumūx** China
28B3 **Kumwha** S Korea
42C2 **Kunar** *R* Afghanistan
29F2 **Kunashir, Ostrov** *I* Russian Federation
12K7 **Kunda** Estonia
42C4 **Kundla** India
42B1 **Kunduz** Afghanistan
Kunene *R* **= Cunene R**
12G7 **Kungsbacka** Sweden
20K4 **Kungur** Russian Federation
30B1 **Kunhing** Burma
39G2 **Kunlun Shan** *Mts* China
31A4 **Kunming** China
20M3 **Kunovat** *R* Russian Federation
28B3 **Kunsan** S Korea
12K6 **Kuopio** Finland
16D1 **Kupa** *R* Bosnia-Herzegovina/Croatia
32B2 **Kupang** Indonesia
32D2 **Kupiano** Papua New Guinea
54E4 **Kupreanof I** USA
21F6 **Kupyansk** Ukraine
39G1 **Kuqa** China
21H8 **Kura** *R* Azerbaijan
29C3 **Kurabe** Japan
29C4 **Kurashiki** Japan
29B3 **Kurayoshi** Japan
41E2 **Kurdistan** *Region* Iran
17F2 **Kŭrdzhali** Bulgaria
28C4 **Kure** Japan
20C4 **Kuressaare** Estonia
25L3 **Kureyka** *R* Russian Federation
24H4 **Kurgan** Russian Federation
24H4 **Kurgan** *Division* Russian Federation
12J6 **Kurikka** Finland
25Q5 **Kuril Is** Russian Federation
Kuril'skiye Ostrova *Is* **= Kuril Islands**
36J2 **Kuril Trench** Pacific Ocean
21H8 **Kurinskaya Kosa** *Sand Spit* Azerbaijan
44B2 **Kurnool** India
29D2 **Kuroishi** Japan
29D3 **Kuroiso** Japan
35B2 **Kurow** New Zealand
34D2 **Kurri Kurri** Australia
21F5 **Kursk** Russian Federation
21F5 **Kursk** *Division* Russian Federation
26B2 **Kuruktag** *R* China
47C2 **Kuruman** South Africa
47C2 **Kuruman** *R* South Africa
28C4 **Kurume** Japan
44C3 **Kurunegala** Sri Lanka
24K5 **Kurunktag** *R* China
20K3 **Kur'ya** Russian Federation
20K4 **Kusa** Russian Federation
17F3 **Kuşadası Körfezi** *B* Turkey
17F2 **Kus Golü** *L* Turkey
29D4 **Kushimoto** Japan
29E2 **Kushiro** Japan
38E2 **Kushka** Afghanistan
43F4 **Kushtia** Bangladesh
21J5 **Kushum** *R* Kazakhstan
20K4 **Kushva** Russian Federation
54B3 **Kuskokwim** *R* USA
54C3 **Kuskokwim Mts** USA
43E3 **Kusma** Nepal
28B3 **Kusŏng** N Korea
24H4 **Kustanay** Kazakhstan
27E7 **Kuta** *R* Indonesia
21D8 **Kütahya** Turkey
21G7 **Kutaisi** Georgia
29D2 **Kutchan** Japan
29E2 **Kutcharo-ko** *L* Japan
18D3 **Kutná Hora** Czech Republic
19D2 **Kutno** Poland
50B4 **Kutu** Zaïre
43G4 **Kutubdia I** Bangladesh
50C2 **Kutum** Sudan
55M4 **Kuujjuaq** Canada
55L4 **Kuujjuarapik** Canada
12K5 **Kuusamo** Finland
21K5 **Kuvandyk** Russian Federation
41E4 **Kuwait** Kuwait
38C3 **Kuwait** *Sheikhdom* SW Asia
29C3 **Kuwana** Japan
24J4 **Kuybyshev** Russian Federation
Kuybyshev = Samara
20H5 **Kuybyshevskoye Vodokhranilishche** *Res* Russian Federation
20E2 **Kuyto, Ozero** *L* Russian Federation
25M4 **Kuytun** Russian Federation
21F7 **Kuzey Anadolu Dağları** *Mts* Turkey
20F2 **Kuzomen** Russian Federation
20C2 **Kvænangen** *Sd* Norway
12G5 **Kvigtind** *Mt* Norway
20B2 **Kvikkjokk** Sweden
50D4 **Kwale** Kenya
28B3 **Kwangju** S Korea
50B4 **Kwango** *R* Zaïre
28A3 **Kwangyang** S Korea
28A2 **Kwanmo-bong** *Mt* N Korea

KwaZulu Natal
Lena

51D6 **KwaZulu Natal** *Province* South Africa
51C5 **Kwekwe** Zimbabwe
19D2 **Kwidzyn** Poland
54B4 **Kwigillingok** USA
27G7 **Kwoka** *Mt* Indonesia
34C3 **Kyabram** Australia
30B2 **Kyaikkami** Burma
30B2 **Kyaikto** Burma
26D1 **Kyakhta** Russian Federation
30B1 **Kyaukme** Burma
30B1 **Kyauk-padaung** Burma
30A2 **Kyaukpyu** Burma
20G2 **Kychema** Russian Federation
10B2 **Kyle of Lochalsh** Scotland
13D2 **Kyll** *R* Germany
34B3 **Kyneton** Australia
50D3 **Kyoga, L** Uganda
34D1 **Kyogle** Australia
28B3 **Kyŏngju** S Korea
28A3 **Kyongsang Sanmaek** *Mts* S Korea
28A2 **Kyŏngsŏng** N Korea
29D3 **Kyōto** Japan
45B1 **Kyrenia** Cyprus
24J5 **Kyrgyzstan** *Republic* Asia
20K3 **Kyrta** Russian Federation
20L4 **Kyshtym** Russian Federation
45B1 **Kythrea** Cyprus
28B4 **Kyūshū** *I* Japan
36H4 **Kyushu-Palau Ridge** Pacific Ocean
17E2 **Kyustendil** Bulgaria
25O2 **Kyusyur** Russian Federation
26C1 **Kyzyl** Russian Federation
24H5 **Kyzylkum** *Desert* Uzbekistan
24H5 **Kzyl Orda** Kazakhstan

L

50E3 **Laascaanood** Somalia
50E2 **Laas Dawaco** Somalia
13E2 **Laasphe** Germany
50E2 **Laasqoray** Somalia
72F1 **La Asunción** Venezuela
48A2 **Laâyoune** Morocco
58D2 **La Barge** USA
48A3 **Labé** Guinea
18D2 **Labe** *R* Czech Republic
65E1 **Labelle** Canada
67B3 **La Belle** USA
21G7 **Labinsk** Russian Federation
45D1 **Laboué** Lebanon
55M4 **Labrador** *Region* Canada
55M4 **Labrador City** Canada
55N4 **Labrador S** Canada/Greenland
72F5 **Lábrea** Brazil
27E6 **Labuk B** Malaysia
30A2 **Labutta** Burma
20M2 **Labytnangi** Russian Federation
13B2 **La Capelle** France
Laccadive Is = **Lakshadweep**
39F4 **Laccadive Is** India
70D3 **La Ceiba** Honduras
34A3 **Lacepede B** Australia
14C2 **La Châtre** France
45C3 **Lachish** *Hist Site* Israel
32D4 **Lachlan** *R* Australia
72C2 **La Chorrera** Panama
65E1 **Lachute** Canada
65D2 **Lackawanna** USA
54G4 **Lac la Biche** Canada
55L4 **Lac L'eau Claire** Canada
65E1 **Lac Mégantic** Canada
54G4 **Lacombe** Canada
65E2 **Laconia** USA
15A1 **La Coruña** Spain
57D2 **La Crosse** USA
63D1 **La Cygne** USA
42D2 **Ladākh Range** *Mts* India
27E6 **Ladd Reef** S China Sea
42C3 **Lādnūn** India
20E3 **Ladoga, L** Russian Federation
31B5 **Ladong** China
Ladozhskoye Oz *L* = **Ladoga, L**
55K2 **Lady Ann Str** Canada
34C4 **Lady Barron** Australia
47D2 **Ladybrand** South Africa
47D2 **Ladysmith** South Africa
64A1 **Ladysmith** USA
32D1 **Lae** Papua New Guinea
30C3 **Laem Ngop** Thailand
18C1 **Laesø** *I* Denmark
60B3 **Lafayette** Colorado, USA
57E2 **Lafayette** Indiana, USA
57D3 **Lafayette** Louisiana, USA
13B3 **La Fère** France
13B3 **La-Ferté-sous-Jouarre** France
48C4 **Lafia** Nigeria
48C4 **Lafiagi** Nigeria
14B2 **La Flèche** France
16B3 **La Galite** *I* Tunisia
18C1 **Lagan** *R* Sweden
73L6 **Lagarto** Brazil
8C3 **Laggan, L** Scotland
48C1 **Laghouat** Algeria
72C4 **Lago Agrio** Ecuador
48C4 **Lagos** Nigeria
15A2 **Lagos** Portugal
70B2 **Lagos de Moreno** Mexico
56B2 **La Grande** USA
32B2 **Lagrange** Australia
57E3 **La Grange** Georgia, USA
64B3 **La Grange** Kentucky, USA
67C1 **La Grange** N Carolina, USA
63C3 **La Grange** Texas, USA
72F2 **La Gran Sabana** *Mts* Venezuela
62A2 **Laguna** USA
59C4 **Laguna Beach** USA
56C4 **Laguna Seca** Mexico
28B2 **Lagusha** N Korea
27E6 **Lahad Datu** Malaysia
41F2 **Lāhījān** Iran
13D2 **Lahn** *R* Germany
13D2 **Lahnstein** Germany
42C2 **Lahore** Pakistan
13D3 **Lahr** Germany
12K6 **Lahti** Finland
50B3 **Lai** Chad
31B5 **Laibin** China
30C1 **Lai Chau** Vietnam
13C4 **Laignes** France
12J6 **Laihia** Finland
47C3 **Laingsburg** South Africa
8C2 **Lairg** Scotland
31E2 **Laiyang** China
31D2 **Laizhou Wan** *B* China
74B5 **Laja, Lago de la** Chile
74F3 **Lajes** Brazil
66D4 **La Jolla** USA
56C3 **La Junta** USA
60D2 **Lake Andes** USA
34C2 **Lake Cargelligo** Australia
57D3 **Lake Charles** USA
67B2 **Lake City** Florida, USA
61E2 **Lake City** Minnesota, USA
67C2 **Lake City** S Carolina, USA
6C2 **Lake District** *Region* England
66D4 **Lake Elsinore** USA
32C3 **Lake Eyre Basin** Australia
65D2 **Lakefield** Canada
64B2 **Lake Geneva** USA
68D1 **Lake George** USA
55M3 **Lake Harbour** Canada
59D4 **Lake Havasu City** USA
66C3 **Lake Hughes** USA
68C2 **Lakehurst** USA
66C3 **Lake Isabella** USA
63C3 **Lake Jackson** USA
67B3 **Lakeland** USA
55J5 **Lake of the Woods** Canada
58B1 **Lake Oswego** USA
12K7 **Lake Peipus** Estonia/Russian Federation
59B3 **Lakeport** USA
63D2 **Lake Providence** USA
35B2 **Lake Pukaki** New Zealand
34C3 **Lakes Entrance** Australia
66C2 **Lakeshore** USA
34B1 **Lake Stewart** Australia
65D1 **Lake Traverse** Canada
56A2 **Lakeview** USA
58B1 **Lakeview Mt** Canada
63D2 **Lake Village** USA
67B3 **Lake Wales** USA
66C4 **Lakewood** California, USA
60B3 **Lakewood** Colorado, USA
68C2 **Lakewood** New Jersey, USA
64C2 **Lakewood** Ohio, USA
67B3 **Lake Worth** USA
43E3 **Lakhīmpur** India
42B4 **Lakhpat** India
62B1 **Lakin** USA
42C2 **Lakki** Pakistan
17E3 **Lakonikós Kólpos** *G* Greece
48B4 **Lakota** Ivory Coast
12K4 **Laksefjord** *Inlet* Norway
12K4 **Lakselv** Norway
44A3 **Lakshadweep** *Is, Union Territory* India
72B4 **La Libertad** Ecuador
15A2 **La Linea** Spain
42D4 **Lalitpur** India
54H4 **La Loche** Canada
13C2 **La Louvière** Belgium
69A4 **La Luz** Nicaragua
55L5 **La Malbaie** Canada
56C3 **Lamar** Colorado, USA
63D1 **Lamar** Missouri, USA
63C3 **La Marque** USA
50B4 **Lambaréné** Gabon
72B5 **Lambayeque** Peru
76F10 **Lambert Glacier** Antarctica
47B3 **Lamberts Bay** South Africa
68C2 **Lambertville** USA
54F2 **Lambton,C** Canada
30C2 **Lam Chi** *R* Thailand
15A1 **Lamego** Portugal
72C6 **La Merced** Peru
62B2 **Lamesa** USA
59C4 **La Mesa** USA
17E3 **Lamía** Greece
8D4 **Lammermuir Hills** Scotland
12G7 **Lammhult** Sweden
61E2 **Lamoni** USA
66C3 **Lamont** California, USA
60B2 **Lamont** Wyoming, USA
27H6 **Lamotrek** *I* Pacific Ocean
13B4 **Lamotte-Beuvron** France
60D1 **La Moure** USA
62C2 **Lampasas** USA
7B3 **Lampeter** Wales
50E4 **Lamu** Kenya
66E5 **Lanai** *I* Hawaiian Islands
66E5 **Lanai City** Hawaiian Islands
27F6 **Lanao, L** Philippines
8D4 **Lanark** Scotland
30B3 **Lanbi** *I* Burma
30C1 **Lancang** *R* China
6C3 **Lancashire** *County* England
59C4 **Lancaster** California, USA
6C2 **Lancaster** England
61E2 **Lancaster** Missouri, USA
65E2 **Lancaster** New Hampshire, USA
68A1 **Lancaster** New York, USA
64C3 **Lancaster** Ohio, USA
57F3 **Lancaster** Pennsylvania, USA
67B2 **Lancaster** S Carolina, USA
55K2 **Lancaster Sd** Canada
13E3 **Landan** Germany
18C3 **Landeck** Austria
56C2 **Lander** USA
14B3 **Landes, Les** *Region* France
67B1 **Landrum** USA
18C3 **Landsberg** Germany
54F2 **Lands End** *C* Canada
7B4 **Land's End** *Pt* England
18C3 **Landshut** Germany
12G7 **Làndskrona** Sweden
67A2 **Lanett** USA
43E2 **La'nga Co** *L* China
60D1 **Langdon** USA
47C2 **Langeberg** *Mts* South Africa
18B2 **Langenhagen** Germany
13D1 **Langeoog** *I* Germany
8D4 **Langholm** Scotland
12A2 **Langjökull** *Mts* Iceland
30B4 **Langkawi** *I* Malaysia
34C1 **Langlo** *R* Australia
6B2 **Langness** *Pt* England
14B3 **Langon** France
14D2 **Langres** France
13C4 **Langres, Plateau de** France
27C6 **Langsa** Indonesia
26D2 **Lang Shan** *Mts* China
30D1 **Lang Son** Vietnam
62B3 **Langtry** USA
14C3 **Languedoc** *Region* France
74B5 **Lanin, Vol** Argentina
68C2 **Lansdale** USA
55K4 **Lansdowne House** Canada
68C2 **Lansford** USA
57E2 **Lansing** USA
48A2 **Lanzarote** *I* Canary Islands
31A2 **Lanzhou** China
27F5 **Laoag** Philippines
30C1 **Lao Cai** Vietnam
31D1 **Laoha He** *R* China
9C3 **Laois** *County* Irish Republic
28A2 **Laoling** China
13B3 **Laon** France
72C6 **La Oroya** Peru
30C2 **Laos** *Republic* SE Asia
75C4 **Lapa** Brazil
14C2 **Lapalisse** France
72C2 **La Palma** Panama
48A2 **La Palma** *I* Canary Islands
74C5 **La Pampa** *State* Argentina
66B3 **La Panza Range** *Mts* USA
72F2 **La Paragua** Venezuela
74E4 **La Paz** Argentina
72E7 **La Paz** Bolivia
70A2 **La Paz** Mexico
26H2 **La Perouse Str** Japan/Russian Federation
58B2 **La Pine** USA
45B1 **Lapithos** Cyprus
63D2 **Laplace** USA
60C1 **La Plant** USA
74E4 **La Plata** Argentina
64B2 **La Porte** USA
68B2 **Laporte** USA
12K6 **Lappeenranta** Finland
12H5 **Lappland** *Region* Finland/Sweden
62C3 **La Pryor** USA
25O2 **Laptev S** Russian Federation
12J6 **Lapua** Finland
56B4 **La Purísima** Mexico
50C1 **Laqiya Arbain** *Well* Sudan
74C2 **La Quiaca** Argentina
16C2 **L'Aquila** Italy
41F4 **Lār** Iran
15A2 **Larache** Morocco
56C2 **Laramie** USA
60B2 **Laramie Mts** USA
56C2 **Laramie Range** *Mts* USA
75B4 **Laranjeiras do Sul** Brazil
56D4 **Laredo** USA
41F4 **Larestan** *Region* Iran
Largeau = **Faya**
67B3 **Largo** USA
8C4 **Largs** Scotland
41E2 **Lārī** Iran
74C3 **La Rioja** Argentina
15B1 **La Rioja** *Region* Spain
74C3 **La Rioja** *State* Argentina
17E3 **Lárisa** Greece
42B3 **Larkana** Pakistan
40B3 **Larnaca** Cyprus
45B1 **Larnaca B** Cyprus
9C2 **Larne** Northern Ireland
62C1 **Larned** USA
15A1 **La Robla** Spain
13C2 **La Roche-en-Ardenne** Belgium
14B2 **La Rochelle** France
14B2 **La Roche-sur-Yon** France
15B2 **La Roda** Spain
69D3 **La Romana** Dominican Republic
54H4 **La Ronge** Canada
12F7 **Larvik** Norway
24J3 **Laryak** Russian Federation
15B2 **La Sagra** *Mt* Spain
65E1 **La Salle** Canada
64B2 **La Salle** USA
62B1 **Las Animas** USA
55L5 **La Sarre** Canada
62A2 **Las Cruces** USA
69C3 **La Selle** *Mt* Haiti
31B2 **Lasengmiao** China
74B3 **La Serena** Chile
74E5 **Las Flores** Argentina
30B1 **Lashio** Burma
16D3 **La Sila** *Mts* Italy
41F2 **Lāsjerd** Iran
42A2 **Laskar Gāh** Afghanistan
15A2 **Las Marismas** *Marshland* Spain
48A2 **Las Palmas de Gran Canaria** Canary Islands
16B2 **La Spezia** Italy
74C6 **Las Plumas** Argentina
58B2 **Lassen Peak** *Mt* USA
58B2 **Lassen Volcanic Nat Pk** USA
50B4 **Lastoursville** Gabon
16D2 **Lastovo** *I* Croatia
70B2 **Las Tres Marias** *Is* Mexico
56B3 **Las Vegas** USA
40C2 **Latakia** Syria
16C2 **Latina** Italy
69D4 **La Tortuga, I** Venezuela
34C4 **Latrobe** Australia
45C3 **Latrun** West Bank
55L5 **La Tuque** Canada
44B2 **Lātūr** India
20C4 **Latvia** *Republic* Europe
8D4 **Lauder** Scotland
18B2 **Lauenburg** Germany
33H2 **Lau Group** *Is* Fiji
32D5 **Launceston** Australia
7B4 **Launceston** England
74B6 **La Unión** Chile
70D3 **La Unión** El Salvador
72C5 **La Unión** Peru
32D2 **Laura** Australia
65D3 **Laurel** Delaware, USA
68B3 **Laurel** Maryland, USA
57E3 **Laurel** Mississippi, USA
58E1 **Laurel** Montana, USA
67B2 **Laurens** USA
67C2 **Laurinburg** USA
16B1 **Lausanne** Switzerland
27E7 **Laut** *I* Indonesia
74B7 **Lautaro** Chile
13E2 **Lauterbach** Germany
13D3 **Lauterecken** Germany
65E1 **Laval** Canada
14B2 **Laval** France
66B2 **Laveaga Peak** *Mt* USA
58E1 **Lavina** USA
13C3 **La Vôge** *Region* France
73K8 **Lavras** Brazil
54A3 **Lavrentiya** Russian Federation
47E2 **Lavumisa** Swaziland
30B1 **Lawksawk** Burma
61D3 **Lawrence** Kansas, USA
65E2 **Lawrence** Massachusetts, USA
35A3 **Lawrence** New Zealand
63E1 **Lawrenceburg** USA
64B3 **Lawrenceville** Illinois, USA
68B2 **Lawrenceville** Pennsylvania, USA
56D3 **Lawton** USA
40C4 **Lawz, Jebel al** *Mt* Saudi Arabia
6B2 **Laxey** England
38C3 **Layla'** Saudi Arabia
50D3 **Laylo** Sudan
70B3 **Lázaro Cardenas** Mexico
29C2 **Lazo** Russian Federation
56C2 **Lead** USA
60B3 **Leadville** USA
63E2 **Leaf** *R* USA
62C3 **Leakey** USA
7D5 **Leamington Spa, Royal** England
61E3 **Leavenworth** USA
19D2 **Łeba** Poland
60D3 **Lebanon** Kansas, USA
63D1 **Lebanon** Missouri, USA
58B2 **Lebanon** Oregon, USA
65D2 **Lebanon** Pennsylvania, USA
64B3 **Lebanon** Tennessee, USA
40C3 **Lebanon** *Republic* SW Asia
66C3 **Lebec** USA
51D6 **Lebombo Mts** Mozambique/South Africa/Swaziland
19D2 **Lębork** Poland
74B5 **Lebu** Chile
13B2 **Le Cateau** France
17D2 **Lecce** Italy
16B1 **Lecco** Italy
13D3 **Le Champ du Feu** *Mt* France
14C2 **Le Creusot** France
7C3 **Ledbury** England
43H3 **Ledo** India
68D1 **Lee** USA
61E1 **Leech L** USA
10C3 **Leeds** England
7C3 **Leek** England
18B2 **Leer** Germany
67B3 **Leesburg** Florida, USA
68B3 **Leesburg** Virginia, USA
63D2 **Leesville** USA
34C2 **Leeton** Australia
47C3 **Leeugamka** South Africa
18B2 **Leeuwarden** Netherlands
32A4 **Leeuwin,C** Australia
66C2 **Lee Vining** USA
69E3 **Leeward Is** Caribbean Sea
45B1 **Lefka** Cyprus
45B1 **Lefkara** Cyprus
45B1 **Lefkoniko** Cyprus
27F5 **Legazpi** Philippines
18D2 **Legnica** Poland
73G2 **Leguan Island** Guyana
72D4 **Leguizamo** Peru
42D2 **Leh** India
14C2 **Le Havre** France
59D2 **Lehi** USA
68C2 **Lehigh** *R* USA
68C2 **Lehighton** USA
13D3 **Le Hohneck** *Mt* France
42C2 **Leiah** Pakistan
18D3 **Leibnitz** Austria
7D3 **Leicester** England
7D3 **Leicester** *County* England
32C2 **Leichhardt** *R* Australia
18A2 **Leiden** Netherlands
13B2 **Leie** *R* Belgium
32C4 **Leigh Creek** Australia
7E4 **Leigh on Sea** England
7D4 **Leighton Buzzard** England
18B2 **Leine** *R* Germany
9C3 **Leinster** *Region* Irish Republic
18C2 **Leipzig** Germany
15A2 **Leiria** Portugal
12F7 **Leirvik** Norway
8D4 **Leith** Scotland
31C4 **Leiyang** China
31B5 **Leizhou Bandao** *Pen* China
31C5 **Leizhou Wan** *B* China
18A2 **Lek** *R* Netherlands
16B3 **Le Kef** Tunisia
63D2 **Leland** USA
17D2 **Lelija** *Mt* Bosnia-Herzegovina
16B1 **Léman, Lac** France/Switzerland
14C2 **Le Mans** France
61D2 **Le Mars** USA
13E1 **Lemgo** Germany
58D2 **Lemhi Range** *Mts* USA
55M3 **Lemieux Is** Canada
56C2 **Lemmon** USA
59D4 **Lemmon,Mt** USA
59C3 **Lemoore** USA
14C2 **Lempdes** France
43G4 **Lemro** *R* Burma
16D2 **Le Murge** *Region* Italy
25O3 **Lena** *R* Russian Federation

Lendery Longview

20E3 **Lendery** Russian Federation
13D1 **Lengerich** Germany
31C4 **Lengshuijiang** China
Leningrad = St Petersburg
20D4 **Leningrad** *Division* Russian Federation
76F7 **Leningradskaya** *Base* Antarctica
20J5 **Leninogorsk** Russian Federation
26B1 **Leninogorsk** Kazakhstan
24K4 **Leninsk-Kuznetskiy** Russian Federation
26G2 **Leninskoye** Russian Federation
21H8 **Lenkoran'** Azerbaijan
13E2 **Lenne** *R* Germany
67B1 **Lenoir** USA
68D1 **Lenox** USA
13B2 **Lens** France
25N3 **Lensk** Russian Federation
16C3 **Lentini** Sicily, Italy
30B3 **Lenya** *R* Burma
16C1 **Leoben** Austria
7C3 **Leominster** England
68E1 **Leominster** USA
70B2 **León** Mexico
72A1 **León** Nicaragua
15A1 **León** Spain
47B1 **Leonardville** Namibia
45C1 **Leonarisso** Cyprus
32B3 **Leonora** Australia
75D3 **Leopoldina** Brazil
Léopoldville = Kinshasa
20D5 **Lepel** Belarus
31D4 **Leping** China
14C2 **Le Puy-en-Velay** France
50B3 **Léré** Chad
47D2 **Leribe** Lesotho
15C1 **Lérida** Spain
17F3 **Léros** *I* Greece
68B1 **Le Roy** USA
10C1 **Lerwick** Scotland
69C3 **Les Cayes** Haiti
65F1 **Les Escoumins** Canada
31A4 **Leshan** China
17E2 **Leskovac** Serbia, Yugoslavia
47D2 **Leslie** South Africa
20J4 **Lesnoy** Russian Federation
25L4 **Lesosibirsk** Russian Federation
47D2 **Lesotho** *Kingdom* South Africa
26G2 **Lesozavodsk** Russian Federation
14B2 **Les Sables-d'Olonne** France
76E4 **Lesser Antarctica** *Region* Antarctica
69E3 **Lesser Antilles** *Is* Caribbean Sea
21G7 **Lesser Caucasus** *Mts* Azerbaijan/Georgia
17F3 **Lésvos** *I* Greece
18D2 **Leszno** Poland
47E1 **Letaba** *R* South Africa
43G4 **Letha Range** *Mts* Burma
54G5 **Lethbridge** Canada
73G3 **Lethem** Guyana
19F3 **Letichev** Ukraine
72E4 **Letícia** Colombia
32B1 **Leti, Kepulauan** *I* Indonesia
47D1 **Letlhakeng** Botswana
7E4 **le Touquet-Paris-Plage** France
30B2 **Letpadan** Burma
25N4 **Let Oktyabr'ya** Russian Federation
14C1 **Le Tréport** France
9C2 **Letterkenny** Irish Republic
27C6 **Leuser** *Mt* Indonesia
18A2 **Leuven** Belgium
17E3 **Levádhia** Greece
12G6 **Levanger** Norway
62B2 **Levelland** USA
8D3 **Leven** Scotland
8D3 **Leven, Loch** *L* Scotland
27F8 **Lévêque,C** Australia
13D2 **Leverkusen** Germany
19D3 **Levice** Slovakia
35C2 **Levin** New Zealand
55L5 **Lévis** Canada
65E2 **Levittown** USA
17E3 **Lévka Óri** *Mt* Greece
17E3 **Levkás** Greece
17E3 **Levkás** *I* Greece
32B2 **Lévêque,C** Australia
17F2 **Levski** Bulgaria
7E4 **Lewes** England
62C1 **Lewis** USA
10B2 **Lewis** *I* Scotland
68B2 **Lewisburg** USA
35B2 **Lewis P** New Zealand
56B2 **Lewis Range** *Mts* USA
67A2 **Lewis Smith,L** USA
56B2 **Lewiston** Idaho, USA
57F2 **Lewiston** Maine, USA
56C2 **Lewistown** Montana, USA
65D2 **Lewistown** Pennsylvania, USA
63D2 **Lewisville** USA
57E3 **Lexington** Kentucky, USA
61E3 **Lexington** Missouri, USA
67B1 **Lexington** N Carolina, USA
60D2 **Lexington** Nebraska, USA
65D3 **Lexington** Virginia, USA
65D3 **Lexington Park** USA
6D2 **Leyburn** England
27F5 **Leyte** *I* Philippines
17D2 **Lezhe** Albania
39H3 **Lhasa** China
43F3 **Lhazê** China
27C6 **Lhokseumawe** Indonesia
43G3 **Lhozhag** China
26C4 **Lhunze** China
Liancourt Rocks = Tok-do
28B2 **Liangbingtai** China
31B3 **Liangdang** China
31C5 **Lianjiang** China
31C5 **Lianping** China
31C5 **Lian Xian** China
31D3 **Lianyungang** China
31E1 **Liaodong Bandao** *Pen* China
31E1 **Liaodong Wan** *B* China
31E1 **Liao He** *R* China
28A2 **Liaoning** *Province* China
31E1 **Liaoyang** China
28A2 **Liaoyangwopu** China
31E1 **Liaoyuan** China
28A2 **Liaozhong** China
54F3 **Liard** *R* Canada
54F4 **Liard River** Canada
13C3 **Liart** France
45C2 **Liban, Jebel** *Mts* Lebanon
58C1 **Libby** USA
50B3 **Libenge** Zaïre
56C3 **Liberal** USA
18C2 **Liberec** Czech Republic
48A4 **Liberia** *Republic* Africa
61E3 **Liberty** Missouri, USA
65E2 **Liberty** New York, USA
68B2 **Liberty** Pennsylvania, USA
63D2 **Liberty** Texas, USA
45B3 **Libni, Gebel** *Mt* Egypt
14B3 **Libourne** France
48C4 **Libreville** Equatorial Guinea
49D2 **Libya** *Republic* Africa
49E2 **Libyan Desert** Egypt/Libya/Sudan
49E1 **Libyan Plat** Egypt
16C3 **Licata** Sicily, Italy
7D3 **Lichfield** England
51D5 **Lichinga** Mozambique
47D2 **Lichtenburg** South Africa
64C3 **Licking** *R* USA
66B2 **Lick Observatory** USA
16C2 **Licosa, Punta** *Pt* Italy
66D2 **Lida** USA
20D5 **Lida** Belarus
12G7 **Lidköping** Sweden
16C2 **Lido di Ostia** Italy
16B1 **Liechtenstein** *Principality* Europe
18B2 **Liège** Belgium
19E1 **Lielupe** *R* Latvia
50C3 **Lienart** Zaïre
18C3 **Lienz** Austria
12J7 **Liepāja** Latvia
13C2 **Lier** Belgium
65E1 **Lièvre** *R* Canada
18C3 **Liezen** Austria
9C3 **Liffey** *R* Irish Republic
9C2 **Lifford** Irish Republic
33F3 **Lifu** *I* Nouvelle Calédonie
34C1 **Lightning Ridge** Australia
13C3 **Ligny-en-Barrois** France
51D5 **Ligonha** *R* Mozambique
16B2 **Ligurian S** Italy
33E1 **Lihir Group** *Is* Papua New Guinea
66E5 **Lihue** Hawaiian Islands
51C5 **Likasi** Zaïre
14C1 **Lille** France
12G6 **Lillehammer** Norway
13B2 **Lillers** France
12G7 **Lillestrøm** Norway
51D5 **Lilongwe** Malawi
17D2 **Lim** *R* Montenegro/Serbia, Yugoslavia
72C6 **Lima** Peru
57E2 **Lima** USA
15A1 **Lima** *R* Portugal
58D2 **Lima Res** USA
40B3 **Limassol** Cyprus
9C2 **Limavady** Northern Ireland
48C4 **Limbe** Cameroon
51D5 **Limbe** Malawi
18B2 **Limburg** Germany
73J8 **Limeira** Brazil
10B3 **Limerick** Irish Republic
18B1 **Limfjorden** *L* Denmark
32C2 **Limmen Bight** *B* Australia
17F3 **Límnos** *I* Greece
73L5 **Limoeiro** Brazil
14C2 **Limoges** France
70D4 **Limón** Costa Rica
56C3 **Limon** USA
14C2 **Limousin** *Region* France
14C2 **Limousin, Plateaux de** France
47E1 **Limpopo** *R* Mozambique
74B5 **Linares** Chile
56D4 **Linares** Mexico
15B2 **Linares** Spain
26C4 **Lincang** China
74D4 **Lincoln** Argentina
7D3 **Lincoln** England
64B2 **Lincoln** Illinois, USA
65F1 **Lincoln** Maine, USA
56D2 **Lincoln** Nebraska, USA
65E2 **Lincoln** New Hampshire, USA
35B2 **Lincoln** New Zealand
7D3 **Lincoln** *County* England
58B2 **Lincoln City** USA
64C2 **Lincoln Park** USA
76A2 **Lincoln Sea** Greenland
16B2 **L'Incudine** *Mt* Corsica, France
18B3 **Lindau** Germany
73G2 **Linden** Guyana
12F7 **Lindesnes** *C* Norway
51D4 **Lindi** Tanzania
50C3 **Lindi** *R* Zaïre
47D2 **Lindley** South Africa
17F3 **Lindos** Greece
66C2 **Lindsay** California, USA
65D2 **Lindsay** Canada
60B1 **Lindsay** Montana, USA
37M4 **Line Is** Pacific Ocean
31C2 **Linfen** China
30D2 **Lingao** China
27F5 **Lingayen** Philippines
18B2 **Lingen** Germany
27D7 **Lingga** *I* Indonesia
60C2 **Lingle** USA
31C4 **Lingling** China
31B5 **Lingshan** China
31C2 **Lingshi** China
48A3 **Linguère** Senegal
31E4 **Linhai** Zhejiang, China
73L7 **Linhares** Brazil
31B1 **Linhe** China
28B2 **Linjiang** China
28A2 **Linjiatai** China
12H7 **Linköping** Sweden
8C3 **Linnhe, Loch** *Inlet* Scotland
31D2 **Linqing** China
75C3 **Lins** Brazil
31A2 **Lintao** China
60C1 **Linton** USA
26E2 **Linxi** China
31A2 **Linxia** China
18C3 **Linz** Austria
14C3 **Lion, Golfe du** *G* France
16C3 **Lipari** *I* Italy
16C3 **Lipari, Isole** *Is* Italy
21F5 **Lipetsk** Russian Federation
21F5 **Lipetsk** *Division* Russian Federation
17E1 **Lipova** Romania
18B2 **Lippe** *R* Germany
13E2 **Lippstadt** Germany
50D3 **Lira** Uganda
50B4 **Liranga** Congo
50C3 **Lisala** Zaïre
Lisboa = Lisbon
15A2 **Lisbon** Portugal
61D1 **Lisbon** USA
9C2 **Lisburn** Northern Ireland
31D4 **Lishui** China
31C4 **Li Shui** *R* China
21F6 **Lisichansk** Ukraine
14C2 **Lisieux** France
21F5 **Liski** Russian Federation
13B3 **L'Isle-Adam** France
33E3 **Lismore** Australia
9C3 **Lismore** Irish Republic
31B5 **Litang** China
45C2 **Lītāni** *R* Lebanon
73H3 **Litani** *R* Surinam
64B3 **Litchfield** Illinois, USA
61E1 **Litchfield** Minnesota, USA
32E4 **Lithgow** Australia
20C4 **Lithuania** *Republic* Europe
68B2 **Lititz** USA
26G2 **Litovko** Russian Federation
63C2 **Little** *R* USA
57F4 **Little Abaco** *I* The Bahamas
44E3 **Little Andaman** *I* Andaman Islands
67C3 **Little Bahama Bank** Bahamas
35C1 **Little Barrier I** New Zealand
58D1 **Little Belt Mts** USA
45B3 **Little Bitter L** Egypt
70D3 **Little Cayman** *I* Cayman Is, Caribbean Sea
68C3 **Little Egg Harbor** *B* USA
61E1 **Little Falls** Minnesota, USA
68C1 **Little Falls** New York, USA
62B2 **Littlefield** USA
61E1 **Littlefork** USA
61E1 **Little Fork** *R* USA
7D4 **Littlehampton** England
69C2 **Little Inagua** *I* The Bahamas
47C3 **Little Karoo** *Mts* South Africa
66D3 **Little Lake** USA
60C1 **Little Missouri** *R* USA
30A4 **Little Nicobar** *I* Nicobar Is, India
57D3 **Little Rock** USA
66D3 **Littlerock** USA
68B3 **Littlestown** USA
60B3 **Littleton** Colorado, USA
65E2 **Littleton** New Hampshire, USA
28B2 **Liuhe** China
31B2 **Liupan Shan** *Upland* China
31B5 **Liuzhou** China
17E3 **Livanátais** Greece
19F1 **Līvāni** Latvia
67B2 **Live Oak** USA
59B3 **Livermore** USA
62B2 **Livermore,Mt** USA
55M5 **Liverpool** Canada
7C3 **Liverpool** England
54E2 **Liverpool B** Canada
7C3 **Liverpool B** England
55L2 **Liverpool,C** Canada
34D2 **Liverpool Range** *Mts* Australia
56B2 **Livingston** Montana, USA
67A1 **Livingston** Tennessee, USA
63D2 **Livingston** Texas, USA
8D4 **Livingstone** Scotland
51C5 **Livingstone** Zambia
63C2 **Livingston,L** USA
16D2 **Livno** Bosnia-Herzegovina
21F5 **Livny** Russian Federation
64C2 **Livonia** USA
16C2 **Livorno** Italy
75D1 **Livramento do Brumado** Brazil
51D4 **Liwale** Tanzania
7B5 **Lizard Pt** England
16C1 **Ljubljana** Slovenia
12G6 **Ljungan** *R* Sweden
12G7 **Ljungby** Sweden
12H6 **Ljusdal** Sweden
20B3 **Ljusnan** *R* Sweden
7C4 **Llandeilo** Wales
7C4 **Llandovery** Wales
7C3 **Llandrindod Wells** Wales
7C3 **Llandudno** Wales
7D4 **Llanelli** Wales
7C3 **Llangollen** Wales
62C2 **Llano** USA
62C2 **Llano** *R* USA
56C3 **Llano Estacado** *Plat* USA
72D2 **Llanos** *Region* Colombia/Venezuela
72F7 **Llanos de Chiquitos** *Region* Bolivia
7C4 **Llantrisant** Wales
7C3 **Llanwrst** Wales
Lleida = Lérida
15A2 **Llerena** Spain
7B3 **Lleyn** *Pen* Wales
54F4 **Lloyd George,Mt** Canada
54H4 **Lloydminster** Canada
74C2 **Llullaillaco** *Mt* Argentina/Chile
74C2 **Loa** *R* Chile
50B4 **Loange** *R* Zaïre
47D2 **Lobatse** Botswana
50B3 **Lobaye** *R* Central African Republic
51B5 **Lobito** Angola
8B3 **Lochboisdale** Scotland
8C3 **Lochearnhead** Scotland
14C2 **Loches** France
8C3 **Lochgoilhead** Scotland
8C2 **Lochinver** Scotland
8D4 **Lochmaben** Scotland
8B3 **Lochmaddy** Scotland
8D3 **Lochnagar** *Mt* Scotland
8C3 **Loch Ness** Scotland
58C1 **Lochsa** *R* USA
8C3 **Lochy, Loch** *L* Scotland
8D4 **Lockerbie** Scotland
65D2 **Lock Haven** USA
65D2 **Lockport** USA
30D3 **Loc Ninh** Vietnam
16D3 **Locri** Italy
45C3 **Lod** Israel
34B3 **Loddon** *R* Australia
20E3 **Lodeynoye Pole** Russian Federation
58E1 **Lodge Grass** USA
42C3 **Lodhran** Pakistan
16B1 **Lodi** Italy
59B3 **Lodi** USA
50C4 **Lodja** Zaïre
50D3 **Lodwar** Kenya
19D2 **Łódź** Poland
47B3 **Loeriesfontein** South Africa
12G5 **Lofoten** *Is* Norway
6D2 **Loftus** England
62B1 **Logan** New Mexico, USA
56B2 **Logan** Utah, USA
54D3 **Logan,Mt** Canada
64B2 **Logansport** Indiana, USA
15D3 **Logansport** Louisiana, USA
68B2 **Loganton** USA
50B2 **Logone** *R* Cameroon/Chad
15B1 **Logroño** Spain
43E4 **Lohārdaga** India
12J6 **Lohja** Finland
30B2 **Loikaw** Burma
12J6 **Loimaa** Finland
13B3 **Loing** *R* France
14C2 **Loir** *R* France
14C2 **Loire** *R* France
13B4 **Loiret** *Department* France
72C4 **Loja** Ecuador
15B2 **Loja** Spain
12K5 **Lokan Tekojärvi** *Res* Finland
13B2 **Lokeren** Belgium
27F7 **Lokialaki, G** *Mt* Indonesia
50D3 **Lokitaung** Kenya
19F1 **Loknya** Russian Federation
50C4 **Lokolo** *R* Zaïre
50C4 **Lokoro** *R* Zaïre
55M3 **Loks Land** *I* Canada
18C2 **Lolland** *I* Denmark
58D1 **Lolo P** USA
17E2 **Lom** Bulgaria
51C4 **Lomami** *R* Zaïre
48A4 **Loma Mts** Guinea/Sierra Leone
27F7 **Lomblen** *I* Indonesia
27E7 **Lombok** *I* Indonesia
48C4 **Lomé** Togo
50C4 **Lomela** Zaïre
50C4 **Lomela** *R* Zaïre
8C3 **Lomond, Loch** *L* Scotland
20D4 **Lomonosov** Russian Federation
59B4 **Lompoc** USA
19E2 **Łomza** Poland
44A2 **Lonāvale** India
74B5 **Loncoche** Chile
55K5 **London** Canada
7D4 **London** England
64C3 **London** USA
9C2 **Londonderry** Northern Ireland
9C2 **Londonderry** *County* Northern Ireland
74B9 **Londonderry** *I* Chile
32B2 **Londonderry,C** Australia
74C3 **Londres** Argentina
74F2 **Londrina** Brazil
66D1 **Lone Mt** USA
66C2 **Lone Pine** USA
27H7 **Long** *I* Papua New Guinea
57F4 **Long** *I* The Bahamas
25T2 **Longa, Proliv** *Str* Russian Federation
69H2 **Long B** Jamaica
67C2 **Long B** USA
56B3 **Long Beach** California, USA
65E2 **Long Beach** New York, USA
65E2 **Long Branch** USA
31D5 **Longchuan** China
58C2 **Long Creek** USA
7D3 **Long Eaton** England
34C4 **Longford** Australia
9C3 **Longford** Irish Republic
9C3 **Longford** *County* Irish Republic
8E3 **Long Forties** *Region* N Sea
28B2 **Longgang Shan** *Mts* China
31D1 **Longhua** China
57F4 **Long I** Bahamas
55L4 **Long I** Canada
32D1 **Long I** Papua New Guinea
57F2 **Long I** USA
68D2 **Long Island Sd** USA
28B2 **Longjing** China
64B1 **Long L** Canada
60C1 **Long L** USA
55K4 **Longlac** Canada
31B5 **Longlin** China
8C3 **Long, Loch** *Inlet* Scotland
7E3 **Long Melford** England
56C2 **Longmont** USA
13C3 **Longny** France
61E1 **Long Prairie** USA
32D3 **Longreach** Australia
31A2 **Longshou Shan** *Upland* China
60B2 **Longs Peak** *Mt* USA
7E3 **Long Sutton** England
6C2 **Longtown** England
65E1 **Longueuil** Canada
13C3 **Longuyon** France
57D3 **Longview** Texas, USA

105

Marquette **Metz**

57E2 **Marquette** USA
37N5 **Marquises, Îles** Pacific Ocean
34C2 **Marra** *R* Australia
47E2 **Marracuene** Mozambique
50C2 **Marra, Jebel** *Mt* Sudan
48B1 **Marrakech** Morocco
32C3 **Marree** Australia
63D3 **Marrero** USA
51D5 **Marromeu** Mozambique
51D5 **Marrupa** Mozambique
40B4 **Marsa Alam** Egypt
50D3 **Marsabit** Kenya
16C3 **Marsala** Sicily, Italy
13E2 **Marsberg** Germany
14D3 **Marseilles** France
75D3 **Mar, Serra do** *Mts* Brazil
64B3 **Marshall** Illinois, USA
64C2 **Marshall** Michigan, USA
61D2 **Marshall** Minnesota, USA
61E3 **Marshall** Missouri, USA
57D3 **Marshall** Texas, USA
68B3 **Marshall** Virginia, USA
37K4 **Marshall Is** Pacific Ocean
61E2 **Marshalltown** USA
63D1 **Marshfield** Missouri, USA
64A2 **Marshfield** Wisconsin, USA
69B1 **Marsh Harbour** The Bahamas
63D3 **Marsh I** USA
30B2 **Martaban,G of** Burma
65E2 **Martha's Vineyard** *I* USA
14D2 **Martigny** Switzerland
14D3 **Martigues** France
19D3 **Martin** Slovakia
60C2 **Martin** S Dakota, USA
63E1 **Martin** Tennessee, USA
35C2 **Martinborough** New Zealand
69E4 **Martinique** *I* Caribbean Sea
67A2 **Martin,L** USA
65D3 **Martinsburg** USA
64C2 **Martins Ferry** USA
65D3 **Martinsville** USA
52G6 **Martin Vaz** *I* Atlantic Ocean
35C2 **Marton** New Zealand
15B2 **Martos** Spain
54G3 **Martre, Lac la** Canada
42B2 **Maruf** Afghanistan
29B4 **Marugame** Japan
59D3 **Marvine,Mt** USA
42C3 **Mārwār** India
24H6 **Mary** Turkmenistan
33E3 **Maryborough** Queensland, Australia
34B3 **Maryborough** Victoria, Australia
54F4 **Mary Henry,Mt** Canada
57F3 **Maryland** *State* USA
6C2 **Maryport** England
59B3 **Marysville** California, USA
61D3 **Marysville** Kansas, USA
58B1 **Marysville** Washington, USA
57D2 **Maryville** Iowa, USA
61D2 **Maryville** Missouri, USA
67B1 **Maryville** Tennessee, USA
49D2 **Marzuq** Libya
45A3 **Masabb Dumyât** *C* Egypt
Masada = Mezada
45C2 **Mas'adah** Syria
50D4 **Masai Steppe** *Upland* Tanzania
50D4 **Masaka** Uganda
41E2 **Masally** Azerbaijan
28B3 **Masan** S Korea
51D5 **Masasi** Tanzania
70D3 **Masaya** Nicaragua
27F5 **Masbate** Philippines
27F5 **Masbate** *I* Philippines
15C2 **Mascara** Algeria
36D5 **Mascarene Ridge** Indian Ocean
75E2 **Mascote** Brazil
47D2 **Maseru** Lesotho
42B2 **Mashaki** Afghanistan
41G2 **Mashhad** Iran
50B4 **Masi-Manimba** Zaïre
50D3 **Masindi** Uganda
38D3 **Maşīrah** *I* Oman
50C4 **Masisi** Zaïre
41E3 **Masjed Soleyman** Iran
51F5 **Masoala, C** Madagascar
66C1 **Mason** Nevada, USA
62C2 **Mason** Texas, USA
57D2 **Mason City** USA
Masqat = Muscat
16C2 **Massa** Italy
57F2 **Massachusetts** *State* USA
65E2 **Massachusetts B** USA
50B2 **Massakori** Chad
51D6 **Massangena** Mozambique
50D2 **Massawa** Eritrea
65E2 **Massena** USA
50B2 **Massénya** Chad
64C1 **Massey** Canada
14C2 **Massif Central** *Mts* France
51E6 **Massif de l'Isalo** *Upland* Madagascar
51E5 **Massif du Tsaratanana** *Mts* Madagascar
64C2 **Massillon** USA
48B3 **Massina** *Region* Mali
51D6 **Massinga** Mozambique
47E1 **Massingir** Mozambique
21J6 **Masteksay** Kazakhstan
33G5 **Masterton** New Zealand
28C4 **Masuda** Japan
50B4 **Masuku** Gabon
40C2 **Maşyāf** Syria
64C1 **Matachewan** Canada
62A3 **Matachie** Mexico
50B4 **Matadi** Zaïre
72A1 **Matagalpa** Nicaragua
55L5 **Matagami** Canada
56D4 **Matagorda B** USA
63C3 **Matagorda I** USA
35C1 **Matakana I** New Zealand
51B5 **Matala** Angola
44C4 **Matale** Sri Lanka
48A3 **Matam** Senegal
48C3 **Matameye** Niger
70C2 **Matamoros** Mexico
49E2 **Ma'tan as Sarra** *Well* Libya
55M5 **Matane** Canada
70D2 **Matanzas** Cuba
65F1 **Matapedia** *R* Canada
44C4 **Matara** Sri Lanka
32A1 **Mataram** Indonesia
72D7 **Matarani** Peru
75E1 **Mataripe** Brazil
15C1 **Mataró** Spain
47D3 **Matatiele** South Africa
35A3 **Mataura** New Zealand
70B2 **Matehuala** Mexico
69L1 **Matelot** Trinidad
16D2 **Matera** Italy
19E3 **Mátészalka** Hungary
16B3 **Mateur** Tunisia
66C2 **Mather** USA
64C1 **Matheson** Canada
63C3 **Mathis** USA
42D3 **Mathura** India
7D3 **Matlock** England
73G6 **Mato Grosso** *State* Brazil
73G7 **Mato Grosso do Sul** *State* Brazil
47E2 **Matola** Mozambique
49E1 **Matrûh** Egypt
28C3 **Matsue** Japan
29E2 **Matsumae** Japan
29D3 **Matsumoto** Japan
29D4 **Matsusaka** Japan
28C4 **Matsuyama** Japan
55K5 **Mattagami** *R* Canada
65D1 **Mattawa** Canada
16B1 **Matterhorn** *Mt* Italy/Switzerland
58C2 **Matterhorn** *Mt* USA
69C2 **Matthew Town** The Bahamas
68D2 **Mattituck** USA
64B3 **Mattoon** USA
42B2 **Matun** Afghanistan
69L1 **Matura B** Trinidad
72F2 **Maturín** Venezuela
43E3 **Mau** India
51D5 **Maúa** Mozambique
14C1 **Maubeuge** France
34B2 **Maude** Australia
52J8 **Maud Seamount** Atlantic Ocean
26H4 **Maug Is** Marianas
66E5 **Maui** *I* Hawaiian Islands
64C2 **Maumee** USA
64C2 **Maumee** *R* USA
51C5 **Maun** Botswana
66E5 **Mauna Kea** *Vol* Hawaiian Islands
66E5 **Mauna Loa** *Vol* Hawaiian Islands
54F3 **Maunoir,L** Canada
14C2 **Mauriac** France
48A2 **Mauritania** *Republic* Africa
46K10 **Mauritius** *I* Indian Ocean
64A2 **Mauston** USA
51C5 **Mavinga** Angola
47E1 **Mavue** Mozambique
43G4 **Mawlaik** Burma
Mawlamyine = Moulmein
76G10 **Mawson** *Base* Antarctica
60C1 **Max** USA
47E1 **Maxaila** Mozambique
27D7 **Maya** *I* Indonesia
25P4 **Maya** *R* Russian Federation
40D2 **Mayādīn** Syria
57F4 **Mayaguana** *I* The Bahamas
69D3 **Mayagüez** Puerto Rico
48C3 **Mayahi** Niger
50B4 **Mayama** Congo
41G2 **Mayamey** Iran
8C4 **Maybole** Scotland
57F3 **May,C** USA
34C4 **Maydena** Australia
13D2 **Mayen** Germany
14B2 **Mayenne** France
59D4 **Mayer** USA
64B3 **Mayfield** USA
62A2 **Mayhill** USA
21G7 **Maykop** Russian Federation
30B1 **Maymyo** Burma
54E3 **Mayo** Canada
68B3 **Mayo** USA
15C2 **Mayor** *Mt* Spain
35C1 **Mayor I** New Zealand
74D1 **Mayor P Lagerenza** Paraguay
51E5 **Mayotte** *I* Indian Ocean
69H2 **May Pen** Jamaica
68C3 **May Point,C** USA
68C3 **Mays Landing** USA
64C3 **Maysville** USA
50B4 **Mayumba** Gabon
61D1 **Mayville** USA
60C2 **Maywood** USA
51C5 **Mazabuka** Zambia
42D1 **Mazar** China
45C3 **Mazār** Jordan
16C3 **Mazara del Vallo** Sicily, Italy
42B1 **Mazar-i-Sharif** Afghanistan
15B2 **Mazarrón, Golfo de** *G* Spain
70B2 **Mazatlán** Mexico
20C4 **Mazeikiai** Lithuania
45C3 **Mazra** Jordan
51D6 **Mbabane** Swaziland
50B3 **Mbaïki** Central African Republic
51D4 **Mbala** Zambia
51C6 **Mbalabala** Zimbabwe
50D3 **Mbale** Uganda
50B3 **Mbalmayo** Cameroon
50B3 **Mbam** *R* Cameroon
51D5 **Mbamba Bay** Tanzania
50B3 **Mbandaka** Zaïre
50B4 **Mbanza Congo** Angola
50B4 **Mbanza-Ngungu** Zaïre
50D4 **Mbarara** Uganda
50C3 **M'Bari,R** Central African Republic
50B3 **Mbèndza** Congo
50B3 **Mbére** *R* Cameroon/Central African Republic/Chad
51D4 **Mbeya** Tanzania
50B4 **Mbinda** Congo
48A3 **Mbout** Mauritius
50C4 **Mbuji-Mayi** Zaïre
50D4 **Mbulu** Tanzania
48B2 **Mcherrah** *Region* Algeria
51D5 **Mchinji** Malawi
30D3 **Mdrak** Vietnam
62B1 **Meade** USA
56B3 **Mead,L** USA
54H4 **Meadow Lake** Canada
64C2 **Meadville** USA
29D2 **Me-akan dake** *Mt* Japan
55N4 **Mealy Mts** Canada
34C1 **Meandarra** Australia
54G4 **Meander River** Canada
9C3 **Meath** Irish Republic
14C2 **Meaux** France
50E1 **Mecca** Saudi Arabia
59C4 **Mecca** USA
68D1 **Mechanicville** USA
24G2 **Mechdusharskiy, O** *I* Russian Federation
18A2 **Mechelen** Belgium
48B1 **Mecheria** Algeria
18C2 **Meckenburg-Vorpommern** *State* Germany
18C2 **Mecklenburger Bucht** *B* Germany
51D5 **Meconta** Mozambique
51D5 **Mecuburi** Mozambique
51E5 **Mecufi** Mozambique
51D5 **Mecula** Mozambique
27C6 **Medan** Indonesia
74C7 **Médanosa, Puerta** *Pt* Argentina
15C2 **Médéa** Algeria
72C2 **Medellín** Colombia
13C1 **Medemblik** Netherlands
48D1 **Medenine** Tunisia
56A2 **Medford** USA
17F2 **Medgidia** Romania
17E1 **Mediaş** Romania
58C1 **Medical Lake** USA
60B2 **Medicine Bow** USA
60B2 **Medicine Bow Mts** USA
60B2 **Medicine Bow Peak** *Mt* USA
54G5 **Medicine Hat** Canada
62C1 **Medicine Lodge** USA
75D2 **Medina** Brazil
60D1 **Medina** N Dakota, USA
68A1 **Medina** New York, USA
40C5 **Medina** Saudi Arabia
15B1 **Medinaceli** Spain
15A1 **Medina del Campo** Spain
15A1 **Medina de Rioseco** Spain
62C3 **Medina L** USA
43F4 **Medinīpur** India
46E4 **Mediterranean S** Europe
16B3 **Medjerda** *R* Algeria/Tunisia
16B3 **Medjerda, Mts de la** Algeria/Tunisia
21K5 **Mednogorsk** Russian Federation
25S4 **Mednyy, Ostrov** *I* Russian Federation
43H3 **Mêdog** China
50B3 **Medouneu** Gabon
21G5 **Medvedista** *R* Russian Federation
25S2 **Medvezh'i Ova** *Is* Russian Federation
20E3 **Medvezh'yegorsk** Russian Federation
32A3 **Meekatharra** Australia
60B2 **Meeker** USA
42D3 **Meerut** India
58E2 **Meeteetse** USA
50D3 **Mēga** Ethiopia
17E3 **Megalópolis** Greece
17E3 **Mégara** Greece
43G3 **Meghālaya** *State* India
43G4 **Meghna** *R* Bangladesh
45C2 **Megiddo** *Hist Site* Israel
42D4 **Mehekar** India
43M2 **Mehndawal** India
41F4 **Mehrān** *R* Iran
41F3 **Mehriz** Iran
75C2 **Meia Ponte** *R* Brazil
50B3 **Meiganga** Cameroon
30B1 **Meiktila** Burma
31A4 **Meishan** China
18C2 **Meissen** Germany
31D5 **Mei Xian** China
31D5 **Meizhou** China
72D8 **Mejillones** Chile
50B3 **Mekambo** Gabon
50D2 **Mek'elē** Ethiopia
48B1 **Meknès** Morocco
30D3 **Mekong** *R* Cambodia
30D4 **Mekong, Mouths of the** Vietnam
48C3 **Mekrou** *R* Benin
30C5 **Melaka** Malaysia
36J5 **Melanesia** *Region* Pacific Ocean
32D4 **Melbourne** Australia
57E4 **Melbourne** USA
56C4 **Melchor Muźguiz** Mexico
20K5 **Meleuz** Russian Federation
50B2 **Melfi** Chad
54H4 **Melfort** Canada
15B2 **Melilla** NW Africa
74B6 **Melimoyu** *Mt* Chile
60C1 **Melita** Canada
21F6 **Melitopol'** Ukraine
50D3 **Melka Guba** Ethiopia
13E1 **Melle** Germany
16B3 **Mellégue** *R* Algeria/Tunisia
47E2 **Melmoth** South Africa
74F4 **Melo** Uruguay
75A3 **Melo** *R* Brazil
66B2 **Melones Res** USA
8D4 **Melrose** Scotland
61E1 **Melrose** USA
7D3 **Melton Mowbray** England
14C2 **Melun** France
54H4 **Melville** Canada
55M2 **Melville Bugt** *B* Greenland
69Q2 **Melville,C** Dominica
54F3 **Melville Hills** Canada
32C2 **Melville I** Australia
54G2 **Melville I** Canada
55N4 **Melville,L** Canada
55K3 **Melville Pen** Canada
51E5 **Memba** Mozambique
32A1 **Memboro** Indonesia
18C3 **Memmingen** Germany
57E3 **Memphis** Tennessee, USA
62B2 **Memphis** Texas, USA
63D2 **Mena** USA
19G2 **Mena** Ukraine
7B3 **Menai Str** Wales
48C3 **Ménaka** Mali
64B2 **Menasha** USA
27E7 **Mendawai** *R* Indonesia
14C3 **Mende** France
50D3 **Mendebo Mts** Ethiopia
32D1 **Mendi** Papua New Guinea
7C4 **Mendip Hills** *Upland* England
58B2 **Mendocino,C** USA
37M3 **Mendocino Seascarp** Pacific Ocean
66B2 **Mendota** California, USA
64B2 **Mendota** Illinois, USA
74C4 **Mendoza** Argentina
74C5 **Mendoza** *State* Argentina
17F3 **Menemen** Turkey
13B2 **Menen** Belgium
31D3 **Mengcheng** China
30B1 **Menghai** China
31A5 **Mengla** China
30B1 **Menglian** China
31A5 **Mengzi** China
32D4 **Menindee** Australia
34B2 **Menindee L** Australia
34A3 **Meningie** Australia
64B1 **Menominee** USA
64B2 **Menomonee Falls** USA
64A2 **Menomonie** USA
51B5 **Menongue** Angola
Menorca *I* **= Minorca**
27C7 **Mentawi, Kepulauan** *Is* Indonesia
62A1 **Mentmore** USA
27D7 **Mentok** Indonesia
64C2 **Mentor** USA
27E6 **Menyapa** *Mt* Indonesia
31A2 **Menyuan** China
16B3 **Menzel** Tunisia
20J4 **Menzelinsk** Russian Federation
13D1 **Meppel** Netherlands
18B2 **Meppen** Germany
15B1 **Mequinenza, Embalse de** *Res* Spain
63D1 **Meramec** *R* USA
16C1 **Merano** Italy
27E7 **Meratus, Pegunungan** *Mts* Indonesia
32D1 **Merauke** Indonesia
56A3 **Merced** USA
66B2 **Merced** *R* USA
74B4 **Mercedario** *Mt* Argentina
74E4 **Mercedes** Buenos Aires, Argentina
74E3 **Mercedes** Corrientes, Argentina
74C4 **Mercedes** San Luis, Argentina
74E4 **Mercedes** Uruguay
35C1 **Mercury B** New Zealand
35C1 **Mercury Is** New Zealand
54F2 **Mercy B** Canada
55M3 **Mercy,C** Canada
62B1 **Meredith,L** USA
30B3 **Mergui** Burma
30B3 **Mergui Arch** Burma
70D2 **Mérida** Mexico
15A2 **Mérida** Spain
72D2 **Mérida** Venezuela
72D2 **Mérida, Cordillera de** Venezuela
57E3 **Meridian** USA
34C3 **Merimbula** Australia
34B2 **Meringur** Australia
27G6 **Merir** *I* Pacific Ocean
62B2 **Merkel** USA
50D2 **Merowe** Sudan
32A4 **Merredin** Australia
8C4 **Merrick** *Mt* Scotland
64B1 **Merrill** USA
64B2 **Merrillville** USA
68E1 **Merrimack** *R* USA
60C2 **Merriman** USA
67B3 **Merritt Island** USA
34D2 **Merriwa** Australia
50E3 **Mersa Fatma** Eritrea
7E4 **Mersea** *I* England
15B2 **Mers el Kebir** Algeria
7C3 **Mersey** *R* England
7C3 **Merseyside** *Metropolitan County* England
21E8 **Mersin** Turkey
30C5 **Mersing** Malaysia
42C3 **Merta** India
7C4 **Merthyr Tydfil** Wales
7C4 **Merthyr Tydfil** *County* Wales
15A2 **Mertola** Portugal
13B3 **Méru** France
50D4 **Meru** *Mt* Tanzania
21F7 **Merzifon** Turkey
13D3 **Merzig** Germany
56B3 **Mesa** USA
62A1 **Mesa Verde Nat Pk** USA
13E2 **Meschede** Germany
40D1 **Mescit Dağ** *Mt* Turkey
50C3 **Meshra'er Req** Sudan
17E3 **Mesolóngion** Greece
59D3 **Mesquite** Nevada, USA
63C2 **Mesquite** Texas, USA
51D5 **Messalo** *R* Mozambique
47D1 **Messina** South Africa
16D3 **Messina** Sicily, Italy
16D3 **Messina, Stretto de** *Str* Italy/Sicily
17E3 **Messíni** Greece
17E3 **Messiniakós Kólpos** *G* Greece
Mesta *R* **= Néstos**
17E2 **Mesta** *R* Bulgaria
16C1 **Mestre** Italy
72D3 **Meta** *R* Colombia/Venezuela
20E4 **Meta** *R* Russian Federation
55M3 **Meta Incognita Pen** Canada
63D3 **Metairie** USA
58C1 **Metaline Falls** USA
74D3 **Metán** Argentina
51D5 **Metangula** Mozambique
16D2 **Metaponto** Italy
8D3 **Methil** Scotland
68E1 **Methuen** USA
35B2 **Methven** New Zealand
54E4 **Metlakatla** USA
64B3 **Metropolis** USA
44B3 **Mettūr** India
14D2 **Metz** France

Mont-de-Marsan **Murgab**

14B3 **Mont-de-Marsan** France
14C2 **Montdidier** France
72F7 **Monteagudo** Bolivia
73H4 **Monte Alegre** Brazil
75D2 **Monte Azul** Brazil
65D1 **Montebello** Canada
32A3 **Monte Bello Is** Australia
14D3 **Monte Carlo** Monaco
75C2 **Monte Carmelo** Brazil
69C3 **Montecristi** Dominican Republic
16C2 **Montecristo** *I* Italy
69H1 **Montego Bay** Jamaica
14C3 **Montélimar** France
75A3 **Montelindo** *R* Paraguay
70C2 **Montemorelos** Mexico
15A2 **Montemor-o-Novo** Portugal
17D2 **Montenegro** *Republic* Yugoslavia
51D5 **Montepuez** Mozambique
13B3 **Montereau-Faut-Yonne** France
56A3 **Monterey** California, USA
65D3 **Monterey** Virginia, USA
56A3 **Monterey B** USA
72C2 **Montería** Colombia
72F7 **Montero** Bolivia
70B2 **Monterrey** Mexico
73K7 **Montes Claros** Brazil
15B2 **Montes de Toledo** *Mts* Spain
74E4 **Montevideo** Uruguay
61D2 **Montevideo** USA
62A1 **Monte Vista** USA
62B1 **Montezuma** USA
66D2 **Montezuma Peak** *Mt* USA
57E3 **Montgomery** Alabama, USA
68B2 **Montgomery** Pennsylvania, USA
7C3 **Montgomery** Wales
66C2 **Montgomery P** USA
13C3 **Monthermé** France
63D2 **Monticello** Arkansas, USA
64A2 **Monticello** Iowa, USA
61E1 **Monticello** Minnesota, USA
68C2 **Monticello** New York, USA
56C3 **Monticello** Utah, USA
13C3 **Montier-en-Der** France
55L5 **Mont-Laurier** Canada
14C2 **Montluçon** France
55L5 **Montmagny** Canada
13C3 **Montmédy** France
13B3 **Montmirail** France
Mont, Monte : see also individual mt. names
65E1 **Montmorency** Canada
15B2 **Montoro** Spain
68B2 **Montoursville** USA
58D2 **Montpelier** Idaho, USA
64C2 **Montpelier** Ohio, USA
57F2 **Montpelier** Vermont, USA
14C3 **Montpellier** France
55L5 **Montréal** Canada
14C1 **Montreuil** France
16B1 **Montreux** Switzerland
56C3 **Montrose** Colorado, USA
68C2 **Montrose** Pennsylvania, USA
10C2 **Montrose** Scotland
8F3 **Montrose** *Oilfield* N Sea
14B2 **Mont-St-Michel** France
69E3 **Montserrat** *I* Caribbean Sea
57F1 **Monts Otish** Canada
56B3 **Monument V** USA
50C3 **Monveda** Zaïre
30B1 **Monywa** Burma
16B1 **Monza** Italy
51C5 **Monze** Zambia
47E2 **Mooi** *R* South Africa
47D2 **Mooi River** South Africa
34B1 **Moomba** Australia
34D2 **Moonbi Range** *Mts* Australia
34B1 **Moonda L** Australia
34D1 **Moonie** Australia
34C1 **Moonie** *R* Australia
34A2 **Moonta** Australia
32A4 **Moora** Australia
34B1 **Mooraberree** Australia
60C2 **Moorcroft** USA
32A3 **Moore,L** Australia
8D4 **Moorfoot Hills** Scotland
56D2 **Moorhead** USA
66C3 **Moorpark** USA
47B3 **Moorreesburg** South Africa
55K4 **Moose** *R* Canada
65F1 **Moosehead L** USA
54H4 **Moose Jaw** Canada
61E1 **Moose Lake** USA
54H4 **Moosomin** Canada
55K4 **Moosonee** Canada
68E2 **Moosup** USA
51D5 **Mopeia** Mozambique
48B3 **Mopti** Mali
72D7 **Moquegua** Peru
12G6 **Mora** Sweden
61E1 **Mora** USA
42D3 **Morādābād** India
73L5 **Morada Nova** Brazil
75C2 **Morada Nova de Minas** Brazil
51E5 **Morafenobe** Madagascar
51E5 **Moramanga** Madagascar
58D2 **Moran** USA
69J2 **Morant Bay** Jamaica
69J2 **Morant Pt** Jamaica
8C3 **Morar, Loch** *L* Scotland
44B4 **Moratuwa** Sri Lanka
18D3 **Morava** *R* Austria/Czechoslovakia
17E2 **Morava** *R* Serbia, Yugoslavia
41G2 **Moraveh Tappeh** Iran
8D3 **Moray** *Division* Scotland
10C2 **Moray Firth** *Estuary* Scotland
42C4 **Morbi** India
41D2 **Mor Dağ** *Mt* Turkey
54J5 **Morden** Canada
20G5 **Mordoviya** *Division* Russian Federation
60C1 **Moreau** *R* USA
7C2 **Morecambe** England
7C2 **Morecambe B** England
32D3 **Moree** Australia
64C3 **Morehead** USA
67C2 **Morehead City** USA
70B3 **Morelia** Mexico
42D3 **Morena** India
15A2 **Morena, Sierra** *Mts* Spain
54E4 **Moresby I** Canada
34D1 **Moreton I** Australia
13B3 **Moreuil** France
63D3 **Morgan City** USA
66B2 **Morgan Hill** USA
66C2 **Morgan,Mt** USA
67B1 **Morganton** USA
65D3 **Morgantown** USA
47D2 **Morgenzon** South Africa
13D3 **Morhange** France
29E2 **Mori** Japan
69K1 **Moriah** Tobago
62A2 **Moriarty** USA
29E3 **Morioka** Japan
34D2 **Morisset** Australia
25N3 **Morkoka** *R* Russian Federation
14B2 **Morlaix** France
69Q2 **Morne Diablotin** *Mt* Dominica
34B1 **Morney** Australia
32C2 **Mornington** *I* Australia
42B3 **Moro** Pakistan
32D1 **Morobe** Papua New Guinea
48B1 **Morocco** *Kingdom* Africa
27F6 **Moro G** Philippines
51D4 **Morogoro** Tanzania
51E6 **Morombe** Madagascar
69B2 **Morón** Cuba
51E6 **Morondava** Madagascar
15A2 **Moron de la Frontera** Spain
51E5 **Moroni** Comoros
27F6 **Morotai** *I* Indonesia
50D3 **Moroto** Uganda
21G6 **Morozovsk** Russian Federation
6D2 **Morpeth** England
45B1 **Morphou** Cyprus
45B1 **Morphou B** Cyprus
60C2 **Morrill** USA
63D1 **Morrilton** USA
75C2 **Morrinhos** Brazil
35C1 **Morrinsville** New Zealand
61D1 **Morris** Canada
61D1 **Morris** USA
68C2 **Morristown** New Jersey, USA
65D2 **Morristown** New York, USA
67B1 **Morristown** Tennessee, USA
68C1 **Morrisville** New York, USA
68C2 **Morrisville** Pennsylvania, USA
66B3 **Morro Bay** USA
51D5 **Morrumbala** Mozambique
51D6 **Morrumbene** Mozambique
20G5 **Morshansk** Russian Federation
Mortes *R* **= Manso**
73H6 **Mortes** *R* Mato Grosso, Brazil
75D3 **Mortes** *R* Minas Gerais, Brazil
34B3 **Mortlake** Australia
62B2 **Morton** USA
69L1 **Moruga** Trinidad
34D3 **Moruya** Australia
34C1 **Morven** Australia
8C3 **Morvern** *Pen* Scotland
34C3 **Morwell** Australia
13E3 **Mosbach** Germany
30B3 **Moscos Is** Burma
58C1 **Moscow** Idaho, USA
68C2 **Moscow** Pennsylvania, USA
42F4 **Moscow** Russian Federation
18B2 **Mosel** *R* Germany
47C2 **Moselebe** *R* Botswana
13D3 **Moselle** *Department* France
13D3 **Moselle** *R* France
58C1 **Moses Lake** USA
35B3 **Mosgiel** New Zealand
50D4 **Moshi** Tanzania
64B2 **Mosinee** USA
12G5 **Mosjøen** Norway
25Q4 **Moskal'vo** Russian Federation
Moskva = Moscow
20F4 **Moskva** *Division* Russian Federation
62B1 **Mosquero** USA
75D2 **Mosquito** *R* Brazil
72B2 **Mosquitos, Golfo de los** Panama
12G7 **Moss** Norway
50B4 **Mossaka** Congo
Mossâmedes = Namibe
47C3 **Mossel Bay** South Africa
50B4 **Mossendjo** Congo
34B2 **Mossgiel** Australia
73L5 **Mossoró** Brazil
18C2 **Most** Czech Republic
15C2 **Mostaganem** Algeria
17D2 **Mostar** Bosnia-Herzegovina
19E2 **Mosty** Belarus
41D2 **Mosul** Iraq
12H7 **Motala** Sweden
8D4 **Motherwell** Scotland
43E3 **Motihāri** India
15B2 **Motilla del Palancar** Spain
47D1 **Motloutse** *R* Botswana
15B2 **Motril** Spain
60C1 **Mott** USA
35B2 **Motueka** New Zealand
35B2 **Motueka** *R* New Zealand
50B4 **Mouila** Gabon
34B2 **Moulamein** Australia
54G2 **Mould Bay** Canada
69P2 **Moule à Chique, Cap** St Lucia
14C2 **Moulins** France
30B2 **Moulmein** Burma
48B1 **Moulouya** *R* Morocco
67B2 **Moultrie** USA
67C2 **Moultrie,L** USA
64B3 **Mound City** Illinois, USA
61D2 **Mound City** Missouri, USA
50B3 **Moundou** Chad
64C3 **Moundsville** USA
67A2 **Mountain Brook** USA
63D1 **Mountain Grove** USA
63D1 **Mountain Home** Arkansas, USA
58C2 **Mountain Home** Idaho, USA
66A2 **Mountain View** USA
54B3 **Mountain Village** USA
68B3 **Mount Airy** Maryland, USA
67B1 **Mount Airy** N Carolina, USA
47D3 **Mount Ayliff** South Africa
68B2 **Mount Carmel** USA
65F2 **Mount Desert I** USA
47D3 **Mount Fletcher** South Africa
34B3 **Mount Gambier** Australia
32D1 **Mount Hagen** Papua New Guinea
68C3 **Mount Holly** USA
68B2 **Mount Holly Springs** USA
32C3 **Mount Isa** Australia
68A3 **Mount Jackson** USA
68A2 **Mount Jewett** USA
34A2 **Mount Lofty Range** *Mts* Australia
32A3 **Mount Magnet** Australia
34B2 **Mount Manara** Australia
9C3 **Mountmellick** Irish Republic
32E3 **Mount Morgan** Australia
68B1 **Mount Morris** USA
34D1 **Mount Perry** Australia
63D2 **Mount Pleasant** Texas, USA
59D3 **Mount Pleasant** Utah, USA
68C2 **Mount Pocono** USA
58B1 **Mount Rainier Nat Pk** USA
7B4 **Mounts B** England
58B2 **Mount Shasta** USA
68B2 **Mount Union** USA
63E2 **Mount Vernon** Alabama, USA
64B3 **Mount Vernon** Illinois, USA
63D1 **Mount Vernon** Missouri, USA
58B1 **Mount Vernon** Washington, USA
50C2 **Mourdi, Dépression du** *Desert Region* Chad
9C2 **Mourne Mts** Northern Ireland
50B2 **Moussoro** Chad
48C2 **Mouydir, Mts du** Algeria
50B4 **Mouyondzi** Congo
13C3 **Mouzon** France
18D3 **M'óvár** Hungary
9C2 **Moville** Irish Republic
9B2 **Moy** *R* Irish Republic
50D3 **Moyale** Kenya
48A4 **Moyamba** Sierra Leone
48B1 **Moyen Atlas** *Mts* Morocco
47D3 **Moyeni** Lesotho
25M3 **Moyero** *R* Russian Federation
50D3 **Moyo** Uganda
72C5 **Moyobamba** Peru
42D1 **Moyu** China
51D6 **Mozambique** *Republic* Africa
51D6 **Mozambique Chan** Madagascar/Mozambique
20J4 **Mozhga** Russian Federation
12K8 **Mozyr'** Belarus
50D4 **Mpanda** Tanzania
51D5 **Mpika** Zambia
51D4 **Mporokosa** Zambia
51C5 **Mposhi** Zambia
48B4 **Mpraeso** Ghana
51D4 **Mpulungu** Zambia
51C6 **Mpumalanga** *Province* South Africa
50D4 **Mpwapwa** Tanzania
16C3 **M'saken** Tunisia
15C2 **M'Sila** Algeria
19G2 **Mstislavl'** Belarus
20F5 **Mtsensk** Russian Federation
47E2 **Mtubatuba** South Africa
51E5 **Mtwara** Tanzania
30C2 **Muang Chainat** Thailand
30C2 **Muang Chiang Rai** Thailand
30C2 **Muang Kalasin** Thailand
30C2 **Muang Khon Kaen** Thailand
30B2 **Muang Lampang** Thailand
30B2 **Muang Lamphun** Thailand
30C2 **Muang Loei** Thailand
30C2 **Muang Lom Sak** Thailand
30C2 **Muang Nakhon Phanom** Thailand
30B2 **Muang Nakhon Sawan** Thailand
30C2 **Muang Nan** Thailand
30C2 **Muang Phayao** Thailand
30C2 **Muang Phetchabun** Thailand
30C2 **Muang Phichit** Thailand
30C2 **Muang Phitsanulok** Thailand
30C2 **Muang Phrae** Thailand
30C2 **Muang Roi Et** Thailand
30C2 **Muang Sakon Nakhon** Thailand
30C3 **Muang Samut Prakan** Thailand
30C2 **Muang Uthai Thani** Thailand
30C2 **Muang Yasothon** Thailand
30C5 **Muar** Malaysia
27D7 **Muara** Indonesia
30A2 **Muaungmya** Burma
50D3 **Mubende** Uganda
49D3 **Mubi** Nigeria
45C3 **Mubrak, Jebel** *Mt* Jordan
51D5 **Muchinga Mts** Zambia
7C3 **Much Wenlock** England
8B3 **Muck** *I* Scotland
34C1 **Muckadilla** Australia
9B2 **Muckros Hd,** *Pt* Irish Republic
51C5 **Muconda** Angola
75E2 **Mucuri** Brazil
75D2 **Mucuri** *R* Brazil
51C5 **Mucusso** Angola
26F2 **Mudanjiang** China
60B2 **Muddy Gap P** USA
45D3 **Mudeisisat, Jebel** *Mt* Jordan
34C2 **Mudgee** Australia
66D2 **Mud L** USA
30B2 **Mudon** Burma
20F3 **Mud'yuga** Russian Federation
51D5 **Mueda** Mozambique
33F3 **Mueo** New Caledonia (Nouvelle Calédonie)
51C5 **Mufulira** Zambia
31C4 **Mufu Shan** *Hills* China
40C4 **Mughayra** Saudi Arabia
40A2 **Muğla** Turkey
21K5 **Mugodzhary** *Mts* Kazakhstan
43E3 **Mugu** Nepal
31A3 **Muguaping** China
40D3 **Muhaywir** Iraq
13E3 **Mühlacker** Germany
18C3 **Mühldorf** Germany
18C2 **Mühlhausen** Germany
12K6 **Muhos** Finland
30C4 **Mui Bai Bung** *C* Cambodia
9C3 **Muine Bheag** Irish Republic
45C3 **Mujib, Wadi** Jordan
51C5 **Mujimbeji** Zambia
19E3 **Mukachevo** Ukraine
27E6 **Mukah** Malaysia
29D2 **Mukawa** Japan
26H4 **Muko-jima** *I* Japan
43E3 **Muktinath** Nepal
42B2 **Mukur** Afghanistan
63D1 **Mulberry** USA
18C2 **Mulde** *R* Germany
60C2 **Mule Creek** USA
62B2 **Muleshoe** USA
27H8 **Mulgrave I** Australia
15B2 **Mulhacén** *Mt* Spain
13D2 **Mülheim** Germany
13D4 **Mulhouse** France
31A4 **Muli** China
8C3 **Mull** *I* Scotland
44C4 **Mullaittvu** Sri Lanka
34C2 **Mullaley** Australia
27E6 **Muller, Pegunungan** *Mts* Indonesia
9A2 **Mullet, The** *Pt* Irish Republic
32A3 **Mullewa** Australia
13D4 **Müllheim** Germany
68C3 **Mullica** *R* USA
9C3 **Mullingar** Irish Republic
8C4 **Mull of Kintyre** *Pt* Scotland
8B4 **Mull of Oa** *C* Scotland
34D1 **Mullumbimby** Australia
51C5 **Mulobezi** Zambia
42C2 **Multan** Pakistan
51C5 **Mumbwa** Zambia
21H6 **Mumra** Russian Federation
27F7 **Muna** Indonesia
München = Munich
28A3 **Munchŏn** N Korea
64B2 **Muncie** USA
34A1 **Muncoonie,L** Australia
68B2 **Muncy** USA
18B2 **Münden** Germany
34D1 **Mundubbera** Australia
34C1 **Mungallala** Australia
34C1 **Mungallala** *R* Australia
50C3 **Mungbere** Zaïre
43E4 **Mungeli** India
43F3 **Munger** India
34C1 **Mungindi** Australia
18C3 **Munich** Germany
64B1 **Munising** USA
74B8 **Muñoz Gamero,Pen** Chile
28A3 **Munsan** S Korea
13D3 **Munster** France
18B2 **Münster** Germany
13D2 **Münsterland** *Region* Germany
17E1 **Munţii Apuseni** *Mts* Romania
17E1 **Munţii Călimani** *Mts* Romania
17E1 **Munţii Carpaţii Meridionali** *Mts* Romania
17E1 **Munţii Rodnei** *Mts* Romania
17E1 **Munţii Zarandului** *Mts* Romania
40C2 **Munzur Silsilesi** *Mts* Turkey
30C1 **Muong Khoua** Laos
30D3 **Muong Man** Vietnam
30D2 **Muong Nong** Laos
30C1 **Muong Ou Neua** Laos
30C1 **Muong Sai** Laos
30C2 **Muong Sen** Vietnam
30C1 **Muong Sing** Laos
30C1 **Muong Son** Laos
12J5 **Muonio** Finland
12J5 **Muonio** *R* Finland/Sweden
28A3 **Muping** China
Muqdisho = Mogadishu
16C1 **Mur** *R* Austria
29D3 **Murakami** Japan
74B7 **Murallón** *Mt* Argentina/Chile
20H4 **Murashi** Russian Federation
40D2 **Murat** *R* Turkey
16B3 **Muravera** Sardinia, Italy
29D3 **Murayama** Japan
41F3 **Murcheh Khvort** Iran
35B2 **Murchison** New Zealand
32A3 **Murchison** *R* Australia
15B2 **Murcia** Spain
15B2 **Murcia** *Region* Spain
60C2 **Murdo** USA
17E1 **Mureş** *R* Romania
67C1 **Murfreesboro** N Carolina, USA
67A1 **Murfreesboro** Tennessee, USA
13E3 **Murg** *R* Germany
24H6 **Murgab** *R* Turkmenistan

Nerchinsk Northfield

26E1 **Nerchinsk** Russian Federation
17D2 **Neretva** *R* Bosnia-Herzegovina/Croatia
27H5 **Nero Deep** Pacific Ocean
20G2 **Nes'** Russian Federation
12C1 **Neskaupstaður** Iceland
13B3 **Nesle** France
62C1 **Ness City** USA
8C3 **Ness, Loch** *L* Scotland
17E2 **Néstos** *R* Greece
45C2 **Netanya** Israel
68C2 **Netcong** USA
18B2 **Netherlands** *Kingdom* Europe
53M7 **Netherlands Antilles** *Is* Caribbean Sea
43G4 **Netrakona** Bangladesh
55L3 **Nettilling L** Canada
18C2 **Neubrandenburg** Germany
16B1 **Neuchâtel** Switzerland
13C3 **Neufchâteau** Belgium
13C3 **Neufchâteau** France
14C2 **Neufchâtel** France
18B2 **Neumünster** Germany
16D1 **Neunkirchen** Austria
13D3 **Neunkirchen** Germany
74C5 **Neuquén** Argentina
74C5 **Neuquén** *R* Argentina
74B5 **Neuquén** *State* Argentina
18C2 **Neuruppin** Germany
67C1 **Neuse** *R* USA
13D2 **Neuss** Germany
18C2 **Neustadt** Germany
13E3 **Neustadt an der Weinstrasse** Germany
13E1 **Neustadt a R** Germany
13E4 **Neustadt im Schwarzwald** Germany
18C2 **Neustrelitz** Germany
13E1 **Neuwerk** *I* Germany
13D2 **Neuwied** Germany
63D1 **Nevada** USA
56B3 **Nevada** *State* USA
15B2 **Nevada, Sierra** *Mts* Spain
45C3 **Nevatim** Israel
20D4 **Nevel'** Russian Federation
14C2 **Nevers** France
34C2 **Nevertire** Australia
Nevis = St Kitts-Nevis
40B2 **Nevşehir** Turkey
20L4 **Nev'yansk** Russian Federation
64C3 **New** *R* USA
51D5 **Newala** Tanzania
64B3 **New Albany** Indiana, USA
63E2 **New Albany** Mississippi, USA
73G2 **New Amsterdam** Guyana
34C1 **New Angledool** Australia
65D3 **Newark** Delaware, USA
57F2 **Newark** New Jersey, USA
68B1 **Newark** New York, USA
64C2 **Newark** Ohio, USA
7D3 **Newark-upon-Trent** England
65E2 **New Bedford** USA
58B1 **Newberg** USA
67C1 **New Bern** USA
67B2 **Newberry** USA
47C3 **New Bethesda** South Africa
69B2 **New Bight** The Bahamas
64C3 **New Boston** USA
62C3 **New Braunfels** USA
68D2 **New Britain** USA
32E1 **New Britain** *I* Papua New Guinea
32E1 **New Britain Trench** Papua New Guinea
68C2 **New Brunswick** USA
55M5 **New Brunswick** *Province* Canada
68C2 **Newburgh** USA
7D4 **Newbury** England
68E1 **Newburyport** USA
33F3 **New Caledonia** *I* SW Pacific Ocean
68D2 **New Canaan** USA
34D2 **Newcastle** Australia
64B3 **New Castle** Indiana, USA
9D2 **Newcastle** Northern Ireland
64C2 **New Castle** Pennsylvania, USA
47D2 **Newcastle** South Africa
60C2 **Newcastle** Wyoming, USA
8D4 **New Castleton** Scotland
7C3 **Newcastle under Lyme** England
6D2 **Newcastle upon Tyne** England
32C2 **Newcastle Waters** Australia
66C3 **New Cuyama** USA
42D3 **New Delhi** India
34D2 **New England Range** *Mts* Australia
68A1 **Newfane** USA
7D4 **New Forest,The** England
55N5 **Newfoundland** *I* Canada
55M4 **Newfoundland** *Province* Canada
52F2 **Newfoundland Basin** Atlantic Ocean
61E3 **New Franklin** USA
8C4 **New Galloway** Scotland
33E1 **New Georgia** *I* Solomon Islands
55M5 **New Glasgow** Canada
32D1 **New Guinea** *I* SE Asia
66C3 **Newhall** USA
57F2 **New Hampshire** *State* USA
61E2 **New Hampton** USA
47E2 **New Hanover** South Africa
32E1 **New Hanover** *I* Papua New Guinea
7E4 **Newhaven** England
65E2 **New Haven** USA
33F3 **New Hebrides Trench** Pacific Ocean
63D2 **New Iberia** USA
32E1 **New Ireland** *I* Papua New Guinea
57F2 **New Jersey** *State* USA
62B2 **Newkirk** USA
55L5 **New Liskeard** Canada
68D2 **New London** USA
32A3 **Newman** Australia
66B2 **Newman** USA
7E3 **Newmarket** England
65D3 **New Market** USA
58C2 **New Meadows** USA
56C3 **New Mexico** *State* USA
68D2 **New Milford** Connecticut, USA
68C2 **New Milford** Pennsylvania, USA
67B2 **Newnan** USA
34C4 **New Norfolk** Australia
57D3 **New Orleans** USA
68C2 **New Paltz** USA
64C2 **New Philadelphia** USA
35B1 **New Plymouth** New Zealand
63D1 **Newport** Arkansas, USA
7D4 **Newport** England
7C4 **Newport** *County* Wales
64C3 **Newport** Kentucky, USA
68D1 **Newport** New Hampshire, USA
58B2 **Newport** Oregon, USA
68B2 **Newport** Pennsylvania, USA
65E2 **Newport** Rhode Island, USA
65E2 **Newport** Vermont, USA
7C4 **Newport** Wales
58C1 **Newport** Washington, USA
66D4 **Newport Beach** USA
57F3 **Newport News** USA
69B1 **New Providence** *I* The Bahamas
7B4 **Newquay** England
7B3 **New Quay** Wales
55L3 **New Quebec Crater** Canada
7C3 **New Radnor** Wales
7E4 **New Romney** England
9C3 **New Ross** Irish Republic
9C2 **Newry** Northern Ireland
New Siberian Is = Novosibirskye Ostrova
67B3 **New Smyrna Beach** USA
32D4 **New South Wales** *State* Australia
61E2 **Newton** Iowa, USA
63C1 **Newton** Kansas, USA
68E1 **Newton** Massachusetts, USA
63E2 **Newton** Mississippi, USA
68C2 **Newton** New Jersey, USA
9D2 **Newtonabbey** Northern Ireland
7C4 **Newton Abbot** England
9C2 **Newton Stewart** Northern Ireland
8C4 **Newton Stewart** Scotland
60C1 **New Town** USA
7C3 **Newtown** Wales
9D2 **Newtownards** Northern Ireland
61E2 **New Ulm** USA
68B2 **Newville** USA
54F5 **New Westminster** Canada
57F2 **New York** USA
57F2 **New York** *State* USA
33G5 **New Zealand** *Dominion* SW Pacific Ocean
37K7 **New Zealand Plat** Pacific Ocean
20G4 **Neya** Russian Federation
41F4 **Neyrīz** Iran
41G2 **Neyshābūr** Iran
21E5 **Nezhin** Ukraine
50B4 **Ngabé** Congo
51C6 **Ngami, L** Botswana
49D4 **Ngaoundéré** Cameroon
30A1 **Ngape** Burma
35C1 **Ngaruawahia** New Zealand
35C1 **Ngaruroro** *R* New Zealand
35C1 **Ngauruhoe,Mt** New Zealand
50B4 **Ngo** Congo
30D2 **Ngoc Linh** *Mt* Vietnam
50B3 **Ngoko** *R* Cameroon/Central African Republic/Congo
26C3 **Ngoring Hu** *L* China
50D4 **Ngorongoro Crater** Tanzania
50B4 **N'Gounié** *R* Gabon
50B2 **Nguigmi** Niger
27G6 **Ngulu** *I* Pacific Ocean
48D3 **Nguru** Nigeria
30D3 **Nha Trang** Vietnam
75A2 **Nhecolândia** Brazil
34B3 **Nhill** Australia
47E2 **Nhlangano** Swaziland
30D2 **Nhommarath** Laos
32C2 **Nhulunbuy** Australia
48B3 **Niafounké** Mali
64B1 **Niagara** USA
65D2 **Niagara Falls** Canada
65D2 **Niagara Falls** USA
27E6 **Niah** Malaysia
48B4 **Niakaramandougou** Ivory Coast
48C3 **Niamey** Niger
50C3 **Niangara** Zaïre
50C3 **Nia Nia** Zaïre
27E6 **Niapa** *Mt* Indonesia
27C6 **Nias** *I* Indonesia
70D3 **Nicaragua** *Republic* Central America
70D3 **Nicaragua, L de** Nicaragua
16D3 **Nicastro** Italy
14D3 **Nice** France
69B1 **Nicholl's Town** The Bahamas
68C2 **Nicholson** USA
39H5 **Nicobar Is** India
45B1 **Nicosia** Cyprus
72A2 **Nicoya, Golfo de** Costa Rica
70D3 **Nicoya,Pen de** Costa Rica
6D2 **Nidd** *R* England
13E2 **Nidda** *R* Germany
19E2 **Nidzica** Poland
13D3 **Niederbronn** France
18B2 **Niedersachsen** *State* Germany
50C4 **Niemba** Zaïre
18B2 **Nienburg** Germany
13D2 **Niers** *R* Germany
48B4 **Niete,Mt** Liberia
73G2 **Nieuw Amsterdam** Surinam
73G2 **Nieuw Nickerie** Surinam
47B3 **Nieuwoudtville** South Africa
13B2 **Nieuwpoort** Belgium
40B2 **Niğde** Turkey
48B3 **Niger** *R* W Africa
48C3 **Niger** *Republic* Africa
48C4 **Nigeria** *Federal Republic* Africa
48C4 **Niger, Mouths of the** Nigeria
43L1 **Nighasan** India
64C1 **Nighthawk L** Canada
17E2 **Nigríta** Greece
29D3 **Nihommatsu** Japan
29D3 **Niigata** Japan
29C4 **Niihama** Japan
29C4 **Nii-jima** *I* Japan
29B4 **Niimi** Japan
29D3 **Niitsu** Japan
45C3 **Nijil** Jordan
18B2 **Nijmegen** Netherlands
20E2 **Nikel'** Russian Federation
48C4 **Nikki** Benin
29D3 **Nikko** Japan
21E6 **Nikolayev** Ukraine
21H6 **Nikolayevsk** Russian Federation
25Q4 **Nikolayevsk-na-Amure** Russian Federation
20H5 **Nikol'sk** Penza, Russian Federation
20H4 **Nikol'sk** Russian Federation
21E6 **Nikopol** Ukraine
40C1 **Niksar** Turkey
17D2 **Nikšić** Montenegro, Yugoslavia
33G1 **Nikunau** *I* Kiribati
27F7 **Nila** *I* Indonesia
38B3 **Nile** *R* NE Africa
64B2 **Niles** USA
44B3 **Nilgiri Hills** India
42C4 **Nimach** India
14C3 **Nîmes** France
34C3 **Nimmitabel** Australia
50D3 **Nimule** Sudan
39F5 **Nine Degree Chan** Indian Ocean
36F5 **Ninety-East Ridge** Indian Ocean
34C3 **Ninety Mile Beach** Australia
31D4 **Ningde** China
31D4 **Ningdu** China
26C3 **Ningjing Shan** *Mts* China
30D1 **Ningming** China
31A4 **Ningnan** China
31B2 **Ningxia** *Province* China
31B2 **Ning Xian** China
31B5 **Ninh Binh** Vietnam
32D1 **Ninigo Is** Papua New Guinea
75A3 **Nioaque** Brazil
60C2 **Niobrara** *R* USA
50B4 **Nioki** Zaïre
48B3 **Nioro du Sahel** Mali
14B2 **Niort** France
54H4 **Nipawin** Canada
55K5 **Nipigon** Canada
64B1 **Nipigon B** Canada
55K5 **Nipigon,L** Canada
64C1 **Nipissing,L** Canada
66B3 **Nipomo** USA
59C3 **Nipton** USA
75C1 **Niquelândia** Brazil
44B2 **Nirmal** India
43F3 **Nirmāli** India
17E2 **Niš** Serbia, Yugoslavia
38C4 **Nişāb** Yemen
26H4 **Nishino-shima** *I* Japan
28C3 **Nishino-shima** *I* Japan
28A4 **Nishi-suidō** *Str* S Korea
29B4 **Nishiwaki** Japan
33E1 **Nissan Is** Papua New Guinea
55L4 **Nitchequon** Canada
73K8 **Niterói** Brazil
8D4 **Nith** *R* Scotland
19D3 **Nitra** Slovakia
64C3 **Nitro** USA
33J2 **Niue** *I* Pacific Ocean
33G2 **Niulakita** *I* Tuvalu
27E6 **Niut** *Mt* Indonesia
33G1 **Niutao** *I* Tuvalu
28A2 **Niuzhuang** China
13C2 **Nivelles** Belgium
14C2 **Nivernais** *Region* France
12L5 **Nivskiy** Russian Federation
44B2 **Nizāmābād** India
45C3 **Nizana** *Hist Site* Israel
26C1 **Nizhneudinsk** Russian Federation
20K4 **Nizhniye Sergi** Russian Federation
20G5 **Nizhniy Lomov** Russian Federation
20G4 **Nizhniy Novgorod** Russian Federation
20G5 **Nizhniy Novgorod** *Division* Russian Federation
20J3 **Nizhniy Odes** Russian Federation
20K4 **Nizhniy Tagil** Russian Federation
25L3 **Nizhnyaya Tunguska** *R* Russian Federation
20G2 **Nizhnyaya Zolotitsa** Russian Federation
40C2 **Nizip** Turkey
12C1 **Njarðvik** Iceland
51C5 **Njoko** *R* Zambia
51D4 **Njombe** Tanzania
50B3 **Nkambé** Cameroon
51D5 **Nkhata Bay** Malawi
50B3 **Nkongsamba** Cameroon
48C3 **N'Konni** Niger
43G4 **Noakhali** Bangladesh
54B3 **Noatak** USA
54B3 **Noatak** *R* USA
28C4 **Nobeoka** Japan
29D2 **Noboribetsu** Japan
75A1 **Nobres** Brazil
63C2 **Nocona** USA
70A1 **Nogales** Sonora, Mexico
59D4 **Nogales** USA
28B4 **Nogata** Japan
13C3 **Nogent-en-Bassigny** France
13B3 **Nogent-sur-Seine** France
20F4 **Noginsk** Russian Federation
42C3 **Nohar** India
29D2 **Noheji** Japan
14B2 **Noirmoutier, Ile de** *I* France
47C1 **Nojane** Botswana
29C4 **Nojima-zaki** *C* Japan
50B3 **Nola** Central African Republic
20H4 **Nolinsk** Russian Federation
68E2 **Nomans Land** *I* USA
54B3 **Nome** USA
13D3 **Nomeny** France
31B1 **Nomgon** Mongolia
28A4 **Nomo-saki** *Pt* Japan
54H3 **Nonacho L** Canada
30C2 **Nong Khai** Thailand
47E2 **Nongoma** South Africa
33G1 **Nonouti** *I* Kiribati
28A3 **Nonsan** S Korea
13C1 **Noord Holland** *Province* Netherlands
47B2 **Noordoewer** Namibia
13C1 **Noordoost Polder** Netherlands
13C1 **Noordzeekanal** Netherlands
54B3 **Noorvik** USA
50B4 **Noqui** Angola
55L5 **Noranda** Canada
13B2 **Nord** *Department* France
24D2 **Nordaustlandet** *I* Svalbard
13D1 **Norden** Germany
13E1 **Nordenham** Germany
13D1 **Norderney** *I* Germany
12F6 **Nordfjord** *Inlet* Norway
12F8 **Nordfriesische** *Is* Germany
18C2 **Nordhausen** Germany
13D1 **Nordhorn** Germany
18B2 **Nordrhein Westfalen** *State* Germany
12J4 **Nordkapp** *C* Norway
55N3 **Nordre Strømfyord** *Fyord* Greenland
12G5 **Nord Storfjället** *Mt* Sweden
25N2 **Nordvik** Russian Federation
9C3 **Nore** *R* Irish Republic
61D2 **Norfolk** Nebraska, USA
65D3 **Norfolk** Virginia, USA
7E3 **Norfolk** *County* England
33F3 **Norfolk I** Pacific Ocean
37K6 **Norfolk I Ridge** Pacific Ocean
63D1 **Norfolk L** USA
25K3 **Noril'sk** Russian Federation
64B2 **Normal** USA
63C1 **Norman** USA
14B2 **Normandie** *Region* France
67B1 **Norman,L** USA
32D2 **Normanton** Australia
54F3 **Norman Wells** Canada
20B2 **Norra Storfjället** *Mt* Sweden
67B1 **Norris L** USA
65D2 **Norristown** USA
12H7 **Norrköping** Sweden
12H6 **Norrsundet** Sweden
12H7 **Norrtälje** Sweden
32B4 **Norseman** Australia
26F1 **Norsk** Russian Federation
75A1 **Nortelândia** Brazil
6D2 **Northallerton** England
32A4 **Northam** Australia
47D2 **Northam** South Africa
52E3 **North American Basin** Atlantic Ocean
32A3 **Northampton** Australia
7D3 **Northampton** England
65E2 **Northampton** USA
7D3 **Northampton** *County* England
44E3 **North Andaman** *I* Indian Ocean
54G3 **North Arm** *B* Canada
67B2 **North Augusta** USA
55M4 **North Aulatsivik** *I* Canada
8C4 **North Ayrshire** *Division* Scotland
54H4 **North Battleford** Canada
55L5 **North Bay** Canada
58B2 **North Bend** USA
8D3 **North Berwick** Scotland
68E1 **North Berwick** USA
55M5 **North,C** Canada
62B1 **North Canadian** *R* USA
57E3 **North Carolina** *State* USA
58B1 **North Cascades Nat Pk** USA
64C1 **North Chan** Canada
6B2 **North Chan** Ire/Scotland
56C2 **North Dakota** *State* USA
7E4 **North Downs** England
65D2 **North East** USA
52H2 **North East Atlantic Basin** Atlantic Ocean
54B3 **Northeast C** USA
51C6 **Northern Cape** *Province* South Africa
10B3 **Northern Ireland** UK
61E1 **Northern Light L** Canada/USA
27H5 **Northern Mariana Is** Pacific Ocean
51C6 **Northern Province** *Province* South Africa
69L1 **Northern Range** *Mts* Trinidad
32C2 **Northern Territory** Australia
Northern Transvaal = Northern Province
8D3 **North Esk** *R* Scotland
68D1 **Northfield** Massachusetts, USA

Old Town
Paisley

65F2 **Old Town** USA
31B1 **Öldziyt**
68A1 **Olean** USA
25O4 **Olekma** *R* Russian Federation
25O3 **Olekminsk** Russian Federation
20E2 **Olenegorsk** Russian Federation
25N3 **Olenek** Russian Federation
25O2 **Olenek** *R* Russian Federation
19F2 **Olevsk** Ukraine
29D2 **Ol'ga** Russian Federation
47C3 **Olifants** *R* Cape Province, South Africa
47B1 **Olifants** *R* Namibia
47E1 **Olifants** *R* Transvaal, South Africa
47C2 **Olifantshoek** South Africa
17E2 **Ólimbos** *Mt* Greece
75C3 **Olímpia** Brazil
73M5 **Olinda** Brazil
74C4 **Olivares** *Mt* Argentina/Chile
75D3 **Oliveira** Brazil
61E2 **Olivia** USA
74C2 **Ollagüe** Chile
74C2 **Ollagüe, Vol** Bolivia
7D3 **Ollerton** England
64B3 **Olney** Illinois, USA
62C2 **Olney** Texas, USA
26E1 **Olochi** Russian Federation
12G7 **Olofström** Sweden
50B4 **Olombo** Congo
18D3 **Olomouc** Czech Republic
20E3 **Olonets** Russian Federation
14B3 **Oloron-Ste-Marie** France
26E1 **Olovyannaya** Russian Federation
13D2 **Olpe** Germany
19E2 **Olsztyn** Poland
16B1 **Olten** Switzerland
17E2 **Olt** *R* Romania
58B1 **Olympia** USA
58B1 **Olympic Nat Pk** USA
Olympus *Mt* = **Ólimbos**
45B1 **Olympus,Mt** Cyprus
58B1 **Olympus,Mt** USA
25T4 **Olyutorskiy, Mys** *C* Russian Federation
29C3 **Omachi** Japan
29C4 **Omae-zaki** *C* Japan
9C2 **Omagh** Northern Ireland
61D2 **Omaha** USA
58C1 **Omak** USA
38D4 **Oman** *Sultanate* Arabian Pen
38D3 **Oman,G of** UAE
47B1 **Omaruru** Namibia
47A1 **Omaruru** *R* Namibia
29D2 **Ōma-saki** *C* Japan
50A4 **Omboué** Gabon
50D2 **Omdurman** Sudan
50D2 **Om Häjer** Eritrea
29D2 **Ōminato** Japan
54F4 **Omineca Mts** Canada
29C3 **Omiya** Japan
54H2 **Ommanney B** Canada
50D3 **Omo** *R* Ethiopia
16B2 **Omodeo, L** Sardinia, Italy
25R3 **Omolon** *R* Russian Federation
25P3 **Omoloy** *R* Russian Federation
29D3 **Omono** *R* Japan
24J4 **Omsk** Russian Federation
24J4 **Omsk** *Division* Russian Federation
29D2 **Ōmu** Japan
28C4 **Omura** Japan
47C1 **Omuramba Eiseb** *R* Botswana
28C4 **Ōmuta** Japan
20J4 **Omutninsk** Russian Federation
64A2 **Onalaska** USA
65D3 **Onancock** USA
43K1 **Onandausi** India
64C1 **Onaping L** Canada
61D2 **Onawa** USA
51B5 **Oncócua** Angola
51B5 **Ondangua** Namibia
19E3 **Ondava** *R* Slovakia
48C4 **Ondo** Nigeria
26E2 **Öndörhaan** Mongolia
39F5 **One and Half Degree Chan** Indian Ocean
42F3 **Onega** Russian Federation
20F3 **Onega** *R* Russian Federation
20F3 **Onega, L** Russian Federation
68C1 **Oneida** USA
68B1 **Oneida L** USA
60D2 **O'Neill** USA
26J2 **Onekotan** *I* Kuril Is, Russian Federation
50C4 **Onema** Zaïre
68C1 **Oneonta** USA
17F1 **Oneşti** Romania
20F3 **Onezhskaya Guba** *B* Russian Federation
Onezhskoye, Oz *L* = **Onega, L**
47C3 **Ongers** *R* South Africa
51B5 **Ongiva** Angola
28B3 **Ongjin** N Korea
31D1 **Ongniud Qi** China
44C2 **Ongole** India
51E6 **Onilahy** *R* Madagascar
48C4 **Onitsha** Nigeria
26D2 **Onjüül** Mongolia
29C3 **Ono** Japan
29C4 **Ōnohara-jima** *I* Japan
29C4 **Onomichi** Japan
33G1 **Onotoa** *I* Kiribati
32A3 **Onslow** Australia
67C2 **Onslow B** USA
29C3 **Ontake-san** *Mt* Japan
66D3 **Ontario** California, USA
58C2 **Ontario** Oregon, USA
55J4 **Ontario** *Province* Canada
65D2 **Ontario,L** Canada/USA
15B2 **Onteniente** Spain
33E1 **Ontong Java Atoll** Solomon Islands
28A3 **Onyang** S Korea
66C3 **Onyx** USA
32C3 **Oodnadatta** Australia
32C4 **Ooldea** Australia
63C1 **Oologah L** USA
13C1 **Oostelijk Flevoland** *Polder* Netherlands
13B2 **Oostende** Belgium
13B2 **Oosterschelde** *Estuary* Netherlands
44B3 **Ootacamund** India
25R4 **Opala** Russian Federation
50C4 **Opala** Zaïre
44C4 **Opanake** Sri Lanka
20H4 **Oparino** Russian Federation
19D3 **Opava** Czech Republic
67A2 **Opelika** USA
63D2 **Opelousas** USA
60B1 **Opheim** USA
19F1 **Opochka** Russian Federation
19D2 **Opole** Poland
15A1 **Oporto** Portugal
35C1 **Opotiki** New Zealand
67A2 **Opp** USA
12F6 **Oppdal** Norway
35B1 **Opunake** New Zealand
17E1 **Oradea** Romania
12B2 **Öræfajökull** *Mts* Iceland
42D3 **Orai** India
15B2 **Oran** Algeria
72F8 **Orán** Argentina
28A2 **Orang** N Korea
34C2 **Orange** Australia
66D4 **Orange** California, USA
14C3 **Orange** France
63D2 **Orange** Texas, USA
47B2 **Orange** *R* South Africa
67B2 **Orangeburg** USA
73H3 **Orange, Cabo** *C* Brazil
61D2 **Orange City** USA
Orange Free State = **Free State**
67B2 **Orange Park** USA
64C2 **Orangeville** Canada
18C2 **Oranienburg** Germany
47B2 **Oranjemund** Namibia
47D1 **Orapa** Botswana
27F5 **Oras** Philippines
17E1 **Orăştie** Romania
17E1 **Oraviţa** Romania
16C2 **Orbetello** Italy
68B2 **Orbisonia** USA
34C3 **Orbost** Australia
13B2 **Orchies** France
66B3 **Orcutt** USA
60D2 **Ord** USA
32B2 **Ord** *R* Australia
59D3 **Orderville** USA
32B2 **Ord,Mt** Australia
25M6 **Ordos** *Desert* China
40C1 **Ordu** Turkey
62B1 **Ordway** USA
12H7 **Örebro** Sweden
64C2 **Oregon** USA
56A2 **Oregon** *State* USA
58B1 **Oregon City** USA
12H6 **Öregrund** Sweden
20F4 **Orekhovo Zuyevo** Russian Federation
21F5 **Orel** Russian Federation
21F5 **Orel** *Division* Russian Federation
59D2 **Orem** USA
21J5 **Orenburg** Russian Federation
20J5 **Orenburg** *Division* Russian Federation
15A1 **Orense** Spain
18C1 **Oresund** *Str* Denmark/Sweden
35A3 **Oreti** *R* New Zealand
19F3 **Orgeyev** Moldavia
17F3 **Orhaneli** *R* Turkey
26D2 **Orhon Gol** *R* Mongolia
34B1 **Orientos** Australia
15B2 **Orihuela** Spain
65D2 **Orillia** Canada
72F2 **Orinoco** *R* Venezuela
68C1 **Oriskany Falls** USA
43E4 **Orissa** *State* India
16B3 **Oristano** Sicily, Italy
16B3 **Oristano, G. di** Sardinia, Italy
12K6 **Orivesi** *L* Finland
73G4 **Oriximiná** Brazil
70C3 **Orizaba** Mexico
75C2 **Orizona** Brazil
8D2 **Orkney** *Is, Division* Scotland
75C3 **Orlândia** Brazil
67B3 **Orlando** USA
14C2 **Orléanais** *Region* France
14C2 **Orléans** France
68E2 **Orleans** USA
25L4 **Orlik** Russian Federation
67B3 **Ormond Beach** USA
7C3 **Ormskirk** England
13C3 **Ornain** *R* France
14B2 **Orne** *R* France
12H6 **Örnsköldsvik** Sweden
28A2 **Oro** N Korea
72D3 **Orocué** Colombia
58C1 **Orofino** USA
45C3 **Oron** Israel
8B3 **Oronsay, I** Scotland
Orontes = **Asi**
19E3 **Orosháza** Hungary
25R3 **Orotukan** Russian Federation
59B3 **Oroville** California, USA
58C1 **Oroville** Washington, USA
19G2 **Orsha** Belarus
21K5 **Orsk** Russian Federation
12F6 **Ørsta** Norway
14B3 **Orthez** France
15A1 **Ortigueira** Spain
14E2 **Ortles** *Mt* Italy
69L1 **Ortoire** *R* Trinidad
61D1 **Ortonville** USA
25O3 **Orulgan, Khrebet** *Mts* Russian Federation
72E7 **Oruro** Bolivia
7E3 **Orwell** *R* England
20K4 **Osa** Russian Federation
61E2 **Osage** Iowa, USA
60C2 **Osage** Wyoming, USA
63D1 **Osage** *R* USA
29D4 **Ōsaka** Japan
70D4 **Osa,Pen de** Costa Rica
63E1 **Osceola** Arkansas, USA
61E2 **Osceola** Iowa, USA
58C2 **Osgood Mts** USA
29D2 **Oshamambe** Japan
65D2 **Oshawa** Canada
29D4 **Ō-shima** *I* Japan
60C2 **Oshkosh** Nebraska, USA
55K5 **Oshkosh** USA
64B2 **Oshkosh** Wisconsin, USA
21H8 **Oshnovīyeh** Iran
48C4 **Oshogbo** Nigeria
50B4 **Oshwe** Zaïre
17D1 **Osijek** Croatia
24K4 **Osinniki** Russian Federation
19F2 **Osipovichi** Belarus
61E2 **Oskaloosa** USA
20B4 **Oskarshamn** Sweden
12G6 **Oslo** Norway
40C2 **Osmaniye** Turkey
18B2 **Osnabrück** Germany
74B6 **Osorno** Chile
15B1 **Osorno** Spain
58C1 **Osoyoos** Canada
32D5 **Ossa,Mt** Australia
64A2 **Osseo** USA
68D2 **Ossining** USA
25S4 **Ossora** Russian Federation
20E4 **Ostashkov** Russian Federation
13E1 **Oste** *R* Germany
Ostend = **Oostende**
12G6 **Østerdalen** *V* Norway
13E1 **Osterholz-Scharmbeck** Germany
12G6 **Östersund** Sweden
13D1 **Ostfriesland** *Region* Germany
12H6 **Östhammär** Sweden
16C2 **Ostia** Italy
19D3 **Ostrava** Czech Republic
19D2 **Ostróda** Poland
19E2 **Ostrołęka** Poland
20D4 **Ostrov** Russian Federation
19D2 **Ostrów Wlkp** Poland
19E2 **Ostrowiec** Poland
19E2 **Ostrów Mazowiecka** Poland
15A2 **Osuna** Spain
65D2 **Oswego** USA
68B1 **Oswego** *R* USA
7C3 **Oswestry** England
19D3 **Oświęcim** Poland
29C3 **Ota** Japan
35B3 **Otago Pen** New Zealand
35C2 **Otaki** New Zealand
29E2 **Otaru** Japan
72C3 **Otavalo** Ecuador
51B5 **Otavi** Namibia
29D3 **Otawara** Japan
68C1 **Otego** USA
58C1 **Othello** USA
17E3 **Óthris** *Mt* Greece
60C2 **Otis** Colorado, USA
68D1 **Otis** Massachusetts, USA
68C2 **Otisville** USA
47B1 **Otjimbingwe** Namibia
51B6 **Otjiwarongo** Namibia
6D3 **Otley** England
31B2 **Otog Qi** China
29D2 **Otoineppu** Japan
35C1 **Otorohanga** New Zealand
12F7 **Otra** *R* Norway
17D2 **Otranto** Italy
17D2 **Otranto,Str of** *Chan* Albania/Italy
64B2 **Otsego** USA
68C1 **Otsego L** USA
29C3 **Ōtsu** Japan
12F6 **Otta** Norway
65D1 **Ottawa** Canada
64B2 **Ottawa** Illinois, USA
63C1 **Ottawa** Kansas, USA
65D1 **Ottawa** *R* Canada
55K4 **Ottawa Is** Canada
13E1 **Otterndorf** Germany
55K4 **Otter Rapids** Canada
55K1 **Otto Fjord** Canada
47D2 **Ottosdal** South Africa
64A2 **Ottumwa** USA
13D3 **Ottweiler** Germany
48C4 **Oturkpo** Nigeria
72C5 **Otusco** Peru
34B3 **Otway,C** Australia
19E2 **Otwock** Poland
30C1 **Ou** *R* Laos
63D2 **Ouachita** *R* USA
63D2 **Ouachita,L** USA
63D2 **Ouachita Mts** USA
48A2 **Ouadane** Mauritius
50C3 **Ouadda** Central African Republic
50C2 **Ouaddai** *Desert Region* Chad
48B3 **Ouagadougou** Burkina
48B3 **Ouahigouya** Burkina
50C3 **Ouaka** *R* Central African Republic
48C3 **Oualam** Niger
48C2 **Ouallen** Algeria
50C3 **Ouanda Djallé** Central African Republic
13B4 **Ouanne** *R* France
48A2 **Ouarane** *Region* Mauritius
48C1 **Ouargla** Algeria
48B2 **Ouarkziz, Jbel** *Mts* Morocco
50C3 **Ouarra** *R* Central African Republic
15C2 **Ouarsenis, Massif de l'** *Mts* Algeria
48B1 **Ouarzazate** Morocco
15C2 **Ouassel** *R* Algeria
50B3 **Oubangui** *R* Central African Republic/Congo/Zaïre
13B2 **Oudenaarde** Belgium
47C3 **Oudtshoorn** South Africa
15B2 **Oued Tlělat** Algeria
48B1 **Oued Zem** Morocco
40B4 **Ouena, Wadi** *Watercourse* Egypt
14A2 **Ouessant, Ile d'** *I* France
50B3 **Ouesso** Congo
48B1 **Ouezzane** Morocco
9C2 **Oughter, L** Irish Republic
50B3 **Ouham** *R* Chad
48C4 **Ouidah** Benin
48B1 **Oujda** Morocco
12J6 **Oulainen** Finland
15C3 **Ouled Nail, Monts des** Algeria
12K5 **Oulu** Finland
12K6 **Oulu** *R* Finland
12K6 **Oulujärvi** *L* Finland
50C2 **Oum Chalouba** Chad
16B3 **Oumel Bouaghi** Algeria
50B2 **Oum Hadjer** Chad
50C2 **Oum Haouach** *Watercourse* Chad
12K5 **Ounas** *R* Finland
20C2 **Ounastunturi** *Mt* Finland
50C2 **Ounianga Kebir** Chad
13D2 **Our** *R* Germany
62A1 **Ouray** USA
13C3 **Ource** *R* France
13B3 **Ourcq** *R* France
Ourense = **Orense**
73K5 **Ouricurí** Brazil
75C3 **Ourinhos** Brazil
75D3 **Ouro Prêto** Brazil
13C2 **Ourthe** *R* Belgium
7E3 **Ouse** *R* Norfolk, England
6D2 **Ouse** *R* N Yorks, England
10B2 **Outer Hebrides** *Is* Scotland
66C4 **Outer Santa Barbara** *Chan* USA
51B6 **Outjo** Namibia
12K6 **Outokumpu** Finland
34B3 **Ouyen** Australia
16B2 **Ovada** Italy
74B4 **Ovalle** Chile
51B5 **Ovamboland** *Region* Namibia
13D1 **Overijssel** *Province* Netherlands
59D3 **Overton** USA
12J5 **Övertorneå** Sweden
60C2 **Ovid** Colorado, USA
68B1 **Ovid** New York, USA
15A1 **Oviedo** Spain
12F6 **Øvre** Norway
21D5 **Ovruch** Ukraine
25O4 **Ovsyanka** Russian Federation
35A3 **Owaka** New Zealand
68B1 **Owasco L** USA
29C4 **Owase** Japan
61E2 **Owatonna** USA
68B1 **Owego** USA
66C2 **Owens** *R* USA
64B3 **Owensboro** USA
66D2 **Owens L** USA
64C2 **Owen Sound** Canada
32D1 **Owen Stanley Range** *Mts* Papua New Guinea
48C4 **Owerri** Nigeria
58E2 **Owl Creek Mts** USA
48C4 **Owo** Nigeria
64C2 **Owosso** USA
58C2 **Owyhee** USA
58C2 **Owyhee** *R* USA
58C2 **Owyhee Mts** USA
72C6 **Oxapampa** Peru
12H7 **Oxelösund** Sweden
7D3 **Oxford** England
68E1 **Oxford** Massachusetts, USA
63E2 **Oxford** Mississippi, USA
68C1 **Oxford** New York, USA
7D4 **Oxford** *County* England
66C3 **Oxnard** USA
29D3 **Oyama** Japan
50B3 **Oyen** Gabon
8C3 **Oykel** *R* Scotland
25Q3 **Oymyakon** Russian Federation
34C4 **Oyster B** Australia
27F6 **Ozamiz** Philippines
19F2 **Ozarichi** Belarus
67A2 **Ozark** USA
63D1 **Ozark Plat** USA
63D1 **Ozarks,L of the** USA
19E3 **Ózd** Hungary
62B2 **Ozona** USA
40D1 **Ozurgety** Georgia

P

47B3 **Paarl** South Africa
8B3 **Pabbay** *I* Scotland
19D2 **Pabianice** Poland
43F4 **Pabna** Bangladesh
19F1 **Pabrade** Lithuania
72F3 **Pacaraima, Serra** *Mts* Brazil/Venezuela
72C5 **Pacasmayo** Peru
70C2 **Pachuca** Mexico
66B1 **Pacific** USA
37N7 **Pacific-Antarctic Ridge** Pacific Ocean
66B2 **Pacific Grove** USA
37L4 **Pacific O**
75D2 **Pacuí** *R* Brazil
27D7 **Padang** Indonesia
20E3 **Padany** Russian Federation
18B2 **Paderborn** Germany
54J3 **Padlei** Canada
43G4 **Padma** *R* Bangladesh
16C1 **Padova** Italy
50B4 **Padrão, Ponta do** *Pt* Angola
56D4 **Padre I** USA
7B4 **Padstow** England
34B3 **Padthaway** Australia
Padua = **Padova**
64B3 **Paducah** Kentucky, USA
62B2 **Paducah** Texas, USA
12L5 **Padunskoye More** *L* Russian Federation
28A2 **Paegam** N Korea
35C1 **Paeroa** New Zealand
47E1 **Pafuri** Mozambique
16C2 **Pag** *I* Croatia
27D7 **Pagai Selatan** *I* Indonesia
27C7 **Pagai Utara** *I* Indonesia
27H5 **Pagan** *I* Pacific Ocean
59D3 **Page** USA
27F8 **Pago Mission** Australia
17F3 **Pagondhas** Greece
62A1 **Pagosa Springs** USA
66E5 **Pahala** Hawaiian Islands
35C2 **Pahiatua** New Zealand
66E5 **Pahoa** Hawaiian Islands
67B3 **Pahokee** USA
12K6 **Päijänne** *L* Finland
66E5 **Pailola Chan** Hawaiian Islands
64C2 **Painesville** USA
59D3 **Painted Desert** USA
64C3 **Paintsville** USA
8C4 **Paisley** Scotland

País Vasco

Perryton

15B1 **País Vasco** *Region* Spain
72B5 **Paita** Peru
12J5 **Pajala** Sweden
38E3 **Pakistan** *Republic* Asia
30C2 **Pak Lay** Laos
43H4 **Pakokku** Burma
16D1 **Pakrac** Croatia
17D1 **Paks** Hungary
30C2 **Pak Sane** Laos
30D2 **Pakse** Laos
50D3 **Pakwach** Uganda
50B3 **Pala** Chad
16D2 **Palagruža** *I* Croatia
13B3 **Palaiseau** France
47D1 **Palala** *R* South Africa
44E3 **Palalankwe** Andaman Islands
25S4 **Palana** Russian Federation
27E7 **Palangkaraya** Indonesia
44B3 **Palani** India
42C4 **Pālanpur** India
47D1 **Palapye** Botswana
67B3 **Palatka** USA
36H4 **Palau** *Republic* Pacific Ocean
30B3 **Palaw** Burma
27E6 **Palawan** *I* Philippines
44B4 **Palayankottai** India
12J7 **Paldiski** Estonia
27D7 **Palembang** Indonesia
15B1 **Palencia** Spain
45B1 **Paleokhorio** Cyprus
16C3 **Palermo** Sicily, Italy
63C2 **Palestine** USA
43G4 **Paletwa** Burma
44B3 **Pālghāt** India
42C3 **Pāli** India
60B3 **Palisade** USA
42C4 **Pālitāna** India
44B4 **Palk Str** India/Sri Lanka
21H5 **Pallasovka** Russian Federation
12J5 **Pallastunturi** *Mt* Finland
35B2 **Palliser B** New Zealand
35C2 **Palliser,C** New Zealand
51E5 **Palma** Mozambique
15C2 **Palma de Mallorca** Spain
73L5 **Palmares** Brazil
69A5 **Palmar Sur** Costa Rica
75B4 **Palmas** Brazil
48B4 **Palmas,C** Liberia
75D1 **Palmas de Monte Alto** Brazil
69B2 **Palma Soriano** Cuba
67B3 **Palm Bay** USA
67B3 **Palm Beach** USA
66C3 **Palmdale** USA
59C4 **Palm Desert** California, USA
75C4 **Palmeira** Brazil
73L5 **Palmeira dos Indos** Brazil
54D3 **Palmer** USA
76G3 **Palmer** *Base* Antarctica
76G3 **Palmer Arch** Antarctica
76F3 **Palmer Land** *Region* Antarctica
35B3 **Palmerston** New Zealand
35C2 **Palmerston North** New Zealand
68C2 **Palmerton** USA
67B3 **Palmetto** USA
16D3 **Palmi** Italy
72C3 **Palmira** Colombia
32D2 **Palm Is** Australia
59C4 **Palm Springs** USA
64A3 **Palmyra** Missouri, USA
68B1 **Palmyra** New York, USA
68B2 **Palmyra** Pennsylvania, USA
43F4 **Palmyras Pt** India
66A2 **Palo Alto** USA
27D6 **Paloh** Indonesia
50D2 **Paloích** Sudan
59C4 **Palomar Mt** USA
27F7 **Palopo** Indonesia
15B2 **Palos, Cabo de** *C* Spain
27E7 **Palu** Indonesia
40C2 **Palu** Turkey
42D3 **Palwal** India
48C3 **Pama** Burkina
27E7 **Pamekasan** Indonesia
14C3 **Pamiers** France
39F2 **Pamir** *Mts* Tajikistan
67C1 **Pamlico** *R* USA
67C1 **Pamlico Sd** USA
62B1 **Pampa** USA
74C4 **Pampa de la Salinas** *Plain* Argentina
74D5 **Pampas** *Plains* Argentina
72D2 **Pamplona** Colombia
15B1 **Pamplona** Spain
64B3 **Pana** USA
59D3 **Panaca** USA
17E2 **Panagyurishte** Bulgaria
44A2 **Panaji** India
72C2 **Panamá** Panama
72B2 **Panama** *Republic* Central America
69B5 **Panama Canal** Panama
67A2 **Panama City** USA
70E4 **Panamá, G de** Panama
59C3 **Panamint Range** *Mts* USA
66D2 **Panamint V** USA
27F5 **Panay** *I* Philippines
17E2 **Pancevo** Serbia, Yugoslavia
27F5 **Pandan** Philippines
44B2 **Pandharpur** India
34A1 **Pandie Pandie** Australia
19E1 **Panevežys** Lithuania
24K5 **Panfilov** Kazakhstan
30B1 **Pang** *R* Burma
50D4 **Pangani** Tanzania
50D4 **Pangani** *R* Tanzania
50C4 **Pangi** Zaïre
27D7 **Pangkalpinang** Indonesia
55M3 **Pangnirtung** Canada
30B1 **Pangtara** Burma
59D3 **Panguitch** USA
62B1 **Panhandle** USA
42D3 **Pānīpat** India
42B2 **Panjao** Afghanistan
28B3 **P'anmunjom** S Korea
43E4 **Panna** India
75B3 **Panorama** Brazil
28A2 **Panshan** China
28B2 **Panshi** China
75A2 **Pantanal de São Lourenço** *Swamp* Brazil
75A2 **Pantanal do Rio Negro** *Swamp* Brazil
75A2 **Pantanal do Taquari** *Swamp* Brazil
16C3 **Pantelleria** *I* Italy
31A4 **Pan Xian** China
16D3 **Paola** Italy
63D1 **Paola** USA
64B3 **Paoli** USA
18D3 **Pápa** Hungary
72A1 **Papagaya, Golfo del** Nicaragua
70D3 **Papagayo, G de** Costa Rica
66E5 **Papaikou** Hawaiian Islands
35B1 **Papakura** New Zealand
70C2 **Papantla** Mexico
8E1 **Papa Stour** *I* Scotland
35B1 **Papatoetoe** New Zealand
8D2 **Papa Westray** *I* Scotland
13D1 **Papenburg** Germany
45B1 **Paphos** Cyprus
8B4 **Paps of Jura** Scotland
32D1 **Papua,G of** Papua New Guinea
32D1 **Papua New Guinea** *Republic* SE Asia
30B2 **Papun** Burma
73J4 **Pará** *R* Brazil
73H4 **Pará** *State* Brazil
32A3 **Paraburdoo** Australia
72C6 **Paracas,Pen de** Peru
75C2 **Paracatu** Brazil
75C2 **Paracatu** *R* Brazil
30E2 **Paracel Is** SE Asia
34A2 **Parachilna** Australia
42C2 **Parachinar** Pakistan
17E2 **Paracin** Serbia, Yugoslavia
75D2 **Pará de Minas** Brazil
59B3 **Paradise** California, USA
59D3 **Paradise** Nevada, USA
66D1 **Paradise Peak** *Mt* USA
63D1 **Paragould** USA
72F6 **Paraguá** *R* Bolivia
72F2 **Paragua** *R* Venezuela
75D1 **Paraguaçu** *R* Brazil
73G7 **Paraguai** *R* Brazil
75A4 **Paraguarí** Paraguay
74E2 **Paraguay** *R* Paraguay
74E2 **Paraguay** *Republic* S America
75C3 **Paraíba** *R* Brazil
73L5 **Paraíba** *State* Brazil
75D3 **Paraíba do Sul** *R* Brazil
48C4 **Parakou** Benin
44B4 **Paramakkudi** India
73G2 **Paramaribo** Surinam
75D1 **Paramirim** Brazil
26J1 **Paramushir** *I* Russian Federation
74D4 **Paraná** Argentina
74E4 **Paraná** *R* Argentina
75B3 **Paraná** *R* Brazil
73J6 **Paranã** *R* Brazil
74F2 **Paraná** *State* Brazil
75C4 **Paranaguá** Brazil
75B2 **Paranaíba** Brazil
75B2 **Paranaíba** *R* Brazil
75B3 **Paranapanema** *R* Brazil
75C3 **Paranapiacaba, Serra do** *Mts* Brazil
75B3 **Paranavaí** Brazil
75D2 **Paraope** *R* Brazil
35B2 **Paraparaumu** New Zealand
75D1 **Paratinga** Brazil
44B2 **Parbhani** India
45C2 **Pardes Hanna** Israel
75E2 **Pardo** *R* Bahia, Brazil
75B3 **Pardo** *R* Mato Grosso do Sul, Brazil
75C2 **Pardo** *R* Minas Gerais, Brazil
75C3 **Pardo** *R* São Paulo, Brazil
18D2 **Pardubice** Czech Republic
26G4 **Parece Vela** *Reef* Pacific Ocean
75A1 **Parecis** Brazil
72F6 **Parecis, Serra dos** *Mts* Brazil
57F2 **Parent** Canada
65D1 **Parent,L** Canada
32A1 **Parepare** Indonesia
69E4 **Paria, G de** Trinidad/Venezuela
27D7 **Pariaman** Indonesia
69E4 **Paria, Península de** Venezuela
72F3 **Parima, Serra** *Mts* Brazil
14C2 **Paris** France
64C3 **Paris** Kentucky, USA
63E1 **Paris** Tennessee, USA
63C2 **Paris** Texas, USA
59D4 **Parker** USA
64C3 **Parkersburg** USA
34C2 **Parkes** Australia
68C3 **Parkesburg** USA
64A1 **Park Falls** USA
66B3 **Parkfield** USA
64B2 **Park Forest** USA
61D1 **Park Rapids** USA
61D2 **Parkston** USA
58B1 **Parksville** Canada
58D2 **Park Valley** USA
44C2 **Parlākimidi** India
44B2 **Parli** India
16C2 **Parma** Italy
64C2 **Parma** USA
73K4 **Parnaiba** Brazil
73K4 **Parnaiba** *R* Brazil
17E3 **Párnon Óros** *Mts* Greece
20C4 **Pärnu** Estonia
43F3 **Paro** Bhutan
34B1 **Paroo** *R* Australia
34B2 **Paroo Channel** *R* Australia
17F3 **Páros** *I* Greece
59D3 **Parowan** USA
34D2 **Parramatta** Australia
56C4 **Parras** Mexico
55K3 **Parry B** Canada
54G2 **Parry Is** Canada
55L2 **Parry, Kap** *C* Canada
55L5 **Parry Sound** Canada
18C3 **Parsberg** Germany
54F4 **Parsnip** *R* Canada
63C1 **Parsons** Kansas, USA
65D3 **Parsons** West Virginia, USA
14B2 **Parthenay** France
16C3 **Partinico** Italy
28C2 **Partizansk** Russian Federation
9B3 **Partry** *Mts* Irish Republic
73H4 **Paru** *R* Brazil
44C2 **Parvatipuram** India
47D2 **Parys** South Africa
63C3 **Pasadena** Texas, USA
66C3 **Pasadena** USA
30B2 **Pasawing** Burma
63E2 **Pascagoula** USA
17F1 **Paşcani** Romania
58C1 **Pasco** USA
75E2 **Pascoal, Monte** Brazil
Pascua, Isla de = Easter I
13B2 **Pas-de-Calais** *Department* France
12G8 **Pasewalk** Germany
41G4 **Pashū'īyeh** Iran
32B4 **Pasley,C** Australia
74E3 **Paso de los Libres** Argentina
74E4 **Paso de los Toros** Uruguay
74B6 **Paso Limay** Argentina
66B3 **Paso Robles** USA
68C2 **Passaic** USA
18C3 **Passau** Germany
74F3 **Passo Fundo** Brazil
75C3 **Passos** Brazil
72C4 **Pastaza** *R* Peru
72C3 **Pasto** Colombia
19E1 **Pasvalys** Lithuania
74B8 **Patagonia** *Region* Argentina
42C4 **Pātan** India
43F3 **Patan** Nepal
43J1 **Patandi** India
34B3 **Patchewollock** Australia
35B1 **Patea** New Zealand
35B2 **Patea** *R* New Zealand
6D2 **Pateley Bridge** England
16C3 **Paterno** Sicily, Italy
68C2 **Paterson** USA
35A3 **Paterson Inlet** *B* New Zealand
42D2 **Pathankot** India
60B2 **Pathfinder Res** USA
42D2 **Patiāla** India
72C6 **Pativilca** Peru
17F3 **Pátmos** *I* Greece
43F3 **Patna** India
40D2 **Patnos** Turkey
25N4 **Patomskoye Nagor'ye** *Upland* Russian Federation
73L5 **Patos** Brazil
75C2 **Patos de Minas** Brazil
74F4 **Patos, Lagoa dos** *Lg* Brazil
17E3 **Pátrai** Greece
20L3 **Patrasuy** Russian Federation
75C2 **Patrocínio** Brazil
50E4 **Patta I** Kenya
30C4 **Pattani** Thailand
30C3 **Pattaya** Thailand
66B2 **Patterson** California, USA
63D3 **Patterson** Louisiana, USA
66C2 **Patterson Mt** USA
68A2 **Patton** USA
73L5 **Patu** Brazil
43G4 **Patuakhali** Bangladesh
70D3 **Patuca** *R* Honduras
14B3 **Pau** France
54F3 **Paulatuk** Canada
73K5 **Paulistana** Brazil
47E2 **Paulpietersburg** South Africa
63C2 **Pauls Valley** USA
30B2 **Paungde** Burma
42D2 **Pauri** India
75D2 **Pavão** Brazil
16B1 **Pavia** Italy
24J4 **Pavlodar** Kazakhstan
20K4 **Pavlovka** Russian Federation
20G4 **Pavlovo** Russian Federation
21G5 **Pavlovsk** Russian Federation
63C1 **Pawhuska** USA
68A3 **Paw Paw** USA
68E2 **Pawtucket** USA
60C2 **Paxton** USA
58C2 **Payette** USA
55L4 **Payne,L** Canada
61E1 **Paynesville** USA
74E4 **Paysandú** Uruguay
17E2 **Pazardzhik** Bulgaria
54G4 **Peace** *R* Canada
67B3 **Peace** *R* USA
54G4 **Peace River** Canada
59D3 **Peach Springs** USA
7D3 **Peak District Nat Pk** England
65F1 **Peaked Mt** USA
34C2 **Peak Hill** Australia
7D3 **Peak,The** *Mt* England
59E3 **Peale,Mt** USA
63D2 **Pearl** *R* USA
66E5 **Pearl City** Hawaiian Islands
66E5 **Pearl Harbor** Hawaiian Islands
62C3 **Pearsall** USA
47D3 **Pearston** South Africa
54H2 **Peary Chan** Canada
51D5 **Pebane** Mozambique
17E2 **Peć** Serbia, Yugoslavia
75D2 **Peçanha** Brazil
63D3 **Pecan Island** USA
12L5 **Pechenga** Russian Federation
20K2 **Pechora** Russian Federation
20J2 **Pechora** *R* Russian Federation
20J2 **Pechorskaya Guba** *G* Russian Federation
20J2 **Pechorskoye More** *S* Russian Federation
16D3 **Pecoraro** *Mt* Italy
62B2 **Pecos** USA
62B2 **Pecos** *R* USA
19D3 **Pécs** Hungary
45B1 **Pedhoulas** Cyprus
75D2 **Pedra Azul** Brazil
75C3 **Pedregulho** Brazil
69B3 **Pedro Cays** *Is* Caribbean Sea
74C2 **Pedro de Valdivia** Chile
75B2 **Pedro Gomes** Brazil
75A3 **Pedro Juan Caballero** Paraguay
44C4 **Pedro,Pt** Sri Lanka
34B2 **Peebinga** Australia
8D4 **Peebles** Scotland
67C2 **Pee Dee** *R* USA
68D2 **Peekskill** USA
6B2 **Peel** Isle of Man, British Islands
54E3 **Peel** *R* Canada
54J2 **Peel Sd** Canada
Pefos = Paphos
27G7 **Peg Arfak** *Mt* Indonesia
35B2 **Pegasus B** New Zealand
30B2 **Pegu** Burma
32C1 **Pegunungan Maoke** *Mts* Indonesia
30B2 **Pegu Yoma** *Mts* Burma
74D5 **Pehuajó** Argentina
Peipsi Järv = Lake Peipus
75B1 **Peixe** *R* Mato Grosso, Brazil
75B3 **Peixe** *R* São Paulo, Brazil
31D3 **Pei Xian** China
30C5 **Pekan** Malaysia
27D6 **Pekanbaru** Indonesia
64B2 **Pekin** USA
Peking = Beijing
30C5 **Pelabohan Kelang** Malaysia
14D3 **Pelat, Mont** France
17E1 **Peleaga** *Mt* Romania
25N4 **Peleduy** Russian Federation
64C2 **Pelee I** Canada
32B1 **Peleng** *I* Indonesia
61E1 **Pelican L** USA
47A1 **Pelican Pt** South Africa
17D2 **Pelješac** *Pen* Croatia
12J5 **Pello** Finland
55K3 **Pelly Bay** Canada
54E3 **Pelly Mts** Canada
74F4 **Pelotas** Brazil
74F3 **Pelotas** *R* Brazil
45B3 **Pelusium** *Hist Site* Egypt
14D2 **Pelvoux, Massif du** *Mts* France
20L3 **Pelym** *R* Russian Federation
51E5 **Pemba** Mozambique
51E5 **Pemba, Baiá de** *B* Mozambique
50D4 **Pemba I** Tanzania
61D1 **Pembina** USA
65D1 **Pembroke** Canada
7B4 **Pembroke** *County* Wales
67B2 **Pembroke** USA
7B4 **Pembroke** Wales
68E1 **Penacook** USA
75B3 **Penápolis** Brazil
15A2 **Peñarroya** Spain
15B1 **Peñarroya** *Mt* Spain
7C4 **Penarth** Wales
15A1 **Peñas, Cabo de** *C* Spain
74B7 **Penas, Golfo de** *G* Chile
15A1 **Peña Trevinca** *Mt* Spain
50B3 **Pende** *R* Central African Republic/Chad
58C1 **Pendleton** USA
58C1 **Pend Oreille** *R* USA
73L6 **Penedo** Brazil
42D5 **Penganga** *R* India
31D5 **Pengho Lieh Tao** *Is* Taiwan
31E2 **Penglai** China
31B4 **Pengshui** China
8D4 **Penicuik** Scotland
30C5 **Peninsular Malaysia** Malaysia
7D3 **Penistone** England
44B3 **Penner** *R* India
6C2 **Pennine Chain** *Mts* England
68C3 **Penns Grove** USA
57F2 **Pennsylvania** *State* USA
68B1 **Penn Yan** USA
55M3 **Penny Highlands** *Mts* Canada
65F1 **Penobscot** *R* USA
65F2 **Penobscot B** USA
34B3 **Penola** Australia
32C4 **Penong** Australia
69A5 **Penonomé** Panama
6C2 **Penrith** England
63E2 **Pensacola** USA
76E2 **Pensacola Mts** Antarctica
33F2 **Pentecost** *I* Vanuatu
54G5 **Penticton** Canada
8D2 **Pentland Firth** *Chan* Scotland
8D4 **Pentland Hills** Scotland
6C2 **Pen-y-ghent** *Mt* England
20H5 **Penza** Russian Federation
21G5 **Penza** *Division* Russian Federation
7B4 **Penzance** England
25S3 **Penzhina** *R* Russian Federation
25S3 **Penzhinskaya Guba** *B* Russian Federation
64B2 **Peoria** USA
30C5 **Perak** *R* Malaysia
75A3 **Perdido** *R* Brazil
72C3 **Pereira** Colombia
75B3 **Pereira Barreto** Brazil
21G6 **Perelazovskiy** Russian Federation
19G2 **Pereyaslav** Ukraine
74D4 **Pergamino** Argentina
40B2 **Perge** Turkey
55L4 **Péribonca** *R* Canada
14C2 **Périgueux** France
72C2 **Perlas, Archipiélago de las** Panama
69A4 **Perlas, Laguna de** Nicaragua
20K4 **Perm'** Russian Federation
20K4 **Perm'** *Division* Russian Federation
Pernambuco = Recife
73L5 **Pernambuco** *State* Brazil
17E2 **Pernik** Bulgaria
13B3 **Péronne** France
14C3 **Perpignan** France
66D4 **Perris** USA
67B2 **Perry** Florida, USA
67B2 **Perry** Georgia, USA
68A1 **Perry** New York, USA
63C1 **Perry** Oklahoma, USA
54H3 **Perry River** Canada
64C2 **Perrysburg** USA
62B1 **Perryton** USA

Red Wing **Ruapehu,Mt**

61E2 **Red Wing** USA
66A2 **Redwood City** USA
61D2 **Redwood Falls** USA
64B2 **Reed City** USA
66C2 **Reedley** USA
58B2 **Reedsport** USA
65D3 **Reedville** USA
35B2 **Reefton** New Zealand
10B3 **Ree, Lough** *L* Irish Republic
6D2 **Reeth** England
40C2 **Refahiye** Turkey
63C3 **Refugio** USA
75E2 **Regência** Brazil
18C3 **Regensburg** Germany
48C2 **Reggane** Algeria
16D3 **Reggio di Calabria** Italy
16C2 **Reggio nell'Emilia** Italy
17E1 **Reghin** Romania
54H4 **Regina** Canada
42A2 **Registan** *Region* Afghanistan
47B1 **Rehoboth** Namibia
65D3 **Rehoboth Beach** USA
45C3 **Rehovot** Israel
67C1 **Reidsville** USA
7D4 **Reigate** England
14B2 **Ré, Ile de** *I* France
13B3 **Reims** France
74B8 **Reina Adelaida, Archipiélago de la** Chile
61E2 **Reinbeck** USA
54H4 **Reindeer L** Canada
15B1 **Reinosa** Spain
68B3 **Reisterstown** USA
47D2 **Reitz** South Africa
54H3 **Reliance** Canada
58E2 **Reliance** USA
15C2 **Relizane** Algeria
34A2 **Remarkable,Mt** Australia
27E7 **Rembang** Indonesia
13D3 **Remiremont** France
13D2 **Remscheid** Germany
68C1 **Remsen** USA
12G6 **Rena** Norway
64B3 **Rend L** USA
18B2 **Rendsburg** Germany
65D1 **Renfrew** Canada
8C4 **Renfrew** Scotland
8C4 **Renfrewshire** *Division* Scotland
27D7 **Rengat** Indonesia
19F3 **Reni** Ukraine
50D2 **Renk** Sudan
55Q2 **Renland** *Pen* Greenland
34B2 **Renmark** Australia
33F2 **Rennell** *I* Solomon Islands
14B2 **Rennes** France
59C3 **Reno** USA
16C2 **Reno** *R* Italy
68B2 **Renovo** USA
68D1 **Rensselaer** USA
58B1 **Renton** USA
27F7 **Reo** Indonesia
19G2 **Repki** Ukraine
75C3 **Reprêsa de Furnas** *Dam* Brazil
75C2 **Reprêsa Três Marias** *Dam* Brazil
58C1 **Republic** USA
60D2 **Republican** *R* USA
55K3 **Repulse Bay** Canada
41F2 **Reshteh-ye Alborz** *Mts* Iran
31A2 **Reshui** China
74E3 **Resistencia** Argentina
17E1 **Reşiţa** Romania
55J2 **Resolute** Canada
35A3 **Resolution I** New Zealand
55M3 **Resolution Island** Canada
47E2 **Ressano Garcia** Mozambique
13C3 **Rethel** France
17E3 **Réthimnon** Greece
36D6 **Réunion** *I* Indian Ocean
15C1 **Reus** Spain
18B3 **Reutlingen** Germany
20K4 **Revda** Russian Federation
54G4 **Revelstoke** Canada
13C3 **Revigny-sur-Ornain** France
70A3 **Revillagigedo** *Is* Mexico
37O4 **Revilla Gigedo, Islas** Pacific Ocean
13C3 **Revin** France
45C3 **Revivim** Israel
43E4 **Rewa** India
42D3 **Rewāri** India
58D2 **Rexburg** USA
12A2 **Reykjavik** Iceland
70C2 **Reynosa** Mexico
14B2 **Rezé** France
19F1 **Rezekne** Latvia
20L4 **Rezh** Russian Federation
7C3 **Rhayader** Wales
45C1 **Rhazīr** Lebanon
13E2 **Rheda Wiedenbrück** Germany
18B2 **Rhein** *R* W Europe
18B2 **Rheine** Germany
14D2 **Rheinland Pfalz** *Region* Germany
Rhine *R* = **Rhein**
68D2 **Rhinebeck** USA
64B1 **Rhinelander** USA
65E2 **Rhode Island** *State* USA
68E2 **Rhode Island Sd** USA
17F3 **Rhodes** Greece
17F3 **Rhodes** *I* Greece
47D1 **Rhodes Drift** *Ford* Botswana/South Africa
58D1 **Rhodes Peak** *Mt* USA
7C4 **Rhondda** Wales
7C4 **Rhondda Cynon Taff** *County* Wales
14C3 **Rhône** *R* France
7C3 **Rhyl** Wales
73L6 **Riachão do Jacuipe** Brazil
75D1 **Riacho de Santana** Brazil
15A1 **Ria de Arosa** *B* Spain
15A1 **Ria de Betanzos** *B* Spain
15A1 **Ria de Corcubion** *B* Spain
15A1 **Ria de Lage** *B* Spain
15A1 **Ria de Sta Marta** *B* Spain
15A1 **Ria de Vigo** *B* Spain
42C2 **Riāsi** Pakistan
27D6 **Riau, Kepulauan** *Is* Indonesia
15A1 **Ribadeo** Spain
75B3 **Ribas do Rio Pardo** Brazil
51D5 **Ribauè** Mozambique
6C3 **Ribble** *R* England
75C3 **Ribeira** Brazil
75C3 **Ribeirão Prêto** Brazil
72E6 **Riberalta** Bolivia
65D2 **Rice L** Canada
64A1 **Rice Lake** USA
47E2 **Richard's Bay** South Africa
63C2 **Richardson** USA
54E3 **Richardson Mts** Canada
59D3 **Richfield** USA
68C1 **Richfield Springs** USA
66C3 **Richgrove** USA
58C1 **Richland** USA
64C3 **Richlands** USA
66A2 **Richmond** California, USA
47C3 **Richmond** Cape Province, South Africa
6D2 **Richmond** England
64C3 **Richmond** Kentucky, USA
47E2 **Richmond** Natal, South Africa
34D2 **Richmond** New South Wales, Australia
35B2 **Richmond** New Zealand
32D3 **Richmond** Queensland, Australia
65D3 **Richmond** Virginia, USA
35B2 **Richmond Range** *Mts* New Zealand
68C1 **Richmondville** USA
7D4 **Rickmansworth** England
65D2 **Rideau Lakes** Canada
67B2 **Ridgeland** USA
68A2 **Ridgway** USA
69D4 **Riecito** Venezuela
18C2 **Riesa** Germany
74B8 **Riesco** *I* Chile
47C2 **Riet** *R* South Africa
16C2 **Rieti** Italy
15B2 **Rif** *Mts* Morocco
48B1 **Rif** *R* Morocco
60B3 **Rifle** USA
19E1 **Riga** Latvia
11H2 **Riga,G of** Estonia/Latvia
Rīgas Jūrās Līcis = Gulf of Riga
58D2 **Rigby** USA
58C1 **Riggins** USA
55N4 **Rigolet** Canada
Riia Laht = Gulf of Riga
12J6 **Riihimaki** Finland
16C1 **Rijeka** Croatia
29D3 **Rikuzen-Tanaka** Japan
12H7 **Rimbo** Sweden
16C2 **Rimini** Italy
17F1 **Rîmnicu Sărat** Romania
17E1 **Rîmnicu Vîlcea** Romania
57G2 **Rimouski** Canada
12F7 **Ringkøbing** Denmark
27E7 **Rinjani** *Mt* Indonesia
8B4 **Rinns Point** Scotland
13E1 **Rinteln** Germany
72C4 **Riobamba** Ecuador
48C4 **Rio Benito** Equatorial Guinea
72E5 **Rio Branco** Brazil
75C4 **Rio Branco do Sul** Brazil
62C3 **Rio Bravo** Mexico
70B1 **Rio Bravo del Norte** *R* Mexico/USA
75B3 **Rio Brilhante** Brazil
75C3 **Rio Claro** Brazil
69L1 **Rio Claro** Trinidad
74D4 **Ríocuarto** Argentina
75D3 **Rio de Janeiro** Brazil
75D3 **Rio de Janeiro** *State* Brazil
48A2 **Rio de Oro, Bahia de** *B* Morocco
74C8 **Río Gallegos** Argentina
74C8 **Río Grande** Argentina
74F4 **Rio Grande** Brazil
69A4 **Rio Grande** Nicaragua
70B2 **Rio Grande** *R* Mexico/USA
70D3 **Rio Grande** *R* Nicaragua
62C3 **Rio Grande City** USA
70B2 **Rio Grande de Santiago** *R* Mexico
73L5 **Rio Grande do Norte** *State* Brazil
74F3 **Rio Grande Do Sul** *State* Brazil
52G6 **Rio Grande Rise** Atlantic Ocean
69C4 **Ríohacha** Colombia
14C2 **Riom** France
72E7 **Rio Mulatos** Bolivia
75C4 **Rio Negro** Brazil
74C5 **Río Negro** *State* Argentina
74E4 **Rio Negro, Embalse de** *Res* Uruguay
74F3 **Rio Pardo** Brazil
74B8 **Rio Turbio** Argentina
75B2 **Rio Verde** Brazil
75B2 **Rio Verde de Mato Grosso** Brazil
7D3 **Ripley** England
64C3 **Ripley** Ohio, USA
63E1 **Ripley** Tennessee, USA
64C3 **Ripley** West Virginia, USA
6D2 **Ripon** England
66B2 **Ripon** USA
29E1 **Rishiri-tō** *I* Japan
45C3 **Rishon le Zion** Israel
68B3 **Rising Sun** USA
12F7 **Risør** Norway
44E3 **Ritchie's Arch** *Is* Andaman Islands
55N2 **Ritenbenk** Greenland
66C2 **Ritter,Mt** USA
58C1 **Ritzville** USA
74B3 **Rivadavia** Chile
72A1 **Rivas** Nicaragua
74E4 **Rivera** Uruguay
66B2 **Riverbank** USA
48B4 **River Cess** Liberia
66C2 **Riverdale** USA
68D2 **Riverhead** USA
34B3 **Riverina** *Region* Australia
35A3 **Riversdale** New Zealand
47C3 **Riversdale** South Africa
66D4 **Riverside** USA
35A3 **Riverton** New Zealand
58E2 **Riverton** USA
67B3 **Riviera Beach** USA
65F1 **Riviére-du-Loup** Canada
28A2 **Riwon** N Korea
41E5 **Rīyadh** Saudi Arabia
40D1 **Rize** Turkey
31D2 **Rizhao** China
45C1 **Rizokaipaso** Cyprus
16D3 **Rizzuto, C** Italy
12F7 **Rjukan** Norway
8B2 **Roag, Loch** *Inlet* Scotland
55K2 **Roanes Pen** Canada
14C2 **Roanne** France
67A2 **Roanoke** Alabama, USA
65D3 **Roanoke** Virginia, USA
65D3 **Roanoke** *R* USA
67C1 **Roanoke Rapids** USA
59D3 **Roan Plat** USA
58D2 **Roberts** USA
59C3 **Roberts Creek Mt** USA
12J6 **Robertsfors** Sweden
63D1 **Robert S Kerr Res** USA
47B3 **Robertson** South Africa
48A4 **Robertsport** Liberia
55L5 **Roberval** Canada
6D2 **Robin Hood's Bay** England
34B2 **Robinvale** Australia
63C3 **Robstown** USA
15A2 **Roca, Cabo de** *C* Portugal
70A3 **Roca Partida** *I* Mexico
73M4 **Rocas** *I* Brazil
74F4 **Rocha** Uruguay
7C3 **Rochdale** England
75B2 **Rochedo** Brazil
14B2 **Rochefort** France
64B2 **Rochelle** USA
54G3 **Rocher River** Canada
34B3 **Rochester** Australia
55L5 **Rochester** Canada
7E4 **Rochester** England
61E2 **Rochester** Minnesota, USA
68E1 **Rochester** New Hampshire, USA
68B1 **Rochester** New York, USA
64B2 **Rock** *R* USA
52H2 **Rockall** *I* UK
64B2 **Rockford** USA
67B2 **Rock Hill** USA
67C2 **Rockingham** USA
64A2 **Rock Island** USA
64B1 **Rockland** Michigan, USA
34B3 **Rocklands Res** Australia
67B3 **Rockledge** USA
63C3 **Rockport** USA
61D2 **Rock Rapids** USA
60B2 **Rock River** USA
60B1 **Rock Springs** Montana, USA
62B2 **Rocksprings** Texas, USA
58E2 **Rock Springs** Wyoming, USA
35B2 **Rocks Pt** New Zealand
34C3 **Rock,The** Australia
68D2 **Rockville** Connecticut, USA
64B3 **Rockville** Indiana, USA
68B3 **Rockville** Maryland, USA
65F1 **Rockwood** USA
62B1 **Rocky Ford** USA
64C1 **Rocky Island L** Canada
67C1 **Rocky Mount** USA
60B2 **Rocky Mountain Nat Pk** USA
56B1 **Rocky Mts** Canada/USA
18C2 **Rødbyhavn** Denmark
14C3 **Rodez** France
Ródhos = Rhodes
16D2 **Rodi Garganico** Italy
17E2 **Rodopi Planina** *Mts* Bulgaria
32A3 **Roebourne** Australia
47D1 **Roedtan** South Africa
13D2 **Roer** *R* Netherlands
13C2 **Roermond** Netherlands
13B2 **Roeselare** Belgium
55K3 **Roes Welcome Sd** Canada
19F2 **Rogachev** Belarus
72E6 **Rogaguado, Lago** Bolivia
63D1 **Rogers** USA
64C1 **Rogers City** USA
66D3 **Rogers L** USA
64C3 **Rogers,Mt** USA
58D2 **Rogerson** USA
47B3 **Roggeveldberge** *Mts* South Africa
58B2 **Rogue** *R* USA
42B3 **Rohri** Pakistan
42D3 **Rohtak** India
19E1 **Roja** Latvia
70C2 **Rojo, Cabo** *C* Mexico
75B3 **Rolândia** Brazil
63D1 **Rolla** USA
58D1 **Rollins** USA
Roma = Rome
34C1 **Roma** Australia
67C2 **Romain,C** USA
17F1 **Roman** Romania
52H5 **Romanche Gap** Atlantic Ocean
27F7 **Romang** *I* Indonesia
21C6 **Romania** *Republic* E Europe
67B3 **Romano,C** USA
14D2 **Romans-sur-Isère** France
27F5 **Romblon** Philippines
67A2 **Rome** Georgia, USA
16C2 **Rome** Italy
68C1 **Rome** New York, USA
65D2 **Rome** USA
14C2 **Romilly-sur-Seine** France
65D3 **Romney** USA
21E5 **Romny** Ukraine
18B1 **Rømø** *I* Denmark
14C2 **Romorantin** France
8C3 **Rona, I** Scotland
8B3 **Ronay, I** Scotland
75B1 **Roncador, Serra do** *Mts* Brazil
15A2 **Ronda** Spain
15A2 **Ronda, Sierra de** *Mts* Spain
72F6 **Rondônia** Brazil
72F6 **Rondônia** *State* Brazil
75B2 **Rondonópolis** Brazil
31B4 **Rong'an** China
31B4 **Rongchang** China
31E2 **Rongcheng** China
54H4 **Ronge, Lac la** Canada
31B4 **Rongjiang** China
31B4 **Rong Jiang** *R* China
30A1 **Rongklang Range** *Mts* Burma
12G7 **Rønne** Denmark
12H7 **Ronneby** Sweden
76F2 **Ronne Ice Shelf** Antarctica
13B2 **Ronse** Belgium
13D1 **Roodeschool** Netherlands
56C3 **Roof Butte** *Mt* USA
42D3 **Roorkee** India
13C2 **Roosendaal** Netherlands
59D2 **Roosevelt** USA
76E6 **Roosevelt I** Antarctica
61E2 **Root** *R* USA
32C2 **Roper** *R* Australia
8D2 **Rora Head** *Pt* Scotland
72F2 **Roraima** *Mt* Brazil/Guyana/Venezuela
72F3 **Roraima** *State* Brazil
12G6 **Røros** Norway
12G6 **Rorvik** Norway
19G3 **Ros'** *R* Ukraine
69Q2 **Rosalie** Dominica
66C3 **Rosamond** USA
66C3 **Rosamond L** USA
74D4 **Rosario** Argentina
73K4 **Rosário** Brazil
75A3 **Rosario** Paraguay
75A1 **Rosário Oeste** Brazil
68C2 **Roscoe** USA
14B2 **Roscoff** France
10B3 **Roscommon** Irish Republic
9C3 **Roscrea** Irish Republic
69Q2 **Roseau** Dominica
34C4 **Rosebery** Australia
60B1 **Rosebud** USA
58B2 **Roseburg** USA
63C3 **Rosenberg** USA
18C3 **Rosenheim** Germany
54H4 **Rosetown** Canada
66B1 **Roseville** USA
12G7 **Roskilde** Denmark
20E5 **Roslavl'** Russian Federation
20G4 **Roslyatino** Russian Federation
17E2 **Roşorii de Vede** Romania
35B2 **Ross** New Zealand
16D3 **Rossano** Italy
10B3 **Rossan Pt** Irish Republic
63E2 **Ross Barnett Res** USA
65D1 **Rosseau L** Canada
33E2 **Rossel** *I* Papua New Guinea
76E6 **Ross Ice Shelf** Antarctica
58B1 **Ross L** USA
9C3 **Rosslare** Irish Republic
35C2 **Ross,Mt** New Zealand
48A3 **Rosso** Mauritius
16B2 **Rosso, C** Corsica, France
7C4 **Ross-on-Wye** England
21F5 **Rossosh** Russian Federation
54E3 **Ross River** Canada
76F6 **Ross S** Antarctica
41F4 **Rostāq** Iran
18C2 **Rostock** Germany
20F4 **Rostov** *Division* Russian Federation
20F4 **Rostov** Russian Federation
21F6 **Rostov-na-Donu** Russian Federation
67B2 **Roswell** Georgia, USA
62B2 **Roswell** New Mexico, USA
27H5 **Rota** *I* Pacific Ocean
27F8 **Rote** *I* Indonesia
18B2 **Rotenburg** Niedersachsen, Germany
13E2 **Rothaar-Geb** *Region* Germany
6D2 **Rothbury** England
76G3 **Rothera** *Base* Antarctica
7D3 **Rotherham** England
8C4 **Rothesay** Scotland
8D3 **Rothes-on-Spey** Scotland
34C2 **Roto** Australia
35B2 **Rotoiti,L** New Zealand
35B2 **Rotoroa,L** New Zealand
35C1 **Rotorua** New Zealand
35C1 **Rotorua,L** New Zealand
13E3 **Rottenburg** Germany
18A2 **Rotterdam** Netherlands
13E3 **Rottweil** Germany
33G2 **Rotuma** *I* Fiji
13B2 **Roubaix** France
14C2 **Rouen** France
6E3 **Rough** *Oilfield* N Sea
Roulers = Roeselare
51F6 **Round I** Mauritius
66D1 **Round Mountain** USA
34D2 **Round Mt** Australia
58E1 **Roundup** USA
8D2 **Rousay** *I* Scotland
14C3 **Roussillon** *Region* France
47D3 **Rouxville** South Africa
65D1 **Rouyn** Canada
12K5 **Rovaniemi** Finland
16C1 **Rovereto** Italy
16C1 **Rovigo** Italy
16C1 **Rovinj** Croatia
19F2 **Rovno** Ukraine
41E2 **Row'ān** Iran
34C1 **Rowena** Australia
55L3 **Rowley I** Canada
32A2 **Rowley Shoals** Australia
27F5 **Roxas** Philippines
67C1 **Roxboro** USA
35A3 **Roxburgh** New Zealand
58E1 **Roy** USA
9C3 **Royal Canal** Irish Republic
64B1 **Royale, Isle** USA
7D3 **Royal Leamington Spa** England
64C2 **Royal Oak** USA
7E4 **Royal Tunbridge Wells** England
14B2 **Royan** France
13B3 **Roye** France
7D3 **Royston** England
19E3 **Rožňava** Slovakia
13B3 **Rozoy** France
21G5 **Rtishchevo** Russian Federation
7C3 **Ruabon** Wales
51D4 **Ruaha Nat Pk** Tanzania
35C1 **Ruahine Range** *Mts* New Zealand
35C1 **Ruapehu,Mt** New Zealand

Salon-de-Provence São Vicente

14D3 **Salon-de-Provence** France
Salonica = Thessaloníki
17E1 **Salonta** Romania
12K6 **Salpausselkä** *Region* Finland
21G6 **Sal'sk** Russian Federation
45C2 **Salt** Jordan
47C3 **Salt** *R* South Africa
59D4 **Salt** *R* USA
74C2 **Salta** Argentina
74C2 **Salta** *State* Argentina
7B4 **Saltash** England
9C3 **Saltee, I** Irish Republic
70B2 **Saltillo** Mexico
58D2 **Salt Lake City** USA
72D3 **Salto Angostura** *Waterfall* Colombia
75E2 **Salto da Divisa** Brazil
75B3 **Salto das Sete Quedas** Brazil
72F2 **Salto del Angel** *Waterfall* Venezuela
74E2 **Salto del Guaíra** *Waterfall* Brazil
72D4 **Salto Grande** *Waterfall* Colombia
59C4 **Salton S** USA
75B4 **Saltos do Iguaçu** *Waterfall* Argentina
74E4 **Salto Tacuarembó** Uruguay
42C2 **Salt Range** *Mts* Pakistan
69H2 **Salt River** Jamaica
67B2 **Saluda** USA
44C2 **Sālūr** India
73L6 **Salvador** Brazil
63D3 **Salvador,L** USA
41F5 **Salwah** Qatar
30B1 **Salween** *R* Burma
21H8 **Sal'yany** Azerbaijan
64C3 **Salyersville** USA
18C3 **Salzburg** Austria
18C2 **Salzgitter** Germany
18C2 **Salzwedel** Germany
26C1 **Samagaltay** Russian Federation
69D3 **Samaná** Dominican Republic
40C2 **Samandaği** Turkey
42B1 **Samangan** Afghanistan
29D2 **Samani** Japan
45A3 **Samannûd** Egypt
27F5 **Samar** *I* Philippines
20J5 **Samara** *Division* Russian Federation
20J5 **Samara** Russian Federation
32E2 **Samarai** Papua New Guinea
27E7 **Samarinda** Indonesia
38E2 **Samarkand** Uzbekistan
41D3 **Sāmarrā'** Iraq
43E4 **Sambalpur** India
27D6 **Sambas** Indonesia
51F5 **Sambava** Madagascar
42D3 **Sambhal** India
19E3 **Sambor** Ukraine
13B2 **Sambre** *R* France
28B3 **Samch'ŏk** S Korea
28A4 **Samch'ŏnp'o** S Korea
28A3 **Samdŭng** N Korea
50D4 **Same** Tanzania
51C5 **Samfya** Zambia
30B1 **Samka** Burma
30C1 **Sam Neua** Laos
33H2 **Samoan Is** Pacific Ocean
17F3 **Sámos** *I* Greece
17F2 **Samothráki** *I* Greece
27E7 **Sampit** Indonesia
63D2 **Sam Rayburn Res** USA
30C3 **Samrong** Cambodia
18C1 **Samsø** *I* Denmark
28A2 **Samsu** N Korea
40C1 **Samsun** Turkey
48B3 **San** Mali
30D3 **San** *R* Cambodia
19E2 **San** *R* Poland
50E2 **San'ā** Yemen
50B3 **Sanaga** *R* Cameroon
74C4 **San Agustín** Argentina
52D6 **San Ambrosia, Isla** Pacific Ocean
41E2 **Sanandaj** Iran
66B1 **San Andreas** USA
69A4 **San Andres, Isla de** Caribbean Sea
62A2 **San Andres Mts** USA
70C3 **San Andrés Tuxtla** Mexico
62B2 **San Angelo** USA
16B3 **San Antioco** Sardinia, Italy
16B3 **San Antioco** *I* Sardinia, Italy
56B4 **San Antonia, Pt** Mexico
74B4 **San Antonio** Chile
62A2 **San Antonio** New Mexico, USA
62C3 **San Antonio** Texas, USA
66B2 **San Antonio** *R* California, USA
63C3 **San Antonio** *R* Texas, USA
15C2 **San Antonio Abad** Spain
69A2 **San Antonio, Cabo** *C* Cuba
62B2 **San Antonio de Bravo** Mexico
69A2 **San Antonio de los Banos** Cuba
66D3 **San Antonio,Mt** USA
74D6 **San Antonio Oeste** Argentina
66B3 **San Antonio Res** USA
66B2 **San Ardo** USA
42D4 **Sanāwad** India
70A3 **San Benedicto** *I* Mexico
63C3 **San Benito** USA
66B2 **San Benito** *R* USA
66B2 **San Benito Mt** USA
66D3 **San Bernardino** USA
74B4 **San Bernardo** Chile
59C4 **San Bernardo Mts** USA
67A3 **San Blas,C** USA
70E4 **San Blas, Puerta** *Pt* Panama
74E3 **San Borja** Brazil
74B5 **San Carlos** Chile
72B1 **San Carlos** Nicaragua
59D4 **San Carlos** USA
74B6 **San Carlos de Bariloche** Argentina
20H4 **Sanchursk** Russian Federation
66D4 **San Clemente** USA
59C4 **San Clemente I** USA
70C3 **San Cristóbal** Mexico
72D2 **San Cristóbal** Venezuela
33F2 **San Cristobal** *I* Solomon Islands
70E2 **Sancti Spíritus** Cuba
14C2 **Sancy, Puy de** *Mt* France
47D1 **Sand** *R* South Africa
8C4 **Sanda, I** Scotland
27E6 **Sandakan** Malaysia
8D2 **Sanday** *I* Scotland
62B2 **Sanderson** USA
7E4 **Sandgate** England
59C4 **San Diego** USA
74C8 **San Diego, Cabo** Argentina
40B2 **Sandıklı** Turkey
43E3 **Sandīla** India
12F7 **Sandnes** Norway
12G5 **Sandnessjøen** Norway
51C4 **Sandoa** Zaïre
19E2 **Sandomierz** Poland
43G5 **Sandoway** Burma
7D4 **Sandown** England
12D3 **Sandoy** *I* Faeroes
58C1 **Sandpoint** USA
63C1 **Sand Springs** USA
32A3 **Sandstone** Australia
61E1 **Sandstone** USA
31C4 **Sandu** China
64C2 **Sandusky** USA
12H6 **Sandviken** Sweden
68E2 **Sandwich** USA
55J4 **Sandy L** Canada
75A3 **San Estanislao** Paraguay
56B3 **San Felipe** Baja Cal, Mexico
74B4 **San Felipe** Chile
69D4 **San Felipe** Venezuela
15C1 **San Felíu de Guixols** Spain
52D6 **San Felix, Isla** Pacific Ocean
74B4 **San Fernando** Chile
27F5 **San Fernando** Philippines
15A2 **San Fernando** Spain
69L2 **San Fernando** Trinidad
66C3 **San Fernando** USA
72E2 **San Fernando** Venezuela
67B3 **Sanford** Florida, USA
65E2 **Sanford** Maine, USA
67C1 **Sanford** N Carolina, USA
57E4 **Sanford** USA
54D3 **Sanford, Mt** USA
74D4 **San Francisco** Argentina
69C3 **San Francisco** Dominican Republic
66A2 **San Francisco** USA
66A2 **San Francisco B** USA
70B2 **San Francisco del Oro** Mexico
66D3 **San Gabriel Mts** USA
42C5 **Sangamner** India
64B3 **Sangamon** *R* USA
25O3 **Sangar** Russian Federation
44B2 **Sangāreddi** India
66C2 **Sanger** USA
31C2 **Sanggan He** *R* China
27E6 **Sanggau** Indonesia
50B3 **Sangha** *R* Congo
42B3 **Sanghar** Pakistan
27F6 **Sangir** *I* Indonesia
27F6 **Sangir, Kepulauan** *Is* Indonesia
30B3 **Sangkhla Buri** Thailand
27E6 **Sangkulirang** Indonesia
44A2 **Sāngli** India
50B3 **Sangmélima** Cameroon
56B3 **San Gorgonio Mt** USA
62A1 **Sangre de Cristo Mts** USA
66A2 **San Gregorio** USA
42D2 **Sangrūr** India
47E1 **Sangutane** *R* Mozambique
74E3 **San Ignacio** Argentina
72D2 **San Jacinto** Colombia
59C4 **San Jacinto Peak** *Mt* USA
28A2 **Sanjiangkou** China
29D3 **Sanjō** Japan
74H2 **San João del Rei** Brazil
66B2 **San Joaquin** *R* USA
66B2 **San Joaquin Valley** USA
62B1 **San Jon** USA
74C7 **San Jorge, Golfo** *G* Argentina
15C1 **San Jorge, Golfo de** *G* Spain
72B1 **San José** Costa Rica
70C3 **San José** Guatemala
66B2 **San Jose** USA
56B4 **San José** *I* Mexico
72F7 **San José de Chiquitos** Bolivia
56C4 **San José del Cabo** Mexico
74G2 **San José do Rio Prêto** Brazil
70B2 **San Joseé del Cabo** Mexico
28A3 **Sanju** S Korea
74C4 **San Juan** Argentina
69D3 **San Juan** Puerto Rico
69L1 **San Juan** Trinidad
72E2 **San Juan** Venezuela
69B2 **San Juan** *Mt* Cuba
66B3 **San Juan** *R* California, USA
70D3 **San Juan** *R* Costa Rica/ Nicaragua
59D3 **San Juan** *R* Utah, USA
74C4 **San Juan** *State* Argentina
74E3 **San Juan Bautista** Paraguay
66B2 **San Juan Bautista** USA
70D3 **San Juan del Norte** Nicaragua
69D4 **San Juan de los Cayos** Venezuela
70D3 **San Juan del Sur** Nicaragua
58B1 **San Juan Is** USA
62A1 **San Juan Mts** USA
74C7 **San Julián** Argentina
50C4 **Sankuru** *R* Zaïre
66A2 **San Leandro** USA
40C2 **Sanliurfa** Turkey
72C3 **San Lorenzo** Colombia
72B4 **San Lorenzo, Cabo** *C* Ecuador
15B1 **San Lorenzo de Escorial** Spain
66B2 **San Lucas** USA
74C4 **San Luis** Argentina
59D4 **San Luis** USA
74C4 **San Luis** *State* Argentina
66B2 **San Luis Canal** USA
66B3 **San Luis Obispo** USA
66B3 **San Luis Obispo B** USA
70B2 **San Luis Potosí** Mexico
66B2 **San Luis Res** USA
16B3 **Sanluri** Sardinia, Italy
72E2 **San Maigualida** *Mts* Venezuela
63C3 **San Marcos** USA
76G3 **San Martin** *Base* Antarctica
74B7 **San Martin, Lago** Argentina/Chile
66A2 **San Mateo** USA
73G7 **San Matías** Bolivia
74D6 **San Matías, Golfo** *G* Argentina
31C3 **Sanmenxia** China
70D3 **San Miguel** El Salvador
66B3 **San Miguel** USA
66B3 **San Miguel** *I* USA
74C3 **San Miguel de Tucumán** Argentina
74F3 **San Miguel d'Oeste** Brazil
31D4 **Sanming** China
74D4 **San Nicolas** Argentina
56B3 **San Nicolas** *I* USA
47D2 **Sannieshof** South Africa
48B4 **Sanniquellie** Liberia
19E3 **Sanok** Poland
69B5 **San Onofore** Colombia
66D4 **San Onofre** USA
27F5 **San Pablo** Philippines
66A1 **San Pablo B** USA
48B4 **San Pédro** Ivory Coast
74D2 **San Pedro** Jujuy, Argentina
74E2 **San Pedro** Paraguay
59D4 **San Pedro** *R* USA
66C4 **San Pedro Chan** USA
56C4 **San Pedro de los Colonias** Mexico
70D3 **San Pedro Sula** Honduras
16B3 **San Pietro** *I* Sardinia, Italy
8D4 **Sanquar** Scotland
70A1 **San Quintin** Mexico
74C4 **San Rafael** Argentina
66A2 **San Rafael** USA
66C3 **San Rafael Mts** USA
16B2 **San Remo** Italy
62C2 **San Saba** *R* USA
71B2 **San Salvador** El Salvador
69C2 **San Salvador** *I* The Bahamas
74C2 **San Salvador de Jujuy** Argentina
15B1 **San Sebastián** Spain
16D2 **San Severo** Italy
66B3 **San Simeon** USA
72E7 **Santa Ana** Bolivia
70C3 **Santa Ana** Guatemala
66D4 **Santa Ana** USA
66D4 **Santa Ana Mts** USA
62C2 **Santa Anna** USA
70B2 **Santa Barbara** Mexico
66C3 **Santa Barbara** USA
66C4 **Santa Barbara** *I* USA
66B3 **Santa Barbara Chan** USA
66C3 **Santa Barbara Res** USA
66C4 **Santa Catalina** *I* USA
66C4 **Santa Catalina,G of** USA
74F3 **Santa Catarina** *State* Brazil
74G3 **Santa Catarina, Isla de** Brazil
69B2 **Santa Clara** Cuba
66B2 **Santa Clara** USA
66C3 **Santa Clara** *R* USA
74C8 **Santa Cruz** Argentina
72F7 **Santa Cruz** Bolivia
27F5 **Santa Cruz** Philippines
66A2 **Santa Cruz** USA
66C4 **Santa Cruz** *I* USA
59D4 **Santa Cruz** *R* USA
74B7 **Santa Cruz** *State* Argentina
75E2 **Santa Cruz Cabrália** Brazil
66C3 **Santa Cruz Chan** USA
48A2 **Santa Cruz de la Palma** Canary Islands
69B2 **Santa Cruz del Sur** Cuba
48A2 **Santa Cruz de Tenerife** Canary Islands
51C5 **Santa Cruz do Cuando** Angola
75C3 **Santa Cruz do Rio Pardo** Brazil
33F2 **Santa Cruz Is** Solomon Islands
66A2 **Santa Cruz Mts** USA
72F3 **Santa Elena** Venezuela
74D4 **Santa Fe** Argentina
62A1 **Santa Fe** USA
74D3 **Santa Fe** *State* Argentina
75B2 **Santa Helena de Goiás** Brazil
31B3 **Santai** China
74B8 **Santa Inés** *I* Chile
33E1 **Santa Isabel** *I* Solomon Islands
66B2 **Santa Lucia Range** *Mts* USA
48A4 **Santa Luzia** *I* Cape Verde
66B3 **Santa Margarita** USA
66D4 **Santa Margarita** *R* USA
70A2 **Santa Margarita, Isla** Mexico
74F3 **Santa Maria** Brazil
66B3 **Santa Maria** USA
48A1 **Santa Maria** *I* Azores
62A2 **Santa María** *R* Chihuahua, Mexico
47E2 **Santa Maria, Cabo de** *C* Mozambique
75D1 **Santa Maria da Vitória** Brazil
17D3 **Santa Maria di Leuca, Capo** *C* Italy
62A2 **Santa María Laguna de** *L* Mexico
69C4 **Santa Marta** Colombia
72D1 **Santa Marta, Sierra Nevada de** *Mts* Colombia
66C3 **Santa Monica** USA
66C4 **Santa Monica B** USA
75D1 **Santana** Brazil
74E4 **Santana do Livramento** Brazil
72C3 **Santander** Colombia
15B1 **Santander** Spain
15C2 **Santañy** Spain
66C3 **Santa Paula** USA
73K4 **Santa Quitéria** Brazil
73H4 **Santarém** Brazil
15A2 **Santarém** Portugal
75B2 **Santa Rita do Araguaia** Brazil
74D5 **Santa Rosa** Argentina
66A1 **Santa Rosa** California, USA
70D3 **Santa Rosa** Honduras
62B2 **Santa Rosa** New Mexico, USA
66B3 **Santa Rosa** *I* USA
70A2 **Santa Rosalía** Mexico
58C2 **Santa Rosa Range** *Mts* USA
73L5 **Santa Talhada** Brazil
75D2 **Santa Teresa** Brazil
16B2 **Santa Teresa di Gallura** Sardinia, Italy
66B3 **Santa Ynez** *R* USA
66B3 **Santa Ynez Mts** USA
67C2 **Santee** *R* USA
74B4 **Santiago** Chile
69C3 **Santiago** Dominican Republic
72B2 **Santiago** Panama
72C4 **Santiago** *R* Peru
15A1 **Santiago de Compostela** Spain
69B2 **Santiago de Cuba** Cuba
74D3 **Santiago del Estero** Argentina
74D3 **Santiago del Estero** *State* Argentina
66D4 **Santiago Peak** *Mt* USA
33F2 **Santo** Vanuatu
75C3 **Santo Amaro, Ilha** Brazil
75B3 **Santo Anastatácio** Brazil
74F3 **Santo Angelo** Brazil
48A4 **Santo Antão** *I* Cape Verde
75B3 **Santo Antônio da Platina** Brazil
75E1 **Santo Antônio de Jesus** Brazil
75A2 **Santo Antônio do Leverger** Brazil
69D3 **Santo Domingo** Dominican Republic
75C3 **Santos** Brazil
75D3 **Santos Dumont** Brazil
59C4 **Santo Tomas** Mexico
74E3 **Santo Tomé** Argentina
74B7 **San Valentin** *Mt* Chile
16C3 **San Vito, C** Sicily, Italy
28B2 **Sanyuanpu** China
51B4 **Sanza Pomba** Angola
75C3 **São Carlos** Brazil
75C1 **São Domingos** Brazil
73H5 **São Félix** Mato Grosso, Brazil
75D3 **São Fidélis** Brazil
75D2 **São Francisco** Brazil
73L5 **São Francisco** *R* Brazil
74G3 **São Francisco do Sul** Brazil
75C4 **São Francisco, Ilha de** Brazil
75C2 **São Gotardo** Brazil
51D4 **Sao Hill** Tanzania
75A2 **São Jerônimo, Serra de** *Mts* Brazil
75D3 **São João da Barra** Brazil
75C3 **São João da Boa Vista** Brazil
75C1 **São João d'Aliança** Brazil
75D2 **São João da Ponte** Brazil
75D3 **São João del Rei** Brazil
75D2 **São João do Paraíso** Brazil
75C3 **São Joaquim da Barra** Brazil
48A1 **São Jorge** *I* Azores
75C3 **São José do Rio Prêto** Brazil
75C3 **São José dos Campos** Brazil
75C4 **São José dos Pinhais** Brazil
75A2 **São Lourenço** *R* Brazil
73K4 **São Luís** Brazil
75C2 **São Marcos** *R* Brazil
73K4 **São Marcos, Baia de** *B* Brazil
75D2 **São Maria do Suaçui** Brazil
75E2 **São Mateus** Brazil
75D2 **São Mateus** *R* Brazil
48A1 **São Miguel** *I* Azores
75B1 **São Miguel de Araguaia** Brazil
14C2 **Saône** *R* France
48A4 **São Nicolau** *I* Cape Verde
75D1 **São Onofre** *R* Brazil
75C3 **São Paulo** Brazil
75B3 **São Paulo** *State* Brazil
71H3 **São Pedro e São Paulo** *Is* Atlantic Ocean
73K5 **São Raimundo Nonato** Brazil
75C2 **São Romão** Brazil
75C3 **São Sebastia do Paraíso** Brazil
75C3 **São Sebastião, Ilha de** Brazil
75B2 **São Simão,Barragem de** Brazil
75B2 **São Simão** Goias, Brazil
75C3 **São Simão** São Paulo, Brazil
48A4 **São Tiago** *I* Cape Verde
48C4 **São Tomé** *I* W Africa
48C4 **Sao Tome and Principe** *Republic* W Africa
75D3 **São Tomé, Cabo de** *C* Brazil
48B2 **Saoura** *Watercourse* Algeria
75A1 **Saouriuiná** *R* Brazil
75C3 **São Vicente** Brazil

Shangsi Slutsk

31B5 **Shangsi** China
31C3 **Shang Xian** China
7D4 **Shanklin** England
9B3 **Shannon** *R* Irish Republic
28B2 **Shansonggang** China
26G1 **Shantarskiye Ostrova** *I* Russian Federation
31D5 **Shantou** China
31C2 **Shanxi** *Province* China
31D3 **Shan Xian** China
31C5 **Shaoguan** China
31E4 **Shaoxing** China
31C4 **Shaoyang** China
8D2 **Shapinsay** *I* Scotland
45D2 **Shaqqā** Syria
41E4 **Shaqra'** Saudi Arabia
31A1 **Sharhulsan** Mongolia
29D2 **Shari** Japan
41G2 **Sharifābād** Iran
41G4 **Sharjah** UAE
32A3 **Shark B** Australia
41G2 **Sharlauk** Turkmenistan
45C2 **Sharon,Plain of** Israel
68B3 **Sharpsburg** USA
40C3 **Sharqi, Jebel esh** *Mts* Lebanon/Syria
20H4 **Sharya** Russian Federation
50D3 **Shashamenē** Ethiopia
47D1 **Shashani** *R* Zimbabwe
47D1 **Shashe** *R* Botswana
31C3 **Shashi** China
58B2 **Shasta L** USA
58B2 **Shasta,Mt** USA
45D1 **Shaṭḥah at Taḥtā** Syria
41E3 **Shaṭṭ al Gharraf** *R* Iraq
45C3 **Shaubak** Jordan
66C2 **Shaver L** USA
68C2 **Shawangunk Mt** USA
64B2 **Shawano** USA
65E1 **Shawinigan** Canada
63C1 **Shawnee** Oklahoma, USA
60B2 **Shawnee** Wyoming, USA
31D4 **Sha Xian** China
32B3 **Shay Gap** Australia
45D2 **Shaykh Miskīn** Syria
50E2 **Shaykh 'Uthmān** Yemen
21F5 **Shchigry** Russian Federation
21E5 **Shchors** Ukraine
24J4 **Shchuchinsk** Kazakhstan
50E3 **Shebele** *R* Ethiopia
64B2 **Sheboygan** USA
50B3 **Shebshi Mts** Nigeia
9C3 **Sheelin, L** Irish Republic
9C2 **Sheep Haven** *Estuary* Irish Republic
7E4 **Sheerness** England
45C2 **Shefar'am** Israel
63E2 **Sheffield** Alabama, USA
7D3 **Sheffield** England
62B2 **Sheffield** Texas, USA
8C3 **Sheil, Loch** *L* Scotland
42C2 **Shekhupura** Pakistan
25T2 **Shelagskiy, Mys** *C* Russian Federation
68D1 **Shelburne Falls** USA
64B2 **Shelby** Michigan, USA
58D1 **Shelby** Montana, USA
67B1 **Shelby** N Carolina, USA
64B3 **Shelbyville** Indiana, USA
67A1 **Shelbyville** Tennessee, USA
61D2 **Sheldon** USA
54C4 **Shelikof Str** USA
58D2 **Shelley** USA
34D2 **Shellharbour** Australia
35A3 **Shelter Pt** New Zealand
58B1 **Shelton** USA
41E1 **Shemakha** Azerbaijan
61D2 **Shenandoah** USA
65D3 **Shenandoah** *R* USA
65D3 **Shenandoah Nat Pk** USA
48C4 **Shendam** Nigeria
50D2 **Shendi** Sudan
20G3 **Shenkursk** Russian Federation
31C2 **Shenmu** China
31E1 **Shenyang** China
31C5 **Shenzhen** China
42D3 **Sheopur** India
19F2 **Shepetovka** Ukraine
68B3 **Shepherdstown** USA
34C3 **Shepparton** Australia
7E4 **Sheppey** *I* England
55K2 **Sherard,C** Canada
7C4 **Sherborne** England
48A4 **Sherbro I** Sierra Leone
65E1 **Sherbrooke** Canada
68C1 **Sherburne** USA
42C3 **Shergarh** India
63D2 **Sheridan** Arkansas, USA
60B2 **Sheridan** Wyoming, USA
7E3 **Sheringham** England
63C2 **Sherman** USA
18B2 **'s-Hertogenbosch** Netherlands
10C1 **Shetland** *Division* Scotland
10C1 **Shetland** *Is* Scotland
21J7 **Shevchenko** Kazakhstan
60D1 **Sheyenne** USA
60D1 **Sheyenne** *R* USA
41F4 **Sheyk Sho'eyb** *I* Iran
8B3 **Shiant, Sd of** Scotland
26J2 **Shiashkotan** *I* Kuril Is, Russian Federation
42B1 **Shibarghan** Afghanistan
29D3 **Shibata** Japan
29D2 **Shibetsu** Japan
49F1 **Shibîn el Kom** Egypt
45A3 **Shibîn el Qanâtir** Egypt
29C3 **Shibukawa** Japan
68B2 **Shickshinny** USA
28A3 **Shidao** China
31C2 **Shijiazhuang** China
42B3 **Shikarpur** Pakistan
26G3 **Shikoku** *I* Japan
29B4 **Shikoku-sanchi** *Mts* Japan
26H2 **Shikotan** *I* Russian Federation
29D2 **Shikotsu-ko** *L* Japan
20G3 **Shilega** Russian Federation
43F3 **Shiliguri** India
26E1 **Shilka** Russian Federation
26E1 **Shilka** *R* Russian Federation
68C2 **Shillington** USA
43G3 **Shillong** India
20G5 **Shilovo** Russian Federation
28B4 **Shimabara** Japan
29C4 **Shimada** Japan
26F1 **Shimanovsk** Russian Federation
29D3 **Shimizu** Japan
29C4 **Shimoda** Japan
44B3 **Shimoga** India
28C4 **Shimonoseki** Japan
29C3 **Shinano** *R* Japan
41G5 **Shināş** Oman
38E2 **Shindand** Afghanistan
68A2 **Shinglehouse** USA
29D4 **Shingū** Japan
29D3 **Shinjō** Japan
8C2 **Shin, Loch** *L* Scotland
29D3 **Shinminato** Japan
45D1 **Shinshār** Syria
50D4 **Shinyanga** Tanzania
29E3 **Shiogama** Japan
29C4 **Shiono-misaki** *C* Japan
31A5 **Shiping** China
68B2 **Shippensburg** USA
62A1 **Shiprock** USA
31B3 **Shiquan** China
29D3 **Shirakawa** Japan
29C3 **Shirane-san** *Mt* Japan
41F4 **Shīraz** Iran
45A3 **Shirbîn** Egypt
29F2 **Shiretoko-misaki** *C* Japan
29D2 **Shiriya-saki** *C* Japan
41F3 **Shīr Kūh** *Mt* Iran
29C3 **Shirotori** Japan
41G2 **Shirvān** Iran
54B3 **Shishmaref** USA
31B2 **Shitanjing** China
64B3 **Shively** USA
42D3 **Shivpuri** India
45C3 **Shivta** *Hist Site* Israel
59D3 **Shivwits Plat** USA
51D5 **Shiwa Ngandu** Zambia
31C3 **Shiyan** China
31B2 **Shizuishan** China
29C3 **Shizuoka** Japan
17D2 **Shkodër** Albania
19G2 **Shkov** Belarus
25L1 **Shmidta, Ostrov** *I* Russian Federation
34D2 **Shoalhaven** *R* Australia
28B4 **Shobara** Japan
44B3 **Shoranūr** India
44B2 **Shorāpur** India
59C3 **Shoshone** California, USA
58D2 **Shoshone** Idaho, USA
58E2 **Shoshone** *R* USA
58D2 **Shoshone L** USA
59C3 **Shoshone Mts** USA
58E2 **Shoshoni** USA
21E5 **Shostka** Ukraine
59D4 **Show Low** USA
63D2 **Shreveport** USA
7C3 **Shrewsbury** England
7C3 **Shropshire** *County* England
31E1 **Shuangliao** China
28B2 **Shuangyang** China
26G2 **Shuangyashan** China
21K6 **Shubar-Kuduk** Kazakhstan
20N2 **Shuga** Russian Federation
31D2 **Shu He** *R* China
31A4 **Shuicheng** China
42C3 **Shujaabad** Pakistan
42D4 **Shujālpur** India
26C2 **Shule He** *R* China
17F2 **Shumen** Bulgaria
20H4 **Shumerlya** Russian Federation
31D4 **Shuncheng** China
54C3 **Shungnak** USA
31C2 **Shuo Xian** China
38D3 **Shūr Gaz** Iran
51C5 **Shurugwi** Zimbabwe
20G4 **Shuya** Russian Federation
30B1 **Shwebo** Burma
30B2 **Shwegyin** Burma
42A2 **Siah Koh** *Mts* Afghanistan
42C2 **Sialkot** Pakistan
Sian = Xi'an
27F6 **Siargao** *I* Philippines
27F6 **Siaton** Philippines
19E1 **Šiauliai** Lithuania
20K5 **Sibay** Russian Federation
47E2 **Sibayi L** South Africa
16D2 **Šibenik** Croatia
25L5 **Siberia** Russian Federation
27C7 **Siberut** *I* Indonesia
42B3 **Sibi** Pakistan
50B4 **Sibiti** Congo
50D4 **Sibiti** *R* Tanzania
17E1 **Sibiu** Romania
61D2 **Sibley** USA
27C6 **Sibolga** Indonesia
43G3 **Sibsāgar** India
27E6 **Sibu** Malaysia
50B3 **Sibut** Central African Republic
31A3 **Sichuan** *Province* China
Sicilia = Sicily
16C3 **Sicilian Chan** Italy/Tunisia
16C3 **Sicily** *I* Medit Sea
72D6 **Sicuani** Peru
42C4 **Siddhapur** India
44B2 **Siddipet** India
43E4 **Sidhi** India
49E1 **Sidi Barrani** Egypt
15B2 **Sidi-bel-Abbès** Algeria
48B1 **Sidi Kacem** Morocco
8D3 **Sidlaw Hills** Scotland
76F5 **Sidley,Mt** Antarctica
7C4 **Sidmouth** England
58B1 **Sidney** Canada
60C1 **Sidney** Montana, USA
60C2 **Sidney** Nebraska, USA
68C1 **Sidney** New York, USA
64C2 **Sidney** Ohio, USA
67B2 **Sidney Lanier,L** USA
45C2 **Sidon** Lebanon
75B3 **Sidrolândia** Brazil
19E2 **Siedlce** Poland
13D2 **Sieg** *R* Germany
13D2 **Siegburg** Germany
13D2 **Siegen** Germany
30C3 **Siem Reap** Cambodia
16C2 **Siena** Italy
19D2 **Sierpc** Poland
62A2 **Sierra Blanca** USA
70B2 **Sierra de los Alamitos** *Mts* Mexico
48A4 **Sierra Leone** *Republic* Africa
48A4 **Sierra Leone,C** Sierra Leone
70B3 **Sierra Madre del Sur** Mexico
66B3 **Sierra Madre Mts** USA
70B2 **Sierra Madre Occidental** *Mts* Mexico
70B2 **Sierra Madre Oriental** *Mts* Mexico
56C4 **Sierra Mojada** Mexico
59B3 **Sierra Nevada** *Mts* USA
59D4 **Sierra Vista** USA
75A3 **Siete Puntas** *R* Paraguay
17E3 **Sífnos** *I* Greece
15B2 **Sig** Algeria
20E2 **Sig** Russian Federation
19E3 **Sighetu Marmaţiei** Romania
17E1 **Sighişoara** Romania
12B1 **Siglufjörður** Iceland
72A1 **Siguatepeque** Honduras
15B1 **Sigüenza** Spain
48B3 **Siguiri** Guinea
30C3 **Sihanoukville** Cambodia
42D4 **Sihora** India
40D2 **Siirt** Turkey
43J1 **Sikandarabad** India
42D3 **Sīkar** India
42B2 **Sikaram** *Mt* Afghanistan
48B3 **Sikasso** Mali
63E1 **Sikeston** USA
26G2 **Sikhote-Alin'** *Mts* Russian Federation
17F3 **Síkinos** *I* Greece
17E3 **Sikionía** Greece
43F3 **Sikkim** *State* India
25O3 **Siktyakh** Russian Federation
15A1 **Sil** *R* Spain
43G4 **Silchar** India
48C2 **Silet** Algeria
43E3 **Silgarhi** Nepal
40B2 **Silifke** Turkey
45D1 **Şilinfah** Syria
39G2 **Siling Co** *L* China
17F2 **Silistra** Bulgaria
20A3 **Siljan** *L* Sweden
12F7 **Silkeborg** Denmark
6C2 **Silloth** England
63D1 **Siloam Springs** USA
63D2 **Silsbee** USA
50B2 **Siltou** *Well* Chad
19E1 **Šilute** Lithuania
40D2 **Silvan** Turkey
75C2 **Silvania** Brazil
42C4 **Silvassa** India
61E1 **Silver Bay** USA
59C3 **Silver City** Nevada, USA
62A2 **Silver City** New Mexico, USA
58B2 **Silver Lake** USA
66D2 **Silver Peak Range** *Mts* USA
68B3 **Silver Spring** USA
34B2 **Silverton** Australia
62A1 **Silverton** USA
27E6 **Simanggang** Malaysia
30C1 **Simao** China
65D1 **Simard,L** Canada
41E3 **Simareh** *R* Iran
17F3 **Simav** Turkey
17F3 **Simav** *R* Turkey
65D2 **Simcoe,L** Canada
27C6 **Simeulue** *I* Indonesia
21E7 **Simferopol'** Ukraine
17F3 **Sími** *I* Greece
43E3 **Simikot** Nepal
42D2 **Simla** India
60C3 **Simla** USA
13D2 **Simmern** Germany
66C3 **Simmler** USA
47B3 **Simonstown** South Africa
14D2 **Simplon** *Mt* Switzerland
16B1 **Simplon** *Pass* Italy/Switzerland
54C2 **Simpson,C** USA
32C3 **Simpson Desert** Australia
55K3 **Simpson Pen** Canada
12G7 **Simrishamn** Sweden
26J2 **Simushir** *I* Kuril Is, Russian Federation
50E3 **Sina Dhaga** Somalia
40B4 **Sinai** *Pen* Egypt
72C2 **Sincelejo** Colombia
67B2 **Sinclair,L** USA
75D1 **Sincora, Serra do** *Mts* Brazil
42D3 **Sind** *R* India
42B3 **Sindh** *Province* Pakistan
17F3 **Sindirği** Turkey
43F4 **Sindri** India
15A2 **Sines** Portugal
15A2 **Sines, Cabo de** *C* Portugal
50D2 **Singa** Sudan
30C5 **Singapore** *Republic* SE Asia
30C5 **Singapore,Str of** SE Asia
27E7 **Singaraja** Indonesia
13E4 **Singen** Germany
50D4 **Singida** Tanzania
43H3 **Singkaling Hkamti** Burma
27D6 **Singkawang** Indonesia
27D7 **Singkep** *I* Indonesia
34D2 **Singleton** Australia
30B1 **Singu** Burma
47E1 **Singuédeze** *R* Mozambique
28A3 **Sin'gye** N Korea
28A2 **Sinhŭng** N Korea
16B2 **Siniscola** Sardinia, Italy
40D2 **Sinjár** Iraq
42B2 **Sinkai Hills** *Mts* Afghanistan
50D2 **Sinkat** Sudan
39G1 **Sinkiang** *Autonomous Region* China
43K2 **Sinkobabad** India
73H2 **Sinnamary** French Guiana
45B4 **Sinn Bishr, Gebel** *Mt* Egypt
28A3 **Sinnyong** S Korea
40C1 **Sinop** Turkey
28A2 **Sinpa** N Korea
28A2 **Sinp'o** N Korea
28A3 **Sinp'yong** N Korea
17E1 **Sîntana** Romania
27E6 **Sintang** Indonesia
63C3 **Sinton** USA
15A2 **Sintra** Portugal
72C2 **Sinú** *R* Colombia
28A2 **Sinŭiju** N Korea
19D3 **Siófok** Hungary
16B1 **Sion** Switzerland
61D2 **Sioux City** USA
61D2 **Sioux Falls** USA
69L1 **Siparia** Trinidad
28A2 **Siping** China
76F3 **Siple** *Base* Antarctica
76F5 **Siple I** Antarctica
27C7 **Sipora** *I* Indonesia
63E2 **Sipsey** *R* USA
45B4 **Sîq, Wadi el** Egypt
44B3 **Sira** India
Siracusa = Syracuse
43F4 **Sirajganj** Bangladesh
41F5 **Şīr Banī Yās** *I* UAE
32C2 **Sir Edward Pellew Group** *Is* Australia
17F1 **Siret** *R* Romania
40C3 **Sirhān, Wādi as** *V* Jordan/Saudi Arabia
40D2 **Şirnak** Turkey
42C4 **Sirohi** India
44C2 **Sironcha** India
42D4 **Sironj** India
17E3 **Síros** *I* Greece
66C3 **Sirretta Peak** *Mt* USA
41F4 **Sīrrī** *I* Iran
42C3 **Sirsa** India
44A3 **Sirsi** India
49D1 **Sirt** Libya
49D1 **Sirte Desert** Libya
49D1 **Sirte,G of** Libya
21H9 **Sirvan** *R* Iran
16D1 **Sisak** Croatia
30C2 **Sisaket** Thailand
30C3 **Sisophon** Cambodia
66B3 **Sisquoc** USA
66C3 **Sisquoc** *R* USA
61D1 **Sisseton** USA
13B3 **Sissonne** France
14D3 **Sisteron** France
25L4 **Sistig Khem** Russian Federation
43E3 **Sītāpur** India
17F3 **Sitía** Greece
75C1 **Sítio d'Abadia** Brazil
54E4 **Sitka** USA
30B2 **Sittang** *R* Burma
13C2 **Sittard** Netherlands
43G4 **Sittwe** Burma
40C2 **Sivas** Turkey
40C2 **Siverek** Turkey
40B2 **Sivrihisar** Turkey
25S4 **Sivuchiy, Mys** *C* Russian Federation
49E2 **Siwa** Egypt
42D2 **Siwalik Range** *Mts* India
43E3 **Siwalik Range** *Mts* Nepal
20G3 **Siya** Russian Federation
31D3 **Siyang** China
18C1 **Sjaelland** *I* Denmark
12G7 **Skagen** Denmark
12F7 **Skagerrak** *Str* Denmark/Norway
58B1 **Skagit** *R* USA
58B1 **Skagit Mt** Canada
54E4 **Skagway** USA
68B1 **Skaneateles** USA
68B1 **Skaneateles L** USA
12G7 **Skara** Sweden
19E2 **Skarzysko-Kamienna** Poland
54F4 **Skeena** *R* Canada
54F4 **Skeene Mts** Canada
54D3 **Skeenjek** *R* USA
7E3 **Skegness** England
20B2 **Skellefte** *R* Sweden
12J6 **Skellefteå** Sweden
9C3 **Skerries** Irish Republic
17E3 **Skíathos** *I* Greece
54E4 **Skidegate** Canada
19E2 **Skiemiewice** Poland
12F7 **Skien** Norway
16B3 **Skikda** Algeria
6D3 **Skipton** England
17E3 **Skíros** *I* Greece
12F7 **Skive** Denmark
18B1 **Skjern** Denmark
55O3 **Skjoldungen** Greenland
64B2 **Skokie** USA
17E3 **Skópelos** *I* Greece
17E2 **Skopje** Macedonia, Yugoslavia
12G7 **Skövde** Sweden
25O4 **Skovorodino** Russian Federation
65F2 **Skowhegan** USA
47E1 **Skukuza** South Africa
54C3 **Skwentna** USA
18D2 **Skwierzyna** Poland
10B2 **Skye** *I* Scotland
12G7 **Slagelse** Denmark
27D7 **Slamet** *Mt* Indonesia
9C3 **Slaney** *R* Irish Republic
17E2 **Slatina** Romania
54G3 **Slave** *R* Canada
19G2 **Slavgorod** Belarus
24J4 **Slavgorod** Russian Federation
19F2 **Slavuta** Ukraine
21F6 **Slavyansk** Ukraine
18D2 **Sławno** Poland
7D3 **Sleaford** England
8C3 **Sleat,Sound of** *Chan* Scotland
54C3 **Sleetmute** USA
63E2 **Slidell** USA
68C2 **Slide Mt** USA
9B3 **Slieve Aughty Mts** Irish Republic
9C3 **Slieve Bloom** *Mts* Irish Republic
10B3 **Sligo** Irish Republic
10B3 **Sligo B** Irish Republic
17F2 **Sliven** Bulgaria
59C3 **Sloan** USA
17F2 **Slobozia** Romania
19F2 **Slonim** Belarus
7D4 **Slough** England
66B2 **Slough** *R* USA
19D3 **Slovakia** *Republic* Europe
16C1 **Slovenia** *Republic* Europe
18C2 **Słubice** Poland
19F2 **Sluch'** *R* Ukraine
18D2 **Słupsk** Poland
19F2 **Slutsk** Belarus
19F2 **Slutsk** *R* Belarus

60C2 Thedford USA
48A3 The Gambia *Republic* W Africa
41F4 The Gulf SW Asia
18A2 The Hague Netherlands
54H3 Thelon *R* Canada
7E4 The Naze *Pt* England
32E3 Theodore Australia
59D4 Theodore Roosevelt L USA
72F6 Theodore Roosevelt, R Brazil
54H4 The Pas Canada
17E2 Thermaïkós Kólpos *G* Greece
58E2 Thermopolis USA
54F2 Thesiger B Canada
64C1 Thessalon Canada
17E2 Thessaloníki Greece
7E3 Thetford England
65E1 Thetford Mines Canada
47D2 Theunissen South Africa
63D3 Thibodaux USA
54J4 Thicket Portage Canada
61D1 Thief River Falls USA
58B2 Thielsen,Mt USA
14C2 Thiers France
48A3 Thiès Senegal
50D4 Thika Kenya
43F3 Thimphu Bhutan
14D2 Thionville France
17F3 Thira *I* Greece
6D2 Thirsk England
44B4 Thiruvananthapuram India
12F7 Thisted Denmark
27E5 Thitu S China Sea
17E3 Thívai Greece
14C2 Thiviers France
66C2 Thomas A Edison,L USA
67B2 Thomaston Georgia, USA
65F2 Thomaston Maine, USA
9C3 Thomastown Irish Republic
63E2 Thomasville Alabama, USA
67B2 Thomasville Georgia, USA
67C1 Thomasville N Carolina, USA
55J2 Thom Bay Canada
54J4 Thompson Canada
61E2 Thompson *R* USA
58C1 Thompson Falls USA
54G3 Thompson Landing Canada
68D2 Thompsonville USA
67B2 Thomson USA
32D3 Thomson *R* Australia
30C3 Thon Buri Thailand
30B2 Thongwa Burma
62A1 Thoreau USA
6D2 Thornaby England
7D3 Thorne England
8D4 Thornhill Scotland
14B2 Thouars France
65D2 Thousand Is Canada/USA
58D1 Three Forks USA
64B1 Three Lakes USA
30B2 Three Pagodas P Thailand
48B4 Three Points, C Ghana
66C2 Three Rivers California, USA
64B2 Three Rivers Michigan, USA
62C3 Three Rivers Texas, USA
58B2 Three Sisters *Mt* USA
55M2 Thule Greenland
16B1 Thun Switzerland
64B1 Thunder Bay Canada
30B4 Thung Song Thailand
18C2 Thüringen *State* Germany
18C2 Thüringer Wald *Upland* Germany
9C3 Thurles Irish Republic
8D2 Thurso Scotland
76F4 Thurston I Antarctica
34B1 Thylungra Australia
31B5 Tiandong China
31B5 Tian'e China
31D2 Tianjin China
31B5 Tianlin China
28B2 Tianqiaoling China
24J5 Tian Shan *Mts* China/Kirgizia
31B3 Tianshui China
31A2 Tianzhu China
15C2 Tiaret Algeria
75B3 Tibagi *R* Brazil
48D4 Tibati Cameroon
45C2 Tiberias Israel
45C2 Tiberias,L Israel
Tiber,R = Tevere,R
58D1 Tiber Res USA
50B1 Tibesti *Mountain Region* Chad
39G2 Tibet *Autonomous Region* China
34B1 Tibooburra Australia
43E3 Tibrikot Nepal
70A2 Tiburón I Mexico
48B3 Tichitt Mauritius

48A2 Tichla Morocco
65E2 Ticonderoga USA
70D2 Ticul Mexico
48C2 Tidikelt, Plaine du *Desert Region* Algeria
48A3 Tidjikja Mauritius
48A3 Tidra, Isla Mauritius
13C2 Tiel Netherlands
28A2 Tieling China
13B2 Tielt Belgium
13C2 Tienen Belgium
13E4 Tiengen Germany
Tientsin = Tianjin
12H6 Tierp Sweden
62A1 Tierra Amarilla USA
70C3 Tierra Blanca Mexico
71C9 Tierra del Fuego *I* Argentina/Chile
74C8 Tierra del Fuego *Territory* Argentina
74C8 Tierra del Fuego, Isla Grande de Argentina/Chile
75C3 Tietê Brazil
75B3 Tiete *R* Brazil
64C2 Tiffin USA
67B2 Tifton USA
25R4 Tigil Russian Federation
72C4 Tigre *R* Peru
72F2 Tigre *R* Venezuela
50D2 Tigre *Region* Ethiopia
41E3 Tigris *R* Iraq
45B4 Tîh, Gebel el *Upland* Egypt
59C4 Tijuana Mexico
42D4 Tikamgarh India
21G6 Tikhoretsk Russian Federation
20E4 Tikhvin Russian Federation
33F2 Tikopia *I* Solomon Islands
41D3 Tikrît Iraq
25O2 Tiksi Russian Federation
13C2 Tilburg Netherlands
7E4 Tilbury England
74C2 Tilcara Argentina
34B1 Tilcha Australia
48C3 Tilemis, Vallée du Mali
43K2 Tilhar India
30A1 Tilin Burma
48C3 Tillabéri Niger
58B1 Tillamook USA
44E4 Tillanchong *I* Nicobar Is, Indian Ocean
48C3 Tillia Niger
6D2 Till, R England
17F3 Tílos *I* Greece
34B2 Tilpa Australia
8D3 Tilt *R* Scotland
20H2 Timanskiy Kryazh *Mts* Russian Federation
35B2 Timaru New Zealand
21F6 Timashevsk Russian Federation
17E3 Timbákion Greece
63D3 Timbalier B USA
48B3 Timbédra Mauritius
Timbuktu = Tombouctou
48B3 Timétrine Monts *Mts* Mali
48C3 Timia Niger
17E1 Timiş *R* Romania
48C2 Timimoun Algeria
17E1 Timişoara Romania
64C1 Timmins Canada
32B1 Timor *I* Indonesia
32B2 Timor S Australia/Indonesia
45B3 Timsâh,L Egypt
67A1 Tims Ford L USA
27F6 Tinaca Pt Philippines
69D5 Tinaco Venezuela
44B3 Tindivanam India
48B2 Tindouf Algeria
66C2 Tinemaha Res USA
48B2 Tinfouchy Algeria
48C2 Tin Fouye Algeria
55O3 Tingmiarmiut Greenland
72C5 Tingo María Peru
48B3 Tingrela Ivory Coast
43F3 Tingri China
75E1 Tinharé, Ilha de Brazil
27H5 Tinian Pacific Ocean
74C3 Tinogasta Argentina
17F3 Tínos *I* Greece
43H3 Tinsukia India
7B4 Tintagel Head *Pt* England
48C2 Tin Tarabine *Watercourse* Algeria
34B3 Tintinara Australia
48C2 Tin Zaouaten Algeria
60C1 Tioga USA
68B2 Tioga *R* USA
66C2 Tioga P USA
30C5 Tioman *I* Malaysia
68B1 Tioughnioga *R* USA
10B3 Tipperary Irish Republic
9C3 Tipperary *County* Irish Republic
66C2 Tipton California, USA
61E3 Tipton Missouri, USA
44B3 Tiptūr India

17D2 Tiranë Albania
19F3 Tiraspol Moldavia
45A3 Tir'at el Ismâiliya *Canal* Egypt
17F3 Tire Turkey
40C1 Tirebolu Turkey
8B3 Tiree *I* Scotland
17F2 Tîrgovişte Romania
17E1 Tîrgu Jiu Romania
17E1 Tîrgu Mureş Romania
42C1 Tirich Mir *Mt* Pakistan
48A2 Tiris *Region* Morocco
20K5 Tirlyanskiy Russian Federation
17E1 Tîrnãveni Romania
17E3 Tírnavos Greece
42D4 Tirodi India
16B2 Tirso *R* Sardinia, Italy
44B4 Tiruchchendŭr India
44B3 Tiruchchirãppalli India
44B4 Tirunelveli India
44B3 Tirupati India
44B3 Tiruppattŭr India
44B3 Tiruppur India
44B3 Tiruvannãmalai India
63C2 Tishomingo USA
45D2 Tisīyah Syria
19E3 Tisza *R* Hungary
72E7 Titicaca, Lago Bolivia/Peru
43E4 Titlagarh India
17E2 Titov Veles Macedonia, Yugoslavia
50C3 Titule Zaire
67B3 Titusville USA
8B2 Tiumpan Head *Pt* Scotland
7C4 Tiverton England
16C2 Tivoli Italy
70D2 Tizimín Mexico
15C2 Tizi Ouzou Algeria
48B2 Tiznit Morocco
48B1 Tlemcen Algeria
51E5 Toamasina Madagascar
29C4 Toba Japan
42B2 Toba and Kakar Ranges *Mts* Pakistan
69E4 Tobago *I* Caribbean Sea
27F6 Tobelo Indonesia
64C1 Tobermory Canada
8B3 Tobermory Scotland
27G6 Tobi *I* Pacific Ocean
59C2 Tobin,Mt USA
29C3 Tobi-shima *I* Japan
27D7 Toboah Indonesia
24H4 Tobol *R* Russian Federation
27F7 Toboli Indonesia
24H4 Tobol'sk Russian Federation
Tobruk = Tubruq
20J2 Tobseda Russian Federation
73J4 Tocantins *R* Brazil
73J6 Tocantins *State* Brazil
67B2 Toccoa USA
74B2 Tocopilla Chile
74C2 Tocorpuri Bolivia/Chile
72E1 Tocuyo *R* Venezuela
42D3 Toda India
28B3 Todong S Korea
73L6 Todos os Santos, Baia de *B* Brazil
56B4 Todos Santos Mexico
59C4 Todos Santos,B de Mexico
33H2 Tofua *I* Tonga
32B1 Togian, Kepulauan *I* Indonesia
48C4 Togo *Republic* W Africa
31C1 Togtoh China
62A1 Tohatchi USA
29E2 Tokachi *R* Japan
29C3 Tokamachi Japan
50D2 Tokar Sudan
26F4 Tokara Retto *Arch* Japan
40C1 Tokat Turkey
28B3 Tok-do *I* S Korea
33H1 Tokelau Is Pacific Ocean
39F1 Tokmak Kirgizia
35C1 Tokomaru Bay New Zealand
26F4 Tokuno *I* Ryukyu Is, Japan
29C4 Tokushima Japan
28B4 Tokuyama Japan
29D3 Tōkyō Japan
35C1 Tolaga Bay New Zealand
51E6 Tôlañaro Madagascar
73H8 Toledo Brazil
15B2 Toledo Spain
64C2 Toledo USA
63D2 Toledo Bend Res USA
51E6 Toliara Madagascar
72C2 Tolina *Mt* Colombia
19F2 Tolochin Belarus
15B1 Tolosa Spain
28A4 Tolsan-do *I* S Korea
74B5 Toltén Chile
70C3 Toluca Mexico
20H5 Tol'yatti Russian Federation
64A2 Tomah USA
64B1 Tomahawk USA

29E2 Tomakomai Japan
15A2 Tomar Portugal
19E2 Tomaszów Mazowiecka Poland
63E2 Tombigbee *R* USA
51B4 Tomboco Angola
75D3 Tombos Brazil
48B3 Tombouctou Mali
59E4 Tombstone USA
51B5 Tombua Angola
47D1 Tomburke South Africa
74B5 Tomé Chile
15B2 Tomelloso Spain
28A4 Tomie Japan
8D3 Tomintoul Scotland
32B3 Tomkinson Range *Mts* Australia
25O4 Tommot Russian Federation
17E2 Tomorrit *Mt* Albania
24J4 Tomsk *Division* Russian Federation
24K4 Tomsk Russian Federation
68C3 Toms River USA
70C3 Tonalá Mexico
58C1 Tonasket USA
7E4 Tonbridge England
33H3 Tonga *Is, Kingdom* Pacific Ocean
47E2 Tongaat South Africa
33H3 Tongatapu *I* Tonga
33H3 Tongatapu Group *Is* Tonga
33H3 Tonga Trench Pacific Ocean
28A2 Tongchang N Korea
31D3 Tongcheng China
31B2 Tongchuan China
31A2 Tongde China
13C2 Tongeren Belgium
30E2 Tonggu Jiao *I* China
31A5 Tonghai China
28B2 Tonghua China
28B3 Tongjosŏn-Man *S* N Korea
30D1 Tongkin,G of China/Vietnam
31E1 Tongliao China
31D3 Tongling China
28A3 Tongnae S Korea
34B2 Tongo Australia
31B4 Tongren Guizhou, China
31A2 Tongren Qinghai, China
43G3 Tongsa Bhutan
30B1 Tongta Burma
26C3 Tongtian He *R* China
8C2 Tongue Scotland
60B1 Tongue *R* USA
31D2 Tong Xian China
31B2 Tongxin China
28A2 Tongyuanpu China
31B4 Tongzi China
25L5 Tonhil Mongolia
56C4 Tónichi Mexico
50C3 Tonj Sudan
42D3 Tonk India
63C1 Tonkawa USA
30C3 Tonle Sap *L* Cambodia
13C4 Tonnerre France
29D3 Tono Japan
59C3 Tonopah USA
58D2 Tooele USA
34D1 Toogoolawah Australia
34B1 Toompine Australia
34D1 Toowoomba Australia
66C1 Topaz L USA
61D3 Topeka USA
59D4 Topock USA
56C4 Topolobampo Mexico
20E2 Topozero, Ozero *L* Russian Federation
58B1 Toppenish USA
68E1 Topsfield USA
50D3 Tor Ethiopia
17F3 Torbalı Turkey
41G2 Torbat-e-Heydariyeh Iran
15A1 Tordesillas Spain
7C4 Torfaen *County* Wales
18C2 Torgau Germany
13B2 Torhout Belgium
26H3 Tori *I* Japan
Torino = Turin
50D3 Torit Sudan
75B2 Torixoreu Brazil
15A1 Tormes *R* Spain
12J5 Torne *R* Sweden
12H5 Torneträsk *L* Sweden
55M4 Torngat *Mts* Canada
12J5 Tornio Finland
74C3 Toro, Cerro del *Mt* Argentina/Chile
65D2 Toronto Canada
20E4 Toropets Russian Federation
50D3 Tororo Uganda
Toros, Dağlari = Taurus Mts
7C4 Torquay England
66C4 Torrance USA
15A2 Torrão Portugal
15C1 Torreblanca Spain
16C2 Torre del Greco Italy
15B1 Torrelavega Spain

15B2 Torremolinos Spain
32C4 Torrens, L Australia
56C4 Torreón Mexico
33F2 Torres Is Vanuatu
32D2 Torres Str Australia
15A2 Torres Vedras Portugal
7B4 Torridge *R* England
8C3 Torridon, Loch *Inlet* Scotland
68D2 Torrington Connecticut, USA
60C2 Torrington Wyoming, USA
12D3 Tórshavn Faeroes
15C1 Tortosa Spain
15C1 Tortosa, Cabo de *C* Spain
72C3 Tortugas, Golfo de Colombia
41G2 Torūd Iran
19D2 Toruń Poland
10B2 Tory I Irish Republic
9B2 Tory Sol Irish Republic
20E4 Torzhok Russian Federation
29B4 Tosa Japan
28C4 Tosashimizu Japan
29C4 Tosa-Wan *B* Japan
29C4 To-shima *I* Japan
12L7 Tosno Russian Federation
28B4 Tosu Japan
40B1 Tosya Turkey
15B2 Totana Spain
20G4 Tot'ma Russian Federation
7C4 Totnes England
73G2 Totness Surinam
34C2 Tottenham Australia
29C3 Tottori Japan
48B4 Touba Ivory Coast
48A3 Touba Senegal
48B1 Toubkal *Mt* Morocco
13B4 Toucy France
48B3 Tougan Burkina
48C1 Touggourt Algeria
48A3 Tougué Guinea
13C3 Toul France
14D3 Toulon France
14C3 Toulouse France
48B4 Toumodi Ivory Coast
30B2 Toungoo Burma
13B2 Tourcoing France
48A2 Tourine Mauritius
13B2 Tournai Belgium
14C2 Tours France
47C3 Touws River South Africa
29E2 Towada Japan
29E2 Towada-ko *L* Japan
68B2 Towanda USA
66D2 Towne P USA
60C1 Towner USA
58D1 Townsend USA
32D2 Townsville Australia
68B3 Towson USA
7C4 Towy *R* Wales
62B2 Toyah USA
29D2 Toya-ko *L* Japan
29D3 Toyama Japan
29C3 Toyama-wan *B* Japan
29C4 Toyohashi Japan
29C4 Toyonaka Japan
29B3 Toyooka Japan
29D3 Toyota Japan
48C1 Tozeur Tunisia
13D3 Traben-Trarbach Germany
Trâblous = Tripoli
40C1 Trabzon Turkey
61D2 Tracy Minnesota, USA
66B2 Tracy USA
15A2 Trafalgar, Cabo *C* Spain
54G5 Trail Canada
10B3 Tralee Irish Republic
9C3 Tramore Irish Republic
12G7 Tranås Sweden
30B4 Trang Thailand
27G7 Trangan *I* Indonesia
34C2 Trangie Australia
76E3 Transantarctic Mts Antarctica
Transylvanian Alps *Mts* = Munţii Carpaţii Meridionali
16C3 Trapani Italy
34C3 Traralgon Australia
48A3 Trarza *Region* Mauritius
30C3 Trat Thailand
34B2 Traveller's L Australia
18C2 Travemünde Germany
64B2 Traverse City USA
35B2 Travers,Mt New Zealand
62C2 Travis,L USA
18D3 Třebíč Czech Republic
17D2 Trebinje Bosnia-Herzegovina
18C3 Trebon Czech Republic
74F4 Treinta y Tres Uruguay
74C6 Trelew Argentina
12G7 Trelleborg Sweden
7B3 Tremadog B Wales
65E1 Tremblant,Mt Canada
16D2 Tremiti, Is Italy
68B2 Tremont USA

Tremonton Uniontown

58D2 **Tremonton** USA
19D3 **Trenčín** Slovakia
74D5 **Trenque Lauquén** Argentina
7D3 **Trent** *R* England
16C1 **Trento** Italy
65D2 **Trenton** Canada
61E2 **Trenton** Missouri, USA
68C2 **Trenton** New Jersey, USA
55N5 **Trepassey** Canada
74D5 **Tres Arroyos** Argentina
75C3 **Três Corações** Brazil
15B2 **Tres Forcas, Cabo** *C* Morocco
75B2 **Três Irmãos, Represa** *Res* Brazil
74F2 **Três Lagoas** Brazil
66B2 **Tres Pinos** USA
74C7 **Tres Puntas, Cabo** Argentina
75D3 **Três Rios** Brazil
16C1 **Treviso** Italy
7B4 **Trevose Hd** *Pt* England
13E2 **Treysa** Germany
62B1 **Tribune** USA
44B3 **Trichūr** India
34C2 **Trida** Australia
13D3 **Trier** Germany
16C1 **Trieste** Italy
45B1 **Trikomo** Cyprus
9C3 **Trim** Irish Republic
44C4 **Trincomalee** Sri Lanka
52G6 **Trindade** *I* Atlantic Ocean
72F6 **Trinidad** Bolivia
74E4 **Trinidad** Uruguay
62B1 **Trinidad** USA
69E4 **Trinidad** *I* Caribbean Sea
69E4 **Trinidad & Tobago** *Is Republic* Caribbean Sea
63C2 **Trinity** USA
56D3 **Trinity** *R* USA
55N5 **Trinity B** Canada
67A2 **Trion** USA
45C1 **Tripoli** Lebanon
49D1 **Tripoli** Libya
17E3 **Trípolis** Greece
43G4 **Tripura** *State* India
52H6 **Tristan da Cunha** *Is* Atlantic Ocean
19D3 **Trnava** Slovakia
32E1 **Trobriand Is** Papua New Guinea
65F1 **Trois Pistoles** Canada
65E1 **Trois-Riviéres** Canada
20L5 **Troitsk** Russian Federation
20K3 **Troitsko Pechorsk** Russian Federation
12G7 **Trollhättan** Sweden
12F6 **Trollheimen** *Mt* Norway
46K9 **Tromelin** *I* Indian Ocean
47D3 **Trompsburg** South Africa
12H5 **Tromsø** Norway
66D3 **Trona** USA
12G6 **Trondheim** Norway
12G6 **Trondheimfjord** *Inlet* Norway
45B1 **Troödos Range** *Mts* Cyprus
8C4 **Troon** Scotland
52J3 **Tropic of Cancer**
52K6 **Tropic of Capricorn**
48B2 **Troudenni** Mali
55J4 **Trout L** Ontario, Canada
58E2 **Trout Peak** *Mt* USA
68B2 **Trout Run** USA
7C4 **Trowbridge** England
67A2 **Troy** Alabama, USA
58C1 **Troy** Montana, USA
68D1 **Troy** New York, USA
64C2 **Troy** Ohio, USA
68B2 **Troy** Pennsylvania, USA
17E2 **Troyan** Bulgaria
13C3 **Troyes** France
59C3 **Troy Peak** *Mt* USA
41F5 **Trucial Coast** *Region* UAE
59B3 **Truckee** *R* USA
70D3 **Trujillo** Honduras
72C5 **Trujillo** Peru
15A2 **Trujillo** Spain
72D2 **Trujillo** Venezuela
59D3 **Trumbull,Mt** USA
34C2 **Trundle** Australia
55M5 **Truro** Canada
7B4 **Truro** England
62A2 **Truth or Consequences** USA
26C2 **Tsagaan Nuur** *L* Mongolia
26C1 **Tsagan-Tologoy** Russian Federation
51E5 **Tsaratanana** Madagascar
51C6 **Tsau** Botswana
50D4 **Tsavo** Kenya
50D4 **Tsavo Nat Pk** Kenya
60C1 **Tschida,L** USA
24J4 **Tselinograd** Kazakhstan
47B2 **Tses** Namibia
26D2 **Tsetserleg** Mongolia
48C4 **Tsévié** Togo
47C2 **Tshabong** Botswana
47C1 **Tshane** Botswana
21F6 **Tshchikskoye Vdkhr** *Res* Russian Federation
50B4 **Tshela** Zaïre
51C4 **Tshibala** Zaïre
50C4 **Tshikapa** Zaïre
50C4 **Tshuapa** *R* Zaïre
21G6 **Tsimlyanskoye Vodokhranilishche** *Res* Russian Federation
Tsinan = Jinan
Tsingtao = Qingdao
51E6 **Tsiombe** Madagascar
51E5 **Tsiroanomandidy** Madagascar
19F2 **Tsna** *R* Belarus
31B1 **Tsogt Ovoo** Mongolia
47D3 **Tsomo** South Africa
26D2 **Tsomog** Mongolia
29C4 **Tsu** Japan
29C3 **Tsubata** Japan
29E3 **Tsuchiura** Japan
29E2 **Tsugarū-kaikyō** *Str* Japan
51B5 **Tsumeb** Namibia
51B6 **Tsumis** Namibia
29D3 **Tsuruga** Japan
29C3 **Tsurugi** Japan
29D3 **Tsuruoka** Japan
29C3 **Tsushima** Japan
28B4 **Tsushima** *Is* Japan
Tsushima-Kaikyō = Korea Str
29C3 **Tsuyama** Japan
15A1 **Tua** *R* Portugal
37M5 **Tuamotu, Îles** Pacific Ocean
21F7 **Tuapse** Russian Federation
35A3 **Tuatapere** New Zealand
59D3 **Tuba City** USA
37M6 **Tubai, Îles** Pacific Ocean
74G3 **Tubarão** Brazil
45C2 **Tubas** West Bank
18B3 **Tübingen** Germany
49E1 **Tubruq** Libya
68C3 **Tuckerton** USA
59D4 **Tucson** USA
74C3 **Tucumán** *State* Argentina
62B1 **Tucumcari** USA
72F2 **Tucupita** Venezuela
15B1 **Tudela** Spain
40C3 **Tudmur** Syria
47E2 **Tugela** *R* South Africa
34D2 **Tuggerah L** Australia
27F5 **Tuguegarao** Philippines
25P4 **Tugur** Russian Federation
31D2 **Tuhai He** *R* China
27F7 **Tukangbesi, Kepulauan** *Is* Indonesia
54E3 **Tuktoyaktuk** Canada
19E1 **Tukums** Latvia
25O4 **Tukuringra, Khrebet** *Mts* Russian Federation
51D4 **Tukuyu** Tanzania
42B1 **Tukzar** Afghanistan
20F5 **Tula** *Division* Russian Federation
20F5 **Tula** Russian Federation
66C2 **Tulare** USA
66C2 **Tulare Lake Bed** USA
62A2 **Tularosa** USA
72C3 **Tulcán** Ecuador
21D6 **Tulcea** Romania
19F3 **Tul'chin** Ukraine
66C2 **Tule** *R* USA
51C6 **Tuli** Zimbabwe
47D1 **Tuli** *R* Zimbabwe
62B2 **Tulia** USA
45C2 **Tulkarm** West Bank
67A1 **Tullahoma** USA
9C3 **Tullarnore** Irish Republic
14C2 **Tulle** France
63D2 **Tullos** USA
9C3 **Tullow** Irish Republic
68B1 **Tully** USA
63C1 **Tulsa** USA
72C3 **Tuluá** Colombia
40C3 **Tulūl ash Shāmīyah** *Desert Region* Iran/Syria
25M4 **Tulun** Russian Federation
72C3 **Tumaco** Colombia
25R3 **Tumany** Russian Federation
34C3 **Tumbarumba** Australia
72B4 **Tumbes** Ecuador
28B2 **Tumen** China
28B2 **Tumen R** China/N Korea
44B3 **Tumkūr** India
30C4 **Tumpat** Malaysia
42D4 **Tumsar** India
48B3 **Tumu** Ghana
73H3 **Tumucumaque, Serra** *Mts* Brazil
34C3 **Tumut** Australia
34C3 **Tumut** *R* Australia
69L1 **Tunapuna** Trinidad
7E4 **Tunbridge Wells, Royal** England
40C2 **Tunceli** Turkey
51D4 **Tunduma** Zambia
51D5 **Tunduru** Tanzania
17F2 **Tundzha** *R* Bulgaria
44B2 **Tungabhadra** *R* India
26E4 **Tungkang** Taiwan
12B2 **Tungnafellsjökull** *Mts* Iceland
25M3 **Tunguska** *R* Russian Federation
44C2 **Tuni** India
16C3 **Tunis** Tunisia
16C3 **Tunis, G de** Tunisia
48C1 **Tunisia** *Republic* N Africa
72D2 **Tunja** Colombia
68C2 **Tunkhannock** USA
Tunxi = Huangshan
66C2 **Tuolumne Meadows** USA
75B3 **Tupã** Brazil
75C2 **Tupaciguara** Brazil
63E2 **Tupelo** USA
19G1 **Tupik** Russian Federation
72E8 **Tupiza** Bolivia
66C3 **Tupman** USA
65E2 **Tupper Lake** USA
74C4 **Tupungato** *Mt* Argentina
43L3 **Tura** India
25L3 **Tura** Russian Federation
20L4 **Tura** *R* Russian Federation
41G2 **Turān** Iran
25L4 **Turan** Russian Federation
40C3 **Turayf** Saudi Arabia
38E3 **Turbat** Pakistan
72C2 **Turbo** Colombia
17E1 **Turda** Romania
24K5 **Turfan Depression** China
24H5 **Turgay** Kazakhstan
25L5 **Turgen Uul** *Mt* Mongolia
40A2 **Turgutlu** Turkey
40C1 **Turhal** Turkey
12K7 **Türi** Estonia
15B2 **Turia** *R* Spain
16B1 **Turin** Italy
20L4 **Turinsk** Russian Federation
26G2 **Turiy Rog** Russian Federation
50D3 **Turkana, L** Ethiopia/Kenya
38E1 **Turkestan** *Region* C Asia
40C2 **Turkey** *Republic* W Asia
38D1 **Turkmenistan** *Republic* Asia
41F2 **Turkmenskiy Zaliv** *B* Turkmenistan
69C2 **Turks Is** Caribbean Sea
12J6 **Turku** Finland
50D3 **Turkwel** *R* Kenya
66B2 **Turlock** USA
66B2 **Turlock L** USA
35C2 **Turnagain,C** New Zealand
70D3 **Turneffe I** Belize
68D1 **Turners Falls** USA
13C2 **Turnhout** Belgium
17E2 **Turnu Măgurele** Romania
17E2 **Turnu-Severin** Romania
25K5 **Turpan** China
69B2 **Turquino** *Mt* Cuba
8D3 **Turriff** Scotland
38E1 **Turtkul'** Uzbekistan
61D3 **Turtle Creek Res** USA
25K3 **Turukhansk** Russian Federation
26D1 **Turuntayevo** Russian Federation
75B2 **Turvo** *R* Goias, Brazil
75C3 **Turvo** *R* São Paulo, Brazil
19E2 **Tur'ya** *R* Ukraine
63E2 **Tuscaloosa** USA
68B2 **Tuscarora Mt** USA
64B3 **Tuscola** Illinois, USA
62C2 **Tuscola** Texas, USA
63E2 **Tuscumbia** USA
41G3 **Tusharīk** Iran
68A2 **Tussey Mt** USA
Tutera = Tudela
44B4 **Tuticorin** India
17F2 **Tutrakan** Bulgaria
18B3 **Tuttlingen** Germany
33H2 **Tutuila** *I* American Samoa
26D2 **Tuul Gol** *R* Mongolia
33G1 **Tuvalu** *Is* Pacific Ocean
45C4 **Tuwayīlel Hāj** *Mt* Jordan
70B2 **Tuxpan** Mexico
70C2 **Tuxpan** Mexico
70C3 **Tuxtla Gutiérrez** Mexico
15A1 **Túy** Spain
30D3 **Tuy Hoa** Vietnam
40B2 **Tuz Gölü** *Salt L* Turkey
41D3 **Tuz Khurmātū** Iraq
17D2 **Tuzla** Bosnia-Herzegovina
20E4 **Tver'** *Division* Russian Federation
20F4 **Tver'** Russian Federation
8D4 **Tweed** *R* England/Scotland
34D1 **Tweed Heads** Australia
8D4 **Tweedsmuir Hills** Scotland
59C4 **Twentynine Palms** USA
55N5 **Twillingate** Canada
58D1 **Twin Bridges** USA
62B2 **Twin Buttes Res** USA
58D2 **Twin Falls** USA
35B2 **Twins,The** *Mt* New Zealand
66B3 **Twitchell Res** USA
64A1 **Two Harbors** USA
58D1 **Two Medicine** *R* USA
64B2 **Two Rivers** USA
25O4 **Tygda** Russian Federation
63C2 **Tyler** USA
26H1 **Tymovskoye** Russian Federation
26F1 **Tynda** Russian Federation
6D2 **Tyne** *R* England
6D2 **Tynemouth** England
12G6 **Tynset** Norway
Tyr = Tyre
45C2 **Tyre** Lebanon
62A2 **Tyrone** New Mexico, USA
68A2 **Tyrone** Pennsylvania, USA
9C2 **Tyrone** *County* Northern Ireland
34B3 **Tyrrell,L** Australia
16C2 **Tyrrhenian S** Italy
21J7 **Tyuleni, Ova** *Is* Kazakhstan
24H4 **Tyumen'** *Division* Russian Federation
24H4 **Tyumen'** Russian Federation
25O3 **Tyung** *R* Russian Federation
25L4 **Tyva** *Division* Russian Federation
7B3 **Tywyn** Wales
47E1 **Tzaneen** South Africa
17E3 **Tzoumérka** *Mt* Greece

U

75D3 **Ubá** Brazil
75D2 **Ubaí** Brazil
75E1 **Ubaitaba** Brazil
50B3 **Ubangi** *R* Central African Republic/Congo/Zaïre
40D3 **Ubayyid, Wadi al** *Watercourse* Iraq
28B4 **Ube** Japan
15B2 **Ubeda** Spain
55N2 **Ubekendt Ejland** *I* Greenland
75C2 **Uberaba** Brazil
75A2 **Uberaba, Lagoa** Brazil
75C2 **Uberlândia** Brazil
30D2 **Ubon Ratchathani** Thailand
19F2 **Ubort** *R* Belarus
50C4 **Ubundu** Zaïre
72D5 **Ucayali** *R* Peru
42C3 **Uch** Pakistan
25P4 **Uchar** *R* Russian Federation
29E2 **Uchiura-wan** *B* Japan
13E1 **Uchte** Germany
58A1 **Ucluelet** Canada
25L4 **Uda** *R* Russian Federation
42C4 **Udaipur** India
43F3 **Udaipur Garhi** Nepal
12G7 **Uddevalla** Sweden
12H5 **Uddjaur** *L* Sweden
44B2 **Udgir** India
42D2 **Udhampur** India
16C1 **Udine** Italy
30C2 **Udon Thani** Thailand
25P4 **Udskaya Guba** *B* Russian Federation
44A3 **Udupi** India
25N2 **Udzha** Russian Federation
29C3 **Ueda** Japan
50C3 **Uele** *R* Zaïre
25U3 **Uelen** Russian Federation
18C2 **Uelzen** Germany
50C3 **Uere** *R* Zaïre
20K5 **Ufa** Russian Federation
20K4 **Ufa** *R* Russian Federation
51B6 **Ugab** *R* Namibia
50D4 **Ugaila** *R* Tanzania
50D3 **Uganda** *Republic* Africa
45C3 **'Ugeiqa, Wadi** Jordan
26H2 **Uglegorsk** Russian Federation
20F4 **Uglich** Russian Federation
28C2 **Uglovoye** Russian Federation
20F5 **Ugra** *R* Russian Federation
8B3 **Uig** Scotland
51B4 **Uige** Angola
28A3 **Ŭijŏngbu** S Korea
21J6 **Uil** Kazakhstan
58D2 **Uinta Mts** USA
28A3 **Ŭiryŏng** S Korea
28A3 **Uisŏng** S Korea
47D3 **Uitenhage** South Africa
19E3 **Újfehértó** Hungary
29C4 **Uji** Japan
50C4 **Ujiji** Tanzania
74C2 **Ujina** Chile
42D4 **Ujjain** India
32A1 **Ujung Pandang** Indonesia
50D4 **Ukerewe I** Tanzania
43G3 **Ukhrul** India
20J3 **Ukhta** Russian Federation
59B3 **Ukiah** California, USA
58C1 **Ukiah** Oregon, USA
56A3 **Ukiah** USA
19E1 **Ukmerge** Lithuania
21D6 **Ukraine** *Republic* Europe
28A4 **Uku-jima** *I* Japan
26D2 **Ulaanbaatar** Mongolia
26C2 **Ulaangom** Mongolia
31C1 **Ulaan Uul** Mongolia
Ulan Bator = Ulaanbaatar
39G1 **Ulangar Hu** *L* China
26F2 **Ulanhot** China
26D1 **Ulan Ude** Russian Federation
26C3 **Ulan Ul Hu** *L* China
25Q3 **Ul'beya** *R* Russian Federation
28B3 **Ulchin** S Korea
17D2 **Ulcinj** Montenegro, Yugoslavia
26E2 **Uldz** Mongolia
26C2 **Uliastay** Mongolia
27G5 **Ulithi** *I* Pacific Ocean
19F1 **Ulla** Belarus
34D3 **Ulladulla** Australia
8C3 **Ullapool** Scotland
12H5 **Ullsfjorden** *Inlet* Norway
6C2 **Ullswater** *L* England
28C3 **Ullung-do** *I* Japan
18C3 **Ulm** Germany
34A1 **Uloowaranie,L** Australia
28B3 **Ulsan** S Korea
9C2 **Ulster** *Region* Northern Ireland
24K5 **Ulungur He** *R* China
24K5 **Ulungur Hu** *L* China
8B3 **Ulva** *I* Scotland
6C2 **Ulverston** England
34C4 **Ulverstone** Australia
25Q4 **Ulya** *R* Russian Federation
19G3 **Ulyanovka** Ukraine
20H5 **Ul'yanovsk** *Division* Russian Federation
20H5 **Ul'yanovsk** Russian Federation
62B1 **Ulysses** USA
21E6 **Uman'** Ukraine
55N2 **Umanak** Greenland
43E4 **Umaria** India
42B3 **Umarkot** Pakistan
58C1 **Umatilla** USA
20E2 **Umba** Russian Federation
50D4 **Umba** *R* Kenya/Tanzania
32D1 **Umboi I** Papua New Guinea
12H6 **Ume** *R* Sweden
12J6 **Umea** Sweden
45C2 **Um ed Daraj, Jebel** *Mt* Jordan
45C4 **Um el Hashīm, Jebel** *Mt* Jordan
47E2 **Umfolozi** *R* South Africa
54C3 **Umiat** USA
45C4 **Um Ishrīn, Jebel** *Mt* Jordan
47E3 **Umkomaas** *R* South Africa
41G4 **Umm al Qaiwain** UAE
50C2 **Umm Bell** Sudan
50C2 **Umm Keddada** Sudan
40C4 **Umm Lajj** Saudi Arabia
50D2 **Umm Ruwaba** Sudan
41F5 **Umm Sa'id** Qatar
51C5 **Umniati** *R* Zimbabwe
58B2 **Umpqua** *R* USA
42D4 **Umred** India
Umtali = Mutare
47D3 **Umtata** South Africa
75B3 **Umuarama** Brazil
47D3 **Umzimkulu** South Africa
47E3 **Umzimkulu** *R* South Africa
47D3 **Umzimvubu** *R* South Africa
47D1 **Umzingwane** *R* Zimbabwe
75E2 **Una** Brazil
16D1 **Una** *R* Bosnia-Herzegovina/Croatia
68C1 **Unadilla** USA
68C1 **Unadilla** *R* USA
75C2 **Unaí** Brazil
54B3 **Unalakleet** USA
41D4 **Unayzah** Saudi Arabia
68D2 **Uncasville** USA
60B3 **Uncompahgre Plat** USA
47D2 **Underberg** South Africa
60C1 **Underwood** USA
20E5 **Unecha** Russian Federation
45C3 **Uneisa** Jordan
55M4 **Ungava B** Canada
28C2 **Unggi** N Korea
74F3 **União de Vitória** Brazil
63D1 **Union** Missouri, USA
67B2 **Union** S Carolina, USA
65D2 **Union City** Pennsylvania, USA
63E1 **Union City** Tennessee, USA
47C3 **Uniondale** South Africa
67A2 **Union Springs** USA
65D3 **Uniontown** USA

Vienna Waterville

64B3 **Vienna** Illinois, USA
64C3 **Vienna** W Virginia, USA
14C2 **Vienne** France
14C2 **Vienne** *R* France
30C2 **Vientiane** Laos
14C2 **Vierzon** France
16D2 **Vieste** Italy
27D5 **Vietnam** *Republic* SE Asia
30D1 **Vietri** Vietnam
69P2 **Vieux Fort** St Lucia
27F5 **Vigan** Philippines
14B3 **Vignemale** *Mt* France/Spain
15A1 **Vigo** Spain
44C2 **Vijayawāda** India
17D2 **Vijosë** *R* Albania
17E2 **Vikhren** *Mt* Bulgaria
12G6 **Vikna** *I* Norway
51D5 **Vila da Maganja** Mozambique
51D5 **Vila Machado** Mozambique
51D6 **Vilanculos** Mozambique
Vilanova i la Geltrú = Villanueva-y-Geltrú
15A1 **Vila Real** Portugal
51D5 **Vila Vasco da Gama** Mozambique
75D3 **Vila Velha** Brazil
19F2 **Vileyka** Belarus
12H6 **Vilhelmina** Sweden
73G6 **Vilhena** Brazil
19F2 **Viliya** Belarus
20D4 **Viljandi** Estonia
47D2 **Viljoenskroon** South Africa
25L2 **Vilkitskogo, Proliv** *Str* Russian Federation
19F3 **Vilkovo** Ukraine
62A2 **Villa Ahumada** Mexico
15A1 **Villaba** Spain
16C1 **Villach** Austria
74C4 **Villa Dolores** Argentina
74E5 **Villa Gesell** Argentina
75A4 **Villa Hayes** Paraguay
70C3 **Villahermosa** Mexico
74D4 **Villa Huidobro** Argentina
74D4 **Villa María** Argentina
72F8 **Villa Montes** Bolivia
15A1 **Villa Nova de Gaia** Portugal
15A2 **Villanueva de la Serena** Spain
15C1 **Villanueva-y-Geltrú** Spain
15B2 **Villarreal** Spain
74E3 **Villarrica** Paraguay
15B2 **Villarrobledo** Spain
62B3 **Villa Unión** Coahuila, Mexico
72D3 **Villavicencio** Colombia
14C2 **Villefranche** France
55L5 **Ville-Marie** Canada
15B2 **Villena** Spain
13B3 **Villeneuve-St-Georges** France
14C3 **Villeneuve-sur-Lot** France
13B3 **Villeneuve-sur-Yonne** France
63D2 **Ville Platte** USA
13B3 **Villers-Cotterêts** France
14C2 **Villeurbanne** France
47D2 **Villiers** South Africa
13E3 **Villingen-Schwenningen** Germany
44B3 **Villupuram** India
19F2 **Vilnius** Lithuania
25N3 **Vilyuy** *R* Russian Federation
25O3 **Vilyuysk** Russian Federation
15C1 **Vinaroz** Spain
64B3 **Vincennes** USA
12H5 **Vindel** *R* Sweden
42D4 **Vindhya Range** *Mts* India
68C3 **Vineland** USA
68E2 **Vineyard Haven** USA
30D2 **Vinh** Vietnam
30D3 **Vinh Cam Ranh** *B* Vietnam
30D4 **Vinh Loi** Vietnam
30D3 **Vinh Long** Vietnam
63C1 **Vinita** USA
17D1 **Vinkovci** Croatia
19F3 **Vinnitsa** Ukraine
76F3 **Vinson Massif** *Upland* Antarctica
61E2 **Vinton** USA
74B4 **Viõna del Mar** Chile
51B5 **Virei** Angola
75D2 **Virgem da Lapa** Brazil
59D3 **Virgin** *R* USA
47D2 **Virginia** South Africa
61E1 **Virginia** USA
57F3 **Virginia** *State* USA
65D3 **Virginia Beach** USA
59C3 **Virginia City** USA
69E3 **Virgin Is** Caribbean Sea
64A2 **Viroqua** USA
16D1 **Virovitica** Croatia
13C3 **Virton** Belgium
44B4 **Virudunagar** India
16D2 **Vis** *I* Croatia
66C2 **Visalia** USA
12H7 **Visby** Sweden
54H2 **Viscount Melville Sd** Canada
17D2 **Višegrad** Bosnia-Herzegovina
15A1 **Viseu** Portugal
44C2 **Vishākhapatnam** India
20K3 **Vishera** *R* Russian Federation
16B2 **Viso, Monte** *Mt* Italy
59C4 **Vista** USA
Vistula *R* = **Wisła**
44A2 **Vite** India
19G1 **Vitebsk** Belarus
16C2 **Viterbo** Italy
15A1 **Vitigudino** Spain
25N4 **Vitim** *R* Russian Federation
73K8 **Vitória** Brazil
15B1 **Vitoria** Spain
73K6 **Vitória da Conquista** Brazil
14B2 **Vitré** France
13C3 **Vitry-le-François** France
12J5 **Vittangi** Sweden
13C3 **Vittel** France
16C3 **Vittoria** Sicily, Italy
26J2 **Vityaz Depth** Pacific Ocean
Viviero = Vivero
15A1 **Vivero** Spain
25L3 **Vivi** *R* Russian Federation
15B1 **Vizcaya, Golfo de** Spain
25M4 **Vizhne-Angarsk** Russian Federation
44C2 **Vizianagaram** India
20J3 **Vizinga** Russian Federation
17E1 **Vlădeasa** *Mt* Romania
21G7 **Vladikavkaz** Russian Federation
20G4 **Vladimir** *Division* Russian Federation
20G4 **Vladimir** Russian Federation
19E2 **Vladimir Volynskiy** Ukraine
28C2 **Vladivostok** Russian Federation
18A2 **Vlieland** *I* Netherlands
13B2 **Vlissingen** Netherlands
47B2 **Vloosdrift** South Africa
17D2 **Vlorë** Albania
18C3 **Vltara** *R* Czech Republic
18C3 **Vöcklabruck** Austria
30D3 **Voeune Sai** Cambodia
13E2 **Vogelsberg** *Region* Germany
Vohemar = Vohimarina
Vohibinany = Ampasimanolotra
51F5 **Vohimarina** Madagascar
50D4 **Voi** Kenya
48B4 **Voinjama** Liberia
14D2 **Voiron** France
17D1 **Vojvodina** *Region* Serbia, Yugoslavia
60B1 **Volborg** USA
69A5 **Volcán Barú** *Mt* Panama
Volcano Is = Kazan Retto
20K4 **Volchansk** Russian Federation
21H6 **Volga** *R* Russian Federation
21G6 **Volgodonsk** Russian Federation
21G6 **Volgograd** *Division* Russian Federation
21G6 **Volgograd** Russian Federation
21H5 **Volgogradskoye Vodokhranilishche** *Res* Russian Federation
20E4 **Volkhov** Russian Federation
20E4 **Volkhov** *R* Russian Federation
19E2 **Volkovysk** Belarus
47D2 **Volksrust** South Africa
25L2 **Volochanka** Russian Federation
20G3 **Vologda** *Division* Russian Federation
20G4 **Vologda** Russian Federation
17E3 **Vólos** Greece
21H5 **Vol'sk** Russian Federation
66B2 **Volta** USA
48B3 **Volta Blanche** *R* Burkina/Ghana
48B4 **Volta, L** Ghana
48B4 **Volta Noire** *R* W Africa
75D3 **Volta Redonda** Brazil
48B3 **Volta Rouge** *R* Burkina/Ghana
21G6 **Volzhskiy** Russian Federation
20F3 **Vonguda** Russian Federation
55R3 **Vopnafjörður** Iceland
18C1 **Vordingborg** Denmark
21C8 **Voriái** *I* Greece
20L2 **Vorkuta** Russian Federation
12G6 **Vorma** *R* Norway
21F5 **Voronezh** *Division* Russian Federation
21F5 **Voronezh** Russian Federation
12M5 **Voron'ya** *R* Russian Federation
21F6 **Voroshilovgrad** Ukraine
12K7 **Võru** Estonia
13D3 **Vosges** *Department* France
14D2 **Vosges** *Mts* France
12F6 **Voss** Norway
25L4 **Vostochnyy Sayan** *Mts* Russian Federation
76F9 **Vostok** *Base* Antarctica
20J4 **Votkinsk** Russian Federation
13C3 **Vouziers** France
61E1 **Voyageurs Nat Pk** USA
20K3 **Voy Vozh** Russian Federation
21E6 **Voznesensk** Ukraine
17E2 **Vranje** Serbia, Yugoslavia
17E2 **Vratsa** Bulgaria
17D1 **Vrbas** Serbia, Yugoslavia
16D2 **Vrbas** *R* Bosnia-Herzegovina
16C1 **Vrbovsko** Croatia
47D2 **Vrede** South Africa
47B3 **Vredendal** South Africa
73G2 **Vreed en Hoop** Guyana
44B3 **Vriddhāchalam** India
17E1 **Vršac** Serbia, Yugoslavia
16D2 **Vrtoče** Bosnia-Herzegovina
47C2 **Vryburg** South Africa
47E2 **Vryheid** South Africa
17D1 **Vukovar** Croatia
20K3 **Vuktyl'** Russian Federation
7F3 **Vulcan** *Oilfield* N Sea
16C3 **Vulcano** *I* Italy
30D3 **Vung Tau** Vietnam
12J5 **Vuollerim** Sweden
20E3 **Vyartsilya** Russian Federation
20J4 **Vyatka** *R* Russian Federation
26G2 **Vyazemskiy** Russian Federation
20E4 **Vyaz'ma** Russian Federation
20G4 **Vyazniki** Russian Federation
20D3 **Vyborg** Russian Federation
20F3 **Vygozero, Ozero** *L* Russian Federation
20J3 **Vym** *R* Russian Federation
7C3 **Vyrnwy** *R* Wales
20E4 **Vyshniy-Volochek** Russian Federation
18D3 **Vyškov** Czech Republic
20F3 **Vytegra** Russian Federation

W

48B3 **Wa** Ghana
13C2 **Waal** *R* Netherlands
54G4 **Wabasca** *R* Canada
64B2 **Wabash** USA
64B3 **Wabash** *R* USA
64C1 **Wabatongushi L** Canada
54J4 **Wabowden** Canada
55M4 **Wabush** Canada
67B3 **Waccasassa B** USA
68E1 **Wachusett Res** USA
63C2 **Waco** USA
42B3 **Wad** Pakistan
49D2 **Waddān** Libya
13C1 **Waddenzee** *S* Netherlands
54F4 **Waddington,Mt** Canada
7B4 **Wadebridge** England
61D1 **Wadena** USA
45C3 **Wadi es Sir** Jordan
50D1 **Wadi Halfa** Sudan
45C3 **Wādi Mūsā** Jordan
50D2 **Wad Medani** Sudan
28A3 **Waegwan** S Korea
28A2 **Wafang** China
41E4 **Wafra** Kuwait
13C2 **Wageningen** Netherlands
55K3 **Wager B** Canada
55J3 **Wager Bay** Canada
34C3 **Wagga Wagga** Australia
32A4 **Wagin** Australia
61D2 **Wagner** USA
66E5 **Wahiawa** Hawaiian Islands
61D2 **Wahoo** USA
61D1 **Wahpeton** USA
44A2 **Wai** India
66E5 **Waialua** Hawaiian Islands
35B2 **Waiau** New Zealand
35B2 **Waiau** *R* New Zealand
27G6 **Waigeo** *I* Indonesia
35C1 **Waihi** New Zealand
35C1 **Waikaremoana,L** New Zealand
35C1 **Waikato** *R* New Zealand
34A2 **Waikerie** Australia
35B3 **Waikouaiti** New Zealand
66E5 **Wailuku** Hawaiian Islands
35B2 **Waimakariri** *R* New Zealand
35B2 **Waimate** New Zealand
66E5 **Waimea** Hawaiian Islands
32B1 **Waingapu** Indonesia
54G4 **Wainwright** Canada
54B2 **Wainwright** USA
35C1 **Waioura** New Zealand
35B2 **Waipara** New Zealand
35C2 **Waipukurau** New Zealand
35C2 **Wairarapa,L** New Zealand
35B2 **Wairau** *R* New Zealand
35C1 **Wairoa** New Zealand
35C1 **Wairoa** *R* New Zealand
35B2 **Waitaki** *R* New Zealand
35B1 **Waitara** New Zealand
35C1 **Waitomo** New Zealand
35B1 **Waiuku** New Zealand
29C3 **Wajima** Japan
50E3 **Wajir** Kenya
29C3 **Wakasa-wan** *B* Japan
35A3 **Wakatipu,L** New Zealand
29D4 **Wakayama** Japan
60D3 **Wa Keeney** USA
7D3 **Wakefield** England
69H1 **Wakefield** Jamaica
64B1 **Wakefield** Michigan, USA
68E2 **Wakefield** Rhode Island, USA
30B2 **Wakema** Burma
29E1 **Wakkanai** Japan
34B3 **Wakool** *R* Australia
18D2 **Wałbrzych** Poland
34D2 **Walcha** Australia
18D2 **Wałcz** Poland
13D2 **Waldbröl** Germany
68C2 **Walden** USA
13E4 **Waldshut** Germany
54B3 **Wales** USA
7C3 **Wales** *Principality* U K
55K3 **Wales I** Canada
34C2 **Walgett** Australia
76F4 **Walgreen Coast** *Region* Antarctica
50C4 **Walikale** Zaïre
61E1 **Walker** USA
66C1 **Walker L** USA
66C3 **Walker Pass** USA
64C2 **Walkerton** Canada
60C2 **Wall** USA
58C1 **Wallace** USA
32C4 **Wallaroo** Australia
34C3 **Walla Walla** Australia
58C1 **Walla Walla** USA
68D2 **Wallingford** USA
37K5 **Wallis and Futuna** *Is* Pacific Ocean
33H2 **Wallis, Îles** Pacific Ocean
58C1 **Wallowa** USA
58C1 **Wallowa Mts** USA
34C1 **Wallumbilla** Australia
6C2 **Walney** *I* England
63D1 **Walnut Ridge** USA
68D1 **Walpole** USA
7D3 **Walsall** England
62B1 **Walsenburg** USA
67B2 **Walterboro** USA
67A2 **Walter F George Res** USA
62C2 **Walters** USA
68E1 **Waltham** USA
68C1 **Walton** USA
7E4 **Walton-on-the Naze** England
47A1 **Walvis Bay** Namibia
52J6 **Walvis Ridge** Atlantic Ocean
48C4 **Wamba** Nigeria
50B4 **Wamba** *R* Zaïre
61D3 **Wamego** USA
58E2 **Wamsutter** USA
42B2 **Wana** Pakistan
34B1 **Wanaaring** Australia
35A2 **Wanaka** New Zealand
35A2 **Wanaka,L** New Zealand
64C1 **Wanapitei L** Canada
28A4 **Wando** S Korea
34C1 **Wandoan** Australia
34B3 **Wanganella** Australia
35B1 **Wanganui** New Zealand
35C1 **Wanganui** *R* New Zealand
34C3 **Wangaratta** Australia
13D1 **Wangerooge** *I* Germany
28B2 **Wangqing** China
28A3 **Wanjialing** China
Wankie = Hwange
50E3 **Wanleweyne** Somalia
30E2 **Wanning** China
44B2 **Wanparti** India
6D2 **Wansbeck, R** England
7D4 **Wantage** England
31B3 **Wanxian** China
31B3 **Wanyuan** China
63D1 **Wappapello,L** USA
68D2 **Wappingers Falls** USA
61E2 **Wapsipinicon** *R* USA
44B2 **Warangal** India
34C4 **Waratah** Australia
34C3 **Waratah B** Australia
13E2 **Warburg** Germany
34C3 **Warburton** Australia
34C1 **Ward** *R* Australia
47D2 **Warden** South Africa
42D4 **Wardha** India
35A3 **Ward,Mt** New Zealand
54F4 **Ware** Canada
68D1 **Ware** USA
7C4 **Wareham** England
68E2 **Wareham** USA
13D2 **Warendorf** Germany
34D1 **Warialda** Australia
30D2 **Warin Chamrap** Thailand
47B2 **Warmbad** Namibia
51C6 **Warmbad** South Africa
7C4 **Warminster** England
68C2 **Warminster** USA
59C3 **Warm Springs** USA
18C2 **Warnemünde** Germany
58B2 **Warner Mts** USA
67B2 **Warner Robins** USA
34B3 **Warracknabeal** Australia
32D3 **Warrego** *R* Australia
63D2 **Warren** Arkansas, USA
34C2 **Warren** Australia
61D1 **Warren** Minnesota, USA
64C2 **Warren** Ohio, USA
65D2 **Warren** Pennsylvania, USA
68E2 **Warren** Rhode Island, USA
9C2 **Warrenpoint** Northern Ireland
61E3 **Warrensburg** USA
47C2 **Warrenton** South Africa
65D3 **Warrenton** USA
48C4 **Warri** Nigeria
7C3 **Warrington** England
63E2 **Warrington** USA
34B3 **Warrnambool** Australia
61D1 **Warroad** USA
19E2 **Warsaw** Poland
68A1 **Warsaw** USA
50E3 **Warshiikh** Somalia
Warszawa = Warsaw
19D2 **Warta** *R* Poland
34D1 **Warwick** Australia
7D3 **Warwick** England
68C2 **Warwick** New York, USA
68E2 **Warwick** Rhode Island, USA
7D3 **Warwick** *County* England
59D3 **Wasatch Range** *Mts* USA
47E2 **Wasbank** South Africa
66C3 **Wasco** USA
61E2 **Waseca** USA
64A1 **Washburn** USA
54H2 **Washburn L** Canada
58D2 **Washburn,Mt** USA
42D4 **Wāshīm** India
57F3 **Washington** District of Columbia, USA
67B2 **Washington** Georgia, USA
64B3 **Washington** Indiana, USA
61E2 **Washington** Iowa, USA
61E3 **Washington** Missouri, USA
67C1 **Washington** N Carolina, USA
68C2 **Washington** New Jersey, USA
64C2 **Washington** Pennsylvania, USA
59D3 **Washington** Utah, USA
56A2 **Washington** *State* USA
64C3 **Washington Court House** USA
55M1 **Washington Land** *Region* Canada
65E2 **Washington,Mt** USA
62C1 **Washita** *R* USA
7E3 **Wash,The** *B* England
42A3 **Washuk** Pakistan
51L4 **Waskaganish** Canada
69A4 **Waspán** Nicaragua
66C1 **Wassuk Range** *Mts* USA
13C3 **Wassy** France
27F7 **Watampone** Indonesia
47D3 **Waterberge** *Mts* South Africa
68D2 **Waterbury** USA
10B3 **Waterford** Irish Republic
9C3 **Waterford** *County* Irish Republic
9C3 **Waterford Harbour** Irish Republic
13C2 **Waterloo** Belgium
61E2 **Waterloo** USA
64B1 **Watersmeet** USA
58D1 **Waterton-Glacier International Peace Park** USA
65D2 **Watertown** New York, USA
61D2 **Watertown** S Dakota, USA
64B2 **Watertown** Wisconsin, USA
47E2 **Waterval-Boven** South Africa
65F2 **Waterville** Maine, USA

Woodlark Yuzh Ural

33E1 **Woodlark** *I* Papua New Guinea
32C3 **Woodroffe,Mt** Australia
61E1 **Woods,L of the** Canada/USA
64B2 **Woodstock** Illinois, USA
65F1 **Woodstock** New Brunswick, Canada
64C2 **Woodstock** Ontario, Canada
68A3 **Woodstock** Virginia, USA
68C3 **Woodstown** USA
35C2 **Woodville** New Zealand
63D2 **Woodville** USA
62C1 **Woodward** USA
6D2 **Wooler** England
32C4 **Woomera** Australia
65E2 **Woonsocket** USA
64C2 **Wooster** USA
7D4 **Wootton Bassett** England
7C3 **Worcester** England
47B3 **Worcester** South Africa
68E1 **Worcester** USA
6C2 **Workington** England
7D3 **Worksop** England
58E2 **Worland** USA
13E3 **Worms** Germany
7B4 **Worms Head** *Pt* Wales
7D4 **Worthing** England
61D2 **Worthington** USA
64C2 **Worthington** USA
60C2 **Wounded Knee** USA
27F7 **Wowoni** Indonesia
25T2 **Wrangel I** Russian Federation
54E4 **Wrangell** USA
54D3 **Wrangell Mts** USA
10B2 **Wrath,C** Scotland
60C2 **Wray** USA
7C3 **Wrexham** Wales
59D4 **Wrightson, Mt** USA
67B2 **Wrightsville** USA
66D3 **Wrightwood** USA
54F3 **Wrigley** Canada
18D2 **Wrocław** Poland
19D2 **Września** Poland
26F2 **Wuchang** China
30E1 **Wuchuan** China
31E2 **Wuda** China
31C2 **Wuding He** *R* China
31A3 **Wudu** China
31C4 **Wugang** China
31B2 **Wuhai** China
31C3 **Wuhan** China
31D3 **Wuhu** China
31D5 **Wuhua** China
42D2 **Wūjang** China
31B1 **Wujia He** *R* China
31B4 **Wu Jiang** *R* China
48C4 **Wukari** Nigeria
31B4 **Wuling Shan** *Mts* China
31A4 **Wumeng Shan** *Upland* China
13E1 **Wümme** *R* Germany
13E1 **Wunstorf** Germany
43H4 **Wuntho** Burma
13D2 **Wuppertal** Germany
31B2 **Wuqi** China
31D2 **Wuqing** China
18B3 **Würzburg** Germany
18C2 **Wurzen** Germany
31C2 **Wutai Shan** *Mt* China
27H7 **Wuvulu** *I* Pacific Ocean
31A2 **Wuwei** China
31E3 **Wuxi** China
31E3 **Wuxing** China
31C2 **Wuyang** China
31D4 **Wuyi Shan** *Mts* China
31B1 **Wuyuan** China
30D2 **Wuzhi Shan** *Mts* China
31B2 **Wuzhong** China
31C5 **Wuzhou** China
64C2 **Wyandotte** USA
34C1 **Wyandra** Australia
7C4 **Wye** *R* England
7C4 **Wylye** *R* England
7E3 **Wymondham** England
32B2 **Wyndham** Australia
63D1 **Wynne** USA
54G2 **Wynniatt B** Canada
34C4 **Wynyard** Australia
64B2 **Wyoming** USA
56C2 **Wyoming** *State* USA
58D2 **Wyoming Peak** *Mt* USA
58D2 **Wyoming Range** *Mts* USA
34D2 **Wyong** Australia
64C3 **Wytheville** USA

X

42D1 **Xaidulla** China
47E2 **Xai Xai** Mozambique
51B5 **Xangongo** Angola
13D2 **Xanten** Germany
17E2 **Xánthi** Greece
31D1 **Xar Moron He** *R* China
47C1 **Xau,L** Botswana
64C3 **Xenia** USA
Xiaguan = Dali
31A2 **Xiahe** China
31D5 **Xiamen** China
31B3 **Xi'an** China
31B4 **Xianfeng** China
31C3 **Xiangfan** China
31C4 **Xiang Jiang** *R* China
31C4 **Xiangtan** China
31C4 **Xianning** China
31B3 **Xianyang** China
26F2 **Xiao Hinggan Ling** *Region* China
31C4 **Xiao Shui** *R* China
31D4 **Xiapu** China
31A4 **Xichang** China
30C2 **Xieng Khouang** Laos
31B4 **Xifeng** China
28A2 **Xifeng** China
43F3 **Xigazê** China
31A1 **Xi He** *R* China
28A2 **Xi He** *R* China
31B2 **Xiji** China
31C5 **Xi Jiang** *R* China
31E1 **Xiliao He** *R* China
31B5 **Xilin** China
28A2 **Xinbin** China
28A2 **Xinchengzi** China
31D4 **Xinfeng** China
31C1 **Xinghe** China
31D5 **Xingning** China
31B4 **Xingren** China
31C2 **Xingtai** China
73H4 **Xingu** *R* Brazil
26C2 **Xingxingxia** China
31A4 **Xingyi** China
31A2 **Xining** China
31E2 **Xinjin** Liaoning, China
31A3 **Xinjin** Sichuan, China
28A2 **Xinlitun** China
28A2 **Xinmin** China
31D2 **Xinwen** China
31C2 **Xin Xian** China
31C2 **Xinxiang** China
31C3 **Xinyang** China
31C5 **Xinyi** Guangdong, China
31D3 **Xinyi** Jiangsu, China
28B2 **Xinzhan** China
28A2 **Xiongyuecheng** China
31D1 **Xi Ujimqin Qi** China
28A2 **Xiuyan** China
31D3 **Xuancheng** China
31B3 **Xuanhan** China
31D1 **Xuanhua** China
31A4 **Xuanwei** China
31C3 **Xuchang** China
50E3 **Xuddur** Somalia
28A2 **Xujiatun** China
31A2 **Xunhua** China
31C5 **Xun Jiang** *R* China
26F2 **Xunke** China
31D5 **Xunwu** China
31C4 **Xupu** China
43N1 **Xurgru** China
30E1 **Xuwen** China
31B4 **Xuyong** China
31D3 **Xuzhou** China

Y

31A4 **Ya'an** China
34B3 **Yaapeet** Australia
50B3 **Yabassi** Cameroon
26D1 **Yablonovyy Khrebet** *Mts* Russian Federation
45D2 **Yabrūd** Syria
58B2 **Yachats** USA
72F8 **Yacuiba** Bolivia
44B2 **Yādgīr** India
49D1 **Yafran** Libya
29D2 **Yagishiri-tō** *I* Japan
19G2 **Yagotin** Ukraine
50C3 **Yahuma** Zaïre
29C3 **Yaita** Japan
29C4 **Yaizu** Japan
31A4 **Yajiang** China
54D3 **Yakataga** USA
58B1 **Yakima** USA
58B1 **Yakima** *R* USA
48B3 **Yako** Burkina
50C3 **Yakoma** Zaïre
29E2 **Yakumo** Japan
54E4 **Yakutat** USA
54E4 **Yakutat B** USA
Yakutia = Sakha
25O3 **Yakutsk** Russian Federation
30C4 **Yala** Thailand
58B1 **Yale** Canada
50C3 **Yalinga** Central African Republic
34C3 **Yallourn** Australia
26C3 **Yalong** *R* China
31A4 **Yalong Jiang** *R* China
17F2 **Yalova** Turkey
21E7 **Yalta** Ukraine
28B2 **Yalu Jiang** *R* China/N Korea
29D3 **Yamada** Japan
29E3 **Yamagata** Japan
28C4 **Yamaguchi** Japan
20M2 **Yamalo-Nenetskiy Avt. Okrug** *Division* Russian Federation
24J2 **Yamal, Poluostrov** *Pen* Russian Federation
26E1 **Yamarovka** Russian Federation
34D1 **Yamba** New S Wales, Australia
34B2 **Yamba** S Australia, Australia
50C3 **Yambio** Sudan
17F2 **Yambol** Bulgaria
27G7 **Yamdena** *I* Indonesia
30B1 **Yamethin** Burma
Yam Kinneret = Tiberias,L
34B1 **Yamma Yamma,L** Australia
48B4 **Yamoussoukro** Ivory Coast
60B2 **Yampa** *R* USA
25R4 **Yamsk** Russian Federation
42D3 **Yamuna** *R* India
43G3 **Yamzho Yumco** *L* China
25P3 **Yana** *R* Russian Federation
34B3 **Yanac** Australia
28B4 **Yanagawa** Japan
44C2 **Yanam** India
31B2 **Yan'an** China
40C5 **Yanbu'al Bahr** Saudi Arabia
34B2 **Yancannia** Australia
31E3 **Yancheng** China
31B2 **Yanchi** China
34B1 **Yandama** *R* Australia
50C3 **Yangambi** Zaïre
28A3 **Yanggu** S Korea
31C1 **Yang He** *R* China
31C5 **Yangjiang** China
Yangon = Rangoon
31C2 **Yangquan** China
28A3 **Yangsan** S Korea
31C5 **Yangshan** China
31C3 **Yangtze Gorges** China
31E3 **Yangtze,Mouths of the** China
28A3 **Yangyang** S Korea
31D3 **Yangzhou** China
31B4 **Yanhe** China
28B2 **Yanji** China
34C3 **Yanko** Australia
61D2 **Yankton** USA
26B2 **Yanqqi** China
39G1 **Yanqqi** China
31D1 **Yan Shan** *Hills* China
25P2 **Yanskiy Zaliv** *B* Russian Federation
34B1 **Yantabulla** Australia
31E2 **Yantai** China
28B2 **Yantongshan** China
31D2 **Yanzhou** China
50B3 **Yaoundé** Cameroon
27G6 **Yap** *I* Pacific Ocean
27G7 **Yapen** *I* Indonesia
70B2 **Yaqui** *R* Mexico
20H4 **Yaransk** Russian Federation
7E3 **Yare** *R* England
20H3 **Yarenga** Russian Federation
20H3 **Yarensk** Russian Federation
72D3 **Yari** *R* Colombia
29D3 **Yariga-take** *Mt* Japan
39F2 **Yarkant He** *R* China
43G3 **Yarlung Zangbo Jiang** *R* China
55M5 **Yarmouth** Canada
45C2 **Yarmūk** *R* Jordan/Syria
20F4 **Yaroslavl'** *Division* Russian Federation
20F4 **Yaroslavl'** Russian Federation
45C2 **Yarqon** *R* Israel
34C3 **Yarram** Australia
34D1 **Yarraman** Australia
34C3 **Yarrawonga** Australia
20N2 **Yar Sale** Russian Federation
20E4 **Yartsevo** Russian Federation
25L3 **Yartsevo** Russian Federation
72C2 **Yarumal** Colombia
48C3 **Yashi** Nigeria
48C4 **Yashikera** Nigeria
21G6 **Yashkul'** Russian Federation
42C1 **Yasin** Pakistan
19E3 **Yasinya** Ukraine
34C2 **Yass** Australia
34C2 **Yass** *R* Australia
28B3 **Yasugi** Japan
63C1 **Yates Center** USA
54J3 **Yathkyed L** Canada
50C3 **Yatolema** Zaïre
45C3 **Yatta** West Bank
72D4 **Yavari** Peru
42D4 **Yavatmāl** India
28C4 **Yawatahama** Japan
30D2 **Ya Xian** China
41F3 **Yazd** Iran
41F3 **Yazd-e Khvāst** Iran
63D2 **Yazoo** *R* USA
63D2 **Yazoo City** USA
30B2 **Ye** Burma
19F3 **Yedintsy** Moldavia
20F5 **Yefremov** Russian Federation
21G6 **Yegorlyk** *R* Russian Federation
50D3 **Yei** Sudan
20L4 **Yekaterinburg** Russian Federation
21F5 **Yelets** Russian Federation
25Q4 **Yelizavety, Mys** *C* Russian Federation
10C1 **Yell** *I* Scotland
44C2 **Yellandu** India
56B1 **Yellowhead P** Canada
54G3 **Yellowknife** Canada
34C2 **Yellow Mt** Australia
Yellow R = Huang He
26F3 **Yellow Sea** China Korea
56C2 **Yellowstone** *R* USA
58D2 **Yellowstone L** USA
58D2 **Yellowstone Nat Pk** USA
8E1 **Yell Sd** Scotland
19G2 **Yel'nya** Russian Federation
19F2 **Yel'sk** Belarus
55K1 **Yelverton B** Canada
48C3 **Yelwa** Nigeria
38C4 **Yemen** *Republic* Arabian Pen
30C1 **Yen Bai** Vietnam
48B4 **Yendi** Ghana
30B1 **Yengan** Burma
24K3 **Yenisey** *R* Russian Federation
25L4 **Yeniseysk** Russian Federation
25L3 **Yeniseyskiy Kryazh** *Ridge* Russian Federation
24J2 **Yeniseyskiy Zaliv** *B* Russian Federation
7C4 **Yeo** *R* England
34C2 **Yeoval** Australia
7C4 **Yeovil** England
25M3 **Yerbogachen** Russian Federation
21G7 **Yerevan** Armenia
59C3 **Yerington** USA
20J2 **Yermitsa** Russian Federation
59C4 **Yermo** USA
25O4 **Yerofey-Pavlovich** Russian Federation
45C3 **Yeroham** Israel
25S3 **Yeropol** Russian Federation
21H5 **Yershov** Russian Federation
Yerushalayim = Jerusalem
40C1 **Yeşil** *R* Turkey
25M3 **Yessey** Russian Federation
45C2 **Yesud Hama'ala** Israel
34D1 **Yetman** Australia
48B2 **Yetti** Mauritius
43H4 **Yeu** Burma
14B2 **Yeu, Ile d'** *I* France
21H7 **Yevlakh** Azerbaijan
21E6 **Yevpatoriya** Ukraine
25P5 **Yevreyskaya Avt. Oblast** *Division* Russian Federation
31E2 **Ye Xian** China
21F6 **Yeysk** Russian Federation
45B3 **Yi'allaq, Gebel** *Mt* Egypt
45C1 **Yialousa** Cyprus
17E2 **Yiannitsá** Greece
31A4 **Yibin** China
31C3 **Yichang** China
26F2 **Yichun** China
31B2 **Yijun** China
17F2 **Yıldız Dağları** *Upland* Turkey
40C2 **Yıldızeli** Turkey
31A5 **Yiliang** China
31B2 **Yinchuan** China
31D3 **Ying He** *R* China
28A2 **Yingkou** China
31D3 **Yingshan** Hubei, China
31B3 **Yingshan** Sichuan, China
31D4 **Yingtan** China
39G1 **Yining** China
31B1 **Yin Shan** *Upland* China
50D3 **Yirga' Alem** Ethiopia
50D3 **Yirol** Sudan
25N5 **Yirshi** China
31B5 **Yishan** China
31D2 **Yishui** China
17E3 **Yíthion** Greece
28B2 **Yitong** China
28A2 **Yi Xian** China
31C4 **Yiyang** China
20D2 **Yli-Kitka** *L* Finland
12J5 **Ylitornio** Sweden
12J6 **Ylivieska** Finland
63C3 **Yoakum** USA
27E7 **Yogyakarta** Indonesia
50B3 **Yokadouma** Cameroon
29C4 **Yokkaichi** Japan
29D3 **Yokobori** Japan
29C3 **Yokohama** Japan
29C3 **Yokosuka** Japan
29D3 **Yokote** Japan
48D4 **Yola** Nigeria
29C3 **Yonago** Japan
28A3 **Yŏnan** N Korea
29E3 **Yonezawa** Japan
28A4 **Yongam** S Korea
31D4 **Yong'an** China
31A2 **Yongchang** China
28B3 **Yŏngch'ŏn** S Korea
31B4 **Yongchuan** China
31A2 **Yongdeng** China
31D5 **Yongding** China
31D2 **Yongding He** *R* China
28B3 **Yŏngdŏk** S Korea
28A3 **Yŏnggwang** S Korea
28B3 **Yŏnghŭng** N Korea
28A3 **Yŏnghŭng-man** *I* N Korea
28A3 **Yŏngil-man** *B* S Korea
28B2 **Yongji** China
28B3 **Yongju** S Korea
31B2 **Yongning** China
28A3 **Yŏngsanp'o** S Korea
28A3 **Yŏngyang** S Korea
68D2 **Yonkers** USA
13B4 **Yonne** *Department* France
14C2 **Yonne** *R* France
6D3 **York** *County* England
6D3 **York** England
61D2 **York** Nebraska, USA
68B3 **York** Pennsylvania, USA
32D2 **York,C** Australia
55J4 **York Factory** Canada
55M2 **York, Kap** *C* Greenland
27F8 **York Sd** Australia
6C4 **Yorkshire Dales Nat Pk** England
10C3 **Yorkshire Moors** England
7D2 **Yorkshire Wolds** *Upland* England
56C1 **Yorkton** Canada
65D3 **Yorktown** USA
68E1 **York Village** USA
66B2 **Yosemite L** USA
66C1 **Yosemite Nat Pk** USA
29B3 **Yoshii** *R* Japan
29B4 **Yoshino** *R* Japan
20H4 **Yoshkar Ola** Russian Federation
28B4 **Yŏsu** S Korea
45C4 **Yotvata** Israel
10B3 **Youghal** Irish Republic
31B5 **You Jiang** *R* China
34C2 **Young** Australia
35A2 **Young Range** *Mts* New Zealand
68A1 **Youngstown** New York, USA
64C2 **Youngstown** Ohio, USA
66A1 **Yountville** USA
31B4 **Youyang** China
40B2 **Yozgat** Turkey
75A3 **Ypané** *R* Paraguay
58B2 **Yreka** USA
12G7 **Ystad** Sweden
7C3 **Ystwyth** *R* Wales
8D3 **Ythan** *R* Scotland
31C4 **Yuan Jiang** *R* Hunan, China
31A5 **Yuan Jiang** *R* Yunnan, China
31A4 **Yuanmu** China
31C2 **Yuanping** China
59B3 **Yuba City** USA
29E2 **Yūbari** Japan
48A2 **Yubi,C** Morocco
70D3 **Yucatan** *Pen* Mexico
70D2 **Yucatan Chan** Cuba/Mexico
59D4 **Yucca** USA
31C2 **Yuci** China
25P4 **Yudoma** *R* Russian Federation
31D4 **Yudu** China
31A4 **Yuexi** China
31C4 **Yueyang** China
20L2 **Yugorskiy Poluostrov** *Pen* Russian Federation
17D2 **Yugoslavia** *Federal Republic* Europe
31B5 **Yu Jiang** *R* China
54D3 **Yukon** *R* Canada/USA
54E3 **Yukon Territory** Canada
30E1 **Yulin** Guangdong, China
31C5 **Yulin** Guangxi, China
31B2 **Yulin** Shaanxi, China
59D4 **Yuma** USA
26C3 **Yumen** China
31C5 **Yunkai Dashan** *Hills* China
34A2 **Yunta** Australia
31C3 **Yunxi** China
31C3 **Yun Xian** China
31B3 **Yunyang** China
72C5 **Yurimaguas** Peru
31E5 **Yu Shan** *Mt* Taiwan
20E3 **Yushkozero** Russian Federation
39H2 **Yushu** Tibet, China
31D2 **Yutian** China
75A4 **Yuty** Paraguay
31A5 **Yuxi** China
29D3 **Yuzawa** Japan
19F3 **Yuzhnyy Bug** *R* Ukraine
26H2 **Yuzhno-Sakhalinsk** Russian Federation
20K5 **Yuzh Ural** *Mts* Russian Federation